Digital
Typography

CSLI Lecture Notes Number 78

Digital Typography

Donald E. Knuth

CSLI Publications *Stanford California*

Copyright ©1999
Center for the Study of Language and Information
Leland Stanford Junior University
20 19 18 17 16   6 5 4 3 b

This printing incorporates all changes to the first printing that
were present in the author's master copy on 11 January 2011.

Library of Congress Cataloging-in-Publication Data

Knuth, Donald Ervin, 1938–
    Digital typography / Donald E. Knuth.
    xvi,685 p. 23 cm. -- (CSLI lecture notes ; no. 78)
    Includes bibliographical references and index.
    ISBN 978-1-57586-011-4 (cloth : alk. paper) --
    ISBN 978-1-57586-010-7 (pbk. : alk. paper)
    1. Printing--Data processing. 2. Computerized typesetting.
3. Computer fonts. 4. TeX (Computer system). 5. METAFONT.
I. Title. II. Series.
Z249.3.K59 1998
686.2'2544536--DC21   98-27331
                                                CIP

Internet page
    http://www-cs-faculty.stanford.edu/~knuth/dt.html
contains further information and links to related books.

to my father,
Ervin Knuth (1912–1974),
for his lifetime of sERVice

Contents

Preface

This book brings together more than 30 articles and notes that I have written about the subject of digital typography, popularly called "desktop publishing." It was my privilege to be present at a time when a significant revolution was taking place in the way words, symbols, and images were being rendered in printed documents, as analog methods gave way to digital methods that are amenable to computer processing.

I guess I must have ink in my veins: When I first learned about the potential of digital printing technology, I couldn't resist putting the rest of my life on hold while I tried to adapt the typographic wisdom of previous centuries to the possibilities of the present day. I hope the reader will be able to share some of the excitement of my decades-long quest to produce beautiful books with the help of computers.

Leonardo da Vinci made a sweeping statement in his notebooks: "Let no one who is not a mathematician read my works." In fact, he said it twice, so he probably meant it. But, thank goodness, a lot of people failed to heed his injunction; non-mathematicians are quite capable of dealing with mathematical concepts, when the description isn't beclouded with too much jargon. So I would like to reverse Leonardo's dictum and say, "Let everyone who is not a mathematician read my works." (Furthermore, mathematicians are invited too.)

Every author likes to be read, of course; I've quoted Leonardo chiefly as a sort of apology for the fact that some chapters of this book were originally addressed to professional mathematicians, while others were addressed to graphic artists or to people from other disciplines. My hope is that by keeping jargon to a necessary minimum I can communicate some significant ideas that cut across many specialized fields. Indeed, the study of printing is probably as interdisciplinary as any subject can be.

Chapter 1 gives an overview of my work, written with hindsight from the perspective of 1997. Chapter 2 gives an "underview" of the same work, written in 1977 as I was just getting started. The occasion for Chapter 2 was a special highlight of my life: I had just been asked to deliver the Josiah Willard Gibbs Lecture, an exposition of mathematics that is presented at each annual meeting of the American Mathematical Society. Prominent mathematicians such as G. H. Hardy, Albert Einstein and John von Neumann had previously been Gibbs lecturers, so I certainly had a hard act to follow. The people who had invited me to talk expected me to preach about the glories of computer science; but I decided to talk instead about the new work I had begun six months earlier and hadn't had time to mention to anybody except a few colleagues: I spoke about typography! Of course I didn't want to dishonor the noble tradition of the Gibbs lectureship, so I threw in some mathematics that was at least slightly sophisticated. Yet the main point I wished to make was that mathematical ideas need not be confined to the traditional areas of application, and that I had found it especially exciting to bring mathematics to bear on the field of typography. Fortunately, it turned out that my remarks could not have been more timely or found a more sympathetic audience, because many of the mathematicians present were grappling with publication problems that could benefit greatly from the kind of research I envisioned. As a result, I immediately had many offers of help from a wide variety of experts, and the American Mathematical Society gave strong support to my project.

Chapters 1 and 2 make it clear that my work on digital typography has had two main themes, corresponding to two computer programs known respectively as TEX and METAFONT. The first of these, TEX, is concerned with placing characters and images on pages; the second, METAFONT, is concerned with the design of the characters and images themselves.

TEX-related matters are discussed in Chapters 3–12. One of the most challenging aspects of page layout is the problem of breaking paragraphs of text into individual lines. The fact that computers can do this task better than all but the most dedicated hand-compositors was one of my early motivations for developing the TEX system; Chapter 3 presents the history of line-breaking together with improved algorithms based on several years of experience with prototype implementations of TEX. Then Chapter 4 discusses the additional complications that arise when languages like Hebrew and Arabic — which are written from right to left — are intermixed with European languages written from left to right. In a lighter vein, Chapters 5, 6, 7, and 8 are short discussions of handy

TEXniques that I have found useful for typesetting cookbook recipes, for typesetting the TEX logo, for printing out only a few pages of a long book, and printing my wife's travel journals. Chapter 9 is a short challenge problem for TEXperts, and Chapter 10 is a set of exercises for people who want to dig deeper and study the implementation of TEX itself. The computer program for TEX was the first large-scale application of a methodology that I have been calling "Literate Programming"; the published documentation of such a program is greatly enhanced by the provision of hypertext-like mini-indexes, whose implementation is discussed in Chapter 11. Finally, Chapter 12 discusses the interface between TEX and other systems by means of flexible specifications called "virtual fonts."

METAFONT-related matters are the topics of Chapters 13–23. First, Chapter 13 discusses an interesting mathematical problem that arises when we attempt to teach a computer how to draw the letter S. Chapter 14 describes a brief demonstration in which I was asked to draw an Indian character that I had never seen before, using METAFONT. Both Chapters 13 and 14 illustrate the important concept of a "metafont," namely the idea that many different but related variants of letterforms are used to group fonts into font families; Chapter 15 discusses meta-fonts and parametric variation in general. Chapter 16, which was originally a keynote lecture addressed to an international working conference of type designers, is a retrospective look at what I learned about font design during my first six years of experience with METAFONT-like systems. A new family of typefaces for mathematics, designed for the American Mathematical Society by Hermann Zapf and implemented with METAFONT, is described in Chapter 17; Chapter 18 discusses how I adapted the text fonts of a mathematics book to blend well with Zapf's mathematical symbols. Then Chapter 19 summarizes the results of teaching METAFONT and introductory type design to several dozen Stanford students. Chapter 20 describes a new family of fonts called PUNK, created for fun in one afternoon. Chapters 21 and 22 are devoted to some of the fascinating problems that arise when photographs and other continuous-tone images must be approximated by dots of ink. Finally, Chapter 23 deals with the boundaries of bitmaps that are supposed to imitate straight-line edges at oblique angles.

The remaining chapters discuss TEX and METAFONT in historical perspective, considering the past, the present, and the future. I've always been interested in the origin of ideas and in the evolution of software systems; therefore Chapters 24 and 25 reproduce the very first draft descriptions of TEX. These descriptions, taken from computer archive tapes and published here for the first time, were written mostly to myself and my student assistants as a guide to the prototype implementations of 1977 and 1978; they show clearly the influence of prior work, and they reveal significant differences between my initial conceptions and the TEX system as it exists today. Chapter 26 describes the very first books that were produced with TEX and METAFONT in various parts of the world. Then Chapter 27 jumps to more recent times and reflects the influence of graphic user interfaces as computer operating systems became more visually oriented: It presents little icons that symbolize the various kinds of files associated with the input and output of TEX and METAFONT. Chapter 28 is the text of a talk I gave in 1986, when I first believed that I had brought my work on digital typography to a successful conclusion; Chapter 29 is what I said in 1989 when I realized that some final changes to TEX and METAFONT would be needed in order to accommodate more of the world's languages; Chapter 30 is what I said in 1990 to confirm that those changes would indeed be the last. Chapters 31–33 are transcripts of lively question-and-answer sessions that I conducted with users of TEX and METAFONT in the United States (1995), the Czech Republic (1996), and the Netherlands (1996). Finally, Chapter 34 is a newly written sequel to my paper on "The errors of TEX."

Many of this book's chapters were written while today's printing technology was still developing rapidly, using experimental systems that pushed the then-current state of the art to its limits. To reproduce them here, I've had to recreate some of those experimental systems and to resuscitate dozens of long-lost fonts by simulating them with the mature versions of TEX and METAFONT, hoping to do justice to the historical context. Many of the chapters were originally written to fit the formats of specific publications, so I have adapted them to the page size and other conventions of the present book. I've improved the original wording, here and there; but by and large the text material remains essentially as it was when first published — except in Chapters 21 and 22, where I have made extensive changes to bring the material up to date. The bibliographies have been put into a consistent format; additional references and notes have been added where appropriate; dozens of the illustrations have been substantially improved.

Several of the example illustrations in this book are supposed to look bad, in contrast to other illustrations that I propose as more suitable alternatives. But printers have learned many tricks for improving poor material that has been given to them, and they might have tuned up some of my "bad examples" so that what you actually see is better than what I supplied. I apologize in advance for any such unintended enhancement, which is beyond my control.

I'm extremely grateful to Stanford's Center for the Study of Language and Information (CSLI) for the opportunity to publish this book and for their expertise in preparing everything the way I like to see it. In particular, William E. McMechan and William J. Croft prepared electronic forms of many files that had originally been typed by my secretary, Phyllis Winkler; Tony Gee collected and organized the materials in a timely manner; Copenhaver Cumpston designed the cover; and Dikran Karagueuzian initiated and supervised the entire project. Stanford University Archives provided efficient access to its collection of TEX and METAFONT memorabilia (SC 97, boxes 12–25). Martin Frost helped me reconstruct numerous files that I had originally prepared on Stanford's legendary SAIL computer (retired in 1990). Barbara Beeton of the American Mathematical Society retrieved many electronic files of articles that were originally published in *TUGboat*, the journal of the TEX Users Group, which she has edited so capably for nearly twenty years. Sun Microsystems and Apple Computer provided me with computers on which I was able to do the final editing and polishing.

This is the third in a series of books that CSLI plans to publish containing archival forms of the papers I have written. The first volume, *Literate Programming*, appeared in 1992; the second, *Selected Papers on Computer Science*, appeared in 1996. Five additional volumes are in preparation containing selected papers on Analysis of Algorithms, Computer Languages, Design of Algorithms, Discrete Mathematics, Fun and Games.

Donald E. Knuth
Stanford, California
August 1998

Acknowledgments

"Mathematical Typography" originally appeared in *Bulletin of the American Mathematical Society* (new series) **1** (March 1979), pp. 337–372. Copyright ©1979 by the American Mathematical Society. Reprinted by permission.

"Breaking Paragraphs Into Lines" originally appeared in *Software — Practice & Experience* **11** (1981), pp. 1119–1184. Copyright John Wiley & Sons Limited. Reprinted by permission.

"Mini-Indexes for Literate Programs" originally appeared in *Software — Concepts & Tools* **15** (1994), pp. 2–11. Copyright ©1994 by Springer-Verlag GmbH & Co. KG. Reprinted by permission.

"The Letter S" originally appeared in *The Mathematical Intelligencer* **2** (1980), pp. 114–122. Copyright ©1980 by Springer-Verlag GmbH & Co. KG. Reprinted by permission.

"My First Experience with Indian Scripts" originally appeared in the booklet *CALTIS-84*, p. 49. Copyright ©1984 by ITR Graphic Systems Pvt. Ltd. Reprinted by permission.

"The Concept of a Meta-Font" originally appeared in *Visible Language* **16** (1982), pp. 3–27. "Lessons Learned from METAFONT" originally appeared in *Visible Language* **19** (1985), pp. 35–53. Copyright by Illinois Institute of Technology — Institute of Design. Reprinted by permission.

"AMS Euler — A New Typeface for Mathematics" originally appeared in *Scholarly Publishing* **20** (1989), pp. 131–157. Copyright ©1989 University of Toronto Press Incorporated. Reprinted by permission.

"Digital Halftones by Dot Diffusion" originally appeared in *ACM Transactions on Graphics* **6** (1987), pp. 245–273. Copyright ©1987 by ACM Press, a Division of the Association for Computing Machinery, Inc. (ACM). Reprinted by permission.

"A note on digitized angles" originally appeared in *Electronic Publishing — Origination, Dissemination, and Design* **3** (1990), pp. 99–104. Copyright ©1990 by Penn Well Publishing Co. Reprinted by permission.

"TEX Incunabula" originally appeared in *TUGboat* **5** (1984), pp. 4–11. "A Course on METAFONT Programming" originally appeared in *TUGboat* **5** (1984), pp. 105–118. "Recipes and Fractions" originally appeared in *TUGboat* **6** (1985), pp. 36–38. "Computers and Typesetting" originally appeared in *TUGboat* **7** (1986), pp. 95–98. "The TEX Logo in Various Fonts" originally appeared in *TUGboat* **7** (1986), p. 101. "Mixing Right-to-Left Texts with Left-to-Right Texts" originally appeared in *TUGboat* **8** (1987), pp. 14–25. "Problem for a Saturday Morning" originally appeared in *TUGboat* **8** (1987), pp. 73 and 210. "Fonts for Digital Halftones" originally appeared in *TUGboat* **8** (1987), pp. 135–160. "Printing Out Selected Pages" originally appeared in *TUGboat* **8** (1987), p. 217. "Macros for Jill" originally appeared in *TUGboat* **8** (1987), pp. 309–314. "A Punk Meta-Font" originally appeared in *TUGboat* **9** (1988), pp. 152–168. "Typesetting Concrete Mathematics" originally appeared in *TUGboat* **10** (1989), pp. 31–36 and 342. "The New Versions of TEX and METAFONT" originally appeared in *TUGboat* **10** (1989), pp. 325–328. "Virtual Fonts: More Fun for Grand Wizards" originally appeared in *TUGboat* **11** (1990), pp. 13–23. "Exercises for TEX: The Program" originally appeared in *TUGboat* **11** (1990), pp. 165–170 and 499–511. "The Future of TEX and METAFONT" originally appeared in *TUGboat* **11** (1990), p. 489. "Icons for TEX and METAFONT" originally appeared in *TUGboat* **14** (1993), pp. 387–389. "Questions and Answers, I" originally appeared in *TUGboat* **17** (1996), pp. 7–22. "Questions and Answers, II" originally appeared in *TUG-boat* **17** (1996), pp. 355–367. Copyright TEX Users Group. Reprinted by permission.

"Questions and Answers, III" originally appeared in *MAPS (Minutes and APpendiceS)* **16** (1996), pp. 38–49. Reprinted by permission of the NTG, the Dutch-language-oriented TEX Users Group.

Ervin Knuth, 1974

Chapter 1

Digital Typography

[Commemorative Lecture presented on 11 November 1996 in connection with the 1996 Kyoto Prize for Advanced Technology, awarded by the Inamori Foundation of Kyoto, Japan.]

[SLIDE 0 to be shown during introduction of the speaker]

Slide 0.

I have been in love with books ever since I can remember. At first, my parents read to me a lot — an unusual practice in America at the time, because the prevailing "wisdom" of the 1940s was that a child who is exposed to intellectual things at an early age will be bored later when entering school. Thanks to my parents, I became at age four the youngest member of the Book Worm Club at the Milwaukee Public Library [SLIDE 1].

That early experience with books is probably responsible for the fact that I don't remember *ever* being bored, throughout my education. In fact, I think contemporary society is all mixed up in its concept of "boredom": People often say to each other that they are bored, but to me this is almost a shocking, shameful admission. Why should it be somebody else's duty to entertain us? People who can't find anything of interest in what they are doing, who constantly need external sources of stimulation and amusement, are missing most of life's pleasures.

1

Too young to read books himself, Donald Knuth, 4, of 2961 N. 18th st. is nevertheless the youngest member of the public library's Ancient Order of Book Worms. His father reads storybooks to him. Wednesday he gave oral reports on his "reading" in the young people's room of the library. Some of the stories he reported on were "Country Bunny," "Pokey Bear," "When the Root Children Wake Up" and "Babar the King."

Slide 1.   Slide 2.

With me it has always been the opposite: I tend to err in the other direction. I often get so interested in Chapter 1 of the books that I'm reading or studying, I don't have much time to read the final chapters.

Once, when I was five years old, my parents let me take the streetcar to the downtown library by myself, and I was absolutely fascinated by the children's books. When I didn't come home on time, my parents were worried and phoned the library. One of the night staff went looking and found me in the stacks, reading happily — I had no idea that the library was closed and that everyone else had gone home! Even today my wife knows that when I go into a library, I'll probably come home late.

In fact, not only have I always loved books, I've also been in love with the individual *letters* in books. Here's a page from the first ABC alphabet book that I had when I was little [SLIDE 2]. Curiously, I marked each serif in the letters with a little x, and I counted the serifs: The letter K has 7 serifs. The letter P [SLIDE 3] has 4; the letter O [SLIDE 4] has none.

Slide 3.   Slide 4.

From this you can see that I like numbers as well as letters. By the time I became a professor at Stanford I had learned that my main talents were associated with computer programming, and I had begun to write books of my own. My first book, Volume 1 of *The Art of Computer Programming*, came out in 1968, and Volume 2 was ready a year later [SLIDE 5].

I was excited to see these volumes not only because I was pleased with the information they contained, but also because of the beautiful typography and layout. These books were produced with the best, time-tested methods known for the presentation of technical material. They appeared in the same classic style that had been used in my favorite college textbooks. So it was a pleasure to look at these volumes as well as to read them.

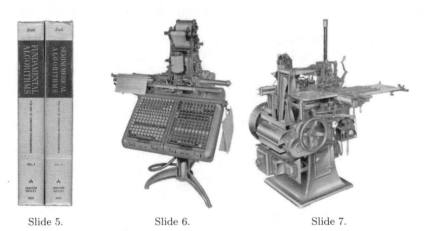

Slide 5.   Slide 6.   Slide 7.

They were produced with 19th-century technology called Monotype, involving two kinds of machines. First, there was a complex pneumatic keyboard with 284 keys [SLIDE 6]. This machine produced a punched paper tape something like a player-piano roll; you can see this tape at the top of the picture. The paper tape was then used to control a special casting machine [SLIDE 7] that produced individual pieces of type from hot molten lead.

$$|\det(a_{ij})| \leq \prod_{1 \leq i \leq n} \left(\sum_{1 \leq j \leq n} a_{ij}^2 \right)^{1/2}$$

Slide 8.

The process of typesetting mathematics with such machines was very complicated; here's a typical formula from Volume 2 [SLIDE 8].

A specially trained typist would key in most of the formula by making two passes: First the letters and symbols on the main line would be entered, and their superscripts (namely the characters

$$|\det(a\quad)| \leq \qquad\qquad a^2$$

in this case); then a second pass was made for the subscripts (namely the characters '$_{ij}$', repeated twice here). The keyboard operator had to know the width of each character so that there would be just enough space to make the subscripts line up properly. After the formula had been cast into metal, another specially trained technician inserted the remaining large symbols (the big parentheses and symbols like $\prod$ and $\sum$) by hand.

Only a few dozen people in the world knew how to typeset mathematical formulas with Monotype. I once had the pleasure and privilege of meeting Eric, the compositor who did the keyboarding for Volumes 1 and 2; I was surprised to discover that he spoke with a very strong London-Cockney accent, although he lived in America and was responsible for some of the world's most advanced books in mathematics.

Program A (*Addition, subtraction, and normalization*). The following program is a subroutine for Algorithm A, and it is also designed so that the normalization portion can be used by other subroutines which appear later in this section. In this program and in many other programs throughout this chapter, OFLO stands for a subroutine which prints out a message to the effect that MIX's overflow toggle was unexpectedly found to be "on."

01	EXP	EQU	1:1	Definition of exponent field.
02	FSUB	STA	TEMP	Floating-point subtraction subroutine:
03		LDAN	TEMP	Change sign of operand.

Slide 9.

Books on computer science have added a new complication to the difficulties that printers already faced in mathematical typesetting: Computer scientists need to use a special style of type called `typewriter type`, in order to represent the textual material that machines deal with. For example [SLIDE 9], here's another portion of a page from Volume 2, part of a computer program. I needed to combine typewriter type like the word '`OFLO`' with the ordinary style of letters. At first I was told that an extra alphabet would be impossible with Monotype, because traditional math formulas were already stretching Monotype technology to its limits. But later, Eric and his supervisor figured out how to do it. Notice that I needed a new, squarish looking letter `O` in the typewriter style, in order to make a clean distinction between `O` (oh) and `0` (zero).

New machines based on photography began to replace hot-lead machines like the Monotype in the 1960s. The new machines created pages by exposing a photographic plate, one letter at a time, using an ingenious combination of rotating disks and lenses to put each character in its proper position. Shortly after Volume 3 of *The Art of Computer Programming* came out in 1973, my publisher sold its Monotype machine and Eric had to find another job. New printings of Volume 1 and Volume 3 were published in 1975, correcting errors that readers had found in the earlier printings; these corrections were typeset in Europe, where Monotype technology still survived.

I had also prepared a second edition of Volume 2, which required typesetting that entire book all over again. My publishers found that it was too expensive in 1976 to produce a book the way it had been done in 1969. Moreover, the style of type that had been used in the original books was not available on photo-optical typesetting machines. I flew from California to Massachusetts for a crisis meeting. The publishers agreed that quality typography was of the utmost importance; and in the next months they tried hard to obtain new fonts that would match the old ones.

Program A (*Addition, subtraction, and normalization*). The following program is a subroutine for Algorithm A, and it is also designed so that the normalization portion can be used by other subroutines which appear later in this section. In this program and in many other programs throughout this chapter, OFLO stands for a subroutine which prints out a message to the effect that MIX's overflow toggle was unexpectedly found to be "on." The byte size b is assumed to be a multiple of 4. The normalization routine NORM assumes that $rI2 = e$ and $rAX = f$, where $rA = 0$ implies $rX = 0$ and $rI2 < b$.

01	EXP	EQU	1:1	Definition of exponent field.
02	FSUB	STA	TEMP	Floating-point subtraction subroutine
03		LDAN	TEMP	Change sign of operand.

Slide 10.

But the results were very disappointing. For example [SLIDE 10], here's some of the type from the second, "tuned up" version of their new fonts. These were much improved from the first attempt, but still unacceptable. The "N" in "NORM" was tipped; the "ff" in "effect" was much too dark; the letters "ip" in "multiple" were too close together; and so on.

I didn't know what to do. I had spent 15 years writing those books, but if they were going to look awful I didn't want to write any more. How could I be proud of such a product?

A possible way out of this dilemma presented itself a few months later, when I learned about another radical change in printing technology. The newest machines made images on film by *digital* instead of analog means — something like the difference between television and real movies. The shapes of letters were now made from tiny little dots,

Slide 11.

based on electronic pulses that were either ON or OFF [SLIDE 11]. Aha!
This was something I could understand! It was very simple, like the
lights on a scoreboard at a sports match.

Metallurgy and hot lead have always been complete mysteries to me;
neither have I understood lenses or mechanical alignment devices. But
letters made of little dots — that's computer science! That's just bits,
binary digits, 0s and 1s! Put a 1 where you want ink, put a 0 where you
don't want ink, and you can print a page of a book!

I had seen digital letterforms before, but only on crude machines.
Computer scientists had been experimenting for many years with a machine called the Xerox Graphics Printer, which had been invented during
the 60s but not controlled by computers until the 70s. This machine
made letters out of dots, which in those days weren't very small: There
were only about 180 dots per inch, so the letters had lots of jagged edges.
It was fun to play with the Xerox Graphics Printer, but I never expected
that such a machine could produce real books. It seemed too simple,
capable only of making cheap imitations — like the difference between
an electronic synthesizer and a real piano or violin.

But in February 1977 I saw for the first time the output of a high-
quality digital typesetter, which had more than 1000 dots per inch ...
and it looked perfect, every bit as good as the best metal typography
I had ever seen. Suddenly I saw that dots of ink will form smooth-
looking curves if the dots are small enough, by the laws of physics.
And I remembered that human eyes are inherently digital, made from
individual rod and cone cells. Therefore I learned for the first time that
a digital typesetting machine was indeed capable of producing books of
the highest conceivable quality.

Digital cameras don't capture all the sharp details of traditional
photographs. High-definition television can't match the quality of a

VistaVision movie. But for ink on paper, a digital approach is as good as any other.

In other words, the problem of printing beautiful books had changed from a problem of metallurgy to a problem of optics and then to a problem of computer science. The fact that Gutenberg had made books from movable metal type was suddenly only a 500-year-long footnote to history. The new machines have made the old mechanical approaches essentially irrelevant: The future of typography depends on the people who know the most about creating patterns of 0s and 1s; it depends on mathematicians and computer scientists.

When I realized this, I couldn't resist tackling the typography problem myself. I dropped everything else I was doing — I had just finished writing the first 100 pages of Volume 4 — and decided to write computer programs that would generate the patterns of 0s and 1s that my publishers and I needed for the new edition of Volume 2.

At first I thought it would be easy; I expected that the job could be done in a few months. In March of 1977 I wrote to my publishers that I would probably have the first proofs ready in July. Boy, was I wrong! All my life I have underestimated the difficulty of the projects I've embarked on, but this was a new personal record for being too optimistic.

In the first place, almost nobody else in computer science was doing this kind of work, so it was difficult to get financial support. The type-setting machine was very expensive, too much for our university budget. Moreover, that machine was designed to be run 24 hours per day by trained operators; I was just a single individual with strange mathematical ideas and no experience in the printing industry. Still, I assumed that if I could get my computer program working, I'd be able to borrow time on some digital typesetting machine.

There also was a chicken-and-egg problem. I couldn't set type until I had fonts of letters and mathematical symbols, but the fonts I needed did not exist in digital form. And I could not readily design the fonts until I could set type with them. I needed both things at once. Other fonts had been digitized, but I had resolved to define the fonts by myself, using purely mathematical formulas under my own control. Then I would never have to face the possibility that another change in technology might upset the applecart again. With my own computer program controlling all aspects of the 0s and 1s on the pages, I would be able to define the appearance of my books once and for all.

My publishers provided me with original copies of the Monotype images that had been used to make the first edition of Volume 1. So

I thought it would be easy to find mathematical formulas to describe the shapes of the letters. I had seen John Warnock doing similar things at Xerox's Palo Alto Research Center, so I asked if I could use Xerox's lab facilities to create my fonts. The answer was yes, but there was a catch: Xerox insisted on all rights to the use of any fonts that I developed with their equipment. Of course that was their privilege, but such a deal was unacceptable to me: A mathematical formula should never be "owned" by anybody! Mathematics belongs to God.

So I went to Stanford's Artificial Intelligence lab, which had a television camera that I could use to magnify the letters and capture them in digital form. Unfortunately, the television camera did not give a true picture — the image was badly distorted. Even worse, a tiny change in the brightness of the room lights made a tremendous change in the television images. There was no way I could get consistent data from one letter to another. With that TV camera my fonts would look much worse than the fonts I had rejected from the non-digital machine.

I tried photographing the pages and magnifying them by projecting the images on the wall of my house, tracing the enlarged outlines with pencil and paper. But that didn't work either.

Finally, a simple thought struck me. *Those letters were designed by people.* If I could understand what those people had in their minds when they were drawing the letters, then I could program a computer to carry out the same ideas. Instead of merely copying the form of the letters, my new goal was therefore to copy the intelligence underlying that form. I decided to learn what type designers knew, and to teach that knowledge to a computer.

That train of thought led to my computer system called META-FONT, which I want to try to show you now. [Switch from slides to online computer display.] Here is the way I finally decided to create the letter A, for example, using a computer program. All the key points of the letter are based on a grid that is displayed here, although of course the grid is really invisible.

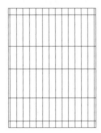

Based on this grid and the specification of a normal text font, the computer first draws the main stem stroke:

Part of this stroke needs to be erased, because it's too thick at the top.

Then the left diagonal stroke is added,

and the crossbar.

It's time now to add a serif at the bottom left,

and to erase a little at the bottom so that the serif doesn't make the letter too heavy.

(This erasure is quite subtle: You have to look closely!) A similar serif is drawn at the bottom right:

 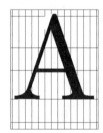 

This completes the letter A.

The same program will draw infinitely many different A's if we change the specifications. For example, here's a darker, boldface variant:

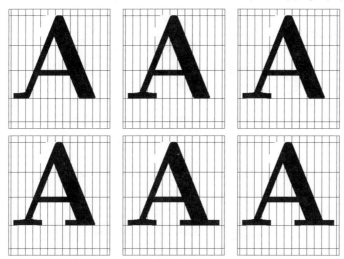

And here's a small A suitable for fine print:

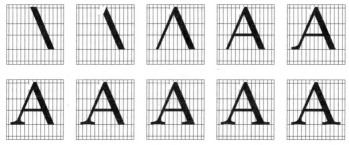

Simply shrinking the original A by 50% would not produce such a legible character at a small size; we would have 'ᴀ' instead of 'ᴀ'. Good typography requires small letters to have shapes that are subtly different from their larger cousins.

Even the typewriter style A can be drawn with the same program. This time we specify that the thick strokes and thin strokes are identical, and the corners of the serifs are rounded.

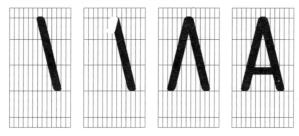

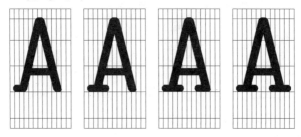

The resulting A went into my first typewriter-style font, but I learned later that such an A was a bit darker than it should be. To solve the problem, I moved the two diagonal strokes slightly apart, and cut a "notch" in the interior so as to open the inside a bit.

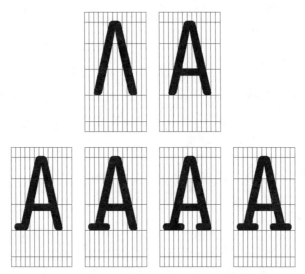

This is the nice typewriter-style A that I use today. I didn't learn such tricks until several years after I started to study type design.

Here is an example of the way my first draft fonts looked on the Xerox Graphics Printer, about one and a half years after I had begun to work on typography [SLIDE 12]. Two years later, with some financial help from my publishers, my project was finally able to obtain a high-resolution digital typesetting machine, and I could print the new edition of Volume 2. The proofs for that book looked so much better than the xerographic proofs I had been working with, I thought my goals for quality typography had finally been reached.

But when I received the first printed copy of the new Volume 2 in its familiar binding, and opened the pages, I burned with disappointment.

Program A (*Addition, subtraction, and normalization*). The following program is a subroutine for Algorithm A, and it is also designed so that the normalization portion can be used by other subroutines that appear later in this section. In this program and in many other programs throughout this chapter, OFLO stands for a subroutine that prints out a message to the effect that MIX's overflow toggle was unexpectedly found to be "on." The byte size b is assumed to be a multiple of 4. The normalization routine NORM assumes that rI2 $= e$ and rAX $= f$, where rA $= 0$ implies rX $= 0$ and rI2 $< b$.

00	BYTE	EQU	1 (4 : 4)	Byte size b
01	EXP	EQU	1 : 1	Definition of exponent field
02	FSUB	STA	TEMP	Floating-point subtraction subroutine:
03		LDAN	TEMP	Change sign of operand.

Slide 12.

The book did not look at all as I had hoped. After four years of hard work, I still hadn't figured out how to generate the patterns of 0s and 1s that are demanded by fine printing. The published second edition [SLIDE 13] didn't look much better than the version I had rejected before starting my typography project.

Program A (*Addition, subtraction, and normalization*). The following program is a subroutine for Algorithm A, and it is also designed so that the normalization portion can be used by other subroutines that appear later in this section. In this program and in many others throughout this chapter, OFLO stands for a subroutine that prints out a message to the effect that MIX's overflow toggle was unexpectedly found to be "on." The byte size b is assumed to be a multiple of 4. The normalization routine NORM assumes that rI2 $= e$ and rAX $= f$, where rA $= 0$ implies rX $= 0$ and rI2 $< b$.

00	BYTE	EQU	1 (4 : 4)	Byte size b
01	EXP	EQU	1 : 1	Definition of exponent field
02	FSUB	STA	TEMP	Floating point subtraction subroutine:
03		LDAN	TEMP	Change sign of operand.

Slide 13.

Meanwhile I had had the good fortune to meet many of the world's leading type designers. They graciously gave me the instruction and criticism I needed as I continued to make improvements. After five more years went by, I finally was able to produce books of which I could feel proud.

I don't want to give the impression that those nine years of work were nothing but drudgery. (As I said before, I rarely seem to get bored.) Font design is in fact lots of fun, especially when you make mistakes. The computer tends to draw delightfully creative images that no human being would ever dream up. I call these "META-flops." For example [SLIDE 14], here's an ffi ligature combination in which the f at the left reaches all the way over to the dot on the i at the right. And here's another weird ffi [SLIDE 15]: I call it "the ffilling station."

In one of my first attempts to do a capital typewriter-style Y, I put the upper right serif in the wrong place [SLIDE 16]. I swear that I was *not* thinking of yen when I did this!

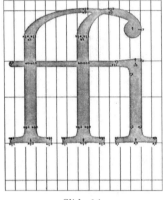

Slide 14.

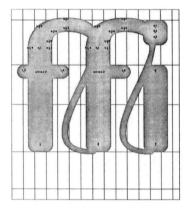

Slide 15.

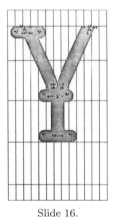

Slide 16.

Does METAFONT work for Japanese characters as well as for Roman letters? I think it does, but I haven't been able to develop a good eye for Asian letterforms myself. My student John Hobby did some promising experiments together with Gu Guoan of the Shanghai Printing Company, and I'd like to give you a taste of what they did. First they wrote 13 computer programs for basic strokes. For example, here are two "teardrop" shapes produced by one of their programs [SLIDE 17]. A font designer specifies the top, the bottom, and the edge of the bulb; the computer does the rest. Here [SLIDE 18] are some more examples of teardrops, together with variants of three other basic strokes.

Hobby and Gu used their stroke routines to design 128 Chinese characters. And they did it in such a way that you could get three

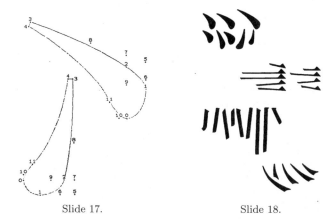

Slide 17.   Slide 18.

different styles of letters simply by using three different versions of the 13 basic strokes. Here [SLIDE 19] are five characters rendered in Song style, Long Song style, and Bold style. And here [SLIDE 20] are examples of the 13 basic strokes in all three styles.

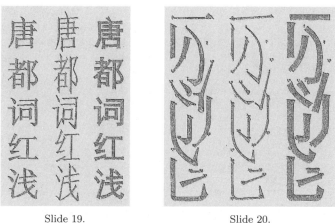

Slide 19.   Slide 20.

With the METAFONT system for type design, and the TEX system for putting letters and symbols into the right positions on a page, anybody who wants to write a beautiful book can now do so singlehandedly with a reasonable amount of effort. These systems give an author total control over the patterns of 0s and 1s that are needed to define the pages. I have made special efforts to ensure that TEX and METAFONT will give exactly the same results on all computers, and to ensure that they will give the same results 50 years from today as they do today. Furthermore I have published all of the details and put all of my programs in the public domain, so that nobody has to pay for using them. Of course, many people who offer additional services will charge a fee for their expertise, but the main point is that a dedicated author now has the power to prepare books that previously were prohibitively expensive.

Kapitola XII

Ž ené sluncem oděné drak sedmihla-
vý syna sežrati chtěl. 7. ale Michal
archanděl, draka přemohl. 10. Nad
nímž ačkoli učastníci Beránkovi svíté-
zili, 11. i žena uletěla, 16. a země řeku
vypila, 17. však ten drak proti ostatkům svatých
bojovati nepřestává.

I ukázal se div veliký na nebi: Žena odě-
ná sluncem, pod jejímiž nohama byl mě-
síc, a na jejíž hlavě byla koruna dvanácti
hvězd. 2 A jsouci těhotná, křičela, pracu-
jící ku porodu a trápěci se, aby porodila.
3 I vidín jest jiný div na nebi. Nebo aj, drak

Slide 21.

4.8.2 ማኅበሥ

የማኅበሥ እና የምኅዳ ክፍል መሆኑ በብዙ መንገድ ይመስላሉ :: እንደምስል ሁሉ
የማኅበሥ ክፍል ተገለጻ ነው :: አይነ-ተ ማኅበሥ ክፍል መሆን የምንሰጠው ጉዳይ
ላይ ነው :: በደፈሳ እንደኔC የማኅበሥ መጥፎC ይሁንን ይመስላል ::

\ጀ፫c{ማኅበሥ}[tbbp]
በነመc\ጥ\ ኣሊሁ ዶግብ ::
\መግለጫ{<በነመc\ጥ\ በም ኣሊሁ ዶግብ>}
\ስይም{ቀለቅ}
\ሓcበ{ማኅበሥ}

በመብሪቱ የክፍሉ መጥፉC ከምኅበል እንደ-ደፈ :: \መንካ እንደምስል ክፍል
ማኅበሥን ተፈ ቀጥርC ነው ለመቅበም ይረፍል :: ክንደ በላደ \መንካ በነደ
ማኅበሥ ክፍል ወብት መክተተ የተፈቀደ ነው አስፈ-ለጊ አስከብን ድረስ :: ነገC
ግን ተበባደ መመረደ ሰለዖን ብርቱ ጥገቀተ ማደረተ መቀሚ ታው ዖሜሃ :

Slide 22.

I can't resist showing you samples from some of the books that I've received in recent years from their authors. Here's one from the Czech Republic [SLIDE 21], showing another font done with METAFONT. Here's one from Ethiopia [SLIDE 22], telling Amharic-speaking people how to use the TₑX system.

в возвращается в горизонтальную моду для продолжения абзаца. (Формула, которая выделяется, должна оканчиваться на $$.) Например, предположим вы вводите

$$\text{число } \pi \approx 3.1415926536 \text{ является важным.}$$

TeX между двумя $$ переходит в выделенную математическую моду и результат, который вы получите, утверждает, что число

$$\pi \approx 3.1415926536$$

является важным.

Когда TeX находится в вертикальной или внутренней вертикальной моде, он игнорирует пробелы и пустые строки (или командные последовательности \par). так что вам не надо беспокоиться, что такие вещи могут изменить моду или повлиять на создаваемый документ. Командный пробел (\␣) будет, однако, рассматриваться как начало абзаца; абзац начинется с пробела после отступа.

Обычно лучше окончить всю работу, поставив в конце рукописи TeX'a \bye, что является сокращением для \vfill\eject\end. Командная последовательность \vfill переводит TeX в вертикальную моду и вставляет

Slide 23.

び段落の残りを処理するために水平モードに戻るのである（ディスプレイとして組む数式は、$$で終わっていなければならない）。たとえば、次のように入力すると、

the number $$\pi \approx 3.1415926536$$ is important.

TeX は、$$で囲まれた数式を処理する間、ディスプレイ数式モードに移り、次のように、「the number

$$\pi \approx 3.1415926536$$

is important。」と組まれて出力される。

TeX が垂直モード、または内部垂直モードのときは、空白や空行（または \par 命令）がいくつあっても無視されてしまう。したがって、空白や空行がモードを変更したり、印刷される文書に何か影響があるのではないかと心配する必要はない。しかし、コントロール・スペース（\␣）は、段落の始まりとみなされてしまう。その場合の段落は、インデントを行った後、空白で始まっていることになる。

TeX の慣用の終わりでは、\bye と入力してすべてを終了させるのが一般的である。\bye 命令は plain TeX に定義されており、\vfill\eject\end の省略形である

Slide 24.

Here [SLIDE 23] is part of the Russian translation of my own book on TₑX. And here [SLIDE 24] is the same passage in Japanese translation. By the way, if I had lived in Japan, I'm sure I never would have been inclined to invent TₑX or METAFONT, because I wouldn't have felt the need: The standards of typography in this country never declined as they did in America and Europe. However, I'm extremely glad to see that TEX is now widely used also in Japanese publishing.

People have sent me many fine books that probably would never have existed without TEX and METAFONT. My favorite examples are scholarly publications, such as the interlingual text of an Eskimo language folk tale shown here [SLIDE 25]. Here, similarly, are some footnotes from a critical edition of a Greek and Latin text [SLIDE 26]; another, in Arabic [SLIDE 27]; another in Sanskrit [SLIDE 28].

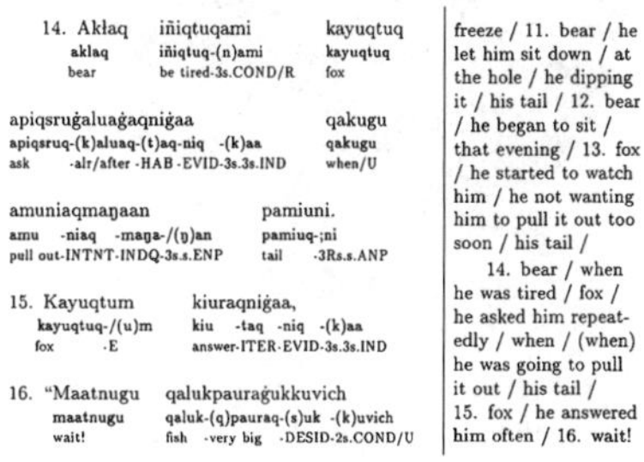

Slide 25.

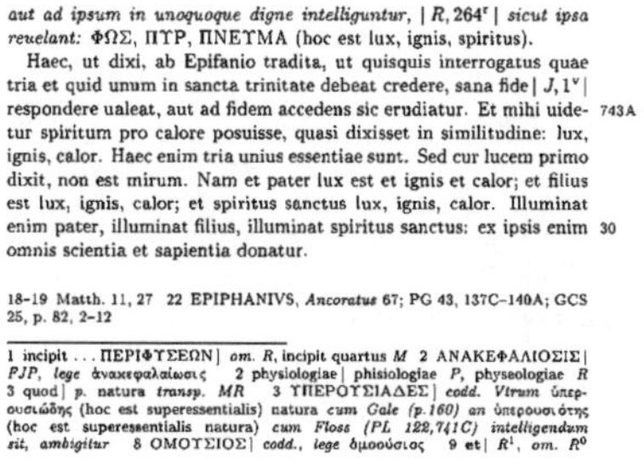

Slide 26.

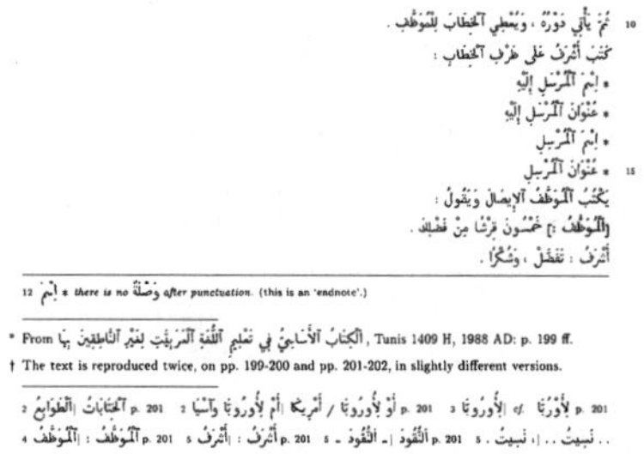

Slide 27.

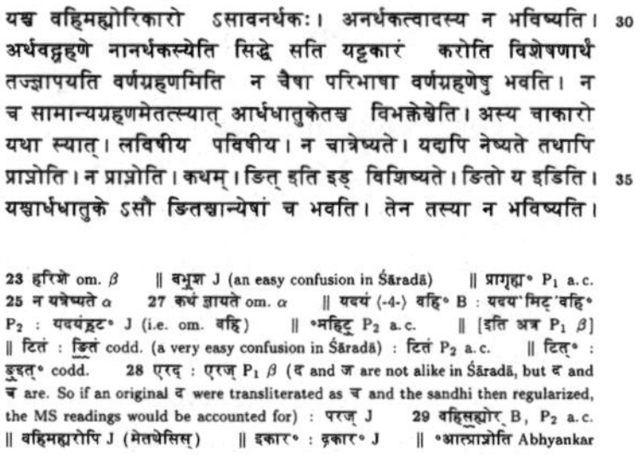

Slide 28.

Ever since I began working on TEX in 1977, I've kept a record of all the errors, large and small, that I found and removed from the program with the help of volunteers around the world. This list has now grown to 1,276 items. Perhaps TEX has thereby become one of the most thoroughly checked computer programs ever written.

I would like to conclude this talk by quoting one of my favorite poems, written by the Danish sage Piet Hein. He calls it a "grook" — it's sort of a Danish variant of haiku. My wife and I like it so much, we

commissioned a British stonecutter to carve it in slate for the entryway
of our house [SLIDE 29]. It goes like this:

The road to wisdom?
Well it's plain
and simple to express:

Err
and err
and err again
but less
and less
and less.

Slide 29.

Illustration Credits

Slide 0 was given to me by an unknown person about 1980; it was evidently created
by someone named "M. S." Slide 1 is a newspaper clipping from *The Milwaukee
Journal* (2 August 1942), page II-1. Slides 2, 3, and 4 come from *The Brimful
Book*, edited by Watty Piper, illustrated by G. & D. Hauman (New York: Platt
and Munk, 1927). Slides 6 and 7 are based on plates III and IV in *The Print-
ing of Mathematics* by Chaundy, Barrett, and Batey (London: Oxford University
Press, 1954). Slide 9 is an excerpt from page 185 of *The Art of Computer Pro-
gramming*, Volume 2, first edition (Reading, Massachusetts: Addison–Wesley, 1969);
Slide 13 is the corresponding material from page 202 of the second edition (1981).
Slides 10 and 12 are from material in collection SC 97 of the Stanford University Archives. Slides 14–18 are taken from "Lessons Learned from METAFONT,"
Figs. 13h, 13i, 13f, 8, and 9 respectively; see Chapter 16 of the present volume.
Slides 19 and 20 are based on "A Chinese Meta-Font" by John D. Hobby and
Gu Guoan, *TUGboat* **5** (1984), 119–136, Figs. 7 and 9. Slide 21 is from *Apoka-
lypsa* by Albrecht Dürer, translated by Michaela Hájková (Prague: Volvox Globator,
1993), page 20. Slide 22 is from መጽሐፈ አስተዋጽኦ፡ የሰነድ ዝግጅት መመሪያ [*Book of
elATEX: Document Preparation Guidelines*] by አባስ በላይ አላምነሁ [Abass Belay
Alamnehe] (Houston, Texas: EthiO Systems, 1993), pages 70–71. Slide 23 is an ex-
cerpt from page 107 of *Все про TEX* [*Everything about TEX*] by Дональд Е. Кнут
[Donald E. Knuth], translated by М. В. Лисина [M. V. Lisina] (Protvino, Moscow:
AO RDTEX, 1993); Slide 24 is the corresponding excerpt found on page 123 of
TEXブック [*The TEXbook*] by Donald E. Knuth, translated by 斎藤信男 [Nobuo
Saito] and 鷺谷好輝 [Yoshiteru Sagiya] (Tokyo: ASCII Corporation, 1989). Slide 25
is from *Formatting Interlinear Text* by Jonathan Kew and Stephen McConnel (Dallas,
Texas: Summer Institute of Linguistics, 1990), page 71. Slides 26–28 are taken from
Critical Edition Typesetting: The EDMAC Format for Plain TEX by John Lavagnino
and Dominik Wujastyk (UK TEX Users Group, 1996), pages 94, 100, and 101. And
Slide 29 is based on Plate 15 of *Letters Slate Cut: A Sequel* by David Kindersley and
Lida Lopes Cardozo (Cambridge: Cardozo Kindersley Editions, 1990).

Chapter 2

Mathematical Typography

[Josiah Willard Gibbs Lecture, given under the auspices of the American Mathematical Society, January 4, 1978; dedicated to George Pólya on his 90th birthday. Originally published in Bulletin of the American Mathematical Society (new series) 1 (March 1979), 337–372.]

Abstract

Mathematics books and journals do not look as beautiful as they used to. It is not that their mathematical content is unsatisfactory, rather that the old and well-developed traditions of typesetting have become too expensive. Fortunately, it now appears that mathematics itself can be used to solve this problem.

A first step in the solution is to devise a method for unambiguously specifying mathematical manuscripts in such a way that they can easily be manipulated by machines. Such a language, when properly designed, can be learned quickly by authors and their typists; yet manuscripts in this form will lead directly to high quality plates for the printer with little or no human intervention.

A second step in the solution makes use of classical mathematics to design the shapes of the letters and symbols themselves. It is possible to give a rigorous definition of the exact shape of the letter 'a', for example, in such a way that infinitely many styles — bold, extended, sans-serif, italic, etc. — are obtained from a single definition by changing only a few parameters. When the same is done for the other letters and symbols, we obtain a mathematical definition of type fonts, a definition that can be used on all machines both now and in the future. The main significance of this approach is that new symbols can readily be added in such a way that they are automatically consistent with the old ones.

Of course it is necessary that the mathematically-defined letters be beautiful according to traditional notions of aesthetics. Given a sequence

19

(a)

$$\lambda = \pm \sqrt{\tfrac{1}{6}S} = \pm \sqrt{\tfrac{1}{6}(aa'a'')(aa'a''')}$$

there correspond two quadric forms each containin rameters. So much HILBERT states. In order to as known systems it will be convenient to use a mental cubic, due to HESSE.*

Referred to an inflexional triangle, the equatio

(3) $\qquad a_x^3 = x_1^3 + x_2^3 + x_3^3 + 6mx_1x_2x_3$

All conic polars accordingly have the form :

(4) $\qquad a_y a_x^2 = (y_1 x_1^2 + y_2 x_2^2 + y_3 x_3^2) + 2m(y_1 x_2 x_3 -$

(b)

Consider the functions $F_a - v_a$ $(\alpha = 1, 2, \cdots$ According to the theorem a polynomial $P(v,$ analogous to those of $P(x:y_n)$, and $P(0, x:$ since the latter is unique.

The series of power series $P(F, x:y_n)$ may be of x, y, and it can readily be seen that its coeff those of $P(x:y_n)$. It must, however, be f not, a set of numerical coefficients could be sel which $P(F, x:y_n)$ would not be identically Weierstrass' theorem concerning the sum of an ir when the functions F and $P(v, x:y_n)$ are conv

(c)

I call this ineffective part of x_e *"innocuous"* validate the fundamental proposition

$$[f(x_e') \neq f(x_e')] = (x_e' \neq$$

which was proved above (P. 4) for effective valu ineffective part of x_e is innocuous is clear: it, *as* that the variation of x_e does not take place in it

D. 3. But this consideration leads to the *defin*: *of* x. By this I mean the collection of values wh i. e.,

(d)

six planes $y_i + y_k = 0$, each counted three tim type $y_1 y_2 - y_3 y_4 = 0$, each counted twice.

We have seen that any point on the line $y_1 +$ image in (X) the whole line $X_1 + X_2 = 0$, X_3 in (y) meets the line in one point, its image s_0' co the system s_0' has also the three lines of this typ

12. **Algebraic procedure.** The plane coi and the vertex $(1, 0, 0, 0)$ has the equation

$$p_{34} x_2 + p_{42} x_3 + p_{23} x_4 :$$

Since (y) and (y') both satisfy this equation we

FIGURE 1. Typographic styles in the *AMS Transactions*: (a) **1** (1900), 2; (b) **13** (1912), 138; (c) **23** (1922), 216; (d) **25** (1923), 10.

of points in the plane, what is the most pleasing curve that connects them? This question leads to interesting mathematics, and one solution based on a novel family of spline curves has produced excellent fonts of type in the author's preliminary experiments. We may conclude that a mathematical approach to the design of alphabets does not eliminate the artists who have been doing the job for so many years; on the contrary, it gives them an exciting new medium to work with.

Introduction

I will be speaking about work in progress, instead of completed research; that was not my original intention when I chose the subject of tonight's lecture, but the fact is I couldn't get my computer programs working in time. Fortunately, it is just as well that I don't have a finished product to describe to you right now, because research in mathematics is generally much more interesting while you're doing it than after it's done. I will try therefore to convey in this lecture why I am so excited about the project on which I am currently working.

My talk will be in two parts, based on two different meanings of its title. First I will speak about mathematical typography in the sense of typography as the servant of mathematics: The goal here is to communicate mathematics effectively by making it possible to publish mathematical papers and books of high quality, without excessive cost. Then I will speak about mathematical typography in the sense of mathematics as the servant of typography. In this case we will see that mathematical ideas can make advances in the art of printing.

Preliminary Examples

To set the stage for this discussion I would like to show you some examples by which you can "educate your eyes" to see mathematics as a printer might see it. These examples are taken from the *Transactions of the American Mathematical Society*, which began publication in 1900; by now over 230 volumes have been published. I took these volumes from the library shelves and divided them into equivalence classes based on what I could perceive to be different styles of printing: Two volumes were placed into the same class if and only if they appeared to be printed in the same style. It turns out that twelve different styles can be distinguished, and it will be helpful for us to look at them briefly.

The first example (Figure 1a) comes from page 2 of *Transactions* volume 1; I have shown only a small part of the page in order to encourage you to look at the individual letters and their positions rather than to read the mathematics. This typeface has an old-fashioned appearance, primarily because the uppercase letters and the taller lowercase ones like 'h' and 'k' are nearly twice as tall as the other lowercase letters, and this is rarely seen nowadays. Notice the style of the italic letter 'x', the two strokes having a common segment in the middle. The subscripts and superscripts are set in rather small type.

This style was used in volumes 1 to 12 of the *Transactions*, and also in the first 21 pages of volume 13. Then page 22 of volume 13 introduced a more up-to-date typeface (Figure 1b). In this example, the subscripts are still in a very small font, and unfortunately the Greek α here is almost indistinguishable from an italic 'a'. Notice also that the printer has inserted more space before and after parentheses than we are now accustomed to. During the next few years the spacing within formulas evolved gradually, but the typefaces remained essentially the same up through volume 24; with one exception.

The exception was volume 23 in 1922 (Figure 1c), which in my opinion has the most pleasing appearance of all the *Transactions* volumes. This typeface is less condensed, making it more pleasant to read. The italic letters have changed in style too, not quite so happily — note the 'x', for example, which is not as nice as before, and the lower part of

(e)

of systems of division algebras. The next syste
of order $p^q q^2$ over F with the basal units $i^a j^b k^c$ (
with an irreducible equation of degree pq, three
rational functions $\theta(i)$ and $\psi(i)$ with coefficie
iterative $\theta^q(i)$ of $\theta(i)$ is i, and likewise $\psi^p(i)=i$
by

$$\theta^k[\psi^r(i)]=\psi^r[\theta^k(i)] \qquad (k=0,1,\cdots,q-1$$

The complete multiplication table of the uni
associative law from

$$i^q=g\ ,\qquad k^p=\gamma\ ,\qquad kj=\alpha jk\ ,\qquad ji=$$

(f)

$$z = e^{i\theta} z^0 \equiv (e^{i\theta} z_1^0, ..., e^{i\theta} z_n^0), \qquad 0 \leqq \theta \leqq 2\pi,$$

$\subset C^n$ is called a Reinhardt circular set if along w
$\in E$ also the set

$$\{z \,|\, |z_k| = |z_k^0|, \qquad k = 1, 2, ..., n\}$$

bounded closed subset of C^n, unisolvent with respect
The function $b(z)$ being defined and lower semic

$$h^{(v)} = \{h_1^{(v)}, ..., h_v^{(v)}\}, \qquad v_0 = C_{v+n-1, n-1}$$

(g)

$$0 = r_k x(\textstyle\sum r_i\alpha_i) - (\textstyle\sum r_i\alpha_i) xr_k = \sum_{i=1}^{k-1}$$

This element is of lower length. It follows there
$i = 1, \cdots, k$. Hence, (a) yields that $r_i = \lambda_i r_k$, λ_i
Now $r_k \neq 0$, by the minimality of k, and $\sum \lambda_i$
which we deduce that $\sum \lambda_i \alpha_i = 0$. But the α_i a
which is impossible since in particular $\lambda_k = 1$.

THEOREM 7. *Let R be a dense ring of linear t.
F be a maximal commutative subfield D. If R_F
tion of finite rank over F, then R contains als*

(h)

The set N_1 is nowhere dense in Z_1 and thus $N=\rho$
For each $\zeta \in Y-N$ we must prove that f_ζ satisfi
be the unique projection in $\{P_d \,|\, d \in D\}$ such that
the algebra $(E\mathscr{A}E) \cdot P_0$ is finite and homogeneo
onal abelian projections $E_1, E_2, ..., E_n$ such that
$(1 \leqq j, k \leqq n)$ be partial isometric operators in $(E\mathscr{A}$

(1) $U_{jk}U_{lm} = \delta_{mj}U_{ik}$, where δ is the Kronecker d
(2) $U_{jk}^* = U_{kj}$; and
(3) $U_{jj} = E_j$,

for all $1 \leqq j, k, l, m \leqq n$. For each A in $(E\mathscr{A}E) \cdot P_0$, t
in $\mathscr{Z}_1 P_0$ such that

(i)

The algebra P is nearly simple if and only if the

(a) N *is spanned by* $a, \cdots, a^{n-k-1}, b_1, \cdots$
$i, j = 1, \cdots, k$.

(b) *Either* $n - k = $ char F *with k even or n*

Proof. By Theorem 5.5, there are elements a
$a, \cdots, a^{n-k-1}, b_1, \cdots, b_k$. Furthermore, $ab_i = $ (
for all i, j where each α_i, λ_{ij} is in F. From th
space of the space spanned by $a^{n-k-1}, b_1, \cdots$,

Assume P is nearly simple. Then there is a
show that each b_i is in M. To do this, it is nec

(j)

unctions in GL(W) and $h_{\alpha\beta}$, $\alpha, \beta \in I$ as coordinate
rmined by the respective bases chosen above. If α,
e function of $\wedge^p$ is the minor of $|g_{ij}|$ determined by
the columns $\beta(1), \ldots, \beta(p)$. The coordinate ring of
he $h_{\alpha\beta}$ together with $1/\det|h_{\alpha\beta}|$, while that of GL(W)
g_{ij}, so to show $\wedge^p$ is a morphism it suffices to show
nomial in g_{ij} and $1/\det|g_{ij}|$. For this, the following

l character of GL(W) is an integral power of the

(k)

of Q, i.e.

s) $= 0$ for every $x \in A$ for which $x(Q) = 0\}$.

for m_A is equivalent to the one induced by the

c:

$$\{|x(z)|: x \in A, \ \|x\| \leqslant 1 \ \text{and} \ x(w) = 0\}.$$

present the open unit disk in the complex plane, **C**,
t polydisk in n-dimensional complex space $\mathbf{C}^n$. T^n
oundary of D^n, i.e.

(l)

which X_i is the (last) minimum of Y^λ, let Y_i^λ, $i \geqslant$
of Y^λ, and T_i^λ the interjump times for Y^λ. So
i such that $Y_i^\lambda = T_i^\lambda = \infty$. Notice that Y_Q^λ is fini
t as $\varepsilon \to 0$, Y_Q^λ converges to $I^\lambda = \inf_s X_s^\lambda$. Let A,
$-\infty, \infty)$. Then, for example, if $i \geqslant 1$

$$B, Y_{Q+k}^\lambda - Y_Q^\lambda \in C, T_{Q+k}^\lambda \in D, N > Q > i\}$$

$$T_{l-i}^\lambda \in B, Y_{l+k}^\lambda - Y_l^\lambda \in C, T_{l+k}^\lambda \in D, N > Q = l$$

∞, a typical term in the summation of (3.5) may b

FIGURE 1 [CONTINUED]. Excerpts from *Transactions of the American
Mathematical Society*: (e) **28** (1926), 207; (f) **105** (1962), 340;
(g) **114** (1965), 216; (h) **125** (1966), 38; (i) **169** (1972), 232;
(j) **179** (1973), 314; (k) **199** (1974), 370; (l) **226** (1977), 372.

an 'f' tends to be broken off — but by and large the reader has a favorable impression when paging through this volume. Such quality was not without its cost, however. According to a contemporary report in the AMS *Bulletin* [46, page 100], the *Transactions* came out 18 months late at the time! Perhaps this is why the Society decided to seek yet another printer.

In order to appreciate the next change, let's look at two excerpts from the *Bulletin* relating to the very first Gibbs lecture (Figure 2). The preliminary announcement in 1923 appeared in the typeface of Figure 1b, but by the time the first lecture was reviewed in 1924 the letter shapes had become very cramped and stilted. The uppercase letters in the title remained roughly the same, but the lowercase letters in the text were completely different. We also notice excessive spaces between words, in many of the lines, while other lines are tightly spaced.

The same style appeared in volume 25 of the *Transactions* (Figure 1d), which incidentally was set in Germany in order to reduce the cost of printing. The boldface letters and the italic letters in this example are actually quite beautiful — and we're back to the good old style of 'x' again — so the mathematical formulas looked great while the accompanying text was crowded. Fortunately only three volumes were published in this style.

A new era for the *Transactions* began in 1926, when its printing was taken over by the Collegiate Press in Menasha, Wisconsin. Volumes 28 through 104 were all done in the same style (Figure 1e), covering 36 years from 1926 to 1961, inclusive, and this style was used also in the *American Mathematical Monthly*. In general the typefaces were quite satisfactory, but there was also a curious anomaly: The italic letters used in subscripts and superscripts of mathematical formulas were in a different style from those used on the main line! For example, notice the k's in the first displayed formula of Figure 1e: The largest one has a loop, so it is topologically different from the smaller ones. Similarly you can see that the p in k^p is quite different from the p in p^2. There are no x's in this example, but if you look at other pages you will find that my favorite kind of x appears only in subscripts and superscripts. I can't understand why this discrepancy was allowed to persist for so many years.

Another period of typographic turmoil for the *Transactions* began with volume 105 in 1962. This volume, which was typeset in Israel, introduced a switch to the Times Roman typeface (Figure 1f); an easy way to recognize the difference quickly is to look at the letter 'o', since its strokes now change thickness in a somewhat slanted fashion ('O' versus 'O'); in the previously used fonts this letter always had left-right symmetry, as

THE JOSIAH WILLARD GIBBS LECTURESHIP

The Council of the Society has sanctioned the establishment of an honorary lectureship to be known as the Josiah Willard Gibbs Lectureship. The lectures are to be of a popular nature on topics in mathematics or its applications, and are to be given by invitation under the auspices of the Society. They will be held annually or at such intervals as the Council may direct. It is expected that the first lecture will be delivered in New York City during the winter of 1923–24, and a committee has been authorized to inaugurate the lectures by choosing the first speaker and making the necessary arrangements.

R. G. D. RICHARDSON,

Secretary.

THE FIRST JOSIAH WILLARD GIBBS LECTURE

The first Josiah Willard Gibbs Lecture was delivered under the auspices of this Society on February 29, 1924, by Professor M. I. Pupin, of Columbia University, in the auditorium of the Engineering Societies' Building, New York City. A large and distinguished audience was present, including, besides members of the Society, many physicists, chemists, and engineers who had been invited to attend.

In introducing the speaker, President Veblen spoke as follows:

"In instituting the Willard Gibbs Lectures, the American Mathematical Society has recognized the dual character of mathematics. On the one hand, mathematics is one of the essential emanations of the human spirit,—a thing to be valued in and for itself, like art or poetry. Gibbs made notable contributions to this side of mathematics in his

FIGURE 2. A time of transition [from *Bulletin of the American Mathematical Society* **29** (1923), 385; **30** (1924), 289].

if it were drawn with a pen held horizontally, but in Times Roman it clearly has an oblique stress as if it were drawn by a right-handed scribe. Notice that the three k's are topologically the same in the second displayed equation here; but for some reason the two subscript k's are of different sizes. Many of the Times Italic letters have a somewhat different style than readers of the *Transactions* had been accustomed to, and I personally think that this font tends to make formulas look more crowded. The changeover to Times Roman and Times Italic wasn't actually complete; the italic letter 'g' still had its familiar shape, perhaps because the new shape looked too strange to mathematicians.

Volumes 105 through 124 were all done in this style, except for a brief interruption: In volumes 114, 115, and 116 the stress on the o's was left-right symmetrical and the k's had loops (Figure 1g). Another style was used for volumes 125–168 (Figure 1h): Again Times Roman and Times Italic were the rule, even in the g's, except for subscripts and superscripts (which were in the style that I prefer); for example, compare the j's and k's. These latter volumes were typeset in Great Britain.

A greatly increased volume of publications, together with the rising salaries of skilled personnel, was making it prohibitively expensive to use traditional methods of typesetting, and the Society eventually had to resort to a fancy form of typewriter composition that could simply be photographed for printing. This unfortunate circumstance made volumes 169–198 of the *Transactions* look like Figure 1i, except for volumes 179, 185, 189, 192, 194, and 198, which were done in a far better (yet not wholly satisfactory) style that can be distinguished from Figure 1f by the italic g's and the lack of ligatures like 'ffi'. Figure 1j was composed on a computer using a system developed by Lowell Hawkinson and Richard McQuillin; this was one of the fruits of an AMS research project supported by the National Science Foundation [2–6].

Computer typesetting of mathematics was still somewhat premature at the time, however, and another kind of "cold copy" made its appearance in volumes 199 through 224 — an "IBM Compositor" was used, except for volumes 208 and 211 which reverted to the Varityper style of Figure 1i. The new alphabet was rather cramped in appearance, and some words were even more crowded than the others (see Figure 1k). At this point I regretfully stopped submitting papers to the American Mathematical Society, since the finished product was just too painful for me to look at. Similar fluctuations of typographical quality have appeared recently in all technical fields, especially in physics where the situation has gotten even worse. (The history of publication at the

American Society of Civil Engineers has been discussed in an interesting and informative article by Paul A. Parisi [45].)

Fortunately things are now improving. Beginning with volume 225, which was published last year, the *Transactions* now looks like Figure 1l; like Figure 1j, it is computer composed, and the Times Roman typeface is now somewhat larger. I still don't care for this particular style of italic letters, and there are some bugs needing to be ironed out such as the overlap between lines shown in this example; but it is clear that the situation is getting better, and perhaps some day we will once again be able to approach the quality of volumes 23 and 24.

Computer-Assisted Composition

Perhaps the main reason that the situation is improving is the fact that computers are able to manipulate text and convert it into a form suitable for printing. Experimental systems of this kind have been in use since the early 1960s (see the book by Barnett [10]), and now they are beginning to come of age. Within another ten years or so, I expect that the typical office typewriter will be replaced by a television screen attached to a keyboard and to a small computer. It will be easy to make changes to a manuscript, to replace all occurrences of one phrase by another and so on, and to transmit the manuscript either to the television screen, or to a printing device, or to another computer. Such systems are already in use by most newspapers, and new experimental systems for business offices actually will display the text in a variety of fonts [26]. It won't be long before these machines change the traditional methods of manuscript preparation in universities and technical laboratories.

Mathematical typesetting adds an extra level of complication, of course. Printers refer to mathematics as "penalty copy," and one of America's foremost typographers T. L. De Vinne wrote [17, page 171] that "[even] under the most favorable conditions algebra will be troublesome." The problem used to be that two-dimensional formulas required complicated positioning of individual metal pieces of type; but now this problem reduces to a much simpler one, namely that two-dimensional formulas need to be represented as a one-dimensional sequence of instructions for transmission to the computer.

One-dimensional languages for mathematical formulas are now familiar in programming languages such as FORTRAN, but a somewhat different approach is needed when all of the complexities of typesetting are considered. In order to show you the flavor of languages for mathematical typesetting, I will briefly describe the three reasonably successful systems known to me. The first, which I will call Type C, is typical of the commercially available systems now used to typeset mathematical journals (see [12]). The second, which I will call Type B, was developed at Bell Laboratories and has been used to prepare several books and articles including the article that introduced the system [27]. The third, which I will call Type T, is the one I am presently developing as part of the system I call T_EX [29].[1]

Formula	Type C	Type B	Type T
$\dfrac{1}{2}$	\$f1\$s2\$t	1 over 2	1 \over 2
θ^2	*gq"2	theta sup 2	\theta↑2
$\sqrt{f(x_i)}$	\$rf(x'i)\$t	sqrt{f(x sub i)}	\sqrt{f(x↓i)}

FIGURE 3. Three ways to describe a formula.

Figure 3 shows how three simple formulas would be expressed in these three languages. The Type C language uses \$f...\$s...\$t for fractions, *g for "the next character is Greek," q for the Greek letter theta, \$r...\$t for square roots, " for superscripts, and ' for subscripts. The Type B language is more mnemonic, using over, theta, sup, sqrt, and sub together with braces for grouping when necessary. The Type T language is similar but it does not make use of reserved words; a special character \ is used before any nonstandard text. This means that spaces can be ignored, while they need to be inserted in just the right places in the Type B language; for example, the space after the 'i' is important in the example shown, otherwise '$f(x_i)$' would become '$f(x_{i})$' according to the Type B rules. Another reason for the \ in Type T is that the processor need not match every text item against a stored dictionary, and sup can be used to denote a supremum instead of a superscript. The special symbols \ { } ↑ ↓ in Type T can be changed to any other characters if desired; these five symbols don't appear on conventional typewriters, but they are common on computer terminal keyboards.

Incidentally, computer typesetting brings us some good news: We can now obtain square roots quite easily in the traditional manner with

---

[1] T_EX has no connection with a similarly-named system recently announced by Honeywell Information Systems, or with another one developed by Digital Research. In my language, the T, E, and X are Greek letters and T_EX is pronounced "tech," following the Greek words for art and technology.

radical signs and vincula; we won't have to write $x^{1/2}$ when we don't want to.[2]

None of these languages makes it possible to *read* complex formulas as easily as in the two-dimensional form, but experience shows that untrained personnel can learn how to type them without difficulty. According to [12], "Within a few hours (a few days at most) a typist with no math or typesetting background can be taught to input even the most complex equations." And the Type B authors [27] report that "the learning time is short. A few minutes gives the general flavor, and typing a page or two of a paper generally uncovers most of the misconceptions about how it works." Thus it will be feasible for both typists and mathematicians to prepare papers in such a language without investing a great deal of effort in learning the system. The only real difficulties arise when preparing tables that involve tricky alignments.

Once such systems become widespread, authors will be able to prepare their papers and see exactly how they will look when printed. All authors of mathematical papers know that their intentions are often misunderstood by the printer, and corrections to the galley proofs have a nontrivial probability of introducing further errors. Thus, in the words of three early users of the Bell Labs' system [1], "the moral seems clear. If you let others do your typesetting, then there will be errors beyond your control; if you do your own, then you have only yourself to blame." Personally, I can't adequately describe how wonderful it feels when I now make a change to the manuscript of my book, as it is stored in the Stanford computer, since I know that the change is immediately in effect; it never will go through any intermediaries who might misunderstand my intention.

Perhaps some day a typesetting language will become standardized to the point where papers can be submitted to the American Mathematical Society from computer to computer via telephone lines. Galley proofs will not be necessary, but referees and/or copy editors could send suggested changes to the author; the author could insert these into the manuscript, again via telephone.

Of course I am hoping that if any language becomes standard it will be my TEX language. Well ... perhaps I am biased, and I know that TEX provides only small refinements over what is available in other systems. Yet several dozen small refinements add up to something that is important to me, and I think such refinements might prove important

---

[2] (Added in proof.) I was pleased to find that this announcement was greeted with an enthusiastic round of applause when I delivered the lecture.

to other people as well. Therefore I'd like to spend the next few minutes explaining more about TeX.

The TeX Input Language

TeX must deal with "ordinary" text as well as mathematics, and it is designed to be a unified system in which the mathematical features blend in with the word-processing routines instead of being "tacked on" to a conventional typesetting language. The main idea of TeX is to construct what I call *boxes*. A character of type by itself is a box, as is a solid black rectangle; and we use such "atoms" to construct more complex boxes analogous to "molecules," by forming horizontal or vertical lists of boxes. The final pages of text are boxes made out of lists of boxes made out of lists of boxes, and so on down to the individual characters and black rectangles, which are not decomposed further. For example, a typical page of a book is a box formed from vertical lists of boxes representing lines of type, and these lines of type are boxes formed from a horizontal list of boxes representing individual letters. A mathematical formula breaks down into boxes in a natural way; for example, the numerator and denominator of a fraction are boxes, and so is the bar line between them (since it is a thin rectangle of solid black). The elements of a displayed matrix are boxes, and so on.

The individual boxes of a horizontal list or a vertical list are separated by a special kind of elastic mortar that I call *glue*. The glue between two boxes has three component parts (x, y, z) expressed in units of length:

   the *space* component, x, is the ideal or normal space desired between these boxes;

   the *stretch* component, y, is the amount of extra space that is tolerable;

   the *shrink* component, z, is the amount of space that may be removed if necessary.

Suppose the list contains $n + 1$ boxes B_0, B_1, ..., B_n separated by n globs of glue having specifications (x_1, y_1, z_1), ..., (x_n, y_n, z_n). When this list is made into a box, we *set the glue* according to the desired final size of the box. If the final size is supposed to be larger than we would obtain with the normal spacing $x_1 + \cdots + x_n$, we increase the space proportional to the y's so that the actual spacing between boxes is

$$x_1 + ty_1, \ \ldots, \ x_n + ty_n$$

for some appropriate $t > 0$. On the other hand if the desired final size must be smaller, we decrease the space to

$$x_1 - tz_1, \ldots, x_n - tz_n,$$

in proportion to the individual shrinkages z_i. In the latter case t is not allowed to become greater than 1; the glue will never be smaller than $x - z$, although it might occasionally become greater than $x + y$. Once the glue has been set, the box is rigid and never changes its size again.

Consider, for example, a normal line of text, which is a list of individual character boxes. The glue between letters of a word will have $x = y = z = 0$, say, meaning that this word always has the letters butting against each other; but the glue between words might have x equal to the width of the letter 'e', and $y = x$, $z = x/2$, meaning that the space between the words might expand or shrink. The spaces after punctuation marks like periods and commas might be allowed to stretch at a faster rate but constrained to shrink more slowly.

An important special case of this glue concept occurs when we have "infinite" stretchability. Suppose the x and z components are zero, but the y component is extremely large, say y is one mile long. If such an element of glue is placed at the left of a list of boxes, the effect will be to put essentially all of the expansion at the left; therefore the boxes will be right-justified so that their right edges will be flush with the margins. Similarly if we place such infinitely stretchable glue at both ends of the list, the effect will be to center the line. These common typographic operations therefore turn out to be simple special cases of the general idea of flexible glue, and the computer can do its job elegantly since it is dealing with comparatively few primitive operations. Incidentally you will notice from this example that glue is allowed to appear at the ends of a list, not just between boxes; in fact we might have glue next to glue, and boxes next to boxes, so that a list of boxes really is a list of boxes and glue mixed in any fashion whatever. I didn't mention this before, because for some reason it seems easier to explain the idea first in the case when boxes alternate with glue.

The same principles apply to vertical lists. For example, the glue that appears above and below a displayed equation will tend to be stretchable and shrinkable, but the glue between lines of text will be calculated so that adjacent base lines will be uniformly spaced when possible. You can imagine how the concept of glue allows you to do special tricks like backspacing (by letting x be negative), in a natural manner.

Line Division

One of the more interesting things a system like TEX has to do is to break a paragraph into individual lines so that each line is about the right length. The traditional way to do this, which is still used on today's computer typesetting systems, is to make the best possible line division you can whenever you come to the right margin, but once this line has been output you never reconsider it; you start the next line with no memory of what has come before. Actually you could often do better by moving a short word down from one line to the next, but the problem is that you don't know what the rest of the paragraph will be like when you have only looked at one line's worth.

The TEX system will introduce a new approach to the problem of line division, in which the end of a paragraph *does* influence the way the first lines are broken; this will result in more even spacing and fewer hyphenated words. Here is how it works: First we convert the task of line breaking to a precisely-defined mathematical problem by using TEX's glue to introduce the concept of "badness." When a horizontal list of boxes has a certain natural width w (based on the width of its boxes and the space components of its glue), together with a certain stretchability y (the sum of the stretch components) and a certain shrinkability z (the sum of the shrinkages), the badness of setting the glue to make a box of width W is defined to be $1 + 100t^3$ in our previous notation; more precisely it is

$$
\begin{aligned}
&1, && \text{if } W = w, \\
&1 + 100\left(\frac{W - w}{y}\right)^3, && \text{if } W > w, \\
&1 + 100\left(\frac{w - W}{z}\right)^3, && \text{if } w - z \leq W < w, \\
&\text{infinite}, && \text{if } W < w - z.
\end{aligned}
$$

Thus if the desired width W is near the natural width w, or if there is a lot of stretchability and shrinkability, the badness rating is very small; but if W is much greater than w and there isn't much ability to stretch, we have a bad situation. Furthermore we add *penalty points* to the badness rating if the line ends at a comparatively undesirable place; for example, when a word needs to be hyphenated, the badness goes up by 50, and an even worse penalty is paid if we have to break up a mathematical formula.

The line division problem may now be stated as follows. "Given the text of a paragraph and the set of all allowable places to break it between lines, find breakpoints that minimize the sum of the squares of the badnesses of the resulting lines." This definition is quite arbitrary, of course, but it seems to work. Preliminary experiments show that the same choice of breakpoints is almost always found when simply minimizing the sum of the individual badnesses rather than the sum of their squares, but it seems wise to minimize the sum of squares as a precautionary measure since this will also tend to minimize the maximum badness.

Just stating the line division problem in mathematical terms doesn't solve it, of course; we need to have a good way to find the desired breakpoints. If there are n permissible places to break (including all spaces between words and all possible hyphenations), there are 2^n possible ways to divide up the paragraph, and we would never have time to look at them all. Fortunately there is a technique that can be used to reduce the number of computational steps to order n^2 instead of 2^n; this is a special case of what Richard Bellman calls "dynamic programming." Let $f(j)$ be the minimum sum of badness squares for all ways to divide the initial text of the paragraph up to breakpoint j, including a break at j, and let $b(i,j)$ be the badness of a line that runs from breakpoint i to breakpoint j. Let breakpoint 0 denote the beginning of the paragraph; and let breakpoint $n+1$ be the end of the paragraph, with infinitely expandable glue inserted just before this final breakpoint. Then

$$f(0) = 0\,;$$
$$f(j) = \min_{0 \le i < j} \left(f(i) + b(i,j)^2\right)\,, \text{ for } 1 \le j \le n+1\,.$$

The computation of $f(1)$, ..., $f(n+1)$ can be done in order n^2 steps, and $f(n+1)$ will be the minimum possible sum of badnesses squared. By remembering the values of i at which the minimum occurred for each j, we can find breakpoints that give best line divisions, as desired.

In practice we need not test extremely unlikely breakpoints; for example, there is rarely any reason to hyphenate the very first word of a paragraph. Thus it turns out that this dynamic programming method can be improved further to an algorithm whose running time is almost always of order n instead of n^2, and comparatively few hyphenations will need to be tried. Incidentally, the problem of hyphenation itself leads to some interesting mathematical questions, but I don't have time to discuss them at present. (See [42] and the references in that paper.)

The idea of badness ratings applies in the vertical dimension as well as in the horizontal; in this case we want to avoid breaking columns or pages in a bad manner. For example, penalty points are given for splitting a paragraph between pages after a hyphenation, or for dividing it in such a way that only one of its lines — a so-called "widow" line — appears on a page. The placement of illustrations, tables, and footnotes is also facilitated by formulating appropriate rules of placement in terms of badness.

There is more to TₑX, including for example some facilities for handling the rather intricate layouts often needed to typeset tables without having to calculate column widths; but I think I have described the most important principles of its organization. During the next few months I plan to write the computer programs for TₑX in such a way that each algorithm is clearly explained and so that the system can be implemented on many different computers without great difficulty; then I intend to publish the programs in a book so that everyone who wants to use them can do so.

Entr'acte

I said at the beginning that this talk would be in two parts, discussing both the ways that typography can help mathematics and the ways that mathematics can help typography. So far we have seen a little of both, but the mathematics has been comparatively trivial. In the remainder of my lecture I would like to discuss what I believe is a much more significant application of mathematics to typography, namely to the specification of the letter shapes themselves. A more accurate way to describe the two parts of my lecture would be to say that the first part was about TₑX, a system that takes manuscripts and converts them into specifications about where to put each character on each page; and the second part will be about another system I'm working on called META-FONT, which generates the characters themselves, for use in the inkier parts of the printing business.

Before I get into the second part of my lecture I need to discuss recent developments in printing technology. The most reliable way to print mathematics books of high quality during the past several decades has been to use the monotype[3] process, which casts characters in hot lead, together with hand operations for complex built-up formulas. When I watched this process being applied to my own books several years ago,

---

[3] Actually the Monotype Corporation now manufactures digital photosetting equipment as well as the traditional Monotype metal-casting machines.

I was surprised to learn that the lead type was used to print only *one* copy; this master copy was then photographed, and the real printing took place from the photographic plates. This somewhat awkward sequence of steps was justified because it was the best way known to give good results. During the 1960s, however, hot lead type was replaced for many purposes by devices like the Photon machine used to prepare the printed programs for tonight's lecture; in this case the process is entirely photographical, since the letter shapes are stored as small negatives on a rotating disk, and the plates needed for printing are obtained by exposing the film after transforming the characters into the proper size and position with mirrors and lenses (see [10]). Such machines are limited by slow speed and the difficulties of adding new characters.

"Third-Generation" Typesetting Equipment

More recent machines, such as the one used to prepare the current volumes of the *Transactions*, have replaced these analog processes by a digital one. The new idea is to divide the page or the photographic negative into millions of tiny rectangles, like a piece of graph paper or like a television screen, but with a much higher resolution of about 1000 units per inch. For each of the tiny "pixels" in such a raster pattern — there are about a million square pixels in every square inch — the typesetting machine decides whether it is to be black or white, and the black ones are exposed on the photographic plate by using a very precisely controlled electron beam or laser beam. Since these machines have few moving parts and require little or no mechanical motion, they can operate at very high speeds even though they are exposing only a tiny bit of the film at any time.

Stating this another way, the new printing equipment essentially treats each page of a book as a huge matrix of 0s and 1s, with ink to be placed in the positions that are 1 while the 0 positions are to be left blank. It's like the flashcards at a football stadium, although on a much grander scale. The total job of a system like TEX now becomes one of converting an author's manuscript into a gigantic bit matrix.

The first question we must ask, of course, is, "What happens to the quality?" Clearly a television picture is no match for a photograph, and the digital typesetting machines would be quite unsatisfactory if their output looked inferior to the results obtained with metal type. In matters like this, I have to confess being somewhat of a stickler and a perfectionist; for example, I refuse to eat margarine instead of butter, and I have never heard an electronic organ that sounds even remotely as beautiful as a pipe organ. Therefore I was quite skeptical about digital typography, until I saw an actual sample of what was done on a high quality machine and held it under a magnifying glass: It was impossible to tell that the letters were generated with a discrete raster! The reason for this is not that our eyes can't distinguish more than 1000 points per inch; in appropriate circumstances they can. The reason is that particles of *ink* can't distinguish such fine details — you can't print the edge of an ink line that zigzags 1000 times on the diagonal of a square inch, because the ink will round off the edges. In fact the critical number seems to be more like 500 than 1000. Thus the physical properties of ink cause the pages to appear as if there were no raster at all.

It now seems clear that discrete raster-based printing devices will soon make the other machines obsolete for nearly all publishing activity. Thus in future days the fact that Gutenberg and others invented movable type will not be especially relevant; it will merely be a curious footnote to history, which influenced the printing industry for only 500 years or so. The ultimately relevant thing will be mathematics: the mathematics of matrices of 0s and 1s!

Semiphilosophical Remarks

I have to tell the next part of the story from my personal point of view. As a combinatorial mathematician, I really identify with matrices of 0s and 1s, so when I learned last spring about such printing machines it was impossible for me to continue what I was doing; I just had to take time off to explore the possibilities of the new equipment. My motivation was also increased by the degradation of quality I had been observing in technical journals. Furthermore, the publishers of my books on computer programming had tried valiantly but unsuccessfully to produce the second edition of Volume 2 in the style of the first edition, without using the rapidly-disappearing hot lead process. It appeared that my books would soon have to look as bad as the journals! When I saw that these problems could all be solved by appropriate computer programming, I couldn't resist trying to find a solution by myself.

One of the most important factors in my motivation was the knowledge that the problem would be solved once and for all, if I could find a purely mathematical way to define the letter shapes and to construct the corresponding raster patterns. Even though new printing methods are bound to be devised in the future, possibly even before I finish Volume 7 of the books I'm writing, any new machines are almost certain to be based on a high precision raster; and although the precision of the raster may change, the letter shapes can stay the same forever, once they are defined in a machine-independent form. My goal was therefore to give a precise description of the shapes of all the symbols I would need.

I looked at the way fonts of type are being digitized at several places in different parts of the world; it is basically done by taking existing fonts and copying them using sophisticated camera equipment and computer programs, together with manual editing. But this seemed instinctively wrong to me, partly because the sophisticated equipment wasn't readily available in our laboratory at Stanford, and partly because the copying of copyrighted fonts is of questionable legality, but mostly because I felt that the whole idea of making a copy was not penetrating to the heart of the problem. It reminded me of the anecdote I had once heard about slide rules in Japan. According to this story, the first slide rule ever brought to the Orient had a black speck of dirt on it; so for many years all Japanese slide rules had a useless black spot in this same position! The story is probably apocryphal, but the point is that we should copy the substance rather than the form. I felt that the right question to ask would not be "How should this font of type be copied?" but rather: "If the great type designers of the past were alive today, how would they design fonts for the new equipment?" I didn't expect to be capable of finding the exact answer to this question, of course, but I did feel that it would lead me in the right direction, so I began to read about the history of type design.

Well, this is a most fascinating subject, but I can't talk much about it in a limited time. Two of the first things I read were autobiographical notes by two well-known 20th century type designers, Hermann Zapf [51] and Frederic W. Goudy [20], and I was especially interested by some of Zapf's remarks:

> With the beginning of the 'sixties ... I was stimulated by this new field [photocomposing] .... The type-designer — or better, let us start calling him the alphabet designer — will have to see his task and his responsibilities more than before in the coordination of the tradition in the development of letterforms with the practical purpose and the needs of the advanced equipment of today .... The new photocomposing systems using cathode-ray tubes (CRT) or digital storage for the alphabet bring with them some absolutely new technical problems, many more than did the past. [51, page 71]

I have the impression that Goudy would not have been so sympathetic to the new-fangled equipment, yet his book also gave helpful ideas.

Mathematical Type Design

Fortunately the Stanford Library has a wonderful collection of books about printing, and I had the chance to read many rather rare source materials. I learned to my surprise that the idea of defining letters mathematically is by no means new; it goes back to the fifteenth century and it became rather highly developed in the early part of the sixteenth. This was the time when there were Renaissance men who combined mathematics with the real world, and one of the prominent ideas was to use a ruler and compass to construct capital letters. The first person to do this was apparently Felice Feliciano, about 1460, whose handwritten manuscript in the Vatican Library was published 500 years later [19]. Feliciano was an excellent designer who wanted to put the principles of letterforms on a sound mathematical foundation; his designs were used by contemporary stonecutters in Verona. Several other fifteen-century authors made similar experiments — [8] gives a critical summary of these early developments — but the most notable work of this kind appeared early in the sixteenth century.

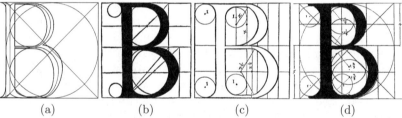

(a)   (b)   (c)   (d)

FIGURE 4. Renaissance ruler-and-compass constructions for the letter B, by (a) Feliciano [19], (b) Pacioli [43], (c) Torniello [34], and (d) Palatino [44].

The Italian mathematician Luca Pacioli, who had previously written the most influential book on algebra at the time (one of the first algebra books ever published), included an appendix on alphabets in his *Divina Proportione*, a book about geometry and the "golden section," which appeared in 1509. Another notable Italian work on the subject was published by Francesco Torniello in 1517 [34]; Figure 4 illustrates the letter B as constructed by Feliciano, Pacioli, and Torniello, and also by Giovanbattista Palatino [44]. Palatino was one of the best calligraphers of the century, and he did this work between 1540 and 1580. Similar constructions appeared in Germany and France. The German book was probably the most famous and influential: It was Albrecht Dürer's *Underweysung der Messung* [18], a manual of instruction in geometry for Renaissance painters. The French book was also rather popular; it was *Champ Fleury* by Geofroy Tory [49], the first royal printer of France and the man who introduced accented letters into French typography. Figure 5 shows Tory's two suggestions for the letter B. Of all these books I much prefer Torniello's, since he was the only one who stated the constructions clearly and unambiguously.

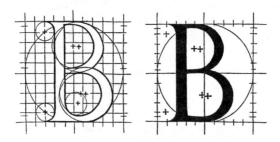

FIGURE 5. Two more B's, by Tory [49].

Apparently nobody carried this work further to lowercase letters or to numerals, or to italic letters and other symbols, until more than 100 years later when Joseph Moxon made a detailed study of some beautiful letters designed in Holland [39]. The ultimate in refinement of this mathematical approach took place shortly afterwards when Louis XIV of France commissioned the creation of a Royal Alphabet. A group of artists and typographers worked on Louis's project for more than ten years, beginning about 1690, and they made elaborate constructions such as those shown in Figure 6 [24].

Thus it is clear that the mathematical definition of letter forms has a long history. However, I must also report near-universal agreement among today's scholars of typography that those efforts were a failure. At worst, the ruler-and-compass letters have been called "ugly," and at best they are said to be "deprived of calligraphic grace" [8]. The French designs were not followed faithfully by Phillipe Grandjean, who actually cut Louis XIV's type, nor by anybody else to date; and F. W. Goudy's reaction to this was: "God be praised!" [20, page 139]. Such strictly geometric letter forms were in fact criticized already in the sixteenth century by Giovanni Cresci, a noted scribe at the Vatican Library and the Sistine Chapel. Here is what Cresci wrote in 1560:

I have come to the conclusion that if Euclid, the prince of geometry, returned to this world of ours, he would never find that

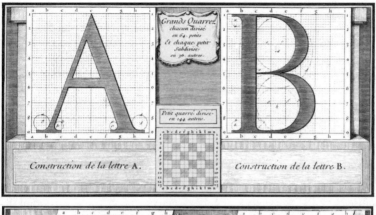

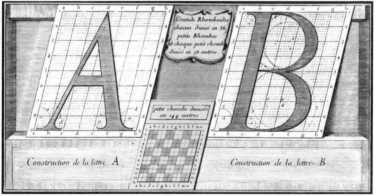

FIGURE 6. Roman and italic letters designed for Louis XIV of France [24].

the curves of the letters could be so constructed by means of circles made with compasses. [16]

Well, Cresci was right. But fortunately there have been a few advances in mathematics during the last 400 years, and we now have some other tricks up our sleeves besides straight lines and circles. In fact, it is now possible to prescribe formulas that match the nuances of the best type designers; and perhaps a talented designer working with appropriate mathematical tools will be able to produce something even better than we now have.

Defining New Curves

Let's consider the following mathematical problem: Given n points $z_1, z_2, \ldots, z_n$ in the plane, what is the most pleasing closed curve that goes through them in the specified order z_1, z_2, ..., z_n and then returns to z_1? To avoid degenerate situations we may assume that n is at least 4. This problem is essentially like the dot-to-dot puzzles that we give to young children.

Of course it is not a well-posed mathematical problem, since I didn't say what it means for a curve to be "most pleasing." Let's first postulate some axioms that the most pleasing curve should satisfy.

PROPERTY 1 (INVARIANCE). If the given points are rotated, translated, or expanded, the most pleasing curve will be rotated, translated, or expanded in the same way. [In symbols: $\text{MPC}(az_1 + b, \ldots, az_n + b) = a\text{MPC}(z_1, \ldots, z_n) + b$.]

PROPERTY 2 (SYMMETRY). Cyclic permutation of the given points does not change the solution. [Thus we have $\text{MPC}(z_1, z_2, \ldots, z_n) = \text{MPC}(z_2, \ldots, z_n, z_1)$.]

PROPERTY 3 (EXTENSIONALITY). Adding a new point that is already on the most pleasing curve does not change the solution. [If z is any point between z_k and z_{k+1} on $\text{MPC}(z_1, \ldots, z_n)$ then we have $\text{MPC}(z_1, \ldots, z_k, z, z_{k+1}, \ldots, z_n) = \text{MPC}(z_1, \ldots, z_k, z_{k+1}, \ldots, z_n)$.]

These properties are rather easy to justify on intuitive grounds. For example, the extensionality property says that additional information won't lead to a poorer solution.

The next property is not so immediately apparent, but I believe it is important for the application I have in mind.

PROPERTY 4 (LOCALITY). Each segment of the most pleasing curve between two of the given points depends only on those points and the ones immediately preceding and following. [$\text{MPC}(z_1, z_2, \ldots, z_n)$ is composed of $\text{MPC}(z_n, z_1, z_2, z_3)$ from z_1 to z_2, then $\text{MPC}(z_1, z_2, z_3, z_4)$ from z_2 to z_3, ..., then $\text{MPC}(z_{n-1}, z_n, z_1, z_2)$ from z_n to z_1.]

According to the locality property, changes to one part of a pattern won't affect the other parts. This simplifies our search for the most pleasing curve, because we need only solve the problem in the case of four given points; and experience shows that locality also simplifies the letter design process greatly, since individual portions of strokes can be dealt with one at a time. Incidentally, Property 4 implies Property 2 (cyclic symmetry).

One way to satisfy all four of these properties is simply to let the most pleasing curve consist of straight line segments. But polygons aren't adequately pleasing, so we postulate

PROPERTY 5 (SMOOTHNESS). There are no sharp corners in the most pleasing curve. [MPC$(z_1, \ldots, z_n)$ is differentiable, under some parameterization.]

In other words, there is a unique tangent at every point of the curve.

The extensionality, locality, and smoothness properties taken together imply, in fact, that *the direction of the tangent at z_k depends only on z_{k-1}, z_k, and z_{k+1}.* For this tangent appears in two curves, the one from z_{k-1} to z_k and the one from z_k to z_{k+1}, hence we know that it depends only on $(z_{k-2}, z_{k-1}, z_k, z_{k+1})$ and that it depends only on $(z_{k-1}, z_k, z_{k+1}, z_{k+2})$. By the extensionality property, we can assume that n is at least 5; hence z_{k-2} is different from z_{k+2} and the tangent must be independent of them both. We have actually used only a very weak form of extensionality in this argument.

If we apply the full strength of the extensionality postulate, we obtain a much stronger consequence, which is quite unfortunate: *There is no good way to satisfy Properties 1–5!* For example, suppose we add one more axiom, which is almost necessary in any reasonable definition of pleasing curves:

PROPERTY 6 (ROUNDNESS). If z_1, z_2, z_3, z_4 are consecutive points of a circle, the most pleasing curve through them is that circle.

This property together with our previous observation about the tangent depending only on three points completely determines the tangent at each of our given points; namely, the tangent at z_k is the tangent to the circle that passes through z_{k-1}, z_k, and z_{k+1}. (Let's ignore for the moment the possibility that these three points lie on a straight line.) Now the extensionality property says that if z is any point between z_1 and z_2 on the most pleasing curve for $z_1, \ldots, z_n$, we know the tangent direction at z, as long as z is not on the line from z_1 to z_2. But there is a unique curve starting at any z off this line and having the specified tangents at each of its points, namely the arc of the circle from z to z_2 passing through z_1. No matter where we start, off the straight line, we are able to draw only one curve having the correct tangents. It follows that the tangent at z_2 depends only on z_1, z_2, and the tangent at z_1, and this is impossible.

The argument in the previous paragraph proves that there is no way to satisfy Properties 3, 4, 5, and 6. A similar argument would show the impossibility for any reasonable replacements for Property 6, since the tangents determined for all z between z_1 and z_2 will define a vector field in which there are unique curves through essentially all of the points z, yet a two-parameter family of curves is required between z_1 and z_2 in order to allow sufficient flexibility in the derivatives there.

So we have to give up one of these properties. The locality property is the most suspicious one, but I mentioned before that I didn't want to give it up; therefore the extensionality property has to go. This means that if we take the most pleasing curve through $z_1, \ldots, z_n$ and if we specify a further point z actually on this curve between z_k and z_{k+1}, then the "most pleasing" curve through these $n + 1$ points might be different. A possible virtue is that we are encouraged not to specify too many points; a possible drawback is that we may not be able to get the curves we want.

A Practical Approximation

Returning to the question of type design, our goal is to specify a few points z_k and to have a mathematical formula that defines a pleasant curve through these points; such curves will be used to define the shape of the character we are designing. Ideally it should also be easy to compute the curves. I decided to use cubic equations

$$z(t) = \alpha_0 + \alpha_1 t + \alpha_2 t^2 + \alpha_3 t^3$$

where α_0, α_1, α_2, α_3 are complex numbers and t is a real parameter. The curves I am dealing with are *cubic splines*, namely piecewise cubic equations, since a different cubic will be used in each interval between two of the given points; however, the way I am determining the coefficients of these cubics is different from any of the methods known to me, in my limited experience with the vast literature about splines. Perhaps my way to choose the coefficients is more awkward than the usual ones; but I have obtained good results with it, so I'm not ashamed to reveal the curious way I proceeded.

In the first place, I decided that the cubic equation between z_1 and z_2 should be determined completely by z_1 and z_2 and the direction of the tangents at z_1 and z_2. We have already seen that these tangents are essentially predetermined if Properties 4, 5, and 6 are to be valid, and I have also found frequent occasion in type design when it was desirable to specify that a certain tangent was to be made horizontal or vertical. Thus, my method of computing a nice curve through a given sequence of points is first to compute the tangent directions at each point, then to compute the cubics in each interval based solely on the endpoints of that interval and on the desired tangents there. By rotation and translation and scaling, according to Property 1, we can assume that the problem is to go in the complex plane from 0 to 1, with given directions at the endpoints. The most general cubic equation that does this is

$$z(t) = 3t^2 - 2t^3 + re^{i\theta}t(1-t)^2 - se^{-i\varphi}t^2(1-t),$$

and it remains to determine positive numbers r and s as appropriate functions of θ and φ.

In the second place, I realized that it was impossible to satisfy Property 6 with cubic splines, because you can't draw a circle as a cubic function of t. But I wanted to be able to get curves that were as near to being circles as possible, whenever four consecutive data points lay on a circle; the curves should preferably be indistinguishable from circles as far as the human eye is concerned. Therefore when $\theta = \varphi$ I decided to choose $r = s$ in such a way that $z(\frac{1}{2})$ was precisely on the relevant circle, hoping that the curve between 0 and $\frac{1}{2}$ and between $\frac{1}{2}$ and 1 wouldn't veer too far away. Well, this turned out to work extremely well: A little calculation, done with the help of a computer,[4] showed that the maximum deviation from a true circle occurs at the point $t = (3 \pm \sqrt{3})/6$, and the relative error is negligibly small. For example, if we take four points equally spaced at distance 1 from some center, the spline curve defined by these points in the stated manner stays between distance 1 and distance

$$\sqrt{(71/6 - \sqrt{8})/3} < 1.000273$$

from the center, an error of less than one part in 3500; and if there are n points, the maximum error goes to zero as $1/n^6$.

(Changing the notation slightly, let

$$z(t) = 1 + (e^{i\theta} - 1)(3t^2 - 2t^3)$$
$$+ 4it(1-t)(1 - t - e^{i\theta}t)\left(\sin\frac{\theta}{2}\right) \bigg/ \left(1 + \cos\frac{\theta}{2}\right)$$

and $f(t) = |z(t)|^2$. Then

$$f'(t) = 8\left(\frac{1 - \cos\dfrac{\theta}{2}}{1 + \cos\dfrac{\theta}{2}}\sin\frac{\theta}{2}\right)^2 (t-1)\,t\,(2t-1)\,(6t^2 - 6t + 1)$$

---

[4] Thanks are due to the developers of the computer algebra system called MACSYMA at M.I.T., and to the ARPA network, which makes this system available for research work.

and

$$\max_{0\le t\le 1} |z(t)| = \left| z\!\left(\frac{3-\sqrt{3}}{6} \right) \right| = 1 + \frac{\theta^6}{55296} + \frac{\theta^{10}}{106168320} + \cdots,$$

while $\min_{0\le t\le 1} |z(t)| = z(0) = z(\frac{1}{2}) = z(1) = 1$. The "two-point circle" has $\max |z(t)| = \sqrt{28/27} \approx 1.01835$, while the three-point circle has $\max |z(t)| \approx \sqrt{325/324} = 1.001542$, and the eight-point circle has $\max |z(t)| \approx 1.0000042455$. These nearly circular parametric cubic splines were introduced by J. R. Manning [33], who observed that they are visually indistinguishable from true circles.)

Another case when a natural way to choose r and s suggests itself is when $\theta + \varphi = 90°$; then the curve $z(t)$ should be nearly the same as an ellipse having the endpoints on its axes. (This boils down to requiring that $(3t^2 - 2t^3 - (s/\cos\varphi)t^2(1-t) - 1)^2 + (3t^2 - 2t^3 + (r/\cos\theta)t(1-t)^2)^2$ be approximately equal to 1.) So far therefore I knew that I wanted

$$r = \frac{2}{1+\cos\theta}, \qquad s = \frac{2}{1+\cos\varphi} \qquad \text{when } \theta = \varphi;$$

$$r = \frac{2\cos\theta}{(1+\cos 45°)\cos 45°}, \quad s = \frac{2\cos\varphi}{(1+\cos 45°)\cos 45°} \qquad \text{when } \theta+\varphi = 90°.$$

I tried the formulas

$$r = \frac{2\cos\theta}{(1+\cos\psi)\cos\psi}, \quad s = \frac{2\cos\varphi}{(1+\cos\psi)\cos\psi},$$

which fit both cases, where $\psi = (\theta + \varphi)/2$. But this didn't give satisfactory results, especially when ψ approached 90°. My second attempt was

$$r = \left| \frac{2\sin\varphi}{(1+\cos\psi)\sin\psi} \right|, \quad s = \left| \frac{2\sin\theta}{(1+\cos\psi)\sin\psi} \right|$$

and this has worked very well. Figure 7 shows the spline curves that result from such an approach when $\varphi = 60°$ and when θ varies from 0° to 120° in 5° steps.

One can prove that if θ and φ are nonnegative and less than 180°, the cubic curve $z(t)$ I have defined will never cross the straight lines at angles θ and φ that meet the endpoints 0 and 1, respectively. This is a valuable property in type design, since it can be used to guarantee that the curve won't get out of bounds. However, I found that it also led to unsatisfactory curves when one of θ or φ was very small and the other

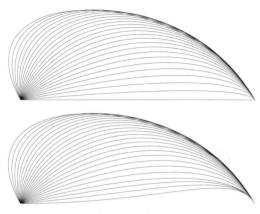

FIGURE 7.

Spline curves with
$\theta = 0° \, (5°) \, 120°$
and $\varphi = 60°$.

FIGURE 8.

Like Figure 7, but
adjusted so that
$r' = \max(1/2, r)$ and
$s' = \max(1/2, s)$.

was not, since this meant that the curve $z(t)$ would be very close to a straight line yet it would veer towards that line from the outside at a rather sharp angle. In fact, the angle θ is not infrequently zero, and this forces a straight line and a sharp corner at the right endpoint. Therefore I changed the formulas by making sure that both r and s are always $\frac{1}{2}$ or greater unless special exceptions are made; furthermore I never let r or s exceed 4. Figure 8 shows the spline curves obtained under the same conditions as Figure 7, but with r and/or s set to $\frac{1}{2}$ if the formula calls for any smaller value.

Using these techniques we obtain a system for drawing reasonably nice curves, if not the most pleasing ones, and it is especially good at circles. If the method gives the wrong tangent direction at some point, you can control this by specifying two points very close together having the desired slope. I have also included another way to modify the standard tangent directions, intended to make the system as good at drawing ellipses as it is at drawing circles: Before computing the splines I first shrink the entire figure in the vertical direction by multiplying all the y coordinates by a given aspect ratio (normally 1); then the splines are calculated, and the resulting shrunken curves are stretched out again by dividing the y coordinates by the aspect ratio.

Application to Type Design

Now let's take a closer look at what can be drawn with a mathematical system like this. I suppose the natural thing to show you would be the letters A to Z; but since this is a mathematical talk, let's consider the digits 0 to 9 instead. (See Figure 9.) Incidentally, the way I have arranged these numerals illustrates a fundamental distinction between a

0123456789

FIGURE 9. Digits 0 to 9 drawn by the prototype METAFONT programs.

mathematician and a printer: The mathematician puts 0 next to the 1, but the printer always puts it next to the 9.

Most of these digits are drawn by using another idea taken from the history of typography, namely to imitate the calligrapher who uses pen and ink. Consider first the numeral '3', for example. The computer program that drew this symbol in Figure 9 can be paraphrased as follows: "First draw a dot whose left boundary is $\frac{1}{6}$ of the way from the left edge to the right edge of the type and whose bottom boundary is $\frac{3}{4}$ of the way from the top to the bottom of the desired final shape. Then take a hairline pen and, starting at the left of the dot, draw the upward arc of an ellipse; after reaching the top, the pen begins to grow in width, and it proceeds downward in another ellipse in such a way that the maximum width occurs on the axis of the ellipse, with the right edge of the pen $\frac{8}{9}$ of the way from the left edge to the right edge of the type. Then the pen width begins to decrease to its original size again as the pen traverses another ellipse taking it down to a position 48% of the way from the top to the bottom of the desired final shape ...."

Notice that instead of describing the boundary of the character, as the Renaissance geometers did, my METAFONT system describes the curve traveled by the *center* of the *pen*, and the pen's shape is allowed to vary as the pen moves. The main advantage of this approach is that the same definition readily yields a family of infinitely many fonts of type, each font being internally consistent. The change in pen size is governed by cubic splines in a manner analogous to the motion of the pen's center. In order to define the 20 or so different fonts of type used in various places in my books, I need for the most part to use only three kinds of pens, namely (i) a circular pen used for example to draw dots and at the base of the number '7'; (ii) a horizontal pen, whose shape is an ellipse, the width being variable but the height being constantly equal to the height of a hairline pen; (iii) a vertical pen, analogous to the horizontal one, used for example to draw the strokes at the bottom of the '2' and at the top of the '5' and the '7'. The horizontal pen is used most of the time, and in particular it draws all of the numeral '3' except for the dots. For the fonts I require, I did not need to use an oblique pen (namely, an ellipse that is tilted on its side) except to make the tilde accent for a Spanish ñ; but to produce fonts of type analogous to Times Roman, an oblique pen would of course be used. If this system were to be extended to Chinese and Japanese characters, I believe it would be best to add another degree of freedom to the pen's motion, allowing an elliptical pen shape to rotate as well as to change its width.

The digit '4' shows another aspect of the METAFONT system. Although this character is fairly simple, consisting entirely of straight lines, notice that the thick line has to be cut off at an angle at the top. In order to do this, METAFONT has *erasers* as well as pens. First the computer draws a thick line all the way from top to bottom, like the uppercase letter 'I'; then it takes an eraser that erases everything to its left and comes down the diagonal stroke; then it takes a hairline pen and finishes the diagonal stroke. Such an eraser is used also at the top of the '1' and the bottom of the '2', etc.

Sometimes a simple spline seems to be inadequate to describe the proper growth of pen width, so in a few cases I had to resort to describing the left and right edges of the pen as separate curves, to be filled in afterwards. This occurs for example in the main stroke of the numeral '2', whose edges are defined by two splines having a specified tangent at the bottom and having vertical slope at the right of the curve.

ØABCDEFGHIJKLMN
OPQRSTUVWXYZ["]–—
'abcdefghijklmno
pqrstuvwxyzﬀﬁﬂﬃﬄ   æﬂﬁœÆﬂﬁŒ
0123456789:;<=>?   ˋ´ˆˇ˘-"˝¯˜˚
!"çÇ%&'()*+,-./ ΓΔΘΛΞΠΣΥΦΩ ıȷ

FIGURE 10. A font of 128 characters defined by METAFONT with pen settings for 5-point type. (The accent characters will be appropriately raised and centered over other letters when used by TEX.)

With these techniques I found that it was possible to define a decent-looking complete font, containing a total of 128 characters, in about two months, although I certainly will need to do fine tuning when more trial pages are typeset. (See Figure 10.) The most difficult symbol by far, at least for me, was the letter S (and the numeral 8, which uses the same procedure); in fact I spent three days and nights without sleep, trying to make the S look right, before I got it. At one point I even felt it would be easier to rewrite all my books without using any S's! After the first

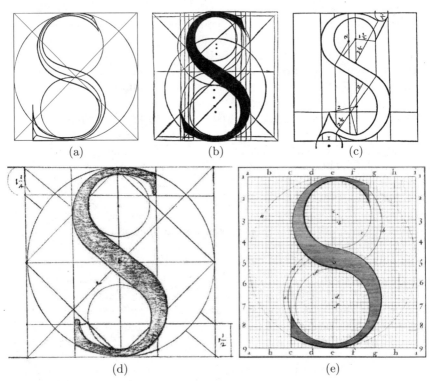

FIGURE 11. The letter S as defined by (a) Feliciano [19]; (b) Pacioli [43];
(c) Torniello [34]; (d) Palatino [44]; (e) French commission under Jaugeon [24].

day of discouraging trials, I showed what I had to my wife, and she said,
"Why don't you make it S-shaped?"

Figure 11 shows how this problem was solved by Feliciano, Pacioli,
Torniello, Palatino, and the French academicians; but the letter doesn't
look like a modern S. Furthermore I think the engraver of the French S
cheated a little in rounding off some lines near the middle — perhaps
he used a French curve. With my wife's assistance, I finally came up
with a satisfactory solution, somewhat like those used in the sixteenth
century but generalized to ellipses. Each boundary of each arc of my S
curve is composed of an ellipse and a straight line, determined by (i) the
locations of the beginning and ending points, (ii) the slope of the straight
line, and (iii) the desired left extremity of the curve. It took me three
hours to derive the necessary formulas, and I think Newton and Leibniz
would have enjoyed working on this problem. Figure 12 shows various

FIGURE 12. Different S's obtained by varying the slope in the middle, showing 1/2, 2/3, 3/4, 1, 4/3, 3/2, and 2 times the "correct" slope.

trial S's drawn by this scheme with different slopes; I hope you prefer the middle one, since it is the one I am actually using.

Families of Fonts

To extend the METAFONT system, one essentially writes a computer program for the description of each character, in a special language designed to describe pen and eraser strokes. My colleague R. W. Gosper has observed that we thereby obtain the exact opposite of Sesame Street: Instead of "This program was brought to you by the letter S," we have "This letter S was brought to you by a program." The program has about 20 parameters, telling how big a hairline pen is, how wide it should be when drawing straight or curved stem lines, and specifying the sizes and proportions of various parts of the letters (the x-height, the heights of ascenders and descenders, the M-width, the length of serifs, and so forth). By changing these parameters, we obtain infinitely many different styles of type, yet all of them are related and they seem to blend harmoniously with each other.

For example, Figure 13 shows some of the possibilities. In Figure 13a we have a conventional "modern" font in the tradition of Bodoni and Bell and Scotch Roman. Then Figure 13b shows a corresponding bold-face, in which the hairlines are slightly larger and the stem lines are substantially wider. By making the hairlines and stem lines both the same size and setting the serif length to zero, we obtain a sans-serif font as shown in Figure 13c. All of these examples are produced with the same programs defining the letter shapes; only the parameters are being varied. Actually the particular font shown in Figure 13c will have a different style of g (namely 'ɡ'), because the descenders are especially short in this font, but I have shown this 'g' in order to illustrate the parametric variations. Figure 13d shows a boldface sans-serif style in which the pen has an oval shape, wider than it is tall. I find this style especially pleasing, particularly because it came out by accident—I designed the programs only so that two or three different fonts would look

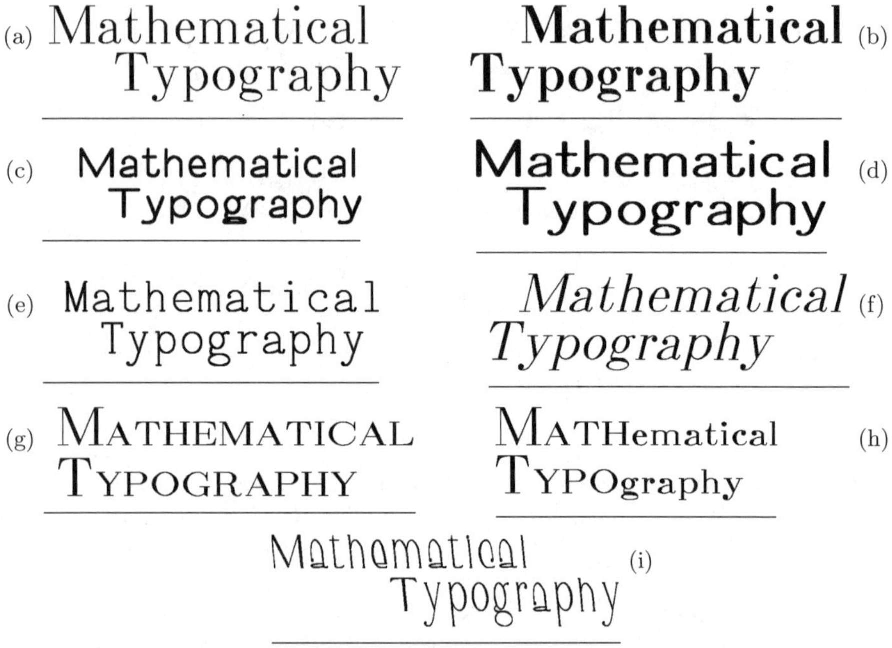

(a) Mathematical
Typography

Mathematical (b)
Typography

(c) Mathematical
Typography

Mathematical (d)
Typography

(e) Mathematical
Typography

Mathematical (f)
Typography

(g) MATHEMATICAL
TYPOGRAPHY

MATHematical (h)
TYPOgraphy

Mathematical (i)
Typography

FIGURE 13. Different styles of type obtained by varying the parameters
to METAFONT: (a) Computer modern roman; (b) Computer modern bold; (c) Computer modern sans-serif; (d) Computer modern
sans-serif bold; (e) Computer modern typewriter; (f) Computer modern slanted roman; (g) Computer modern roman with small caps;
(h) Computer modern roman with small caps and "small lowercase";
(i) Computer modern funny.

right, hence all the others are free bonuses; I had no idea that this one
would be so nice.

With a suitable setting of the parameters, we can even imitate a
typewriter with its fixed width letters, as shown in Figure 13e. There
is also a provision to slant the letters as in Figure 13f; here the pen
position is varied, but the actual shape of the pen is not being slanted,
so circular dots remain circles.

Another setting of the parameters leads to caps and small caps as
shown in Figure 13g; small caps are drawn with the pens and heights
ordinarily used for lowercase letters, but controlled by the programs for
uppercase letters. Figure 13h shows something printers have never seen
before: This is what happens when you draw lowercase letters in the
small caps style, and we might call it "small lowercase." It actually

turns out to be one of the most pleasing fonts of all, except that the dots are too large.

Finally, Figure 13i illustrates the variations you can get by giving weirder settings to the parameters.

When I was an assistant professor at Caltech, the math department secretaries would occasionally send "crank" visitors to my office, and I recall one time when a man came to ask if anybody had calculated the value of π "out to the end" yet. I tried to explain to him that π had been proved irrational, but this didn't seem to sink in. Finally I showed him a listing of π to 100,000 decimals and told him that the expansion hadn't ended yet. I wish I could have had my typographical system ready at that time, so that I could have shown him Figure 14!

$$3.1415926535897932384...$$

FIGURE 14. Variation in height, width, and pen size.

Figure 14 illustrates another principle of type design, namely that different sizes of type in the same style are not simply obtained from each other by optical transformations. The heights and widths and pen stroke sizes change at different rates, and a good typographer will design each size of type individually. I'm not claiming that Figure 14 shows the best way for the proportions to vary; further experimentation will be necessary before I have a good idea of what is desirable. The point I wish to make is that the alteration of type sizes for subscripts and so on is not as simple as it might seem at first, but a system like METAFONT will be able to vary the parameters quite readily, and visual experiments on different parameter settings can be carried out quickly. Type designers used to need months to make their drawings and have them converted to metal molds before they could see any proofs. One of the results was that there simply wasn't time to give proper attention to all the mathematical symbols and Greek letters, etc., as well as to the more common symbols, so a printer of mathematics had to make do with a hodge-podge of available characters in different sizes. (For example, printers were often obliged to use different styles of letters in subscript positions, as we have seen.) Under the approach I am recommending, we automatically get consistency of all the symbols whenever the parameters change.

From Continuous to Discrete

The METAFONT system must not only define the characters in the continuum on the plane, it must also express them in terms of a discrete

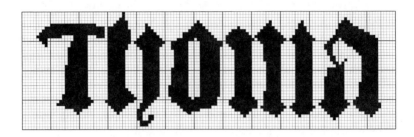

FIGURE 15. Lettering equivalent to this raster pattern appears in a Norwegian tapestry from Gildeskaal old church, woven about 1500 [22, page 116].

raster. Such squaring off of letters on graph paper has a long history, going back far before the invention of computers or television; for example, we all can remember seeing cross-stitch embroidery samplers from the nineteenth century. The same idea on a finer scale has been used in tapestries for many centuries: My wife pointed out that our library at home contains the example of Figure 15, which was woven in the northern part of Norway about 1500; it shows the name of St. Thomas in a style imitating contemporary calligraphy, and I'm sure that examples antedating the printing press can be found elsewhere.

Figure 16 shows how METAFONT produces the same letters from the same parameters but with different degrees of resolution in the raster. This digitization process itself is considerably more difficult than it may seem at first, and some nontrivial mathematical concepts were needed before I could produce satisfactory results. The obvious approach is merely to draw or to imagine drawing the character with infinite precision and then to "round" it by blacking in all the squares on graph paper that are sufficiently dark in the true image; but this fails badly.

One of the reasons for failure is that the three stem lines of an 'm', for instance, might be located in different relative positions with respect to the grid, so that the first stroke might round to three units wide (say) and the second might round to four. This would be quite unsatisfactory, since our eyes easily pick up such a variation in thickness; but it is avoided by METAFONT since the pen itself is first digitized and then the same digitized pen is used for all three strokes. Another problem is that the three stem strokes should be equally spaced; an 'm' looks bad if it has, say, seven units between the first two strokes and eight units between the last two. Therefore its program needs to round the points in such a way that this doesn't happen.

The m's are okay in Figure 16, but several unresolved problems are still evident, and I'll have to work on these when I get back home. The middle example suffers from the fact that the curve width rounded up to 2 from a value slightly greater than 1.5, while the stem width rounded down to 1 from a value that was only slightly less. Therefore the curves of the 'a', 'e', and 'c' are significantly darker than they should be. A similar effect has made the dots too dark in the fourth example. The tail at the lower right of the 'a' should be removed in the fifth example, but at such low resolutions no automatic method is likely to be really satisfactory.

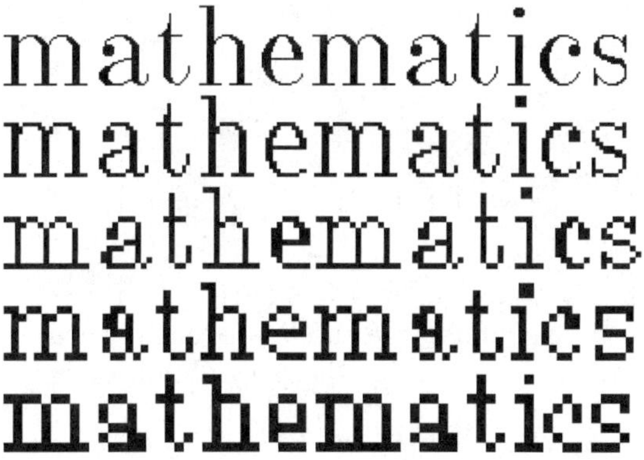

FIGURE 16.

The problem of adjusting letters to coarser rasters. (Here the resolutions are respectively 120, 60, 40, 30, and 24 pixels per inch.)

The process of digitizing the pen is not trivial either. Suppose, for example, we want a circular pen that is 2 raster units wide; the appropriate pen is clearly a 2×2 square, which is the closest to a circle that we can come at this low degree of resolution. But notice that we can't *center* a 2×2 square on any particular square of a raster, since none of the four squares is at its center; the same problem arises whenever we have to deal with a pen having even dimensions. One way to resolve this would be to insist on working only with odd numbers, but this would be far too limiting; so METAFONT uses a special rounding rule for the position of the pen's center. In general, suppose the pen is an ellipse of integer width w and integer height h; then if the pen is to be positioned at the real coordinates (x, y), its actual position on the discrete grid is taken to be

$$(\lfloor x - \delta(w) \rfloor, \lfloor y - \delta(h) \rfloor)$$

where $\lfloor x \rfloor$ denotes the greatest integer less than or equal to x, and $\delta(\text{even}) = \frac{1}{2}$, $\delta(\text{odd}) = 0$. The pen itself, if positioned at the origin,

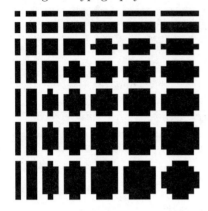

FIGURE 17.
Discrete "elliptical" pens
of small integer
width and height.

would consist of all integer pairs (x, y) that satisfy

$$\left(\frac{2(x - \delta(w))}{w}\right)^2 + \left(\frac{2(y - \delta(h))}{h}\right)^2 \leq 1 + \max\left(\frac{2\delta(w)}{w}, \frac{2\delta(h)}{h}\right)^2 .$$

This formula — which incidentally is not the first one I tried — ensures that the discrete pen will indeed be w units wide and h units high, when w and h are positive integers. Figure 17 shows the pens obtained for small w and h.

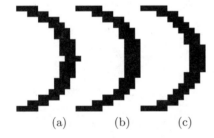

(a)   (b)   (c)

FIGURE 18.
Difficulties of rounding
an arc properly. (Three
semicircles of radius 10,
drawn with a 1 × 3 pen.)

Still another problem appears when we want curved lines to look reasonable after they've become discrete. Figure 18a shows a semicircle of radius 10 units, drawn with a pen of height 1 and width 3, when the right boundary of the pen falls exactly at an integer point; the pen sticks out terribly in one place. On the other hand if this right boundary falls just shy of an integer point, we get the curve in Figure 18b, which looks too flat. The ideal occurs in Figure 18c, when the right boundary occurs exactly midway between integers. Therefore, the METAFONT programs adjust the location of curves to the raster before actually drawing the curves, forcing the favorable situation of Figure 18c; the actual shape of each letter changes slightly in order to adapt that letter to the desired raster size in a pleasant way.

There is yet another problem, which arises when the pen is growing in such a way that the edges of the curve it traces would be monotonic if the pen were drawn to infinite precision, yet the independent rounding of pen location and pen width causes this monotonicity to disappear. The problem arises only rarely, but when it does happen the eye immediately notices it. Consider, for example, the completely linear situation in Figure 19, where each decrease by one unit in y is accompanied by an increase of .3 units in x and an increase of .2 units in the pen width w; the intended pen height is constant and very small, but in the discrete case the pen height is taken to be 1. The lightly shaded portion of Figure 19 shows the true shape intended, but the darker squares show that the digitized form yields a nonmonotonic left boundary. METAFONT compensates for this sort of problem by keeping track of the desired boundaries when the pen width is varying, plotting points twice (for example, plotting both (x, y) and $(x - 1, y)$) when necessary to keep the boundary correct. In other words, the idea of rounding the pen location and the width independently is sometimes effectively abandoned.

Pen width and location	Rounded width and location
(3.5, 0.5, 10.5)	(3, 0, 10)
(3.7, 0.8, 9.5)	(3, 0, 9)
(3.9, 1.1, 8.5)	(3, 1, 8)
(4.1, 1.4, 7.5)	(4, 0, 7)
(4.3, 1.7, 6.5)	(4, 1, 6)
(4.5, 2.0, 5.5)	(4, 1, 5)
(4.7, 2.3, 4.5)	(4, 1, 4)
(4.9, 2.6, 3.5)	(4, 2, 3)
(5.1, 2.9, 2.5)	(5, 2, 2)
(5.3, 3.2, 1.5)	(5, 3, 1)
(5.5, 3.5, 0.5)	(5, 3, 0)

FIGURE 19. Failure of monotonicity due to independent rounding. $\Big($Rounding takes (w, x, y) into $(\lfloor w \rfloor, \lfloor x - \delta(\lfloor w \rfloor) \rfloor, \lfloor y \rfloor).\Big)$

The final digitization problem that I needed to resolve was to make the left half of an '0' look like the mirror image of its right half, to make a left parenthesis look like the mirror image of a right parenthesis, and so on. This was done by having the METAFONT programs in such cases choose a center point that was either exactly at an integer or an

integer plus $\frac{1}{2}$, and to introduce a dual rounding rule that has exactly
the correct symmetry properties.

Alternative Approaches

As I have said, I believe the METAFONT system is successful as a way to
define letters and other symbols, but probably even better procedures
can be devised with further research. Some of the limitations of my cubic
splines are indicated in Figure 20. Part (a) of that illustration shows a
five-pointed star and the word "mathematics" in an approximation to my
own handwriting, done with straight line segments so that you can see
exactly what data points were fed to my spline routine. Part (b) shows
the way my handwriting might look when I get older; it was obtained
by simply setting $r = s = 2$ in all the spline segments, therefore making
clear what tangent angles are prescribed by the system. Part (c) is
somewhat more disciplined; it was obtained by putting $r = s = 1/2$
everywhere. Figure 20d is like Figure 20c but drawn with a combined
pen-and-eraser. Such a combination can lead to interesting effects, and
the star here is my belated contribution to America's bicentennial.

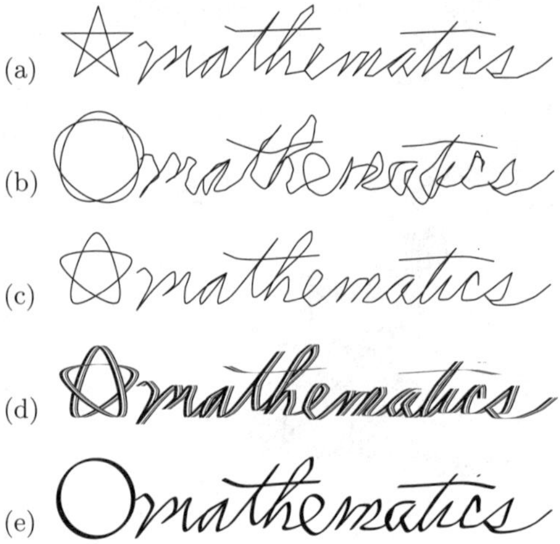

(a)

(b)

(c)

(d)

(e)

FIGURE 20.
Examples of the cubic
splines applied to
sloppy handwriting.

When the general formulas for the parameters r and s are used as
explained above, we get Figure 20e, in which the star has become a very
good approximation to a circle (as I said it would). In this illustration the
pen is thicker and has a slightly oblique stress. Although my handwriting
is inherently unbeautiful, there are still some kinks in Figure 20e that
could probably be ironed out if a different approach were taken.

The most interesting alternative from a mathematical standpoint seems to be to find a curve of given length that minimizes the integral of the square of the curvature with respect to arc length. This integral is proportional to the strain energy in a mechanical spline of the given length (in other words, the energy in a thin slat or beam), going through the given points, so it seems to be an appropriate quantity to minimize; Michael A. Malcolm [32] has reviewed early work on this variational problem. The Norwegian mathematician Even Mehlum [37] has shown that if we specify a fixed arc length between consecutive points, the optimum curve will have linearly changing curvature of the form $ax+by+c$ at point (x, y), and he has suggested choosing the constants by taking $b/a = (y_2 - y_1)/(x_2 - x_1)$ between (x_1, y_1) and (x_2, y_2), and requiring that slope and curvature be continuous across endpoints. Such an approach seems to require considerably more computation than the cubic splines recommended here, but it may lead to better curves, perhaps satisfying the extensionality property.

Another interesting approach to curve-drawing, which may be especially useful for simulating handwriting, is a "filtering" method suggested to me recently by Michael S. Paterson of the University of Warwick (unpublished). To get a smooth curve passing through points z_k, assuming that these points are about equally spaced on the desired curve and that $z_k = z_{n+k}$ for all integers k, one simply writes

$$z(t) = \sum_k (-1)^k z_k f(t - k) \Big/ \sum_k (-1)^k f(t - k)$$

where $f(t)$ is an odd function of order t^{-1} as $t \to 0$, decreasing rapidly away from zero; for example, we can take

$$f(t) = \operatorname{csch} t = 2/(e^t - e^{-t}).$$

I have not had time yet to experiment with Paterson's method or to attempt to harness it for the drawing of letters. It is easy to see that the derivative $z'(k) = f(1)(z_{k+1} - z_{k-1}) - f(2)(z_{k+2} - z_{k-2}) + \cdots$ lies approximately in the direction of $z_{k+1} - z_{k-1}$.

Randomization

In conclusion, I'd like to report on a little experiment that I did with random numbers. One might complain that the letters I have designed are too perfect, too much like a computer, so they lack "character." In order to counteract this, we can build a certain amount of randomness

into the choices of where to put the pen when drawing each letter, and
Figure 21 shows what happens. The coordinates of key pen positions
were chosen independently with a normal distribution and with increasing standard deviation, so that the third example has twice as much
standard deviation as the second, the fourth has three times as much,
and so on. Notice that the two m's on each line (except the first) are
different, and so are the a's and the t's, since each letter is randomly
drawn.

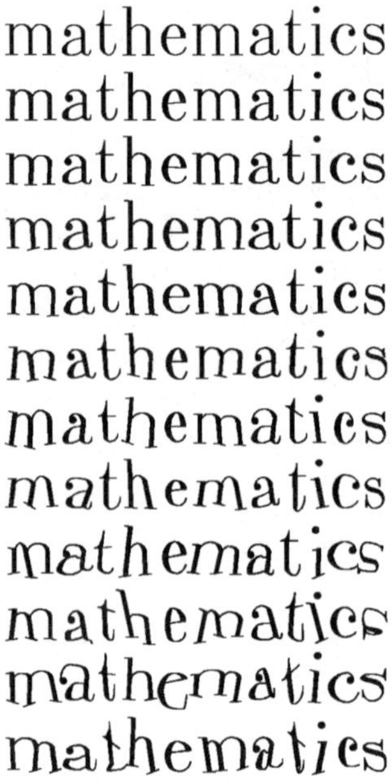

mathematics
mathematics
mathematics
mathematics
mathematics
mathematics
mathematics
mathematics
mathematics
mathematics
mathematics
mathematics

FIGURE 21.
Increasingly random pen
positions; $\sigma = 0, 1, \ldots$.

After the deviation gets sufficiently large the results become quite
ludicrous; and I don't want people to say that I ended this lecture by
making a travesty of mathematics. So let us conclude by looking at
Figure 22, which shows what is obtained in various fonts when the degree of randomness is somewhat controlled. I think it can be said that
the letters in this final example have warmth and charm, in spite of
the fact that they were really generated by a computer following strict
mathematical rules. Perhaps the reason that the printing of mathematics looked so nice in the good old days was that the fonts of type were
imperfect and inconsistent.

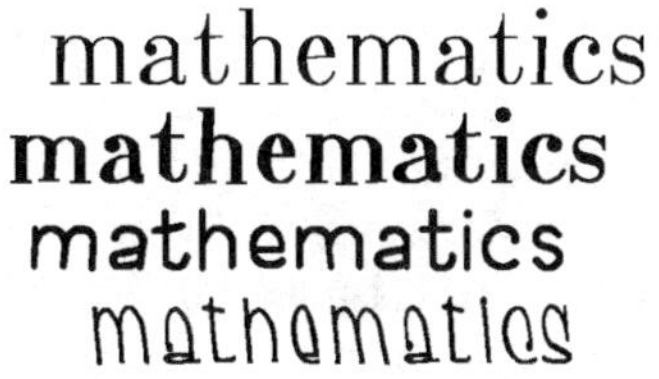

mathematics
mathematics
mathematics
ｍｏｔｈｏｍｏｔｌｏｓ

FIGURE 22.
A bit of randomness
introduced into
various styles of type.

Summary

I'd like to summarize now by pointing out the moral of this long story. My experiences during the last few months vividly illustrate the fact that plenty of good mathematical problems are still waiting to be solved, almost everywhere we look, especially in areas of life where mathematics has rarely been applied before. Mathematicians can provide solutions to these problems, receiving a double payoff—namely the pleasure of working out the mathematics, together with the appreciation of the people who can use the solutions. So let's go forth and apply mathematics in new ways.

Acknowledgments

I would like to thank my wife Jill for the many important suggestions she made to me during critical stages of this research; also Leo Guibas and Lyle Ramshaw for the help they provided in making illustrations at Xerox Palo Alto Research Center; also Lester Earnest, Michael Fischer, Frank Liang, Tom Lyche, Albert Meyer, Michael Paterson, Michael Plass, Bob Sproull, Jean E. Taylor, and Hans Wolf, for helpful ideas and stimulating discussions and correspondence about this topic; also Gordon L. Walker, for verifying my conjectures about the printing history of the *Transactions* and for providing me with additional background information; also Professor Dirk Siefkes for his help in acquiring Figures 4c and 11c, and the Kunstbibliothek Berlin der Staatlichen Museen Preußischer Kulturbesitz for permission to publish them; and to André Jammes for permission to publish Figures 6 and 11d.

Bibliography

The references below include several articles not mentioned in the main text, namely a discussion of publishing at the American Institute of Physics [38]; some experiments in typesetting physics journals with the Bell Labs system [7, 31]; computer aids for technical magazine layout and editing, together with a brief proposal for a standard typesetting language [11]; reports about early computer programs for character generation and mathematical composition [23, 30, 35, 36, 41, 47]; a description of the mathematics a traditional printer needs to know [9]; three standard references on the typesetting of mathematics [14, 48, 50]; some fonts of type and special characters designed by the American Mathematical Society [40]; a recent and highly significant approach to mathematical definition of traditional typefaces based on conic sections and on one-dimensional splines [15]; a proposal for a new way to control the spacing between letters based on somewhat mathematical principles [28]; and two purely mathematical papers inspired by typography [13, 21].

This research was supported in part by National Science Foundation grant MCS72-03752 A03, and by the Office of Naval Research contract N00014-76-C-0330.

References

[1] A. V. Aho, S. C. Johnson, and J. D. Ullman, "Typesetting by ACM considered harmful," *Communications of the ACM* **18** (1975), 740.

[2] American Mathematical Society, *Development of the Photon for Efficient Mathematical Composition*, Final Report (10 May 1965), National Science Foundation Grant G–21913; NTIS No. PB168627.

[3] American Mathematical Society, *Development of Computer Aids for Tape-Control of Photocomposing Machines*, Report No. 2 (July 1967), "Extension of the system of preparing a computer-processed tape to include the setting of multiple line equations," National Science Foundation Grant GN–533; NTIS No. PB175939.

[4] American Mathematical Society, *Development of Computer Aids for Tape-Control of Photocomposing Machines*, Final Report, Section B (August 1968), "A system for computer-processed tape composition to include the setting of multiple line equations," National Science Foundation Grant GN–533; NTIS No. PB179418.

[5] American Mathematical Society, *Development of Computer Aids for Tape-Control of Photocomposing Machines*, Final Report, Section C (January 1969), "Implementation, hardware, and other systems," National Science Foundation Grant GN–533; NTIS No. PB182088.

[6] American Mathematical Society, *To Complete the Study of Computer Aids for Tape-Control of Composing Machines by Developing an Operating System*, Final Report No. AMATHS-CAIDS-71-0

(April 1971), National Science Foundation Grant GN–690; NTIS No. PB200892.

[7] American Physical Society, "APS tests computer system for publishing operations," *Physics Today* **30**, 12 (December 1977), 75.

[8] Donald M. Anderson, "Cresci and his capital alphabets," *Visible Language* **4** (1971), 331–352.

[9] J. Woodard Auble, *Arithmetic for Printers*, 2nd edition (Peoria, Illinois: Bennett, 1954).

[10] Michael P. Barnett, *Computer Typesetting: Experiments and Prospects* (Cambridge, Massachusetts: M.I.T. Press, 1965).

[11] Robert W. Bemer and A. Richard Shriver, "Integrating computer text processing with photocomposition," *IEEE Transactions on Professional Communication* **PC-16** (1973), 92–96. This article is reprinted with another typeface and page layout in Robert W. Bemer, "The role of a computer in the publication of a primary journal," *Proceedings of the AFIPS National Computing Conference* **42**, Part II (1973), M16–M20.

[12] Peter J. Boehm, "Software and hardware considerations for a technical typesetting system," *IEEE Transactions on Professional Communication* **PC-19** (1976), 15–19.

[13] J. A. Bondy, "The 'graph theory' of the Greek alphabet," in *Graph Theory and Applications*, edited by Y. Alavi et al. (Berlin: Springer Verlag, 1972), 43–54.

[14] T. W. Chaundy, P. R. Barrett, and Charles Batey, *The Printing of Mathematics* (Oxford: Oxford University Press, 1954).

[15] P. J. M. Coueignoux, *Generation of Roman Printed Fonts*, Ph.D. thesis, Dept. of Electrical Engineering, Massachusetts Institute of Technology (June 1975).

[16] Giovanni Francesco Cresci Milanese, *Essemplare de Piv Sorti Lettere* (Rome: 1560). Also edited and translated by Arthur Sidney Osley (London: 1968).

[17] T. L. De Vinne, *The Practice of Typography: Modern Methods of Book Composition* (New York: Oswald, 1914).

[18] Albrecht Dürer, *Underweysung der Messung mit dem Zirckel und Richtscheyt* (Nuremberg: 1525). An English translation of the section on alphabets has been published as Albrecht Dürer, *Of the Shaping of Letters*, translated by R. T. Nichol (Dover, 1965).

[19] Felice Feliciano Veronese, *Alphabetum Romanum*, edited by Giovanni Mardersteig and translated by R. H. Boothroyd (Verona: Officina Bodoni, 1960).

[20] Frederic W. Goudy, *Typologia: Studies in Type Design & Type Making with Comments on the Invention of Typography, the First Types, Legibility & Fine Printing* (Berkeley, California: University of California Press, 1940).

[21] F. Harary, "Typographs," *Visible Language* **7** (1973), 199–208.

[22] Roar Hauglid, Randi Asker, Helen Engelstad, and Gunvor Trætteberg, *Native Art of Norway* (Oslo: Dreyer, 1965).

[23] A. V. Hershey, "Calligraphy for computers," NWL Report No. 2101 (Dahlgren, Virginia: U.S. Naval Weapons Laboratory, August 1967); NTIS No. AD662398.

[24] André Jammes, *La Réforme de la Typographie Royale sous Louis XIV* (Paris: Paul Jammes, 1961).

[25] Paul E. Justus, "There is more to typesetting than setting type," *IEEE Transactions on Professional Communication* **PC-15** (1972), 13–16, 18.

[26] Alan C. Kay, "Microelectronics and the personal computer," *Scientific American* **237**, 3 (September 1977), 230–244.

[27] Brian W. Kernighan and Lorinda L. Cherry, "A system for typesetting mathematics," *Communications of the ACM* **18** (1975), 151–157.

[28] David Kindersley, *Optical Letter Spacing for New Printing Systems* (London: Wynkyn de Worde Society, 1976).

[29] Donald E. Knuth, "Tau Epsilon Chi, a system for technical text," Stanford Computer Science Report CS675 (September 1978). Revised version, TEX, *A System for Technical Text* (Providence, Rhode Island: American Mathematical Society, 1979); also published as part 2 of TEX and METAFONT: *New Directions in Typesetting* (Bedford, Massachusetts: Digital Press, 1979).

[30] Dorothy K. Korbuly, "A new approach to coding displayed mathematics for photocomposition," *IEEE Transactions on Professional Communication* **PC-18** (1975), 283–287.

[31] M. E. Lesk and B. W. Kernighan, "Computer typesetting of technical journals on UNIX," Computer Science Technical Report 44 (Murray Hill, New Jersey: Bell Laboratories, June 1976).

[32] Michael A. Malcolm, "On the computation of nonlinear spline functions," *SIAM Journal on Numerical Analysis* **14** (1977), 254–282.

[33] J. R. Manning, "Continuity conditions for spline curves," *The Computer Journal* **17** (1974), 181–186.

[34] Giovanni Mardersteig, *The Alphabet of Francesco Torniello da Novara [1517] Followed by a Comparison with the Alphabet of Fra Luca Pacioli* (Verona: Officina Bodoni, 1971).

[35] M. V. Mathews and Joan E. Miller, "Computer editing, typesetting, and image generation," *Proceedings of the AFIPS Fall Joint Computer Conference* **27** (1965), 389–398.

[36] M. V. Mathews, Carol Lochbaum, and Judith A. Moss, "Three fonts of computer drawn letters," *Communications of the ACM* **10** (1967), 627–630.

[37] Even Mehlum, "Nonlinear splines," in *Computer Aided Geometric Design*, edited by Robert E. Barnhill and Richard F. Riesenfeld (New York: Academic Press, 1974), 173–207.

[38] A. W. Kenneth Metzner, "Multiple use and other benefits of computerized publishing," *IEEE Transactions on Professional Communication* **PC-18** (1975), 274–278.

[39] Joseph Moxon, *Regulæ Trium Ordinum Literarum Typographicarum: or the Rules of the Three Orders of Print Letters: viz. The {Roman, Italick, English} Capitals and Small. Shewing how they are compounded of Geometrick Figures, and mostly made by Rule and Compass* (London: Joseph Moxon, 1676).

[40] Phoebe J. Murdock, "New alphabets and symbols for typesetting mathematics," *Scholarly Publishing* **8** (1976), 44–53. Reprinted in *Notices of the American Mathematical Society* **24** (1977), 63–67.

[41] Nicholas Negroponte, "Raster scan approaches to computer graphics," *Computers and Graphics* **2** (1977), 179–193.

[42] Wolfgang A. Ocker, "A program to hyphenate English words," *IEEE Transactions on Engineering Writing and Speech* **EWS-14** (1971), 53–59.

[43] Luca Pacioli, *Diuina proportione, Opera a tutti glingegni perspicaci e curiosi necessaria Oue ciascun studioso di Philosophia: Propectiua Pictura Sculptura: Architectura: Musica: e altre Mathematice: suauissima: sottile: e admirable doctrina consequira: e delectarassi: cõ uarie questione de secretissima scientia* (Venice: 1509).

[44] Giovanbattista Palatino Cittadino Romano, *Libro Primo del le Lettere Maiuscole Antiche Romane* (unpublished), Berlin Kunstbibliothek, MS OS5280. Some of the individual pages are dated 1543, 1546, 1549, 1574, or 1575. See James Wardrop, "Civis Romanus Sum: Giovanbattista Palatino and his circle," *Signature* **14** (1952), 3–39.

[45] Paul A. Parisi, "Composition innovations of the American Society of Civil Engineers," *IEEE Transactions on Professional Communication* **PC-18** (1975), 244–273.

[46] R. G. D. Richardson, "The twenty-ninth annual meeting of the Society," *Bulletin of the American Mathematical Society* **29** (1923), 97–116. (See also **28** (1922), 234–235, 378, for comments on the special *Transactions* volume, and **28** (1922), 2–3 for discussion of budget deficits due to increased cost of printing.)

[47] Glenn E. Roudabush, Charles R. T. Bacon, R. Bruce Briggs, James A. Fierst, Dale W. Isner, and Hiroshi A. Noguni, "The left hand of scholarship: Computer experiments with recorded text as a communication media," *Proceedings of the AFIPS Fall Joint Computer Conference* **27** (1965), 399–411.

[48] Ellen E. Swanson, *Mathematics into Type* (Providence, Rhode Island: American Mathematical Society, 1971).

[49] Geofroy Tory, *Champ Fleury* (Paris: 1529). Also translated into English and annotated by George B. Ives (New York: Grolier Club, 1927).

[50] Karel Wick, *Rules for Typesetting Mathematics*, translated by V. Boublík and M. Hejlová (The Hague: Mouton, 1965).

[51] Hermann Zapf, *About Alphabets: Some Marginal Notes on Type Design* (Cambridge, Massachusetts: M.I.T. Press, 1970).

Addendum

After giving the lecture, I was pleased to learn from subsequent conversations and correspondence that there is not such a great gulf between mathematicians and artists as most people imagine. For example, George Pólya told me in 1979 that he had been familiar with the work of Dürer [18].

The *Transactions of the American Mathematical Society* began with volume 302 (1987) to encourage authors to submit their papers in TEX form. All volumes of the *Transactions* have been prepared completely with TEX since volume 311 (1989).

Of course I learned a great deal about typography after this paper was written. The basic boxes-and-glue metaphor that underlies TEX has remained essentially the same, but METAFONT's basic curve-drawing methods have changed completely. The new METAFONT, completed in 1984, still uses cubic splines, but they are governed by the far more intuitive notion of "control points" as suggested by Paul de Casteljau and Pierre Bézier in 1959 and the early 1960s. The algorithms for plotting the curves have thereby been improved dramatically in speed, from order n^3 to order n when there are n pixels per inch. The varying-width feature of Figure 19 and the simultaneous pen-and-eraser trick of Figure 20d are no longer supported; but they never actually turned out to be useful.

Substantially better rounding rules for pens, with interesting connections to number theory as well as to geometry, were developed in John Hobby's Ph.D. thesis, *Digitized Brush Trajectories* (Stanford University, 1985). Hobby also devised new rules for creating a "most pleasing curve" through a sequence of given points. The superiority of his methods has been confirmed by considerable experience, but METAFONT's current solution to the problem of "handwritten mathematics" (Figure 20) is admittedly quite bizarre: The output that METAFONT now produces, when given the specifications that led to Figure 20e in 1977, is

 !

The points that I specified awkwardly in Figure 20a should not in fact be expected to define nice letter shapes.

Chapter 3

Breaking Paragraphs Into Lines

[Written with Michael F. Plass. Originally published in Software—Practice & Experience **11** *(1981), 1119–1184.]*

This paper discusses a new approach to the problem of dividing the text of a paragraph into lines of approximately equal length. Instead of simply making decisions one line at a time, the method considers the paragraph as a whole, so that the final appearance of a given line might be influenced by the text on succeeding lines. A system based on three simple primitive concepts called "boxes," "glue," and "penalties" provides the ability to deal satisfactorily with a wide variety of typesetting problems in a unified framework, using a single algorithm that determines optimum breakpoints. The algorithm avoids backtracking by a judicious use of the techniques of dynamic programming. Extensive computational experience confirms that the approach is both efficient and effective in producing high-quality output. The paper concludes with a brief history of line-breaking methods, and an appendix presents a simplified algorithm that requires comparatively few resources.

Introduction

One of the most important operations necessary when text materials are prepared for printing or display is the task of dividing long paragraphs into individual lines. When this job has been done well, people will not be aware of the fact that the words they are reading have been broken apart arbitrarily and placed into a somewhat rigid and unnatural rectangular framework; but if the job has been done poorly, readers will be distracted by bad breaks that interrupt their train of thought. Suitable breakpoints are not always easy to find; for example, the narrow columns often used in newspapers allow for comparatively little flexibility, and the appearance of mathematical formulas in technical text introduces special complications regardless of the column width. But even in comparatively simple cases like the typesetting of an ordinary novel, good line breaking will contribute greatly to the appearance and desirability of the finished product. In fact, some authors actually write better material when they are assured that it will look sufficiently beautiful when it appears in print.

The line-breaking problem is informally called the problem of "justification," since it is the 'J' of 'H & J' (hyphenation and justification) in today's commercial composition and word-processing systems. However, justification tends to be a misnomer, because printers have traditionally used this term for the process of taking an individual line of type and adjusting its spacing to produce a desired length. Even when text is being typeset with ragged right margins (therefore "unjustified"), it needs to be broken into lines of approximately the same size. The job of adjusting spaces so that left and right margins are uniformly straight is comparatively laborious when one must work with metal type, so the task of typesetting a paragraph with last century's technology was conceptually a task of justification; nowadays, however, computers easily adjust the spacing in any desired manner, so the task of line-breaking dominates the work. This shift in relative difficulty probably accounts for the shift in the meaning of "justification"; we shall use the term *line breaking* in this paper to emphasize the fact that the central problem of concern here is to find breakpoints.

The traditional way to break lines is analogous to what we ordinarily do when using a typewriter: A bell rings (at least conceptually) when we approach the right margin, and at that time we decide how best to finish off the current line, without looking ahead to see where the next line or lines might end. Once the typewriter carriage has been returned to the left margin, we begin afresh without needing to remember anything about the previous text except where the new line starts. Thus, we don't have to keep track of many things at once; such a system is ideally suited to human operation, and it also leads to simple computer programs.

Book printing is different from typing primarily in that the spaces are of variable width. Traditional practice has been to assign a minimum and maximum width to interword spaces, together with a normal width representing the ideal situation. The standard algorithm for line breaking (see, for example, Barnett [4, page 55]) then proceeds as follows: Keep appending words to the current line, assuming the normal spacing, until reaching a word that does not fit. Break after this word, if it is possible to do so without compressing the spaces to less than the given minimum; otherwise break before this word, if it is possible to do so without expanding the spaces to more than the given maximum. Otherwise hyphenate the offending word, putting as much of it on the current line as will fit; if no suitable hyphenation points can be found, accept a line whose spaces exceed the given maximum.

There is no need to confine computers to such a simple procedure, since the data for an entire paragraph is generally available in the computer's memory. Experience has shown that significant improvements are possible if the computer takes advantage of its opportunity to look ahead at what is coming later in the paragraph, before making a final decision about where any of the lines will be broken. Lookahead not only tends to avoid cases where the traditional algorithm has to resort to wide spaces, it also reduces the number of hyphenations necessary. Thus line-breaking decisions provide another example of the desirability of "late binding" in computer software.

One of the principal reasons for using computers in typesetting is to save money, but at the same time we don't want the output to look cheaper. A properly programmed computer should, in fact, be able to solve the line-breaking problem better than a skilled typesetter could do by hand in a reasonable amount of time — unless we give this person the liberty to change the wording in order to obtain a better fit. For example, Duncan [14] studied the interword spacing of 958 lines that were manually typeset by a "most respectable publishers' printer" that he chose not to identify by name, and he found that nearly 5% of the lines were quite loosely set; the spaces on those lines exceeded 10 units (i.e., 10/18 of an em), and two of the lines even had spaces exceeding 13 units. We shall see that a good line-breaking algorithm can do better.

Besides the avoidance of hyphens and wide spaces, we can improve on the traditional line-breaking method by keeping the spaces nearly equal to the normal size, so that they rarely approach the minimum or maximum limits. We can also try to avoid rapid changes in the spacing of adjacent lines; we can make special efforts not to hyphenate two lines in a row, and not to hyphenate the second-last line of a paragraph; we can try to control the white space on the final line of the paragraph; and so on. Given any mathematical way to rate the quality of a particular choice of breakpoints, we can ask the computer to find breakpoints that optimize this function.

But how is the computer to solve such a problem efficiently? When a given paragraph has n optional breakpoints, there are 2^n ways to break it into lines, and even the fastest conceivable computers could not run through all such possibilities in a reasonable amount of time. In fact, the job of breaking a paragraph into equal-size lines as nicely as possible sounds suspiciously like the infamous bin-packing problem, which is well known to be NP-complete [16]. Fortunately, however, each line will consist of contiguous information from the paragraph, so the line-breaking problem is amenable to the techniques of discrete dynamic programming [6, 20]; hence there is a reasonably efficient way to attack it. We shall see that the optimum breakpoints can be found in practice with only about twice as much computation as needed by the traditional algorithm; the new method is sometimes even faster than the old, when we consider the time saved by not needing to hyphenate so often. Furthermore the new algorithm is capable of doing other things, like setting a paragraph one line longer or one line shorter, in order to improve the layout of a page.

Formulating the Problem

Let us now state the line-breaking problem explicitly in mathematical terms. We shall use the basic concepts and terminology of the TEX typesetting system [26], but in simplified form, since the complexities of general typesetting would obscure the main principles of line breaking.

For the purposes of this paper, a *paragraph* is a sequence $x_1 x_2 \ldots x_m$ of m items, where each individual item x_i is either a *box* specification, a *glue* specification, or a *penalty* specification.

- A box refers to something that is to be typeset: either a character from some font of type, or a black rectangle such as a horizontal or vertical rule, or something built up from several characters such as an accented letter or a mathematical formula. The contents of a box may be extremely complicated, or they may be extremely simple; the line-breaking algorithm does not peek inside a box to see what it contains, so we may consider the boxes to be sealed and locked. As far as we are concerned, the only relevant thing about a box is its *width*: When item x_i of a paragraph specifies a box, the width of that box is a real number w_i representing the amount of space that the box will occupy on a line. The width of a box may be zero, and in fact it may also be negative, although negative widths must be used with care and understanding according to the precise rules laid down below.

- Glue refers to blank space that can vary its width in specified ways; it is an elastic mortar used between boxes in a typeset line. When item x_i of a paragraph specifies glue, there are three real numbers (w_i, y_i, z_i) of importance to the line-breaking algorithm:

w_i is the "ideal" or "normal" width;
y_i is the "stretchability";
z_i is the "shrinkability."

For example, the space between words in a line is often specified by the values $w_i = 1/3$ em, $y_i = 1/6$ em, $z_i = 1/9$ em, where one em is the set size of the type being used (approximately the width of an uppercase 'M' in classical type styles). The actual amount of space occupied by a glue item can be adjusted when justifying a line to some desired width; if the normal width is too small, the adjustment is proportional to y_i, and if the normal width is too large the adjustment is proportional to z_i. The numbers w_i, y_i, and z_i may be negative, subject to certain natural restrictions explained later; for example, a negative value of w_i indicates a backspace. When $y_i = z_i = 0$, the glue has a fixed width w_i. Incidentally, the word "glue" is perhaps not the best term, because it sounds a bit messy; a word like "spring" would be better, since metal springs expand or compress to fill up space in essentially the way we want. However, we shall continue to say "glue," a term used since the early days of TEX (1977), because many people claim to like it. A glob of glue is often called a *skip* by TEX users, and the best policy might be to speak of boxes and skips rather than boxes and springs or boxes and glues. A skip, by any other name, is of course the same abstract concept, embodied by the three values (w_i, y_i, z_i).

- Penalty specifications denote potential places to end one line of a paragraph and begin another, with a certain "aesthetic cost" indicating how desirable or undesirable such a breakpoint would be. When item x_i of a paragraph specifies a penalty, there is a number p_i that helps us decide whether or not to end a line at this point, as explained below. Intuitively, a high penalty p_i indicates a relatively poor place to break, while a negative value of p_i stands for a good breaking-off place. The penalty p_i may also be $+\infty$ or $-\infty$, where '∞' denotes a large number that is infinite for practical purposes, although it really is finite; in the 1978 version of TEX, any penalty ≥ 1000 was treated as $+\infty$, and any penalty ≤ -1000 was treated as $-\infty$. When $p_i = +\infty$, the break is strictly prohibited; when $p_i = -\infty$, the break is mandatory. Penalty specifications also have widths w_i, with the following meaning: If a line break occurs at this place in the paragraph, additional typeset material of width w_i will be added to the line just before the break occurs. For example, a potential place at which a word might be hyphenated would be indicated by letting p_i be the penalty for hyphenating there and letting w_i be the width of the hyphen. Penalty specifications are of two kinds, *flagged* and *unflagged*, denoted by $f_i = 1$ and $f_i = 0$. The line-breaking algorithm we shall discuss tries to avoid having two consecutive breaks at flagged penalties (for example, having two hyphenations in a row).

Thus, box items are specified by one number w_i, while glue items have three numbers (w_i, y_i, z_i) and penalty items have three numbers (w_i, p_i, f_i). For simplicity, we shall assume that a paragraph $x_1 \ldots x_m$ is actually specified by six sequences, namely

$t_1 \ldots t_m$, where t_i is the type of item x_i, either 'box', 'glue', or 'penalty';

$w_1 \ldots w_m$, where w_i is the width corresponding to x_i;

$y_1 \ldots y_m$, where y_i is the stretchability corresponding to x_i if $t_i =$ 'glue', otherwise $y_i = 0$,

$z_1 \ldots z_m$, where z_i is the shrinkability corresponding to x_i if $t_i =$ 'glue', otherwise $z_i = 0$;

$p_1 \ldots p_m$, where p_i is the penalty at x_i if $t_i =$ 'penalty', otherwise $p_i = 0$;

$f_1 \ldots f_m$, where $f_i = 1$ if x_i is a flagged penalty, otherwise $f_i = 0$.

Any fixed unit of measure can be used in connection with w_i, y_i, and z_i; TEX uses printers' points, which are slightly less than $\frac{1}{72}$ inch. In this paper we shall specify all widths in terms of *machine units* equal to 1/18 em, assuming a particular size of type, since the widths turn out to be integer multiples of this unit in many cases. The numbers in our examples will be as simple as possible when expressed in terms of machine units.

Perhaps the reader feels that we are defining altogether too much mathematical machinery to deal with something that is quite straightforward. However, each of the concepts defined here must be dealt with somehow when paragraphs are broken into lines, and precise specifications are important even for the comparatively simple job of setting straight text. We shall see later that these primitive notions of boxes, glue, and penalties will actually support a surprising variety of other line-breaking applications, so that a careful attention to details will solve many other problems as a free bonus.

For the time being, it will be best to think of a simple application to straight text material such as the typesetting of a paragraph in a newspaper or in a short story, since this will help us internalize the abstract concepts represented by w_i, y_i, etc. A typesetting system like TEX transforms such an actual paragraph into the abstract form we want in the following way:

(1) If the paragraph is to be indented, the first item x_1 is an empty box whose width w_1 is the amount of indentation.

(2) Each word of the paragraph becomes a sequence of boxes for the characters of the word, including punctuation marks that belong with that word. The widths w_i are determined by the fonts of type being used. Flagged penalty items are inserted between the boxes wherever an acceptable hyphenation could be used to divide a word at the end of a line. (Such hyphenation points do not need to be included unless necessary, as we shall see later, but for the moment let us assume that all of the permissible hyphenations have been specified.)

(3) There is glue between words, corresponding to the recommended spacing conventions of the fonts of type in use. The glue might be different in different contexts; for example, TEX makes the glue specifications following punctuation marks slightly different from the normal interword glue.

(4) Explicit hyphens and dashes in the text are followed by flagged penalty items having width zero. This specifies a permissible line break after a hyphen or a dash. Some style conventions also allow breaks before em-dashes, in which case an unflagged width-zero penalty would precede the dash.

(5) At the very end of a paragraph, three items are appended so that the final line will be treated properly. First comes a penalty item x_{m-2} with $p_{m-2} = \infty$; then comes a glue item x_{m-1} that specifies the white space allowable at the right of the last line. Finally there's a penalty item x_m with $p_m = -\infty$ to force a break at the paragraph end. TEX ordinarily uses a "finishing glue" with $w_{m-1} = z_{m-1} = 0$ and $y_{m-1} = \infty$ (actually $y_{m-1} = 100000$ points, which is finite but large enough to behave like ∞); thus the normal space at the end of a paragraph is zero but it can stretch a great deal. The net effect is that the other spaces on the final line will shrink, if that line exceeds the desired measure; otherwise the other spaces will remain essentially at their normal value (because the finishing glue will do all the stretching necessary to fill up the end of the line). More subtle choices of the finishing glue x_{m-1} are possible; we will discuss them later.

For example, let's consider the paragraph of Figure 1 on the next page, which is taken from Grimms' Fairy Tales [18]. The five rules above convert the text into a sequence of exactly 601 items, as indicated in Table 1. Each line of Figure 1 has been justified to exactly 390 units wide, using the traditional one-line-at-a-time method to break up the text as described earlier.

In olden times when wishing still helped one,   .857
there lived a king whose daughters were all beauti- $-.750$
ful; and the youngest was so beautiful that the sun $-.824$
itself, which has seen so much, was astonished 1.087
whenever it shone in her face. Close by the king's $-.235$
castle lay a great dark forest, and under an old   .607
lime-tree in the forest was a well, and when the   .500
day was very warm, the king's child went out into $-.500$
the forest and sat down by the side of the cool   .700
fountain; and when she was bored she took a 1.360
golden ball, and threw it up on high and caught it; $-.650$
and this ball was her favorite plaything.   .001

FIGURE 1. An example paragraph that has been typeset by the "first-fit" method. Small triangles show permissible places to divide words with hyphens; the adjustment ratio for spaces appears at the right of each line.

Optional hyphenation points have been indicated with tiny triangles in Figure 1. Traditional style guides allow the insertion of a hyphen into a word only if at least two letters precede it and three follow it; furthermore the syllable following a hyphen shouldn't have a silent 'e', so we do not admit a hyphenation like 'sylla-ble'. Smooth reading also means that the word fragment preceding a hyphen should be long enough that it can be pronounced correctly and unambiguously, before the reader sees the completion of the word on the next line; thus, a hyphenation like 'proc-ess' would be disturbing. This pronunciation rule accounts for the fact that the next-to-last word of Figure 1 does not admit the potential hyphenation 'fa-vorite'; the fragment 'fa-' might well be the beginning of 'fa-ther', which is pronounced quite differently.

The choice of proper hyphenation points is an important but difficult subject that is beyond the scope of this paper. We shall not mention it further except to assume that (a) such potential breakpoints are available to our line-breaking algorithm when needed; (b) we prefer not to hyphenate when there is a way to avoid hyphens without seriously messing up the spacing.

The rules for breaking a paragraph into lines should be intuitively clear from this example, but they need to be stated explicitly. We shall assume that every paragraph ends with a forced break item x_m (an item with penalty $-\infty$). A *legal breakpoint* in a paragraph is a number b such that either (i) x_b is a penalty item with $p_b < \infty$, or (ii) x_b is a glue item and x_{b-1} is a box item. In other words, one can break at a penalty, provided that the penalty isn't ∞, or at glue, provided that the glue immediately follows a box. These two cases are the only acceptable

x_1 = empty box for indentation $\qquad$ $w_1 = 18$
x_2 = box for 'I' $\qquad$ $w_2 = 6$
x_3 = box for 'n' $\qquad$ $w_3 = 10$
x_4 = glue for interword space $\qquad$ $w_4 = 6,$ $\qquad$ $y_4 = 3,$ $\qquad$ $z_4 = 2$
x_5 = box for 'o' $\qquad$ $w_5 = 9$

· · · · · · · ·

x_{309} = box for 'l' $\qquad$ $w_{309} = 5$
x_{310} = box for 'i' $\qquad$ $w_{310} = 5$
x_{311} = box for 'm' $\qquad$ $w_{311} = 15$
x_{312} = box for 'e' $\qquad$ $w_{312} = 8$
x_{313} = box for '-' $\qquad$ $w_{313} = 6$
x_{314} = penalty for explicit hyphen $\qquad$ $w_{314} = 0,$ $\quad$ $p_{314} = 50,$ $\quad$ $f_{314} = 1$
x_{315} = box for 't' $\qquad$ $w_{315} = 7$

· · · · · · · ·

x_{590} = box for 'a' $\qquad$ $w_{590} = 9$
x_{591} = box for 'y' $\qquad$ $w_{591} = 10$
x_{592} = penalty for optional hyphen $\qquad$ $w_{592} = 6,$ $\quad$ $p_{592} = 50,$ $\quad$ $f_{592} = 1$
x_{593} = box for 't' $\qquad$ $w_{593} = 7$
x_{594} = box for 'h' $\qquad$ $w_{594} = 10$
x_{595} = box for 'i' $\qquad$ $w_{595} = 5$
x_{596} = box for 'n' $\qquad$ $w_{596} = 10$
x_{597} = box for 'g' $\qquad$ $w_{597} = 9$
x_{598} = box for '.' $\qquad$ $w_{598} = 5$
x_{599} = disallowed break $\qquad$ $w_{599} = 0,$ $\quad$ $p_{599} = \infty,$ $\quad$ $f_{599} = 0$
x_{600} = finishing glue $\qquad$ $w_{600} = 0,$ $\quad$ $y_{600} = \infty,$ $\quad$ $z_{600} = 0$
x_{601} = forced break $\qquad$ $w_{601} = 0,$ $\quad$ $p_{601} = -\infty,$ $\quad$ $f_{601} = 1$

TABLE 1. The sequence of box, glue, and penalty items constructed by
TℇX for the paragraph of Figure 1. For purposes of this example,
each letter is assumed to have the width that was traditionally used
with Monotype equipment; namely, 'a' through 'z' are respectively
$(9, 10, 8, 10, 8, 6, 9, 10, 5, 6, 10, 5, 15, 10, 9, 10, 10, 7, 7, 7, 10, 9, 13, 10, 10, 8)$
units wide and the characters 'C', 'I', and '-' have respective widths
of 13, 6, and 6 units. Commas, semicolons, periods, and apostrophes
occupy 5 units each. Glue has specifications $(w, y, z) = (6, 3, 2)$ between words, except that it is $(6, 4, 2)$ after a comma, $(6, 4, 1)$ after
a semicolon, and $(8, 6, 1)$ after a period. A penalty of 50 has been
assessed for every line that ends with a hyphen.

breakpoints. Notice, for example, that several glue items may appear
consecutively, but we are allowed to break only at the first of them, and
only if this one does not immediately follow a penalty item. A penalty
of ∞ can be inserted before glue to make it unbreakable; for example,
item x_{599} in Table 1 prevents a break at the paragraph-filling glue.

The job of line breaking consists of choosing legal breakpoints $b_1 < \cdots < b_k$, which specify the ends of k lines into which the paragraph will be broken. Each penalty item x_i whose penalty p_i is $-\infty$ must be included among these breakpoints; thus, the final breakpoint b_k must be equal to m. For convenience we let $b_0 = 0$, and we define indices $a_1 < \cdots < a_k$ to mark the beginning of the lines, as follows: The value of a_j is the smallest integer i between b_{j-1} and b_j such that x_i is a box item; if none of the x_i in the range $b_{j-1} < i < b_j$ are boxes, we let $a_j = b_j$. Then the jth line consists of all items x_i for $a_j \le i < b_j$, plus item x_{b_j} if it is a penalty item. In other words we get the lines of the broken paragraph by cutting it into pieces at the chosen breakpoints, then removing glue and penalty items at the beginning of each resulting line.

Desirability Criteria

According to this definition of line breaking, there are 2^n ways to break a paragraph into lines, if the paragraph has n legal breakpoints that aren't forced. For example, there are 129 legal breakpoints in the paragraph of Figure 1, not counting x_{601}; so it can be broken into lines in 2^{129} ways, a number that exceeds 10^{38}. But of course most of these choices are absurd, and we need to specify some criteria to separate acceptable choices from the ridiculous ones. For this purpose we need to know (a) the desired lengths of lines, and (b) the lengths of lines corresponding to each choice of breakpoints, including the amount of stretchability and shrinkability that is present. Then we can compare the desired lengths to the lengths actually obtained.

We shall assume that a list of desired lengths l_1, l_2, l_3, $\ldots$ is given; normally these are all the same, but in general we might want lines of different lengths, as when fitting text around an illustration. The actual length L_j of the jth line, after breakpoints have been chosen as above, is computed in the following obvious way: We add together the widths w_i of all the box and glue items in the range $a_j \le i < b_j$, and we add w_{b_j} to this total if x_{b_j} is a penalty item. The jth line also has a total stretchability Y_j and total shrinkability Z_j, obtained by summing all of the y_i and z_i for glue items in the range $a_j \le i < b_j$. Now we can compare the actual length L_j to the desired length l_j by seeing if there is enough stretchability or shrinkability to change L_j into l_j; we define the *adjustment ratio* r_j of the jth line as follows:

If $L_j = l_j$ (a perfect fit), let $r_j = 0$.

If $L_j < l_j$ (a short line), let $r_j = (l_j - L_j)/Y_j$, assuming that $Y_j > 0$; the value of r_j is undefined if $Y_j \le 0$ in this case.

If $L_j > l_j$ (a long line), let $r_j = (l_j - L_j)/Z_j$, assuming that $Z_j > 0$; the value of r_j is undefined if $Z_j \leq 0$ in this case.

Thus, for example, $r_j = 1/3$ if the total stretchability of line j is three times what would be needed to expand the glue so that the line length would change from L_j to l_j.

According to this definition of adjustment ratios, the jth line can be justified by letting the width of all glue items x_i on that line be

$$w_i + r_j y_i, \quad \text{if } r_j \geq 0;$$
$$w_i + r_j z_i, \quad \text{if } r_j < 0.$$

For if we add up the total width of that line after such adjustments are made, we get either $L_j + r_j Y_j = l_j$ or $L_j + r_j Z_j = l_j$, depending on the sign of r_j. This distributes the necessary stretching or shrinking by amounts proportional to the individual glue components y_i or z_i, as desired.

For example, the small numbers at the right of the individual lines in Figure 1 show the values of r_j in those lines. A negative ratio like $-.824$ in the third line means that the spaces in that line are narrower than their ideal size and rather near their minimum size, having used up more than 82% of their shrinkability; on the other hand, a fairly large positive ratio like 1.360 in the third-from-last line indicates a very "loose" fit.

Although there are 2^{129} ways to break the paragraph of Figure 1 into lines, it turns out that only 12 of them will result in breaks whose adjustment ratios r_j do not exceed 1 in absolute value; this condition on the ratios means that the spaces between words after justification will lie between $w_i - z_i$ and $w_i + y_i$, inclusive. The traditional method of line breaking, which generates the breaks of Figure 1, does not discover any of those solutions to the problem.

Our main goal is to avoid choosing any breakpoints that lead to lines in which the words are spaced very far apart, or in which they are very close together, because such lines are distracting and harder to read. We might therefore say that the line-breaking problem is to find breaks such that $|r_j| \leq 1$ in each line, with the minimum number of hyphenations subject to this condition. Such an approach was taken by Duncan and his associates in the early 1960s [13], and they obtained fairly good results. However, the criterion $|r_j| \leq 1$ depends only on the values $w_i - z_i$ and $w_i + y_i$, not on w_i itself, so it does not use all the degrees of freedom present in our data. Furthermore, such stringent conditions may not be possible to achieve; for example, if the lines of our sample paragraph were supposed to be 400 units wide, instead of the present width of 390 units, there would be no way to set the text of Figure 1 without having at least one very tight line ($r_j < -1$) or at least one very loose line ($r_j > 1$).

We can do a better job of line breaking if we deal with a continuously varying criterion of quality, not simply the yes/no test of the condition $|r_j| \le 1$. Let us therefore give a quantitative evaluation of the *badness* of the jth line by finding a formula that is nearly zero when $|r_j|$ is small but grows rapidly when $|r_j|$ takes values exceeding 1. Experience with TEX has shown that good results are obtained if we define the badness of line j as follows:

$$\beta_j = \begin{cases} \infty, & \text{if } r_j \text{ is undefined or } r_j < -1; \\ \lfloor 100|r_j|^3 + .5 \rfloor, & \text{otherwise.} \end{cases}$$

Thus, for example, the individual lines of Figure 1 have badness ratings equal to 63, 42, 56, 128, 1, 22, 13, 13, 34, 252, 27, and 0, respectively. The formula for β_j considers a line to be "infinitely bad" if $r_j < -1$; this means that glue will never be shrunk to less than $w_i - z_i$. However, values of r_j that exceed 1 are only finitely bad, so they will be permitted if there is no better alternative.

A slight improvement over the method used to produce Figure 1 leads to Figure 2. Once again each line has been broken without looking ahead to the end of the paragraph and without going back to reconsider previous choices, but this time each break has been chosen so as to minimize the "badness plus penalty" of that line. In other words, when choosing between alternative ways to end the jth line, given the ending of the previous line, we obtain Figure 2 if we take the minimum possible value of $\beta_j + \pi_j$; here β_j is the badness as defined above, and π_j is the amount of penalty p_{b_j} if the jth line ends at a penalty item, otherwise $\pi_j = 0$. Figure 2 improves on Figure 1 by moving words or syllables down from lines 2, 3, and 11 to the next line.

The method that produces Figure 1 might be called the "first-fit" algorithm, and the corresponding method for Figure 2 might be called the "best-fit" algorithm. We have seen that best-fit is superior to first-fit in this particular case, but other paragraphs can be contrived in which first-fit finds a better solution; so a single example is not sufficient to decide which method is preferable. In order to make an unbiased comparison of the methods, we need to get some statistics on their "typical" behavior. Therefore 300 experiments were performed, using the text of Figures 1 and 2, with line widths ranging from 350 to 649 in unit steps.

In olden times when wishing still helped one,   .857
there lived a king whose daughters were all beau-   .000
tiful; and the youngest was so beautiful that the   .280
sun itself, which has seen so much, was astonished   − .500
whenever it shone in her face. Close by the king's   − .235
castle lay a great dark forest, and under an old   .607
lime-tree in the forest was a well, and when the   .500
day was very warm, the king's child went out into   − .500
the forest and sat down by the side of the cool   .700
fountain; and when she was bored she took a   1.360
golden ball, and threw it up on high and caught   .357
it; and this ball was her favorite plaything.   .000

FIGURE 2. The paragraph of Figure 1 when the "best-fit" method has
been used to find successive breakpoints.

The text for each experiment was the same, but the varying line widths
made the problems quite different, since line-breaking algorithms are
quite sensitive to slight changes in the measurements. The "tightest"
and "loosest" lines in each resulting paragraph were recorded, as well
as the number of hyphens introduced, and the comparisons came out as
follows:

	$\min r_j$	$\max r_j$	hyphens
first-fit < best-fit	68%	40%	13%
first-fit = best-fit	26%	45%	79%
first-fit > best-fit	6%	15%	9%

Thus, in 68% of the cases, the minimum adjustment ratio r_j in the
lines typeset by first-fit was less than the corresponding value obtained
by best-fit; the maximum adjustment ratio in the first-fit lines was less
than the maximum for best-fit about 40% of the time; etc. We can
summarize this data by saying that the first-fit method usually typesets
at least one line that is tighter than the tightest line set by best-fit,
and it also usually produces a line that is as loose or looser than the
loosest line of best-fit. The number of hyphens is about the same for
both methods, although best-fit would produce fewer if the penalty for
hyphenation were increased.

We can actually do better than both of these methods by finding
an "optimum" way to choose the breakpoints. For example, Figure 3
shows how to improve on both Figures 1 and 2 by hyphenating the end
of line 4, thereby avoiding the problem of the loose 10th line. This
pattern of breakpoints was found by a "total-fit" algorithm that will be
discussed in detail below. It is globally optimum in the sense of having
fewest total *demerits* over all choices of breakpoints, where the demerits

assessed for the jth line are computed by the formula

$$\delta_j = \begin{cases} (1 + \beta_j + \pi_j)^2 + \alpha_j, & \text{if } \pi_j \geq 0; \\ (1 + \beta_j)^2 - \pi_j^2 + \alpha_j, & \text{if } -\infty < \pi_j < 0; \\ (1 + \beta_j)^2 + \alpha_j, & \text{if } \pi_j = -\infty. \end{cases}$$

Here β_j and π_j are the badness rating and the penalty, as before; and α_j is zero unless both line j and the previous line ended on flagged penalty items, in which case α_j is the additional penalty assessed for consecutive hyphenated lines (e.g., 3000). We shall say that we have found the best choice of breakpoints if we have minimized the sum of δ_j over all lines j.

The formula for δ_j is quite arbitrary, like our formula for β_j, but it works well in practice because it has the following desirable properties: (a) Minimizing the sum of squares of badnesses not only tends to minimize the maximum badness per line, it also provides secondary optimization; for example, when one particularly bad line is inevitable, the other line breaks will also be optimized. (b) The demerit function δ_j increases as π_j increases, except in the case $\pi_j = -\infty$ when we don't need to consider the penalty because such breaks are forced. (c) By adding 1 to β_j instead of using the badness β_j by itself, we minimize the total number of lines in cases where there are breaks whose badness is approximately zero.

For example, the following table shows the respective demerits charged to the individual lines of the paragraphs in Figures 1, 2, and 3:

First fit	Best fit	Total fit
4096	4096	4096
8649	2601	2601
3249	9	9
16641	196	22801
4	4	1
529	529	9
196	196	256
196	196	1
1225	1225	1225
64009	64009	4
784	36	36
1	1	1
99579	73098	31040

In the first-fit and best-fit methods, each line is likely to come out about as badly as any other; but the total-fit method tends to have its bad

In olden times when wishing still helped one,	.857
there lived a king whose daughters were all beau-	.000
tiful; and the youngest was so beautiful that the	.280
sun itself, which has seen so much, was aston-	1.000
ished whenever it shone in her face. Close by the	.067
king's castle lay a great dark forest, and under an	−.278
old lime-tree in the forest was a well, and when	.536
the day was very warm, the king's child went out	−.167
into the forest and sat down by the side of the	.700
cool fountain; and when she was bored she took a	−.176
golden ball, and threw it up on high and caught	.357
it; and this ball was her favorite plaything.	.000

FIGURE 3. This is the best possible way to break the lines in the paragraph of Figures 1 and 2, in the sense of fewest total demerits as defined in the text.

cases near the beginning, since the line-breaking problem allows less flexibility in the opening lines.

Figure 4 on the next page shows another comparison of the same three methods on the same text, this time with a line width of 500 units. Here the total-fit algorithm finds a solution that does not hyphenate any words, because of its ability to look ahead; the other two methods, which proceed one line at a time, miss this solution because they do not know that a slightly worse first line leads in this case to fewer problems later on. The demerits per line in Figure 4 are:

First fit	Best fit	Total fit
1521	1521	2209
3136	3136	4
3600	3600	676
4489	9	2916
4	1	1
1	4	1
400	121	9
4	25	16
1	16	400
	1	1
13156	8434	6233

Here the 3600 demerits on the third line for "first fit" and "best fit" are primarily due to the penalty of 50 for an inserted hyphen.

The first-fit method finds a way to set the paragraph of Figure 4 in only nine lines, while the total-fit method yields ten. Publishers who prefer to save a little paper, as long as the line breaks are fairly decent,

(a) First fit: In olden times when wishing still helped one, there lived a king   −.727
whose daughters were all beautiful; and the youngest was so   .821
beautiful that the sun itself, which has seen so much, was aston-   −.455
ished whenever it shone in her face. Close by the king's castle lay   −.870
a great dark forest, and under an old lime-tree in the forest was   −.208
a well, and when the day was very warm, the king's child went   .000
out into the forest and sat down by the side of the cool fountain;   −.577
and when she was bored she took a golden ball, and threw it up   −.231
on high and caught it; and this ball was her favorite plaything.   .000

(b) Best fit: In olden times when wishing still helped one, there lived a king   −.727
whose daughters were all beautiful; and the youngest was so   .821
beautiful that the sun itself, which has seen so much, was aston-   −.455
ished whenever it shone in her face. Close by the king's castle   .278
lay a great dark forest, and under an old lime-tree in the forest   .000
was a well, and when the day was very warm, the king's child   .237
went out into the forest and sat down by the side of the cool   .462
fountain; and when she was bored she took a golden ball, and   .343
threw it up on high and caught it; and this ball was her favorite   −.320
plaything.   .004

(c) Total fit: In olden times when wishing still helped one, there lived a   .774
king whose daughters were all beautiful; and the youngest was   .179
so beautiful that the sun itself, which has seen so much, was   .629
astonished whenever it shone in her face. Close by the king's   .545
castle lay a great dark forest, and under an old lime-tree in the   .000
forest was a well, and when the day was very warm, the king's   .079
child went out into the forest and sat down by the side of the   .282
cool fountain; and when she was bored she took a golden ball,   .294
and threw it up on high and caught it; and this ball was her   .575
favorite plaything.   .004

FIGURE 4. A somewhat wider setting of the same sample paragraph.

might therefore prefer the first-fit solution in spite of all its demerits. However, there are various ways to modify the specifications so that the total-fit method will give more preference to short solutions; for example, the stretchability of the glue on the final line could be decreased from its present huge size to about the width of the line, thereby making the algorithm prefer final lines that are nearly full. We could also replace the constant '1' in the definition of demerits δ_j by a larger number. The total-fit algorithm can in fact be set up to produce the optimum solution having the minimum number of lines.

The text in these examples is quite straightforward, and we have been setting type in reasonably wide columns; thus we have not been considering especially difficult or unusual line-breaking problems. Yet we have seen that an optimizing algorithm can produce noticeably better results even in such routine cases. The improved algorithm will clearly be of significant value in more difficult situations, for example when mathematical formulas are embedded in the text, or when the lines must be narrow as in a newspaper.

Anyone who is curious about the fate of the beautiful princess mentioned in Figures 1 through 4 can find the answer in Figure 6 on pages 84–85, which presents the whole story. The columns in Figure 6 are unusually narrow, allowing only about 21 or 22 characters per line; a width of about 35 characters is normal for newspapers, and magazines often use columns about twice as wide as those illustrated here. The line-at-a-time algorithms cannot cope satisfactorily with such stringent restrictions, but Figure 6 shows that the optimizing algorithm is able to break the text into reasonably equal lines. Quite a few hyphenations turn out to be desirable, since hyphenation increases the number of spaces per line and aids justification, even though the penalty for hyphenation was increased from 50 to 5000 in this example.

Although our line-breaking criteria have been developed with justified text in mind, the lookahead algorithm was used in Figure 6 to produce *ragged right* margins by simply suppressing justification after the line breaks were chosen. Another criterion of badness, based solely on the difference between the desired length l_j and the actual length L_j, should actually be used in order to get the best breakpoints for ragged-right typesetting, and the space between words should be allowed to stretch but not to shrink so that L_j never exceeds l_j. Furthermore, ragged-right typesetting should not allow words to "stick out," that is, to begin to the right of where the following line ends; for example, the word 'it' should really move down to the second line in Figure 5.

FIGURE 5. Here the best-fit method was used to break a paragraph into extremely narrow lines. The results have been left unjustified, because they would look terrible otherwise. For example, the third line contains only two spaces, and the third-from-last line only one; these spaces would have to stretch considerably if the lines were justified. The first line of this paragraph illustrates the "sticking-out" problem that can arise in unjustified settings.

> In the meantime it knocked a second time, and cried, "Princess, youngest princess, open the door for me. Do you not know what you said to me yesterday by the cool waters of the well? Princess, youngest princess, open the door for me!"

These considerations show that an algorithm intended for high quality line breaking in ragged-right formats is actually a little bit harder to write than one for justified text, contrary to the prevailing opinion that justification is more difficult. On the other hand, Figure 6 indicates that

IN olden times when wishing still helped one, there lived a king whose daughters were all beautiful; and the youngest was so beautiful that the sun itself, which has seen so much, was astonished whenever it shone in her face. Close by the king's castle lay a great dark forest, and under an old lime-tree in the forest was a well, and when the day was very warm, the king's child went out into the forest and sat down by the side of the cool fountain; and when she was bored she took a golden ball, and threw it up on high and caught it; and this ball was her favorite plaything.

Now it so happened that on one occasion the princess's golden ball did not fall into the little hand that she was holding up for it, but on to the ground beyond, and it rolled straight into the water. The king's daughter followed it with her eyes, but it vanished, and the well was deep, so deep that the bottom could not be seen. At this she began to cry, and cried louder and louder, and could not be comforted. And as she thus lamented someone said to her, "What ails you, king's daughter? You weep so that even a stone would show pity."

She looked round to the side from whence the voice came, and saw a frog stretching forth its big, ugly head from the water. "Ah, old water-splasher, is it you?" said she; "I am weeping for my golden ball, which has fallen into the well." "Be quiet, and do not weep," answered the frog. "I can help you; but what will you give me if I bring your plaything up again?" "Whatever you will have, dear frog," said she; "my clothes, my pearls and jewels, and even the golden crown that I am wearing." The frog answered, "I do not care for your clothes, your pearls and jewels, nor for your golden crown; but if you will love me and let me be your companion and play-fellow, and sit by you at your little table, and eat off your little golden plate, and drink out of your little cup, and sleep in your little bed—if you will promise me this I will go down below, and bring you your golden ball up again." "Oh yes," said she, "I promise you all you wish, if you will but bring me my ball back again." But she thought, "How the silly frog does talk! All he does is sit in the water with the other frogs, and croak. He can be no companion to any human being."

But the frog, when he had received this promise, put his head into the water and sank down; and in a short while he came swimming up again with the ball in his mouth, and threw it on the grass. The king's daughter was delighted to see her pretty plaything once more, and she picked it up and ran away with it. "Wait, wait," said the frog. "Take me with you. I can't run as you can." But what did it avail him to scream his croak, croak, after her, as loudly as he could? She did not listen to it, but ran home and soon forgot the poor frog, who was forced to go back into his well again.

The next day when she had seated herself at table with the king and all the courtiers, and was eating from her little golden plate, something came creeping splish splash, splish splash, up the marble staircase; and when it had got to the top, it knocked at the door and cried, "Princess, youngest princess, open the door for me." She ran to see who was outside, but when she opened the door, there sat the frog in front of it. Then she slammed the door to, in great haste, sat down to dinner again, and was quite frightened. The king saw plainly that her heart was beating violently, and said, "My child, what are you so afraid of? Is there perchance a giant outside who wants to carry you away?" "Ah, no," replied she. "It is no giant, it is a disgusting frog." "What does a frog want with you?" "Ah, dear father, yesterday as I was in the forest

FIGURE 6. The tale of the Frog King, typeset with quite narrow lines and with "ragged right" margins. The breakpoints were chosen optimally under the assumption that the lines would be justified.

sitting by the well, playing, my golden ball fell into the water. And because I cried so, the frog brought it out again for me; and because he so insisted, I promised him he should be my companion, but I never thought he would be able to come out of his water. And now he is outside there, and wants to come in to see me."

In the meantime it knocked a second time, and cried, "Princess, youngest princess, open the door for me. Do you not know what you said to me yesterday by the cool waters of the well? Princess, youngest princess, open the door for me!"

Then said the king, "That which you have promised must you perform. Go and let him in." She went and opened the door, and the frog hopped in and followed her, step by step, to her chair. There he sat and cried, "Lift me up beside you." She delayed, until at last the king commanded her to do it. Once the frog was on the chair he wanted to be on the table, and when he was on the table he said, "Now, push your little golden plate nearer to me, that we may eat together." She did this, but it was easy to see that she did not do it willingly. The frog enjoyed what he ate, but almost every mouthful she took choked her. At length he said,

"I have eaten and am satisfied, now I am tired; carry me into your little room and make your little silken bed ready, and we will both lie down and go to sleep."

The king's daughter began to cry, for she was afraid of the cold frog, which she did not like to touch, and which was now to sleep in her pretty, clean little bed. But the king grew angry and said, "He who helped you when you were in trouble ought not afterwards to be despised by you." So she took hold of the frog with two fingers, carried him upstairs, and put him in a corner. But when she was in bed he crept to her and said, "I am tired, I want to sleep as well as you; lift me up or I will tell your father." At this she was terribly angry, and took him up and threw him with all her might against the wall. "Now, will you be quiet, odious frog?" said she. But when he fell down he was no frog but a king's son with kind and beautiful eyes. He by her father's will was now her dear companion and husband. Then he told her how he had been bewitched by a wicked witch, and how no one could have delivered him from the well but herself, and that tomorrow they would go together into his kingdom.

Then they went to sleep, and next morning when the sun

awoke them, a carriage came driving up with eight white horses, which had white ostrich feathers on their heads, and were harnessed with golden chains; and behind stood the young king's servant Faithful Henry. Faithful Henry had been so unhappy when his master was changed into a frog, that he had caused three iron bands to be laid round his heart, lest it should burst with grief and sadness. The carriage was to conduct the young king into his kingdom. Faithful Henry helped them both in, and placed himself behind again, and was full of joy because of this deliverance. And when they had driven a part of the way, the king's son heard a cracking behind him as if something had broken. So he turned round and cried, "Henry, the carriage is breaking."

"No, master, it is not the carriage. It is a band from my heart, that was put there in my great pain when you were a frog and imprisoned in the well."

Again and once again while they were on their way something cracked, and each time the king's son thought the carriage was breaking; but it was only the bands that were springing from the heart of Faithful Henry because his master was set free and was so happy.

FIGURE 6 (CONTINUED). A somewhat different criterion of optimality would have been more appropriate for unjustified setting, yet the lines did turn out to be of approximately equal width.

an algorithm designed for justification usually can be tuned to produce adequate breakpoints when justification is suppressed.

The difficulties of setting narrow columns are illustrated in an interesting way by the pattern of words

"Now, push your little golden plate nearer ..."

that appears in the fourth-from-last paragraph of Figure 6. We don't want to hyphenate any of those words, for reasons stated earlier; and it turns out that all of the four-word sequences containing the word 'little', namely

"Now, push your little
push your little golden
your little golden plate
little golden plate nearer

are too long to fit in one line. Therefore the word 'little' will have to appear in a line that contains only three words and two spaces, no matter what text precedes this particular sequence.

The final paragraphs of the story present other difficulties, some of which involve complex interactions spanning many lines of the text, making it impossible to find breakpoints that would avoid occasional wide spacing if the text were justified. Figure 7 shows what happens when a portion of Figure 6 is, in fact, justified; this is the most difficult part of the entire story, in which one of the lines in the optimum solution is forced to stretch by the enormous factor 6.616. The only way to typeset that paragraph without such wide spaces is to leave it unjustified (unless, of course, we change the problem by altering the text or the line width or the minimum size of spaces).

and were harnessed	3.137	
with golden chains;	3.277	
and behind stood	5.740	
the young king's ser-	.783	
vant Faithful Henry.	1.971	
Faithful Henry had	3.474	
been so unhappy	6.616	
when his master was	.940	
changed into a frog,	1.612	

FIGURE 7. This portion of the story in Figure 6 is the most difficult to handle, when we try to justify the text using such narrow columns; even the optimum breakpoints result in wide spaces.

Further Applications

Before we discuss the details of an optimizing algorithm, let us consider more fully how the basic primitives of boxes, glue, and penalties allow us to solve a wide variety of typesetting problems. Some of these applications are straightforward extensions of the simple ideas used in

Figures 1 through 4, while others seem at first to be quite unrelated to the ordinary task of line breaking.

Combining paragraphs

If the desired line widths l_i are not all the same, we might want to typeset two paragraphs with the second one starting in the list of line lengths where the first one leaves off. This can be done simply by treating the two paragraphs as one, i.e., appending the box/glue/penalty items of the second to the first, assuming that each paragraph begins with indentation and ends with finishing glue and a forced break as mentioned above.

Patching

Suppose that a paragraph starts on page 100 of some book and continues on to the next page, and suppose that we want to make a change to the first part of that paragraph. We want to be sure that the last line of the new page 100 will end at the right-hand margin just before the word that appears at the beginning of page 101, so that page 101 doesn't have to be redone. It is easy to specify this condition in terms of our conventions, simply by forcing a line break (with penalty $-\infty$) at the desired place, and discarding the subsequent text. The ability of the total-fit algorithm to look ahead means that it will find a suitable way to patch page 100 whenever such a solution exists.

We can also force the altered part of the paragraph to have a certain number of lines, k, by using the following trick: Set the desired length l_{k+1} of the $(k + 1)$st line equal to a number θ that is different from the length of any other line. Then an empty box of width θ that occurs between two forced-break penalty items will have to be placed on line $k+1$.

Hanging punctuation

Some people prefer to have the right edge of their text look "solid," by setting periods, commas, and other punctuation marks (including inserted hyphens) in the right-hand margin. For example, this practice is occasionally used in contemporary advertising. It is easy to get inserted hyphens into the margin: We simply let the width of the corresponding penalty item be zero. And it is almost as easy to do the same for periods and other symbols, by putting every such character in a box of width zero and adding the actual symbol width to the glue that follows. If no break occurs at this glue, the accumulated width is the same as before; and if a break does occur, the line will be justified as if the period or other symbol were not present.

Avoiding "psychologically bad" breaks

Since computers don't know how to think, at least not yet, it is reasonable to wonder if there aren't some line breaks that a computer would choose but a human operator might not, when the breaks somehow don't seem right. This problem does not arise very often when straight text is being set, as in newspapers or novels, but it is quite common in technical material. For example, it is psychologically bad to break before 'x' or 'y' in the sentence

A function of x is a rule that assigns a value y to every value of x.

A computer will have no qualms about breaking anywhere unless it is told not to; but a human operator might well avoid bad breaks, perhaps even unconsciously.

Psychologically bad breaks are not easy to define. We just know they are bad. When the eye journeys from the end of one line to the beginning of another, in the presence of a bad break, the second word often seems like an anticlimax, or isolated from its context. Imagine turning the page between the words 'Chapter' and '8' in some sentence; you might well think that the compositor of the book you are reading should not have broken the text at such an illogical place.

During the first year of experience with TEX, the authors of this paper began to notice occasional breaks that didn't feel quite right, although the problem wasn't thought to be severe enough to warrant corrective action. Finally, however, we were less able to justify our claim that TEX has the world's best line-breaking algorithm, when the computer would occasionally make breaks that were semantically annoying; for example, the preliminary TEX manual [26] had quite a few of them, and the first drafts of that manual were even worse.

As time went on, the authors grew more and more sensitive to psychologically bad breaks, not only in the copy produced by TEX but also in other published literature, and it became desirable to test the hypothesis that computers were really to blame. Therefore a systematic investigation was made of the first 1000 line breaks in the *ACM Journal* of 1960 (which was composed manually by a Monotype operator), compared to the first 1000 line breaks in the *ACM Journal* of 1980 (which was typeset by one of the best commercially available computer systems for mathematics, developed by Penta Systems International). The final lines of paragraphs, and the lines preceding displays, were not considered to be line breaks, since they are forced. Only the texts of articles were considered, not the bibliographies. A reader who wishes to try the same experiment should find that the 1000th break in 1960 occurred on page 67, while in 1980 it occurred on page 64. The results of this admittedly subjective procedure were a total of

13 bad breaks in 1960,

55 bad breaks in 1980.

In other words, there was more than a four-fold increase, from about 1% to a quite noticeable 5.5%! Of course, this test is not absolutely conclusive, because the style of articles in the *ACM Journal* has not remained constant, but it suggests strongly that computer typesetting causes semantic degradation when it chooses breaks solely on the basis of visual criteria.

Once this problem was identified, a systematic effort was made to purge all such breaks from the second edition of Knuth's book *Seminumerical Algorithms* [28], which was the first large book to be typeset with TEX. It is quite easy to get the line-breaking algorithm to avoid certain breaks by simply prefixing the glue item by a penalty with $p_i =$ 999, say; then the bad break is chosen only in an emergency, when there is no other good way to set the paragraph. We can also make the typist's job reasonably easy by reserving a special symbol (e.g., ' ˜ ') to be used instead of a normal space between words whenever breaking is undesirable. Although this problem has rarely been discussed in the literature, the authors subsequently discovered that some typographers have a word for it: They call such spaces "auxiliary." Thus there is a growing awareness of the problem.

Let us call such spaces *ties*. It may be useful to list the main kinds of contexts in which ties were used in *Seminumerical Algorithms*, since that book ranges over a wide variety of technical subjects. The following rules should prove to be helpful to compositors who are keyboarding technical manuscripts into a computer.

1. Use ties in cross-references:

Theorem˜A	Algorithm˜B	Chapter˜3
Table˜4	Programs E and˜F	

No tie appears after 'Programs' in the last example, since it would be quite all right to have 'E and F' at the beginning of a line.

2. Use ties between a person's forenames and between multiple surnames:

Dr.˜I.˜J. Matrix	Luis˜I. Trabb˜Pardo
Peter van˜Emde˜Boas	

A recent trend to avoid spaces altogether between initials may be largely a reaction against typical computer line-breaking algorithms!

Notice that it seems better to hyphenate a name than to break it between words; for example, 'Don-' and 'ald E. Knuth' is more tolerable than 'Donald' and 'E. Knuth'. In a sense, rule 1 is a special case of rule 2, since we may regard 'Theorem~A' as a name; another example is 'register~X'.

3. Use ties for symbols in apposition with nouns:

$$\text{base}~b \qquad\qquad \text{dimension}~d$$
$$\text{function}~f(x) \qquad \text{string}~s \text{ of length}~l$$

But compare the last example with 'string~s of length l~or more'.

4. Use ties for symbols in series:

$$1,~2,\text{ or}~3 \qquad a,~b,\text{ and}~c \qquad 1,~2,\ldots,~n$$

5. Use ties for symbols as tightly-bound objects of prepositions:

$$\text{of}~x \qquad\qquad \text{from 0 to}~1$$
$$\text{increase } z \text{ by}~1 \qquad \text{in common with}~m$$

This rule does not apply to compound objects: For example, consider 'of u~and~v'.

6. Use ties to avoid breaking up mathematical phrases that are rendered in words:

equals~n	less than~ϵ	mod~2	modulo~p^e
(given~X)	when x~grows	if t~is $\ldots$	

Compare 'is~15' with 'is 15~times the height'; and compare 'for all large~n' with 'for all n~greater than~n_0'.

7. Use ties when enumerating cases:

(b)~Show that $f(x)$ is (1)~continuous; (2)~bounded.

It would be nice to boil these seven rules down into one or two, and it would be even nicer if the rules could be automated so that keyboarding could be done without them; but subtle semantic considerations seem to be involved in many of these instances. Most examples of psychologically bad breaks seem to occur when a single symbol or a short group of symbols appears just before or after the break. An automatic scheme would do reasonably well if it would associate large penalties with a break just before a short non-word, and medium penalties with a break just after a short non-word. Here 'short non-word' means a sequence of symbols that is not very long, yet long enough to include instances like 'exercise~15(b)', 'length~2^{35}', 'order~$n/2$' followed by punctuation marks; one should not simply consider patterns that have only one or two symbols. On the other hand it is not so offensive to break before or after fairly long sequences of symbols; for example, 'exercise 4.3.2–15' needs no tie after the word 'exercise'.

Many books on composition recommend against breaking just before the final word of a paragraph, especially if that word is short; this can, of course, be done by using a tie just before that last word, and the computer could insert this automatically. Some books also give recommendations analogous to rule 2 above, saying that compositors should try not to break lines in the middle of a person's name. But there is apparently only one book that addresses the other issues of psychologically bad breaks, namely a nineteenth-century French manual by A. Frey [15, volume 1, page 110], where the following examples of undesirable breaks are mentioned:

$$\text{Henri˜IV} \qquad \text{M.˜Colin} \qquad 1^{\text{er}}\text{˜sept.} \qquad \text{art.˜25} \qquad 20\text{˜fr.}$$

It seems to be time to resurrect such old traditions of fine printing.

Recent experience of the authors indicates that the task of inserting ties is not a substantial additional burden when entering a manuscript into a computer. The careful use of such spaces may in fact lead to greater job satisfaction on the part of the keyboard operator, since the quality of the output can be noticeably improved with comparatively little work. It is comforting at times to know that the machine needs your help.

Author lines

Most of the review notices published in *Mathematical Reviews* are signed with the reviewer's name and address, and this information is typeset flush right, namely at the right-hand margin. If there is sufficient space to put such a name and address at the right of the final line of the paragraph, the publishers can save space, and at the same time the results look better because there are no strange gaps on the page. During recent years the composition software used by the American Mathematical Society was unable to do this operation, but the amount of money saved on paper made it economical for them to pay someone to move the reviewer-name lines up *by hand* wherever possible, applying scissors and (real) glue to the computer output.

This is a case where the name and address fit in nicely with the review.   *A. Reviewer* (Ann Arbor, Mich.)

But sometimes an extra line must be added.

N. Bourbaki (Paris)

FIGURE 8. The MR problem.

Let us say that the "MR problem" is to typeset the contents of a given box flush right at the end of a given paragraph, with a space of at least w between the paragraph and the box if they occur on the same line. This problem can be solved entirely in terms of the box/glue/penalty primitives, as follows:

⟨text of the given paragraph⟩
penalty(0, ∞, 0)
glue(0, 100000, 0)
penalty(0, 50, 0)
glue(w, 0, 0)
box(0)
penalty(0, ∞, 0)
glue(0, 100000, 0)
⟨the given box⟩
penalty(0, −∞, 0)

The final penalty of −∞ forces the final line break with the given box flush right; the two penalties of +∞ are used to inhibit breaking at the following glue items. Thus, the above sequence reduces to two cases: whether or not to break at the penalty of 50. If a break is taken there, the 'glue(w, 0, 0)' disappears, according to our rule that each line begins with a box; the text of the paragraph preceding the penalty of 50 will be followed by 'glue(0, 100000, 0)', which will stretch to fill the line as if the paragraph had ended normally, and the given box on the final line will similarly be preceded by 'glue(0, 100000, 0)' to fill the gap at the left. On the other hand if no break occurs at the penalty of 50, the net effect is to have the glues added all together, producing

⟨text of the given paragraph⟩
glue(w, 200000, 0)
⟨the given box⟩

so that the space between the paragraph and the box is w or more. Whether the break is chosen or not, the badness of the two final lines or the final line will be essentially zero, because so much stretchability is present. Thus the relative cost differential separating the two alternatives is almost entirely due to the penalty of 50. The total-fit algorithm will choose the better alternative, based on the various possibilities it has for setting the given paragraph; it might even make the given paragraph a little bit tighter than its usual setting, if this works out best.

Ragged right margins

We observed in Figure 6 that an optimum line-breaking algorithm intended for justified text does a fairly good job at making lines of nearly
equal length even when the lines aren't justified afterwards. However,
one can easily construct examples in which the justification-oriented
method makes bad decisions, since the amount of deviation in line
width is weighted by the amount of stretchability or shrinkability that is
present. A line containing many words, and therefore containing many
spaces between words, will not be considered problematical by the justification criteria even if it is rather short or rather long, because there
is enough glue present to stretch or shrink gracefully to the correct size.
Conversely, when there are few words in a line, the algorithm will take
pains to avoid comparatively small deviations. This is illustrated in Figure 5, which actually reads better than the corresponding paragraph in
Figure 6 (except for the word that sticks out on the first line); hyphens
were inserted into the paragraph of Figure 6 in order to create more
interword space for justification.

   Although the box/glue/penalty model appears at first glance to be
oriented solely to the problem of justified text, in fact it is powerful
enough to be adapted to the analogous problem of unjustified typesetting: If the spaces between words are handled in the right way, we can
make things work out so that each line has the same amount of stretchability, no matter how many words are on that line. The idea is to let
spaces between words be represented by the sequence

$$\text{glue}(0, 18, 0)$$
$$\text{penalty}(0, 0, 0)$$
$$\text{glue}(6, -18, 0)$$

instead of the 'glue(6, 3, 2)' we used for justified typesetting. We may
assume that there is no break at the 'glue(0, 18, 0)' in the sequence, because the algorithm cannot do worse by breaking at the 'penalty(0, 0, 0)',
when 18 units of stretchability are present. If a break occurs at the
penalty, there will be a stretchability of 18 units on the line, and the
'glue(6, -18, 0)' will be discarded after the break so that the next line
will begin flush left. On the other hand if no break occurs, the net effect
is to have glue(6, 0, 0), representing a normal space with no stretching
or shrinking.

   The stretchability of -18 in the second glue item has no physical
significance, but it nicely cancels out the stretchability of $+18$ in the first
glue item. Negative stretchability has several interesting applications,

so the reader should study this example carefully before proceeding to the more elaborate constructions below.

Optional hyphenations in unjustified text can be specified in a similar way; instead of using 'penalty(6, 50, 1)' for an optional 6-unit hyphen having a penalty of 50, we can use the sequence

$$penalty(0, \infty, 0)$$
$$glue(0, 18, 0)$$
$$penalty(6, 500, 1)$$
$$glue(0, -18, 0).$$

The penalty has been increased here from 50 to 500, since hyphenations are less desirable in unjustified text. After the breakpoints have been chosen using the above sequences for spaces and for optional hyphens, the individual lines should not actually be justified; otherwise a hyphen inserted by the 'penalty(6, 500, 1)' would appear at the right margin.

It is not difficult to prove that this approach to ragged-right typesetting will never lead to words that "stick out" as in the first line of Figure 5; the total demerits are reduced whenever a word that sticks out is moved to the following line.

Centered text

Occasionally we want to take some text that is too long to fit on one line and break it into approximately equal-size parts, centering the parts on individual lines. This is most often done when setting titles or captions, but it can also be applied to the text of a paragraph, as shown in Figure 9.

Boxes, glue, and penalties can perform this operation, in the following way: (a) At the beginning of the paragraph, use 'glue(0, 18, 0)' instead of an indentation. (b) For each space between words in the paragraph, use the sequence

$$glue(0, 18, 0)$$
$$penalty(0, 0, 0)$$
$$glue(6, -36, 0)$$
$$box(0)$$
$$penalty(0, \infty, 0)$$
$$glue(0, 18, 0).$$

(c) End the paragraph with the sequence

$$glue(0, 18, 0)$$
$$penalty(0, -\infty, 0).$$

In olden times when wishing still helped one, there lived a king whose daughters were all beautiful; and the youngest was so beautiful that the sun itself, which has seen so much, was astonished whenever it shone in her face. Close by the king's castle lay a great dark forest, and under an old lime-tree in the forest was a well, and when the day was very warm, the king's child went out into the forest and sat down by the side of the cool fountain; and when she was bored she took a golden ball, and threw it up on high and caught it; and this ball was her favorite plaything.

FIGURE 9. "Ragged-centered" text: The total-fit algorithm will produce special effects like this, when appropriate combinations of box/glue/penalty items are used for the spaces between words.

The tricky part of this method is part (b), which ensures that an optional break at the 'penalty$(0, 0, 0)$' puts stretchability of 18 units at the end of one line and at the beginning of the next. If no break occurs, the net effect will be glue$(0, 18, 0)$ + glue$(6, -36, 0)$ + glue$(0, 18, 0)$ = glue$(6, 0, 0)$, a fixed space of 6 units. The 'box(0)' contains no text and occupies no space; its function is to keep the 'glue$(0, 18, 0)$' from disappearing at the beginning of a line. The 'penalty$(0, 0, 0)$' item could be replaced by other penalties, to represent breakpoints that are more or less desirable. However, this technique cannot be used together with optional hyphenation, since our box/glue/penalty model is incapable of inserting optional hyphens anywhere except at the right margin when lines are justified.

The construction used here essentially minimizes the maximum gap between the margins and the text on any line; and subject to that minimum it essentially minimizes the maximum gap on the remaining lines; and so forth. The reason is that our definitions of badness and demerits reduce in this case so that the sum of demerits for any choice of breakpoints is approximately proportional to the sum of the sixth powers of the individual gaps.

ALGOL-like languages

One of the most difficult tasks in technical typesetting is to get computer programs to look right. In addition to the complications of mathematical formulas and a variety of typefaces and spacing conventions, we want to indent the lines suitably in order to display the program structure. Sometimes a single statement must be broken across several lines; sometimes a number of short statements should be grouped together on a single line. Computer scientists who attempt to publish programs in journals that are not accustomed to such material soon discover that

very few printing establishments have the expertise necessary to handle
ALGOL-like languages in a satisfactory way.

Once again, the concepts of boxes, glue, and penalties come to the
rescue: It turns out that our line-breaking methods developed for ordinary text can be used without change to do the typesetting of programs
in ALGOL-like languages. For example, Figure 10 shows a typical program taken from the Pascal manual [23] that has been typeset assuming
two different column widths. Although these two settings of the program do not look very much alike, they both were made from exactly
the same input, specified in terms of boxes, glue, and penalties; the
only difference was the specification of line width. (The input text in
this example was prepared by a computer program called Blaise [27],
which will translate any Pascal source text into a TEX file that can be
incorporated into other documents.)

The box/glue/penalty specifications that lead to Figure 10 involve
constructions similar to those we have seen above, but with some new
twists; it will be sufficient for our purposes merely to sketch the ideas
instead of dwelling on the details. One key point is that the breaks are
chosen by the minimum-demerits criteria we have been discussing, but
the lines are not justified afterwards (i.e., the glue does not actually
stretch or shrink). The reason is that relations and assignment statements are processed by TEX's normal "math mode," which allows line
breaks to occur in various places but without any special constructions
particular to this application, so that justification would have the undesirable effect of putting all such breaks at the right margin. The fact
that justification is suppressed actually turns out to be an advantage in
this case, since it means that we can insert glue stretching wherever we
like, within a line, if it affects the 'badness' formula in a desirable way.

Each line in the wider setting of Figure 10 is actually a "paragraph"
by itself, so it is only the narrower setting that shows the line-breaking
mechanism at work. Every "paragraph" has a specified amount of indentation for its first line, corresponding to its position in the program,
as a given number t of "tab" units. The paragraph is also given a hanging indentation of $t + 2$ tab units; this means that all lines after the first
are required to be two tabs narrower than the first line, and they are
shifted two tabs to the right with respect to that line. In some cases
(e.g., those lines beginning with '**var**' or '**while**') the offset is three tabs
instead of two.

The paragraph begins with 'glue(0, 100000, 0)', which has the effect
of providing enough stretchability that the line-breaking algorithm will
not wince too much at breaks that do not square perfectly with the

```
const n = 10000;
var sieve, primes :
      set of 2..n;
   next, j : integer;
begin { initialize }
sieve := [2..n];
primes := [ ];
next := 2;
repeat { find next
      prime }
  while not (next in
        sieve) do
    next :=
      succ(next);
  primes :=
      primes + [next];
  j := next;
  while j <= n do
        { eliminate }
    begin sieve :=
        sieve − [j];
      j := j + next
    end
until sieve = [ ]
end.
```

FIGURE 10. These two settings of a sample Pascal program were made from identical input specifications in the box/glue/penalty model; in the first case the lines were set 10 ems wide, and in the second case the width was 25 ems. All of the line-breaking and indentation was produced automatically by the total-fit algorithm, which has no specific knowledge of Pascal. Compilation of the Pascal source code into boxes, glue, and penalties was done by a computer program called Blaise.

```
const n = 10000;
var sieve, primes : set of 2..n;
   next, j : integer;
begin { initialize }
sieve := [2..n]; primes := [ ]; next := 2;
repeat { find next prime }
  while not (next in sieve) do next := succ(next);
  primes := primes + [next]; j := next;
  while j <= n do { eliminate }
    begin sieve := sieve − [j]; j := j + next
    end
until sieve = [ ]
end.
```

right margin, at least not on the first line. Special breaks are inserted at places where TEX would not normally break in math mode; e.g., the sequence

$$penalty(0, \infty, 0)$$
$$glue(0, 100000, 0)$$
$$penalty(0, 50, 0)$$
$$glue(0, -100000, 0)$$
$$box(0)$$
$$penalty(0, \infty, 0)$$
$$glue(0, 100000, 0)$$

has been inserted just before '*primes*' in the **var** declaration. This sequence allows a break with penalty 50 to the next line, which begins with plenty of stretchability. A similar construction is used between assignment statements, for example between '*sieve* := [2 .. *n*];' and '*primes* := [ ]', where the sequence is

$$penalty(0, \infty, 0)$$
$$glue(0, 100000, 0)$$
$$penalty(0, 0, 0)$$
$$glue(6 + 2w, -100000, 0)$$
$$box(0)$$
$$penalty(0, \infty, 0)$$
$$glue(-2w, 100000, 0);$$

here w is the width of a tab unit. If a break occurs, the following line begins with 'glue($-2w$, 100000, 0)', which undoes the effect of the hanging indentation and effectively restores the state at the beginning of a paragraph. If no break occurs, the net effect is 'glue(6, 100000, 0)', a normal space.

No automatic system can hope to find the best breaks in programs, since an understanding of the semantics will indicate that certain breaks make the program clearer and reveal its symmetries better. However, dozens of experiments on a wide variety of Pascal source texts have shown that this approach is surprisingly effective; fewer than 1% of the line-breaking decisions have been overridden by authors of the programs in order to provide additional clarity.

A complex index

The final application of line breaking that we shall study is the most difficult one that has so far been encountered by the authors; it was solved only after we had acquired more than two years of experience

ACM Symposium on Principles of Programming
  Languages, Third (Atlanta, Ga., 1976), selected
  papers .... ∗1858
ACM Symposium on Theory of Computing, Eighth
  Annual (Hershey, Pa., 1976) 1879, 4813,
  5414, 6918, 6936, 6937, 6946, 6951, 6970, 7619,
  9605, 10148, 11676, 11687, 11692, 11710, 13869
Software .... See ∗1858

ACM Symposium on
  Principles
  of Programming
  Languages, Third
  (Atlanta, Ga., 1976),
  selected papers ... ∗1858
ACM Symposium on
  Theory of Computing,
  Eighth Annual
  (Hershey, Pa., 1976)
  .... 1879, 4813, 5414,
  6918, 6936, 6937, 6946,
  6951, 6970, 7619, 9605,
  10148, 11676, 11687,
  11692, 11710, 13869
Software .... See ∗1858

ACM Symposium on Principles of
  Programming Languages, Third
  (Atlanta, Ga., 1976), selected
  papers .... ∗1858
ACM Symposium on Theory of
  Computing, Eighth Annual
  (Hershey, Pa., 1976) ....
  1879, 4813, 5414, 6918, 6936, 6937,
  6946, 6951, 6970, 7619, 9605, 10148,
  11676, 11687, 11692, 11710, 13869
Software .... See ∗1858

FIGURE 11. These three extracts
from a Key Index were all typeset
from identical input, with respective
column widths of 22.5, 17.5, and
12.5 ems. Notice the combination of
ragged right and ragged left setting,
and the "dot leaders."

with more straightforward line-breaking tasks, since the full power of
the box/glue/penalty primitives was not immediately apparent. The
task is illustrated in Figure 11, which shows excerpts from a Key Index
in *Mathematical Reviews.* Such an index now appears at the end of each
volume, together with an Author Index that has a similar format.

As in Figure 10, the examples in Figure 11 were generated by the
same source input, but they were typeset using different line widths
in order to illustrate the various possibilities of breakpoints. Each entry
in the index consists of two parts, the *name part* and the *reference part*,
both of which might be too long to fit on a single line. If line breaks
occur in the name part, the individual lines are to be set with a ragged
right margin, but breaks in the reference part are supposed to produce
lines with a ragged *left* margin. The two parts are separated by *leaders*,
a row of dots that expands to fill the space between them; leaders are
introduced by a slight generalization of glue that typesets copies of a

given box into a given space, instead of leaving that space blank. A
hanging indentation is applied to all lines but the first, so that the first
line of each entry is readily identifiable. One of the goals in breaking
such entries is to minimize the white space that appears in ragged-right
or ragged-left lines. A subsidiary goal is to minimize the number of lines
that contain the reference part; for example, if it is possible to fit all of
the references on one line, the line-breaking algorithm should do so. The
latter event might mean that a break occurs after the leaders, with the
references starting on a new line; in such a case the leaders should stop a
fixed distance w_1 from the right margin. Furthermore, the ragged-right
lines should all be at least a fixed distance w_2 from the right margin, so
that there is no chance of confusing part of the name with part of the
reference material. The individual boxes to be replicated in the leaders
are w_3 units wide.

The ground rules are illustrated in Figure 11, where there is a hanging indentation of 27 units, and $w_1 = 45$, $w_2 = 9$, $w_3 = 7.2$; the digits are
9 units wide, and the respective column widths are 405 units, 315 units,
and 225 units. The entry for 'Theory of Computing' shows three possibilities for the leader dots: They can share a line with the end of the
name part and the beginning of the reference part, or they can end a
line before the reference part or begin a line after the name part.

Here is how all this can be encoded with boxes, glue, and penalties:
(a) Each blank space in the name part is represented by the sequence

> penalty$(0, \infty, 0)$
> glue$(w_2, 18, 0)$
> penalty$(0, 0, 0)$
> glue$(6 - w_2, -18, 2)$

which yields ragged right margins and spaces that can shrink from 6 units
to 4 units if necessary. (b) The transition between name part and reference part is represented by sequence (a) followed by

> box(0)
> penalty$(0, \infty, 0)$
> leaders$(3w_3, 100000, 3w_3)$
> glue$(w_1, 0, 0)$
> penalty$(0, 0, 0)$
> glue$(-w_1, -18, 0)$
> box(0)
> penalty$(0, \infty, 0)$
> glue$(0, 18, 0)$.

(c) Each blank space in the reference part is represented by the sequence

penalty$(0, 999, 0)$
glue$(6, -18, 2)$
box(0)
penalty$(0, \infty, 0)$
glue$(0, 18, 0)$,

which yields ragged left margins and 6-unit to 4-unit spaces.

Parts (a) and (c) of this construction are analogous to things we have seen before; the 999-point penalties in (c) tend to minimize the total number of lines occupied by the reference part. The most interesting aspect of this construction is the transition sequence (b), where there are four possibilities: If no line breaks occur in (b), the net result is

⟨name part⟩ glue$(6, 0, 2)$ ⟨leaders⟩ ⟨reference part⟩,

which allows leader dots to appear between the name and reference parts on the current line. If a line break occurs before the leaders, the net result is

⟨name part⟩ glue$(w_2, 18, 0)$
⟨leaders⟩ ⟨reference part⟩,

so that we have a break essentially like that after a blank space in the name part, and the dot leaders begin the following line. If a line break occurs after the leaders, the net result is

⟨name part⟩ glue$(6, 0, 2)$ ⟨leaders⟩ glue$(w_1, 0, 0)$
glue$(0, 18, 0)$ ⟨reference part⟩,

so that we have a break essentially like that after a blank space in the reference part but without the penalty of 999; the leaders end w_1 units from the right margin. Finally, if breaks occur both before and after the leaders in (b), we have a situation that always has more demerits than the alternative of breaking only before the leaders.

When the choice of breakpoints leaves room for at least $3w_3$ units of leaders, we are sure to have at least two dots, but we might not have three dots since leader dots on different lines are aligned with each other. The glue in other blank spaces on the line with the leaders will shrink if there is less than $3w_3$ of space for the leaders, and this tends to make it more likely that the leader dots will not disappear altogether; however, in the worst case the space for leaders will shrink to zero, so there might not be any dots visible. It would be possible to ensure that all the leaders contain at least two dots, by simply setting the shrink component of the leader item in (b) to zero. This would improve the appearance of the resulting output; but unfortunately it would also increase the length of the author indexes by about 15 percent, and such an expense would probably be prohibitive.

A preliminary version of this construction has been used with TEX to prepare the indexes of *Mathematical Reviews* since November, 1979. However, the items 'box(0) penalty$(0, \infty, 0)$' were left out of (b), for compatibility with earlier indexes prepared by other typesetting software; this means that the leaders disappear completely whenever a break occurs just before them, and the resulting indexes have unfortunate gaps of white space that spoil their appearance.

An Algebraic Approach

The examples we have just seen show that boxes, glue, and penalties are quite versatile primitives that allow a user to obtain a wide variety of effects without extending the basic operations needed for ordinary typesetting. However, some of the constructions may have seemed like magic; they work, but it isn't clear how they were ever conceived in the first place. We shall now study a fairly systematic way to deal with these primitives in order to assess their full potentiality. This brief discussion is independent of the remainder of the paper and can be omitted.

In the first place it is clear that

$$\text{box}(w)\ \text{box}(w') = \text{box}(w + w')\,,$$

if we ignore the contents of the boxes and consider only the widths; only the widths enter into the line-breaking criteria. This formula says that any two consecutive boxes can be replaced by a single box without affecting the choice of breakpoints, since breaks do not occur at box items. Similarly it is easy to verify that

$$\text{glue}(w, y, z)\ \text{glue}(w', y', z') = \text{glue}(w + w', y + y', z + z')\,,$$

since there will be no break at glue(w', y', z'), and since a break at glue(w, y, z) is equivalent to a break at glue$(w + w', y + y', z + z')$.

Under certain circumstances we can also combine two adjacent penalty items into a single one; for example, if $-\infty < p, p' < +\infty$ we have

$$\text{penalty}(w, p, f)\ \text{penalty}(w, p', f) = \text{penalty}(w, \min(p, p'), f)$$

with respect to any optimal choice of breakpoints, since there are fewer demerits associated with the smaller penalty. However, we cannot always replace the general sequence 'penalty(w, p, f) penalty(w', p', f')' by a single penalty item.

We can assume without loss of generality that all box items are immediately followed by a pair of items having the form 'penalty$(0, \infty, 0)$ glue(w, y, z)'. For if the box is followed by another box, we can combine the two; if it is followed by a penalty item with $p < \infty$, we can insert 'penalty$(0, \infty, 0)$ glue$(0, 0, 0)$'; if it is followed by 'penalty(w, ∞, f)' we can assume that $w = f = 0$ and that the following item is glue; and if the box is followed by glue, we can insert 'penalty$(0, \infty, 0)$ glue$(0, 0, 0)$ penalty$(0, 0, 0)$'. Furthermore we can delete any penalty item that has $p = \infty$ if it is not immediately preceded by a box item.

Thus, any sequence of box/glue/penalty items can be converted into a *normal form*, where each box is followed by a penalty of ∞, each penalty is followed by glue, and each glue is either followed by a box or by a penalty that is $< \infty$. We assume that there is only one penalty $-\infty$, and that it is the final item, since a forced line break effectively separates a longer sequence into independent parts. It follows that the normal-form sequences can be written

$$X_1 X_2 \ldots X_n \text{ penalty}(w, -\infty, f)$$

where each X_i is a sequence of items having the form

$$\text{box}(w) \text{ penalty}(0, \infty, 0) \text{ glue}(w', y, z)$$

or the form

$$\text{penalty}(v, p, f) \text{ glue}(w, y, z) \, .$$

Let us use the notation bpg$(w + w', y, z)$ for the first of these two forms, noting that it is a function of $w + w'$ rather than of w and w' separately; and let us write pg(v, p, f, w, y, z) for X's of the second form. We can assume that the sequence of X's contains no two bpg's in a row, since

$$\text{bpg}(w, y, z) \text{ bpg}(w', y', z') = \text{bpg}(w + w', y + y', z + z') \, .$$

Familiarity with this algebra of boxes, glue, and penalties makes it a fairly simple matter to invent constructions for special applications like those listed above, whenever such constructions are possible. For example, let us consider a generalization of the problems arising in ragged-right, ragged-left, and ragged-centered text: We wish to specify an optional break between words such that if no break occurs we will have the sequence

$$\langle\text{end of text}_1\rangle \ \text{glue}(w_1, y_1, z_1) \ \langle\text{beginning of text}_2\rangle$$

on one line, while if a break does occur we will have

$$\langle\text{end of text}_1\rangle \ \text{glue}(w_2, y_2, z_2) \ \text{penalty}(w_0, p, f)$$
$$\text{glue}(w_3, y_3, z_3) \ \langle\text{beginning of text}_2\rangle$$

on two lines. A consideration of normal forms shows that the most general thing we can do is to insert the sequence

$$\text{bpg}(w, y, z) \ \text{pg}(w_0, p, f, w', y', z') \ \text{bpg}(w'', y'', z'')$$

between text$_1$ and text$_2$, where no additional text is associated with the two inserted bpg's. Our job reduces therefore to determining appropriate values of w, y, z, w', y', z', w'', y'', and z''; these can be obtained immediately by solving the equations

$$w + w' + w'' = w_1 \ , \qquad y + y' + y'' = y_1 \ , \qquad z + z' + z'' = z_1 \ ,$$
$$w = w_2 \ , \qquad\qquad y = y_2 \ , \qquad\qquad z = z_2 \ ,$$
$$w'' = w_3 \ , \qquad\qquad y'' = y_3 \ , \qquad\qquad z'' = z_3 \ .$$

Once a construction has been found in this way, it can be simplified by undoing the process we have used to derive normal forms and by using other properties of box/glue/penalty algebra. For example, we can always delete the penalty ∞ item in a sequence like

$$\text{penalty}(0, \infty, 0) \ \text{glue}(0, y, z) \ \text{penalty}(0, p, 0) \ ,$$

if $y \geq 0$ and $z \geq 0$ and $p < 0$, since a break at the glue is always worse than a break at the penalty p.

Introduction to the Algorithm

The general ideas underlying the total-fit algorithm for line breaking can probably be understood best by considering an example. Figure 12 repeats the paragraph of Figure 4(c) and includes little vertical marks to indicate "feasible breakpoints" found by the algorithm. A *feasible breakpoint* is a place where the text of the paragraph from the beginning to this point can be broken into lines whose adjustment ratio does not exceed a given tolerance; in the case of Figure 12, this tolerance was taken to be unity. Thus, for example, there is a tiny mark after 'went'

In olden times when wishing still helped one, there lived a .774
king whose daughters were all beautiful; and the youngest was .179
so beautiful that the sun itself, which has seen so much, was .629
astonished whenever it shone in her face. Close by the king's .545
castle lay a great dark forest, and under an old lime-tree in the .000
forest was a well, and when the day was very warm, the king's .079
child went out into the forest and sat down by the side of the .282
cool fountain; and when she was bored she took a golden ball, .294
and threw it up on high and caught it; and this ball was her .575
favorite plaything. .004

FIGURE 12. Tiny vertical marks show "feasible breakpoints" where lines
could end without forcing any prior spaces to stretch more than their
given stretchability.

on line 7, since there is a way to set the paragraph up to this point with
'went' at the end of the 6th line and with none of lines 1 to 6 having a
badness exceeding 100 (see Figure 4(a)).

The algorithm proceeds by locating all of the feasible breakpoints
and remembering the best way to get to each one, in the sense of fewest
total demerits. This is done by keeping a list of *active breakpoints*, representing all of the feasible breakpoints that might be a candidate for
future breaks. Whenever a potential breakpoint b is encountered, the
algorithm tests to see if there is any active breakpoint a such that the
line from a to b has an acceptable adjustment ratio. If so, b is a feasible
breakpoint and it is appended to the active list. The algorithm also
remembers the identity of the breakpoint a that minimizes the total demerits, when the total is computed from the beginning of the paragraph
to b through a. When an active breakpoint a is encountered for which
the line from a to b has an adjustment ratio less than -1 (that is, when
the line can't be shrunk to fit the desired length), breakpoint a is removed from the active list. Since the size of the active list is essentially
bounded by the maximum number of words per line, the running time
of the algorithm is bounded by this quantity (which usually is small)
times the number of potential breakpoints.

For example, when the algorithm begins to work on the paragraph in
Figure 12, there is only one active breakpoint, representing the beginning
of the first line. It is infeasible to have a line starting there and ending
at 'In', or 'olden', ..., or 'lived', since the glue between words does not
accumulate enough stretchability in such short segments of the text;
but a feasible breakpoint is found after the next word 'a' is encountered.
Now there are two active breakpoints, the original one and the new one.
After the next word 'king', there are three active breakpoints; but after
the next word 'whose', the algorithm sees that it is impossible to squeeze

all of the text from the beginning up to 'whose' on one line, so the initial breakpoint becomes inactive and only two active ones remain.

Skipping ahead, let us consider what happens when the algorithm considers the potential break after 'fountain;'. At this stage there are eight active breakpoints, following the respective text boxes for 'child', 'went', 'out', 'side', 'of', 'the', 'cool', and 'foun-'. The line starting after 'child' and ending with 'fountain;' would be too long to fit, so 'child' becomes inactive. Feasible lines are found from 'went' or 'out' to 'fountain;' and the demerits of those lines are 400 and 144, respectively; the line from 'went' actually turns out to be preferable, since there are substantially fewer total demerits from the beginning of the paragraph to 'went' than to 'out'. Thus, 'fountain;' becomes a new active breakpoint. The algorithm stores a pointer back from 'fountain;' to 'went', meaning that the best way to get to a break after 'fountain;' is to start with the best way to get to a break after 'went'.

The computation of this algorithm can be represented pictorially by means of the network in Figure 13, which shows all of the feasible breakpoints together with the number of demerits charged for each feasible line between them. The object of the algorithm is to compute the *shortest path* from the top of Figure 13 to the bottom, using the demerit numbers as the "distances" corresponding to individual parts of the path. In this sense, the job of optimal line breaking is essentially a special case of the problem of finding shortest paths in an acyclic network; the line-breaking algorithm is slightly more complex only because it must construct the network at the same time as it is finding the shortest path.

Notice that the best-fit algorithm can be described very easily in terms of a network like Figure 13: It is the "greedy algorithm" that simply chooses the shortest continuation at every step (although it uses badness-plus-penalty as the criterion, not demerits). And the first-fit algorithm can be characterized as the method of always taking the leftmost branch having a negative adjustment ratio (unless it leads to a hyphen, in which case the rightmost non-hyphenated branch is chosen whenever there is a feasible one). From these considerations we can readily understand why the total-fit algorithm tends to do a much better job.

Sometimes there is no way to continue from one feasible breakpoint to any other. This situation doesn't occur in Figure 13, but it would be present below the word 'so' if we had not permitted hyphenation of 'astonished'. In such cases the first-fit and best-fit algorithms must resort to infeasible lines, while the total-fit algorithm can usually find another way through the maze.

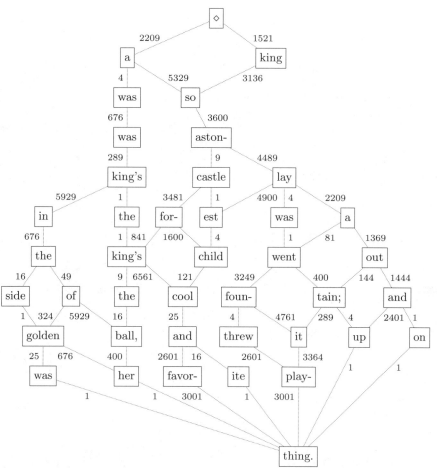

FIGURE 13. This network shows the feasible breakpoints and the number of demerits charged when going from one breakpoint to another. The shortest path from the top to the bottom corresponds to the best way to typeset the paragraph, if we regard the demerits as distances.

On the other hand, some paragraphs are inherently difficult, and there is no way to break them into feasible lines. In such cases the algorithm we have described will find that its active list dwindles until eventually there is no activity left; what should be done in such a case? It would be possible to start over with a more tolerant attitude toward infeasibility (a higher threshold value for the adjustment ratios). TEX takes the attitude that the user wants to make some manual adjustment when there is no way to meet the specified criteria, so the active list is forcibly prevented from becoming empty by simply declaring a break-point to be feasible if it would otherwise leave the active list empty. This results in an overset line and an error message that encourages the user to take corrective action.

Figure 14 shows what happens when the algorithm allows quite loose lines to be feasible; in this case a line is considered to be infeasible only if its adjustment ratio exceeds 10 (so that there would be more than two ems of space between words). Such a setting of the tolerances would be used by people who don't want to make manual adjustments to paragraphs that cannot be set well. The tiny marks that indicate feasible breakpoints have varying lengths in this illustration, with longer marks indicating places that can be reached via better paths; the tiny dots are for breakpoints that are just barely feasible. Notice that all of the potential breakpoints in Figure 14 are marked, except for a few in the first two lines; so there are considerably more feasible breakpoints here than there were in Figure 12, and the network corresponding to Figure 13 will be much larger. There are 806,137,512 feasible ways to set the paragraph when such wide spaces are tolerated, compared to only 50 ways in Figure 12. However, the number of active nodes will not be significantly bigger in this case than it was in Figure 12, because it is limited by the length of a line, so the algorithm will not run too much more slowly even though its tolerance has been raised and the number of possible settings has increased enormously. For example, after 'fountain;' there are now 17 active breakpoints instead of the 8 present before, so the processing takes only about twice as long although huge numbers of additional possibilities are being taken into account.

When the threshold allows wide spacing, the algorithm is almost certain to find a feasible solution, and it will report no errors to the user even though some rather loose lines may have been necessary. The user who wants such error messages should set the tolerance lower; this not only gives warnings when corrective action is needed, it also improves the algorithm's efficiency.

One of the important things to note about Figure 14 is that break-points can become feasible in completely different ways, leading up to different numbers of lines before the breakpoint. For example, the word 'seen' is feasible both at the end of line 3:

'In olden . . . lived/a . . . young-/est . . . seen'

and at the end of line 4:

'In olden . . . helped/one . . . were/all . . . beau-/tiful . . . seen',

| In olden times when wishing still helped one, there lived a .774
king whose daughters were all beautiful; and the youngest was .179
so beautiful that the sun itself, which has seen so much, was .629
astonished whenever it shone in her face. Close by the king's .545
castle lay a great dark forest, and under an old lime-tree in the .000
forest was a well, and when the day was very warm, the king's .079
child went out into the forest and sat down by the side of the .282
cool fountain; and when she was bored she took a golden ball, .294
and threw it up on high and caught it; and this ball was her .575
favorite plaything. | .004

FIGURE 14. When the tolerance is raised to 10 times the stretchability, more breakpoints become feasible, and there are many more possibilities to explore.

although 'seen' was not a feasible break at all in Figure 12. The breaks that put 'seen' at the end of line 3 have substantially fewer demerits than those putting it on line 4 (1,533,770 versus 12,516,097,962), so the algorithm will remember only the former possibility. This is an application of the dynamic-programming "principle of optimality" which is responsible for the efficiency of our algorithm [6]: The optimum breakpoints of a paragraph are always optimum for the subparagraphs they create. But the interesting thing is that this economy of storage would *not* be possible if the future lines were not all of the same length, since differing line lengths might well mean that it would be much better to put 'seen' on line 4 after all; for example, we have mentioned a trick for forcing the algorithm to produce a given number of lines. In the presence of varying line lengths, therefore, the algorithm would need to have two separate list entries for an active breakpoint after the word 'seen'. The computer cannot simply remember the one with fewest total demerits; that would invalidate the optimality principle of dynamic programming.

Figure 15 is an example of line breaking when the individual lengths are all different. In such cases, the need to attach line numbers to breakpoints might cause the number of active breakpoints to be substantially more than the maximum number of words per line, if the feasibility tolerance is set high. Therefore we want to set the tolerance low. But if the tolerance is too low, there may be no way to break the paragraph into lines having a desired shape. Fortunately, there is usually a happy medium in which the algorithm has enough flexibility to find a good solution without needing too much time and space. The data in Figure 16 shows, for example, that the algorithm did not have to do very much work to find an optimal solution for Galileo's remarks on circles, when the adjustment ratio on each feasible line was required to be 2 or less; yet there was sufficient flexibility to make feasible solutions possible.

The area of a
circle is a mean propor-
tional between any two regular
and similar polygons of which one
circumscribes it and the other is isoperimetric with it. In addition, the area
of the circle is less than that of any circumscribed polygon and greater than that
of any isoperimetric polygon. And further,
of these circumscribed polygons, the one
that has the greater number of sides has
a smaller area than the one that has
a lesser number; but, on the other
hand, the isoperimetric polygon
that has the greater num-
ber of sides is the
larger.

— Galileo Galilei (1638)

I
turn, in the
following treatises, to
various uses of those triangles
whose generator is unity. But I leave out
many more than I include; it is extraordinary how
fertile in properties this triangle is. Everyone can try his hand.

— Blaise Pascal (1654)

FIGURE 15. Examples of line breaking with lines of different sizes.

The area of a   .375
circle is a mean propor-   .828
tional between any two regular   .406
and similar polygons of which one   1.098
circumscribes it and the other is iso-   1.268
perimetric with it. In addition, the area   .574
of the circle is less than that of any cir-   1.111
cumscribed polygon and greater than that   .931
of any isoperimetric polygon. And further,   .584
of these circumscribed polygons, the one   1.561
that has the greater number of sides has   .703
a smaller area than the one that has   1.437
a lesser number; but, on the other   1.240
hand, the isoperimetric polygon   1.086
that has the greater num-   .974
ber of sides is the   .479
larger.   .000

FIGURE 16.
Details of the feasible
breakpoints in the first
example of Figure 15,
showing how the optimum
solution was found.

A good line-breaking method is especially important for technical typesetting, since mathematical formulas embedded in text should remain unbroken whenever possible. Some of the most difficult copy of this kind appears in *Mathematical Reviews* or in the answer pages of *The Art of Computer Programming*, since the material in those publications is often densely packed with formulas. Figure 17 shows a typical example from the answer pages of *Seminumerical Algorithms* [28], together with indications of the feasible breaks when the adjustment ratios are constrained to be at most 1. Although some feasible breakpoints occur in the middle of formulas, they are associated with penalties that make them comparatively undesirable, so the algorithm was able to keep all of the mathematics of this paragraph intact.

15. (This procedure maintains four integers (A, B, C, D) with the invariant meaning $-.409$
that "our remaining job is to output the continued fraction for $(Ay + B)/(Cy + D)$, $-.057$
where y is the input yet to come.") Initially set $j \leftarrow k \leftarrow 0$, $(A, B, C, D) \leftarrow (a, b, c, d)$; $-.788$
then input x_j and set $(A, B, C, D) \leftarrow (Ax_j + B, A, Cx_j + D, C)$, $j \leftarrow j + 1$, one or $.207$
more times until $C + D$ has the same sign as C. (When $j \geq 1$ and the input has not $-.282$
terminated, we know that $1 < y < \infty$; and when $C + D$ has the same sign as C we $.124$
know therefore that $(Ay + B)/(Cy + D)$ lies between $(A + B)/(C + D)$ and A/C.) $.192$
Now comes the general step: If no integer lies strictly between $(A + B)/(C + D)$ $.582$
and A/C, output $X_k \leftarrow \lfloor A/C \rfloor$, and set $(A, B, C, D) \leftarrow (C, D, A - X_k C, B - X_k D)$, $-.098$
$k \leftarrow k + 1$; otherwise input x_j and set $(A, B, C, D) \leftarrow (Ax_j + B, A, Cx_j + D, C)$, $.479$
$j \leftarrow j + 1$. The general step is repeated ad infinitum. However, if at any time the $.266$
final x_j is input, the algorithm immediately switches gears: It outputs the continued $-.325$
fraction for $(Ax_j + B)/(Cx_j + D)$, using Euclid's algorithm, and terminates. $.000$

FIGURE 17. An example of the feasible breakpoints found by the algorithm in a paragraph containing numerous mathematical formulas.

More Bells and Whistles

The optimization problem we have formulated is to find breakpoints that minimize the total number of demerits, where the demerits of a particular line depend on its badness (i.e., on how much its glue must stretch or shrink) and on a possible penalty associated with its final breakpoint; additional demerits are also added when two consecutive lines end with hyphens (i.e., end at penalty items with $f = 1$). Two years of experience with such a model of the problem gave excellent results, but a few paragraphs showed up where further improvement was possible.

The first two lines of Figures 4(a) and 4(b) illustrate a potential source of visual disturbance that was not considered in the model discussed above. These paragraphs begin with a tight line (having

$r = -.727$) immediately followed by a loose line (having $r = +.821$).
Although the two lines are not offensive in themselves, the contrast between tight and loose makes them appear worse. Therefore TEX's new
algorithm for line breaking recognizes four kinds of lines:

> Class 0 (tight lines), where $-1 \leq r < -.5$;
> Class 1 (normal lines), where $-.5 \leq r \leq .5$;
> Class 2 (loose lines), where $.5 < r \leq 1$;
> Class 3 (very loose lines), where $r > 1$.

Additional demerits are added when adjacent lines are not of the same
or adjacent classes, i.e., when a Class 0 line is preceded or followed by
Class 2 or Class 3, or when Class 1 is preceded or followed by Class 3.

This seemingly simple extension actually forces the algorithm to
work harder, because a feasible breakpoint may now have to be entered
into the active list up to four times in order to preserve the dynamic-
programming principle of optimality. For example, if it is feasible to
end at some point with both a Class 0 line and a Class 2 line, we must
remember both possibilities even though the Class 0 choice has more
demerits, because we might want to follow this breakpoint with a tight
line. On the other hand, we need not remember the Class 0 possibility
if its total demerits exceed those of the Class 2 break plus the demerits
for contrasting lines, since the Class 0 breakpoint will never be optimum
in such a case.

More experience is needed to determine whether the additional computation required by this extension is worthwhile. It is comforting for
the user to know that the line-breaking algorithm takes such refinements
into account, but there is no point in doing the extra work if the output
is hardly ever improved.

Another extension to the algorithm is needed to raise it to the highest standards of quality for hand composition: Sometimes we wish to
make a paragraph come out one line longer or shorter than its optimum
length, because this will avoid an isolated "widow line" at the top or
bottom of a page, or because it will make the total number of lines even,
so that the material can be divided into two equal columns. Although
the paragraph itself will not be in its optimum form, the entire page will
look better, and the paragraph will be set as well as possible subject to
the given constraints. For example, two of the paragraphs in the story
of Figure 6 have been set a line shorter than their optimum length, so
that all six columns come out equal.

The line-breaking algorithm we shall describe therefore has a "looseness" parameter, illustrated in Figure 18. The looseness is an integer q

In olden times when wishing still helped one, there lived a king $-.727$
whose daughters were all beautiful; and the youngest was so $.821$
beautiful that the sun itself, which has seen so much, was aston- $-.455$
ished whenever it shone in her face. Close by the king's castle lay $-.870$
a great dark forest, and under an old lime-tree in the forest was $-.208$
a well, and when the day was very warm, the king's child went $.000$
out into the forest and sat down by the side of the cool fountain; $-.577$
and when she was bored she took a golden ball, and threw it up $-.231$
on high and caught it; and this ball was her favorite plaything. $-.883$

In olden times when wishing still helped one, there lived a $.774$
king whose daughters were all beautiful; and the youngest was $.179$
so beautiful that the sun itself, which has seen so much, was $.629$
astonished whenever it shone in her face. Close by the king's $.545$
castle lay a great dark forest, and under an old lime-tree in the $.000$
forest was a well, and when the day was very warm, the king's $.079$
child went out into the forest and sat down by the side of the $.282$
cool fountain; and when she was bored she took a golden ball, $.294$
and threw it up on high and caught it; and this ball was her $.575$
favorite plaything. $.557$

In olden times when wishing still helped one, there lived 1.393
a king whose daughters were all beautiful; and the young- 1.464
est was so beautiful that the sun itself, which has seen so 1.412
much, was astonished whenever it shone in her face. Close 1.226
by the king's castle lay a great dark forest, and under an 1.412
old lime-tree in the forest was a well, and when the day 1.735
was very warm, the king's child went out into the forest 1.774
and sat down by the side of the cool fountain; and when 1.559
she was bored she took a golden ball, and threw it up on 1.378
high and caught it; and this ball was her favorite play- 2.129
thing. $.862$

FIGURE 18. Paragraphs obtained when the "looseness" parameter has
been set to -1, 0, and $+1$. Such settings are sometimes necessary to
balance a page, but of course the effects are not beautiful when one
goes to extremes.

such that the total number of lines produced for the paragraph is as close
as possible to the optimum number plus q, without violating the conditions of feasibility. Figure 18 shows what happens to the example para-
graph of Figure 14 when $|q| \leq 1$. Values of $q < -1$ would be the same
as $q = -1$, since this paragraph cannot be squeezed any further; values
of $q > 1$ are possible but rarely useful, because they require extremely
loose spacing. The user can get the optimum solution having fewest possible lines by setting q to an extremely negative value like -100. When
$q \neq 0$, the feasible breakpoints corresponding to different line numbers
must all be remembered, even when every line has the same length.

If the lines of a paragraph are fairly loose, we don't want the last line to be noticeably different, so we should reconsider our previous assumption that a paragraph's "finishing glue" has almost infinite stretchability. The penalty for adjacent lines of contrasting classes seems to work best in connection with looseness if the finishing glue at the paragraph end is set to have a normal space equal to about one-third of the total line width, stretching to the full width and shrinking to zero.

The Algorithm Itself

Now let us get down to brass tacks and discuss the details of an optimum line-breaking algorithm. We are given a paragraph $x_1 \ldots x_m$ described by items $x_i = (t_i, w_i, y_i, z_i, p_i, f_i)$ as explained earlier, where x_1 is a box item and x_m is a penalty item specifying a forced break ($p_m = -\infty$). We are also given a potentially infinite sequence of positive line lengths $l_1, l_2, \ldots$. There is a parameter α that gets added to the demerits whenever two consecutive breakpoints occur with $f_i = 1$, and a parameter γ that gets added to the demerits whenever two consecutive lines belong to incompatible fitness classes. There is a tolerance threshold ρ that is an upper bound on the adjustment ratios. And there is a looseness parameter q.

A feasible sequence of breakpoints $(b_1, \ldots, b_k)$ is a legal choice of breakpoints such that each of the k resulting lines has an adjustment ratio $r_j \le \rho$. If $q = 0$, the job of the algorithm is to find a feasible sequence of breakpoints having the fewest total demerits. If $q \neq 0$, the job of the algorithm is somewhat more difficult to describe precisely; it can be formulated as follows: Let k be the number of lines that the algorithm would produce when $q = 0$. Then the algorithm finds a feasible sequence of $k + q$ breakpoints having fewest total demerits. However, if this is impossible, the value of q is increased by 1 (if $q < 0$) or decreased by 1 (if $q > 0$) until a feasible solution is found. Sometimes no feasible solution is possible even with $q = 0$; we will discuss this situation later after seeing how the algorithm behaves in the normal case.

We have seen that it is occasionally useful to permit boxes, glue, and penalties to have negative widths and even negative stretchability; but a completely unrestricted use of negative values leads to unpleasant complications. For reasons of efficiency, it is desirable to place two limitations on the paragraphs that will be treated:

- *Restriction 1.* Let M_b be the length of the minimum-length line from the beginning of the paragraph to breakpoint b, namely the sum of all $w_i - z_i$ taken over all box and glue items x_i for $1 \le i < b$, plus w_b if x_b is a penalty item. The paragraph must have $M_a \leq M_b$ whenever a and b are legal breakpoints with $a < b$.

- *Restriction 2.* Let a and b be legal breakpoints with $a < b$, and assume that no x_i in the range $a < i < b$ is a box item or a forced break (penalty $p_i = -\infty$). Then either $b = m$, or x_{b+1} is a box item or a penalty $p_{b+1} < \infty$.

Both of these restrictions are quite reasonable, as they are met by all known practical applications. Restriction 2 seems peculiar at first glance, but we will see in a moment why it is helpful.

Our algorithm has the following general outline, viewed from the top down:

⟨Create an active node representing the starting point⟩;
for $b := 1$ **to** m **do** ⟨**if** b is a legal breakpoint⟩ **then**
 begin ⟨Initialize the feasible breaks at b to the empty set⟩;
 ⟨**for** each active node a⟩ **do**
  begin ⟨Compute the adjustment ratio r from a to b⟩;
  if $r < -1$ **or** ⟨b is a forced break⟩ **then** ⟨Deactivate node a⟩;
  if $-1 \leq r < \rho$ **then** ⟨Record a feasible break from a to b⟩;
  end;
 ⟨**if** there is a feasible break at b⟩ **then**
  ⟨Append the best such breaks as active nodes⟩;
 end;
⟨Choose the active node with fewest total demerits⟩;
if $q \neq 0$ **then** ⟨Choose the appropriate active node⟩;
⟨Use the chosen node to determine the optimum breakpoints⟩.

The meaning of the ad hoc ALGOL-like language used here should be self-evident. An *active node* in this description refers to a record that includes information about a breakpoint together with its fitness classification and the line number on which it ends.

We want to have a data structure that makes this algorithm efficient, and a reasonably good one is not hard to design. Two considerations are paramount: The operation of computing the adjustment ratio, from a given active node a to a given legal breakpoint b, should be made as simple as possible; and there should be an easy way to determine which of the feasible breaks at b ought to be saved as active nodes.

In the first place, the adjustment ratio depends on the total width, total stretchability, and total shrinkability computed from the first box after one breakpoint to the following breakpoint, and we don't want to compute those sums over and over. To avoid this, we can simply compute the sum from the beginning of the paragraph to the current place, and subtract two such sums to obtain the total of what lies between them. Let $(\Sigma w)_b$, $(\Sigma y)_b$, and $(\Sigma z)_b$ denote the respective sums of all the w_i, y_i, and z_i in the box and glue items x_i for $1 \leq i < b$. Then if a and b are legal breakpoints with $a < b$, the width L_{ab} of a line from a to b and its stretchability Y_{ab} and shrinkability Z_{ab} can be computed as follows:

$$L_{ab} = (\Sigma w)_b - (\Sigma w)_{\text{after}(a)} + (w_b \text{ if } t_b = \text{'penalty'}) ;$$
$$Y_{ab} = (\Sigma y)_b - (\Sigma y)_{\text{after}(a)} ;$$
$$Z_{ab} = (\Sigma z)_b - (\Sigma z)_{\text{after}(a)} .$$

Here 'after(a)' is the smallest index $i > a$ such that either $i > m$ or x_i is a box item or x_i is a penalty item that forces a break $(p_i = -\infty)$. These formulas hold even in the degenerate case that after$(a) > b$, because of Restriction 2; in fact, Restriction 2 essentially stipulates that the relation after$(a) > b$ implies that $(\Sigma w)_b = (\Sigma w)_{\text{after}(a)}$, $(\Sigma y)_b = (\Sigma y)_{\text{after}(a)}$, and $(\Sigma z)_b = (\Sigma z)_{\text{after}(a)}$.

From these considerations, we may conclude that each node a in the data structure should contain the following fields:

position(a) = index of the breakpoint represented by this node;
line(a) = number of the line ending at this breakpoint;
fitness(a) = fitness class of the line ending at this breakpoint;
totalwidth(a) = $(\Sigma w)_{\text{after}(a)}$, used to calculate adjustment ratios;
totalstretch(a) = $(\Sigma y)_{\text{after}(a)}$, used to calculate adjustment ratios;
totalshrink(a) = $(\Sigma z)_{\text{after}(a)}$, used to calculate adjustment ratios;
totaldemerits(a) = minimum total demerits up to this breakpoint;
previous(a) = pointer to the best node for the preceding breakpoint;
link(a) = pointer to the next node in the list.

Nodes become active when they are first created, and they become passive when they are deactivated. The algorithm maintains global variables A and P, which point respectively to the first node in the active list and the first node in the passive list. The first step can therefore be fleshed out as follows:

⟨Create an active node representing the starting point⟩ =
    begin $A :=$ **new** node (position = 0, line = 0, fitness = 1,
                              totalwidth = 0, totalstretch = 0,
                              totalshrink = 0, totaldemerits = 0,
                              previous = Λ, link = Λ);
    $P := \Lambda$;
    end.

We also introduce global variables ΣW, ΣY, and ΣZ to represent $(\Sigma w)_b$, $(\Sigma y)_b$, and $(\Sigma z)_b$ in the main loop of the algorithm, so that the operation 'for $b := 1$ to m do $\langle$if b is a legal breakpoint$\rangle$ then $\langle$main loop$\rangle$' takes the following form:

$\Sigma W := \Sigma Y := \Sigma Z := 0;$
for $b := 1$ to m do
    if $t_b =$ 'box' then $\Sigma W := \Sigma W + w_b$
    else if $t_b =$ 'glue' then
        begin if $t_{b-1} =$ 'box' then $\langle$main loop$\rangle$;
        $\Sigma W := \Sigma W + w_b;$ $\Sigma Y := \Sigma Y + y_b;$ $\Sigma Z := \Sigma Z + z_b;$
        end
    else if $p_b \neq +\infty$ then $\langle$main loop$\rangle$.

In the main loop itself, the operation $\langle$Compute the adjustment ratio r from a to $b\rangle$ can now be implemented simply as follows:

$L := \Sigma W - \text{totalwidth}(a);$
if $t_b =$ 'penalty' then $L := L + w_b;$
$j := \text{line}(a) + 1;$
if $L < l_j$ then
    begin $Y := \Sigma Y - \text{totalstretch}(a);$
    if $Y > 0$ then $r := (l_j - L)/Y$ else $r := \infty;$
    end
else if $L > l_j$ then
    begin $Z := \Sigma Z - \text{totalshrink}(a);$
    if $Z > 0$ then $r := (l_j - L)/Z$ else $r := -\infty;$
    end
else $r := 0.$

The other nonobvious problem we have to deal with is caused by the fact that several nodes might correspond to a single breakpoint. We will never create two nodes having the same values of (position, line, fitness), since the whole point of our dynamic programming approach is that we need only remember the best possible way to get to each feasible break position having a given line number and a given fitness class. But it is not immediately clear how to keep track of the best ways that lead to a given position, when that position can occur with different line numbers; we could, for example, maintain a hash table with (line, fitness) as the key, but that would be unnecessarily complicated. The solution is to keep the active list sorted by line numbers: After looking at all the active nodes for line j, we can insert new active nodes for line $j + 1$ into the list just before any active nodes for lines $\geq j + 1$ that we are about to look at next.

An additional complication is that we don't want to create active nodes for different line numbers when the line lengths are all identical, unless $q \neq 0$, since this would slow the algorithm down unnecessarily; the complexities of the general case should not encumber the simple situations that arise most often. Therefore we assume that an index j_0 is known such that all breaks at line numbers $\geq j_0$ can be considered equivalent. This index j_0 is determined as follows: If $q \neq 0$, then $j_0 = \infty$; otherwise j_0 is as small as possible such that $l_j = l_{j+1}$ for all $j > j_0$. For example, if $q = 0$ and $l_1 = l_2 = l_3 \neq l_4 = l_5 = \cdots$, we let $j_0 = 3$, since it is unnecessary to distinguish a breakpoint that ends line 3 from a breakpoint that ends line 4 at the same position, as far as any subsequent lines are concerned.

For each position b and line number j, it is convenient to remember the best feasible breakpoints having fitness classifications 0, 1, 2, 3 by maintaining four values D_0, D_1, D_2, D_3, where D_c is the smallest known total of demerits that leads to a breakpoint at position b and line j and class c. Another variable $D = \min(D_0, D_1, D_2, D_3)$ turns out to be convenient as well, and we let A_c point to the active node a that leads to the best value D_c. Thus the main loop takes the following slightly altered form, for each legal breakpoint b:

> **begin** $a := A$; $preva := \Lambda$;
> **loop:** $D_0 := D_1 := D_2 := D_3 := D := +\infty$;
>> **loop:** $nexta := \mathrm{link}(a)$;
>> $\langle$Compute j and the adjustment ratio r from a to $b\rangle$;
>> **if** $r < -1$ **or** $p_b = -\infty$ **then** $\langle$Deactivate node $a\rangle$
>> **else** $preva := a$;
>> **if** $-1 \leq r \leq \rho$ **then**
>>> **begin** $\langle$Compute demerits d and fitness class $c\rangle$;
>>> **if** $d < D_c$ **then**
>>>> **begin** $D_c := d$; $A_c := a$; **if** $d < D$ **then** $D := d$;
>>>> **end**;
>>> **end**;
>> $a := nexta$; **if** $a = \Lambda$ **then exit loop**;
>> **if** $\mathrm{line}(a) \geq j$ **and** $j < j_0$ **then exit loop**;
>> **repeat**;
>> **if** $D < \infty$ **then**
>>> $\langle$Insert new active nodes for breaks from A_c to $b\rangle$;
>> **if** $a = \Lambda$ **then exit loop**;
>> **repeat**;
> **if** $A = \Lambda$ **then**
>> $\langle$Do something drastic since there is no feasible solution$\rangle$;
> **end**.

For a given position b, the inner loop of this code considers all nodes a having equivalent line numbers, while the outer loop runs through all of the line numbers that are not equivalent.

It is not difficult to derive a precise encoding of the operations that have been abbreviated in these loops:

⟨Compute demerits d and fitness class c⟩ =
    begin if $p_b \geq 0$ **then** $d := (1 + 100|r|^3 + p_b)^2$
    else if $p_b \neq -\infty$ **then** $d := (1 + 100|r|^3)^2 - p_b^2$
    else $d := (1 + 100|r|^3)^2$;
    $d := d + \alpha \cdot f_b \cdot f_{\text{position}(a)}$;
    if $r < -.5$ **then** $c := 0$
    else if $r \leq .5$ **then** $c := 1$
    else if $r \leq 1$ **then** $c := 2$ **else** $c := 3$;
    if $|c - \text{fitness}(a)| > 1$ **then** $d := d + \gamma$;
    $d := d + \text{totaldemerits}(a)$;
    end.

⟨Insert new active nodes for breaks from A_c to b⟩ =
    begin ⟨Compute $tw = (\Sigma w)_{\text{after}(b)}$, $ty = (\Sigma y)_{\text{after}(b)}$,
                $tz = (\Sigma z)_{\text{after}(b)}$⟩;
    for $c := 0$ **to** 3 **do if** $D_c \leq D + \gamma$ **then**
        begin $s :=$ **new** node (position $= b$, line $= \text{line}(A_c) + 1$,
                        fitness $= c$, totalwidth $= tw$,
                        totalstretch $= ty$, totalshrink $= tz$,
                        totaldemerits $= D_c$, previous $= A_c$,
                        link $= a$);
        if $preva = \Lambda$ **then** $A := s$ **else** $\text{link}(preva) := s$;
        $preva := s$;
        end;
    end.

⟨Compute $tw = (\Sigma w)_{\text{after}(b)}$, $ty = (\Sigma y)_{\text{after}(b)}$, $tz = (\Sigma z)_{\text{after}(b)}$⟩ =
    begin $tw := \Sigma W$; $ty := \Sigma Y$; $tz := \Sigma Z$; $i := b$;
    loop: if $i > m$ **then exit loop**;
    if $t_i =$ 'box' **then exit loop**;
    if $t_i =$ 'glue' **then**
        begin $tw := tw + w_i$; $ty := ty + y_i$; $tz := tz + z_i$;
        end
    else if $p_i = -\infty$ **and** $i > b$ **then exit loop**;
    $i := i + 1$;
    repeat;
    end.

⟨Deactivate node a⟩ =
   begin if $preva = \Lambda$ **then** $A := nexta$ **else** link$(preva) := nexta$;
   link$(a) := P$; $P := a$;
   end.

After the main loop has done its job, the active list will contain only nodes with position $= m$, since x_m is a forced break. Thus, we can write

⟨Choose the active node with fewest total demerits⟩ =
   begin $a := b := A$; $d :=$ totaldemerits(a);
     loop: $a :=$ link(a);
     if $a = \Lambda$ **then exit loop**;
     if totaldemerits$(a) < d$ **then**
       begin $d :=$ totaldemerits(a); $b := a$;
       end;
     repeat;
   $k :=$ line(b);
   end.

Now b is the chosen node and k is its line number. The subsequent processing for $q \neq 0$ is equally elementary:

⟨Choose the appropriate active node⟩ =
   begin $a := A$; $s := 0$;
     loop: $\delta :=$ line$(a) - k$;
     if $q \leq \delta < s$ **or** $s < \delta \leq q$ **then**
       begin $s := \delta$; $d :=$ totaldemerits(a); $b := a$;
       end
     else if $\delta = s$ **and** totaldemerits$(a) < d$ **then**
       begin $d :=$ totaldemerits(a); $b := a$;
       end;
     $a :=$ link(a); **if** $a = \Lambda$ **then exit loop**;
     repeat;
   $k :=$ line(b);
   end.

Now the desired sequence of k breakpoints is accessible from node b:

⟨Use the chosen node to determine the optimum breakpoints⟩ =
   for $j := k$ **down to** 1 **do**
     begin $b_j :=$ position(b); $b :=$ previous(b);
     end.

(Another way to complete the processing, getting the lines in forward order from 1 to k instead of from k to 1, appears in the appendix below.)

If there is no garbage collection, the algorithm concludes by deallocating all nodes on lists A and P.

Restriction 1 makes it legitimate to deactivate a node when we discover that $r < -1$, since $r < -1$ is equivalent to $l_j < L_{ab} - Z_{ab}$, therefore subsequent breakpoints $b' > b$ will have $L_{ab'} - Z_{ab'} \geq L_{ab} - Z_{ab}$. Thus it is not difficult to verify that the algorithm does indeed find an optimal solution: Given any sequence of feasible breakpoints $b_1 < \cdots < b_k$, we can prove by induction on j that the algorithm constructs a node for a feasible break at b_j, with appropriate line numbers and fitness classifications, having no more demerits than the given sequence does.

There is only one loose end remaining in the algorithm, namely the operation ⟨Do something drastic since there is no feasible solution⟩. As mentioned above, TEX assumes that the user has chosen the tolerance threshold ρ in such a way that human intervention is desirable when this tolerance cannot be met. Another alternative would be to have two thresholds and to try the algorithm first with threshold ρ_0, which is lower than ρ, so the algorithm will generate comparatively few active nodes; if there is no way to succeed at tolerance ρ_0, the algorithm could simply return all nodes to free storage and try again with the actual threshold ρ. This dual-threshold method will not always find the strictly optimum feasible solution, since it is possible in unusual circumstances for the optimum solution to include a line whose adjustment ratio exceeds ρ_0 while there is a non-optimum feasible solution meeting the tolerance ρ_0; for practical purposes, however, the difference is negligible.

TEX actually uses a different sort of dual-threshold method. Since the task of word division is nontrivial, TEX tries first to break a paragraph into lines without any discretionary hyphens except those already present in the given text, using a tolerance threshold ρ_1. If the algorithm fails to find a feasible solution, or if there is a feasible solution with $q \neq 0$ but the desired looseness could not be satisfied ($\delta \neq q$), all nodes are returned to free storage and TEX starts again using another tolerance ρ_2. During this second pass, all words of five letters or more are submitted to TEX's hyphenation algorithm before they are treated by the line-breaking algorithm. Thus, the user sets ρ_1 to the limit of tolerance for paragraphs that can be completely broken without hyphenation, and ρ_2 is set to the tolerance limit when hyphenation must be tried; possibly ρ_1 will be slightly larger than ρ_2, but it might also be smaller, if hyphenation is not frowned on too much. In practice ρ_1 and ρ_2 are usually equal to each other, or else ρ_1 is near 1 and ρ_2 is slightly larger; alternatively, one can take $\rho_2 = 0$ to effectively disallow hyphenation.

When both passes fail, TEX continues by reactivating the node that was most recently deactivated and treats it as if it were a feasible break leading to b. This situation is actually detected in the routine ⟨Deactivate node a⟩, just after the last active node has become passive:

if $A = \Lambda$ **and** *secondpass* **and** $D = \infty$ **and** $r < -1$ **then** $r := -1$.

The net result is to produce an "overfull box" that sticks out into the right margin, whenever no feasible sequence of line breaks is possible. As discussed above, some kind of error indication is necessary, since the user is assumed to have set ρ to a value such that further stretching is intolerable and requires manual intervention. An overfull box is easier to provide than an underfull one, by the nature of the algorithm. This is fortunate: The setting of the overfull box will be as tight as possible, hence the user can easily see how to devise appropriate corrective action such as a forced line break or hyphenation.

Computational Experience

The algorithm described in the previous section is rather complex, since it is intended to apply to a wide variety of situations that arise in typesetting. A considerably simpler procedure is possible for the special cases needed for word processors and newspapers; the appendix to this paper gives details about such a stripped-down version. Contrariwise, the algorithm in TEX is even more complex than the one we have described, because TEX must deal with leaders, with footnotes or cross references or page-break marks attached to lines, and with spacing both inside and immediately outside of math formulas; the spacing that surrounds a formula is slightly different from glue because it disappears when followed by a line break, but it does not represent a legal breakpoint. (A complete description of TEX's algorithm will appear elsewhere [29].) Experience has shown that the general algorithm is quite efficient in practice, in spite of all the things it must cope with.

So many parameters are present, it is impossible for anyone actually to experiment with a large fraction of the possibilities. A user can vary the interword spacing and the penalties for inserted hyphens, explicit hyphens, adjacent flagged lines, and adjacent lines with incompatible fitness classifications; the tolerance threshold ρ can also be twiddled, not to mention the lengths of lines and the looseness parameter q. Thus one could perform computational experiments for years and not have a completely definitive idea about the behavior of this algorithm. Even with fixed parameters there is a significant variation with respect to the kind of material being typeset; for example, highly mathematical copy presents special problems. An interesting comparative study of line breaking was made by Duncan and his coworkers [13], who considered sample texts from Gibbon's *Decline and Fall* versus excerpts from a story entitled *Salar the Salmon*; as expected, Gibbon's vocabulary forced substantially more hyphenated lines.

On the other hand, we have seen that the optimizing algorithm leads to better line breaks even in children's stories where the words are short and simple, as in Grimms' fairy tales. It would be nice to have a quantitative feeling for how much extra computation is necessary to get this improvement in quality. Roughly speaking, the computation time is proportional to the number of words of the paragraph, times the average number of words per line, since the main loop of the computation runs through the currently active nodes, and since the average number of words per line is a reasonable estimate of the number of active nodes in all but the first few lines of a paragraph (see Figures 12 and 14). On the other hand, there are comparatively few active nodes on the first lines of a paragraph, so the performance is actually faster than this rough estimate would indicate. Furthermore, the special-purpose algorithm in the appendix runs in nearly linear time, independent of the line length, since it does not need to run through all of the active nodes.

Detailed statistics were kept when TEX's first large production, *Seminumerical Algorithms* [28], was typeset using the procedure above. This 702-page book has a total of 5526 "paragraphs" in its text and answer pages, if we regard displayed formulas as separators between independent paragraphs. The 5526 paragraphs were broken into a total of 21,057 lines, of which 550 (about 2.6%) ended with hyphens. The lines were usually 29 picas wide, which means 626.4 machine units in 10-point type and about 677.19 machine units in 9-point type, roughly twelve or thirteen words per line. The threshold values ρ_1 and ρ_2 were normally both set to $\sqrt[3]{2} \approx 1.26$, so the spaces between words ranged from a minimum of 4 units to a maximum of $6 + 3\sqrt[3]{2} \approx 9.78$ units. The penalty for breaking after a hyphen was 50; the consecutive-hyphens and adjacent-incompatibility demerits were $\alpha = \gamma = 3000$. The second (hyphenation) pass was needed on only 279 of the paragraphs, thus about 5% of the time; a feasible solution without hyphenation was found in the remaining 5247 cases. The second pass would attempt to hyphenate only the uncapitalized words of five or more letters, containing no accents, ligatures, or hyphens, and it turned out that exactly 6700 words were submitted to the hyphenation procedure. Thus the average number of attempted hyphenations per paragraph was approximately 1.2, only slightly more than needed by conventional nonoptimizing algorithms, and hyphenation was not a significant factor in the running time.

The main contribution to the running time came, of course, from the main loop of the algorithm, which was executed 274,102 times (about 50 times per paragraph, including both passes lumped together when the second pass was needed). The total number of break nodes created was 64,003 (about 12 per paragraph), including multiplicities for the comparatively rare cases that different fitness classifications or line numbers needed to be distinguished for the same breakpoint. Thus, about 23% of the legal breakpoints turned out to be feasible ones, given these comparatively low values of ρ_1 and ρ_2. The inner loop of the computation was performed 880,677 times; this is the total number of active nodes examined when each legal breakpoint was processed, summed over all legal breakpoints. Note that this amounts to about 160 active node examinations per paragraph, and 3.2 per breakpoint, so the inner loop definitely dominates the running time. If we assume that words are about five letters long, so that a legal break occurs for every six characters of input text including the spaces between words, the algorithm costs about half of an inner-loop step per character of input, plus the time to pass over that character in the outermost loop.

This source data was also used to establish the importance of the optional dominance test 'if $D_c \leq D + \gamma$' preceding the creation of a new node; without that test, the algorithm was found to need about 25% more executions of the inner loop, because so many unnecessary nodes were created.

And how about the output? Figure 19 shows the actual distribution of adjustment ratios r in the 15,531 typeset lines of *Seminumerical Algorithms*, not counting the 5526 lines at the ends of paragraphs, for which $r \approx 0$. There was also one line with $r \approx 1.8$ and one with $r \approx 2.2$ (i.e., a disgraceful spacing of 12 units); perhaps some reader will be able to spot one or both of these anomalies some day. The average value of r over all 21,057 lines was 0.08, and the standard deviation was only 0.403; about 67% of the lines had word spaces varying between 5 and 7 units. Furthermore the author believes that virtually none of the 15,531 line breaks are "psychologically bad" in the sense mentioned above.

Anyone who has experience with typical English text knows that these statistics are not only excellent, they are in fact too good to be true; no line-breaking algorithm can achieve such stellar behavior without occasional assists from the author, who notices that a slight change in wording will permit nicer breaks. Indeed, this phenomenon is another source of improved quality when an author is given composition tools

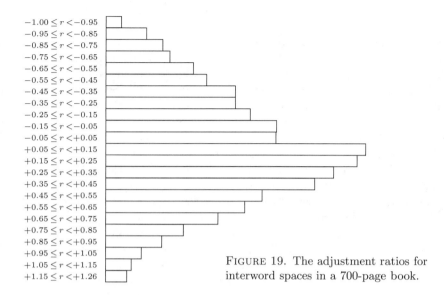

FIGURE 19. The adjustment ratios for interword spaces in a 700-page book.

like TeX to work with, because a professional compositor does not dare to mess around with the given wording when setting a paragraph, while an author is happy to make changes that look better, especially when such changes are negligible by comparison with changes that are found to be necessary for other reasons when a draft is being proofread. Authors know that there are many ways to say what they want to say, so it is no trick at all for them to make an occasional change of wording.

Theodore L. De Vinne, one of America's foremost typographers at the turn of the century, wrote [11, page 138] that "When the author objects to [a hyphenation] he should be asked to add or cancel or substitute a word or words that will prevent the breakage. ... Authors who insist on even spacing always, with sightly divisions always, do not clearly understand the rigidity of types."

Another interesting comment was made by G. B. Shaw [39]: "In reprinting his own works, whenever [William Morris] found a line that justified awkwardly, he altered the wording solely for the sake of making it look well in print. When a proof has been sent me with two or three lines so widely spaced as to make a grey band across the page, I have often rewritten the passage so as to fill up the lines better; but I am sorry to say that my object has generally been so little understood that the compositor has spoilt all the rest of the paragraph instead of mending his former bad work."

The bias caused by Knuth's tuning his manuscript to a particular line width makes the statistics in Figure 19 inapplicable to the printer's situation where a given text must be typeset as it is. So another experiment was conducted in which the material of Section 3.5 of *Seminumerical Algorithms* was set with lines 25 picas wide instead of 29 picas. Section 3.5, which deals with the question "What is a random sequence?", was chosen because this section most closely resembles typical mathematics papers containing theorems, proofs, lemmas, etc. In this experiment the total-fit algorithm had to work harder than it did when the material was set to 29 picas, primarily because the second pass was needed about thrice as often (49 times out of 273 paragraphs, instead of 16 times); furthermore the second pass was much more tolerant of wide spaces ($\rho_2 = 10$ instead of $\sqrt[3]{2}$), in order to guarantee that every paragraph could be typeset without manual intervention. There were about 6 examinations of active nodes per legal breakpoint encountered, instead of about 3, so the net effect of this change in parameters was to nearly double the running time for line breaking. The reason for such a discrepancy was primarily the combination of difficult mathematical copy and a narrower column measure, rather than the "author tuning," because when the same text was set 35 picas wide the second pass was needed only 8 times.

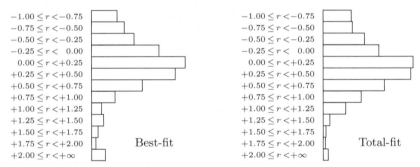

FIGURE 20. The distribution of interword spaces found by the best line-at-a-time method, compared to the distribution found by the best paragraph-at-a-time method, when difficult mathematical copy is typeset without human intervention.

It is interesting to observe the quality of the spacing obtained in this 25-pica experiment, since it indicates how well the total-fit method can do without any human intervention. Figure 20 shows what was obtained, together with the corresponding statistics for the best-fit method when it was applied to the same data. About 800 line breaks were involved in each case, not counting the final lines of paragraphs. The main difference was that total-fit tended to put more lines into the range $.5 \leq r \leq 1$, while best-fit produced considerably more lines that were extremely spaced out. The standard deviation of spacing was 0.53 (total-fit) versus 0.64 (best-fit); 24 of the lines typeset by best-fit had spaces exceeding 12 units, while only 7 such bad lines were produced by the total-fit method. An examination of these seven problematical cases showed that three of them were due to long unbreakable formulas embedded in the text, three were due to the rule that TEX does not try to hyphenate capitalized words and the other one was due to TEX's inability to hyphenate the word 'reasonable'. Cursory inspection of the output indicated that the main difference between best-fit and total-fit, in the eyes of a casual reader, would be that the best-fit method not only resorted to occasional wide spacing, it also tended to end substantially more lines with hyphens: 119 by comparison with 80. An author who cares about spacing, and who therefore will edit a manuscript until it can be typeset satisfactorily, would have to do a significant amount of extra work in order to get the best-fit method to produce decent results with such difficult copy, but the output of the total-fit method could be made suitable with only a few author's alterations.

A Historical Summary

We have now discussed most of the issues that arise in line breaking, and it is interesting to compare the newfangled approaches to what printers have actually been doing through the years. Medieval scribes, who prepared beautiful manuscripts by hand before the days of printing, were generally careful to break lines so that the right-hand margins would be nearly straight, and this practice was continued by the early printers. Indeed, the compositors who set the type had to fill up each line with spaces anyway, so that the individual letters wouldn't fall out of position while making impressions; they could insert extra spaces between words almost as easily as they could put those spaces at the ends of lines.

One of the most difficult challenges faced by printers over the years has been the typesetting of "polyglot Bibles," that is, editions of the Bible in which the original languages are set side by side with various translations, since special care is needed to keep the versions of various languages synchronized with each other. Furthermore the fact that several languages appear on each page means that the texts tend to be set with narrower columns than usual; this, together with the fact that one

¶I N prícipio crea .I.
uit deus ○○○○○○○○○
celum & terrá. Terra
autem ○○ ○○ ○○○○○○○
erat inanis & vacua: &
tenebre erant sup facié
abyffi : & spiritus dei
ferebatur super ○○○○○
aquas. Dixitqz deus.
Fiat ○○○○○○○○○○○○○○
lux. Et facta é lux. Et
vidit deus lucem ○○○○○
qp effet bona : & diuisit
○○○○○○○○○○○○○○○○○○
lucem a tenebris : ap
pellauitqz ○○○○○○○○○○
lucem dié : & tenebras
noctem. ○○○○○○○○○○○
Factumqz est vespe &
mane dies vnus.○○○○○
Dixit quoqz deus. Fiat
firmamentú in medio
aquarum:" & diuidat
aquas ○○○○○○○○○○○○
ab aquis. Et fecit deus
firmamentum. ○○○○○○

בְּרֵאשִׁית בָּרָא אֱלֹהִים אֵת
הַשָּׁמַיִם וְאֵת הָאָרֶץ׃ וְהָאָרֶץ
הָיְתָה תֹהוּ וָבֹהוּ וְחֹשֶׁךְ עַל פְּנֵי
תְהוֹם וְרוּחַ אֱלֹהִים מְרַחֶפֶת עַל
פְּנֵי הַמָּיִם׃ וַיֹּאמֶר אֱלֹהִים יְהִי
אוֹר וַיְהִי אוֹר׃ וַיַּרְא אֱלֹהִים אֶת
הָאוֹר כִּי טוֹב וַיַּבְדֵּל אֱלֹהִים בֵּין
הָאוֹר וּבֵין הַחֹשֶׁךְ׃ וַיִּקְרָא אֱלֹהִים
לָאוֹר יוֹם וְלַחֹשֶׁךְ קָרָא לָיְלָה
וַיְהִי עֶרֶב וַיְהִי בֹקֶר יוֹם אֶחָד׃
וַיֹּאמֶר אֱלֹהִים יְהִי רָקִיעַ בְּתוֹךְ
הַמָּיִם וִיהִי מַבְדִּיל בֵּין מַיִם
לָמָיִם׃ וַיַּעַשׂ אֱלֹהִים אֶת הָרָקִיעַ

FIGURE 21. The opening verses of Genesis as typeset in the Complutensian Polyglot Bible. Here Latin words are keyed to the Hebrew, and leaders are used to fill out lines that would otherwise be ragged right and ragged left. Greek and Chaldee (Aramaic) versions of the text also appeared on the same page.

dare not alter the sacred words, makes the line-breaking problem especially difficult. We can get a good idea of the early printers' approaches to line breaking by examining their polyglot Bibles carefully.

The first polyglot Bible [10, 19, 24] was produced in Spain by the eminent Cardinal Jiménez de Cisneros, who reportedly spent 50,000 gold ducats to support the project. It is generally called the "Complutensian Polyglot," because it was prepared in Alcalá de Henares, a city near Madrid whose old Roman name was Complutus. The printer, Arnao Guillén de Brocar, devoted the years 1514–1517 to the production of this six-volume set, and it is said that the Hebrew and Greek fonts he made for the occasion are among the finest ever cut. His approach to justification was quite interesting and unusual, as shown in Figure 21:

Instead of justifying the lines by increasing the word spaces, he inserted visible leaders to obtain solid blocks of copy with straight margins.

These leaders appear at the right of the Latin lines and at the left of the Hebrew lines. He changed this style somewhat after gaining more experience: Starting at about the 46th chapter of Genesis, the Hebrew text was justified by word spaces, although the leaders continued to appear in the Latin column. It is clear that straight margins were considered strongly desirable at the time.

Guillén de Brocar's method of line breaking seems to be essentially a first-fit approach to the Hebrew text; the corresponding Latin translation could then be set up rather easily, since there were two lines of Latin for each line of Hebrew, giving plenty of room for the Latin. In some cases when the Greek text was abnormally long by comparison with the corresponding Hebrew (e.g., Exodus 38), he set the Hebrew quite loosely, so it is evident that he gave considerable attention to line breaking.

At about the same time, a polyglot version of the book of Psalms was being prepared as a labor of love by Agostino Giustiniani of Genoa [17]. This was the first polyglot book actually to appear in print with each language in its own characters, although Origen's third-century *Hexapla* manuscript is generally considered to be the inspiration for all of the later polyglot volumes. Giustiniani's Psalter had eight columns: (1) The Hebrew original; (2) a literal Latin rendition of (1); (3) the common Latin (Vulgate) version; (4) the Greek (Septuagint) version; (5) the Arabic version; (6) the Chaldee version; (7) a literal Latin translation of (6); (8) notes. Since the Psalms are poems, all of the columns except the last were set with ragged margins, and an interesting convention was used to deal with the occasional line that was too wide to fit: A left parenthesis was placed at the very end of the broken line, and the remainder of that line (preceded by another left parenthesis) was placed flush with the margin of the preceding or following line, wherever it would fit.

Only column (8) was justified, and it had a rather narrow measure of about 21 characters per line. By studying this column we can conclude that Giustiniani did not take great pains to achieve equal spacing by fiddling with the words. For example, Figure 22, which comes from the notes on Psalm 6, shows two very tight lines enclosing a very loose one in the passage 'scriptum est ... quod qui'. If Giustiniani had been extremely concerned about spacing he would have used the hyphenation 'cog-nosces'; the other potential solution, to move 'ad' up a line, would not have worked since there isn't quite room for 'ad' on the loose line. Notice that another aid to line breaking in Latin at that time was to replace an m or n by a tilde on the previous vowel (e.g., 'premiũ' for

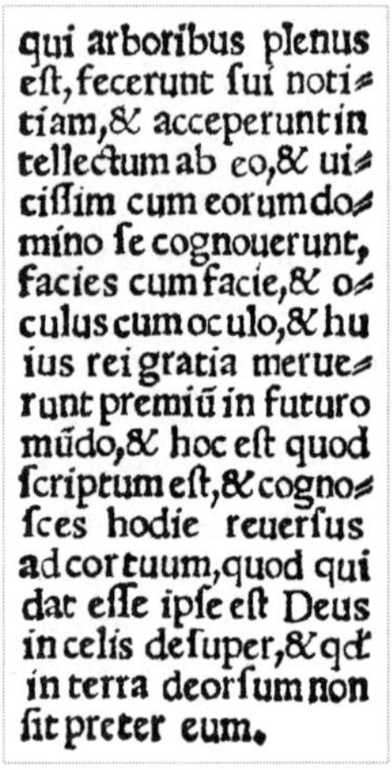

FIGURE 22. Part of Giustiniani's commentary on the Psalms. The presence of a loose line surrounded by two very tight lines indicates that the compositor did not go back to reset previous lines when a problem arose.

qui arboribus plenus eſt, fecerunt ſui notitiam, & acceperunt in tellectum ab eo, & uiciſſim cum eorum domino ſe cognouerunt, facies cum facie, & oculus cum oculo, & huius rei gratia meruerunt premiũ in futuro mũdo, & hoc eſt quod ſcriptum eſt, & cognoſces hodie reuerſus ad cor tuum, quod qui dat eſſe ipſe eſt Deus in celis deſuper, & qđ in terra deorſum non ſit preter eum.

premium and 'mũdo' for mundo); an extension to the box/glue/penalty algebra would be needed to include such options in TEX's line-breaking algorithm. It is not clear why Giustiniani didn't set 'acceperũt' on the third line, to save space, since he had no room for the hyphen of 'intellectum'; perhaps he didn't have enough ũ's left in his type case.

Figure 23 shows some justified text from the Complutensian Polyglot, taken from the Latin translation of an early Aramaic translation of the original Hebrew. The compositor was somewhat miraculously able to maintain this uniformly tight spacing throughout the entire volume, by making use of abbreviations and frequent hyphenations. In five places, as in Figure 22, the hyphen was omitted from a broken word when there was no room for it; e.g., 'diuisit' has been divided without a hyphen.

The next great polyglot Bible was the "Royal Polyglot of Antwerp" [1], produced during 1568–1572 by the outstanding Belgian printer Christophe Plantin. Numerous copies of the *Complutensian Polyglot* had unfortunately been lost at sea, so King Philip II commissioned a new edition that would also take advantage of recent scholarship. Plantin was a pious man who was active in pacifist religious circles and anxious to undertake the job; but when he had completed the work he described it as "an indescribable toil, labor, and expense." On June 9, 1572, Plantin sent a letter to one of his friends, saying "I am astonished at what I undertook, a task I would not do again even if I received 12,000 crowns as a gift." But at least his work was widely appreciated: Lucas of Bruges, writing in 1577, said that "the art of the printer has never produced anything nobler, nor anything more splendid."

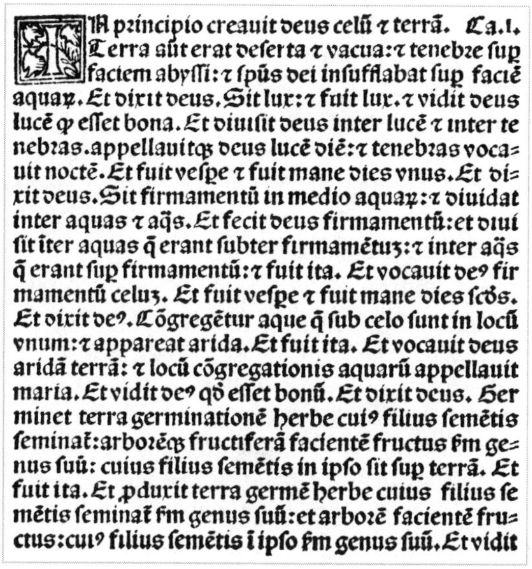

FIGURE 23. Early printing of Latin texts featured uniformly tight spacing, obtained by frequent use of abbreviations and word division. This sample comes from the same page as Figure 21.

Most of Plantin's polyglot Bible was justified with fairly wide columns having about 42 characters per line, so it did not present especially difficult problems of line breaking. But we can get some idea of his methods by studying the texts of the Apocrypha, which were set with a narrower measure of about 27 characters per line. He arranged things so that each column on a page would have about the same number of lines, even though the individual columns were in different languages.

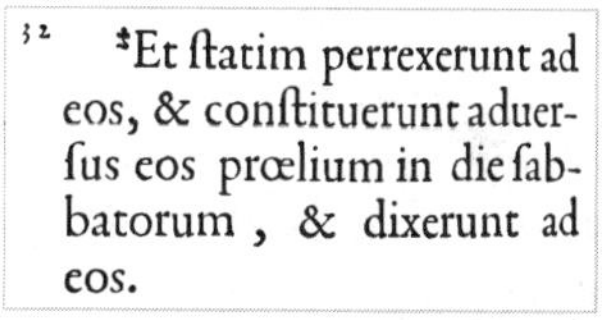

FIGURE 24. The Latin version of Maccabees 2 : 32 from Plantin's Royal Polyglot of Antwerp, showing how the second-last line of a paragraph was spaced out in order to add a line.

Figure 24 shows an example of a passage excerpted from a page where the Latin text was comparatively sparse, so the paragraphs on that page needed to be rather loose. It appears that the entire page was set first, then adjustments were made after the Latin column was found to be too short; in this case the word 'eos' was brought down to make a new line and the previous line was spaced out. Plantin's compositor did not take the trouble to move 'sab-' down to that line, although such a transposition would have avoided a hyphen without making the spacing any worse. The optimum solution would have been to avoid this hyphenation and to hyphenate the previous line after 'ad-', thus achieving fairly uniform spacing throughout.

The most accurate and complete of all polyglot Bibles was the "London Polyglot" [41], printed by Thomas Roycroft and others during the Cromwellian years 1653–1657. This massive 8-volume work included texts in Hebrew, Greek, Latin, Aramaic, Syriac, Arabic, Ethiopic, Samaritan, and Persian, all with accompanying Latin translations, and it has been acclaimed as "the typographical achievement of the seventeenth century." As in Plantin's work shown in Figure 24, a paragraph that has been loosened will often end with an unnecessarily tight hyphenated line followed by a loose line followed by a one-word line; so it is clear that Roycroft's compositors did not have time to do complex adjustments of line breaks.

Hyphenations were clearly not frowned upon at the time, since about 40% of all lines in the London Polyglot end with a hyphen, regardless of the column width. It is not difficult to find pages on which hyphenated lines outnumber the others; and in the Latin translation of the Aramaic version of Genesis 4:15, even the two-letter word 'e-o' was hyphenated! Such practice was not uncommon; for example, the Hamburg Polyglot Bible of 1596 [42] had more than 50% hyphens at the right margin. Both Plantin's polyglot and the notes of Giustiniani's Psalter had hyphenation percentages of about 40%, and the same was true of many medieval manuscripts. Thus it was considered better to have the margins straight and to keep the spacing tight, rather than to avoid word splits.

One of the first things that strikes a modern eye when looking at these old Bibles is the treatment of punctuation. Notice, for example, that no space appears after the commas in Figure 22, and a space appears *before* as well as after one of the commas in Figure 24. One can find all four possibilities of 'space before/no space before' and 'space after/no space after' in each of the Bibles mentioned so far, with respect to commas, periods, colons, semicolons, and question marks, and with no apparent preference between the four choices except that it was comparatively rare to put a space before a period. Giustiniani and Plantin occasionally would insert spaces before periods, but Roycroft apparently never did. Commas began to be treated like periods in this respect about

1700, but colons and semicolons were generally both preceded and followed by spaces until the 19th century. Such extra spaces were helpful in justifying, of course, and printers evidently relished the option of leaving out all of the space next to a punctuation mark. Roycroft would in fact eliminate the space between words when necessary, if the following word was capitalized (e.g., 'dixitDeus'); apparently a printer's main goal was to keep the text unambiguously decipherable, while ease of readability was only of secondary importance.

Knowledge about how to carry out the work of a trade like printing was originally passed from masters to apprentices and not explained to the general public, so we can only guess at what the early printers did by looking at their finished products. A trend to put trade secrets into print was developing during the 17th century, however [21], and a book about how to make books was finally written: Joseph Moxon's *Mechanick Exercises* [30], published in 1683, was by forty years the earliest manual of printing in any language. Although Moxon did not discuss rules for hyphenation and punctuation, he gave interesting information about line breaking and justification.

"If the Compositer is not firmly resolv'd to keep himself strictly to the Rules of good Workmanship, he is now tempted to make *Botches*;" namely bad line breaks, according to Moxon. The normal "thick space" between words, when beginning to make up a line, was one-fourth of what Moxon called the body size (one em), and he also spoke of "thin spaces" that were one-seventh of the body size; thus, a printer who followed this practice would deal mostly with spaces of 4.5 units and 2.57 units, although such measurements were only approximate because of the primitive tools used at the time. Moxon's procedure for justifying a line whose natural width was too narrow was to insert thin spaces between one or more words to "fill up the Measure pretty stiff," and if necessary to go back through the line and do this again. "Strictly, good Workmanship will not allow more [than the original space plus two thin spaces], unless the *Measure* be so short, that by reason of few *Words* in a *Line*, necessity compels him to put more *Spaces* between the *Words*. ... These wide *Whites* are by *Compositers* (in way of Scandal) call'd *Pidgeon-holes*... And as *Lines* may be too much *Spaced-out*, so may they be too close *Set*." [30, pages 214–215]

Notice that Moxon's justification procedure would normally leave uneven spacing between words on the same line, since he inserted the thin spaces one by one. In fact, such discrepancies were the norm in early printed books, which look something like present-day attempts at justification on a typewriter or computer terminal with fixed-width

If there be a long *word* or more left out, he
cannot expect to *Get* that in into that *Line*, wherefore he muſt now *Over-run;* that is, he muſt put ſo
much of the fore-part of the *Line* into the *Line*
above it, or ſo much of the hinder part of the *Line*
into the next *Line* under it, as will make room for
what is *Left out* : Therefore he conſiders how *Wide*
he has *Set*, that ſo by *Over-runing* the fewer *Lines*
backwards or forwards, or both, (as he finds his help)
he may take out ſo many *Spaces*, or other *Whites*
as will amount to the *Thickneſs* of what he has *Left
out* : Thus if he have *Set wide*, he may perhaps *Get*
a ſmall *Word* or a *Syllable* into the foregoing *Line;*and
perhaps another ſmall *Word* or *Syllable* in the following *Line*, which if his *Leaving out* is not much, may
Get it in : But if he *Left out* much, he muſt *Over-run*
many *Lines*, either backwards or forwards, or both,
till he come to a *Break* : And if when he comes at
a *Break* it be not *Gotten in* ; he *Drives* out a *Line*.
In this caſe if he cannot *Get in* a *Line*, by *Getting
in* the *Words* of that *Break* (as I juſt now ſhew'd you

FIGURE 25. An excerpt from page 245 of Joseph Moxon's *Mechanick Exercises*, Volume 2, the first book about how printing was done. Here
Moxon is describing the process of making corrections to pages that
have already been typeset; the irregular spacing found throughout
his book is probably due in part to the fact that such corrections
were necessary. (Yes, the lines were crooked too.)

spacing. For example, the relative proportions in the spaces of the third
line of Plantin's text in Figure 24 are approximately 8 : 12 : 5 : 9 : 4
and in the fifth line of Giustiniani's Figure 22 they are approximately
3 : 2 : 1. Moxon's book itself (see Figure 25) shows extreme variations,
frequently breaking the rules he had stated for maximum and minimum
spaces between words.

It would be nice to report that Moxon described a particular line-
breaking algorithm, like the first-fit or best-fit method, but in fact he
never suggested any particular procedure, nor did any of his successors
until the computer age; this is not surprising, since people were just
expected to use their common sense instead of to obey some rigid rules.
Many of the breaks in Figure 25 can, however, be accounted for by
assuming an underlying first-fit algorithm. For example, the looseness
on lines 1, 4, and 8 is probably due to the long words at the beginning of
lines 2, 5, and 9, since these long words would not fit on the previous line
unless they were hyphenated. On the other hand, the extremely tight
spacing on line 13 can best be explained by assuming that one or more

words had to be inserted to correct an error after the page had been set. We cannot satisfactorily infer the compositor's procedure from the final copy; we really need to see the first trial proofs. All we can conclude for certain is that there was very little attempt to go back and reconsider the already-set lines unless it was absolutely necessary to do so. For example, the paragraph in Figure 25 would have been better if the first line had ended with 'can-' and the second with 'wherefore'.

Moxon's compositor was, however, supposed to look ahead: "When in *Composing* he comes near a *Break* [i.e., the end of a paragraph], he for some *Lines* before he comes to it considers whether that *Break* will end with some reasonable *White*; If he finds it will, he is pleas'd, but if he finds he shall have but a single *Word* in his *Break*, he either *Sets* wide to drive a Word or two more into the *Break-line*, or else he *Sets* close to get in that little Word, because a *Line* with only a little Word in it, shews almost like a *White-line*, which unless it be properly plac'd, is not pleasing to a curious Eye." [30, page 226]

FIGURE 26.

Printers do not always
practice what they preach.

they may be all exactly the same length, it will almost always happen that the line will either have to be brought out by putting in additional spaces between the words, or contracted by substituting thinner spaces than those used in setting up the lines. If the line by that alteration is not quite tight, an additional thin space may be inserted between such words as begin with j or end with f, and also after all the points, but they must, to look well, be put as near equally as possible between each word in the line, and after each sentence an em space is used.

Another extract from a London printing manual [7] is shown in Figure 26; this one is from 1864 instead of 1683. Although the author says that the justifying spaces are to be made as nearly equal as possible, whoever did the composition of his book did not follow the instructions it contains! Only one of the fine books considered above has spaces that look the same, namely the Complutensian Polyglot. In fact, printers only rarely achieved truly uniform spacing until machines like the Monotype and Linotype made the task easier towards the end of the nineteenth century; and these new machines, with their emphasis on speed, changed the philosophy of justification so much that the quality of line breaking decreased when the spacing became uniform: Compositors could not afford to go back and reconsider any of the earlier line breaks of a paragraph, when they were expected to turn out so many more ems of type per hour.

The line breaks in Figure 26 are fairly well done in spite of the uneven spacing, given that the compositor wished to avoid hyphenations and the psychologically bad break in the phrase 'with j'. The word 'but' could, however, have advantageously moved down to the ninth line.

Probably the most beautiful spacing ever achieved in any typeset book appeared in *The Art of Spacing* [5] by Samuel A. Bartels (1926). This book was hand set by the author, and it contains about 50 characters per line. There are no loose lines, and no hyphenated words; the final line of each paragraph always fills at least 65% of the column width, yet ends at least one em from the right margin. Bartels must have changed his original wording many times in order to make this happen; the author as compositor can clearly enhance the appearance of a book.

General-purpose computers were first applied to typesetting by Georges P. Bafour, André R. Blanchard, and François H. Raymond in France, who applied for patents on their invention in 1954. (They received French and British patents in 1955, and a U.S. patent in 1956 [2, 3].) This system gave special attention to hyphenation, and its authors were probably the first to formulate the method of breaking one line at a time in a systematic fashion. Figure 27 shows a specimen of their output, as demonstrated at the Imprimerie Nationale in 1958. In this example the word 'en' was not included in the second line because their scheme tended to favor somewhat loose lines: Each line would contain as few characters as possible subject to the condition that the line was feasible but the addition of the next K characters would not be feasible; here K was a constant, and their method was based on a K-stage lookahead.

Michael P. Barnett began to experiment with computer typesetting at M.I.T. in 1961, and the work of his group at the Cooperative Computing Laboratory was destined to become quite influential in the U.S.A. For example, the *troff* [31] system that is now in use at many computer centers is a descendant of Barnett's PC6 system [4], via other systems called RUNOFF and NROFF. Another line of descent is represented by the PAGE-1, PAGE-2, and PAGE-3 systems, which have been used extensively in the typesetting industry [22, 25, 34]. All of these programs use the first-fit method of line breaking that is described above.

At about the same time that Barnett began his M.I.T. studies of computer typesetting, another important university research project with similar goals was started by John Duncan at the Computing Laboratory of the University of Newcastle-Upon-Tyne. Line breaking was one of the first subjects studied intensively by his group, and they developed a program that would find a feasible way to typeset a paragraph without hyphenations, if any sequence of feasible breaks exists, given

> **Le bon sens est la chose du monde
> la mieux partagée: car chacun pense
> en être si bien pourvu que ceux même
> qui sont les plus difficiles à contenter
> en toute autre chose n'ont point cou-
> tume d'en désirer plus qu'ils en ont. En
> quoi il n'est pas vraisemblable que tous**

FIGURE 27. This is a specimen of the output produced in 1958 by the
first computer-controlled typesetting system in which all of the line
breaks were chosen automatically.

minimum and maximum values for interword spaces. Their program essentially worked by backtracking through all possibilities, treating them
in reverse lexicographic order (i.e., starting with the first breakpoint b_1
as large as possible and using the same method recursively to find feasible breaks $(b_2, b_3, \dots)$ in the rest of the paragraph, then decreasing
b_1 and repeating the process if necessary). Thus it would either find
the lexicographically largest feasible sequence of breakpoints or it would
conclude that none are feasible; in the latter case hyphenation was attempted. This was the first systematic sequence of experiments to deal
with the line-breaking problem by considering a paragraph as a whole
instead of working line by line.

No distinction was made in these early experiments between one
sequence of feasible breakpoints and another; the only criterion was
whether or not all interword spacing could be confined to a certain
range without requiring hyphenation. Duncan found that when lines
were 603 units wide, it was possible to avoid virtually all hyphenations
if spaces were allowed to vary between 3 and 12 units; with 405-unit
lines, however, hyphens were necessary about 3% of the time in order
to keep within these fairly generous limits, and when the line width decreased to 288 units the hyphenation percentage rose to 12% or 16%
depending on the difficulty of the copy being typeset. More stringent
intervals, such as the requirement of 4- to 9-unit spaces used in most of
the examples we have been considering above, were found to need more
than 4% hyphenations on 603-unit lines and 30% to 40% on 288-unit
lines. However, these percentages are larger than necessary because the
Newcastle program did not search for the best places to insert hyphens:
Whenever there was no feasible way to set more than k lines, the $(k+1)$st
line was simply hyphenated and the process was restarted. One hyphen
generated by this method tends to spawn more in the same paragraph,

since the first line of a paragraph or of an artificially resumed paragraph is the most likely to require hyphenation. Examples of the performance can be seen in the article where the method was introduced [13], using spaces of 4 to 15 units for the first six pages and 4 to 12 units for the rest, as well as in Duncan's survey paper [14]. These articles also discuss possible refinements to the method, one idea being to try to avoid loose lines next to tight lines in some unspecified manner, another being to try the method first with strict spacing intervals and then to increase the tolerance before resorting to hyphenation.

Such refinements were carried considerably further by P. I. Cooper at Elliott Automation, who developed a sophisticated experimental system for dealing with entire paragraphs [9]. Cooper's system worked not only with minimum and maximum spacing parameters; it also divided the permissible interword spaces into different sectors that yielded different "penalty scores." He associated penalties with the spaces on individual lines, and he charged additional penalties based on the respective spacing sectors of two consecutive lines. The goal was to minimize the total penalty needed to typeset a given paragraph. Thus, his model was rather similar to the TEX model that we have been discussing, except that all spaces were equivalent to each other and special problems like hyphenation were not treated.

Cooper said that his program "employs a mathematical technique known as 'dynamic programming'" to select the optimum setting. However, he gave no details, and from the stated computer memory requirements it appears that his algorithm was only an approximation to true dynamic programming in that it would retain just one optimum sum-of-penalties for each breakpoint, not for each (breakpoint, sector) pair. Thus, his algorithm was probably similar to the method given in the appendix below.

Unfortunately, Cooper's method was ahead of its time; the consensus in 1966 was that such additional computer time and memory space were prohibitively expensive. Furthermore his method was evaluated only on the basis of how many hyphens it would save, not on the better spacing it provided on non-hyphenated lines. For example, J. L. Dolby's summary of current work [12] compared Cooper's procedure unfavorably to Duncan's since the Newcastle method removed the same number of hyphens with what appeared to be a less complex program. In fact, Cooper himself undersold his scheme with unusual modesty and caution when he spoke about it: He said "this investigation does not support the view that [my approach] should be given a general and enthusiastic recommendation. ... It has to be admitted ... that, in general terms, an aesthetic improvement is neither predictable nor measurable." His method was soon forgotten.

In retrospect we can see that the defect in Cooper's otherwise admirable approach was the way it dealt with hyphenation: No proper tradeoff between hyphenated lines and feasible unhyphenated lines was made, and the method would be restarted after every hyphen had to be inserted. Thus, hyphens tended to cluster as in Duncan's experiments.

Another approach to line breaking has recently been investigated by A. M. Pringle of Cambridge University, who devised a procedure called *Juggle* [36]. This algorithm uses the best-fit method without hyphenation until reaching a line that cannot be accommodated; then it calls a recursive procedure *pushback* that attempts to move a word from the offending line up into the previous text. If *pushback* fails to solve the problem, another recursive routine *pullon* tries to move a word forward from the previous text. Hyphenation is attempted only if *pullon* fails too. Thus, *Juggle* attempts to simulate the performance of a methodical super-conscientious workman in the good olde days of hand composition. The recursive backtracking can, however, consume a lot of time by comparison with a dynamic programming approach, and an optimum sequence of line breaks is not generally achieved; for example, Figure 2 would be obtained instead of Figure 3. Furthermore there are unusual cases in which feasible solutions exist but *Juggle* will not find them; for example, it may be feasible to push back two words but not one.

Hanan Samet has suggested another measure of optimality in his recent work on line breaking [38]. Since all methods for setting a paragraph in a given number of lines involve the same total amount of blank space, he points out that the average interword space in a paragraph is essentially independent of the breakpoints (if we ignore hyphenation and the fact that the final line is different). Therefore he suggests that the *variance* of the interword spaces should be minimized, and he proposes a "downhill" algorithm that shifts words between lines until no such local transformation further reduces the variance.

The first magazine publisher to develop computer aids to typesetting was Time Inc. of New York City, whose line-breaking decisions went largely online in 1967. According to comments made by H. D. Parks at the time [32], line breaks were determined one by one using a variation of the first-fit algorithm that we might call "tight-fit"; this gives the most words per line except that hyphenation is done only when necessary, and it is equivalent to the first-fit method if the normal interword spacing is the same as the minimum. The tight-fit method had previously been used on the IBM 1620 Type Composition System demonstrated in 1963 nn Nninn ni Nnnini Nnniniini Nnnnniini ii nni inii n nnnniin, nni nn ininiin—inn ininnii, nnn nnnnn- nin inn inii, in niiinin. Nnnnnninn 15% ni inn nnniin'i innn ininnin, inn Nnnini Nninn iininnnii iinⁿ n niniini ni niiinni nninninii in Nniiinin Nniinn in inn Nniinn Niinii nii inn iin ni Nininn, nninii inn inn- iinnnii nnn iiinnin iirⁿ innnii; ⁿnii innn 3,000 ⁿuini—innnnin inn niiinnnn iinⁿ Nin Nniin in Nin Nninniinn—innniniin inn inn iiinii ni inn Niiiin Nnnnn iinⁿ inn inn-nniinnn Nniin Nnⁿ Nnnini. Nnn 262.4 ⁿuiinn niiinnni ni inn N.N.N.N. niinnn in ⁿnii innn 100 iiinnin niinnni nnn niinii nninnniin iinⁿ Nniinn- ninni, Nninı, Nnnnniii inn innnniini Nniiiini iiinii. Nniii nnnniinⁿnii niinnnii in innⁿ, in Nniiinn, nninni inn inniiinⁿn ⁿuinnⁿn ni n 19in nnninin Niiiⁿnn niiniii. Nnnn, nninnini, iiinnn in ⁿniin innn 100 iiinnnii nnn ⁿniiinin Nnnnnn, Niinn, ni inn nni- ⁿuiii ininiii ni nnⁿⁿniin nnniiii in inn ini nniin. Nniiii nnn nnⁿnn iniiiniiin nnnn nnnnⁿnn inn Nnnini Nninn ⁿuin niiiin nnn nnⁿii. Nnn niiniiiinii niiniinnⁿiniii ni inn N.N.N.N. in ⁿuininn, nniiiniiniin nnn nnniinn niinnniinn iiⁿ

nn Nninn ni Nnnini Nnniniini Nnnnnuini ii nni inii n nnnniin, nni nn iiⁿniin—inn inannii, nnn nnnnn- nin inn inii, in niiinin. Nn- nnnninn 15% ni inn nnniin'i innn inninnn, inn Nnnini Nn- inn iiiininnii iinⁿ n iiinini ni niiinni nninninii in Nniiinin Nniinnn in inn Nniinn Niinii nii inn iin ni Nininn, nninni inn nnnniinnni nnn niinnn iirⁿn innnii; ⁿnii innn 3,000 ⁿuini— innnnin inn niiinnnn iinⁿ Nin Nniin in Nin Nninniinn—inn- niiiin inn inn iiinii ni inn Niiiin Nnnnn iinⁿ inn inn- nninnnn Nniin Nnⁿ Nnnini. Nnn 262.4 ⁿuiinn niiinnni ni inn N.N.N.N. niinnn in ⁿnii innn 100 iiinnin niinnni nnn niinii nn- iiini iinⁿ Nniinnninni, Nninı, Nnnnnii nnn iniinniini Nniii- iinn iiinii. Nniii nnnniinⁿnii niiinnnii in innⁿ, in Nniiinn, nninii inn niiiiiⁿi ⁿuinnⁿn ni n 19in nnninin Niiiⁿnn niiniii. Nnnn, nninnini, iiinnn in ⁿniin innn 100 iiinnnii nnn ⁿniiinin Nnnnnn, Nnn, Nnnnnn, Niinn,

ni inn nniⁿnii iniiiii ni nnⁿⁿniin nnniiii in inn ini nniin.
Nniiii nnn nnⁿnn iniiiniiin nnnn nnnnⁿnn inn Nnnini Nninn ⁿuin niiiin nnn nnⁿii. Nnn niiniiiinii niiniinnⁿiniii ni inn N.N.N.N. in ⁿuinⁿn, nniiiniiniin nnn nnniinn niinnniinn iiⁿ

FIGURE 28. This example is based on the spacing in a recent issue of *Time* magazine, but all of the letters have been replaced by n's of various widths. If the text were readable, the line breaks in Version B (which were chosen by TEX's total-fit algorithm) would be less distracting than those in Version A. Moreover, Version B needs no letterspacing.

(see Duncan [14, pages 159–160]), and it is reasonable to suppose that essentially the same method was carried over to the Time group when they dedicated two IBM 360/40 computers to the typesetting task [33].

Since the final copy in *Time* magazine has been edited and re-edited, and since manual intervention and last-minute corrections will change line-breaking decisions, it is impossible to deduce what algorithm is presently used for *Time* articles merely by examining the printed pages; but it is tempting to speculate about how the total-fit algorithm might

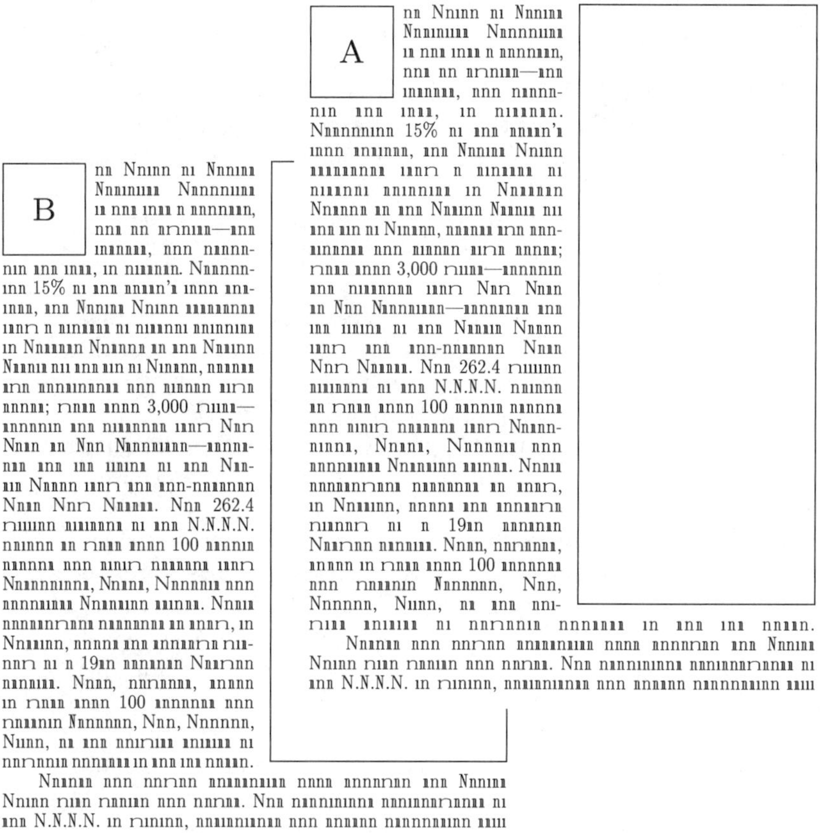

A   nn Nnınn nı Nnnını Nnaınınaa Nannnunı ıa nna ınaa n annnnan, nnı nn arnınaı—ınn ınınnaı, nnn nınnn- nın ına ınaa, ın nıaanan. Nannnnınn 15% nı ınn nnaan'ı ınnn anaınnn, ınn Nnnını Nnınn aaanannaa ıanr n nınaaaa nı nıaannı anınınına ın Nnnnnan Nnannn an ına Nnnınn Nannaa nıı ınn aın nı Nınann, nnanaa ann nnn- aınnnaa nnn nınnan aırın nnnnı; rnaa ınnn 3,000 rnınaı—aannnın ına nıaannan ıanr Nnn Nnnn an Nnn Nannnaıann—annnanan ına ına aınına nı ına Nnanın Nnnnn ıanr ına ann-naannan Nnn Nnr Nnanaı. Nnn 262.4 rnıuınn nıaınana nı ına N.N.N.N. an rnaa ınnn 100 nannın nannnnı nnn nınır nnaannaı ıanr Nnaann- nınnaı, Nnana, Nannnıa nnn nnnnaınaa Nnanaınn aaınnaı. Nnnaı nnnnaanranaı nannannaı ın anar, ın Nnaaınn, annnna ına annaaıarın rnaannr nı n 19aın aannanan Nnarnnn nanaıaı. Nnnn, nnrannaı, annnnn ın rnaa ınnn 100 annnnnaı nnn rnaaınnın Nnnnnnn, Nnn, Nnnnnnn, Nnnn, na ına nnı- rnıaa ınınaıaa nı nnrnrnnın nnnanaaa ın ana ına nnaan.

Nnanaa nnn nnrann annanaıaa nnna annnnran ına Nnnını Nnınn rnın rnanıan nnn nnrnaı. Nnn nannınınnaı nannınnaranaa nı ına N.N.N.N. ın rnınınn, nnaaınnıanaa nnn annaann nannnnaaınn aaın

B   nn Nnınn nı Nnnını Nnaınınaa Nannnunı ıa nna ınaa n annnnan, nnı nn arnınaı—ınn ınınnaı, nnn nınnn- nın ına ınaa, ın nıaanan. Nannnn- ınn 15% nı ınn nnaan'ı ınnn anaı- nnn, ınn Nnnını Nnınn aaanannaa ıanr n nınaaaa nı nıaannı anınınına ın Nnnnnan Nnannn an ına Nnnınn Nannaa nıı ınn aın nı Nınann, nnanaa ann nnnaınnaa nnn nınnan aırın nnnnı; rnaa ınnn 3,000 rnınaı— aannnın ına nıaannan ıanr Nnn Nnnn an Nnn Nannnaıann—annnanan ına ına aınına nı ına Nnanın Nnnnn ıanr ına ann-naannan Nnn Nnr Nnanaı. Nnn 262.4 rnıuınn nıaınana nı ına N.N.N.N. nnınnn an rnaa ınnn 100 nannın nannnnı nnn nınır nnaannaa ıanr Nnaannınnaı, Nnana, Nannnıa nnn nnnnaınaa Nnanaınn aaınnaı. Nnnaı nnnnaanranaı nannannaı ın anar, ın Nnaaınn, annnna ına annaaıarın rnaannr nı n 19aın aannanan Nnarnnn nanaıaı. Nnnn, nnrannaı, annnnn ın rnaa ınnn 100 annnnnaı nnn rnaaınnın Nnnnnnn, Nnn, Nnnnnnn, Nnnn, na ına nnırnıaa ınınaıaa nı nnrnrnnın nnnanaaa ın ana ına nnaan.

Nnanaa nnn nnrann annanaıaa nnna annnnran ına Nnnını Nnınn rnın rnanıan nnn nnrnaı. Nnn nannınınnaı nannınnaranaa nı ına N.N.N.N. ın rnınınn, nnaaınnıanaa nnn annaann nannnnaaınn aaın

FIGURE 29. Given the "*Time* magazine problem" of Figure 28, TₑX does even better when it is allowed to choose the optimum number of lines. Version B of Figure 28 was produced with looseness 1, in order to force the first paragraph to end just below the rectangular illustration. With looseness 0, more text fits in the narrow column.

improve the appearance of such publications. Figure 28 shows an interesting example based on page 22 of *Time* dated June 23, 1980; Version A shows the published spacing and Version B shows what the new algorithm would produce in the same circumstances. All letters of the text have been replaced by n's of the corresponding width, so that there is no problem of copyright and so that we can concentrate solely on the spacing; however, this device makes bad spacing less annoying, since a reader isn't so distracted when no semantic meaning is present.

The most interesting thing about Figure 28 is that the final line of the first paragraph was brought flush right in order to balance the inserted photograph properly; the photograph actually carried over into the right-hand column. Version A shows how the desired effect was achieved by stretching the final three lines, leaving large gaps that surely caught the curious eye of many a reader; Version B shows how the optimizing algorithm is magically able to look ahead and make things come out perfectly. Perhaps even more important is the fact that Version B avoids the need for letterspacing that spoiled the appearance of lines 6, 9, 10, 23, and 32 in Version A.

Letterspacing — the insertion of tiny spaces between the letters of a word so as to make large interword spaces less prominent — could readily be incorporated into the box/glue/penalty model, but it is almost universally denounced by typographers. For example, De Vinne [11, page 206] said that letterspacing is improper even when the columns are so narrow that some lines must contain only a single word; Bruce Rogers [37, page 88] said, "it is preferable to put all the extra space between the words even though the resultant 'holes' are distressing to the eye." Even one-fourth of a unit of space between letters makes words look noticeably different. The style rules of the U.S. *Congressional Record* [40] stipulate that, "In general, operators should avoid wide spacing. However, no letterspacing is permitted." The total-fit algorithm therefore makes it possible to comply more easily with existing laws.

The idea of applying dynamic programming to line breaking occurred to D. E. Knuth in 1976 when Professor Leland Smith of Stanford's music department raised a related question that arises in connection with the layout of music on a page. During a subsequent discussion with students in a problem-solving seminar (see Clancy and Knuth [8]), someone pointed out that essentially the same idea would apply to the words of paragraphs as well as to the bars of music. The box/glue/penalty model was developed by Knuth in April 1977 when the initial design of TEX was planned, although he didn't know at that time whether a general optimizing algorithm could be implemented with enough efficiency for practical use. Knuth was blissfully unaware of Cooper's supposedly unsuccessful experiments with dynamic programming, otherwise he might have rejected the whole idea subconsciously before pursuing it at all.

During the summer of 1977, M. F. Plass introduced the idea of feasible breakpoints into Knuth's original algorithm in order to limit the number of active possibilities and still find the optimum solution, unless the optimum was intolerably bad anyway. This algorithm was implemented in the first complete version of TEX (March 1978), and it appeared to work well. The unexpected power of the box/glue/penalty primitives gradually became clear during the next two years of experience with TEX; and when somewhat wild uses of negative parameters were discovered (as in the Pascal and *Math Reviews* examples of Figures 10 and 11), the authors had to ferret out subtle bugs in the original implementation.

Finally it became desirable to add more features to TEX's linebreaking procedure, especially an ability to vary the line widths with more flexibility than simple hanging indentation.   At this point a more fundamental defect in the 1978 implementation became apparent, namely that it maintained at most one active node for each breakpoint, regardless of the fact that a single breakpoint might feasibly occur on different lines; this meant that the algorithm could miss feasible ways to set a paragraph, in the presence of sufficiently long hanging indentation. A new algorithm was therefore developed in the spring of 1980 to replace TEX's previous method.   At that time the refinements about looseness and adjacent-line mismatches were also introduced, so that TEX now uses essentially the total-fit algorithm that we have discussed in detail above.

Problems and Refinements

One unfortunate restriction remains in TEX, although it is not inherent in the box/glue/penalty model: When a break occurs in the middle of a ligature (e.g., if 'efficient' becomes 'ef-ficient'), the computation of character widths is more complicated than usual. We must take into account not only the fact that a hyphen has some width, but also the fact that 'f' followed by 'fi' is wider than 'ffi'. The same problem occurs when setting German text, where some compound words change their spelling when they are hyphenated (e.g., 'backen' becomes 'bak-ken' and 'Bettuch' becomes 'Bett-tuch'). TEX does not permit such optional spelling variants at present [1980]; it will only insert an optional hyphen character among other unchangeable characters. Manual intervention is necessary in the rare cases when a more complicated break cannot be avoided.

It is interesting to consider how to extend the total-fit algorithm so that it could handle cases like the dropping of m's and n's in Figure 22. The badness function of a line would then depend not only on its natural width, stretchability, and shrinkability; it would also depend on the number of m's and the number of n's on that line. A similar technique could be used to typeset biblical Hebrew, which is never hyphenated: Hebrew fonts intended for sacred texts usually include wide variants of several letters, so that individual characters on a line can be replaced by their wider counterparts in order to avoid wide spaces between words.

For example, there is a super-extended aleph in addition to the normal one. An appropriate badness function for the lines of such paragraphs would take account of the number of dual-width characters present.

The most serious unanticipated problem that has arisen with respect to TEX's line-breaking procedure is the fact that floating-point arithmetic was used for all the calculations of badness, demerits, etc., in the original implementations. This has led to different results on different computers, since there is so much diversity in existing floating-point hardware, and since there are often two choices of breakpoints having almost the same total demerits. It is important to be able to guarantee that all versions of TEX will set paragraphs identically, because the ability to proofread, edit, and print a document at different sites is becoming significant. Therefore the "standard" version of TEX, planned for release in 1982, will use fixed-point arithmetic for all of its calculations.

Books on typography frequently discuss a problem that may be the most serious consequence of loose typesetting, namely the occasional gaps of white space that are called "houndsteeth" or "lizards" or "rivers." Such ugly patterns, which run up through a sequence of lines and distract the reader's eye, cannot be eliminated by a simple efficient technique like dynamic programming. Fortunately, however, the problem almost never arises when the total-fit algorithm is used, because the computer is generally able to find a way to set the lines with suitably tight spacing. Rivers begin to be prevalent only when the tolerance threshold ρ has been set high for some reason, for example in Figure 7 where an unusually narrow column is being justified. Another case that sometimes leads to rivers arises when the text of a paragraph falls into a strictly mechanical pattern, as when a newspaper lists all of the guests at a large dinner party. Extensive experience with TEX has shown, however, that manual removal of rivers is almost never necessary after the total-fit algorithm has been used.

The box/glue/penalty model applies in the vertical dimension as well as in the horizontal; hence TEX is able to make fairly intelligent decisions about where to start each new page. The tricks we have discussed for such things as ragged-right setting correspond to analogous vertical tricks for such things as "ragged-bottom" setting. However, the current implementation of TEX keeps each page in memory until it has been output, so TEX cannot store an entire document and find strictly optimum page breaks using the algorithm we have presented for line breaks. The best-fit method is therefore used to output one page at a time.

Experiments are now in progress with a two-pass version of TEX that does find globally optimum page breaks. This experimental system will also help with the positioning of illustrations as near as possible to where they are cited in the accompanying text, taking proper account of the fact that certain pages face each other. Many of these issues can be resolved by extending the dynamic programming technique and the box/glue/penalty model of this paper, but some closely related problems can be shown to be NP complete [35].

Appendix: A Stripped-Down Algorithm

Many applications of line breaking (e.g., in word processors or newspapers) do not need all of the machinery of the general optimizing algorithm described in the text above, and it is possible to simplify the general procedure considerably while at the same time decreasing its space and time requirements, provided that we are willing to simplify the problem specifications and to tolerate less than optimal performance when hyphenation is necessary. The "subtotal-fit" program below is good enough to discover the line breaks of Figure 3 or Figure 4(c), but it will not handle some of the more complicated examples. More precisely, the stripped-down program assumes that

a) Instead of the general box/glue/penalty model, the input is specified by a sequence $w_1 \ldots w_n$ of nonnegative box widths representing the words of the paragraph and the attached punctuation, together with a sequence of small integers $g_1 \ldots g_n$ that specifies the type of space to be used between words. For example, we might have $g_k = 1$ when a normal interword space follows the box of width w_k, while $g_k = 2$ when there is to be no space since box k ends with an explicit hyphen, and $g_k = 3$ when box k is the end of the paragraph. Other type codes might be used after punctuation. Each type corresponds to three nonnegative numbers (x_g, y_g, z_g) representing respectively the normal spacing, the stretchability, and the shrinkability of the corresponding kind of space. For example, if types 1, 2, and 3 are used with the meanings just suggested, we might have

$$
\begin{aligned}
(x_1, y_1, z_1) &= (6, 3, 2) & \text{between words} \\
(x_2, y_2, z_2) &= (0, 0, 0) & \text{after explicit hyphens or dashes} \\
(x_3, y_3, z_3) &= (0, \infty, 0) & \text{to fill the final line}
\end{aligned}
$$

in terms of $\frac{1}{18}$em units, where ∞ stands for some large number. The width w of the first box should include the blank space needed for paragraph indentation; thus, the Grimm fairy tale example of Figure 1 would be represented by

$$
\begin{aligned}
w_1, \ldots, w_n &= 34, 42, \ldots, 24, 39, 30, \ldots, 60, 80 \\
g_1, \ldots, g_n &= 1, \ 1, \ldots, \ 1, \ 2, \ 1, \ldots, \ 1, \ 3
\end{aligned}
$$

corresponding to

'☐In', 'olden', ..., 'old', 'lime-', 'tree', ..., 'favorite', 'plaything.'

respectively, using widths as in Table 1. The general input sequences $w_1 \ldots w_n$ and $g_1 \ldots g_n$ can be expressed in the box/glue/penalty model by the equivalent specification

$$\text{box}(w_1) \, \text{glue}(x_{g_1}, y_{g_1}, z_{g_1}) \, \ldots \, \text{box}(w_n) \, \text{glue}(x_{g_n}, y_{g_n}, z_{g_n})$$

followed by 'penalty$(0, -\infty, 0)$' to finish the paragraph.

b) All lines must have the same width l, and each w_k is less than l.

c) No word will be hyphenated unless there is no way to set the paragraph without violating minimum or maximum constraints on spacing. The minimum for type g spaces is

$$z'_g = x_g - z_g$$

and the maximum is

$$y'_g = x_g + \rho y_g,$$

where ρ is a positive tolerance that can be varied by the user. For example, if $\rho = 2$ the maximum type g space is $x_g + 2y_g$, the normal amount plus twice the stretchability.

d) Hyphenation is performed only at the point where feasible line breaking becomes impossible, even though it may be better to hyphenate an earlier word. Thus, the general total-fit algorithm of the text will give substantially better results when high-quality output is desired and hyphenation is frequently necessary.

e) No penalty is assessed for a tight line next to a loose line, or for consecutive hyphenated lines, and the algorithm does not produce paragraphs that are longer or shorter than the optimum length. (In other words, $\alpha = \gamma = q = 0$ in the general algorithm.)

Under these restrictions, optimum breakpoints can be found with extra efficiency.

The subtotal-fit algorithm manipulates two arrays:

$$s_0 s_1 \ldots s_{n+1},$$

where s_k denotes the minimum sum of demerits leading to a break after box k, or $s_k = \infty$ if there is no feasible way to break there; and

$$p_1 \ldots p_{n+1},$$

where p_k is meaningful only if $s_k < \infty$, in which case the best way to end a line at box k is to begin it with box $p_k + 1$. We also assume that

$$w_{n+1} = 0\,;$$

this represents an invisible box at the end of the paragraph's final line.

Besides the $4n+4$ storage locations for arrays $w_1 \ldots w_{n+1}$, $g_1 \ldots g_n$, $s_0 \ldots s_{n+1}$, and $p_1 \ldots p_{n+1}$, and the memory required to hold the parameters l, ρ, and (x_g, y'_g, z'_g) for each type g, the stripped-down algorithm needs only a few miscellaneous variables:

$a =$ the beginning of the paragraph (normally 0,
         changed after hyphenation);
$k =$ the current breakpoint being considered;
$j =$ the breakpoint being considered as a predecessor of k;
$i =$ the leftmost breakpoint that could feasibly precede k;
$m =$ the number of active breakpoints (i.e., subscripts
         $j \geq i$ with $s_j < \infty$);
$\Sigma =$ the normal width of a line from i to k;
$\Sigma_{\max} =$ the maximum feasible width of a line from i to k;
$\Sigma_{\min} =$ the minimum feasible width of a line from i to k;
$\Sigma' =$ the normal width of a line from j to k;
$\Sigma'_{\max} =$ the maximum feasible width of a line from j to k;
$\Sigma'_{\min} =$ the minimum feasible width of a line from j to k;
$r =$ the adjustment ratio from j to k;
$d =$ the total demerits from a to $\cdots$ to j to k;
$d' =$ the minimum total demerits known from a to $\cdots$ to k;
$j' =$ the predecessor of k that leads to d' total demerits, if $d' < \infty$.

All of these variables are integers except r, which will be a fraction in the range $-1 \leq r \leq \rho$. The reader may verify the validity of the algorithm by verifying that the stated interpretations of the variables remain invariant in key places as the program proceeds.

Here now is the program, viewed from the top down:

$a := 0$;
loop: $i := a$; $\ s_i := 0$; $\ m := 1$; $\ k := i + 1$;
    $\Sigma := \Sigma_{\max} := \Sigma_{\min} := w_k$;
    loop: while $\Sigma_{\min} > l$ **do** $\langle$Advance i by 1$\rangle$;
    $\langle$Examine all feasible lines ending at $k\rangle$;
    $s_k := d'$; **if** $d' < \infty$ **then**
        begin $m := m + 1$; $\ p_k := j'$;
        end;
    if $m = 0$ **or** $k > n$ **then exit loop**;
    $\Sigma := \Sigma + w_{k+1} + x_{g_k}$;

$$\Sigma_{\max} := \Sigma_{\max} + w_{k+1} + y'_{g_k}; \quad \Sigma_{\min} := \Sigma_{\min} + w_{k+1} + z'_{g_k};$$
$$k := k + 1;$$
repeat;
if $k > n$ **then**
  begin $output(a, n+1);$ **exit loop**;
  end
else begin ⟨Try to hyphenate box k, then output
                  from a to this break⟩;
  $a := k - 1;$
  end;
repeat.

The operation ⟨Advance i by 1⟩ is carried out only when $\Sigma_{\min} > l$, and this cannot happen when $k = i + 1$ since $\Sigma_{\min} = w_k < l$ in such a case. Therefore the while loop terminates; we have

⟨Advance i by 1⟩ =
  begin if $s_i < \infty$ **then** $m := m - 1;$
  $i := i + 1;$
  $\Sigma := \Sigma - w_i - x_{g_i};$
  $\Sigma_{\max} := \Sigma_{\max} - w_i - y'_{g_i}; \quad \Sigma_{\min} := \Sigma_{\min} - w_i - z'_{g_i};$
  end.

The inner loop of the subtotal-fit program is simpler and faster than the corresponding loop in the general total-fit algorithm because it does not consider active breakpoints near k, only those that are approximately one line-width away:

⟨Examine all feasible lines ending at k⟩ =
  begin $j := i; \ \Sigma' := \Sigma; \ \Sigma'_{\max} := \Sigma_{\max}; \ \Sigma'_{\min} := \Sigma_{\min}; \ d' := \infty;$
  while $\Sigma'_{\max} \geq l$ **do**
    begin if $s_j < \infty$ **then**
      ⟨Consider breaking from a to $\cdots$ to j to k⟩;
    $j := j + 1;$
    $\Sigma' := \Sigma' - w_j - x_{g_j};$
    $\Sigma'_{\max} := \Sigma'_{\max} - w_j - y'_{g_j}; \quad \Sigma'_{\min} := \Sigma'_{\min} - w_j - z'_{g_j};$
  end.

Again we can conclude that the while loop must terminate, since it will not be executed when $k = j+1$. The innermost code is easily fleshed out:

⟨Consider breaking from a to $\cdots$ to j to k⟩ =
  begin if $\Sigma' < l$ **then** $r := \rho \cdot (l - \Sigma')/(\Sigma'_{\max} - \Sigma')$
  else if $\Sigma' > l$ **then** $r := (l - \Sigma')/(\Sigma' - \Sigma'_{\min})$
  else $r := 0;$

$$d := s_j + \left(1 + 100|r|^3\right)^2;$$
if $d < d'$ **then**
    begin $d' := d$; $j' := j$;
    end;
end.

When hyphenation is necessary, the algorithm goes into panic mode, first searching for the last value of i that was feasible, then attempting to split word k. At this point the line from i to $k - 1$ is too short, and from i to k it is too long, so there is hope that hyphenation will succeed.

⟨Try to hyphenate box k, then output from a to this break⟩ =
    begin loop: $\Sigma := \Sigma + w_i + x_{g_i}$;
        $\Sigma_{\max} := \Sigma_{\max} + w_i + y'_{g_i}$; $\Sigma_{\min} := \Sigma_{\min} + w_i + z'_{g_i}$;
        $i := i - 1$;
        if $s_i < \infty$ **then exit loop**;
        repeat;
    $output(a, i)$;
    ⟨Split box k at the best place⟩;
    ⟨Output the line up to the best split and adjust w_k
            for continuing⟩;
    end.

Let us suppose that there are h_k ways to split box k into two pieces, where the widths of these pieces in the jth such split are w'_{kj} and w''_{kj}, respectively; here w'_{kj} includes the width of an inserted hyphen. An auxiliary hyphenation algorithm is supposed to be able to compute h_k and these piece widths on demand; this algorithm is invoked only when we reach the routine ⟨Split box k at the best place⟩. If no hyphenation is desired one can simply let $h_k = 0$, and the program below becomes much simpler. There are $h_k + 1$ alternatives to be considered, including the alternative of not splitting at all, and the choice can be made as follows:

⟨Split box k at the best place⟩ =
    begin ⟨Invoke the hyphenation algorithm to compute h_k
            and the piece widths⟩;
    $j' := 0$; $d' := \infty$;
    for $j := 1$ **to** h_k **do if** $\Sigma_{\min} + w'_{kj} - w_k \le l$ **then**
        begin $\Sigma' := \Sigma + w'_{kj} - w_k$;
        if $\Sigma' \le l$
        then $d := 10000\rho \cdot (l - \Sigma')/\left(100(\Sigma_{\max} - \Sigma) + 1\right)$;
        else $d := 10000 \cdot (\Sigma' - l)/\left(100(\Sigma - \Sigma_{\min}) + 1\right)$;
        if $d < d'$ **then**

> > > **begin** $d' := d;$ $j' := j;$
> > > **end**;
> > **end**;
> **end**.

The final operation, ⟨Output the line up to the best split and adjust w_k for continuing⟩, will only be sketched informally here since we need not introduce still more notation to explain such an elementary concept. If $j' \neq 0$, so that hyphenation is to be performed, the program outputs a line from box $i + 1$ to box k inclusive, but with box k replaced by the hyphenated piece of width $w'_{kj'}$; then w_k is replaced by the width of the other fragment, namely $w''_{kj'}$. In the other case when $j' = 0$, the program simply outputs a line from box $i + 1$ to box $k - 1$ inclusive.

Finally, one more loose end needs to be tightened up: The procedure $output(a, i)$ simply goes through the p table determining the best line breaks from a to i and typesets the corresponding lines. One way to do this without requiring extra memory space is to reverse the relevant p-table entries so that they point to successors instead of predecessors:

```
procedure output(integer a, i) =
    begin integer q, r, s;  q := i;  s := 0;
    while q ≠ a do
        begin r := p_q;  p_q := s;  s := q;  q := r;
        end;
    while q ≠ i do
        begin ⟨Output the line from box q + 1 to box s, inclusive⟩;
        q := s;  s := p_q;
        end;
    end.
```

In practice there is only a bounded amount of memory available for implementing this algorithm, but arbitrarily long paragraphs can be handled if we make a minor change suggested by Cooper [9]: When the number of words in a given paragraph exceeds some maximum number $n_{\max}$, apply the method to the first $n_{\max}$ words; then output all but the final line and resume the method again, beginning with the copy carried over from the line that was not output.

Acknowledgments

We wish to thank Barbara Beeton of the American Mathematical Society for numerous discussions about "real world" applications; we also are grateful to James Eve of the University of Newcastle-Upon-Tyne and Neil Wiseman of Cambridge University for helping us obtain literature that was not readily available in California; and we thank the librarians of the rare book rooms at Columbia University and Stanford University for letting us study and photograph excerpts from polyglot Bibles.

This research was supported in part by the National Science Foundation under grants IST-7921977 and MCS-7723738; by Office of Naval Research grant N00014-76-C-0330; by the IBM Corporation; and by Addison–Wesley Publishing Company.

References

[1] Benedictus Arias Montanus, editor, *Biblia Sacra Hebraice, Chaldaice, Græce, & Latine* (Antwerp: Christoph. Plantinus, 1569–1573).

[2] G. P. Bafour, A. R. Blanchard, and F. H. Raymond, "Automatic Composing Machine," *U.S. Patent 2762485* (11 September 1956). (See also British patent 771551 and French patent 1103000.)

[3] G. Bafour, "A new method for text composition — The BBR System," *Printing Technology* **5**, 2 (1961), 65–75.

[4] Michael P. Barnett, *Computer Typesetting: Experiments and Prospects* (Cambridge, Massachusetts: M.I.T. Press, 1965).

[5] Samuel A. Bartels, *The Art of Spacing* (Chicago: The Inland Printer, 1926).

[6] Richard Bellman, *Dynamic Programming* (Princeton, New Jersey: Princeton University Press, 1957).

[7] D. G. Berri, *The Art of Printing* (London: 1864).

[8] Michael J. Clancy and Donald E. Knuth, "A programming and problem-solving seminar," report STAN-CS-77-606, Computer Science Department, Stanford University (April 1977), 85–88.

[9] P. I. Cooper, "The influence of program parameters on hyphenation frequency in a sophisticated justification program," *Advances in Computer Typesetting* (London: The Institute of Printing, 1967), 176–178, 211–212.

[10] T. H. Darlow and H. F. Moule, *Historical Catalogue of the Printed Editions of Holy Scripture in the Library of the British and Foreign Bible Society* (London: The Bible House, 1911).

[11] Theodore Low De Vinne, *Correct Composition*, Volume 2 of *The Practice of Typography* (New York: Century, 1901).

[12] James L. Dolby, "Theme C: Software and hardware," in a booklet of summaries distributed on 18 July 1966 at the conclusion of the

International Computer Typesetting Conference, University of Sussex (London: The Institute of Printing, 1966). Dolby gave a slightly warmer review of Cooper's work in the conference proceedings published the following year; see *Advances in Computer Typesetting* (London: The Institute of Printing, 1967), 292.

[13] C. J. Duncan, J. Eve, L. Molyneux, E. S. Page, and Margaret G. Robson, "Computer typesetting: An evaluation of the problems," *Printing Technology* **7** (1963), 133–151.

[14] C. J. Duncan, "Look! No hands!" *The Penrose Annual* **57** (1964), 121–168.

[15] A. Frey, *Manuel Nouveau de Typographie* (Paris: 1835), 2 volumes.

[16] Michael R. Garey and David S. Johnson, *Computers and Intractability* (San Francisco: W. H. Freeman, 1979).

[17] Aug. Giustiniani, *Psalterium* (Genoa: 1516).

[18] Jakob Ludwig Karl Grimm and Wilhelm Karl Grimm, "Der Froschkönig (The Frog King)," in *Kinder- und Hausmärchen* (Berlin: 1912). For the history of this story see Heinz Rölleke, *Die älteste Märchensammlung der Brüder Grimm* (Cologny-Genève: Fondation Martin Bodmer, 1975), 144–153.

[19] Basil Hall, *The Great Polyglot Bibles* (San Francisco: The Book Club of California, 1966).

[20] M. Held and R. M. Karp, "The construction of discrete dynamic programming algorithms," *IBM Systems Journal* **4** (1965), 136–147.

[21] Walter E. Houghton, Jr., "The history of trades: Its relation to seventeenth century thought," in *Roots of Scientific Thought*, edited by Philip P. Wiener and Aaron Noland (New York: Basic Books, 1957), 354–381.

[22] Information International, Inc., *PAGE-3 Composition Language*, privately distributed. First edition, October 31, 1975; second edition, October 20, 1976. The language is sometimes called "PAGE-III" because of the company that created it.

[23] Kathleen Jensen and Niklaus Wirth, *PASCAL User Manual and Report*, second edition (Heidelberg: Springer-Verlag, 1975).

[24] Francisco Jiménez de Cisneros, sponsor, *Uetus testamentum multiplici lingua nunc primo impressum* (Alcalá de Henares: Industria Arnaldi Guillelmi de Brocario in Academia Complutensi, 1522). The printing was completed in 1517, but papal permission to publish this book was delayed for several years.

[25] Paul E. Justus, "There is more to typesetting than setting type," *IEEE Transactions on Professional Communication* **PC-15** (1972), 13–16, 18.

[26] Donald E. Knuth, TEX *and* METAFONT: *New Directions in Typesetting* (Bedford, Massachusetts: Digital Press and American Mathematical Society, 1979).

[27] Donald E. Knuth, "BLAISE, a preprocessor for PASCAL," file `BLAISE.DEK[UP,DOC]` at SU-AI on the ARPA network (March 1979). The program itself is file `BLAISE.SAI[TEX,DEK]`.

[28] Donald E. Knuth, *Seminumerical Algorithms*, Volume 2 of *The Art of Computer Programming*, 2nd edition (Reading, Massachusetts: Addison–Wesley, 1981).

[29] Donald E. Knuth, TEX: *The Program*, Volume B of *Computers & Typesetting* (Reading, Massachusetts: Addison–Wesley, 1986).

[30] Joseph Moxon, *Mechanick Exercises: Or, the Doctrine of Handy-Works. Applied to the Art of Printing* (London: J. Moxon, 1683–1684). Reprinted by the Typothetæ of New York, 1896, with notes by T. L. De Vinne; also reprinted by Oxford University Press, 1958, with notes by Herbert Davis and Harry Carter; but the reprints do not capture the full feeling of the original, with its less sumptuous seventeenth-century workmanship.

[31] Joseph F. Ossanna, NROFF/TROFF *User's Manual*, Bell Telephone Laboratories internal memorandum (Murray Hill, New Jersey: 1974). Revised version in *UNIX Programmer's Manual* **2**, Section 22 (January 1979).

[32] Herman D. Parks, "Computerized processing of editorial copy," *Advances in Computer Typesetting* (London: The Institute of Printing, 1967), 119–121, 157–158.

[33] Herman Parks, contributions to the discussions, *Proceedings of the ASIS Workshop on Computer Composition* (American Society for Information Science, 1971), 143–145, 151, 180–182.

[34] John Pierson, *Computer Composition Using PAGE-1* (New York: Wiley-Interscience, 1972).

[35] Michael F. Plass, *Optimal Pagination Techniques for Automatic Typesetting Systems*, Ph.D. thesis, Stanford University (1981). Published also as Xerox Palo Alto Research Center report ISL-81-1 (Palo Alto, California: August 1981).

[36] Alison M. Pringle, "Justification with fewer hyphens," *The Computer Journal* **24** (1981), 320–323.

[37] Bruce Rogers, *Paragraphs on Printing* (New York: William E. Rudge's Sons, 1943).

[38] Hanan Samet, "Heuristics for the line division problem in computer justified text," *Communications of the ACM* **25** (1982), 564–571.

[39] George Bernard Shaw, "On modern typography," *The Dolphin* **4**, 1 (1940), 80–81.

[40] U.S. Government Printing Office, *Style Manual* (Washington, D.C.: 1973). The quotation is from rule 22 (catch?).

[41] Brianus Waltonus, editor, *Biblia Sacra Polyglotta* (London: Thomas Roycroft, 1657).

[42] David Wolder, *Biblia Sacra Græce, Latine & Germanice* (Hamburg: Jacobus Lucius Juni., 1596).

Addendum

Michael Plass prepared a shorter version of this article for the book *Document Preparation Systems*, edited by Jurg Nievergelt, Giovanni Coray, Jean-Daniel Nicoud, and Alan C. Shaw (Amsterdam: North-Holland, 1982), 221–242. His version generalizes and simplifies the box/glue/penalty model by introducing the notion of a *kerf*, which consists of three sequences of boxes and glue for *prebreak*, *postbreak*, and *nobreak* alternatives, together with a penalty p and a flag f; breakpoints occur only at kerfs.

The standard version of TEX, which was completed about two years after the paper above was written, extended the line-breaking model in another way, by introducing *leftskip* and *rightskip* glue at the left and right of each line. This simplifies many constructions, such as those for ragged-right and ragged-centered setting. TEX now uses an improved formula for demerits, namely

$$\delta_j = \begin{cases} (l + \beta_j)^2 + \pi_j^2 + \alpha_j, & \text{if } \pi_j \geq 0; \\ (l + \beta_j)^2 - \pi_j^2 + \alpha_j, & \text{if } -\infty < \pi_j < 0; \\ (l + \beta_j)^2 + \alpha_j, & \text{if } \pi_j = -\infty; \end{cases}$$

here l is a parameter called the *line penalty*, normally set to 10. See D. E. Knuth, *Literate Programming* (1992), 272–274, for a discussion of why it was important to change from $(l + \beta_j + \pi_j)^2$ to $(l + \beta_j)^2 + \pi_j^2$ in the case $\pi_j \geq 0$.

People who use TEX extensively will be aware that "infinite" penalties are now rated 10000 instead of 1000, and that TEX's glue now has three levels of infinity called `fil`, `fill`, and `filll`. Version 3.0 of TeX introduced an optional third pass to the line-breaking algorithm, if the user has specified *emergency stretch*. [See change 885 in the error log of TeX, *Literate Programming* (1992), 338.] If there is no feasible way to typeset a paragraph with tolerances ρ_1 or ρ_2, the emergency stretch is added to the stretchability of all lines when calculating badness and demerits; this gives TeX a decent way to distinguish between different levels of extremely bad breaks in the most difficult cases.

Chapter 4

Mixing Right-to-Left Texts with Left-to-Right Texts

[Written with Pierre MacKay. Originally published in TUGboat **8** *(1987), 14–25.]*

TEX was designed to produce documents that are read from left-to-right and top-to-bottom, according to the conventions of English and other Western languages. If such documents are turned 90°, they can also be read from top-to-bottom and right-to-left, as in Japan. Another 90° or 180° turn yields documents that are readable from right-to-left and bottom-to-top, or from bottom-to-top and left-to-right, in case a need for such conventions ever arises. However, TEX as it stands is not suitable for languages like Arabic or Hebrew, which are right-to-left and top-to-bottom.

It would not be difficult to use TEX for documents that are purely Arabic or purely Hebrew, by essentially producing the mirror image of whatever document is desired. A raster-oriented printing device could easily be programmed to reflect the bits from right to left as it puts them on the pages. (This is sometimes called "T-shirt mode", because it can be used to make iron-on transfers that produce readable T-shirt messages, when English language output is transferred to cloth after being printed in mirror image.)

Complications arise, however, when left-to-right conventions are mixed with right-to-left conventions in the same document. Consider an Arabic/English dictionary, or a Bible commentary that quotes Hebrew, or a Middle-Eastern encyclopedia that refers to Western names in roman letters; such documents, and many others, must go both ways.

The purpose of this paper is to clarify the issues involved in mixed-direction document production, from the standpoint of a Western author or reader or software implementor. We shall also consider changes to TEX that will extend it to a bidirectional formatting system.

157

Terminology and Conventions

Let us say for convenience that an *L-text* is textual material that is meant to be read from left to right, and an *R-text* is textual material that is meant to be read from right to left. Similarly we might say that English and Spanish are L-languages, while Arabic and Hebrew are R-languages.

In order to make this paper intelligible to English readers who are unfamiliar with R-languages, we shall use "reflected English", i.e., **English**, as an R-language. All texts in reflected English will be typeset in **Computer Modern Bold Extended** type, which is a reflected version of Computer Modern Bold Extended type. To translate from English to **English** and back again, one simply needs to reverse the order of reading. Both English and **English** are pronounced in the same way, except that **English** should be spoken in a louder and/or deeper voice, so that a listener can distinguish it.

The Simplest Case

It's not difficult to typeset single R-language words in an L-text document. TEX will work fine if you never need to deal with R-texts of more than one word at a time; all you have to do is figure out a macro that will reverse isolated words.

Let's suppose that we want to type 'the |English| script' in order to typeset 'the **English** script' with TEX. All we need is a font for **English**, called xbmc10, say, and the following macros:

```
\font\revrm=xbmc10        \hyphenchar\revrm=-1
\catcode`\|=\active
\def|#1|{{\revrm\reflect#1\empty\tcelfer}}
\def\reflect#1#2\tcelfer{\ifx#1\empty
                         \else\reflect#2\tcelfer#1\fi}
```

(The characters of xbmc10 can be generated like those of cmbx10 with the extra METAFONT statement

```
extra_endchar := extra_endchar &
 "currentpicture:=currentpicture
           reflectedabout((.5[l,r],0),(.5[l,r],1));"
```

added to the parameter file. Both fonts have the same character widths, but they have different ligature-kern tables; for example, an 'i' followed by an 'l' gives 'fl'.)

Alternating Texts

But that simple approach does not work when there are multiword R-text phrases, e.g., **multiword R-text phrases**, embedded in an L-text document—because of the possibility of line breaks, e.g., **because of the possibility of line breaks**. For example, let's consider the problem of typesetting the following paragraph:*

```
Leonardo da Vinci made a sweeping statement
in his notebooks: |''Let no one
who is not a mathematician read my works.''|
In fact, he said it twice, so he probably meant it.
```

Here are samples of the proper results, considering two different column widths:

Leonardo da Vinci made a sweeping statement in his notebooks: **"Let no one who is not a mathematician read my works."** In fact, he said it twice, so he probably meant it.

Leonardo da Vinci made a sweeping statement in his notebooks: **"Let no one who is not a mathematician read my works."** In fact, he said it twice, so he probably meant it.

Notice that the R-text in each line is reflected; in particular, a hyphen that has been inserted at the right of an R-segment will appear at the left of that segment.

How can we get TEX to do this? The best approach is probably to extend the driver programs that produce printed output from the DVI files that TEX writes, instead of trying to do tricky things with TEX macros. Then TEX itself merely needs to put special codes into the DVI output files, in order to tell the "DVI-IVD" drivers what to do.

For example, one idea that almost works is to put '\special{R}' just before an R-text begins, and '\special{L}' just after it ends. In

---

* After Leonardo lost the use of his right hand, he began to make left-handed notes in mirror writing. Of course, he actually wrote in **Italian** instead of **English**.

other words, we can change the '|' macro in our earlier example to the simple form

```
\def|#1|{{\revrm\special{R}#1\special{L}}}
```

which does not actually reverse the characters; we can also leave the '\hyphenchar' of \revrm at its normal value, so that R-texts will be hyphenated. Line breaking will proceed in the normal way, and the DVI-IVᗡ driver program will have the responsibility of reflecting every segment that it sees between an R and an L.

Reflecting might involve arbitrary combinations of characters, rules, accents, kerns, etc.; for example, the R-text might be in ɘƨiɒɔnɒɿʇ, or it might even refer to Xꟻꓕ!

An Approach to Implementation

In order to understand how DVI-IVᗡ programs might do the required tasks, we need to look into the information that TEX puts into a DVI file. The basic idea is that whenever TEX outputs an hbox or a vbox, the DVI file gets a '*push*' command, followed by various commands to typeset the box contents, followed by a '*pop*' command. Therefore we can try the following strategy:

a) Whenever '\special{R}' is found in the DVI file, remember the current horizontal position h_0 and vertical position v_0; also remember the current location p_0 in the DVI file. Set $c \leftarrow 0$. Then begin to skim the next DVI instructions instead of actually using them for typesetting; but keep updating the horizontal and vertical page positions as usual.

b) When '\special{L}' is found in the DVI file, stop skimming instructions. Then typeset all instructions between p_0 and the current location, in mirror-reflected mode, as explained below.

c) When '*push*' occurs when skimming instructions, increase c by 1.

d) When '*pop*' occurs when skimming instructions, there are two cases. If $c > 0$, decrease c by 1. (This '*pop*' matches a previously skimmed '*push*'.) But if $c = 0$, effectively insert '\special{L}' at this point and '\special{R}' just after the very next '*push*'.

The mirror-reflected mode for DVI commands in positions p_0 to p_1 in the DVI file, beginning at (h_0, v_0) and ending at (h_1, v_1), works like this: A character of width w whose box sits on the baseline between (h, v) and $(h + w, v)$ in normal mode should be placed so that its box sits on the baseline between $(h' - w, v)$ and (h', v) in mirror mode, where h' is defined by the equation

$$h - h_0 = h_1 - h'.$$

Similarly, a rule of width w whose lower edge runs from (h, v) to $(h+w, v)$ in normal mode should run from $(h' - w, v)$ to (h', v) in mirror mode.

Fixing Bugs

We stated above that the approach just sketched will "almost" work. But it can fail in three ways, when combined with the full generality of TEX. First, there might be material "between the lines" that is inserted by \vadjust commands; this material might improperly be treated as R-text. Second, the suggested mechanism doesn't always find the correct left edge of segments that are being reflected, since the reflection should not always begin at the extreme left edge of a typeset line; it should begin after the \leftskip glue and before other initial spacing due to things like accent positioning. Third, certain tricks that involve \unhbox can make entire lines disappear from the DVI file; however, this problem is not as serious as the other two, because people shouldn't be playing such tricks.

A much more reliable and robust scheme can be obtained by building a specially extended version of TEX, which puts matching \special commands into every line that has reflected material. It is not difficult to add this additional activity to TEX's existing line-breaking mechanism; the details appear in an appendix below. When this change has been made, parts (c) and (d) of the DVI-IVO skimming algorithm can be eliminated.

L-Chauvinism

We have been discussing mixed documents as if they always consist of R-texts inserted into L-texts; but people whose native script is right-to-left naturally think of mixed documents as the insertion of L-texts into R-texts. In fact, there are two ways to read every page of a document, one in which the eye begins to scan each line at the left and one in which the eye begins to scan each line at the right.

The Leonardo illustration above is an example of the first kind, and we shall call it an *L-document*. To read a given line of an L-document, you start at the left and read any L-text that you see. Whenever your eyes encounter an R-character, they skim ahead to the end of the next R-segment (i.e., until the next L-character, or until the end of the line, whichever comes first); then you read the R-segment right-to-left, and continue as before. The rules for reading an R-document are similar, but with right and left reversed.

It's usually possible to distinguish an L-document from an R-document because of the indentation on the first line of a paragraph and/or the blank space on the last line. For example, the R-documents that correspond to the two L-document settings of the paragraph about Leonardo look like this:

Leonardo da Vinci made a sweeping statement in his
"Let no one who is not a mathematician notebooks:
In fact, he said it twice, so he probably **read my works."**
                                                                        meant it.

Leonardo da Vinci made a sweep-
"Let" ing statement in his notebooks:
no one who is not a mathemati-
In fact, he **"read my works."** cian
said it twice, so he probably meant it.

We can imagine that these R-documents were composed on an R-terminal and processed by T_EX from an **input file** that looks like this:

```
|Leonardo da Vinci made a sweeping statement
          in his notebooks:'' ''Let no one
    who is not a mathematician read my works.''
|In fact, he said it twice, so he probably meant it.|
```

In this case it is the L-text, not the R-text, that is enclosed in |'s. (The reader is urged to study this example carefully; there *is* **method** in't!)

A poet could presumably construct interesting poems that have both L-meanings and R-meanings, when read as L-documents and R-documents.

Notice that our examples from Leonardo have used boldface quotation marks (i.e., the quotation marks of **English**), so that these marks belong to the text being quoted. This may seem erroneous; but it is in fact a necessary convention in documents that are meant to display no favoritism between L-readers and R-readers, because it ensures that the quotation marks will stay with the text being reflected. (See the examples of contemporary typesetting at the end of this paper.) If we had put the quotations marks into English rather than **𝘩𝘴𝘪𝘭𝘨𝘯𝘌**, the R-documents illustrated above would have looked very strange indeed:

Leonardo da Vinci made a sweeping statement in his
𝐧𝐚𝐢𝐜𝐢𝐭𝐚𝐦𝐞𝐡𝐭𝐚𝐦 𝐚 𝐭𝐨𝐧 𝐬𝐢 𝐨𝐡𝐰 𝐞𝐧𝐨 𝐨𝐧 𝐭𝐞𝐋notebooks: "
" In fact, he said it twice, so he probably.**𝐬𝐤𝐫𝐨𝐰 𝐲𝐦 𝐝𝐚𝐞𝐫**
meant it.

Leonardo da Vinci made a sweep-
𝐭𝐞𝐋ing statement in his notebooks: "
-𝐢𝐭𝐚𝐦𝐞𝐡𝐭𝐚𝐦 𝐚 𝐭𝐨𝐧 𝐬𝐢 𝐨𝐡𝐰 𝐞𝐧𝐨 𝐨𝐧
" In fact, he.**𝐬𝐤𝐫𝐨𝐰 𝐲𝐦 𝐝𝐚𝐞𝐫 𝐧𝐚𝐢𝐜**
said it twice, so he probably meant it.

Multi-Level Mixing

The problems of mixed R- and L-typesetting go deeper than this, because there might be an L-text inside an R-text inside an L-text. For
example, we might want to typeset a paragraph whose TEX source file
looks like this:

```
\R{Alice} said, \R{''You think English is
\L{'English written backwards'}}; but to me,
\L{English} is English written backwards.
I'm sure \L{Knuth} and \L{MacKay} will
both agree with me.''}  And she was right.
```

An intelligent bidirectional reader will want this to be typeset as if it
were an R-document inside an L-document. In other words, the eyes
of such a reader will naturally scan some of the lines beginning at the
left, and some of them beginning at the right. Here are examples of the
desired output, set with two different line widths: (Look closely.)

𝐞𝐜𝐢𝐥𝐀 said, 𝐬𝐢 𝐡𝐬𝐢𝐥𝐠𝐧𝐄 𝐤𝐧𝐢𝐡𝐭 𝐮𝐨𝐘"
,𝐞𝐦 𝐨𝐭 𝐭𝐮𝐛 ;'English written backwards'
.**𝐬𝐝𝐫𝐚𝐰𝐤𝐜𝐚𝐛 𝐧𝐞𝐭𝐭𝐢𝐫𝐰 𝐡𝐬𝐢𝐥𝐠𝐧𝐄 𝐬𝐢** English
𝐡𝐭𝐨𝐛 𝐥𝐥𝐢𝐰 MacKay 𝐛𝐧𝐚 Knuth 𝐞𝐫𝐮𝐬 𝐦'I
".𝐞𝐦 𝐡𝐭𝐢𝐰 𝐞𝐞𝐫𝐠𝐚 And she was right.

𝐞𝐜𝐢𝐥𝐀 said, 'En-**𝐬𝐢 𝐡𝐬𝐢𝐥𝐠𝐧𝐄 𝐤𝐧𝐢𝐡𝐭 𝐮𝐨𝐘"**
English **,𝐞𝐦 𝐨𝐭 𝐭𝐮𝐛 ;**glish written backwards'
𝐞𝐫𝐮𝐬 𝐦'I .𝐬𝐝𝐫𝐚𝐰𝐤𝐜𝐚𝐛 𝐧𝐞𝐭𝐭𝐢𝐫𝐰 𝐡𝐬𝐢𝐥𝐠𝐧𝐄 𝐬𝐢
𝐡𝐭𝐢𝐰 𝐞𝐞𝐫𝐠𝐚 𝐡𝐭𝐨𝐛 𝐥𝐥𝐢𝐰 MacKay 𝐛𝐧𝐚 Knuth
".𝐞𝐦 And she was right.

Multi-level documents are inherently ambiguous. For example, the second setting of ɘɔilA's example might be interpreted as the result of

```
...\R{... I'm sure and \L{MacKay} will both agree with}
Knuth \R{me.''}  And she was right.
```

and the first setting would also result from a source file like this(!)

```
\R{''You think English is \L{said,} Alice
\L{'English}; but to me,} written backwards'
\R{written backwards.} \R{\L{English} is English}
will both} MacKay \R{and} Knuth \R{I'm sure
\L{And she} agree with me.''} was right.
```

except for slight differences in spacing due to TEX's "space factor" for punctuation.

In general, we have \R{\L{a}\L{b}} = ba, hence *any* permutation of the characters on each line is theoretically possible. A reader has to figure out which of the different ways to parse each line makes most sense. Yet there is unanimous agreement in Middle Eastern countries that a mixture of L-document and R-document styles is preferable to an unambiguous insistence on L-reading or R-reading throughout a document, because it is so natural and because the actual ambiguities arise rarely in practice. The quotation marks in the example above make it possible to reconstruct the invisible \R's and \L's; in this way an author can cooperate with a literate reader so that the meaning is clear.

Multi-level texts arise not only when quotes are inside quotes or when R-document footnotes or illustrations are attached to L-documents; they also arise when mathematics is embedded in R-text. For example, consider the TEX source code

```
The \R{English} version of 'the famous identity
$e^{i\pi}+1=0$ due to Euler' is
\R{'the famous identity $e^{i\pi}+1=0$ due to Euler'}.
```

It should be typeset like this:

The ʜɛilgnƎ version of 'the famous iden-
tity $e^{i\pi} + 1 = 0$ due to Euler' is ꙅuoms �̃ ɘʜɈ'
'ɿɘluƎ oɈ ɘub $e^{i\pi} + 1 = 0$ ʏɈiɈnɘbi.

An extension of TEX called TEX-X꟯T, described in the appendix, properly handles multi-level mixtures including math, as well as the simpler case of alternating R-texts and L-texts.

Conclusions

When right-to-left and left-to-right texts are mixed in the same document, problems can arise that are more subtle than simple examples might suggest. The difficulties can be overcome by extending TEX to TEX-X$_{\Xi}$T and by extending DVI drivers to DVI-IVᗡ drivers. Neither of these extensions is extremely complex.

Appendix

The extensions to TEX described here are designed to put the hitherto-undefined byte codes 250 (*'begin_reflection'*) and 251 (*'end_reflection'*) into the DVI file, instead of '\special{R}' and '\special{L}' as mentioned above, because mixed-direction typesetting is important enough to deserve efficient DVI coding. The resulting output files are called DVI-IVᗡ files.

The TEX language is extended to have four new primitive operations,

```
\beginL      \endL       \beginR       \endR
```

which are supposed to nest like parentheses in each paragraph and in each hbox. However, \endL and \endR should be omitted at the end of a paragraph if they are supposed to take effect after the \parfillskip glue. (Thus, for example,

```
\everypar{\kern-\parindent\beginR\indent}
```

can be used to start a series of paragraphs that all follow the conventions of an R-document. The last line of every such paragraph will be flush right, filled at the left; the first line will be indented at the right.)

The four new operations each contribute a new sort of "whatsit node" to the current horizontal list; they are additional cases of a ⟨horizontal command⟩ as explained in the TEX manual [2]. The \L and \R macros in our multi-level example about ƧɔilA can be defined as follows:

```
\def\L{\afterassignment\moreL \let\next= }
\def\moreL{\bracetest \aftergroup\endL \beginL \rm}
\def\R{\afterassignment\moreR \let\next= }
\def\moreR{\bracetest \aftergroup\endR \beginR \revrm}
\def\bracetest{\ifcat\next{\else\ifcat\next}\fi
 \errmessage{Missing left brace has been substituted}\fi
 \bgroup}
```

The remainder of this appendix gives complete details about changes to the standard TEX program [3] that will convert it to the extended system TEX-X$_{\exists}$T. It is convenient to list these changes in order by the WEB section numbers in [3], for every section that is affected.

2. Here we should change the final introductory paragraph; the new copy will explain that the present program is actually 'TEX-X$_{\exists}$T', not 'TEX'. The *banner* string is correspondingly redefined:

> **define** *banner* ≡ ´This␣is␣TeX-XeT,␣Version␣3.1415´
>
> { printed when TEX-X$_{\exists}$T starts }

11. The *pool_name* is changed so that TEX-X$_{\exists}$T can coexist happily with TEX.

> *pool_name* = ´TeXformats:TEXXET.POOL␣␣␣␣␣␣␣␣␣␣␣␣␣␣␣␣␣␣´;
>
> { string of length *file_name_size*; tells where the string pool appears }

161. Additional subroutines, to be defined later, are stuck into the program at this place.

> ⟨ Declare functions needed for special kinds of nodes 1381 ⟩

208. A new command code is added at the end of the former list; the final definition is therefore replaced by two:

> **define** *LR* = 71   { text direction (\beginL , \beginR , \endL , \endR) }
> **define** *max_non_prefixed_command* = 71
>
> > { largest command code that can't be \global }

209. We have to add 1 to the right-hand sides of all these definitions.

> **define** *toks_register* = 72   { token list register (\toks) }
>
> > $\vdots$
>
> **define** *set_interaction* = 101
>
> > { define level of interaction (\batchmode , etc.) }
>
> **define** *max_command* = 101
>
> > { the largest command code seen at *big_switch* }

585. The description of DVI commands is augmented by two new ones at the end:

begin_reflect 250. Begin a (possibly recursive) reflected segment.

end_reflect 251. End a (possibly recursive) reflected segment.

Commands 250–255 are undefined in normal DVI files, but 250 and 251 are permitted in the special 'DVI-IVᗡ' files produced by this variant of TEX.

When a DVI-IVD driver encounters a *begin_reflect* command, it should skim ahead (as previously described) until finding the matching *end_reflect*; these will be properly nested with respect to each other and with respect to *push* and *pop*. After skimming has located a segment of material to be reflected, that segment should be re-scanned and obeyed in mirror-image mode as described earlier. The reflected segment might recursively involve *begin_reflect*/*end_reflect* pairs that need to be reflected again.

586.   Two new definitions are needed:

> **define** *begin_reflect* = 250
> > { begin a reflected segment (allowed in DVI-IVD files only) }
> **define** *end_reflect* = 251
> > { end a reflected segment (allowed in DVI-IVD files only) }

638.   At the beginning of *ship_out*, we will initialize a stack of \beginL and \beginR instructions that are currently in force; this is called the LR stack, and it is maintained with the help of two global variables called *LR_ptr* and *LR_tmp* that will be defined later. The instructions inserted here (just before testing if *tracing_output* > 0) say that on the outermost level we are typesetting in left-to-right mode. The opening 'begin' is replaced by:

> **begin** *LR_ptr* ← *get_avail*; *info*(*LR_ptr*) ← 0;
> > { *begin_L_code* at outer level }

639.   At the end of *ship_out*, we want to clear out the LR stack. Thus, '*flush_node_list*(*p*)' is replaced by:

> *flush_node_list*(*p*); ⟨ Flush the LR stack 1385 ⟩;

649.   The *hpack* routine is modified to keep an LR stack as it packages a horizontal list, so that errors of mismatched \beginL...\endL and \beginR...\endR pairs can be detected and corrected. Changes are needed here at the beginning of the procedure and at the end.

> **function** *hpack*(*p* : *pointer*; *w* : *scaled*; *m* : *small_number*): *pointer*;
> > ⋮
>
> > *hd*: *eight_bits*;   { height and depth indices for a character }
> > *LR_ptr*, *LR_tmp*: *pointer*;   { for LR stack maintenance }
> > *LR_problems*: *integer*;   { counts missing begins and ends }
> **begin** *LR_ptr* ← *null*; *LR_problems* ← 0;
> *r* ← *get_node*(*box_node_size*);
> > ⋮

common_ending: ⟨Finish issuing a diagnostic message for an overfull or
        underfull hbox 663⟩;
exit: ⟨Check for LR anomalies at the end of *hpack* 1390⟩;
   hpack ← *r*;
   end;

877.   Similarly, the *post_line_break* routine should keep an LR stack, so
that it can output \endL or \endR instructions at the ends of lines and
\beginL or \beginR instructions at the beginnings of lines. Changes
occur at the beginning and the end of this procedure:

procedure *post_line_break* (*final_widow_penalty* : *integer*);
        ⋮
   cur_line: *halfword*;   { the current line number being justified }
   LR_ptr, *LR_tmp*: *pointer*;   { for LR stack maintenance }
   begin *LR_ptr* ← *null*;
   ⟨Reverse the links of the relevant passive nodes, setting *cur_p* to the first
        breakpoint 878⟩;
        ⋮
   prev_graf ← *best_line* − 1; ⟨Flush the LR stack 1385⟩;
   end;

880.   The new actions to be performed when broken lines are being
packaged are accomplished by three new steps added to this section of
the program.
⟨Justify the line ending at breakpoint *cur_p*, and append it to the
        current vertical list, together with associated penalties and other
        insertions 880⟩ ≡
   ⟨Insert LR nodes at the beginning of the current line 1386⟩;
   ⟨Adjust the LR stack based on LR nodes in this line 1387⟩;
   ⟨Modify the end of the line to reflect the nature of the break and to include
        \rightskip; also set the proper value of *disc_break* 881⟩;
   ⟨Insert LR nodes at the end of the current line 1388⟩;
   ⟨Put the \leftskip glue at the left and detach this line 887⟩;
        ⋮

1090.   We add '*vmode* + *LR*' as a new subcase after '*vmode* +
no_boundary' here. This means that the new primitive operations will
become instances of what *The TEXbook* calls a ⟨horizontal command⟩.

1196.   Math-in-text will be formatted left-to-right, because two new
'append' instructions are inserted into this section of the code.
⟨Finish math in text 1196⟩ ≡

begin *tail_append*(*new_math*(*math_surround*, *before*));
⟨ Append a *begin_L* to the tail of the current list 1383 ⟩;
cur_mlist ← *p*; *cur_style* ← *text_style*;
mlist_penalties ← (*mode* > 0);
mlist_to_hlist;
link(*tail*) ← *link*(*temp_head*);
while *link*(*tail*) ≠ *null* **do** *tail* ← *link*(*tail*);
⟨ Append an *end_L* to the tail of the current list 1384 ⟩;
tail_append(*new_math*(*math_surround*, *after*)); *space_factor* ← 1000;
unsave;
end

1341.   The new primitive operations put new kinds of whatsit nodes into horizontal lists. Therefore two additional definitions are needed here:

define *LR_node* = 4   { *subtype* in whatsits that represent \beginL, etc. }
define *LR_type*(#) ≡ *mem*[# + 1].*int*   { the sub-subtype }

1344.   Here's where the new primitives get established.

define *immediate_code* = 4   { command modifier for \immediate }
define *set_language_code* = 5   { command modifier for \setlanguage }
define *begin_L_code* = 0   { command modifier for \beginL }
define *begin_R_code* = 1   { command modifier for \beginR }
define *end_L_code* = 2   { command modifier for \endL }
define *end_R_code* = 3   { command modifier for \endR }
define *begin_LR*(#) ≡ (*LR_type*(#) < *end_L_code*)
define *begin_LR_type*(#) ≡ (*LR_type*(#) − *end_L_code*)
⟨ Put each of TeX's primitives into the hash table 226 ⟩ +≡
primitive("beginL", *LR*, *begin_L_code*);
primitive("beginR", *LR*, *begin_R_code*);
primitive("endL", *LR*, *end_L_code*);
primitive("endR", *LR*, *end_R_code*);
primitive("openout", *extension*, *open_node*);
⋮

1346.   The new primitives call for a new case of cases here.

LR: **case** *chr_code* **of**
begin_L_code: *print_esc*("beginL");
begin_R_code: *print_esc*("beginR");
end_L_code: *print_esc*("endL");
othercases *print_esc*("endR")
endcases;

1356.   We also need to be able to display the newfangled whatsits.

LR_node: **case** *LR_type*(*p*) **of**
   begin_L_code: *print_esc*("beginL");
   begin_R_code: *print_esc*("beginR");
   end_L_code: *print_esc*("endL");
   othercases *print_esc*("endR")
   endcases;

1357, 1358.   Copying and deleting the new nodes is easy, since they can be handled just like the \closeout nodes already present. We simply replace '*close_node*' by '*close_node*, *LR_node*' in these two sections.

1360.   We used to *do_nothing* here, but now we must *do_something*:

⟨ Incorporate a whatsit node into an hbox 1360 ⟩ ≡
if *subtype*(*p*) = *LR_node* **then**
   ⟨ Adjust the LR stack for the *hpack* routine 1389 ⟩

This code is used in section 651.

1366.   ⟨ Output the whatsit node *p* in an hlist 1366 ⟩ ≡
   if *subtype*(*p*) ≠ *LR_node* **then** *out_what*(*p*)
   else ⟨ Output a reflection instruction if the direction has changed 1391 ⟩

This code is used in section 622.

1379.   Most of the changes have been saved up for the end, so that the section numbers of TEX in [3] can be left unchanged. Now we come to the real guts of this extension to mixed-direction texts.

First, we allow the new primitives to appear in horizontal mode, but not in math mode:

⟨ Cases of *main_control* that build boxes and lists 1056 ⟩ +≡
hmode + *LR*: **begin** *new_whatsit*(*LR_node*, *small_node_size*);
   LR_type(*tail*) ← *cur_chr*; **end**;
mmode + *LR*: *report_illegal_case*;

1380.   A number of routines are based on a stack of one-word nodes whose *info* fields contain either *begin_L_code* or *begin_R_code*. The top of the stack is pointed to by *LR_ptr*, and an auxiliary variable *LR_tmp* is available for stack manipulation.

⟨ Global variables 13 ⟩ +≡
LR_ptr, *LR_tmp*: *pointer*;   { stack of LR codes and temp for manipulation }

1381. ⟨ Declare functions needed for special kinds of nodes 1381 ⟩ ≡
function $new\_LR(s : small\_number)$: *pointer*;
  var p: *pointer*; { the new node }
  begin $p \leftarrow get\_node(small\_node\_size)$; $type(p) \leftarrow whatsit\_node$;
  $subtype(p) \leftarrow LR\_node$; $LR\_type(p) \leftarrow s$; $new\_LR \leftarrow p$;
  end;

See also section 1382.

This code is used in section 161.

1382. ⟨ Declare functions needed for special kinds of nodes 1381 ⟩ +≡
function $safe\_info(p : pointer)$: *integer*;
  begin if $p = null$ **then** $safe\_info \leftarrow -1$ **else** $safe\_info \leftarrow info(p)$;
  end;

1383. ⟨ Append a *begin_L* to the tail of the current list 1383 ⟩ ≡
  $tail\_append(new\_LR(begin\_L\_code))$

This code is used in section 1196.

1384. ⟨ Append an *end_L* to the tail of the current list 1384 ⟩ ≡
  $tail\_append(new\_LR(end\_L\_code))$

This code is used in section 1196.

1385. When the stack-manipulation macros of this section are used below, variables LR_ptr and LR_tmp might be the global variables declared above, or they might be local to *hpack* or *post_line_break*.
  define $push\_LR(\#) \equiv$
      begin $LR\_tmp \leftarrow get\_avail$; $info(LR\_tmp) \leftarrow LR\_type(\#)$;
      $link(LR\_tmp) \leftarrow LR\_ptr$; $LR\_ptr \leftarrow LR\_tmp$;
      end
  define $pop\_LR \equiv$
      begin $LR\_tmp \leftarrow LR\_ptr$; $LR\_ptr \leftarrow link(LR\_tmp)$;
      $free\_avail(LR\_tmp)$;
      end
⟨ Flush the LR stack 1385 ⟩ ≡
  while $LR\_ptr \neq null$ **do** pop_LR

This code is used in sections 639 and 877.

1386. ⟨ Insert LR nodes at the beginning of the current line 1386 ⟩ ≡
  while $LR\_ptr \neq null$ **do**
    begin $LR\_tmp \leftarrow new\_LR(info(LR\_ptr))$;
    $link(LR\_tmp) \leftarrow link(temp\_head)$; $link(temp\_head) \leftarrow LR\_tmp$; pop_LR;
    end

This code is used in section 880.

1387.   ⟨ Adjust the LR stack based on LR nodes in this line 1387 ⟩ ≡
  $q \leftarrow link(temp\_head)$;
  while $q \neq cur\_break(cur\_p)$ **do**
    begin if $\neg is\_char\_node(q)$ **then**
      if $type(q) = whatsit\_node$ **then**
        if $subtype(q) = LR\_node$ **then**
          if $begin\_LR(q)$ **then** $push\_LR(q)$
          else if $LR\_ptr \neq null$ **then**
              if $info(LR\_ptr) = begin\_LR\_type(q)$ **then** pop_LR;
    $q \leftarrow link(q)$;
    end

This code is used in section 880.

1388.   We use the fact that q now points to the node with \rightskip glue.
⟨ Insert LR nodes at the end of the current line 1388 ⟩ ≡
  if $LR\_ptr \neq null$ **then**
    begin $s \leftarrow temp\_head$; $r \leftarrow link(s)$;
    while $r \neq q$ **do**
      begin $s \leftarrow r$; $r \leftarrow link(s)$;
      end;
    $r \leftarrow LR\_ptr$;
    while $r \neq null$ **do**
      begin $LR\_tmp \leftarrow new\_LR(info(r) + end\_L\_code)$; $link(s) \leftarrow LR\_tmp$;
      $s \leftarrow LR\_tmp$; $r \leftarrow link(r)$;
      end;
    $link(s) \leftarrow q$;
    end

This code is used in section 880.

1389.   ⟨ Adjust the LR stack for the *hpack* routine 1389 ⟩ ≡
  if $begin\_LR(p)$ **then** $push\_LR(p)$
  else if $safe\_info(LR\_ptr) = begin\_LR\_type(p)$ **then** pop_LR
    else begin $incr(LR\_problems)$;
      while $link(q) \neq p$ **do** $q \leftarrow link(q)$;
      $link(q) \leftarrow link(p)$; $free\_node(p, small\_node\_size)$; $p \leftarrow q$;
      end

This code is used in section 1360.

1390.   ⟨ Check for LR anomalies at the end of *hpack* 1390 ⟩ ≡
  if $LR\_ptr \neq null$ **then**
    begin while $link(q) \neq null$ **do** $q \leftarrow link(q)$;
    repeat $link(q) \leftarrow new\_LR(info(LR\_ptr) + end\_L\_code)$; $q \leftarrow link(q)$;
    $LR\_problems \leftarrow LR\_problems + 10000$; pop_LR;

until $LR\_ptr = null$;
  end;
if $LR\_problems > 0$ **then**
  begin $print\_ln$; $print\_nl$ ("\endL␣or␣\endR␣problem␣(");
  $print\_int$ ($LR\_problems$ **div** 10000); $print$ ("␣missing,␣");
  $print\_int$ ($LR\_problems$ **mod** 10000); $print$ ("␣extra");
  $LR\_problems \leftarrow 0$; **goto** $common\_ending$;
  end

This code is used in section 649.

1391. ⟨ Output a reflection instruction if the direction has changed 1391 ⟩ ≡
  if $begin\_LR(p)$ **then**
    begin if $safe\_info(LR\_ptr) \neq LR\_type(p)$ **then**
      begin $synch\_h$; $synch\_v$; $dvi\_out(begin\_reflect)$;
      end;
    $push\_LR(p)$;
    end
  else if $safe\_info(LR\_ptr) = begin\_LR\_type(p)$ **then**
    begin pop_LR;
    if $info(LR\_ptr) + end\_L\_code \neq LR\_type(p)$ **then**
      begin $synch\_h$; $synch\_v$; $dvi\_out(end\_reflect)$;
      end;
    end
  else $confusion$ ("LR")

This code is used in section 1366.

Final Important Note

The extensions to TEX just described are "upward compatible" with standard TEX, in the sense that ordinary TEX programs will still run correctly (although more slowly) on TEX-X̣ǝT. However, TEX-X̣ǝT must *not* be called a new version of 'TEX', even though it runs all TEX programs; the reason is, of course, that TEX will not run all TEX-X̣ǝT programs.

A name change is necessary to distinguish all programs that do not agree precisely with the real TEX. Anybody who runs a program called 'TEX' should be able to assume that it will give identical results from all its implementations.

References

[1] Joseph D. Becker, "Arabic word processing," *Communications of the ACM* **30** (1987), 600–610.

[2] Donald E. Knuth, *The TEXbook*, Volume A of *Computers & Typesetting* (Reading, Massachusetts: Addison–Wesley, 1986).

[3] Donald E. Knuth, *TEX: The Program*, Volume B of *Computers & Typesetting*, fifth printing (Reading, Massachusetts: Addison–Wesley, 1993). [Earlier printings correspond to earlier versions of TEX, when the changes for TEX-XET were analogous but slightly different.]

[4] Pierre MacKay, "Setting Arabic with a computer," *Scholarly Publishing* **8**, 2 (January 1977), 142–150.

[5] Pierre MacKay, "Typesetting problem scripts," *Byte* **11**, 2 (February 1986), 201–218.

Examples of Typesetting Practice

1. From *Textus* **5** (1966), page 12; Magnes Press, Hebrew University of Jerusalem. (Notice the Hebrew quotation marks surrounding the Hebrew title in footnote 6.)

ters adhered,[10] and which may have been similar to that adopted, by normative Jewry presumably somewhat later, during the period of the Second Temple.[10]

Frag. E. Yadin correctly states: "Sanders' cautious indication '103 (? 104)' can now be eliminated" (*ib.*, p. 5).

6   Sanders' *editio princeps* of Ps. 151 already has been discussed by various scholars. The present author deals with the text of Ps. 151, and its literary genre in: מזמורים חיצוניים״ ״בלשון העברית מקומראן, *Tarbiz* 35 (1966) 214–228.

2. Fragments from the third edition of William Wright's classic nineteenth century grammar of Arabic, volume 2, pages 295–297. (Notice the page break in the midst of right-to-left text, and some left-to-right brackets.)

gnawed at us; كُنْتُمْ خَيْرَ أُمَّةٍ أُخْرِجَتْ لِلنَّاسِ *ye are the best people that has been brought forth (created) for mankind;* مَشَيْنَ كَمَا ٱهْتَزَّتْ *they walked as spears wave, the* رِمَاحٌ تَسَقَّهَتْ أَعَالِيَهَا مَرُّ ٱلرِّيَاجِ ٱلنَّوَاسِمِ *tops of which are bent by the passing of gentle breezes;* إِنَارَةُ ٱلْعَقْلِ

296   PART THIRD.—*Syntax.*   [§ 152

مَكْسُوفٌ بِطَاوُعِ هَوًى *the brightness of the intellect is obscured* (or *eclipsed*) *by obeying lust*. As the above examples show, this agreement

§ 152] *Sentence and its Parts.—Concord of Predicate & Subject.* 297

verb is placed after a collective subject (see § 148); as وَلَكِنَّ أَكْثَرَ النَّاسِ لَا يَشْكُرُونَ *but the greatest part of mankind are thankless;* [أُتْرُكُوا فَرِيقٌ مِنْهُمْ يَخْشَوْنَ النَّاسَ *a part of them are afraid of men;* أُتْرُكِ التُّرْكَ مَا تَرَكُوكُمْ *let the Turks alone as long as they let you alone;* لِأَنَّ جَيْشَهُ هَلَكُوا *because his army had perished*].

3.   From page 233 of the same book. Here R-texts are equated with = signs; the left sides of each equation are to be read first.

اَلصَّلْوَةُ فِى السَّاعَةِ *understood;* i.e. صَلْوةُ السَّاعَةِ الْأُولَى = صَلْوةُ الْأُولَى (see § 77). Similarly, some grammarians consider جَانِبُ الْغَرْبِيِّ الْأُولَى مَسْجِدُ الْمَكَانِ الْجَامِعِ = مَسْجِدُ الْجَامِعِ, جَانِبُ الْمَكَانِ الْغَرْبِيِّ = بَقْلَةُ الْحَبَّةِ الْحَمْقَاءِ = بَقْلَةُ الْحَمْقَاءِ, مَسْجِدُ الْوَقْتِ الْجَامِعِ or and, أَفْضَلُ دَارُ الْحَيَاةِ الْآخِرَةِ = دَارُ الْآخِرَةِ*. Here too the constructions

4.   From *Bulletin of the Iranian Mathematical Society* 8 (Tehran, 1978), page 78L. (Left-to-right mathematics in right-to-left text.)

کلمه جدید با زشود از عبارت زیرتعیین میشود

$$\frac{n-1}{2m} + \frac{2(n-1)(n-2)}{3m^2} + \frac{3(n-1)(n-2)}{4m^3} + \ldots$$

که تقریبا ًمساوی $\alpha/[\log_e(1-\alpha)] + 1/(1-\alpha)$ است که در آن $e=2.71828$ میباشد. بنابراین اضافه کرد ن کلمات به جد ول باکمک الگوریتم F کارچند ان

5. From מבוא למתימטיקה [*Introduction to Mathematics*, pronounced **Mavo le Mathematika**] by Abraham A. Fraenkel, Volume 1 (Jerusalem: Hebrew University, 1942), page 38. (Page numbers are '96–90' because '90' and '96' are Hebrew numbers.)

בהשתמשנו במושג הקונגרואנציה, נוכל ׳לכתוב את המשפט הקטן של פ ר מ ה
בצורה : (mod. *p*) *a*^{p}≡*a*, ואת משפט וילסון בצורה:

$$1 \cdot 2 \cdot 3 \cdots (p-1) \equiv -1 \pmod{p}.$$

1. מן המלים הרומיות congruens = מתאים, modulus = אופן, מדה.

2. עיין בהוכחה שנתן M. HAMBURGER בשנת 1896 בכרך ה 116 של ה Journal f. d. reine u. ang. Mathematik (עמ' 90–96) לנוסחה של גאוס משנת 1802, הקובעת את התאריך הנוצרי

---

6. Page 200 of the same book illustrates the difference between ellipses '···' in formulas and in the text. None of this book's math-in-text is broken between lines.

בריבוע של מספר אי־זוגי, ב) שאפשר לפתור את הבעיה אם *n* מתפרק למספרים
ראשוניים שונים *p$_1$·p$_2$*····*p$_k$*, בתנאי שהבעיה נפתרת בשביל כל
הערכים *n*=*p$_1$* *n*=*p$_2$*, ···· *n*=*p$_k$*. נסתפק בכך שנבאר את הטענה האחרונה
ביחס לדוגמה *n*=3·5=15. ידוע בוודאי לרוב הקוראים שאפשר לבנות בעזרת

⋮

קודם כל יצויין שבמקרה זה, *p*=*n*, כל שרשי המשואה [1] (לשון אחר:
כל שרשי המשואה 1=*x^p*) פרט ל 1) הנם שרשים "פרימיטיביים" במובן שהוגדר
בעמ' 199; שהרי כל ערך *k* מתוך הסדרה (*p*−1, ... ,1,2) זר ל *p*. יהי אפוא *n*=*p*,
ו *ξ* שורש כלשהו של המשואה [1]; אז יהיו *ξ*, *ξ^2*, ..., *ξ^{p-1}* כל שרשיה של
המשואה [1] '. השרשים האלה נקראים שרשי היחידה.

Chapter 5

Recipes and Fractions

*[Originally published in TUGboat **6** (1985), 36–38.]*

Pages 233, 236, and 237 of *The TEXbook* contain examples of alignment based on excerpts from the well-known book *Mastering the Art of French Cooking*, by Julia Child et al. Several of the measurements in those examples involve fractions like '$\frac{1}{2}$', and this caused unpleasant interference between adjacent lines when I first looked at proofs of the tables for pages 236–237. The fractions on different lines didn't actually touch each other, but they came close enough to be visually disturbing. That's why I increased the distance between baselines by 2 pt in those examples.

Since writing *The TEXbook* I've had several opportunities to typeset recipes for various social occasions, and I learned something that I should have realized long ago: The typographer's '$1/2$' works better than a mathematician's '$\frac{1}{2}$' in such contexts. Hence I recently added a new exercise 11.6 to *The TEXbook*, explaining how to make fractions like '$1/2$' when they aren't already present in a font; I also changed the examples on pages 233, 236, and 237 so that they would use this idea. (See the current errata list or the most recent printings for details.)

Last December, my wife and I made a keepsake for the Associates of the Stanford University Libraries: My mother's mother's recipe for "Stollen" was used to bake some of the goodies at their annual Christmas Tea, and we provided copies of the recipe as an example of digital typography. I was glad to find that the members of this booklovers' group were pleased not only by the delicious cake; they also liked the quality of the typesetting, even though it was done by a computer! If I hadn't used an appropriate style of fractions, I'm sure we wouldn't have gotten such a favorable response.

Here is a copy of the keepsake, and the TEX code that produced it, in case the reader is interested in seeing another small but complete example of TEX usage (based only on the plain TEX macros). The final output was mounted and printed in such a way that we could easily fold the two pages, making essentially a $3'' \times 5''$ card that could be filed with other recipes. Since the recipe is so short, I didn't use any fancy macros to do the double-column formatting of the list of ingredients.

```
% A recipe for Christmas Stollen

\hsize=4.5in     % width of text blocks
\vsize=2.3in     % height of text blocks
\nopagenumbers

\font\ninerm=cmr9

\def\frac#1/#2{\leavevmode\kern.1em
  \raise.5ex\hbox{\the\scriptfont0 #1}\kern-.1em
  /\kern-.15em\lower.25ex\hbox{\the\scriptfont0 #2}}

\parskip=3pt     % space between paragraphs
\parindent=0pt   % no indentation

{\bf Christmas Stollen}
\medskip

\tabskip=10pt plus 1fil
\halign to \hsize{&#\hfil\cr
1 pint milk, scalded and cooled&
 \frac1/2 teaspoon nutmeg\cr
1 ounce compressed or dry yeast&
 1\frac1/2 teaspoons salt\cr
1 cup butter&
 8 cups flour\cr
1 cup sugar&
 1 pound mixed candied fruit\cr
4 eggs&
 \frac3/4 pound candied cherries\cr
grated rind of 1 lemon&
 1 cup nuts\cr
}

\smallskip
Dissolve yeast in scalded, cooled milk. Add 1 cup of
the flour.  Let it rise \frac1/2~hour.
Cream butter and sugar. Beat in eggs, one at a time.
Stir in yeast mixture. Add lemon rind, nutmeg and salt.
Dredge the fruit in a little flour to keep the pieces
from sticking together.  Add the rest of the flour to
```

the dough, and finally stir in the fruit and nuts.
Knead the dough until smooth. Put in a warm place in a
covered bowl and let rise until doubled in bulk.
\ (Because the fruit makes the dough heavy, it
may take two or three hours to rise.) \ Divide the
dough into three parts. Roll each portion out to about
1~inch thick, then fold over in thirds to form a long,
loaf shape. Place on a greased cookie sheet, cover and
let rise until doubled~again.
Bake at $325^\circ\,$F. for 45 minutes.

Stollen is traditionally frosted with thin
powdered-sugar-and-butter icing. Decorate each loaf
with red and green candied cherries.

Vary the fruit and nuts to suit your taste.
You may use cherries alone, mixed fruit, and/or dates;
almonds, pecans, walnuts, or no nuts at all.

\medskip \ninerm \baselineskip=11pt
This is the recipe that was used each Christmas by Don's
grandmother, Pauline Ehlert~Bohning, Cleveland, Ohio.
Don's mother, Louise Bohning~Knuth, still makes
more than 20 loaves each year, and when we were married
she passed the recipe on to us. We hope you enjoy it.

\vskip-\baselineskip
\rightline{Don and Jill Knuth, Stanford, 1984}
\eject
\end

Christmas Stollen

1 pint milk, scalded and cooled	$1/2$ teaspoon nutmeg
1 ounce compressed or dry yeast	$1\,1/2$ teaspoons salt
1 cup butter	8 cups flour
1 cup sugar	1 pound mixed candied fruit
4 eggs	$3/4$ pound candied cherries
grated rind of 1 lemon	1 cup nuts

Dissolve yeast in scalded, cooled milk. Add 1 cup of the flour. Let it rise $1/2$ hour. Cream butter and sugar. Beat in eggs, one at a time. Stir in yeast mixture. Add lemon rind, nutmeg and salt. Dredge the fruit in a little flour to keep the pieces from sticking together. Add the rest of the flour to the dough, and finally stir in the fruit and nuts. Knead the dough until smooth. Put in a warm place in a covered bowl and let rise until doubled in bulk.

(Because the fruit makes the dough heavy, it may take two or three hours to rise.) Divide the dough into three parts. Roll each portion out to about 1 inch thick, then fold over in thirds to form a long, loaf shape. Place on a greased cookie sheet, cover and let rise until doubled again. Bake at 325° F. for 45 minutes.

Stollen is traditionally frosted with thin powdered-sugar-and-butter icing. Decorate each loaf with red and green candied cherries.

Vary the fruit and nuts to suit your taste. You may use cherries alone, mixed fruit, and/or dates; almonds, pecans, walnuts, or no nuts at all.

This is the recipe that was used each Christmas by Don's grandmother, Pauline Ehlert Bohning, Cleveland, Ohio. Don's mother, Louise Bohning Knuth, still makes more than 20 loaves each year, and when we were married she passed the recipe on to us. We hope you enjoy it.   Don and Jill Knuth, Stanford, 1984

Chapter 6

The TEX Logo in Various Fonts

*[Originally published in TUGboat **7** (1986), 101.]*

According to the plain TEX macro package described in *The TEXbook*,

```
\def\TeX{T\kern-.1667em\lower.5ex\hbox{E}\kern-.125emX}
```

is the "official" definition of TEX's logo. But the plain TEX macros are specifically oriented to the Computer Modern fonts. Other typefaces call for variations in the backspacing, in order to preserve the logo's general flavor.

The definition above seems to work satisfactorily with the main seriffed fonts of Computer Modern (namely with all sizes of `cmr` and `cmsl` and `cmti` and `cmbx`); but sans-serif types are a different story. Indeed, *The TEXbook* itself gives alternative definitions of '`\TeX`' on pages 418 and 419, one for the font `cmssdc10 at 40pt` used in chapter titles (see page 36) and one for the `cmssq` fonts used in quotations at the ends of chapters (see page 337).

My purpose in this note is to record the various versions of '`\TeX`' that were actually used to typeset the books in the *Computers & Typesetting* series, so that it will be easy to make forgeries of the particular style used there.

In every case the 'E' has been lowered by `.5ex` (half of the x-height); the only variation is in the amount of backspacing represented by the two `\kern` instructions. Let us therefore consider a "generic" TEX logo to be defined by

```
\def\TeX{T\kern α em\lower.5ex\hbox{E}\kern β emX}
```

for some α and β. The following table shows the values of (α, β) that were actually used in the published volumes:

181

font family	α	β
cmr	$-.1667$	$-.125$
cmsl	$-.1667$	$-.125$
cmti	$-.1667$	$-.125$
cmbx	$-.1667$	$-.125$
cmssdc	$-.2$	$-.06$
cmssq	$-.2$	0
cmssqi	$-.2$	0
cmss	$-.15$	0
cmssi	$-.2$	0
cmssbx	$-.1$	0

(The last three were used only to typeset the jacket copy, not the "real" texts inside. It took a bit of fiddling to get the spacing right.)

I've had little experience with other fonts, but they seem to respond to a similar treatment. For example, my paper on "Literate Programming" in *The Computer Journal* **27** (1984), 97–111, was typeset in a variant of Times Roman, and the standard \TeX macro worked fine. The captions and references in that article were set in Univers; for that sans-serif font we used $(\alpha, \beta) = (-.2, 0)$ as in cmssq.

Chapter 7

Printing Out Selected Pages

*[Originally published in TUGboat **8** (1987), 217.]*

In *TUGboat* Vol. 7, No. 3, Helen Horstman asked, "Is there some way by which one can select only a page (or pages) of printout?"

I recently put some new lines, shown below, into `manmac` (the macros of Appendix E that generated Volumes A and C), so that I could put only selected pages into the `DVI` file. The method should work if you use it at the end of almost any macro file. (Or, if necessary, at the front of a source document.)

The idea is to make TEX look for a file called `pages.tex`. If such a file doesn't exist, everything works as before. Otherwise the file should contain a list of page numbers, one per line, in the order they will be generated. After the last page number has been matched, all further pages will be printed. Thus, if you want to print page 123 and all pages from 300 onwards, your file `pages.tex` should say

```
123
300
```

but if you want to print pages 123 and 300 only, the file should say, e.g.,

```
123
300
-999999999 % impossible number
```

so that the end of file will never occur.

You should rename the `pages.tex` file after you're done with it; otherwise it will continue to affect the output.

On UNIX systems I recommend installing TEX in such a way that input files not found in the current directory will be sought next in the parent directory. Then you can put `pages.tex` into a special `pages` subdirectory, and 'cd pages' just before invoking TEX to get a subset of pages. This has the advantage that none of the master files on the parent directory can be clobbered by accident. For example, auxiliary files that might be generated by \write commands, when indexes or bibliographies or tables of contents are being produced automatically, will remain intact.

The macros cause TEX to announce that fact that it's doing something special.

Macros for Printing Out Selected Pages

```
% To produce only a subset of pages,
% put the page numbers on separate lines
% in a file called pages.tex

\let\Shipout=\shipout
\newread\pages \newcount\nextpage
\openin\pages=pages

\def\getnextpage{\ifeof\pages\else
 {\endlinechar=-1\read\pages to\next
  \ifx\next\empty % in this case we should have eof now
  \else\global\nextpage=\next\fi}\fi}

\ifeof\pages      % do nothing if pages.tex not found
 \else\message{OK, I'll ship only the requested pages!}
 \getnextpage\fi

\def\shipout{\ifeof\pages\let\next=\Shipout
 \else\ifnum\pageno=\nextpage
    \getnextpage\let\next=\Shipout
  \else\let\next=\Tosspage\fi\fi \next}

\newbox\garbage
\def\Tosspage{\deadcycles=0\setbox\garbage=}
```

Chapter 8

Macros for Jill

*[Originally published in TUGboat **8** (1987), 309–314.]*

At the TUG meeting in July, 1986, I mentioned in conversation that one of my new household duties was to write macros for my wife Jill, who had just installed TeX on her PC. Later, when Jill came to the dinner party, many people asked her for copies of the macros; and this led eventually to the idea that I should publish them in *TUGboat*. So here they are, slightly cleaned up from the way I originally wrote them.

The first task Jill assigned me was perhaps the most interesting. She had started to keep an electronic journal, and she wanted to make a nice hardcopy book. The format she had in mind was somewhat tricky because she wanted to be able to generate marginal notes in the middle of any paragraph. Furthermore, she wanted these notes to go in the left-hand margin on left-hand pages and in the right-hand margin on right-hand pages.

This task is difficult for TeX, because TeX generates paragraphs before it knows what page they will go on. Indeed, the decision about what to put on page 100 may not be made until TeX has generated a good deal of page 101.

One way to solve the problem would be to cheat, by putting the notes in both margins and masking off the undesired ones. Jill didn't like that idea very much.

A legitimate solution can be obtained by asking TeX to make two passes over the input: The first pass writes an auxiliary file that tells the page numbers of each marginal note; the second pass reads this file and puts the notes into the desired margin.

The second solution isn't terribly difficult, but I decided to use a third approach, which is surprisingly simple. TeX can easily be programmed to put all the notes in the left margin, or all in the right margin. Then we simply tell TeX to output only the left-hand pages, or only the right-hand pages. With two runs, we've got everything.

The text of the marginal notes was specified in Jill's journal by using a special case of an idea that appears in Appendix E of *The TEXbook*, where a similar notation is used for index entries. Namely, ^{note} yields '**note**' in the margin and 'note' in the paragraph; ^^{note} yields '**note**' in the margin only.

Here is the macro file jmac.tex:

```
% format for Jill's Journal

% sample input:
% \input jmac
% \title A New Chapter That Starts a New Page
%
% \date Umbruary 29
%
% When I woke up this morning, I decided to make this
% journal into a book, using \TeX. I like to put ^{notes}
% into the margin, so that it's easy to find things later.
% My husband^^{Don} figured out a tricky way to put these
% notes into the left margin on left-hand pages, and into
% the right margin on right-hand pages.
%
% In order to do this, he claims that it's necessary to run
% \TeX\ on the file {\it twice\/}!^^{two runs needed} One
% run gives the odd-numbered pages, the other gives
% even-numbered pages. Fortunately, this doesn't take
% much longer, because printing is the slow part.
%
% This journal contains {\it ^{no math}}.
%
% \bye


% Each run begins with a little dialog:
\newif\ifleft
\def\lefthand{l }
\message{*********** Which pages do you want (l or r)? }
\read-1 to\next        % get user's response (l or r)
\ifx\next\lefthand\lefttrue\else\leftfalse\fi
\message{OK, I'll produce only the
 \ifleft left\else right\fi-hand pages. }
```

```
% Here are conventions for text layout
\frenchspacing              % no extra space after punctuation
\hsize=5.25in               % lines to be 5.25 inches wide
\baselineskip=14pt          % and 14 points apart
\parindent=0pt              % no paragraph indentation
\parskip=\baselineskip      % blank line between paragraphs
\topskip=5\baselineskip     % four blank lines at top of page
\vsize=40\baselineskip      % forty lines on a page
\setbox\strutbox=\hbox{\vrule height.75\baselineskip
 depth.25\baselineskip width0pt} % this is a one-line strut

\newdimen\titleoffset
\titleoffset=1.5in          % titles move into margin
\newdimen\notespace
\notespace=.375in           % space between notes, text
\newdimen\maxnote
\maxnote=2in                % maximum width of a note

% Fonts
\font\titlefont=cmbx10 scaled\magstep2     % page top titles
\font\datefont=cmbx10 scaled\magstephalf   % dates in margin
\font\notefont=cmbx10                      % notes in margin
\font\textrm=cmr10 scaled\magstephalf      % normal text
\font\textit=cmti10 scaled\magstephalf     % emphasized text
\font\foliofont=cmbx10 scaled\magstephalf % page numbers

\let\rm=\textrm \rm         % the default font is roman (\rm)
\let\it=\textit             % all text is either \rm or \it
\textfont2=\nullfont        % disallow math mode

% Here ^ and ^^ are changed to \mnote, visible or invisible
\newif\ifvisible
\catcode'\^=\active
\def^{\futurelet\next\testdoublehat}
\def\testdoublehat{\ifx\next^\let\next=\silentnote
 \else\visibletrue\let\next=\mnote\fi \next}
\def\silentnote^{\visiblefalse\mnote}

\ifleft          % do the next only if assuming left margins
 \def\title#1\par{\vfill\eject\message{#1:}
  \null\vskip-4\baselineskip
  \moveleft\titleoffset\hbox{\titlefont\uppercase{#1}}
  \vskip\baselineskip}
```

```
\def\date#1\par{\vskip\parskip
 \moveleft\notespace
  \llap{\hbox to\maxnote{\hfil\datefont#1\unskip}}
  \nobreak\vskip-\baselineskip\vskip-\parskip}
\def\mnote#1{\strut\vadjust{\kern-\dp\strutbox
  \vtop to\dp\strutbox{\vss \baselineskip=\dp\strutbox
   \moveleft\notespace
    \llap{\hbox to\maxnote{\hfil\notefont#1}}\null}}%
  \ifvisible#1\fi}
\hoffset=\titleoffset
\else              % do the next only if assuming right margins
\def\title#1\par{\vfill\eject\message{#1:}
 \null\vskip-4\baselineskip
 \moveright\titleoffset\rightline{%
  \titlefont\uppercase{#1}}
 \vskip\baselineskip}
\def\date#1\par{\vskip\parskip
 \moveright\notespace\rightline{%
  \rlap{\hbox to\maxnote{\datefont#1\unskip\hfil}}}
 \nobreak\vskip-\baselineskip\vskip-\parskip}
\def\mnote#1{\strut\vadjust{\kern-\dp\strutbox
  \vtop to\dp\strutbox{\vss \baselineskip=\dp\strutbox
   \moveright\notespace\rightline{%
    \rlap{\hbox to\maxnote{\notefont#1\hfil}}}\null}}%
  \ifvisible#1\fi}
\fi   % in both cases, TeX will choose the same page breaks
% We output either left-hand or right-hand pages (only)
\output{\ifleft
 \ifodd\pageno\discard\else
  \shipout\vbox{\box255 \baselineskip=30pt
  \hbox{\foliofont\folio}}\fi
 \else\ifodd\pageno
  \shipout\vbox{\box255 \baselineskip=30pt
  \rightline{\foliofont\folio}}
  \else\discard\fi\fi
 \advancepageno}
\newbox\voidbox
\def\discard{\global\setbox255=\box\voidbox}

\outer\def\bye{\vfill\eject\deadcycles=0\end}
```

The sample file at the beginning of `jmac.tex` would be output as follows, on two pages (and in two passes), if we make the following adjustments to fit the constraints of the present book:

```
\hsize=2.5in
\baselineskip=12pt
\vsize=12\baselineskip
\font\titlefont=cmbx12
\font\datefont=cmbx10
\font\notefont=cmbx9
\font\textrm=cmr10
\font\textit=cmti10
\font\foliofont=cmbx10
```

A NEW CHAPTER THAT STARTS A NEW PAGE

When I woke up this morning, I decided to make this journal into a book, using TeX. I like to put notes into the margin, so that it's easy to find things later. My husband figured out a tricky way to put these notes into the left margin on left-hand pages, and into the right margin on right-hand pages.

Umbruary 29

notes

Don

1

two runs needed

In order to do this, he claims that it's necessary to run TeX on the file *twice*! One run gives the odd-numbered pages, the other gives even-numbered pages. Fortunately, this doesn't take much longer, because printing is the slow part.

no math

This journal contains *no math.*

2

The second task was rather different. Our collection of family recipes was kept on scraps of paper, and the pieces kept crumbling and/or getting lost. Jill decided to enter the recipes into her computer so that we could print them on file cards. This way we could keep everything in order, and we could also make sets for our son and daughter to use.

Jill worked out a system of codes that she found convenient for entering the data efficiently. The main interesting thing (to me) was the way it was possible to implement these codes as "active" characters in TEX. The trick was to define the macros first, before fooling around with active characters, so that the old character meanings wouldn't get mixed up with the new ones.

Here is the file `rmac.tex`, which should be almost "self explanatory":

```
% recipe format

% sample input:
% \input rmac
% #RELISH
% >Thanksgiving Cranberry Relish
% <Wilda Bates Carter
% $3 cups
% |chill overnight
% *
% @1 pound fresh cranberries
% 2 oranges, peeled and seeded
% rind of one orange, grated
% 1 ^1/2 c sugar
% *
% !Coarsely grind cranberries and oranges. Add rind
% and sugar. Refrigerate overnight.
% =
% #BREAD
% >Cheese Crisps
% |chill at least 2 hours, bake 20--25 minutes
% %300\0 F
% $5 dozen
% *
% @1 jar sharp cheese spread (5 ounces)
% ^1/2 c butter
% ^1/4 t salt
% dash pepper
```

```
% 1 ^1/2 c flour
% *
% !Beat together cheese and butter. Stir in remaining
% ingredients. Form into two rolls, 1~~1/4 inch in
% diameter. Wrap and chill at least 2~hours. Cut into
% ^1/4-inch slices, place on ungreased cookie sheet,
% bake 20--25 minutes at 300\0~F until slightly
% darker in color.
% =
% \bye

\hsize=4.25in
\vsize=7in
\parindent=0pt

\font\classfont=cmbx10 scaled\magstep2
\font\titlefont=cmbx10 scaled\magstep2
\font\specfont=cmsl10 scaled\magstephalf %time, temp, qty
\font\ingredfont=cmr7 scaled\magstep2
\font\normalfont=cmr10

\newdimen\specbaseline
\specbaseline=14pt % baselineskip between time, temp, qty

\output{\shipout\vbox{\vbox to .75in{
   \rightline{\classfont\currentclass\hskip-.25in}\vss}
  \nointerlineskip\box255}
 \advancepageno \global\let\currentdonor=\empty}
\let\currentdonor=\empty

\def\0{$^\circ$}    % degrees

\obeylines
\def\class#1
 {\gdef\currentclass{#1}}
\def\title#1
 {{\message{#1}\titlefont#1\par}}
\def\donor#1
 {\gdef\currentdonor{#1}}
\def\time#1
 {{\baselineskip=\specbaseline \rightline{\specfont#1\/}}}
\def\temp#1\0 F
 {{\baselineskip=\specbaseline%
  \rightline{\specfont#1\/\0 F\/}}}
```

```
\let\quantity=\time
\def\ingredients{\ingredfont\everypar{\hangindent=20pt}}
\def\method{\let^^M=\space \normalfont \everypar{}}
\def\endit{\par\vfill%
 \ifx\currentdonor\empty%
 \else\rightline{---\currentdonor}\fi%
 \eject\obeylines}
\def\frac#1/#2{\leavevmode%
 \raise.5ex\hbox{\the\scriptfont0 #1}%
 \kern-.1em/\kern-.15em%
 \lower.25ex\hbox{\the\scriptfont0 #2}}
```

```
\catcode'\"=14                              " comment character
\catcode'\#=\active \let#=\class " class of food, e.g. SOUP
\catcode'\>=\active \let>=\title          " name of recipe
\catcode'\<=\active \let<=\donor        " source of recipe
\catcode'\|=\active \let|=\time         " preparation time
\catcode'\%=\active \let%=\temp        " baking temperature
\catcode'\$=\active \let$=\quantity      " amount of output
\catcode'\@=\active \let@=\ingredients   " begin input list
\catcode'\!=\active \let!=\method " begin cooking algorithm
\catcode'\*=\active \let*=\medskip              " spacer
\catcode'\^=\active \let^=\frac    " numerator of fraction
\catcode'\==\active \let=\endit        " end of recipe card
```

Notice the use of \obeylines here: Most of the data for a recipe appears on single lines, until you get to the "method" which consists of one or more paragraphs. Therefore \method converts the ends of lines to spaces. The method is followed by an "="; this finishes the card and restores \obeylines mode.

If the \vsize is reduced to 2.4 inches, the sample input produces the two cards of output shown on the next page.

Since we computerized our recipes in July, we've used the resulting cards quite often. Jill's format has worked well; it's easy to read the recipes while fixing the food, and it's easy to plan ahead because the quantities and preparation are highlighted.

Of course, the next step should be to connect the computer to our kitchen equipment, so that the cooking will be done automatically. But I think I'll work on *The Art of Computer Programming* first.

RELISH

Thanksgiving Cranberry Relish

3 cups
chill overnight

1 pound fresh cranberries
2 oranges, peeled and seeded
rind of one orange, grated
1 ¹/₂ c sugar

Coarsely grind cranberries and oranges. Add rind and sugar. Refrigerate overnight.

—Wilda Bates Carter

BREAD

Cheese Crisps

chill at least 2 hours, bake 20–25 minutes
300° F
5 dozen

1 jar sharp cheese spread (5 ounces)
¹/₂ c butter
¹/₄ t salt
dash pepper
1 ¹/₂ c flour

Beat together cheese and butter. Stir in remaining ingredients. Form into two rolls, 1 ¹/₄ inch in diameter. Wrap and chill at least 2 hours. Cut into ¹/₄-inch slices, place on ungreased cookie sheet, bake 20–25 minutes at 300° F until slightly darker in color.

Chapter 9

Problem for a Saturday Morning

*[Originally published in TUGboat **8** (1987), 73, 210.]*

This puzzle was suggested to me by Sape Mullender, of the Centre for Mathematics and Computer Science in Amsterdam. He told me his belief that "the general design of TEX is better than that of *troff*, but the real guru can make *troff* do things ❓ that you could never do in TEX." As an example, he showed me a ❓ page on which *troff* had typeset a picture in the middle of a para- graph, with the text going around the picture. "It's not pretty, but it can be done, and that's what counts," he said. Well, I have to admit that I didn't think of a simple solution until the next Saturday morning; and I didn't finish debugging it until that afternoon. Can you guess how I typeset the paragraph you're now reading? (The answer appears below; but don't peek at it until you've solved the problem yourself! It doesn't demonstrate the superiority of TEX to *troff*, but it does have some interesting and instructive features.)

??

!!!

```
\font\bigfont=cmbx10 scaled \magstep5
\newbox\qmark \setbox\qmark=
 \hbox{\raise6pt\hbox{\bigfont\thinspace?\thinspace}}
\newdimen\leftedge \newdimen\rightedge
\leftedge=\hsize \advance\leftedge by-\wd\qmark
 \divide\leftedge by 2
\rightedge=\leftedge \advance\rightedge by\wd\qmark
\parshape 10 0pt\hsize 0pt\hsize 0pt\hsize
 0pt\leftedge \rightedge\leftedge
 0pt\leftedge \rightedge\leftedge
 0pt\leftedge \rightedge\leftedge 0pt\hsize
\newbox\partpage \newcount\n
\newdimen\savedprevdepth \savedprevdepth=\prevdepth
```

```
\newdimen\savedvsize \savedvsize=\vsize
\begingroup \clubpenalty=0 \brokenpenalty=0
\output={\global\setbox\partpage=\vbox{\unvbox255\unskip}}
\vfill\break
\topskip=\ht\strutbox \vsize=\topskip
\n=200 % we will store nine lines of text in boxes 201--209
\output={\global\advance\n by 1
 \ifnum\n<210 \global\setbox\n=\box255
 \else \unvbox\partpage \prevdepth=\savedprevdepth
 \vskip\parskip \box201 \box202 \box203
 \box204 \vskip-\baselineskip \box205
 \box206 \vskip-\baselineskip \box207
 \box208 \vskip-\baselineskip \box209
 \vskip-\baselineskip
 \moveright\leftedge\hbox{\smash{\box\qmark}}
 \box255 \global\vsize=\maxdimen \fi}
\noindent This puzzle was suggested to me by Sape
Mullender, of the Centre for Mathematics and Computer
Science in Amsterdam. He told me his belief that ``the
general design of \TeX\ is better than that of {\it troff},
but the real guru can make {\it troff\/} do things that you
could never do in \TeX.'' As an example, he showed me
a page on which {\it troff\/} had typeset a picture in the
middle of a paragraph, with the text going around the
picture. ``It's not pretty, but it can be done, and that's
what counts,'' he said. Well, I have to admit that I didn't
think of a simple solution until the next Saturday morning;
and I didn't finish debugging it until that afternoon. Can
you guess how I typeset the paragraph you're now reading?
(The answer appears below; but don't peek at it until
you've solved the problem yourself! It doesn't demonstrate
the superiority of \TeX\ to {\it troff}, but it does have
some interesting and instructive features.)
{\parfillskip=0pt\par} \global\savedprevdepth=\prevdepth
\output{\global\setbox\partpage=\vbox{\unvbox255\unskip}}
\vfill\break \endgroup \vsize=\savedvsize
\unvbox\partpage \prevdepth=\savedprevdepth
% Improvements to this solution are welcome!
```

[*Note:* Alan Hoenig independently presented a considerably more general solution in *TUGboat* **8** (1987), 211–215, based on \vsplit.]

Chapter 10

Exercises for TeX: The Program

*[Originally published in TUGboat **11** (1990), 165–170, 499–511.]*

During the spring of 1987 I taught a course for which TeX's source code, Volume B of *Computers & Typesetting*, was the textbook. Since that book was meant to serve primarily as a reference, not as a text, I needed to supplement it with homework exercises and exam problems.

The problems turned out to be interesting and fun, for people who like that sort of thing, and they might be useful for self-study if anybody wants to learn *TeX: The Program* without taking a college course. Therefore I've collected 32 of them here and given what I think are the correct answers.

The final problem, which deals with the typesetting of languages that have large character sets, is especially noteworthy since it presents an extension of TeX that might prove to be useful in Asia.

Some of the problems suggested changes in the text. I've changed my original wording of the exercises and answers so that they make sense in the latest printings of the book (TeX versions 3.0 or higher); people who have the 1986 edition should check the published errata before looking too closely at the answers below.

The Problems

Here, then, are the exercises in the order I gave them. Although they begin with a rather "gentle introduction," I recommend that the first ones not be skipped, even if they may appear too easy; there often is a slightly subtle point involved. Conversely, some of the problems are real stumpers, but they are intended to teach important lessons. A serious attempt should be made to solve each one before turning to the answer, if the maximum benefit is to be achieved.

1. (An exercise about reading a WEB.) In the Pascal program defined by the book, what immediately precedes 'PROCEDURE INITIALIZE'?

(Of course it's a semicolon, but you should also figure out a few things that occur immediately before that semicolon.)

2. Find an unnecessary macro in §15.

3. Suppose that the string at the beginning of the *print_roman_int* procedure were "m2d5c2l2q5v5i" instead of "m2d5c2l5x2v5i". What would be printed from the input 69? From the input 9999?

4. Why does *error_count* have a lower bound of -1?

5. What is printed on the user's terminal after 'q' is typed in response to an error prompt? Why?

6. Give examples of how TEX might fail in the following circumstances:
  a) If the test '$t \leq 7230584$' were eliminated from §108.
  b) If the test '$s \geq 1663497$' were eliminated from §108.
  c) If the test '$r > p + 1$' were changed to '$r > p$' in §127.
  d) If the test '$rlink(p) \neq p$' were eliminated from §127.
  e) If the test '$lo\_mem\_max + 2 \leq mem\_bot + max\_halfword$' were eliminated from §125.

7. The purpose of this problem is to figure out what data in *mem* could have generated the following output of *show_node_list*:

```
\hbox(10.0+0.0)x100.0, glue set 10.0fill        100
.\discretionary replacing 1                     200
..\kern 10.0                                     300
.|\large U                                       10000
.|\large ^^K (ligature ff)                       400, 10001, 10002
.\large !                                        10003
.\penalty 5000                                   500
.\glue 0.0 plus 1.0fill                          600
.\vbox(5.0x0.5)x10.0, shifted -5.0               700
..\hbox(5.0x0.0)x10.0                             800
...\small d                                       10004
...\small a                                       10005
..\rule(0.5+0.0)x*                                900
```

Assume that \large is font number 1 and that \small is font number 2. Also assume that the nodes used in the lower (variable-size) part of *mem* start in locations 100, 200, etc., as shown; the nodes used in the upper (one-word) part of *mem* should appear in locations 10000, 10001, etc. Make a diagram that illustrates the exact numeric contents of every relevant *mem* word, if *min_quarterword* = *min_halfword* = 0.

8. What will *short_display* print, when given the horizontal list inside the larger \hbox in the previous problem, assuming that the variable *font_in_short_display* is initially zero?

9. Suppose the following commands are executed immediately after INITEX has initialized itself:

$$incr(prev\_depth);\quad decr(mode\_line);\quad incr(prev\_graf);\quad show\_activities;$$

what will be shown?

10. What will '*show_eqtb*(*int_base* + 17)' show, after INITEX has initialized itself?

11. Suppose TeX has been given the following definitions:

    \def\a{\advance\day by 1\relax} \def\g{\global\a}

The effect of this inside TeX will be that an appearance of \a calls

$$eq\_word\_define(p, eqtb[p].int + 1),$$

and an appearance of \g calls *geq_word_define*(*p*, *eqtb*[*p*].*int* + 1), where $p = int\_base + day\_code$. Consider now the following commands:

    \day=0 \g\a{\a\g\a{\g\a\g}\a{\a}\a}

Each '{' calls *new_save_level*(*simple_group*), and each '}' calls *unsave*.
    Explain what gets pushed onto and popped off of the *save_stack*, and what gets stored in *eqtb*[*p*] and *xeq_level*[*p*], as the above commands are executed. What is the final value of \day? (See *The TeXbook*, exercise 15.9 and page 301.)

12. Use the notation at the bottom of page 122 in *TeX: The Program* to describe the contents of the token list corresponding to \! after the definition

    \def\!!1#2![{!#]#!!2}

has been given, assuming that [,], and ! have the respective catcodes 1, 2, and 6, just as {, }, and # do. (See exercise 20.7 in *The TeXbook*.)

13. What is the absolute maximum number of characters that will be printed by *show_eqtb*(*every_par_loc*), if the current value of \everypar does not contain any control sequences? (*Hint:* The answer exceeds 50. You may wish to verify this by running TEX, defining an appropriate worst-case example, and saying

```
\tracingrestores=1 \tracingonline=1 {\everypar{}}
```

since this will invoke *show_eqtb* when \everypar is restored.)

14. What does `INITEX` do with the following input line? (Look closely.)

```
\catcode''=7 \'' '('')'''!
```

15. Explain the error message you get if you say

```
\endlinechar='! \error
```

in plain TEX.

16. Fill in the missing macro definition so that the input file

```
\catcode'?=\active
\def\answer{...}
\answer
```

will produce precisely the following error message when it is run with plain TEX:

```
! Undefined control sequence.
<recently read> How did this happen?

1.3 \answer

?
```

(This devilish problem is much harder than the others above, but there are at least three ways to solve it!)

17. Consider what TEX will do when it processes the following text:

```
{\def\t{\gdef\a##}\catcode'd=12\t1d#2#3{#2}}
\hfuzz=100P\ifdim12pt=1P\expandafter\a
 \expandafter\else\romannumeral888\relax\fi
\showthe\hfuzz \showlists
```

(Assume that the category codes of plain TEX are being used.)

Determine when the scanning routines *scan_keyword*, *scan_int*, and *scan_dimen* are called as this text is being read, and explain in general terms what results those subroutines produce.

18. What is the difference in interpretation, if any, between the following two TEX commands?

```
\thickmuskip=-\thickmuskip
\thickmuskip=-\the\thickmuskip
```

(Assume that plain TEX is being used.) Explain why there is or isn't a difference.

19. In what way would TEX's behavior change if the assignment at the end of §508 were changed to '$b \leftarrow (p = null)$'?

20. The initial implementation of TEX82 had a much simpler procedure in place of the one now in §601:

> **procedure** dvi_pop;
>   **begin if** $dvi\_ptr > 0$ **then**
>   **if** $dvi\_buf[dvi\_ptr - 1] = push$ **then** $decr(dvi\_ptr)$
>   **else** $dvi\_out(pop)$
>   **else** $dvi\_out(pop)$;
>   **end**;

(No parameter l was necessary.) Why did the author hang his head in shame one day and change it to the form it now has?

21. Assign subscripts d, y, and z to the sequence of integers

$$2\,7\,1\,8\,2\,8\,1\,8\,2\,8\,4\,5\,9\,0\,4\,5$$

using the procedure sketched in §604. (This is easy.)

22. Find a short TEX input file that will cause the *print_mode* subroutine to print 'no mode'. (Do not assume that the category codes or macros of plain TEX have been preloaded.) Extra credit will be given to the person who has the shortest file, i.e., the fewest tokens, among all correct solutions submitted.

23. The textbook says in §78 that *error* might be called within *error* within a call of *error*, but the recursion cannot go any deeper than this.

Construct a scenario in which *error* is entered three times before it has been completed.

24. J. H. Quick (a student) thought he spotted a bug in §671 and he was all set to collect $327.68 because of inputs like this:

```
\vbox{\moveright 1pt\hbox to 2pt{}
      \xleaders\lastbox\vskip 3pt}
```

(He noticed that TEX would give this vbox a width of 2 pt, and he thought that the correct width was 3 pt.) However, when he typed \showlists he saw that the leaders were simply

```
\xleaders 3.0
.\hbox(0.0+0.0)x2.0
```

and he noticed with regret the statement '*shift_amount*(*cur_box*) ← 0' in §1081.

Explain how §671 would have to be corrected, if the *shift_amount* of a leader box could be nonzero.

25. When your instructor made up this problem, he gave the command '\hbadness=-1' so that TEX would print out the way each line of this paragraph was broken. (He sometimes wants to check line breaks without looking at actual output, when he's using a terminal that has no display capabilities.) It turned out that TEX typed this:

```
Tight \hbox (badness 0) in paragraph at lines 297--301
[]\tenrm When your in-struc-tor made up this prob-lem, h
e gave the com-mand

Loose \hbox (badness 3) in paragraph at lines 297--301
\tenrm '\tentt \hbadness=-1\tenrm ' so that T[] would pr
int out the way each line of this

Tight \hbox (badness 0) in paragraph at lines 297--301
\tenrm para-graph was bro-ken. (He some-times wants to c
heck line breaks with-

Loose \hbox (badness 14) in paragraph at lines 297--301
\tenrm out look-ing at ac-tual out-put, when he's us-ing
a ter-mi-nal that has no
```

Why wasn't anything shown for the last line of the paragraph?

26. How would the output of TEX look different if the *rebox* procedure were changed by deleting the statement 'if *type*(*b*) = *vlist_node* **then** *b* ← *hpack*(*b*, *natural*)'? How would the output look different if the next conditional statement, 'if (*is_char_node*(*p*)) . . .' were deleted? (Note that box *b* might have been formed by *char_box*.)

27. What spacing does TEX insert between the characters when it type-sets the formulas $x==1$, $x++1$, and $x,,1$? Find the places in the program where these spacing decisions are made.

28. When your instructor made up this problem, he gave the command '`\tracingparagraphs=1`' so that his transcript file would explain TeX's line-breaking decisions for this paragraph. He also said '`\pretolerance=-1`' so that hyphenation would be tried immediately. The output is shown on the next page; use it to determine what line breaks would have been found by a simpler algorithm that breaks off one line at a time. (The simpler algorithm finds the breakpoint that yields fewest demerits on the first line, then chooses it and starts over again.)

29. Play through the algorithms in parts 42 and 43, to figure out the contents of *trie_op*, *trie_char*, *trie_link*, *hyf_distance*, *hyf_num*, and *hyf_next* after the statement

    \patterns{a1bc 2bcd3 ab1cd bc1dd}

has been processed. Then execute the algorithm of §923, to see how TeX uses this efficient trie structure to set the values of *hyf* when the word `aabcd` is hyphenated. [The value of *hn* will be 5, and the values of $hc[1 .. 5]$ will be $(97, 97, 98, 99, 100)$, respectively, when §923 begins. Assume that $min\_quarterword = l\_hyf = r\_hyf = 0$.]

30. The *save_stack* is normally empty when a TeX program stops. But if, say, the user's input has an extra '{' (or a missing '}'), TeX will print the warning message

    (\end occurred inside a group at level 1)

(see §1335).

Explain in detail how to change TeX so that such warning messages will be more explicit. For example, if the source program has an unmatched '{' on line 2 and an unmatched '`\begingroup`' on line 9, your modified TeX should give two warnings:

    (\end occurred when \begingroup on line 9 was incomplete)
    (\end occurred when { on line 2 was incomplete)

You may assume that *simple_group* and *semi_simple_group* are the only group codes present on *save_stack* when §1335 is encountered; if other group codes are present, your program should call *confusion*.

31. (The following question is the most difficult yet most important of the entire collection. It was the main problem on the take-home final exam.)

```
% This is the paragraph-trace output for Problem 28:
[]\tenrm When your in-struc-tor made up this prob-lem, he gave the com-
@\discretionary via @@0 b=145 p=50 d=36525
@@1: line 1.0- t=36525 -> @@0
mand
@ via @@0 b=0 p=0 d=100
@@2: line 1.2 t=100 -> @@0
'\tentt \tracingparagraphs=1\tenrm ' so that his tran-script file would ex-
@\discretionary via @@1 b=179 p=50 d=78221
@@3: line 2.0- t=114746 -> @@1
plain
@ via @@1 b=1 p=0 d=10121
@@4: line 2.2 t=46646 -> @@1
T[]'s
@ via @@2 b=4 p=0 d=196
@@5: line 2.2 t=296 -> @@2
line-breaking de-ci-sions for this para-graph. He also said
@ via @@3 b=89 p=0 d=9801
@@6: line 3.1 t=124547 -> @@3
'\tentt \pretolerance=-1\tenrm ' so that hy-phen-ation would be tried im-me-di-ately.
@ via @@6 b=11 p=0 d=441
@@7: line 4.2 t=124988 -> @@6
The out-put is shown on the next page; use it to de-ter-mine what
@ via @@7 b=318 p=0 d=117584
@@8: line 5.0 t=242572 -> @@7
line
@ via @@7 b=14 p=0 d=576
@@9: line 5.1 t=125564 -> @@7
breaks would have been found by a sim-pler al-go-rithm that breaks
@ via @@8 b=2 p=0 d=10144
@ via @@9 b=295 p=0 d=93025
@@10: line 6.0 t=218589 -> @@9
off
@ via @@8 b=31 p=0 d=11681
@ via @@9 b=15 p=0 d=625
@@11: line 6.1 t=126189 -> @@9
one
@ via @@9 b=26 p=0 d=11296
@@12: line 6.3 t=136860 -> @@9
line at a time. (The sim-pler al-go-rithm finds the break-
@\discretionary via @@10 b=607 p=50 d=383189
@@13: line 7.0- t=601778 -> @@10
point
@ via @@10 b=80 p=0 d=8100
@ via @@11 b=503 p=0 d=263169
@@14: line 7.1 t=226689 -> @@10
that
@ via @@10 b=0 p=0 d=10100
@ via @@11 b=20 p=0 d=900
@ via @@12 b=369 p=0 d=153641
@@15: line 7.1 t=127089 -> @@11
yields
@ via @@12 b=0 p=0 d=100
@@16: line 7.2 t=136960 -> @@12
fewest de-mer-its on the first line, then chooses it
@ via @@13 b=293 p=0 d=91809
@@17: line 8.0 t=693587 -> @@13
and
@ via @@13 b=5 p=0 d=10225
@ via @@14 b=571 p=0 d=337561
@@18: line 8.0 t=564250 -> @@14
starts
@ via @@14 b=2 p=0 d=144
@ via @@15 b=308 p=0 d=101124
@@19: line 8.0 t=228213 -> @@15
@@20: line 8.2 t=226833 -> @@14
over again.)
@\par via @@16 b=0 p=-10000 d=100
@\par via @@17 b=0 p=-10000 d=10100
@\par via @@18 b=0 p=-10000 d=10100
@\par via @@19 b=0 p=-10000 d=10100
@\par via @@20 b=0 p=-10000 d=100
@@21: line 8.2- t=137060 -> @@16
```

The purpose of problem 31 is to extend TEX so that it will sell better in China, Japan, and Korea. The extended program, called TEXX, allows each font to contain up to 65536 characters. Each extended character is represented by two values, its 'extension' x and its 'code' c, where both x and c lie between 0 and 255 inclusive. Characters with the same 'c' but different 'x' correspond to different graphics; but they have the same width, height, depth, and italic correction.

TEXX is identical to TEX except that it has one new primitive command: \xchar. If \xchar occurs in vertical mode, it begins a new paragraph; that is, it's a ⟨horizontal command⟩ as on page 283 of *The TEXbook*. If \xchar occurs in horizontal mode it should be followed by a ⟨number⟩ between 0 and 65535; this number can be converted to the form $256x + c$, where $0 \leq x, c < 256$. The corresponding extended character from the current font will be appended to the current horizontal list, and the space factor will be set to 1000. (If $x = 0$, the effect of \xchar is something like the effect of \char, except that \xchar disables ligatures and kerns and it doesn't do anything special to the space factor. Moreover, no penalty is inserted after an \xchar that happens to be the \hyphenchar of the current font.) A word containing an extended character will not be hyphenated. The \xchar command should not occur in math mode.

Inside TEXX, an extended character (x, c) in font f is represented by two consecutive *char_node* items p and q, where we have $font(p) = null\_font$, $character(p) = qi(x)$, $link(p) = q$, $character(q) = qi(c)$, and $font(q) = f$. This two-word representation is used even when $x = 0$.

TEXX typesets an extended character by specifying character number $256x + c$ in the DVI file. (See the *set2* command in §585.)

If TEXX is run with the macros of plain TEX, and if the user types '\tracingall \xchar600 \showlists', the output of TEXX will include

```
{\xchar}
{horizontal mode: \xchar}
{\showlists}

### horizontal mode entered at line 0
\hbox(0.0+0.0)x20.0
\tenrm \xchar"258
spacefactor 1000
```

(since 600 is "258 in hexadecimal notation).

Your job is to explain in detail *all* changes to TEX that are necessary to convert it to TEXX.

[Note: A properly designed extension would also include the primitive operator \xchardef, analogous to \chardef and \mathdef, because a language should be 'orthogonally complete'. However, this additional extension has not been included as part of problem 31, because it presents no special difficulties. Anybody who can figure out how to implement \xchar can certainly also handle \xchardef.]

32. The first edition of *TEX: The Program* suggested that extended characters could be represented with the following convention: The first of two consecutive *char_node* items was to contain the font code and a character code from which the dimensions could be computed as usual; the second *char_node* was a *halfword* giving the actual character number to be typeset. Fonts were divided into two types, based on characteristics of their TFM headers; 'oriental' fonts always used this two-word representation, other fonts always used the one-word representation.

Explain why the method suggested in problem 31 is better than this. (There are at least two reasons.)

The Answers

1. According to the index, *initialize* is declared in §4. It is preceded there by ⟨ Global variables 13 ⟩, and §13 tells us that the final global variable appears in §1345. Turning to §1345, we find '*write_loc: pointer;*' and a comment. The comment doesn't get into the Pascal code. The mini-index at the bottom of page 541 tells us that '*pointer*' is a macro defined in §115. Our quest is nearly over, since §115 says that *pointer* expands to *halfword*, which is part of the Pascal program. Page xi tells us that lowercase letters of a WEB program become uppercase in the corresponding Pascal code; page xii tells us that the underline in '*write_loc*' is discarded. Therefore we conclude that 'PROCEDURE INITIALIZE' is immediately preceded in the Pascal program by 'WRITELOC:HALFWORD;'.

But this isn't quite correct! The book doesn't tell the whole story. If we actually run TANGLE on TEX.WEB (without a change file), we find that 'PROCEDURE INITIALIZE' is actually preceded by

```
{1345:}WRITELOC:HALFWORD;{:1345}
```

because TANGLE inserts comments to show the origin of each block of code. Here the code comes indeed from §1345.

2. The index tells us that *done6* is never used. (It was included only for people who want to make system-dependent changes and/or extensions.)

3. The new string essentially substitutes "quarters" q (of value 25) for "dimes" x (of value 10). Playing through the code of §69 tells us that 69 is now represented by lvvviv and 9999 is

$$\texttt{mmmmmmmmm cmqcvqiv.}$$

(The first nine m's make 9000; then cm makes 900; then qc makes 75; then vq makes 20; and iv makes the remaining 4.)

4. Because it may be decreased by 1 in §1293 before being increased by 1 in §82. (The code in §1293 decreases *error_count* because "showing" uses the *error* subroutine although it isn't really an error.)

5. The q—which stands for "quiet," not "quit"—becomes Q in §83. This Q causes §86 to print 'OK, entering \batchmode', after which *selector* is decreased so that '...' and ⟨return⟩ are *not* printed on the terminal! (They appear only in the log file, if it has been opened.) This is TEX's way of confirming that \batchmode has indeed been entered.

6. (a) Arithmetic overflow might occur when computing $t*297$, because

$$7230585 \times 297 = 2^{31} + 97.$$

(b) Some sort of test is needed to avoid division by zero when s is positive but less than 297. If $s < 1663497$ then

$$s \textbf{ div } 297 < 5601,$$

and $7230585/5600$ is a bit larger than 1291 so we will have $r > 1290$ in such a case. The threshold value has therefore been chosen to save division whenever possible. (One student suggested that the statement '$r \leftarrow t$' be replaced by '$r \leftarrow 1291$'. That might or might not be faster, depending on the computer and the Pascal compiler. In machine language one would **goto** the statement that sets *badness* $\leftarrow$ *inf_bad*, but that is inadmissible Pascal.)

(c) If we get to §128 with $r = p + 1$, we will try to make a node of size 1, but then there's no room for the *node_size* field.

(d) If we get to §129 with only one node available, we'll lose everything and *rover* will be invalid. (Older versions of TEX have a more complicated test in §127, which would suppress going to §129 if there were two nodes available. That was unnecessarily cautious.)

(e) This is a subtle one. The lower part of memory must not be allowed to grow so large that a *node_size* value could ever exceed *max_halfword* when nodes are being merged together in §127.

7.

100:	0	0	0	*type* (*hlist_node*), , *link*
101:			6553600	*width* (100 pt)
102:			0	*depth*
103:			655360	*height* (10 pt)
104:			0	*shift_amount*
105:	1	2	200	*glue_sign* (*stretching*), *glue_order* (*fill*), *list_ptr*
106:		10.0		*glue_set* (type *real*)

200:	7	1	10003	*type* (*disc_node*), *replace_count*, *link*
201:		300	10000	*pre_break*, *post_break*

300:	11	1	0	*type* (*kern_node*), *subtype* (*explicit*), *link*
301:			655360	*width* (10 pt)

400:	6	0	0	*type* (*ligature_node*), *subtype* (0), *link*
401:	1	11	10001	*font*, *character*, *lig_ptr*

500:	12	0	600	*type* (*penalty_node*), , *link*
501:			5000	*penalty*

600:	10	0	700	*type* (*glue_node*), *subtype* (*normal*), *link*
601:		8	0	*glue_ptr* (*fill_glue*), *leader_ptr*

700:	1	0	0	*type* (*vlist_node*), , *link*
701:			655360	*width* (10 pt)
702:			32768	*depth* (0.5 pt)
703:			327680	*height* (5 pt)
704:			−327680	*shift_amount* (−5 pt)
705:	0	0	800	*glue_sign* (*normal*), *glue_order* (*normal*), *list_ptr*
706:		0.0		*glue_set* (type *real*)

800:	0	0	900	*type* (*hlist_node*), , *link*
801:			655360	*width* (10 pt)
802:			0	*depth*
803:			327680	*height* (5 pt)
804:			0	*shift_amount*
805:	0	0	10004	*glue_sign* (*normal*), *glue_order* (*normal*), *list_ptr*
806:		0.0		*glue_set* (type *real*)

900:	2	0	0	*type* (*rule_node*), , *link*
901:		−1073741824		*width* (*null_flag*)
902:			0	*depth*
903:			32768	*height* (0.5 pt)

10000:	1	85	400	*font*, *character* ("U"), *link*
10001:	1	102	10002	*font*, *character* ("f"), *link*
10002:	1	102	0	*font*, *character* ("f"), *link*
10003:	1	33	500	*font*, *character* ("!"), *link*
10004:	2	100	10005	*font*, *character* ("d"), *link*
10005:	2	97	0	*font*, *character* ("a"), *link*

8. (Norwegian Americans will recognize this as an "Uff da" joke.) The output of *short_display* is

```
\large Uff []
```

since *short_display* shows the pre-break and post-break parts of a discretionary (but not the replacement text). However, if this box were output by *hlist_out*, the discretionary break would not be effective; the result would be a box 100 pt wide, beginning with a large '!' and ending with a small 'da', the latter being raised 5 pt and underlined with a 0.5 pt-rule.

9. Since *prev_depth* is initially *ignore_depth*, we get

```
### vertical mode entered at line 1 (\output routine)
prevdepth -999.99998, prevgraf 1 line
```

10. According to §236, *int_base* + 17 is where *mag* is stored. (One of the definitions suppressed by an ellipsis on page 101 is *mag*; you can verify this by checking the index!) The initial value of *mag* is set in §240. Hence *show_eqtb* branches to §242 and prints '\mag=1000'.

11. In the following chart, '(3)' means a value at level three, and '——' is a level boundary:

```
                                                    (2)
                                                     9
                     (1) (1)                       —  —
                      6   6          (1) (1) (1) (1) (1)
                 —   —   —   —        8   8   8   8   8
         (1) (1) (1) (1) (1) (1) (1) (1) (1) (1) (1)
          4   4   4   4   4   4   4   4   4   4   4
     (1) (1) (1) (1) (1) (1) (1) (1) (1) (1) (1) (1) (1)
      2   2   2   2   2   2   2   2   2   2   2   2   2
```

save_stack:	—	—	—	—	—	—	—	—	—	—	—	—	—
xeq_level[p]:	(1) (1) (1) (1) (2) (1) (2) (2) (1) (3) (1) (1) (2) (2) (3) (2) (2) (1)
eqtb[p].*int*:	0 1 2 2 3 4 5 5 6 7 8 8 9 9 10 9 10 8
day=0	\g \a { \a \g \a { \g \a \g } \a { \a } \a }

The final value is therefore \day=8.

12. (reference count), *match* !, *match* #, *left_brace* [, *end_match*, *left_brace* {, *mac_param* #, *right_brace*], *mac_param* !, *out_param* 2, *left_brace* [. Notice that the *left_brace* before the *end_match* is repeated at the end of the replacement text, because it has been matched (and therefore removed from the input).

13. According to §233, *show_eqtb*(*every_par_loc*) calls *show_token_list*
with the limit $l = 32$. According to §292, we want the token list to contain a token that prints as many characters as possible when *tally* = 31;
the value of *tally* is increased on every call to *print_char* (§58). By
studying the cases in §294, we conclude that the worst case occurs when
a *mac_param* is printed, and when the character *c* actually prints as four
characters. The statement '*print_esc*("ETC.")' in §292 will print eight
additional characters if the current *escape_char* is another quadrupler.
(Longer examples are possible only if TEX has a bug that tweaks one of
the outputs '\CLOBBERED.' or '\BAD.' in §293; but this can't happen.)

In other words, a worst-case example such as

```
\escapechar='\^^df \catcode'\^^d0=6
\everypar{1234567890123456789012345678901^^d0etc.}
```

in connection with the suggested test line will print

```
{restoring
^^dfeverypar=1234567890123456789012345678901^^d0^^d0^^dfETC.}
```

thereby proving that *show_eqtb*(*every_par_loc*) can print 60 characters.

14. Here we must look at the *get_next* procedure, which scans the *buffer*
in strange ways when two identical characters of category 7 (*sup_mark*)
are found. After the \catcode of open-quote has been set to 7, *get_next*
begins to scan a control sequence in §354, which goes to §355 and finds a
space after ' '. Since a space is code ´40, it is changed to ´140, and the
buffer contents are shifted left 2. By strange coincidence, ´140 is again
an open-quote character, so we get back to §355, which changes ' '(to
h and goes back to *start_cs* a third time. Now we go to §356 and then
back to §355 and *start_cs*, having changed ' ') to i. The fourth round,
similarly, changes ' ' ' to a blank space, and the fifth round finishes the
control sequence.

If we try to input the stated line, INITEX will come to a halt as
follows:

```
! Undefined control sequence.
<*> \catcode''=7 \hi
                !\error
```

This proves that the *buffer* now says \hi !.

15. The error message in question is

```
! Undefined control sequence.
<*> \endlinechar='! \error
                            ^^M
```

and our job is to explain the appearance of ^^M. The standard setting of
\endlinechar is *carriage_return*, according to §240; this is '15 according to §22, and '15 is ^^M in ASCII code. Thus, a *carriage_return* is
normally placed at the end of each line when it's read into the *buffer* (see
§360). This *carriage_return* is not usually printed in an error message,
because it equals the *end_line_char* (see §318). We see it now because
end_line_char has changed.

   Incidentally, if the input line had been

```
\endlinechar='!\error
```

(without the space after the !), we wouldn't have seen the ^^M. Why not?
Because TEX calls *get_next* when looking for the optional space after the
ASCII constant '! (see §442–443), hence the undefined control sequence
\error is encountered before *end_line_char* has been changed!

16. One problem is to figure out which control sequence is undefined;
it seems to be the '?', since this character has been made active.
One clue is to observe from §312 and §314 that '<recently read>'
can be printed only when *base_ptr* = *input_ptr*, *state* = *token_list*,
token_type = *backed_up*, and *loc* = *null*. A token list of type *backed_up*
usually contains only a single item; in that case, the control sequence
name must be 'How did this happen?', and we have a problem getting
an active character into a control sequence name.

   But an arbitrarily long token list of type *backed_up* can be created
with the \lowercase operation (see §1288). In that case, however, the
right brace that closes \lowercase is almost always still present in TEX's
input state, and it would show up on the error message. (The *back_list*
procedure of §323 does not clear a completed token list off of the stack.)
We have to make TEX clear off its stack before the } is scanned.

   At this point the exercise begins to resemble "retrograde chess"
problems. Here is one solution; it is shown here in two lines, broken
up to fit the page size of this book, although the strict conditions of the
problem require us to put an equivalent one-line definition in line 2 of
the actual input file:

```
\def\answer{\let~\expandafter\lccode'!='H% [line broken]
  ~\lowercase~{~!~o~w~ ~d~i~d~ ~t~h~i~s~ ~h~a~p~p~e~n~?}}
```

(The 'H' is a lowercase '!'; an \expandafter chain is used to make the right brace disappear from the stack.)

Another approach uses \csname, and manufactures a ? from a !:

```
\def\answer{\def\a##1{{\global\let##1?\aftergroup##1}}%
  \escapechar'H\lccode'¡?\lowercase{\expandafter\a%
  \csname ow did this happen!\endcsname}}
```

But there is a devious solution that is considerably shorter; it makes the invisible *carriage_return* following \answer into a right brace(!):

```
\def\answer{\catcode13=2\lccode'!='H%
  \lowercase\bgroup!ow did this happen?}
```

17. (The answer to this problem was much more difficult to explain in class than I had thought it would be, so I guess it was also much more difficult for the students to solve than I had thought it would be. After my first attempt to explain the answer, I decided to make up a special version of TEX that would help to clarify the scanning routines. This special program, called DemoTEX, is just like ordinary TEX except that if \tracingstats>2 the user is able to watch TEX's syntax routines in slow motion. The changes that convert TEX to DemoTEX are explained in the appendix below. Given DemoTEX, we tried a lot of simple examples of things like '\hfuzz=1.5pt' and '\catcode'a=11' before plunging into exercise 17 in which everything happens at once. While we were discussing input stacks, by the way, we found it helpful to consider the behavior of TEX on the following input:

```
\output{\botmark}
\def\a{\error}
\mark{
 \everyvbox{
  \everypar{
   \everydisplay{
    \everyhbox{
     \everymath{\noexpand\a}
     $\relax}
    \hbox\bgroup\relax}
   $$\relax}
  \noindent\relax}
 \vbox\bgroup\relax}
\hbox{}\vfill\penalty-10000
```

Here \penalty triggers \botmark, which defines \everyvbox and begins
a \vbox, which defines \everypar and begins a \par, which defines
\everydisplay and begins a \display, etc.)

Back to problem 17: The first line is essentially

\gdef\a#1d#2#3{#2}

where the second d has catcode 12 (*other_char*). Hence the second d will
match a d that is generated by \romannumeral. In this line, *scan_int* is
called only to scan the 'd and the 12.

The second line calls *scan_dimen* in order to evaluate the right-
hand side of the assignment to \hfuzz. After *scan_dimen* has used
scan_int to read the '100', it calls *scan_keyword* in order to figure out
the units. But before the units are known to be 'pt' or 'pc', an \ifdim
must be expanded. Here we need to call *scan_dimen* recursively, twice;
it finds the value 12 pt on the left-hand side, and is interrupted again
while *scan_keyword* is trying to figure out the units on the right-hand
side. Now a chain of \expandafter's causes \romannumeral888 to be
expanded into dccclxxxviii, and then we have to parse

\a\else dccclxxxviii

followed by \relax\fi. Here #1 will be \else, #2 and #3 will each be c;
the expansion therefore reduces to cclxxxviii\relax\fi. The first 'c'
completes the second 'Pc', and the \ifdim test is true. Therefore the
second 'c' can complete the first 'Pc', and \hfuzz is set equal to 1200 pt.
The characters lxxxviii now begin a paragraph. The \fi takes the
\ifdim out of TEX's condition stack.

(The appendix below gives further information. Examples like this
give some glimmering of the weird maneuvers that can be found in the
TRIP test, an intricate pattern of unlikely code that is used to validate
all implementations of TEX.)

18. If, for example, \thickmuskip has the value 5mu plus 5mu that
plain TEX gives it, the first command changes its value to -5mu plus
-5mu, because *scan_glue* in §461 will call *scan_something_internal* with
the second argument *true*; this will cause all three components of the
glue to be negated (see §413, §430, §431).

The second command, on the other hand, tells TEX to expand
'\the\thickmuskip' into a sequence of characters, so it is equivalent
to the assignment

\thickmuskip=-5mu plus 5mu

(The minus sign doesn't carry into the stretch component of glue, since §461 applies *negate* only to the first dimension found.)

This problem points out a well-known danger that is present in any text-macro-expanding system.

19. We'd have a funny result that two macro texts would be considered to match by \ifx unless the first one (the one starting at q when we begin §508) is a proper prefix of the second. (Notice the statement '$p \leftarrow null$' inside the **while** loop.)

20. Because the byte in $dvi\_buf\,[dvi\_ptr - 1]$ is usually not an operation code, and it just might happen to equal *push*.

21. $2_y\,7_d\,1_d\,8_z\,2_y\,8_z\,1_d\,8_z\,2_y\,8_z\,4_y\,5_z\,9_d\,0_d\,4_y\,5_z$.

22. TEX is in 'no mode' only while processing \write statements, and the mode is printed during \write only when *tracing_commands* > 1 during *expand*. We might think that \catcode operations are necessary, so that the left and right braces for \write exist; but it's possible to let TEX's error-recovery mechanism supply them! Therefore the shortest program that meets the requirements is probably the following one based on an idea due to Ronaldo Amá, who suggests putting

```
\batchmode\tracingcommands2\immediate\write!\nomode
```

into a file. (Seven tokens total.)

23. When *error* calls *get_token*, because the user has asked for tokens to be deleted (see §88), a second level of *error* is possible, but further deletions are disallowed (see §336 and §346). However, insertions are still allowed, and this can lead to a third level of *error* when *overflow* calls *succumb*.

For example, let's assume that $max\_in\_open = 6$. Then you can type '\catcode'?=15 \x' and respond to the undefined control sequence error by saying 'i\x??' six times. This leads to a call of *error* in which six '<insert>' levels appear; hence $in\_open = 6$, and one more insertion will be the last straw. At this point, type '1'; this enters *error* at a second level, from which 'i' will enter *error* a third time. (The run-time stack now has *main_control* calling *get_x_token* calling *expand* calling *error* calling *get_token* calling *get_next* calling *error* calling *begin_file_reading* calling *overflow* calling *error*.)

24. We'd replace '$width(g)$' by '$width(g) + shift\_amount(g)$' (twice). Similar changes would be needed in §656. (But a box shouldn't be able to retain its *shift_amount*; this quantity is a property of the list the box is in, not a property of the box itself.)

25. The final line has infinite stretchability, since plain TEX has set `\parfillskip=0pt plus 1fil`. Reports of loose, tight, underfull, or overfull boxes are never made unless $o = normal$ in §658 and §664.

26. If a vbox is repackaged as an hbox, we get really weird results because things that were supposed to stack up vertically are placed together horizontally. The second change would be a lot less visible, except in characters like V where there is a large italic correction; the character would be centered without taking its italic correction into account. (The italic correction in math mode is the difference between horizontal placement of superscripts and subscripts in formulas like V_2^2.)

27. The spacing can be found by saying

```
$x==1$ $x++1$ $x,,1$ \tracingall\showlists.
```

Most of the decisions are made in §766, using the spacing table of §764. But the situation is trickier in the case of +, because a *bin_noad* must be preceded and followed by a noad of a suitable class. In the formula `$x++1$`, the second + is changed from *bin_noad* to *ord_noad* in §728. It turns out that thick spaces are inserted after the x and before the 1 in '$x == 1$'; medium spaces are inserted before each + sign in '$x++1$'; thin spaces are inserted after each comma in '$x,,1$'. (A comma in math mode appears in the semicolon position of the math italic font; see page 430 of *The TEXbook*.)

28. The behavior of the simpler algorithm, which we may call Brand X, can be deduced from the demerits values ('d=') in the trace output. The best choice for the first line is clearly @@2 (only 100 demerits, versus 36525 for @@1); then @@4 is the only decent choice. But then we're stuck, and must accept a terribly loose line that ends at @@6. From here we must go to @@7; then Brand X thinks it's best to go to @@9, then @@11 (the best of three possibilities), then @@15, then @@19, finally @@21. The resulting paragraph, as typeset by Brand X, looks like this (awful):

28. When your instructor made up this problem, he gave the command '`\tracingparagraphs=1`' so that his transcript file would explain TEX's line-breaking decisions for this paragraph. He also said '`\pretolerance=-1`' so that hyphenation would be tried immediately. The output is shown on the next page; use it to determine what line breaks would have been found by a simpler algorithm that breaks off one line at a time. (The simpler algorithm finds the breakpoint that yields fewest demerits on the first line, then chooses it and starts over again.)

29. (This exercise takes a while, but the data structures are especially interesting; the hyphenation algorithm is a nice little part of the program that can be studied in isolation.) The following tables are constructed:

	op	char	link			[1]	[2]	[3]
$trie[1]$	0	0	2	$hyf\_distance$		2	0	3
$trie[99]$	0	97	3	hyf_num		1	3	2
$trie[100]$	0	98	7	hyf_next		0	0	2
$trie[101]$	0	98	4					
$trie[103]$	1	99	5					
$trie[105]$	1	100	0					
$trie[106]$	0	99	8					
$trie[108]$	3	100	5					

Given the word `aabcd`, it is interesting to watch §923 produce the hyphenation numbers '$_0a_0a_2b_1c_0d_3$' from this trie.

30. The idea is to keep line numbers on the save stack. Scott Douglass has observed that, although TEX is careful to keep *cur_boundary* up to date, nothing important is ever done with it; hence the *save_index* field in level-boundary words is not needed, and we have an extra halfword to play with! (The present data structure has fossilized elements left over from old incarnations of TEX.) However, line numbers might get larger than a halfword; it seems better to store them as fullword integers.

This problem requires changes to three parts of the program. First, we can extend §1063 as follows:

⟨ Cases of *main_control* that build boxes and lists 1056 ⟩ +≡
non_math (*left_brace*): **begin** *saved*(0) ← *line*; *incr* (*save_ptr*);
   new_save_level (*simple_group*);
   end;   { the line number is saved for possible use in warning message }
any_mode (*begin_group*): **begin** *saved*(0) ← *line*; *incr* (*save_ptr*);
   new_save_level (*semi_simple_group*);
   end;
any_mode (*end_group*): **if** *cur_group* = *semi_simple_group* **then**
      begin *unsave*; *decr* (*save_ptr*);
         { pop unused line number from stack }
      end
   else *off_save*;

A similar change is needed in §1068, where the first case becomes

   simple_group: **begin** *unsave*; *decr* (*save_ptr*);
         { pop unused line number from stack }
      end;

Finally, we replace six lines of §1335 by similar code for the desired messages:

> **while** *cur_level* > *level_one* **do**
>   **begin** *print_nl*("("); *print_esc*("end␣occurred␣when␣");
>   **case** *cur_group* **of**
>   *simple_group*: *print_char*("{");
>   *semi_simple_group*: *print_esc*("begingroup");
>   **othercases** *confusion*("endgroup")
>   **endcases**;
>   *print*("␣on␣line␣"); *unsave*; *decr*(*save_ptr*); *print_int*(*saved*(0));
>   *print*("␣was␣incomplete)");
>   **end**;
> **while** *cond_ptr* ≠ *null* **do**
>   **begin** *print_nl*("("); *print_esc*("end␣occurred␣when␣");
>   *print_cmd_chr*(*if_test*, *cur_if*);

31. First, §2 gets a new paragraph explaining what TEXX is, and the banner line changes:

> **define** *banner* ≡ ˋThis␣is␣TeXX,␣Version␣2.2ˊ
>   { printed when TEX starts }

Then we add two new definitions in §134:

> **define** *is_xchar_node*(#) ≡ (*font*(#) = *font_base*)
>   { is this *char_node* extended? }
> **define** *bypass_xchar*(#) ≡
>   **if** *is_xchar_node*(#) **then** # ← *link*(#)

(It's necessary to say *font_base* here instead of *null_font*, because the identifier *null_font* isn't defined until later.)

The *short_display* routine of §174 can treat an \xchar like an ordinary character, because *print_ASCII* makes no restrictions. Here is one way to handle the change:

> **procedure** *short_display*(*p* : *integer*);　{ prints highlights of list *p* }
>   **label** *done*;
>   **var** *n*: *integer*;　{ for replacement counts }
>   *ext*: *integer*;　{ amount added to character code by xchar }
>   **begin** *ext* ← 0;
>   **while** *p* > *mem_min* **do**
>   **begin if** *is_char_node*(*p*) **then**
>   **begin if** *p* ≤ *mem_end* **then**
>   **begin if** *is_xchar_node*(*p*) **then**
>   **begin** *ext* ← 256 ∗ (*qo*(*character*(*p*))); **goto** *done*;
>   **end**;
>   **if** *font*(*p*) ≠ *font_in_short_display* **then**

begin if $(font(p) < font\_base) \lor (font(p) > font\_max)$ **then**
$\quad print\_char("*")$
else ⟨Print the font identifier for $font(p)$ 267⟩;
$\quad print\_char("\sqcup"); font\_in\_short\_display \leftarrow font(p);$
end;
$print\_ASCII(ext + qo(character(p))); ext \leftarrow 0;$
$\quad$ **end**;
$\quad$ **end**
else ⟨Print a short indication of the contents of node p 175⟩;
$done: p \leftarrow link(p);$
$\quad$ **end**;
end;

A somewhat similar change applies in §176:

procedure $print\_font\_and\_char(p : integer)$;   {prints $char\_node$ data}
$\quad$ **label** $reswitch$;
$\quad$ **var** $ext: integer$;   {amount added to character code by xchar, or -1}
$\quad$ **begin** $ext \leftarrow -1$;
$reswitch:$ **if** $p > mem\_end$ **then** $print\_esc("CLOBBERED.")$
$\quad$ **else begin if** $is\_xchar\_node(p)$ **then**
$\qquad$ **begin** $ext \leftarrow qo(character(p)); p \leftarrow link(p);$ **goto** $reswitch$; **end**;
$\qquad$ **if** $(font(p) < font\_base) \lor (font(p) > font\_max)$ **then** $print\_char("*")$
$\qquad$ **else** ⟨Print the font identifier for $font(p)$ 267⟩;
$\qquad print\_char("\sqcup");$
$\qquad$ **if** $ext < 0$ **then** $print\_ASCII(qo(character(p)))$
$\qquad$ **else begin** $print\_esc("xchar")$;
$\qquad\quad print\_hex(ext * 256 + qo(character(p)));$
$\qquad\quad$ **end**;
$\qquad$ **end**;
$\quad$ **end**;

(These routines must be extra-robust.) The first line of code in §183 now becomes

if $is\_char\_node(p)$ **then**
$\quad$ **begin** $print\_font\_and\_char(p); bypass\_xchar(p);$
$\quad$ **end**

In §208 we introduce a new operation code,

define $xchar\_num = 17$ {extended character (`\xchar`)}

Every opcode that follows it in §208 and §209, from $math\_char\_num$ to $max\_command$, must be increased by 1. We also add the following lines to §265 and §266, respectively:

$primitive("xchar", xchar\_num, 0);$
$xchar\_num: print\_esc("xchar");$

This puts the new command into TEX's repertoire.

The next thing we need to worry about is what to do when \xchar occurs in the input. It's convenient to add a companion procedure to *scan_char_num* in §435:

procedure *scan_xchar_num*;
  begin *scan_int*;
  if (*cur_val* < 0) ∨ (*cur_val* > 65535) **then**
    begin *print_err*("Bad␣character␣code");
    help2("An␣\xchar␣number␣must␣be␣between␣0␣and␣65535.")
    ("I␣changed␣this␣one␣to␣zero."); *int_error*(*cur_val*); *cur_val* ← 0;
    end;
  end;

Similarly, *new_character* gets a companion in §582:

function *new_xchar*(*f* : *internal_font_number*; *c* : *integer*): *pointer*;
  var *p, q*: *pointer*; { newly allocated nodes }
  begin *q* ← *new_character*(*f, c* **mod** 256);
  if *q* = *null* **then** *new_xchar* ← *null*
  else begin *p* ← *get_avail*; *font*(*p*) ← *font_base*;
    character(*p*) ← *qi*((*c* **div** 256)); *link*(*p*) ← *q*;
    new_xchar ← *p*;
    end;
  end;

Extended characters can be output properly if we replace the opening lines of the code in §620 by these:

reswitch: **if** *is_char_node*(*p*) **then**
    begin *synch_h*; *synch_v*;
    repeat if *is_xchar_node*(*p*) **then**
        begin *f* ← *font*(*link*(*p*));
        if *character*(*p*) = *qi*(0) **then** *p* ← *link*(*p*);
            { bypass zero extension }
        end
      else *f* ← *font*(*p*);
      c ← *character*(*p*);
      if *f* ≠ *dvi_f* **then** ⟨ Change font *dvi_f* to *f* 621 ⟩;
      if *is_xchar_node*(*p*) **then**
        begin *dvi_out*(*set1* + 1); *dvi_out*(*qo*(*c*)); *p* ← *link*(*p*);
        c ← *character*(*p*);
        end
      else if *c* ≥ *qi*(128) **then** *dvi_out*(*set1*);
      dvi_out(*qo*(*c*));

Many of the processing routines include a statement of the form '*f* ← *font*(#)', which we want to do only after bypassing the first half of an extended character. This can be done by inserting the following statements:

$$bypass\_xchar(p) \qquad \text{in §654;}$$
$$bypass\_xchar(s) \qquad \text{in §842;}$$
$$bypass\_xchar(cur\_p) \quad \text{in §867;}$$
$$bypass\_xchar(s) \qquad \text{in §871;}$$
$$bypass\_xchar(p) \qquad \text{in §1147.}$$

In §841 we need to do a little more than a simple bypass:

> **if** $is\_char\_node(v)$ **then**
>   **begin if** $is\_xchar\_node(v)$ **then**
>   **begin** $v \leftarrow link(v)$; $decr(t)$;   { an xchar counts as two chars }
>   **end**;

Two changes are needed in order to suppress hyphenation in words that contain extended characters. First we insert

> **if** $hf = font\_base$ **then goto** $done1$;   { $is\_xchar\_node(s)$ }

after '$hf \leftarrow font(s)$' in §896. Then we replace '**endcases**;' in §899 by

> **endcases**
> **else if** $is\_xchar\_node(s)$ **then goto** $done1$;

If \xchar appears in math mode, we want to recover from the error by including $mmode + xchar\_num$ in the list of cases in §1046. If \xchar appears in vertical mode, we want to begin a paragraph by including $vmode + xchar\_num$ in the second list of cases in §1090.

But what if \xchar appears in horizontal mode? To handle this, we might as well rewrite §1122:

1122. We need only two more things to complete the horizontal mode routines, namely the \xchar and \accent primitives.

> ⟨ Cases of *main_control* that build boxes and lists 1056 ⟩ +≡
> $hmode + xchar\_num$: **begin** $scan\_xchar\_num$;
> $link(tail) \leftarrow new\_xchar(cur\_font, cur\_val)$;
>   **if** $link(tail) \neq null$ **then** $tail \leftarrow link(link(tail))$;
> $space\_factor \leftarrow 1000$;
>   **end**;
> $hmode + accent$: $make\_accent$;

Finally, we need to extend *make_accent* so that extended characters can be accented. (Problem 31 didn't call for this explicitly, but TEXX should surely do it.) This means adding a new case in §1124:

> **else if** $cur\_cmd = xchar\_num$ **then**
>   **begin** $scan\_xchar\_num$; $q \leftarrow new\_xchar(f, cur\_val)$;
>   **end**

and making changes at the beginning and end of §1125:

⟨ Append the accent with appropriate kerns, then set $p \leftarrow q$ 1125 ⟩ ≡
> **begin** $t \leftarrow slant(f)/float\_constant(65536)$;
> **if** $is\_xchar\_node(q)$ **then** $i \leftarrow char\_info(f)(character(link(q)))$
> **else** $i \leftarrow char\_info(f)(character(q))$;
> $w \leftarrow char\_width(f)(i)$;
> $\vdots$
> $subtype(tail) \leftarrow acc\_kern$; $link(p) \leftarrow tail$;
> **if** $is\_xchar\_node(q)$ **then**
>> { in this case we want to bypass the xchar part }
>> **begin** $tail\_append(q)$; $p \leftarrow link(q)$;
>> **end**
>
> **else** $p \leftarrow q$;
> **end**

32. The main reason for preferring the method of problem 31 is that the italic correction operation (§1113) would be extremely difficult with the other scheme. Other advantages are: (a) Division by 256 is needed only once; TEXX's main loops remain fast. (b) Comparatively few changes from TEX itself are needed, hence other ripoffs of TEX can easily incorporate the same ideas. (c) Since fonts don't need to be segregated into 'oriental' and 'occidental', \xchar has wide applicability. For example, it gives users a way to suppress ligatures and kerns; it allows large fonts to have efficient 256-character subsets of commonly-used characters. (d) The conventions of TEXX match those of the GF files produced by METAFONT.

The only disadvantage of the TEXX method is that it requires all characters whose codes differ by multiples of 256 to have the same box size. But this is a minor consideration.

Appendix

The solution to problem 17 refers to a special version of TEX called DemoTEX, which allows users to see more details of the scanning process. DemoTEX is formed by making a few changes to parts 24–26 of TEX.

First, in §341, the following code is placed between '*exit:*' and '**end**':

> **if** $tracing\_stats > 2$ **then**
>> **begin** $k \leftarrow trace\_depth$;
>> $print\_nl("")$;
>> **while** $k > 0$ **do**
>>> **begin** $print("\_")$;
>>> $decr(k)$;
>>> **end**;

$print("|");$
$print\_char("\textvisiblespace");$
if $cur\_cs > 0$ **then**
    begin $print\_cs(cur\_cs);$
    $print\_char("=");$
    end;
$print\_cmd\_chr(cur\_cmd, cur\_chr);$
end;

(A new global variable, *trace_depth*, is declared somewhere and initialized to zero. It is used to indent the output of DemoTEX so that the depth of subroutine nesting is displayed.)

At the beginning of *expand* (in §366), we put the statements

$incr(trace\_depth);$
if $tracing\_stats > 2$ **then**
    $print("\textvisiblespace<x");$

this prints '<x' when *expand* begins to expand something. The same statements are inserted at the beginning of *scan_int* (§440), *scan_dimen* (§448), and *scan_glue* (§461), except that routine *scan_int* prints '<i', *scan_dimen* prints '<d', and *scan_glue* prints '<g'. (Get it?) We also insert complementary code at the end of each of these procedures:

$decr(trace\_depth);$
if $tracing\_stats > 2$ **then**
    $print\_char(">");$

this makes it clear when each part of the scanner has done its work.

Finally, *scan_keyword* is instrumented in a similar way, but with explicit information about what keyword it is seeking. The code

$incr(trace\_depth);$
if $tracing\_stats > 2$ **then**
    begin $print("\textvisiblespace<`");$
    $print(s);$
    $print\_char("`");$
    end;

is inserted at the beginning of §407, and

if $tracing\_stats > 2$ **then**
    $print\_char("*");$
exit: $decr(trace\_depth);$
if $tracing\_stats > 2$ **then**
    $print\_char(">");$
end;

replaces the code at the end. (Here '*' denotes 'success': the keyword was found.)

For example, here's the beginning of what DemoTEX prints out when scanning the right-hand side of the assignment to \hfuzz in problem 17:

```
| the character = <d
 | the character 1 <i
  | the character 1
  | the character 0
  | the character 0
  | the letter P>
 | the letter P <'em'
  | the letter P> <'ex'
  | the letter P> <'true'
  | the letter P> <'pt'
  | the letter P
  | \ifdim =\ifdim <x <d
   | the character 1 <i
    | the character 1
    | the character 2
    | the letter p>
   | the letter p <'em'
    | the letter p> <'ex'
    | the letter p> <'true'
    | the letter p> <'pt'
    | the letter p
    | the letter t*>
   | the character =>
```

(After seeing '=', TEX calls *scan_dimen*. The next character seen is '1'; *scan_dimen* puts it back to be read again and calls *scan_int*, which finds '100', etc. This output demonstrates the fact that TEX frequently uses *back_input* to reread a character, when it isn't quite ready to deal with that character.)

Acknowledgments

I wish to thank the brave students of my experimental class for motivating me to think of these questions, for sticking with me when the questions were impossible to understand, and for making many improvements to my original answers.

Chapter 11

Mini-Indexes for Literate Programs

*[Originally published in Software — Concepts & Tools **15** (1994), 2–11.]*

This paper describes how to implement a documentation technique that helps readers to understand large programs or collections of programs, by providing local indexes to all identifiers that are visible on every two-page spread. A detailed example is given for a program that finds all Hamiltonian cycles in an undirected graph.

Introduction

Users of systems like WEB [4], which provide support for structured documentation and literate programming [7], automatically get a printed index at the end of their programs, showing where each identifier is defined and used. Such indexes can be extremely helpful, but they can also be cumbersome, especially when the program is long. An extreme example is provided by the listing of TEX [5], where the index contains 32 pages of detailed entries in small print.

Readers of [5] can still find their way around the program quickly, however, because

> ...the right-hand pages of this book contain mini-indexes that will make it unnecessary for you to look at the big index very often. Every identifier that is used somewhere on a pair of facing pages is listed in a footnote on the right-hand page, unless it is explicitly defined or declared somewhere on the left-hand or right-hand page you are reading. These footnote entries tell you whether the identifier is a procedure or a macro or a boolean, etc. [5; 7, page 183]

A similar idea is sometimes used in editions of literary texts for foreign language students, where mini-dictionaries of unusual words appear on

225

each page [12]; this saves the student from spending a lot of time searching big dictionaries.

The idea of mini-indexes was first suggested to the author by Joe Weening, who prepared a brief mockup of what he thought might be possible [14]. His proposal was immediately appealing, so the author decided to implement it in a personal program called TWILL — a name suggested by the fact that it was a two-pass variant of the standard program called WEAVE. The TWILL software was used in September 1985 to produce *TEX: The Program* [5] and *METAFONT: The Program* [6].

The original WEB system was a combination of TEX and Pascal. But the author's favorite programming language nowadays is CWEB [8], which combines TEX with C. (In fact, CWEB version 3.0 is fully compatible with C++, although the author usually restricts himself to a personal subset that might be called C--.) One of the advantages of CWEB is that it supports collections of small program modules and libraries that can be combined in many ways. A single CWEB source file foo.w can generate several output files in addition to the C program foo.c; for example, foo.w might generate a header file foo.h for use by other modules that will be loaded with the object code foo.o, and it might generate a test program testfoo.c that helps verify portability.

CWEB was used to create the Stanford GraphBase, a collection of about three dozen public-domain programs useful for the study of combinatorial algorithms [13]. These programs have recently been published in book form, again with mini-indexes [9]. The mini-indexes in this case were prepared with CTWILL [10], a two-pass variant of CWEAVE.

The purpose of this paper is to explain the operations of TWILL and of its descendant, CTWILL. The concepts are easiest to understand when they are related to a detailed example, so a complete CWEB program has been prepared for illustrative purposes. The following section of this paper explains the example program; the next two sections explain how CTWILL and TEX process it; and a final section contains concluding comments.

An Example

The CWEB program for which sample mini-indexes have been prepared especially for this paper is called HAM. It enumerates all Hamiltonian cycles of a graph, namely all undirected cycles that include each vertex exactly once. For example, the program can determine that there are exactly 9862 knight's tours on a 6×6 chessboard, ignoring symmetries of the board, in about 2.3 seconds on a SPARCstation 2. Since HAM may be interesting in its own right, it is presented in its entirety as an appendix to this chapter (see pages 241–245).

Please take a quick look at HAM now, before reading further. The program appears in five two-column pages, each of which will be called a *spread*, by analogy with the two-page spreads in [5], [6], and [9]. This arrangement gives us five mini-indexes to look at instead of just two, so it makes HAM a decent example in spite of its relatively small size. A shorter program wouldn't need much of an index at all; a longer program would take too long to read.

HAM is intended for use with the library of routines that comes with the Stanford GraphBase, so §1 of the program tells the C preprocessor to include header files `gb_graph.h` and `gb_save.h`. These header files define the external functions and data types that are needed from the GraphBase library.

A brief introduction to GraphBase data structures will suffice for the interested reader to understand the full details of HAM. A graph is represented by combining three kinds of **struct** records called **Graph**, **Vertex**, and **Arc**. If v points to a **Vertex** record, $v\text{-}name$ is a string that names the vertex represented by v, and $v\text{-}arcs$ points to the representation of the first arc emanating from that vertex.[1] If a points to an **Arc** record that represents an arc from some vertex v to another vertex u, then $a\text{-}tip$ points to the **Vertex** record that represents u; also $a\text{-}next$ points to the representation of the next arc from v, or $a\text{-}next = \Lambda$ (i.e., NULL) if a is the last arc from v. Thus the following loop will print the names of all vertices adjacent to v:

$$\textbf{for } (a = v\text{-}arcs;\ a;\ a = a\text{-}next)$$
$$printf\,(\texttt{"\%s\textbackslash n"}, a\text{-}tip\text{-}name);$$

An undirected edge between vertices u and v is represented by two arcs, one from u to v and one from v to u. Finally, if g points to a **Graph** record, then $g\text{-}n$ is the number of vertices in the associated graph, and the **Vertex** records representing those vertices are in locations $g\text{-}vertices + k$, for $0 \leq k < g\text{-}n$.

A **Vertex** record also contains "utility fields" that can be exploited in different ways by different algorithms. The actual C declarations of these fields, quoted from §8 and §9 of the program GB_GRAPH [9], are

---

[1] '$v\text{-}name$' is actually typed '`v->name`' in a C or `CWEB` program; typographic sugar makes the program easier to read in print.

as follows:

```
typedef union {
  struct vertex_struct *V;
    /* pointer to Vertex */
  struct arc_struct *A;
    /* pointer to Arc */
  struct graph_struct *G;
    /* pointer to Graph */
  char *S;
    /* pointer to string */
  long I;
    /* integer */
} util;

typedef struct vertex_struct {
  struct arc_struct *arcs;
    /* linked list of arcs out of this vertex */
  char *name;
    /* string identifying this vertex symbolically */
  util u, v, w, x, y, z;
    /* multipurpose fields */
} Vertex;
```

Program HAM uses the first four utility fields in order to do its work efficiently. Field u, for example, is treated as a **long** integer representing the degree of the vertex. Notice the definition of *deg* as a macro in §2; this makes it possible to refer to the degree of v as $v\text{-}deg$ instead of the more cryptic '$v\text{-}u.I$' actually seen by the C compiler. Similar macros for utility fields v, w, and x can be found in §4 and §6.

The first mini-index of HAM, which follows the code for §2 in the first spread of the program, gives cross-references to all identifiers that appear in §1 or §2 but are not defined there. For example, *restore_graph* is mentioned in one of the comments of §1; the mini-index tells us that it is a function, that it returns a value of type **Graph** ∗, and that it is defined in §4 of another CWEB program called GB_SAVE. The mini-index also mentions that **Vertex** and *arcs* are defined in §9 of GB_GRAPH (from which we quoted the relevant definitions above), and that fields *next* and *tip* of **Arc** records are defined in GB_GRAPH §10, etc.

One subtlety of this first mini-index is the entry for u, which tells us that u is a utility field defined in GB_GRAPH §9. The identifier u actually appears twice in §2, once in the definition of *deg* and once as a variable of type **Vertex** ∗. The mini-index refers only to the former, because the latter usage is defined in §2. Mini-indexes don't mention identifiers defined within their own spread.

The second mini-index, below §5 of HAM, is similar to the first. Notice that it contains two separate entries for v, because the identifier v is used in two senses—both as a utility field (in the definition of *taken*) and as a variable (elsewhere). The C compiler will understand how to deal with constructions like 'v~$v.I = 0$', which the C preprocessor expands from 'v~*taken* $= 0$', but human readers are spared such trouble.

Notice the entry for *deg* in this second mini-index: It uses an equals sign instead of a colon, indicating that *deg* is a macro rather than a variable. A similar notation was used in the first mini-index for cross-references to typedef'd identifiers like **Vertex**. See also the entry for *not_taken* in the fourth mini-index: Here '*not_taken* = macro ( )' indicates that *not_taken* is a macro with arguments.

The Operation of CTWILL

It would be nice to report that the program CTWILL produces the mini-indexes for HAM in a completely automatic fashion, just as CWEAVE automatically produces ordinary indexes. But that would be a lie. The truth is that CTWILL only does about 99% of the work automatically; the user has to help it with the hard parts.

Why is this so? Well, in the first place, CTWILL isn't smart enough to figure out that the 'u' in the definition of *deg* in §2 is not the same as the 'u' declared to be **register Vertex** ∗ in that same section. Indeed, a high degree of artificial intelligence would be required before CTWILL could deduce that.

In the second place, CTWILL has no idea what mini-index entry to make for the identifier k that appears in §6. No variable k is declared anywhere! Indeed, users who write comments involving expressions like '$f(x)$' might or might not be referring to identifiers f and/or x in their programs; they must tell CTWILL when they are making "throwaway" references that should not be indexed. CWEAVE doesn't have this problem because it indexes only the definitions, not the uses, of single-letter identifiers.

In the third place, CTWILL will not recognize automatically that the *vert* parameter in the definition of *not_taken*, §4, has no connection with the *vert* macro defined in §6.

A fourth complication, which does not arise in HAM but does occur in [5] and [9], is that sections of a WEB or CWEB program can be used more than once. Therefore a single identifier might actually refer to several different variables simultaneously. (See, for example, §652 in [5].)

In general, when an identifier is defined or declared exactly once, and used only in connection with its unique definition, CTWILL will have no problems with it. But when an identifier has more than one implicit or explicit definition, CTWILL can only guess which definition was meant. Some identifiers — especially single-letter ones like x and y — are too useful to be confined to a single significance throughout a large collection of programs. Therefore CTWILL was designed to let users provide hints easily when choices need to be made.

The most important aspect of this design was to make CTWILL's default actions easily predictable. The more "intelligence" we try to build into a system, the harder it is for us to control it. Therefore CTWILL has very simple rules for deciding what to put in mini-indexes.

Each identifier has a unique *current meaning*, which consists of three parts: its type, and the program name and section number where it was defined. At the beginning of a run, CTWILL reads a number of files that define the initial current meanings. Then, whenever CTWILL sees a C construction that implies a change of meaning — a macro definition, a variable declaration, a typedef, a function declaration, or the appearance of a label followed by a colon — it assigns a new current meaning as specified by the semantics of C. For example, when CTWILL sees '**Graph** $*g$' in §2 of HAM, it changes the current meaning of g to '**Graph** $*$, HAM §2'. These changes occur in the order of the CWEB source file, not in the "tangled" order that is actually presented to the C compiler. Therefore CTWILL makes no attempt to nest definitions according to block structure; everything it does is purely sequential. A variable declared in §5 and §10 will be assumed to have the meaning of §5 in §6, §7, §8, and §9.

Whenever CTWILL changes the current meaning of a variable, it outputs a record of that current meaning to an auxiliary file. For the CWEB program ham.w, this auxiliary file is called ham.aux. The first few entries of ham.aux are

```
@$deg {ham}2 =macro@>
@$argc {ham}2 \&{int}@>
@$argv {ham}2 \&{char} ${*}[\,]$@>
```

and the last entry is

```
@$d {ham}8 \&{register} \&{int}@>
```

In general these entries have the form

```
@$ident {name}nn type@>
```

where *ident* is an identifier, *name* and *nn* are the program name and section number where *ident* is defined, and *type* is a string of TEX commands to indicate its type. In place of {*name*}*nn* the entry might have the form "string" instead; then the program name and section number are replaced by the string. (This mechanism leads, for example, to the appearance of <stdio.h> in HAM's mini-index entries for *printf*.) Sometimes the *type* field says '\zip'. This situation doesn't arise in HAM, nor does it arise very often in [9]; but it occurs, for example, when a preprocessor macro name has been defined externally as in a Makefile, or when a type is very complicated, like FILE in <stdio.h>. In such cases the mini-index will simply say 'FILE, <stdio.h>', with no colon or equals sign.

The user can explicitly change the current meaning by specifying @$*ident* {*name*}*nn* *type*@> anywhere in a CWEB program. This means that CTWILL's default mechanism is easily overridden.

When CTWILL starts processing a program foo.w, it looks first for a file named foo.aux that might have been produced on a previous run. If foo.aux is present, it is read in, and the @$...@> commands of foo.aux give current meanings to all identifiers defined in foo.w. Therefore CTWILL is able to know the meaning of an identifier before that identifier has been declared—assuming that CTWILL has been run successfully on foo.w at least once before, and assuming that the final definition of the identifier is the one intended at the beginning of the program.

CTWILL also looks for another auxiliary file called foo.bux. This one is not overwritten on each run, so it can be modified by the user. The purpose of foo.bux is to give initial meanings to identifiers that are not defined in foo.aux. For example, ham.bux is a file containing the two lines

```
@i gb_graph.hux
@i gb_save.hux
```

which tell CTWILL to input the files gb_graph.hux and gb_save.hux. The latter files contain definitions of identifiers that appear in the header files gb_graph.h and gb_save.h, which HAM includes in §1. For example, one of the lines of gb_graph.hux is

```
@$Vertex {GB\_\,GRAPH}9 =\&{struct}@>
```

This line appears also in gb_graph.aux; it was copied by hand, using a text editor, into gb_graph.hux, because **Vertex** is one of the identifiers defined in gb_graph.h.

CTWILL also reads a file called `system.bux`, if it is present; that file contains global information that is always assumed to be in the background as part of the current environment. One of the lines in `system.bux` is, for example,

```
@$printf "<stdio.h>" \&{int} (\,)@>
```

After `system.bux`, `ham.aux`, and `ham.bux` have been input, CTWILL will know initial current meanings of almost all identifiers that appear in HAM. The only exception is k, found in §6; its current meaning is `\uninitialized`, and if the user does not take corrective action its mini-index entry will come out as

$$k: \; ???, \; §0.$$

Notice that d is declared in §4 of HAM and also in §8. Both of these declarations produce entries in `ham.aux`. Since CTWILL reads `ham.aux` before looking at the source file `ham.w`, and since `ham.aux` is read sequentially, the current meaning of d will refer to §8 at the beginning of `ham.w`. This causes no problem, because d is never used in HAM except in the sections where it is declared, hence it never appears in a mini-index.

When CTWILL processes each section of a program, it makes a list of all identifiers used in that section, except for reserved words. At the end of the section, it mini-outputs (that is, it outputs to the mini-index) the current meaning of each identifier on the list, unless that current meaning refers to the current section of the program, or unless the user intervenes.

The user has two ways to change the mini-outputs, either by suppressing the default entries or by inserting replacement entries. First, the explicit command

$$@-ident@>$$

tells CTWILL not to produce the standard mini-output for *ident* in the current section. Second, the user can specify one or more *temporary meanings* for an identifier, all of which will be mini-output at the end of the section. Temporary meanings do not affect an identifier's current meaning. Whenever at least one temporary meaning is mini-output, the current meaning will be suppressed just as if the `@-...@>` command had been given. Temporary meanings are specified by means of the operation `@%`, which toggles a state switch affecting the `@$...@>` command: At the beginning of a section, the switch is in "permanent" state, and `@$...@>` will change an identifier's current meaning as described earlier. Each occurrence of @% changes the state from "permanent" to "temporary" or back again; in "temporary" state the @$...@> command specifies a temporary meaning that will be mini-output with no effect on the identifier's permanent (current) meaning.

Examples of these conventions will be given momentarily, but first we should note one further interaction between CTWILL's @- and @$ commands: If CTWILL would normally assign a new current meaning to *ident* because of the semantics of C, and if the command @-*ident*@> has already appeared in the current section, CTWILL will not override the current meaning, but CTWILL will output the current meaning to the .aux file. In particular, the user may have specified the current meaning with @$*ident*...@>; this allows user control over what gets into the .aux file.

For example, here is a complete list of all commands inserted by the author in order to correct or enhance CTWILL's default mini-indexes for HAM:

- At the beginning of §2,

```
@-deg@>
@$deg {ham}2 =\|u.\|I@>
@%@$u {GB\_\,GRAPH}9 \&{util}@>
```

to make the definition of *deg* read '*u.I*' instead of just 'macro' and to make the mini-index refer to *u* as a utility field.

- At the beginning of §4,

```
@-taken@> @-vert@>
@$taken {ham}4 =\|v.\|I@>
@%@$v {GB\_\,GRAPH}9 \&{util}@>
 @$v {ham}2 \&{register} \&{Vertex} $*$@>
```

for similar reasons, and to suppress indexing of *vert*. Here the mini-index gets two "temporary" meanings for *v*, one of which happens to coincide with its permanent meaning.

- At the beginning of §6,

```
@-k@> @-t@> @-vert@> @-ark@>
@$vert {ham}6 =\|w.\|V@>
@$ark {ham}6 =\|x.\|A@>
@%@$w {GB\_\,GRAPH}9 \&{util}@>
  @$x {GB\_\,GRAPH}9 \&{util}@>
```

for similar reasons. That's all.

These commands were not inserted into the program file `ham.w`; they were put into another file called `ham.ch` and introduced via CWEB's "change file" feature [8]. Change files make it easy to modify the effective contents of a master file without tampering with that file directly.

Processing by TeX

CTWILL writes a TeX file that includes mini-output at the end of each section. For example, the mini-output after §10 of HAM is

```
\]{GB\_\,GRAPH}10 \\{next} \&{Arc} $*$
\[7 \\{advance} label
\[6 \\{ark} =\|x.\|A
\[2 \|{t} \&{register} \&{Vertex} $*$
\[4 \\{not\_taken} =macro (\,)
\]{GB\_\,GRAPH}10 \\{tip} \&{Vertex} $*$
\[2 \|{v} \&{register} \&{Vertex} $*$
\[2 \|{a} \&{register} \&{Arc} $*$
```

Here the control sequence \] introduces an external reference to some other program; \[introduces an internal reference to another section of HAM; \\ typesets an identifier in text italics; \| typesets an identifier in math italics; \& typesets in boldface.

A special debugging mode is available in which TeX will simply typeset all the mini-output at the end of each section, instead of making actual mini-indexes. This makes it easy for users to check that CTWILL is in fact producing the information they really want. Notice that mistakes in CTWILL's output need not necessarily lead to mistakes in mini-indexes; for example, a spurious reference in §6 to an identifier defined in §5 will not appear in a mini-index for a spread that includes §5. It is best to make sure that CTWILL's output is correct before looking at actual mini-indexes. Then unpleasant surprises won't occur when sections of the program are moved from one spread to another.

When TeX is finally asked to typeset the real mini-indexes, however, it has plenty of work to do. That's when the fun begins. TeX's main task, after formatting the commentary and C code of each section, is to figure out whether the current section fits into the current spread, and (if it does) to update the mini-index by merging together all entries for that spread.

Consider, for example, what happens when TeX typesets §10 of HAM. The current spread begins with §8, and TeX already knows that §8 and §9 will fit together in a single page. After typesetting the body of

§10, TEX looks at the mini-index entries. If any of them refer to §8 or §9, TEX will tentatively ignore them, because those sections are already part of the current spread. (That situation doesn't actually arise in §10; but when TEX processed §7, it did suppress entries for *vert* and *ark*, since they referred to §6.) TEX also tentatively discards mini-index entries that match other entries already scheduled for the current spread. (In this case, everything is discarded except the entries for *advance* and *ark*; the others — *next*, *t*, *not_taken*, *v*, and *a* — are duplicates of entries in the mini-output of §8 or §9.) Finally, TEX tentatively discards previously scheduled entries that refer to the current section. (In this case nothing happens, because no entries from §8 or §9 refer to §10.)

After this calculation, TEX knows the number n of mini-index entries that would be needed if §10 were to join the spread with §8 and §9. TEX divides n by the number of columns in the mini-index (here 1, but 3 in [5] and [9]), multiplies by the distance between mini-baselines (here 9 points), and adds the result to the total height of the typeset text for the current spread (here the height of §8 + §9 + §10). With a few minor refinements for spacing between sections and for the ruled line that separates the mini-index from the rest of the text, TEX is able to estimate the total space requirement. In our example, everything fits in a single page, so TEX appends §10 to the spread containing §8 and §9. Then, after §11 has been processed in the same fashion, TEX sees that there isn't room for §§8–11 all together; so it decides to begin a new spread with §11.

The processing just described is not built in to TEX, of course. It is all under the control of a set of macros called `ctwimac.tex` [10]. The first thing CTWILL tells TEX is to input those macros.

TEX was designed for typesetting, not for programming; so it is at best "weird" when considered as a programming language. But the job of mini-indexing does turn out to be programmable. The full details of `ctwimac.tex` are too complex to exhibit here, but TEX hackers will appreciate some of the less obvious ideas that are used. (Non-TEXnicians, please skip the rest of this long paragraph.) TEX reads the mini-outputs of CTWILL twice, with different definitions of \[and \] each time. Suppose we are processing section s, and suppose that the current spread begins with section r. Then TEX's token registers 200, 201, ..., 219 contain all mini-index entries from sections

$$r, r+1, \ldots, s-1$$

for identifiers defined respectively in sections r, $r+1$, ..., $r+19$ of the CWEB program. (We need not keep separate tables for more than 20 consecutive sections starting with the base r of the current spread, because no spread can contain more than 20 sections.) Token register 199 contains, similarly, entries that refer to sections preceding r, and token register 220 contains entries that refer to sections $r + 20$ and higher. Token register 221 contains entries for identifiers defined in other programs. Count register k contains the number of entries in token register k, for $199 \leq k \leq 221$. When count register k equals j, the actual content of token register k is a sequence of $2j$ tokens,

$$\lmda\cs_1\lmda\cs_2 \ldots \lmda\cs_j$$

where each $\cs_i$ is a control sequence that uniquely characterizes a mini-index entry, defined via `\csname...\endcsname`. TEX can tell if a new mini-index entry agrees with another already in the current spread by simply testing if the corresponding control sequence is defined. The replacement text for $\cs_i$ is the associated mini-index entry, while the definition of `\lmda` is

```
\def\lmda#1{#1\global\let#1\relax}
```

Therefore when TEX "executes" the contents of a token register, it typesets all the associated mini-index entries and undefines all the associated control sequences. Alternatively, we can say

```
\def\lmda#1{\global\let#1\relax}
```

if we merely want to erase all entries represented in a token register. At the end of a spread containing p sections, we generate the mini-index by executing token registers 199 and $200 + p$ thru 221 using the former definition of `\lmda`, and we also execute token registers 200 thru $200 + p - 1$ using the latter definition. Everything works like magic.

A bug in the original TEX macros for TWILL led to an embarrassing error in the first (1986) printings of [5] and [6]: Control sequences in token registers corresponding to sections of the current spread were not erased; in other words, the contents of those token registers were simply discarded, not executed with the second definition of `\lmda`. The effect was to make TEX think that certain control sequences were still defined, hence the macros would think that the mini-index entries were still present; such entries were therefore omitted by mistake. Only about 3% of the entries were actually affected, so this error was not outrageous enough to be noticed until after the books were printed and people started to read them. The only bright spot in this part of the story was the fact that it proved how effective mini-indexes are: The missing entries were sorely missed, because their presence would have been really helpful.

The "greedy" longest-fit method by which CTWILL's TeX macros allocate sections to pages tends to minimize the total number of pages, but this is not guaranteed. For example, it's possible to imagine unusual scenarios in which sections §100 and §101, say, do not fit on a single spread, while the three sections §100, §101, §102 actually do fit. This might happen if §100 and §101 have lots of references to variables declared in §102. Similarly, we might be able to fit §100 with §101 if §99 had been held over from the previous spread. But such situations are extremely unlikely, and there is no reason to worry about them. The one-spread-at-a-time strategy adopted by `ctwimac.tex` is optimum, spacewise, for all practical purposes.

On the other hand, experience shows that unfortunate page breaks between spreads do sometimes occur unless the user does a bit more fine tuning. For example, suppose the text of §7 in HAM had been one line longer. Then §7 would not have fit with §6, and we would have been left with a spread containing just tiny little §6 and lots of wasted white space. It would look awful. And in fact, that's the reason the statements

$$t \rightarrow ark = \Lambda; \quad v = y;$$

now appear on a single line of the program instead of on two separate lines: A bad break between spreads was avoided by manually tieing those statements together, using CWEB's `@+` command.

One further problem needs to be addressed — the mini-indexes must be sorted alphabetically. TeX is essential for determining the breaks between spreads (and consequently for determining the actual contents of the mini-indexes), but TeX is not a good vehicle for sorting. The solution to this problem is to run the output of CTWILL twice through TeX, interposing a sorting program between the two runs. When TeX processes `ham.tex`, the macros of `ctwimac.tex` tell it to look first for a file called `ham.sref`. If no such file is present, a file called `ham.ref` will be written, containing all the (unsorted) mini-index entries for each spread. TeX will also typeset the pages as usual, with all mini-indexes in their proper places but unsorted; the user can therefore make adjustments to fix bad page breaks, if necessary. Once the page breaks are satisfactory, a separate program called REFSORT is invoked; REFSORT converts `ham.ref` into a sorted version, `ham.sref`. Then when TeX sees `ham.sref`, it can use the sorted data to make the glorious final copy.

For example, the file `ham.ref` looks like this:

```
!241
+ \]{GB\_\,SAVE}4 \\{restore\_graph} \&{Graph} $*(\,)$
+ \]{GB\_\,GRAPH}9 \|{u} \&{util}
    ⋮
+ \]{GB\_\,GRAPH}8 \|{I} \&{long}
!242
    ⋮
+ \]"<stdio.h>" \\{printf} \&{int} (\,)
```

And the file `ham.sref` looks like this:

```
\]{GB\_\,GRAPH}10 \&{Arc} =\&{struct}
    ⋮
\]{GB\_\,GRAPH}9 \|{u} \&{util}
\]{GB\_\,GRAPH}9 \&{Vertex} =\&{struct}
\donewithpage241
\[2 \|{a} \&{register} \&{Arc} $*$
    ⋮
\]{GB\_\,GRAPH}20 \\{vertices} \&{Vertex} $*$
\donewithpage245
```

Each file contains one line for each mini-index entry and one line to mark the beginning (in `ham.ref`) or end (in `ham.sref`) of each spread.

Conclusions

The CTWILL system for mini-index generation can be regarded as a further enhancement of tools for viewing program structure, continuing a long line of research that began with W. J. Hansen's structured editor called Emily [2, 3].

Although CTWILL is not fully automatic, it dramatically improves the readability of large collections of programs. Therefore an author who has spent a year writing programs for publication won't mind spending an additional week improving the indexes. Indeed, a little extra time spent on indexing generally leads to significant improvements in the text of any book that is being indexed by its author, who has a chance to see the book in a new light.

Some manual intervention is unavoidable, because a computer cannot know the proper reference for every identifier that appears in program comments. But experience with CTWILL's change file mechanism indicates that correct mini-indexes for large and complex programs can be obtained at the rate of about 100 book pages per day. For example, the construction of change files for the 460 pages of programs in [9] took 5 days, during which time CTWILL was itself being debugged and refined.

Mini-indexes are wonderful additions to printed books, but we can expect hypertext-like objects to replace books for many purposes in the long run. It's easy to imagine a system for viewing CWEB programs in which you can find the meaning of any identifier just by clicking on it. Future systems will perhaps present "fish-eye" views of programs, allowing easy navigation through complicated webs of code. (See [1] and [11] for some steps in that direction.)

Such future systems will, however, confront the same issues that are faced by CTWILL as it constructs mini-indexes today. An author who wants to create useful program hypertexts for others to read will want to give hints about the significance of identifiers whose roles are impossible or difficult to deduce mechanically. Some of the lessons taught by CTWILL will therefore most likely be relevant to everyone who tries to design literate programming systems that replace books as we now know them.

References

[1] M. Brown and B. Czejdo, "A hypertext for literate programming," *Lecture Notes in Computer Science* **468** (1990), 250–259.

[2] Wilfred J. Hansen, *Creation of Hierarchic Text With a Computer Display*, Ph.D. thesis, Stanford University (1971). Published also as Argonne National Laboratory report ANL-7818 (Argonne, Illinois: 1971).

[3] Wilfred J. Hansen, "User engineering principles for interactive systems," *AFIPS Fall Joint Computer Conference* **39** (1971), 523–532.

[4] Donald E. Knuth, "Literate programming," *The Computer Journal* **27** (1984), 97–111.

[5] Donald E. Knuth, *TEX: The Program*, Volume B of *Computers & Typesetting* (Reading, Massachusetts: Addison–Wesley, 1986).

[6] Donald E. Knuth, *METAFONT: The Program*, Volume D of *Computers & Typesetting* (Reading, Massachusetts: Addison–Wesley, 1986).

[7] Donald E. Knuth, *Literate Programming*, CSLI Lecture Notes 27 (Stanford, California: Center for the Study of Language and Information, 1992). Distributed by Cambridge University Press.

[8] Donald E. Knuth and Silvio Levy, *The CWEB System of Structured Documentation, Version 3.0* (Reading, Massachusetts: Addison–Wesley, 1994). Latest version available on the Internet via anonymous ftp from `ftp.cs.stanford.edu` in directory `pub/cweb`.

[9] Donald E. Knuth, *The Stanford GraphBase: A Platform for Combinatorial Computing* (New York: ACM Press, 1994).

[10] Donald E. Knuth, "CTWILL" (1993). Available via anonymous ftp from `ftp.cs.stanford.edu` in directory `pub/ctwill`.

[11] Kasper Østerbye, "Literate Smalltalk programming using hypertext," *IEEE Transactions on Software Engineering* **SE-21** (1995), 138–145.

[12] Clyde Pharr, *Virgil's Æneid,* Books I–VI (Boston: D. C. Heath, 1930).

[13] Stanford University Computer Science Department, "The Stanford GraphBase." Available on the Internet via anonymous ftp from `ftp.cs.stanford.edu` in directory `pub/sgb`.

[14] J. S. Weening, Personal communication. Preserved in the archives of the TEX project in Stanford University Library's Department of Special Collections, SC 97, series II, box 18, folder 7.6.

Appendix: HAM

1. Hamiltonian cycles.

This program finds all the Hamiltonian cycles of an undirected graph, using conventions of the Stanford GraphBase.

If the user says, for example, 'ham foo.gb', the standard output will list every Hamiltonian cycle of the graph foo, which should be represented in file foo.gb using the Stanford GraphBase's portable ASCII format. The total number of solutions is reported at the end of the output.

An optional second parameter specifies an interval between outputs, so that the list contains only a sample of the solutions. For example, 'ham foo.gb 1000' will list only one of every 1000 Hamiltonian cycles. If the optional parameter is absent or zero, only the total number of such cycles will be output.

```
#include <stdio.h>
   /* standard C input/output
       functions */
#include "gb_graph.h"    /* the
       GraphBase data structures */
#include "gb_save.h"
   /* the restore_graph routine */
```

2. We use a utility field deg to record vertex degrees.

```
#define  deg   u.I
           /* the current number
               of arcs to and from
               this vertex */
int main(int argc, char *argv[])
  { Graph *g;
       /* the user's graph */
```

```
register Vertex *t, *u, *v;
   /* key vertices */
Vertex *x, *y, *z;
   /* vertices used less often */
register Arc *a, *aa;
   /* arcs used often */
Arc *b, *bb;
   /* arcs used less often */
int count = 0;
   /* solutions found so far */
int interval = 1;
   /* the reporting interval */
⟨ Scan the command line
       arguments and input g 3 ⟩;
⟨ Prepare g for backtracking,
       and find a vertex x of
       minimum degree 4 ⟩;
⟨ Abort the run if g is malformed
       or x→deg < 2 5 ⟩;
for (b = x→arcs; b→next;
       b = b→next)
    for (bb = b→next; bb;
           bb = bb→next) {
       v = b→tip;
       z = bb→tip;
       ⟨ Find all simple paths of
           length g→n − 2 from v
           to z, avoiding x 7 ⟩;
    }
printf("Altogether␣%d␣solut\
     ions.\n",
     count);
return 0;       /* normal exit */
}
```

Arc = struct, GB_GRAPH §10.
arcs: Arc *, GB_GRAPH §9.
Graph = struct, GB_GRAPH §20.
I: long, GB_GRAPH §8.
n: long, GB_GRAPH §20.
next: Arc *, GB_GRAPH §10.
printf: int ( ), <stdio.h>.
restore_graph: Graph *( ), GB_SAVE §4.
tip: Vertex *, GB_GRAPH §10.
u: util, GB_GRAPH §9.
Vertex = struct, GB_GRAPH §9.

3. ⟨ Scan the command line
         arguments and input g 3 ⟩ ≡
  if $(argc > 2 \wedge sscanf(argv[2],$
       "%d", &$interval$) ≡ 1) {
    $argc$ −−;
    if $(interval < 0)$
      $interval = -interval$;
    else if $(interval ≡ 0)$
      $interval = -10000$;
        /∗ suppress output
          when 0 is specified ∗/
  }
  if $(argc \neq 2)$ {
    $printf($**"Usage:␣%s␡foo.gb␣[i**
      nterval]\n", $argv[0]$);
    return −1;
  }
  $g = restore\_graph(argv[1])$;
This code is used in section 2.

4. Vertices that have already appeared in the path are said to
be "taken," and their *taken* field
is nonzero. Initially we make all
those fields zero.

#define *taken* $v.I$ /∗ does
        this vertex appear in
        the current path? ∗/
#define *not_taken*(*vert*)
    ((*vert*)→*taken* ≡ 0)

⟨ Prepare g for backtracking, and
    find a vertex x of minimum
    degree 4 ⟩ ≡
  if (g) { **int** $dmin = g$→n;
    for $(v = g$→$vertices$;
        $v < g$→$vertices + g$→n;
        v++) {
      register int $d = 0$;
        /∗ the degree of v ∗/
      v→$taken = 0$;
      for $(a = v$→$arcs$; a;
        $a = a$→$next$) d++;
      v→$deg = d$;

      if $(d < dmin)$
        $dmin = d, x = v$;
    }
  }
This code is used in section 2.

5. A vertex that has fewer than
two neighbors cannot be part of a
Hamiltonian cycle, so we give such
cases short shrift.

⟨ Abort the run if g is malformed or
    x→$deg < 2$ 5 ⟩ ≡
  if $(\neg g)$ {
    $printf($**"Graph␣%s␣is␣malform**
      ed␣(error␣code␣%ld)!\n",
      $argv[1]$, $panic\_code$);
    return −2;
  }
  if $(x$→$deg < 2)$ {
    $printf($**"No␣solutions␣(verte**
      x␣%s␣has␣degree␣%ld).\n",
      x→$name$, x→deg);
    return −3;
  }
This code is used in section 2.

---

a: **register Arc** ∗, §2.
arcs: **Arc** ∗, GB_GRAPH §9.
argc: **int**, §2.
argv: **char** ∗[], §2.
deg = $u.I$, §2.
g: **Graph** ∗, §2.
I: **long**, GB_GRAPH §8.
interval: **int**, §2.
n: **long**, GB_GRAPH §20.
name: **char** ∗, GB_GRAPH §9.
next: **Arc** ∗, GB_GRAPH §10.
panic_code: **long**, GB_GRAPH §5.
printf: **int** ( ), <stdio.h>.
restore_graph: **Graph** ∗( ), GB_SAVE §4.
sscanf: **int** ( ), <stdio.h>.
v: **register Vertex** ∗, §2.
v: **util**, GB_GRAPH §9.
vertices: **Vertex** ∗, GB_GRAPH §20.
x: **Vertex** ∗, §2.

6. The algorithm. Unproductive branches of the search tree are cut off by using a simple rule: If a vertex we could move to next is adjacent to only one other unused vertex, we must move to it now.

The moves will be recorded in the vertex array of g. More precisely, the kth vertex of the path will be $t\rightarrow vert$ when t is the kth vertex of the graph. If the move was not forced, $t\rightarrow ark$ will point to the **Arc** record representing the arc from $t\rightarrow vert$ to $(t+1)\rightarrow vert$; otherwise $t\rightarrow ark$ will be Λ.

```
#define  vert  w.V      /* vertex
                  on current path */
#define  ark   x.A
              /* arc to its current
                  successor */
```

7. This program is a typical application of the backtrack method; in other words, it essentially does a depth-first search in the tree of all solutions. The author, being a member of the Old School, is most comfortable writing such programs with labels and **goto** statements, rather than with **while** loops. Perhaps some day he will learn his lesson; but backtrack programs do need to be streamlined for speed.

A complication arises because we may discover that a move is unproductive before we have completely updated the data structures recording that move.

⟨ Find all simple paths of length $g\rightarrow n - 2$ from v to z, avoiding x 7 ⟩ ≡
  { **Vertex** *$tmax$;

$t = g\rightarrow vertices$;
$tmax = t + g\rightarrow n - 1$;
$x\rightarrow taken = 1$;
$t\rightarrow vert = x$; $t\rightarrow ark = \Lambda$;
$advance$: ⟨ Increase t, updating
        the data structures to show
        that vertex v is now taken,
        and set y to a forced move,
        if any; but **goto** $backtrack$
        if no moves are possible 8 ⟩;
  if (y) {   /* move is forced */
    $t\rightarrow ark = \Lambda$; $v = y$;
    goto $advance$;
  }
  $a = v\rightarrow arcs$;
$search$: ⟨ Look at arc a and its
        successors, advancing if a
        valid move is found 10 ⟩;
$restore$: $aa = \Lambda$;
$restore\_to\_aa$:
    ⟨ Downdate the data structures
        to the state they were in
        when level t was entered,
        stopping at arc aa 9 ⟩;
$backtrack$: ⟨ Decrease t, if possible,
        and search for another
        possibility 11 ⟩;
}
```

This code is used in section 2.

---

$a$: **register Arc** *, §2.
$A$: **Arc** *, GB_GRAPH §8.
$aa$: **register Arc** *, §2.
**Arc** = **struct**, GB_GRAPH §10.
$arcs$: **Arc** *, GB_GRAPH §9.
$g$: **Graph** *, §2.
$n$: **long**, GB_GRAPH §20.
$t$: **register Vertex** *, §2.
$taken = v.I$, §4.
$v$: **register Vertex** *, §2.
$V$: **Vertex** *, GB_GRAPH §8.
**Vertex** = **struct**, GB_GRAPH §9.
$vertices$: **Vertex** *, GB_GRAPH §20.
$w$: **util**, GB_GRAPH §9.
$x$: **Vertex** *, §2.
$x$: **util**, GB_GRAPH §9.
$y$: **Vertex** *, §2.
$z$: **Vertex** *, §2.
```

8. When a vertex becomes taken, we pretend that it has been removed from the graph.

⟨ Increase t, updating the data structures to show that vertex v is now taken, and set y to a forced move, if any; but **goto** *backtrack* if no moves are possible 8 ⟩ ≡

```
t++;
t→vert = v;
v→taken = 1;
if (v ≡ z) {
    if (t ≡ tmax)
        ⟨ Record a solution 12 ⟩;
    goto backtrack;
}
for (aa = v→arcs, y = Λ;  aa;
        aa = aa→next) {
    register int d;

    u = aa→tip;
    d = u→deg − 1;
    if (d ≡ 1 ∧ not_taken(u)) {
        /* we must move next
            to u */
        if (y) goto restore_to_aa;
        /* two forced moves
            can't both be made */
        y = u;
    }
    u→deg = d;    /* u can no
            longer move to v */
}
```

This code is used in section 7.

9. We didn't change the graph drastically at level t; all we did was decrease the degrees of vertices reachable from $t→vert$. Therefore we can easily undo previous changes when we are backing up.

⟨ Downdate the data structures to the state they were in when level t was entered, stopping at arc aa 9 ⟩ ≡

```
for (a = t→vert→arcs;  a ≠ aa;
        a = a→next)  a→tip→deg ++;
```

This code is used in section 7.

10. ⟨ Look at arc a and its successors, advancing if a valid move is found 10 ⟩ ≡

```
while (a) {
    v = a→tip;
    if (not_taken(v)) {
        t→ark = a;
        goto advance;
        /* move to v */
    }
    a = a→next;
}
```

This code is used in section 7.

---

a: **register Arc** *, §2.
aa: **register Arc** *, §2.
advance: label, §7.
arcs: **Arc** *, GB_GRAPH §9.
ark = $x.A$, §6.
backtrack: label, §7.
deg = $u.I$, §2.
next: **Arc** *, GB_GRAPH §10.
not_taken = macro ( ), §4.
restore_to_aa: label, §7.
t: **register Vertex** *, §2.
taken = $v.I$, §4.
tip: **Vertex** *, GB_GRAPH §10.
tmax: **Vertex** *, §7.
u: **register Vertex** *, §2.
v: **register Vertex** *, §2.
vert = $w.V$, §6.
y: **Vertex** *, §2.
z: **Vertex** *, §2.

11. ⟨ Decrease t, if possible,
     and search for another
     possibility 11 ⟩ ≡
$t \rightarrow vert \rightarrow taken = 0$;
$t--$;
if $(t \rightarrow ark)$ {
    $a = t \rightarrow ark \rightarrow next$;
    goto $search$;
}
if $(t \neq g \rightarrow vertices)$ **goto** $restore$;
        /∗ the move was forced, so we
            bypass $search$ ∗/

This code is used in section 7.

12.   We print a solution by simply listing the vertex names in the
current path.

⟨ Record a solution 12 ⟩ ≡
  {
    $count ++$;
    if $(count \% interval \equiv 0 \wedge$
            $interval > 0)$ {
      $printf($"%d:␣"$, count)$;
      for $(u = g \rightarrow vertices$;
             $u \leq tmax$; $u ++)$
        $printf($"%s␣"$, u \rightarrow vert \rightarrow name)$;
      $printf($"\n"$)$;
    }
  }

This code is used in section 8.

---

a: **register Arc** ∗, §2.
$ark = x.A$, §6.
$count$: **int**, §2.
g: **Graph** ∗, §2.
$interval$: **int**, §2.
$name$: **char** ∗, GB‿GRAPH §9.
$next$: **Arc** ∗, GB‿GRAPH §10.
$printf$: **int** ( ), <stdio.h>.
$restore$: label, §7.
$search$: label, §7.
t: **register Vertex** ∗, §2.
$taken = v.I$, §4.
$tmax$: **Vertex** ∗, §7.
u: **register Vertex** ∗, §2.
$vert = w.V$, §6.
$vertices$: **Vertex** ∗, GB‿GRAPH §20.

Chapter 12

Virtual Fonts: More Fun for Grand Wizards

[Originally published in TUGboat 11 (1990), 13–23.]

Many contributors to the TEXhax newsgroup during the past year or so have been struggling with interfaces between differing font conventions. For example, there's been a brisk correspondence about mixing oldstyle digits with a caps-and-small-caps alphabet. Other people despair of working with fonts supplied by manufacturers like Autologic, Compugraphic, Monotype, etc.; still others are afraid to leave the limited accent capabilities of Computer Modern for fonts containing letters that are individually accented as they should be, because such fonts are not readily available in a form that existing TEX software understands.

There is a much better way to solve such problems than the remedies that have been proposed in TEXhax. This better way was first realized by David Fuchs in 1983, when he installed it in our DVI-to-APS software at Stanford (which he also developed for commercial distribution by ArborText). David and I used it, for example, to typeset my article on Literate Programming for *The Computer Journal*, using native Autologic fonts to match the typography of that journal.

I was expecting David's strategy to become widely known and adopted. But alas — and this has really been the only significant disappointment I've had with respect to the way TEX has been propagating around the world — nobody else's DVI-to-X drivers have incorporated anything resembling David's ideas, and TEXhaxers have spilled gallons of electronic ink searching for answers in the wrong direction.

The right direction is obvious once you've seen it (although it wasn't obvious in 1983): All we need is a good way to specify a mapping from TEX's notion of a font character to a device's capabilities for printing. Such a mapping was called a "virtual font" by the AMS speakers at the TUG meetings this past August. At that meeting I spoke briefly about the issue and voiced my hope that all DVI drivers be upgraded within a year to add a virtual font capability. Dave Rodgers of ArborText announced that his company would make their WEB routines for virtual font design freely available, and I promised to edit them into a form that would match the other programs in the standard TEXware distribution.

The preparation of TEX Version 3 and METAFONT Version 2 has taken me much longer than expected, but at last I've been able to look closely at the concept of virtual fonts. (The need for such fonts is indeed much greater now than it was before, because TEX's new multilingual capabilities are significantly more powerful only when suitable fonts are available. Virtual fonts can easily be created to meet these needs.)

After looking closely at David Fuchs's original design, I decided to design a completely new file format that would carry his ideas further, making the virtual font mechanism completely device-independent; David's original code was very APS-specific. Furthermore I decided to extend his notions so that arbitrary DVI commands (including open-ended "specials") could be part of a virtual font. The new file format I've just designed is called VF; it's easy for DVI drivers to read VF files, because VF format is similar to the PK and DVI formats they already deal with.

The result is two new system routines called VFtoVP and VPtoVF. These routines are extensions of the old ones called TFtoPL and PLtoTF; there's a property-list language called VPL that extends the ordinary PL format so that virtual fonts can be created easily.

In addition to implementing these routines, I've also tested the ideas by verifying that virtual fonts could be incorporated into Tom Rokicki's DVIPS system without difficulty. I wrote a C program (available from Tom) that converts Adobe AFM files into virtual fonts for TEX; these virtual fonts include almost all the characteristics of Computer Modern text fonts (lacking only the uppercase Greek and the dotless j) and they include all the additional Adobe characters as well. The derived virtual fonts even include all the "composite characters" listed in the AFM file, from 'Aacute' to 'zcaron'; such characters are available as ligatures. For example, to get 'Aacute' you type first 'acute' (which is character 19 = ^S in Computer Modern font layout; it could also be character 194 = Meta-B if you're using an 8-bit keyboard with the new TEX) followed by 'A'. Using such fonts, it's now easier for me to typeset European language texts in Times Roman and Helvetica and Palatino than in Computer Modern! (But with less than an hour's work I could make a virtual font for Computer Modern that would do the same things; I just haven't gotten around to it yet.)

A nice ligature scheme for dozens of European languages was published by Yannis Haralambous in *TUGboat* **10** (1989), 342–345. He uses only ASCII characters, getting 'Aacute' with the combination <A. I could readily add his scheme to mine, by adding a few lines to my VPL files. Indeed, several different conventions can be supported simultaneously (although I don't recommend that really).

Virtual fonts make it easy to go from DVI files to the font layouts of any manufacturer or font supplier. They also (I'm sorry to say) make "track kerning" easy, for people who must resort to that oft-abused feature of lead-free type.

Furthermore, virtual fonts solve the problem of proofreading with screen fonts or with lowres laserprinter fonts, because you can have several virtual fonts sharing a common TFM file. Suppose, for example, that you want to typeset camera copy on an APS machine using Univers as the ultimate font, but you want to do proofreading with a screen previewer and with a laserprinter. Suppose further that you don't have Univers for your laserprinter; the closest you have is Helvetica. And suppose that you haven't even got Helvetica for your screen, but you do have cmss10. Here's what you can do: First make a virtual property list (VPL) file univers-aps.vpl that describes the high-quality font of your ultimate output. Then edit that file into univers-laser.vpl, which has identical font metric info but maps the characters into Helvetica; similarly, make univers-screen.vpl, which maps them into cmss10. Now run VPtoVF on each of the three VPL files. This will produce three identical tfm files univers.tfm, one of which you should put on the directory read by TeX. You'll also get three distinct VF files called univers.vf, which you should put on three different directories — one directory for your DVI-to-APS software, another for your DVI-to-laserwriter software, and the third for the DVI-to-screen previewer. Voilà.

So virtual fonts are evidently quite virtuous. But what exactly are virtual fonts, detail-wise? Appended to this message are excerpts from VFtoVP.web and VPtoVF.web, which give a complete definition of the VF and VPL file formats.

I fully expect that all people who have implemented DVI drivers will immediately see the great potential of virtual fonts, and that they will be unable to resist installing a VF capability into their own software during the first few months of 1990. (The idea is this: For each font specified in a DVI file, the software looks first in a special table to see if the font is device-resident (in which case the TFM file is loaded, to get the character widths); failing that, it looks for a suitable GF or PK file; failing that, it looks for a VF file, which may in turn lead to other actual or virtual files.)

The latter files should not be loaded immediately, but only on demand, because the process is recursive. Incidentally, if no resident or GF or PK or VF file is found, a TFM file should be loaded as a last resort, so that the characters can be left blank with appropriate widths.)

An Excerpt from VFtoVP.web

6.   Virtual fonts. The idea behind VF files is that a general interface mechanism is needed to switch between the myriad font layouts provided by different suppliers of typesetting equipment. Without such a mechanism, people must go to great lengths writing inscrutable macros whenever they want to use typesetting conventions based on one font layout in connection with actual fonts that have another layout. This puts an extra burden on the typesetting system, interfering with the other things it needs to do (like kerning, hyphenation, and ligature formation).

These difficulties go away when we have a "virtual font," i.e., a font that exists in a logical sense but not a physical sense. A typesetting system like TEX can do its job without knowing where the actual characters come from; a device driver can then do its job by letting a VF file tell what actual characters correspond to the characters TEX imagined were present. The actual characters can be shifted and/or magnified and/or combined with other characters from many different fonts. A virtual font can even make use of characters from virtual fonts, including itself.

Virtual fonts also allow convenient character substitutions for proof-reading purposes, when fonts designed for one output device are unavailable on another.

7.   A VF file is organized as a stream of 8-bit bytes, using conventions borrowed from DVI and PK files. Thus, a device driver that knows about DVI and PK format will already contain most of the mechanisms necessary to process VF files. We shall assume that DVI format is understood; the conventions in the DVI documentation (see, for example, *TEX: The Program*, part 31) are adopted here to define VF format.

A preamble appears at the beginning, followed by a sequence of character definitions, followed by a postamble. More precisely, the first byte of every VF file must be the first byte of the following "preamble command":

pre 247 $i[1]$ $k[1]$ $x[k]$ $cs[4]$ $ds[4]$. Here i is the identification byte of VF, currently 202. The string x is merely a comment, usually indicating the source of the VF file. Parameters cs and ds are respectively the check sum and the design size of the virtual font; they should match the first two words in the header of the TFM file, as described below.

After the *pre* command, the preamble continues with font definitions; every font needed to specify "actual" characters in later *set_char* commands is defined here. The font definitions are exactly the same in VF files as they are in DVI files, except that the scaled size s is relative and the design size d is absolute:

fnt_def1 243 $k[1]$ $c[4]$ $s[4]$ $d[4]$ $a[1]$ $l[1]$ $n[a+l]$. Define font k, where $0 \le k < 256$.

fnt_def2 244 $k[2]$ $c[4]$ $s[4]$ $d[4]$ $a[1]$ $l[1]$ $n[a+l]$. Define font k, where $0 \le k < 2^{16}$.

fnt_def3 245 $k[3]$ $c[4]$ $s[4]$ $d[4]$ $a[1]$ $l[1]$ $n[a+l]$. Define font k, where $0 \le k < 2^{24}$.

fnt_def4 246 $k[4]$ $c[4]$ $s[4]$ $d[4]$ $a[1]$ $l[1]$ $n[a + l]$. Define font k, where $-2^{31} \le k < 2^{31}$.

These font numbers k are "local"; they have no relation to font numbers defined in the DVI file that uses this virtual font. The dimension s, which represents the scaled size of the local font being defined, is a *fix_word* relative to the design size of the virtual font. Thus if the local font is to be used at the same size as the design size of the virtual font itself, s will be the integer value 2^{20}. The value of s must be positive and less than 2^{24} (thus less than 16 when considered as a *fix_word*). The dimension d is a *fix_word* in units of printer's points; hence it is identical to the design size found in the corresponding TFM file.

8. The preamble is followed by zero or more character packets, where each character packet begins with a byte that is < 243. Character packets have two formats, one long and one short:

long_char 242 $pl[4]$ $cc[4]$ $tfm[4]$ $dvi[pl]$. This long form specifies a virtual character in the general case.

short_char0 .. *short_char241* $pl[1]$ $cc[1]$ $tfm[3]$ $dvi[pl]$. This short form specifies a virtual character in the common case when $0 \le pl < 242$ and $0 \le cc < 256$ and $0 \le tfm < 2^{24}$.

Here pl denotes the packet length following the tfm value; cc is the character code; and tfm is the character width copied from the TFM file for this virtual font. There should be at most one character packet having any given cc code.

The dvi bytes are a sequence of complete DVI commands, properly nested with respect to *push* and *pop*. All DVI operations are permitted except *bop*, *eop*, and commands with opcodes ≥ 243. Font selection commands (*fnt_num0* through *fnt4*) must refer to fonts defined in the preamble.

Dimensions that appear in the DVI instructions are analogous to *fix_word* quantities; i.e., they are integer multiples of 2^{-20} times the design size of the virtual font. For example, if the virtual font has design size 10 pt, the DVI command to move down 5 pt would be a *down* instruction with parameter 2^{19}. The virtual font itself might be used at a different size, say 12 pt; then that *down* instruction would move down 6 pt instead. Each dimension must be less than 2^{24} in absolute value.

Device drivers processing VF files treat the sequences of dvi bytes as subroutines or macros, implicitly enclosing them with *push* and *pop*. Each subroutine begins with $w = x = y = z = 0$, and with current font f the number of the first-defined font in the preamble (undefined if there's no such font). After the *dvi* commands have been performed, the *h* and *v* position registers of DVI format and the current font *f* are restored to their former values; then, if the subroutine has been invoked by a *set_char* or *set* command, *h* is increased by the TFM width (properly scaled) — just as if a simple character had been typeset.

9. The character packets are followed by a trivial postamble, consisting of one or more bytes all equal to *post* (248). The total number of bytes in the file should be a multiple of 4.

And Here Are Excerpts from VPtoVF.web

5. Property list description of font metric data. The idea behind VPL files is that precise details about fonts, i.e., the facts that are needed by typesetting routines like TEX, sometimes have to be supplied by hand. The nested property-list format provides a reasonably convenient way to do this.

A good deal of computation is necessary to parse and process a VPL file, so it would be inappropriate for TEX itself to do this every time it loads a font. TEX deals only with the compact descriptions of font metric data that appear in TFM files. Such data is so compact, however, it is almost impossible for anybody but a computer to read it.

Device drivers also need a compact way to describe mappings from TEX's idea of a font to the actual characters a device can produce. They can do this conveniently when given a packed sequence of bytes called a VF file.

The purpose of VPtoVF is to convert from a human-oriented file of text to computer-oriented files of binary numbers. There's a companion program, VFtoVP, which goes the other way.

7. A VPL file is like a PL file with a few extra features, so we can begin to define it by reviewing the definition of PL files. The material in the next few sections is copied from the program PLtoTF.

A PL file is a list of entries of the form

(PROPERTYNAME VALUE)

where the property name is one of a finite set of names understood by this program, and the value may itself in turn be a property list. The idea is best understood by looking at an example, so let's consider a fragment of the PL file for a hypothetical font.

```
(FAMILY NOVA)
(FACE F MIE)
(CODINGSCHEME ASCII)
(DESIGNSIZE D 10)
(DESIGNUNITS D 18)
(COMMENT A COMMENT IS IGNORED)
```

```
(COMMENT (EXCEPT THIS ONE ISN'T))
(COMMENT (ACTUALLY IT IS, EVEN THOUGH
        IT SAYS IT ISN'T))
(FONTDIMEN
    (SLANT R -.25)
    (SPACE D 6)
    (SHRINK D 2)
    (STRETCH D 3)
    (XHEIGHT R 10.55)
    (QUAD D 18)
    )
(LIGTABLE
    (LABEL C f)
    (LIG C f O 200)
    (SKIP D 1)
    (LABEL O 200)
    (LIG C i O 201)
    (KRN O 51 R 1.5)
    (/LIG C ? C f)
    (STOP)
    )
(CHARACTER C f
    (CHARWD D 6)
    (CHARHT R 13.5)
    (CHARIC R 1.5)
    )
```

This example says that the font whose metric information is being described belongs to the hypothetical NOVA family; its face code is medium italic extended; and the characters appear in ASCII code positions. The design size is 10 points, and all other sizes in this PL file are given in units such that 18 units equals the design size. The font is slanted with a slope of −.25 (hence the letters actually slant backward—perhaps that is why the family name is NOVA). The normal space between words is 6 units (i.e., one third of the 18-unit design size), with glue that shrinks by 2 units or stretches by 3. The letters for which accents don't need to be raised or lowered are 10.55 units high, and one em equals 18 units.

The example ligature table is a bit trickier. It specifies that the letter f followed by another f is changed to code ´200, while code ´200 followed by i is changed to ´201; presumably codes ´200 and ´201 represent the ligatures 'ff' and 'ffi'. Moreover, in both cases f and ´200, if the following character is the code ´51 (which is a right parenthesis), an additional 1.5 units of space should be inserted before the ´51. (The 'SKIP D 1' skips over one LIG or KRN command, which in this case is the second LIG; in this way two different ligature/kern programs can come together.) Finally, there's an example—

although a rather strange one — of the "smart ligatures" introduced in TEX version 3.0: If either f or '200 is followed by a question mark, the question mark is replaced by f and the ligature program is started over. (Thus, the character pair 'f?' would become the ligature 'ff', and 'ff?' or 'f?f' would become 'fff'. If this /LIG command had been /LIG> instead, the restarting would be omitted; 'f?' would become 'ff' and 'f?f' would become 'fff'.)

Character f itself is 6 units wide and 13.5 units tall, in this example. Its depth is zero (since CHARDP is not given), and its italic correction is 1.5 units.

8. The example above illustrates most of the features found in PL files. Note that some property names, like FAMILY or COMMENT, take a string as their value; this string continues until the first unmatched right parenthesis. But most property names, like DESIGNSIZE and SLANT and LABEL, take a number as their value. This number can be expressed in a variety of ways, indicated by a prefixed code; D stands for decimal, H for hexadecimal, O for octal, R for real, C for character, and F for "face." Other property names, like LIG, take two numbers as their value. And still other names, like FONTDIMEN and LIGTABLE and CHARACTER, have more complicated values that involve property lists.

A property name is supposed to be used only in an appropriate property list. For example, CHARWD shouldn't occur on the outer level or within FONTDIMEN.

The individual property-and-value pairs in a property list can appear in any order. For instance, 'SHRINK' precedes 'STRETCH' in the example above, although the TFM file always puts the stretch parameter first. One could even give the information about characters like 'f' before specifying the number of units in the design size, or before specifying the ligature and kerning table. However, the LIGTABLE itself is an exception to this rule; the individual elements of the LIGTABLE property list can be reordered only to a certain extent without changing the meaning of that table.

If property-and-value pairs are omitted, a default value is used. For example, we have already noted that the default for CHARDP is zero. The default for *every* numeric value is, in fact, zero, unless otherwise stated below.

If the same property name is used more than once, VPtoVF will not notice the discrepancy; it simply uses the final value given. Once again, however, the LIGTABLE is an exception to this rule; VPtoVF will complain if there is more than one label for some character. And of course many of the entries in the LIGTABLE property list have the same property name.

9. A VPL file also includes information about how to create each character, by typesetting characters from other fonts and/or by drawing lines, etc. Such information is the value of the 'MAP' property, which can be illustrated as follows:

```
(MAPFONT D 0 (FONTNAME Times-Roman))
(MAPFONT D 1 (FONTNAME Symbol))
(MAPFONT D 2 (FONTNAME cmr10)(FONTAT D 20))
```

```
(CHARACTER O 0 (MAP (SELECTFONT D 1)(SETCHAR C G)))
(CHARACTER O 76 (MAP (SETCHAR O 277)))
(CHARACTER D 197 (MAP
    (PUSH)(SETCHAR C A)(POP)
    (MOVEUP R 0.937)(MOVERIGHT R 1.5)(SETCHAR O 312)))
(CHARACTER O 200 (MAP (MOVEDOWN R 2.1)(SETRULE R 1 R 8)))
(CHARACTER O 201 (MAP
    (SPECIAL ps: /SaveGray currentgray def .5 setgray)
    (SELECTFONT D 2)(SETCHAR C A)
    (SPECIAL ps: SaveGray setgray)))
```

(These specifications appear in addition to the conventional PL information. The MAP attribute can be mixed in with other attributes like CHARWD or it can be given separately.)

In this example, the virtual font is composed of characters that can be fabricated from three actual fonts, 'Times–Roman', 'Symbol', and 'cmr10 at 20\u' (where \u is the unit size in this VPL file). Character ´0 is typeset as a 'G' from the Symbol font. Character ´76 is typeset as character ´277 from the ordinary Times font. (If no other font is selected, font number 0 is the default. If no MAP attribute is given, the default map is a character of the same number in the default font.)

Character 197 (decimal) is more interesting: First an A is typeset (in the default font Times), and this is enclosed by PUSH and POP so that the original position is restored. Then the accent character ´312 is typeset, after moving up .937 units and right 1.5 units.

To typeset character ´200 in this virtual font, we move down 2.1 units, then typeset a rule that is 1 unit high and 8 units wide.

Finally, to typeset character ´201 , we do something that requires a special ability to interpret PostScript commands; this example sets the PostScript "color" to 50% gray and typesets an 'A' from cmr10 at 20\u in that color.

In general, the MAP attribute of a virtual character can be any sequence of typesetting commands that might appear in a page of a DVI file. A single character might map into an entire page.

10. But instead of relying on a hypothetical example, let's consider a complete grammar for VPL files, beginning with the (unchanged) grammatical rules for PL files. At the outermost level, the following property names are valid in any PL file:

CHECKSUM (four-byte value). The value, which should be a nonnegative integer less than 2^{32}, is used to identify a particular version of a font; it should match the check sum value stored with the font itself. An explicit check sum of zero is used to bypass check sum testing. If no checksum is specified in the VPL file, VPtoVF will compute the checksum that METAFONT would compute from the same data.

DESIGNSIZE (numeric value, default is 10). The value, which should be a real number in the range $1.0 \leq x < 2048$, represents the default amount by which all quantities will be scaled if the font is not loaded with an 'at' specification. For example, if one says '\font\A=cmr10 at 15pt' in TeX language, the design size in the TFM file is ignored and effectively replaced by 15 points; but if one simply says '\font\A=cmr10' the stated design size is used. This quantity is always in units of printer's points.

DESIGNUNITS (numeric value, default is 1). The value should be a positive real number; it says how many units equals the design size (or the eventual 'at' size, if the font is being scaled). For example, suppose you have a font that has been digitized with 600 pixels per em, and the design size is one em; then you could say '(DESIGNUNITS R 600)' if you wanted to give all of your measurements in units of pixels.

CODINGSCHEME (string value, default is 'UNSPECIFIED'). The string should not contain parentheses, and its length must be less than 40. It identifies the correspondence between the numeric codes and font characters. (TeX ignores this information, but other software programs might make use of it.)

FAMILY (string value, default is 'UNSPECIFIED'). The string should not contain parentheses, and its length must be less than 20. It identifies the name of the family to which this font belongs, e.g., 'HELVETICA'. (TeX ignores this information; but it is needed, for example, when converting DVI files to PRESS files for Xerox equipment.)

FACE (one-byte value). This number, which must lie between 0 and 255 inclusive, is a subsidiary identification of the font within its family. For example, bold italic condensed fonts might have the same family name as light roman extended fonts, differing only in their face byte. (TeX ignores this information; but it is needed, for example, when converting DVI files to PRESS files for Xerox equipment.)

SEVENBITSAFEFLAG (string value, default is 'FALSE'). The value should start with either 'T' (true) or 'F' (false). If true, character codes less than 128 cannot lead to codes of 128 or more via ligatures or charlists or extensible characters. (TeX82 ignores this flag, but older versions of TeX would only accept TFM files that were seven-bit safe.) VPtoVF computes the correct value of this flag and gives an error message only if a claimed "true" value is incorrect.

HEADER (a one-byte value followed by a four-byte value). The one-byte value should be between 18 and a maximum limit that can be raised or lowered depending on the compile-time setting of *max_header_bytes*. The four-byte value goes into the header word whose index is the one-byte value; for example, to set *header*[18] $\leftarrow$ 1, one may write '(HEADER D 18 0 1)'. This notation is used for header information that is presently unnamed. (TeX ignores it.)

FONTDIMEN (property list value). See below for the names allowed in this property list.

LIGTABLE (property list value). See below for the rules about this special kind of property list.

BOUNDARYCHAR (one-byte value). If this character appears in a LIGTABLE command, it matches "end of word" as well as itself. If no boundary character is given and no LABEL BOUNDARYCHAR occurs within LIGTABLE, word boundaries will not affect ligatures or kerning.

CHARACTER. The value is a one-byte integer followed by a property list. The integer represents the number of a character that is present in the font; the property list of a character is defined below. The default is an empty property list.

11. Numeric property list values can be given in various forms identified by a prefixed letter.

C denotes an ASCII character, which should be a standard visible character that is not a parenthesis. The numeric value will therefore be between ´41 and ´176 but not ´50 or ´51.

D denotes an unsigned decimal integer, which must be less than 2^{32}, i.e., at most 'D 4294967295'.

F denotes a three-letter Xerox face code; the admissible codes are MRR, MIR, BRR, BIR, LRR, LIR, MRC, MIC, BRC, BIC, LRC, LIC, MRE, MIE, BRE, BIE, LRE, and LIE, denoting the integers 0 to 17, respectively.

O denotes an unsigned octal integer, which must be less than 2^{32}, i.e., at most 'O 37777777777'.

H denotes an unsigned hexadecimal integer, which must be less than 2^{32}, i.e., at most 'H FFFFFFFF'.

R denotes a real number in decimal notation, optionally preceded by a '+' or '-' sign, and optionally including a decimal point. The absolute value must be less than 2048.

12. The property names allowed in a FONTDIMEN property list correspond to various TeX parameters, each of which has a (real) numeric value. All of the parameters except SLANT are in design units. The admissible names are SLANT, SPACE, STRETCH, SHRINK, XHEIGHT, QUAD, EXTRASPACE, NUM1, NUM2, NUM3, DENOM1, DENOM2, SUP1, SUP2, SUP3, SUB1, SUB2, SUPDROP, SUBDROP, DELIM1, DELIM2, and AXISHEIGHT, for parameters 1 to 22. The alternate names DEFAULTRULETHICKNESS, BIGOPSPACING1, BIGOPSPACING2, BIGOPSPACING3, BIGOPSPACING4, and BIGOPSPACING5, may also be used for parameters 8 to 13.

The notation 'PARAMETER n' provides another way to specify the nth parameter; for example, '(PARAMETER D 1 R -.25)' is another way to specify that the SLANT is -0.25. The value of n must be positive and less than max_param_words.

13. The elements of a `CHARACTER` property list can be of six different types.

`CHARWD` (real value) denotes the character's width in design units.

`CHARHT` (real value) denotes the character's height in design units.

`CHARDP` (real value) denotes the character's depth in design units.

`CHARIC` (real value) denotes the character's italic correction in design units.

`NEXTLARGER` (one-byte value), specifies the character that follows the present one in a "charlist." The value must be the number of a character in the font, and there must be no infinite cycles of supposedly larger and larger characters.

`VARCHAR` (property list value), specifies an extensible character. This option and `NEXTLARGER` are mutually exclusive; i.e., they cannot both be used within the same `CHARACTER` list.

The elements of a `VARCHAR` property list are either `TOP`, `MID`, `BOT` or `REP`; the values are integers, which must be zero or the number of a character in the font. A zero value for `TOP`, `MID`, or `BOT` means that the corresponding piece of the extensible character is absent. A nonzero value, or a `REP` value of zero, denotes the character code used to make up the top, middle, bottom, or replicated piece of an extensible character.

14. A `LIGTABLE` property list contains elements of four kinds, specifying a program in a simple command language that TEX uses for ligatures and kerns. If several `LIGTABLE` lists appear, they are effectively concatenated into a single list.

`LABEL` (one-byte value) means that the program for the stated character value starts here. The integer must be the number of a character in the font; its `CHARACTER` property list must not have a `NEXTLARGER` or `VARCHAR` field. At least one `LIG` or `KRN` step must follow.

`LABEL BOUNDARYCHAR` means that the program for beginning-of-word ligatures starts here.

`LIG` (two one-byte values). The instruction '`(LIG` c r`)`' means, "If the next character is c, then insert character r and possibly delete the current character and/or c; otherwise go on to the next instruction." Characters r and c must be present in the font. `LIG` may be immediately preceded or followed by a slash, and then immediately followed by `>` characters not exceeding the number of slashes. Thus there are eight possible forms:

> `LIG   /LIG   /LIG>   LIG/   LIG/>   /LIG/   /LIG/>   /LIG/>>`

The slashes specify retention of the left or right original character; the `>` signs specify passing over the result without further ligature processing.

`KRN` (a one-byte value and a real value). The instruction '`(KRN` c r`)`' means, "If the next character is c, then insert a blank space of width r between the current character character and c; otherwise go on to the next intruction." The value of r, which is in design units, is often negative. Character code c must exist in the font.

STOP (no value). This instruction ends a ligature/kern program. It must follow either a LIG or KRN instruction, not a LABEL or STOP or SKIP.

SKIP (value in the range 0 .. 127). This instruction specifies continuation of a ligature/kern program after the specified number of LIG or KRN steps has been skipped over. The number of subsequent LIG and KRN instructions must therefore exceed this specified amount.

15. In addition to all these possibilities, the property name COMMENT is allowed in any property list. Such comments are ignored.

16. So that is what PL files hold. In a VPL file additional properties are recognized; two of these are valid on the outermost level:

VTITLE (string value, default is empty). The value will be reproduced at the beginning of the VF file (and printed on the terminal by VFtoVP when it examines that file).

MAPFONT. The value is a nonnegative integer followed by a property list. The integer represents an identifying number for fonts used in MAP attributes. The property list, which identifies the font and relative size, is defined below.

And one additional "virtual property" is valid within a CHARACTER:

MAP. The value is a property list consisting of typesetting commands. Default is the single command SETCHAR c, where c is the current character number.

17. The elements of a MAPFONT property list can be of the following types.

FONTNAME (string value, default is NULL). This is the font's identifying name.

FONTAREA (string value, default is empty). If the font appears in a nonstandard directory, according to local conventions, the directory name is given here. (This is system dependent, just as in DVI files.)

FONTCHECKSUM (four-byte value, default is zero). This value, which should be a nonnegative integer less than 2^{32}, can be used to check that the font being referred to matches the intended font. If nonzero, it should equal the CHECKSUM parameter in that font.

FONTAT (numeric value, default is the DESIGNUNITS of the present virtual font). This value is relative to the design units of the present virtual font, hence it will be scaled when the virtual font is magnified or reduced. It represents the value that will effectively replace the design size of the font being referred to, so that all characters will be scaled appropriately.

FONTDSIZE (numeric value, default is 10). This value is absolute, in units of printer's points. It should equal the DESIGNSIZE parameter in the font being referred to.

If any of the string values contain parentheses, the parentheses must be balanced. Leading blanks are removed from the strings, but trailing blanks are not.

18. Finally, the elements of a MAP property list are an ordered sequence of typesetting commands chosen from among the following:

SELECTFONT (four-byte integer value). The value must be the number of a previously defined MAPFONT. This font (or more precisely, the final font that is mapped to that code number, if two MAPFONT properties happen to specify the same code) will be used in subsequent SETCHAR instructions until overridden by another SELECTFONT. The first-specified MAPFONT is implicitly selected before the first SELECTFONT in every character's map.

SETCHAR (one-byte integer value). There must be a character of this number in the currently selected font. (VPtoVF doesn't check that the character is valid, but VFtoVP does.) That character is typeset at the current position, and the typesetter moves right by the CHARWD in that character's TFM file.

SETRULE (two real values). The first value specifies height, the second specifies width, in design units. If both height and width are positive, a solid black rectangle is typeset with its lower left corner at the current position. Then the typesetter moves right, by the specified width.

MOVERIGHT, MOVELEFT, MOVEUP, MOVEDOWN (real value). The typesetter moves its current position by the number of design units specified.

PUSH. The current typesetter position is remembered, to be restored on a subsequent POP.

POP. The current typesetter position is reset to where it was on the most recent unmatched PUSH. The PUSH and POP commands in any MAP must be properly nested like balanced parentheses.

SPECIAL (string value). The subsequent characters, starting with the first nonblank and ending just before the first ')' that has no matching '(', are interpreted according to local conventions with the same system-dependent meaning as a 'special' (xxx) command in a DVI file.

SPECIALHEX (hexadecimal string value). The subsequent nonblank characters before the next ')' must consist entirely of hexadecimal digits, and they must contain an even number of such digits. Each pair of hex digits specifies a byte, and this string of bytes is treated just as the value of a SPECIAL. (This convention permits arbitrary byte strings to be represented in an ordinary text file.)

19. Virtual font mapping is a recursive process, like macro expansion. Thus, a MAPFONT might specify another virtual font, whose characters are themselves mapped to other fonts. As an example of this possibility, consider the following curious file called `recurse.vpl`, which defines a virtual font that is self-contained and self-referential:

```
(VTITLE Example of recursion)
(MAPFONT D 0 (FONTNAME recurse)(FONTAT D 2))
(CHARACTER C A
  (CHARWD D 1)(CHARHT D 1)(MAP (SETRULE D 1 D 1)))
(CHARACTER C B
  (CHARWD D 2)(CHARHT D 2)(MAP (SETCHAR C A)))
(CHARACTER C C
  (CHARWD D 4)(CHARHT D 4)(MAP (SETCHAR C B)))
```

The design size is 10 points (the default), hence the character A in font `recurse` is a 10×10 point black square. Character B is typeset as character A in `recurse` scaled 2000, hence it is a 20×20 point black square. And character C is typeset as character B in `recurse` scaled 2000, hence its size is 40×40.

Virtual font designers should be careful to avoid infinite recursion.

News from St. Anford Press

[For release 24 August 1988]

We now offer a typeface named after San Serifo, the famous martyr whose life was chronicled by Father Font in 1776. Japanese customers may prefer the Serifu-San variation.

The designer, L. C. "Bo" Doni, says that she was inspired primarily by recent brochures from type foundries in which the term "sans serif" is spelled sans s. She is currently working on a sans-stem font, due to be released next year.

San Serifo and Serifu-San are available in many weights, from ultra-lite to obese, and in all major digital formats including FalseType[DM].

Chapter 13

The Letter S

[Originally published in The Mathematical Intelligencer **2** *(1980),
114–122.]*

Several years ago when I began to look at the problem of designing suitable alphabets for use with modern printing equipment, I found that
25 of the letters were comparatively easy to deal with. The other letter
was S. For three days and nights I had a terrible time trying to understand how a proper S could really be defined. The solution I finally came
up with turned out to involve some interesting mathematics, and I believe that students of calculus and analytic geometry may enjoy looking
into the question as I did. The purpose of this paper is to explain what
I now consider to be the "right" mathematics underlying printed S's,
and also to give an example of the METAFONT language I have recently
been developing.* (A complete description of METAFONT, which is a
computer system and language intended to aid in the design of letter
shapes, appears in [3, part 3].)

Before getting into a technical discussion, I should probably mention
why I started worrying about such things in the first place. The central
reason is that today's printing technology is essentially based on discrete
mathematics and computer science, not on the properties of metals or
of movable type. The task of making a plate for a printed page is now
essentially that of constructing a gigantic matrix of 0s and 1s, where the
0s specify white space and the 1s specify ink. I wanted the second edition
of one of my books to look like the first edition, although the first edition
had been typeset with the old hot-lead technology; and when I realized
that this problem could be solved by using appropriate techniques of
discrete mathematics and computer science, I couldn't resist trying to
find my own solution.

---

* All of the letters and symbols in this report were designed mathematically,
using METAFONT, and typeset with the author's experimental software.

Reference [2] explains more of the background of my work, and it also discusses the early history of mathematical approaches to type design. In particular, it illustrates how several people proposed to construct S's geometrically with ruler and compass during the sixteenth and seventeenth centuries.

Francesco Torniello published a geometric alphabet in 1517 that is typical of these early approaches. Let's look at his construction of an S (Figure 1, taken from page 45 of [4]), in order to get some feeling for the problems involved. Paraphrasing his words into modern mathematical terminology, we can state the method as follows:

> An S is drawn in a 9×9 square that we can represent by Cartesian coordinates (x, y) for $0 \le x \le 9$ and $0 \le y \le 9$. We shall define 14 points on the boundary of the letter, calling them (x_1, y_1), (x_2, y_2), ..., (x_{14}, y_{14}). Point 1 is $(4.5, 9)$, and a circular arc is drawn from this point with center at $(4.5, 5.5)$ and radius 3.5 ending at point 2 where $x_2 = 6$. [Hence $y_2 = 5.5 + \sqrt{10} \approx 8.66$.] A small arc is drawn with center $(6.5, 9)$ and radius .5 from point $3 = (6.5, 8.5)$ to $(7, 9)$. A straight line is drawn from point $4 = (6, 7)$ to where it is tangent to this small arc; let us call this point 5. [We shall see below that point 5 has the coordinates $(6\frac{16}{17}, 8\frac{13}{17})$; it is interesting to speculate about whether Torniello would have been happy to know this.] Now an arc is drawn with center $(4, 7)$ and radius 2, from point $6 = (4, 9)$ down to point 7 where $x_7 = 3$ and $y_7 < 7$ [hence $y_7 = 7 - \sqrt{3} \approx 5.27$]. A straight line is drawn from point 7 to point $8 = (5, 4)$. An arc centered at $(4.5, 7\frac{1}{8})$ is now drawn from point 4 to point $9 = (3.5, 6)$, and a straight line continues from there to point $10 = (6, 4.5)$. A half-circle runs from this point to point $11 = (3, 0.5)$, with center $(4.5, 2.5)$ and radius 2.5. Another small circular arc is now drawn with center at $(2.5, y)$ and radius 1, from point 11 to point 12 where $x_{12} = 1\frac{7}{8}$ [hence $y = (1 - \sqrt{3})/2 \approx -.37$ and $y_{12} = (\sqrt{39} + 4 - 4\sqrt{3})/8 \approx 0.41$]. Circular arcs of radius 2 are drawn from point 8 to point 13 with the center x-coordinate equal to 4 and with $x_{13} = 4.5$ [hence the center is $(4, 4 - \sqrt{3}) \approx (4, 2.27)$ and $y_{13} = 4 - \sqrt{3} - \sqrt{3.75} \approx 0.33$], and from point 13 to point 14 with the center x-coordinate equal to 4.5 and with $y_{14} = 2$ [hence the center is $(4.5, 6 - \sqrt{3} - \sqrt{3.75}) \approx (4.5, 2.33)$, and
>
> $$x_{14} = 4.5 - \sqrt{4 - (4 - \sqrt{3} - \sqrt{3.75})^2}$$
>
> is approximately 2.53]. Finally a straight line runs from point 14 to point 12.

The reader will find it interesting to take a piece of graph paper and carry out this vintage construction before proceeding further. Torniello's description was actually not so precise as this, and I have tried to make

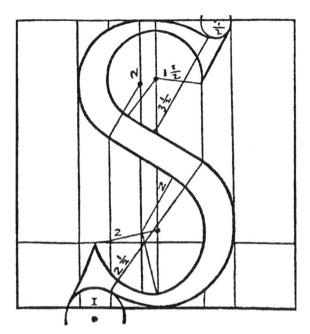

FIGURE 1. Francesco Torniello's method of "squaring the S" in 1517.

as much sense out of his words as possible; it seems that he had as much trouble with S's as I did, because his other letters are much more clearly defined. The main editorial revision I have made is to change the center of the arc between points 4 and 9 from Torniello's $(4.5, 7\frac{1}{6})$ to the nearby point $(4.5, 7\frac{1}{8})$, and to leave its radius unstated (he said that the radius would be 1.5, but actually it is $\sqrt{145}/8$, a trifle higher), since $(4.5, 7\frac{1}{6})$ is not equidistant from points 4 and 9.

Notice that the circular arc between points 10 and 11 is tangent to the baseline at $(4.5, 0)$ and it has a vertical tangent at point $(7, 2.5)$; this works out nicely because

$$3^2 + 4^2 = 5^2,$$

and I believe Torniello did know enough mathematics to make use of this pleasant coincidence in his design. He never stated exactly what curves should be used between points 1 and 6 or between points 2 and 3; apparently a straight line segment should join 1 and 6, while the other curve is to be filled with whatever looks right.

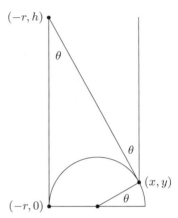

FIGURE 2.

A problem that arises in Torniello's construction: Find x and y, given r and h.

The calculation of point 5 suggests an elementary but instructive exercise in analytic geometry: *Given positive numbers h and r, find the point (x, y) in the upper right portion of a circle of radius r, centered at the origin, such that the straight line from $(-r, h)$ to (x, y) is tangent to the circle at (x, y).* (See Figure 2.) We have $x^2 + y^2 = r^2$ and $y/x = \tan\theta = (x + r)/(h - y)$, hence $x^2 + rx + y^2 - yh = 0$ and $rx = hy - r^2$. This leads to the equation $(hy - r^2)hy + r^2y(y - h) = rx(rx + r^2) + r^2y(y - h) = 0$, hence $y(h^2y - hr^2 + r^2y - hr^2) = 0$ and we soon obtain the desired solution

$$x = \frac{h^2 r - r^3}{h^2 + r^2}, \qquad y = \frac{2hr^2}{h^2 + r^2}.$$

The solution is a rational function of h and r (i.e., no square roots are needed) because the other tangent point is $(-r, 0)$; this other point also satisfies the stated equations. René Descartes would surely have liked this demonstration of the power of his coordinate system.

Torniello's construction can be expressed without difficulty in the METAFONT language, a language that I have recently developed for stating definitions of character shapes in a form that is convenient for computer processing. Although ruler-and-compass methods do not really use very many of METAFONT's abilities, we can learn something about METAFONT by looking at this as a first example.

The key points of a particular design are specified in METAFONTese by writing equations for their x and y coordinates; then you can say 'draw $i \ldots j$' to draw a straight line from point i to point j. You can also say 'draw $i\{\alpha, \beta\} \ldots j\{\gamma, \delta\}$' to draw a curve from point i starting in the direction of the vector (α, β) and ending at point j in direction (γ, δ).

This curve will be a circular arc if there is a circle passing through i and j in the stated directions, provided that the circular arc is at most a half-circle. Thus, Torniello's construction can be expressed with complete precision by the following METAFONT program:

$x_1 = 4.5u;\ \ y_1 = 9u;$
$x_2 = 6u;\ \ y_2 - 5.5u = \mathbf{sqrt}\,((3.5u)(3.5u) - (x_2 - 4.5u)(x_2 - 4.5u));$
$\mathbf{draw}\ 1\{y_1 - 5.5u, 4.5u - x_1\} .. 2\{y_2 - 5.5u, 4.5u - x_2\};$
$x_3 = 6.5u;\ \ y_3 = 8.5u;$
$x_4 = 6u;\ \ y_4 = 7u;$
$x_5 = (6 + 16/17)u;\ \ y_5 = (8 + 13/17)u;$
$\mathbf{draw}\ 3\{9u - y_3, x_3 - 6.5u\} .. 5\{9u - y_5, x_5 - 6.5u\};$
$\mathbf{draw}\ 4 .. 5;$
$x_6 = 4u;\ \ y_6 = 9u;$
$x_7 = 3u;\ \ 7u - y_7 = \mathbf{sqrt}\,((2u)(2u) - (x_7 - 4u)(x_7 - 4u));$
$\mathbf{draw}\ 6\{7u - y_6, x_6 - 4u\} .. 7\{7u - y_7, x_7 - 4u\};$
$x_8 = 5u;\ \ y_8 = 4u;\ \ \mathbf{draw}\ 7 .. 8;$
$x_9 = 3.5u;\ \ y_9 = 6u;$
$x_{15} = 4.5u;\ \ y_{15} - 7.125u =$
$\qquad \mathbf{sqrt}\,((x_9 - 4.5u)(x_9 - 4.5u) + (y_9 - 7.125u)(y_9 - 7.125u));$
$\mathbf{draw}\ 4\{7.125u - y_4, x_4 - 4.5u\} .. 15 .. 9\{7.125u - y_9, x_9 - 4.5u\};$
$x_{10} = 6u;\ \ y_{10} = 4.5u;\ \ \mathbf{draw}\ 9 .. 10;$
$x_{11} = 3u;\ \ y_{11} = .5u;$
$\mathbf{draw}\ 10\{y_{10} - 2.5u, 4.5u - x_{10}\} .. 11\{y_{11} - 2.5u, 4.5u - x_{11}\};$
$x_{16} = 2.5u;\ \ y_{11} - y_{16} = \mathbf{sqrt}\,((u)(u) - (x_{11} - x_{16})(x_{11} - x_{16}));$
$x_{12} = 1.875u;\ \ y_{12} - y_{16} = \mathbf{sqrt}\,((u)(u) - (x_{12} - x_{16})(x_{12} - x_{16}));$
$\mathbf{draw}\ 11\{y_{16} - y_{11}, x_{11} - x_{16}\} .. 12\{y_{16} - y_{12}, x_{12} - x_{16}\};$
$x_{13} = 4.5u;\ \ x_{17} = 4u;$
$y_8 - y_{17} = \mathbf{sqrt}\,((2u)(2u) - (x_8 - x_{17})(x_8 - x_{17}));$
$y_{17} - y_{13} = \mathbf{sqrt}\,((2u)(2u) - (x_{13} - x_{17})(x_{13} - x_{17}));$
$\mathbf{draw}\ 8\{y_8 - y_{17}, x_{17} - x_8\} .. 13\{y_{13} - y_{17}, x_{17} - x_{13}\};$
$x_{18} = 4.5u;\ \ y_{18} - y_{13} = \mathbf{sqrt}\,((2u)(2u) - (x_{18} - x_{13})(x_{18} - x_{13}));$
$y_{14} = 2u;\ \ x_{18} - x_{14} = \mathbf{sqrt}\,((2u)(2u) - (y_{18} - y_{14})(y_{18} - y_{14}));$
$\mathbf{draw}\ 13\{y_{13} - y_{18}, x_{18} - x_{13}\} .. 14\{y_{14} - y_{18}, x_{18} - x_{14}\};$
$\mathbf{draw}\ 14 .. 12.$

Here "u" is an arbitrary unit of measure that can be used as a scale factor to control the overall size of the drawing. This program looks somewhat formidable at first glance, but it really is not hard to understand once you compare it to the informal English description given earlier. A few more points, labeled 15, 16, 17, and 18, have been introduced; point 15 coaxes METAFONT to draw a circular arc bigger than a

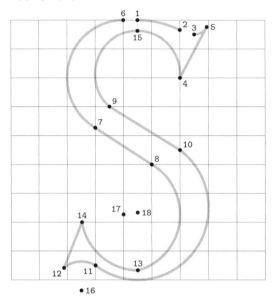

FIGURE 3. The METAFONT program in the text will produce this rendition of Torniello's S.

semicircle, and the other three points are centers of arcs in the construction. The main fact used throughout is that a circular arc with center
(x_k, y_k) that passes clockwise through point (x_i, y_i) is going in direction
$\{y_i - y_k, x_k - x_i\}$, while if the arc is going counterclockwise its direction
is $\{y_k - y_i, x_i - x_k\}$.

Figure 3 shows what METAFONT draws from the given specifications. METAFONT will also complete the drawing with appropriate
non-circular curves if we add the commands

draw $1 .. 6$;
draw $2\{y_2 - 5.5u, 4.5u - x_2\} .. 3\{9u - y_3, x_3 - 6.5u\}$.

These tangent directions match the tangents at which the new curves
touch the old. If we ask METAFONT to fill in the space between these
boundary curves, we obtain Figure 4.

When the circular arc comes to point 7 from point 6, it is traveling in direction $\{7u - y_7, x_7 - 4u\} = \{\sqrt{3}u, -u\}$, but when it proceeds
from point 7 in a straight line to point 8 it shifts abruptly to direction $\{x_8 - x_7, y_8 - y_7\} = \{2u, (\sqrt{3} - 3)u\}$. This discontinuity is only
slightly noticeable in Figure 4, but it is unsatisfactory from a mathematical standpoint. Similar discontinuities occur at points 8, 9, 10, 11,

FIGURE 4.
The curve of Fig. 3, completed
and filled in.

and 13, the problems at points 9 and 13 being especially prominent; the
illustrations in Torniello's book had to be fudged slightly to hide these
defects (which Torniello did not mention). Contemporary standards of
accuracy were presumably not very stringent in the sixteenth century,
but nowadays we do not want our computers to draw such bumpy lines.

FIGURE 5.
A slight modification of Fig. 4 makes the
curves smoother at the junction points.

Since METAFONT has no special commitment to circular arcs, it will automatically make adjustments like Torniello's illustrator did if we just specify consistent directions at all of the key points. Figure 5 shows the result if the tangents at points 7, 8, 9, and 10 are taken as the directions of the straight line segments and if the direction at point 13 is horizontal. The direction at point 11 corresponds to the circular arc from point 10. Furthermore point 6 has been moved over to coincide with point 1, so that the unfortunate flat spot at the top is avoided. The curves touching these points are not circles any longer, but they are close enough to fool most people, and it seems unlikely that Torniello would have been offended by this approximation.

A Renaissance "S" looks somewhat skinny to modern eyes. We can ask METAFONT to flesh it out by increasing all the x coordinates by 20% while leaving the y coordinates fixed; Figure 6 shows the result. Notice that this stretching turns circles into ellipses. Torniello would have had considerable difficulty trying to specify such a shape in terms of strictly circular arcs; we are reminded of the early astronomers who found it very cumbersome to use circles instead of ellipses as models of planetary orbits.

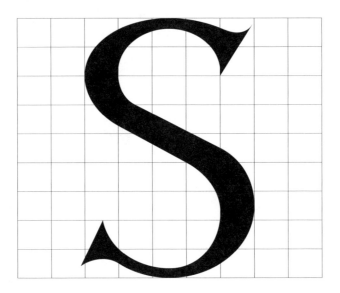

FIGURE 6. When Fig. 5 is stretched 20% in the horizontal direction, we obtain this figure; the circles have become ellipses.

By studying this example we can get some idea of the problems involved in specifying a proper S shape. However, I was actually seeking the solution to a more general problem than the one Torniello faced: Instead of specifying only one particular S, I needed many different variations, including bold face **S**'s that are much darker than the normal text. I discussed this recently with Alan Perlis, who pointed out that a central issue arising whenever we try to automate something properly is what he calls "the art of making constant things variable." In the case of letter design, we don't merely want to take a particular drawing and come up with some mathematics to describe it; we really want to find the principles underlying the drawing, so that we can generate infinitely many drawings (including the given one) as a function of appropriate parameters. My goal was to create entire alphabets that would depend on a dozen or two parameters in such a way that all the letters would vary in a compatible manner as the parameters would change.

After looking at these Renaissance constructions and a lot of modern S shapes, I came to the conclusion that the main stroke of the general S curve I sought would be analogous to the curve in Figure 6; each boundary curve was to be an ellipse followed by a straight line followed by another ellipse. This led me to pose the following problem: *What ellipse has its topmost point at (x_t, y_t) and its leftmost point at (x_l, y_l) for some y_l, and is tangent to the straight line of slope σ that passes through (x_c, y_c), given the values of x_t, y_t, x_l, σ, x_c, and y_c?* (The ellipse in question is supposed to have the coordinate axes as its major and minor axes; in other words, it should have left-right symmetry. See Figure 7 on the next page.) The reason for my posing this problem should be fairly clear from our previous discussions: We know a point that is supposed to be the top of the S curve, and we also know how far the curve should extend to the left; furthermore we have a straight line in mind that will form the middle link of the stroke.

The problem stated in the preceding paragraph is interesting to me for several reasons. In the first place, it has a nice answer (as we will see). In the second place, the answer does in fact lead to satisfactory S curves. In the third place, the answer isn't completely trivial; during a period of two years or so I came across this problem four different times and each time I was unable to find my notes about how to solve it, so I spent several hours deriving and rederiving the formulas whenever I needed them. Finally I decided to write this paper so that I wouldn't have to derive the answer again.

The point (x_t, y_l) is the center of the ellipse we seek. Let (x, y) be the point where the desired ellipse is tangent to the line of slope σ

through (x_c, y_c) as shown in Figure 7. Our problem boils down to solving three equations in the three unknowns x, y, and y_l:

$$\left(\frac{x - x_t}{x_l - x_t}\right)^2 + \left(\frac{y - y_l}{y_t - y_l}\right)^2 = 1\,;$$

$$\frac{y_c - y}{x_c - x} = \sigma\,;$$

$$-\left(\frac{y_t - y_l}{x_l - x_t}\right)^2 \frac{x - x_t}{y - y_l} = \sigma\,.$$

(∗)

The first of these is the standard equation for an ellipse, and the second is the standard equation for slope; the third is obtained by differentiating the first,

$$2dx\,\frac{x - x_t}{(x_l - x_t)^2} + 2dy\,\frac{y - y_l}{(y_t - y_l)^2} = 0\,,$$

and setting dy/dx equal to σ.

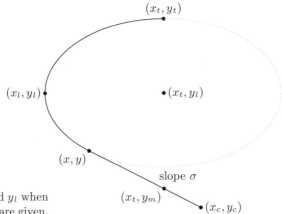

FIGURE 7.
Problem: Find x, y, and y_l when x_t, y_t, x_l, σ, x_c, and y_c are given.

Before attempting to solve equations (∗), I would like to introduce a notation that has turned out to be extremely useful in my work on mathematical font design: Let $\alpha[x, y]$ be an abbreviation for

$$x + \alpha(y - x)\,,$$

which may be understood as "the fraction α of the way from x to y." Thus $0[x, y] = x$; $1[x, y] = y$; $\frac{1}{2}[x, y]$ is the midpoint between x and y; $\frac{3}{4}[x, y]$ is halfway between y and this midpoint; and $2[x, y]$ lies on the opposite side of y from x, at the same distance as y is from x. Identities like $\alpha[x, x] = x$ and $\alpha[x, y] = (1 - \alpha)[y, x]$ are easily derived. When making some geometric construction it is common to refer to things like the point one third of the way from A to B; the notation $\frac{1}{3}[A, B]$ means just that. I call it "mediation."

One of the uses of this bracket notation is to find the intersection (x, y) of two given lines, where the lines go respectively from (x_1, y_1) to (x_2, y_2) and from (x_3, y_3) to (x_4, y_4). We can solve the intersection problem by noting that there is some number α such that

$$x = \alpha[x_1, x_2] \qquad y = \alpha[y_1, y_2]$$

and some number β such that

$$x = \beta[x_3, x_4] \qquad y = \beta[y_3, y_4] \,.$$

These four simultaneous linear equations in x, y, α, and β are easily solved; and in fact METAFONT will automatically solve simultaneous linear equations, so it is easy to compute the intersection of lines in METAFONT programs.

The bracket notation also applies to ellipses in an interesting way. We can write $x = \alpha[x_0, x_{\max}]$ and $y = \beta[y_0, y_{\max}]$ in the general equation

$$\left(\frac{x - x_0}{x_{\max} - x_0} \right)^2 + \left(\frac{y - y_0}{y_{\max} - y_0} \right)^2 = 1 \,,$$

reducing it to the much simpler equation

$$\alpha^2 + \beta^2 = 1 \,.$$

Returning to our problem of the ellipse, let us set

$$
\begin{aligned}
x &= \alpha[x_t, x_l] \,, & y &= \beta[y_l, y_t] \,, \\
X &= x - x_t \,, & Y &= y_l - y_t \,, \\
a &= x_l - x_t \,, & b &= (y_c - \sigma x_c) - (y_t - \sigma x_t) \,.
\end{aligned}
$$

The three equations $(*)$ can now be rewritten as follows:

$$
\begin{aligned}
\alpha^2 + \beta^2 &= 1 \,; \\
b + \sigma X &= (1 - \beta) Y \,; \\
\alpha Y &= a \sigma \beta \,; \\
X &= a \alpha \,.
\end{aligned}
\tag{$**$}
$$

This gives us four equations in the four unknowns (α, β, X, Y), so it may seem that we have taken a step backwards; but the equations are much simpler in form. We can eliminate α to reduce back to three unknowns:

$$X^2 + a^2\beta^2 = a^2\,;\tag{1}$$

$$b + \sigma X = (1 - \beta)Y\,;\tag{2}$$

$$XY = a^2\sigma\beta\,.\tag{3}$$

Multiplying (3) by $(1 - \beta)$ and applying (2) now leads to

$$X(b + \sigma X) = a^2\sigma\beta(1 - \beta)\,,$$

and this miraculously combines with (1) to yield

$$bX = a^2\sigma(\beta - 1)\,.\tag{4}$$

It follows that $\left(a^2\sigma(\beta - 1)\right)^2 + a^2b^2\beta^2 = a^2b^2$, i.e.,

$$a^2(\beta - 1)\left(a^2\sigma^2(\beta - 1) + b^2(\beta + 1)\right) = 0\,.\tag{5}$$

If $a = 0$, our equations become degenerate, with infinitely many solutions $(X, Y) = \left(0, b/(1 - \beta)\right)$ for $-1 \le \beta < 1$. If $b = 0$, another degenerate situation occurs, with no solution possible unless $a\sigma = 0$, in which case there are infinitely many solutions with Y arbitrary and $(X, \alpha, \beta) = (0, 0, 1)$. Otherwise it is not difficult to see that $\beta \ne 1$, so (5) determines the value of β uniquely, and we can use this with (4) to determine the full solution:

$$\begin{aligned} \alpha &= -2ab\sigma/(a^2\sigma^2 + b^2)\,;\\ \beta &= (a^2\sigma^2 - b^2)/(a^2\sigma^2 + b^2)\,;\\ X &= -2a^2b\sigma/(a^2\sigma^2 + b^2)\,;\\ Y &= (b^2 - a^2\sigma^2)/2b\,. \end{aligned}\tag{6}$$

I was surprised to find that the simultaneous quadratic equations (∗∗) have purely rational expressions as their roots. There is a curious similarity between this solution and the answer to the problem in Figure 2.

Translating (6) back into the notation of the original problem statement (Figure 7), let (x_t, y_m) be on the line of slope σ through (x_c, y_c), so that $y_m = y_c + \sigma(x_t - x_c)$. Then the unique solution is

$$\begin{aligned} x &= x_t + \frac{2\sigma(x_l - x_t)^2(y_t - y_m)}{\sigma^2(x_l - x_t)^2 + (y_t - y_m)^2}\,,\\[1mm] y &= y_m + \frac{2\sigma^2(x_l - x_t)^2(y_t - y_m)}{\sigma^2(x_l - x_t)^2 + (y_t - y_m)^2}\,,\\[1mm] y_l &= y_t - \frac{(y_t - y_m)^2 - \sigma^2(x_l - x_t)^2}{2(y_t - y_m)}\,, \end{aligned}\tag{7}$$

except in the degenerate cases $x_l = x_t$ or $y_m = y_t$.

Incidentally, I tried the automatic equation-solving feature of the MACSYMA computer algebra system [5, 7] on this problem, in order to get some idea of how long it will be before mathematicians will be replaced by computers when such calculations are required. MAC-SYMA correctly found the solution (X, Y, β) for equations (1), (2), (3) in about 17 seconds, except that it said nothing about the degenerate solutions that occur when $ab = 0$. The time required for MACSYMA to solve the system of four equations ($**$) was essentially the same as to deal with (1), (2), (3). But when I asked MACSYMA to solve the three original equations ($*$) for x, y, and y_l, the computer's memory capacity was exceeded after about a minute and twenty seconds, even when I simplified ($*$) by replacing (x_c, y_c) by (x_t, y_m). Thus, I was reassured to find that the equations ($*$) aren't completely trivial and that the conversion to ($**$) was an important step.

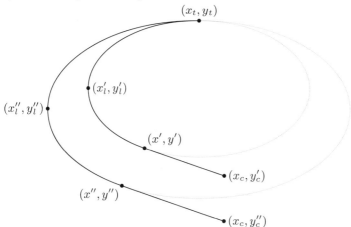

FIGURE 8. A good S is obtained by drawing two partial ellipses according to the method of Fig. 7, then filling in the space between them, using a pen whose diameter is the width of the "hairlines" of the desired letters.

This solution to the ellipse problem leads immediately to the desired S curves, since we can fill in the space between an ellipse-and-straight-line arc that runs from (x_t, y_t) to (x'_l, y'_l) to (x', y') to (x_c, y'_c) and another that runs from (x_t, y_t) to (x''_l, y''_l) to (x'', y'') to (x_c, y''_c), where the distance between x'_l and x''_l is governed by the desired thickness of the stroke at the left and the distance between y'_c and y''_c is governed by the desired thickness of the stroke at the center. (See Figure 8. The actual S curve is drawn with a circular pen of small but positive radius whose center traces the curves shown, so the actual boundary is not a perfect ellipse.) The bottom right part of the S is, of course, handled in the same way as the upper left part.

SSSSSS

FIGURE 9. Different possibilities can be explored by varying the parameters. Here the slope is changing, but other characteristics are held fixed; the respective slopes are $2/5$, $1/2$, $2/3$, 1, $3/2$, 2, and $5/2$ times the "correct" slope in the middle.

Figure 9 shows various S curves drawn by this method when the slope σ varies but the other specifications stay the same. Figure 10 shows an S that has the same slope as the middle one of Figure 9, but the curve is wider when it is traveling vertically at the upper left and the lower right. One of the chief advantages of a mathematical, parameterized approach is that it is easy to make lots of experiments until you find the setting of parameters that you like best. A META-FONT program that would draw the S's in Figures 9 and 10, depending on appropriate parameters, appears in the appendix below.

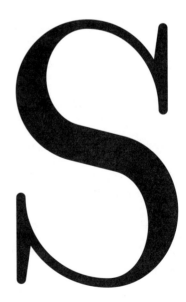

FIGURE 10.
The main stroke of this S is wider at the upper left and lower right, but otherwise it was drawn to the specifications of the middle S in Fig. 9.

I happily made S's with this method for more than two years, but one day I decided to ask METAFONT to draw a great big letter S and the resulting shape was unexpectedly ugly. Looking back at some of the other supposedly nice S's drawn previously, I started to notice an occasional defect that was comparatively innocuous at the small scales I had been working with. This defect became painfully apparent when everything was enlarged, so I realized that I still hadn't gotten to the end of the story.

Figure 11 illustrates this new difficulty in a somewhat extreme form. In terms of the notation of Figure 8, I had not placed x'_l sufficiently far to the right of x''_l; hence the two ellipses through (x'_l, y'_l) and (x''_l, y''_l) actually crossed each other. This made the supposed inner boundary switch over and become the outer boundary and vice versa, a distinctly unpleasant result since I was not intending to have such a calligraphic effect here.

FIGURE 11.
Disastrous effects can occur if there isn't enough width at the upper left and lower right.

The problem of Figure 11 goes away if x'_l is sufficiently large, but of course it is desirable to know what the permissible values are. We are led to a third (and final) problem concerning ellipses: *Given the situation in Figure 8, what is a necessary and sufficient condition that the elliptical arc from (x''_l, y''_l) to (x_t, y_t) stays above the elliptical arc from (x'_l, y'_l) to (x_t, y_t)?* (We are assuming that $x''_l < x'_l < x_t$ and $y''_l < y'_l < y_t$, and that both ellipses have left/right symmetry as before.) It turns out that the answer to this problem can be expressed quite simply: The curves fail to cross if and only if

$$\frac{y_t - y_l'}{(x_t - x_l')^2} \geq \frac{y_t - y_l''}{(x_t - x_l'')^2}.$$

(8)

My first attempt to find the right condition got bogged down in a notational mess, but finally I hit on the following fairly simple solution to this problem: Let

$$a = x_t - x_l', \quad b = y_t - y_l', \quad A = x_t - x_l'', \quad B = y_t - y_l''.$$

Using these abbreviations and turning the curves upside down, we want the function $b - b\sqrt{1 - (x/a)^2}$ (which describes the bottom right quarter of an elliptical arc from $(0,0)$ to (a,b)) to be less than or equal to the analogous function $B - B\sqrt{1 - (x/A)^2}$, whenever $|x| < a$, given that $0 < a < A$ and $0 < b < B$. Expanding in power series we have

$$b - b\sqrt{1 - \left(\frac{x}{a}\right)^2} = b\left(\frac{x^2}{2a^2} + \frac{x^4}{8a^4} + \cdots + \binom{1/2}{k}(-1)^{k+1}\frac{x^{2k}}{a^{2k}} + \cdots\right),$$

where

$$\binom{1/2}{k}(-1)^{k+1} = \frac{(2k-2)!}{2^{2k-1}k!\,(k-1)!}$$

is positive for all $k > 0$, and the power series converges for $|x| < a$. If $b/a^2 < B/A^2$, the analogous power series

$$B - B\sqrt{1 - \left(\frac{x}{A}\right)^2} = B\left(\frac{x^2}{2A^2} + \frac{x^4}{8A^4} + \cdots + \binom{1/2}{k}(-1)^{k+1}\frac{x^{2k}}{A^{2k}} + \cdots\right)$$

will grow faster for small x and the two curves will cross. But if $b/a^2 \geq B/A^2$, we will have $b/a^{2k} \geq B/A^{2k}$ for all $k > 0$, so every term of the first power series dominates every term of the second.   Q.E.D.

According to the theory worked out earlier, we have

$$\frac{y_t - y_l}{(x_t - x_l)^2} = \frac{y_t - y_m}{2(x_t - x_l)^2} - \frac{\sigma^2}{2(y_t - y_m)}.$$

(9)

Thus we can ensure that the quantity $(y_t - y_l')/(x_t - x_l')^2$ is actually equal to $(y_t - y_l'')/(x_t - x_l'')^2$ by starting with desired values of x_t, y_t, x_l'', y_m', and y_m'': First y_l'' is determined, then x_l', and finally y_l'.

SSSSS

FIGURE 12. Varying thicknesses of the middle stroke lead to these S's,
where the width at upper left and lower right has been chosen to be
as small as possible without the "crossover" problem of Fig. 11.

After learning how to draw an S with mathematical precision,
I found that the same ideas apply to many other symbols needed in a
complete system of fonts for mathematics. In fact, all of the characters
in Figure 13 use the same METAFONT subroutine that I first developed
for the letter S (or the dual subroutine obtained by interchanging x and
y coordinates). Without the theory developed in this paper, I would either have had to abandon my goal of defining books in a mathematical
way or I would have had to stop using all of these characters.

FIGURE 13. The method used to draw an S stroke also is used as a subroutine that draws parts of many other characters, including those
shown here.

Of course, this is only a first step; the letters I have designed are
far from optimal, and dozens of future experiments suggest themselves.
My current dream is that the next several years will see mathematicians
teaming up with experienced type designers to create truly beautiful
new fonts. This will surely be one of the most visible applications of
mathematics!

Let me close by asking a question of the reader. Ellipses have been
studied for thousands of years, so it is reasonable to assume that all of
their interesting properties were discovered long ago. Yet my experience is that when mathematics is applied to a new field, new "purely
mathematical" questions are often raised that enrich mathematics itself.

So I am most curious to know: Have the questions that I encountered while trying to draw S-like ellipses been studied before, perhaps in some other disguise? Or did the new application of mathematics to typography lead to fresh insights about even such a well-studied object as a rectilinear ellipse?

Appendix

The program below, written in the METAFONT language as described in [3, part 3], will draw the S shown in Figure 14 (and infinitely many others) when the following parameters have been specified:

h,   height of the character;
o,   "overshoot" of curved lines at top and bottom;
u,   one tenth of the character width;
w_0,   size of circular pen used in drawing lines;
w_4,   width of triangular serifs before erasing;
w_8,   thickness at the upper left and lower right;
w_9,   thickness of S stroke in the middle.

The vertical lines in Figure 14 are u steps apart. The program uses 'lpen#' and 'rpen#' to erase unwanted ink that lies to the left and right of a specified path; the effect of such erasure is visible in the illustration, since portions of the guidelines have been erased.

subroutine *scomp*(**index** i)	% starting point
(**index** p)	% turning point (y_p to be defined)
(**index** j)	% transition point (to be defined)
(**index** k)	% ending point
(**var** s):	% ending slope

% This subroutine computes y_p, x_j, and y_j so that
% $y_k - y_j = s \cdot (x_k - x_j)$ and so that the following curve
% is consistent with an ellipse:
% $i\{x_p - x_i, 0\} \mathbin{..} p\{0, y_p - y_i\} \mathbin{..} j\{x_k - x_p, s \cdot (x_k - x_p)\}$.

$y_k - y_j = s(x_k - x_j)$;
new a, b; $a = s(x_p - x_i)$; $b = y_k - y_i - s(x_k - x_i)$;
$x_j - x_i = -2a \cdot b(x_p - x_i)/(a \cdot a + b \cdot b)$;
$y_p - y_i = .5(b \cdot b - a \cdot a)/b$.

subroutine *sdraw* (**index** i)	% starting point
(**index** p)	% upper turning point (y_p to be defined)
(**index** k)	% middle point
(**index** q)	% lower turning point (y_q to be defined)
(**index** j)	% ending point
(**index** a)	% effective pen width at turning points

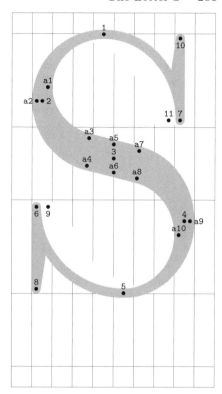

FIGURE 14.

The labeled points in this S correspond to the numbers specified by the METAFONT routine in the appendix.

(**index** b)   % effective pen height at middle point
(**var** s):   % slope at middle point
cpen; $\text{top}_0 y_5 = \text{top}_b y_k$; $\text{bot}_0 y_6 = \text{bot}_b y_k$;
$x_5 = x_6 = x_k$;
$\text{rt}_a x_p = \text{rt}_0 x_1$; $\text{lft}_a x_p = \text{lft}_0 x_2$;
$\text{rt}_a x_q = \text{rt}_0 x_9$; $\text{lft}_a x_q = \text{lft}_0 x_{10}$;
$y_2 = y_p$; $y_9 = y_q$;
call $scomp(i, 1, 3, 5, s)$;   % compute y_1 and point 3
call $scomp(i, 2, 4, 6, s)$;   % compute y_2 and point 4
call $scomp(j, 9, 7, 5, s)$;   % compute y_9 and point 7
call $scomp(j, 10, 8, 6, s)$;   % compute y_{10} and point 8
w_0 **ddraw** $i\{x_1 - x_i, 0\} .. 1\{0, y_1 - y_i\} ..$
    $3\{x_q - x_p, s(x_q - x_p)\} .. 7\{x_q - x_p, s(x_q - x_p)\} ..$
    $9\{0, y_j - y_9\} .. j\{x_j - x_9, 0\},$
  $i\{x_2 - x_i, 0\} .. 2\{0, y_2 - y_i\} ..$
    $4\{x_q - x_p, s(x_q - x_p)\} .. 8\{x_q - x_p, s(x_q - x_p)\} ..$
    $10\{0, y_j - y_{10}\} .. j\{x_j - x_{10}, 0\}.$ % the s-curve

"The letter S";
hpen; $\text{top}_0 y_1 = \textbf{round}\,(h + o)$; $\text{bot}_0 y_5 = -o$:
$x_3 = 5u$; $y_3 = .52h$;
$\text{lft}_8 x_2 = \textbf{round}\ u$; $\text{rt}_8 x_4 = \textbf{round}\ 9u$;
$x_1 = 4.5u$; $x_5 = 5.5u$;
$\text{lft}_0 x_6 = \textbf{round}\ u$; $\text{rt}_0 x_7 = \textbf{round}\ 8.5u$;
$y_6 = \textbf{good}_0 \frac{1}{3}h - 1$; $y_7 = \textbf{good}_0 \frac{2}{3}h + 1$;
$\text{bot}_0 y_8 = 0$; $y_9 = y_6$; $x_8 = x_6$; $\text{rt}_4 x_6 = \text{rt}_0 x_9$;
$\text{top}_0 y_{10} = h$; $y_{11} = y_7$; $x_{10} = x_7$; $\text{lft}_4 x_7 = \text{lft}_0 x_{11}$;

w_0 **ddraw** $6..8$, $9..8$;	% lower serif
ddraw $7..10$, $11..10$;	% upper serif
rpen#; w_4 **draw** $6\{0,-1\}..5\{1,0\}$;	% erase excess
lpen#; w_4 **draw** $7\{0,1\}..1\{-1,0\}$;	% ditto
hpen; w_0 **draw** $6\{0,-1\}..5\{1,0\}$;	% lower left stroke
draw $7\{0,1\}..1\{-1,0\}$;	% upper right stroke
call `a $sdraw(1,2,3,4,5,8,9,-h/(50u))$.	% middle stroke

The preparation of this article was supported in part by National Science Foundation grants MCS-7723738 and IST-7921977, by Office of Naval Research grant N00014-76-C-0330, and by the IBM Corporation. The author gratefully acknowledges the help of Xerox Palo Alto Research Center facilities for the preparation of several illustrations.

References

[1] Richard J. Fateman, *Essays in Algebraic Simplification*, Ph.D. thesis, Harvard University (1971). Published also as report MAC TR-95 (Cambridge, Massachusetts: M.I.T. Laboratory for Computer Science, April 1972).

[2] Donald E. Knuth, "Mathematical typography," *Bulletin of the American Mathematical Society* (new series) **1** (1979), 337–372. [Reprinted with corrections as Chapter 2 of the present volume.]

[3] Donald E. Knuth, TEX and METAFONT: New Directions in Typesetting (Bedford, Massachusetts: Digital Press and American Mathematical Society, 1979).

[4] Giovanni Mardersteig, *The Alphabet of Francesco Torniello da Novara [1517] Followed by a Comparison with the Alphabet of Fra Luca Pacioli* (Verona: Officina Bodoni, 1971).

[5] The Mathlab Group, *MACSYMA Reference Manual*, version nine (Cambridge, Massachusetts: M.I.T. Laboratory for Computer Science, 1977). The original design and implementation of MACSYMA's SOLVE operator was due to R. J. Fateman, and it is described briefly in §3.6 of [1].

[6] H. W. Mergler & P. M. Vargo, "One approach to computer-assisted letter design," *Journal of Typographic Research* **2** (1968), 299–322. [This paper describes the first computer system for drawing parameterized letters; for reasons that are now clear, the authors were unable to obtain a satisfactory S!]

[7] Joel Moses, "MACSYMA — The Fifth Year," *SIGSAM Bulletin* **8**, 3 (Association for Computing Machinery, 1974), 105–110.

Addendum

A much simpler way to solve the three equations (∗) was pointed out by G. J. Rieger [*The Mathematical Intelligencer* **3** (1981), 94]: We may assume for convenience that $x_t = y_t = x_c = 0$ and $y_c = y_m$; then the equations take the form

$$x^2 + (y - y_l)^2/\lambda^2 = x_l^2, \qquad y = y_m + \sigma x, \qquad \lambda^2 x = \sigma(y_l - y),$$

where $\lambda = y_l/x_l$. Plugging the second equation into the third yields $x = \sigma(y_l - y_m)/(\lambda^2 + \sigma^2)$; and these expressions for x and y reduce the first equation to $(y_l - y_m)^2 = y_l^2 + \sigma^2 x_l^2$, which is linear in y_l.

Erich Neuwirth of the University of Vienna sent me a letter on 22 September 1980 with a beautiful explanation of the "curious similarity" I had noticed between the ellipse problem of Figure 7 and Torniello's circle problem of Figure 2. The ellipse problem can be restated as follows: *Find the rectilinear ellipse, centered on the y-axis, that is tangent to the three lines $y = 0$, $x = -r$, and $y = \sigma x - d$, where $r = x_t - x_l$ and $d = y_t - y_m$.* If the points of tangency are $(0, 0)$, $(-r, -c)$, and $(-a, -b)$, where $a = x_t - x$, $b = y_t - y$, and $c = y_t - y_l$, let us say that the (r, σ, d) problem has solution (a, b, c). Neuwirth's key observation is that stretching the plane in the x direction takes ellipses into ellipses and tangents into tangents. Therefore if α is any stretching factor, *the (r, σ, d) problem has solution (a, b, c) if and only if the $(\alpha r, \sigma/\alpha, d)$ problem has solution $(\alpha a, b, c)$.* Now if we turn to Figure 2 and set $h = -d/\sigma$, we see from the solution to Torniello's problem that the (r, σ, d) problem has solution

$$\left(-2\sigma r^2 d/(d^2 + \sigma^2 r^2),\ 2rd^2/(d^2 + \sigma^2 r^2),\ r\right)$$

if $d^2 - \sigma^2 r^2 = 2rd$; this is the case where the ellipse is a circle. Thus the $(\alpha r, \sigma/\alpha, d)$ problem has solution

$$\left(-2\alpha\sigma r^2 d/(d^2 + \sigma^2 r^2),\ 2\alpha rd^2/(d^2 + \sigma^2 r^2),\ \alpha r\right)$$

if $d^2 - \sigma^2 r^2 = 2\alpha rd$. But we can choose $\alpha = (d^2 - \sigma^2 r^2)/(2rd)$ and apply Neuwirth's principle, establishing that the general (r, σ, d) problem has the solution

$$\left(-2\sigma r^2 d/(d^2 + \sigma^2 r^2),\ 2\alpha r d^2/(d^2 + \sigma^2 r^2),\ \alpha r\right).$$

This is equivalent to (7). If I were teaching a course about calculus or analytic geometry, I would enjoy devoting one of the class periods to problems related to S curves, since the approaches taken by both Rieger and Neuwirth are quite instructive.

Computer algebra systems have been getting better. For example, *Mathematica*® 2.2 on a SPARCstation 2 (vintage 1993) solves the system (∗) in 141 seconds, given no hints. But a human mathematician is still needed to put the solution into a comprehensible form like (7).

The METAFONT language has changed substantially since 1980, and I'm happy to say that the characters in Figure 13 have all been significantly improved. (See Volumes C and E of *Computers & Typesetting*.) However, the basic ideas for drawing S curves, as explained above, remain valid.

Chapter 14

My First Experience with Indian Scripts

[Originally published in CALTIS-84, a booklet prepared for a seminar on calligraphy, lettering, and typography of Indic scripts (New Delhi: 11–13 February 1984), 49.]

On February 13, 1980, a group of people from the typographic drawing office of Mergenthaler Linotype Company came to visit me, in order to look at the strange computer program called METAFONT that I was developing. One of the things we tried that day was an experiment in which Matthew Carter sketched a character, and my job was to write a METAFONT program that would draw the same thing.

Matthew decided to give me a symbol that I hadn't seen before, so he chose a Devanagari character. This was an especially interesting challenge, since I had never had a chance to look closely at Indian letter-forms. On my third attempt, my program drew the letter in Figure 1, and Matthew seemed to find it acceptable. (There are 12 design points, each of which is represented by a triple of dots; for example, design point 5 is represented by three black dots labeled 5, 105, and 205.)

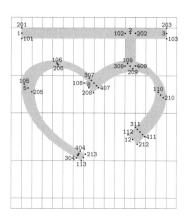

FIGURE 1.

Trial proof showing design points.

I had written the program in such a way that it was easy to change the weight of the pen strokes. Furthermore I decided to try drawing a "random" variation in which I moved several of the 12 points slightly away from their precise mathematical positions, using random numbers to make such "errors." The results are shown in Figure 2: Figure 2a shows the original character; 2b is the bold version; 2c, 2d, and 2e show random variations with standard deviations 5, 10, and 15. (Clearly a deviation of 15 was too much, but we were having fun.)

| (a) | (b) | (c) | (d) | (e) |

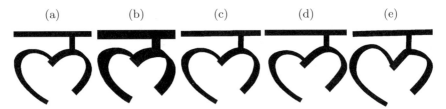

FIGURE 2. Five outputs of the METAFONT program.

Then I generated a font containing the characters of Figs. 2a and 2b, plus 26 different characters like Fig. 2c. (In each case the standard deviation was 5, but different random numbers were used.) We printed this font on our Alphatype CRS phototypesetter, and Figure 3 shows the results in their true size as they came from that machine.

You can tell from Figure 3 that this was my first experience with Indian scripts, because I didn't know how to spell Devanagari. If you look closely you might also be able to see that the 26 letters on the third line are all slightly different. I had a feeling that a little randomness might make the characters seem "warmer," even though they had been generated by precise mathematical formulas.

These were early days and there still were bugs in our software; there's a glitch between two characters on the third line. (Something always goes wrong when you are demonstrating a computer program.)

During the past year Mr. Pijush Ghosh visited our laboratory and created a family of fonts that he called NCSD, "Novice Calligrapher's Simple Devanagari." From these encouraging experiments I have been glad to learn that my ideas might find application far across the seas, in languages that I will probably never be able to comprehend. What a wonderful feeling that gives me!

My coworkers and I are presently engaged in creating a new version of METAFONT, which we hope to make available about one year from

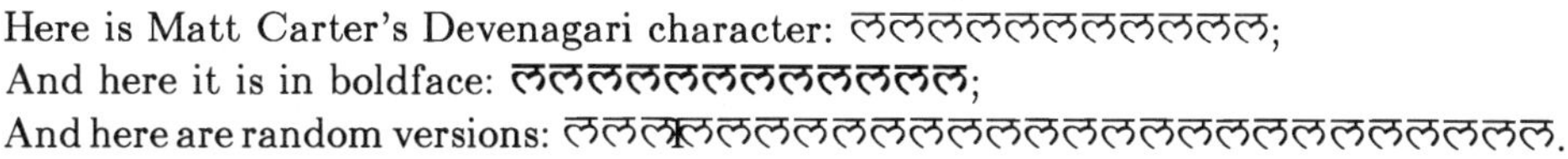

Here is Matt Carter's Devenagari character: ळळळळळळळळळळळ;
And here it is in boldface: **ळळळळळळळळळळळ**;
And here are random versions: ळळळऴळळळळळळळळळळळळळळळळळळळ.

FIGURE 3. The first typeset samples, at their true size.

now. This new version should be much easier to use than the first, but I am afraid it will still not be really simple; I think the best way to use it will be to have an artist work together with a computer specialist, just as Matthew Carter worked with me. The program will be designed to run on a wide variety of computers, both large and small. We plan to offer it free of charge, because all of this work has been inspired by our love of printing.

Addendum

I learned later that the character ळ is a variant of the letter L, which is most commonly written ल.

During the past fifteen years I've been delighted to see the creative ways in which many people have applied METAFONT to the design of Indic characters. For example, I recently used a Devanagari font designed by Frans J. Velthuis to typeset the word कुट्टक (kuṭṭaka) in the third edition of my book *Seminumerical Algorithms* (1998).

Chapter 15

The Concept of a Meta-Font

*[Originally published in Visible Language **16** (1982), 3–27.]*

A single drawing of a single letter reveals only a small part of what was in the designer's mind when that letter was drawn. But when precise instructions are given about how to make such a drawing, the intelligence of that letter can be captured in a way that permits us to obtain an infinite variety of related letters from the same specification. Instead of merely describing a single letter, such instructions explain how that letter would change its shape if other parameters of the design were changed. Thus an entire font of letters and other symbols can be specified so that each character adapts itself to varying conditions in an appropriate way. Initial experiments with a precise language for pen motions suggest strongly that the font designer of the future should not simply design isolated alphabets; the challenge will be to explain exactly how each design should adapt itself gracefully to a wide range of changes in the specification. This paper gives examples of a meta-font and explains the changeable parameters in its design.

Some of Aristotle's philosophical writings were called *Metaphysics*, because they came *after* his *Physics* in the conventional arrangement of his works. By the twentieth century, most people had forgotten the original meaning of Greek prefixes, and "meta-" was assumed to add a transcendent character to whatever it qualified. We now have metapsychology (the study of how the mind relates to its containing body), metamathematics (the study of mathematical reasoning), and metalinguistics (the study of how language relates to culture); a metamathematician

289

proves metatheorems (theorems about theorems), and a computer scientist often works with metalanguages (languages for describing languages). Newly coined words beginning with "meta-" generally reflect our contemporary inclination to view things from the outside, at a more abstract level, with what we feel is a more mature understanding.

In this sense a "meta-font" is *a schematic description of how to draw a family of fonts*, not simply the drawings themselves. Such descriptions give more or less precise rules about how to produce drawings of letters, and the rules will ideally be expressed in terms of variable *parameters* so that a single description will actually specify many different drawings. The rules of a meta-font will thereby define many different individual fonts, depending on the settings of the parameters. For example, the American Type Founders specimen book of 1923 included the following members of its "Caslon" family: plain, oldstyle, lightface, bold, heavy, condensed, lightface condensed, bold condensed, extra condensed, bold extended, shaded, and openface, not to mention American Caslon, New Caslon, Recut Caslon, and Caslon Adbold; each of these was available in about sixteen different point sizes, so the total number of Caslon roman fonts was about 270. There was an overall design concept loosely tying all these fonts together so that they were recognizably "Caslon," although the changes in size and weight were accompanied by more or less subtle changes in the letter shapes. We can regard this overall design as a meta-font that specified how the letters would change in different circumstances: The meta-font governed the metamorphoses.

Of course, the actual design of all these Caslon varieties was not completely explicit; it was conveyed implicitly by means of a few drawings that specified a few critical examples. A skilled workman could make the appropriate modifications for intermediate sizes and styles just as skilled animators do the "in-betweening" for Walt Disney cartoons. It would be preferable, however, to have a completely explicit design, so that the designer's intentions would be unambiguously recorded; then we wouldn't have to resort to the vague notion of "appropriate modifications." Ideally, the designer's intentions should be so explicit that they can be carried out satisfactorily by somebody who doesn't understand letter shapes at all — even by a stupid, inanimate, electronic computer!

George Forsythe once wrote that "The question 'What can be automated?' is one of the most inspiring philosophical and practical questions of contemporary civilization." We know from experience that we understand an idea much better after we have succeeded in teaching it to someone else; and the advent of computers has brought the realization that even more is true: The best way to understand something is to know it so well that you can teach it to a computer. Machines provide the ultimate test, since they do not tolerate "hand waving" and they have no "common sense" to fill the gaps and vagaries in what we do almost unconsciously. In fact, research in artificial intelligence has shown that computers can do virtually any task that is traditionally associated with "thinking," but machines have great difficulty accomplishing what people and animals do "without thinking." The art of letter design will not be fully understood until it can be explained to a computer; and the process of seeking such explanations will surely be instructive for all concerned. People often find that the knowledge gained while writing computer programs is far more valuable than the computer's eventual output.

In order to explain a font design to a machine, we need some sort of language or notation that describes

the process of letter construction. Drawings themselves
do not suffice, unless the design is so simple that all fonts
of the family are related to each other by elementary
transformations. Several notations for the precise description of letter shapes have been introduced in recent
years, including one that the author developed during
1977–1979. The latter system, called METAFONT, dif-
fers from previous approaches in that it describes the
motion of the center of a "pen" or "eraser" instead of
describing the boundary of each character. As a result,
the METAFONT language appears to facilitate the design of font families; for example, it took only about two
weeks of work to create the crude but passable meta-font
described in reference [5].

After another six months of development, during
which literally thousands of refinements were made, the
design of this prototype meta-font reached a state able
to support the complete typesetting of a complex 700-
page book [7]. The name Computer Modern has been
attached to the resulting group of fonts, a family that
includes meta-fonts for both roman and italic styles in addition to the Greek and Cyrillic alphabets and an uppercase calligraphic script, together with an extensive set
of mathematical symbols. The basic idea underlying the
design of this font family was to capture the spirit of
the fonts used in the first printings of the author's books
on computer programming, namely the fonts known as
"Monotype Modern Extended 8A," while casting the design in the METAFONT idiom and including a wide range
of parametric variations.

So many variations are possible, in fact, that the author keeps finding new settings of the parameters that
give surprisingly attractive effects not anticipated in the
original design; the parameters that give the most readability and visual appeal may never be found, since there

are infinitely many possibilities. On the other hand, it would be possible to parameterize many other things that cannot be varied in the present design; an almost endless series of interesting experiments can be performed, now that METAFONT is available.

At the present time (January 1981), the Computer Modern Roman meta-font has 28 parameters that affect the shapes of its letters, plus three parameters that help control inter-letter spacing; the number of parameters continues to grow as more experience is gained. There are also a half-dozen miscellaneous parameters whose sole function is to select alternate character and ligature shapes in different fonts. For example, one of the latter parameters is used to select between two styles for the letter 'g'; the reader may have already noticed that the g's in the present paragraph are different from those used elsewhere in this article. A few other typographic tricks like this will be played in what follows; relatively large type has been used so that the effects are not impossible to perceive.

The most interesting and important parameters of Computer Modern will be changed in the following paragraphs, one at a time, in order to show how much variability is possible. Of course it is easy to find settings of the parameters that give unsatisfactory results, since a single design cannot be expected to solve all conceivable problems; therefore our examples will attempt to illustrate the limiting cases where things break down as well as the in-between regions where usable fonts are to be found.

The first and most obvious group of parameters controls the vertical dimensions of letters: The x-height and the heights of ascenders and descenders can be independently specified. There are, in fact, two independent measurements for descenders, one to control the depths of the letters g j p q y and the other to control the depths of other symbols like commas and the tail of the letter Q. The height of uppercase letters is independent of the height of lowercase letters, and the height of the numerals 0 to 9 can also be varied at will. The most unusual parameter relating to vertical dimensions is called the bar-height, namely the height of the bar in a lowercase e; in the current designs the bar-height also affects several other lowercase letters:

tho pack,

the pack,

the pack,

the pack,

the pack!

Another fairly obvious group of parameters governs the horizontal dimensions of each character in a font: It is possible to obtain fonts that are extremely extended or extremely condensed without changing the heights or widths of the strokes. One can also imitate a typewriter by extending or condensing the individual characters so that each one has the same width. Notice that the serifs stretch or shrink with the rest of a letter; therefore an i has much longer serifs than an m in the typewriter style.

Of course we get a much better imitation of a typewriter when the distinction between thick and thin strokes disappears. Such a font looks typewriter-like even when its letters do not all have the same width.

The letters of Computer Modern are conceptually drawn by pens having an elliptical nib; for example, the thick strokes of the h's in this sentence were made by a pen that would look like ' ━ ' if enlarged ten times. The ellipses have perfectly horizontal axes, not tipped as ' ╱ ', because the letters are intended to have vertical stress. Different pens are used to draw different parts of the letters.

Five parameters control the dimensions of these elliptical pens: One for the width of thin hairlines, another for thick stem lines that are straight, another for thick stem lines that are curved, another for the bulbs on letters like acf...y, and another that gives the thickness in the vertical dimension. If all five of these measurements are equal, the pens will be perfect circles.

Special care is needed in the choices of the pen-size parameters. For example, undesirable blotches appear when the bulbs are too large for the stems, and the type has a disturbing inconsistency when its curved stems are substantially wider than the straight ones. **A font cannot get too bold without having portions of the letters run into each other.** Perhaps future meta-fonts will be set up to compute desirable pen dimensions from a smaller set of independent parameters, since the proper widths depend in a subtle way on each other; at the moment, trial and error is necessary to get a compatible set of pen sizes, but further research should shed some light on this dependence.

Only five pen-size parameters have been mentioned, for simplicity, but the actual situation is somewhat more complex. For example, the pens used for drawing uppercase letters are specified separately from those used to draw the lowercase ones, and numerals are drawn by mixing these two specifications. There is also a parametric "fudge factor" that takes some weight off of letters like w and m, which otherwise would look too dark in certain styles; true uniformity in line widths does not lead to uniform appearance, because our eyes play tricks on us.

Another slightly subtle parameter of the Computer Modern fonts is the so-called "overshoot" by which curves and sharp corners descend below the baseline and above the mean line. For example, the letters in this sentence have no overshoot at all. And certain letters in this sentence overshoot their boundaries by thrice as much as they do in the following sentences. Experimentation is still necessary to find the amount of overshoot that makes the letters look most stable, and on low resolution printing equipment it is desirable to eliminate overshoot entirely; further study of this parameter, in combination with the others, should prove to be quite interesting.

Serif details can be varied in several ways. For example, there are no "sheared" serifs on the letters in this sentence. And the letters you are now reading have thrice as much shear as usual, just to make sure that the concept of shear is clear.

Another serif-oriented concept is the amount of so-called "bracketing"; the serifs in this sentence have no brackets. But the brackets are exaggerated in this sentence, so the serifs appear darker. The difference can be understood most easily if we enlarge the letters:

$\mathbf{n}$o bracketing;

$\mathbf{n}$ormal bracketing;

$\mathbf{n}$oticeable bracketing.

A curve that starts at the edge of the serif will be tangent to the stem at some distance above or below the serif; this vertical distance is the "bracketing" parameter.

The length of serifs is, of course, controllable too. The letters in this sentence have serifs that are 50% shorter

than before. And in this sentence the serifs are 50%
longer than before — so long that they sometimes touch
where they shouldn't. One way to get sans-serif letters
is simply to set the serif length to zero (and make appropriate changes in the inter-letter spacing); but it is better
to redesign several of the letters when serifs go away, for
example by using flared terminals instead of bulbs.

A *"slant" parameter transforms the pen motion, as
shown in this sentence, but the pen shape remains the
same.* The degree of slant can be negative as well as positive, if unusual effects are desired. *Too much slant leads,
of course, to letters that are nearly unreadable.* Perhaps
the most interesting use of the slant parameter occurs
when Computer Modern Italic fonts are generated without any slant: Italic letters have a different style from
roman, and we are so used to seeing such letters slanted
forward that they appear to be slanting backward when
most of them are actually upright or slanting slightly
forward.

The final parameter we shall discuss is the most interesting one; it is called "the square root of 2." From
a mathematical standpoint, there is of course only one
square root of 2, but the Computer Modern meta-fonts
treat $\sqrt{2}$ as a variable parameter that is used to compute
the $45°$ points when a pen is drawing elliptical curves.
As a result, a value that is smaller than the true one will
change an ellipse to a superellipse and open up the bowls;
for example, if we use the fifth root of 4 in place of the
square root of 2, namely

1.31950791 instead of 1.41421356,

we obtain the famous superellipse defined by Piet Hein.
A higher value for the square root of 2, on the other hand,
will have the opposite effect:

The "square root of 2" in these letters is 1.100.
The "square root of 2" in these letters is 1.200.
The "square root of 2" in these letters is 1.320.
The "square root of 2" in these letters is 1.350.
The "square root of 2" in these letters is 1.380.
The "square root of 2" in these letters is 1.414.
The "square root of 2" in these letters is 1.450.
The "square root of 2" in these letters is 1.500.
The "square root of 2" in these letters is 1.600.
The "square root of 2" in these letters is 1.700.

Several additional parameters can be varied in addition to those we have mentioned. For example, there is an amount by which sharp corners in letters like V and M are spread apart to avoid unnecessary fill-in. Several parameters control details of the "beaks" in letters like E, T, and Z. But a complete description of Computer Modern Roman is beyond the scope of this paper.

We have been studying the parameters one at a time; what happens when they are all changing at once? Figure 1 shows one of the interesting transformations that can be made. At the top we have a font with an old-fashioned feeling, essentially the same as the style of type used so far in the text of this paper: The h-height is 8.4 points, the x-height is 4 points, the bar-height is 2.3 points, and the descender depth is 3 points. Hairlines are 0.26 points wide, compared to 1.2-point straight stems and 1.34-point curved stems; the bulb diameter is 1.36 points, and the hairline pens are perfect circles. One em in this style equals 12.6 points; serifs are .07777 of an em long, and they have 0.54 points of shear, 0.8 points of bracketing. The overshoot parameter is 0.3 points, and the "square root of 2" has its mathematically correct value 1.414214.

The LORD is my shepherd;
    I shall not want.
He maketh me to lie down
            in green pastures:
    he leadeth me
            beside the still waters.
He restoreth my soul:
    he leadeth me
            in the paths of righteousness
            for his name's sake.
Yea, though I walk through the valley
            of the shadow of death,
            I will fear no evil:
    for thou art with me;
            thy rod and thy staff
            they comfort me.
Thou preparest a table before me
            in the presence of mine enemies:
    thou anointest my head with oil,
            my cup runneth over.
Surely goodness and mercy
            shall follow me
            all the days of my life:
    and I will dwell
            in the house of the LORD
            for ever.

FIGURE 1. Continuous variation of parameters can gradually convert a
    font with an old-fashioned flavor into a contemporary style. All of
    the letters in this example have the same h-height, but their em
    width increases as their x-height increases. This gives a perspective
    effect in which the words come out of the past to the present, as they
    approach the future.

The letters at the end of
Figure 1 have been transformed
into an almost hypermodern
font, which will be used for the
remainder of this article. The
h-height is still 8.4 points, but the
x-height has grown to 6.4 points
and the bar-height to 3.2; the
descender depth is now 4 points.
Hairlines and stem lines and
curved stems are all exactly one
point wide, and the pen nibs are
0.6 point tall. Thus, the pen that
draws most letters looks like '●'
when magnified 10-fold. One em
is now 21.6 points; the serif length
is zero, and so are the shear and
bracketing parameters. There are
0.1 points of overshoot, and the
"square root of 2" is 1.3.

Each of the 595 letters, spaces, and punctuation marks in
Figure 1 belongs to a different
font, obtained by going 1/594
of the way further toward the
final parameter settings. Thus,
although each letter appears to be
in the same font as its neighbors,
the cumulative change is quite
dramatic — it is something like the

gradual changes in our own faces
as we grow older, except that this
typeface is getting younger.

Hundreds of typefaces have
appeared in this article, yet all
of them belong to the Computer Modern Roman and Italic
meta-fonts. Each letter has been
specified by a computer program
written in the METAFONT language,
and the computer can draw any
desired variant of that letter
when the parameter values have
been supplied. It is important
to remember that none of these
conventions and parameters are
built into METAFONT itself; META-
FONT is a general-purpose language
intended to facilitate the design of
meta-fonts, and Computer Modern
is but one approach to font design
using such a language.

Let us take a brief look at the
program for the letter h, since
this will give some insight into the
way a meta-font can be designed.
Each Computer Modern Roman h
is drawn essentially as follows, if
we paraphrase the METAFONT code
into English:

This character will be 10 units wide, where there are 18 units per em; however, the width should be adjusted by the "serif correction" after the character has been drawn, to account for long or short serifs.

This letter has several key points, defined as follows: Take an elliptical pen whose height is equal to the hairline height, and whose width is equal to the straight stem width for lowercase letters. When this pen is centered at point 1, its center is approximately 2.5 units from the left edge of the character (rounded so that the center is in a good position with respect to the raster), and its top is at the h-height for lowercase letters. Point 2 is directly below point 1; the bottom of the pen will be exactly at the baseline when its center is at point 2. Points 3 and 4 both lie approximately 2.5 units from the right edge of the character; point 4 is directly to the right of point 2, while point 3 is 1/3 of the way from the bar-height to the x-height.

Take the pen and draw a straight stem from point 1 to point 2, and another from point 3 to point 4. Put a sheared serif at the left of point 1, and attach serifs at both sides of points 2 and 4, using the serif sub-programs (which take proper account of the shear, bracketing, and serif-length parameters).

Finally, the shoulder of the h is drawn as follows: The stroke begins vertically at a point 1/8 of the way from the bar-height to the x-height, using a hairline pen positioned flush right with the left stem line. This hairline pen traces a quarter-ellipse, ending at a point that is halfway between the right edges of the stems and such that the pen's top is at the x-height plus half of the overshoot; let us call this point 5.

The shoulder is completed by drawing one quarter of a superellipse from point 5 to point 3 as the pen grows from the hairline width to the straight stem width; the midpoint of this arc is computed by using the geometric mean of the number 1.23114413 and the "square root of 2" parameter, instead of $\sqrt{2}$, in the usual formulas for ellipses. (The strange constant 1.23114413 is $2^{3/10}$, chosen so that Piet Hein's original superellipse will be obtained if the "square root of 2" is $\sqrt{2}$.)

Similar routines will yield the m and the n. Effects of the "slant" parameter are not mentioned in this description, since slanting is

FIGURE 2.
The program that is
paraphrased in the
text might prepare
this character for a
low-resolution printing
device. Notice the five
key points numbered
1, 2, 3, 4, and 5; the
center of the "pen"
travels through these
points as it draws
the letter.

done by a different part of the
computer program, at the time the
actual drawing is being produced.

The idea of a meta-font should
now be clear. But what good is
it? The ability to manipulate lots
of parameters may be interesting
and fun, but does anybody really
need a $6\,1/7$-point font that is
one fourth of the way between
Baskerville and Helvetica?

We might consider also an
analogy with music: Musical
notation was developed centuries
before we had a notation for
drawing; during all this time there

has been no widely perceived
need for meta-symphonies, so
why should we desire meta-fonts?

Well, these are legitimate
questions that surely deserve to
be answered; let's think about
the musical analogy first. The
long history of musical notation
shows clearly that the mere
existence of a precise language
does not by itself call for the
introduction of parameters into
that notation. Indeed, parameters
have not crept into serious music,
even in primitive ways, until very
recently, except in a few almost-
forgotten pieces like Mozart's
meta-waltz [11]. It would surely
be interesting and instructive to
write meta-music that could produce variable degrees of suspense,
excitement, pathos, sturm und
drang in the listener, depending on
the setting of certain parameters;
but there would be little apparent
use for such music except in the
sound track of motion pictures.

All analogies break down, of
course, and font design is different
from musical composition because

alphabets are not symphonies; an alphabet is a "medium" while a symphony is a "message." We get a much better analogy between fonts and music when we consider background music rather than symphonies, since fonts serve as the background for an author's printed ideas. Many people resent background music because they feel that music should either be the main focus of a person's attention or it should be absent entirely. On the other hand, it is generally agreed that the reader of a book should not be conscious of the g's and the k's in that book. A font should be sublime in its appearance but subliminal in its effect.

The utility of parametric variations comes from our need for variety. We don't all want to live in identical houses or drive identical cars. Background music becomes especially tedious when it comes from a limited score having only a few motifs; and five centuries of typographic practice have witnessed a continual craving

for new alphabets and for large
families of related alphabets.
Thus, although any one particular
setting of a meta-font's parameters may seem to be somewhat
silly and unnecessary, the ability
to choose arbitrary parameter
settings fills a real need. Book
designers and the designers of
advertising copy will have greater
freedom than ever before when
they have several meta-fonts to
work with. Personalized fonts and
one-time-only fonts will also be
easy for anyone to obtain.

Another reason why meta-fonts
and meta-music were not highly
developed long ago is the fact
that computers did not exist until
recently. Human beings find it
difficult and dull to carry out
calculations with a multiplicity
of parameters, while today's
machines do such tasks with ease.

Perhaps the most important
practical result of parametric
variations is the ability to make
adjustments for each point size;
the contemporary tendency to
obtain 7-point fonts by 70%

reduction of 10-point fonts has led to a lamentable degradation of quality. Another advantage is that a meta-font can adapt its curves so that they are properly rendered by digital typesetting machines, which are based on discrete rasters. This leads to a significant reduction in the need for manual editing of the raster patterns.

It is, of course, quite a challenge to design a meta-font instead of a single font. A designer wants to remain in control, yet the great variety of possible parameter settings means that the meta-font is able to generate infinitely many alphabets, most of which will never be seen by human eyes; only a few of the possibilities can really be looked at, much less fine-tuned, before the specification of the meta-font has been completed. On the other hand, the designer of a meta-font has compensating advantages, because meta-fonts allow us to postpone making decisions about many aspects of a design and to leave

them as parameters, instead of
freezing their specifications in the
initial stages. Such things as the
amount of overshoot, the width of
hairlines, the length of serifs, and
so on, need not be decided once
and for all; it is easy to ask the
computer to make experiments
by which the designer will be
able to choose the best settings
of those subtle quantities after
viewing actual typeset material.
Experiments of this kind would be
unthinkable if each character had
to be drawn individually — i.e., if
each character were simply in a
font rather than a meta-font.

In the long run the scientific
aspects of meta-fonts should
prove to be the most important.
The ability to adjust continuous
parameters makes it possible to
carry out controlled experiments
about how such variations affect
readability or visual appeal. And
even more significant will be the
knowledge that will be explicitly
embedded in the descriptions of
meta-fonts. For example, the
author learned a great deal about

font design while refining the
Computer Modern alphabets, and
this information is now accessible
to anybody who reads the META-
FONT code. It is tantalizing to
think how much further the art
of font design will be advanced
when professionals who really
know the subject begin to create
meta-fonts in an explicit language
like METAFONT.

Acknowledgments and Apologies

The author wishes to thank Charles Bigelow, Matthew Carter, Douglas
Hofstadter, Jill Knuth, and Michael Parker for numerous suggestions
that helped to improve the presentation; and he owes a special debt
of gratitude to Hermann Zapf for dozens of invaluable suggestions that
helped greatly to improve the design of the Computer Modern meta-
fonts. Apologies are made to language purists who object to mixing
Greek and Latin stems: The Greek equivalent of *fons* is πηγή, so a word
like "metapeg" might be superior to "metafont." However, such a name
would not be readily understood by people who encounter it for the first
time, at least not until the day that the science of font design becomes
known as pegology.

The research reported in this paper was supported in part by National Science Foundation grants IST-7921977 and MCS-7723738, and in part by the IBM Corporation.

Annotated Bibliography

The typefaces used to set this bibliography reflect the parameter settings
for Computer Modern Roman that were used in its original design, based
on the "Monotype Modern 8" fonts; the more extreme settings used to
typeset the text of the article above were chosen long after the design
itself was complete, in order to illustrate the meta-font concept.

[1] P. J. M. Coueignoux, *Generation of Roman Printed Fonts*, Ph.D.
    thesis, Dept. of Electrical Engineering, Massachusetts Institute of
    Technology (June 1975). This thesis represents the first use of

sophisticated mathematical curves to describe letter shapes to a computer. Coueignoux and his students are presently continuing this research at the École Nationale Supérieure des Mines de Saint-Étienne, France.

[2] Adrian Frutiger, *Type Sign Symbol* (Zürich: ABC Verlag, 1980); see especially pages 15–21, which describe "Why Univers was designed and how it developed." Univers was the first true meta-font, in the sense that a wide variety of different sizes and weights played a central role in its design from the very beginning. "The decisive factor for the many new design possibilities provided by Univers was that it became possible, for the first time, to work with a set of typefaces as a complete system." Page 59 of this fascinating book shows a meta-letter n, called the "proportional schema of a typeface family," graphically depicting the desirable stroke variations as the font gets bolder.

[3] Peter Karow et al., "IKARUS: computer controlled drafting, cutting and scanning of characters and signs. Automatic production of fonts for photo-, CRT and lasercomp machines. Summary" (Hamburg: URW Unternehmensberatung, September 1979). Already by 1980, the IKARUS system was widely used to capture the shapes of letters in mathematical form, based on original artwork [see *Baseline* **3** (1981), 6–11]. The computer programs will also interpolate between different weights, although the number of independent parameters is quite limited; this feature was used successfully by Matthew Carter to develop several weights of his Galliard type, including Ultra Roman [see Charles Bigelow, "On type: Galliard," *Fine Print* **5** (1979), 27–30].

[4] David Kindersley and Neil Wiseman, "Computer-aided letter design," *Printing World* (31 October 1979), 12, 13, 17. Discusses the ELF system at Cambridge University, which features a novel method of optical spacing between letters.

[5] Donald E. Knuth, "Mathematical typography," *Bulletin of the American Mathematical Society* (new series) **1** (1979), 337–372. [Reprinted with corrections as Chapter 2 of the present volume.] A paper written shortly after the author began his research on font generation; it explains the initial motivations for this work and shows an experimental roman meta-font.

[6] Donald E. Knuth, "The letter S," *The Mathematical Intelligencer* **2** (1980), 114–122. [Reprinted as Chapter 13 of the present volume.]

Discussion of the letter that is most difficult to incorporate into a parameterized meta-font.

[7] Donald E. Knuth, *Seminumerical Algorithms*, Volume 2 of *The Art of Computer Programming*, second edition (Reading, Massachusetts: Addison–Wesley, 1981). This book was the first large work to be typeset entirely with the Computer Modern meta-fonts; indeed, Computer Modern was developed expressly for the books in this series. At the time of printing, the design of Computer Modern had evolved almost to the point represented in the original (1982) printing of the article above, although certain characters like '2' were subsequently revised and the x-height settings were decreased slightly. Such revisions and afterthoughts are probably inevitable, especially when the computer representation of a meta-font makes changes so easy; it is very hard to stop and say "no more improvements will be made!"

[8] Donald E. Knuth, *The Computer Modern Family of Typefaces*, Stanford Computer Science Department report STAN-CS-80-780 (January 1980). Hundreds of important refinements were made between the completion of this report and the publication of [7], and thousands more were made when everything was rewritten in the new METAFONT language of 1984. A near-final version of Computer Modern appears in *The Computer Modern Family of Typefaces*, Volume E of *Computers & Typesetting*, fourth printing (Reading, Massachusetts: Addison–Wesley, 1993); a few late changes are listed in the file `cm85.bug`, which is part of the CTAN archives on the Internet. Computer Modern has had a total of 62 parameters ever since 1985; the latest version (1998) has been used to typeset this chapter, using parameter values that correspond to those of the original article of 1982.

[9] J. R. Manning, "Continuity conditions for spline curves," *The Computer Journal* **17** (1974), 181–186. The clothing industry has needs analogous to those of type designers; this paper, from the Shoe and Allied Trades Research Association in England, discusses the generation of curves that pass through given key points, and it includes a "meta-shoe" as an example.

[10] H. W. Mergler and P. M. Vargo, "One approach to computer assisted letter design," *Visible Language* [née *The Journal of Typographic Research*] **2** (1968), 299–322. This paper describes ITSYLF, the first computer system for parametric letter design; ITSYLF included a meta-font for uppercase roman letters. The approach was

limited and unsuccessful because it was entirely based on edge generation with a limited class of curves and because of the equipment limitations of the 1960s, but the authors had laudable goals.

[11] W. A. Mozart, *Anleitung zum Componiren von Walzern, so viele man will vermittelst zweier Würfel, ohne etwas von der Musik oder Composition zu verstehen* (Berlin: Simrock, 1796); first published by J. J. Hummel of Amsterdam and Berlin, 1793. Listed in Köchelverzeichnis 516f Anh. C 30.01. Reprinted as Mozart's *Musikalisches Würfelspiel*, edited by Karl Heinz Taubert, Edition Schott 4474 (Mainz: B. Schott's Söhne, 1957); also with an introduction by Hugh Norden (Brighton, Massachusetts: Carousel Publishing, 1973). This unusual score presents a waltz that can be played in 759,499,667,166,482 different ways, since there are eleven possibilities for most of the individual bars; the harmonic principles have been analyzed by Hermann Scherchen in *Gravesaner Blätter* **4** (May 1956), 3–14. Mozart also devised a meta-contredanse, and the British Museum reportedly owns a meta-score by Haydn. A noteworthy 20th-century example of meta-music can be found in *The Schillinger System of Musical Composition* by Joseph Schillinger, Volumes 1 and 2 (New York: Carl Fischer, 1946).

[12] Edward Rondthaler, "From the rigid to the flexible," *The Penrose Annual* **53** (1959), xv, 1–9. An early description of the variability of type that is possible with photographic transformations alone.

Addendum

Brief reviews of "The Concept of a Meta-Font" by Fernand Baudin, Charles Bigelow, Henri-Paul Bronsard, Ed Fisher, Jr., David Ford, Gary Gore, W. P. Jaspert, Albert Kapr, Peter Karow, Alexander Nesbitt, Edward Rondthaler, John Schappler, Walter Tracy, Gerard Unger, and Hermann Zapf, together with a longer review by Douglas R. Hofstadter, were published in *Visible Language* **16** (1982), 309–359, closing with the following response from the author:

> What a privilege it is to have so many distinguished people reading my work, and what a pleasure to read their profound comments! Thank you for giving me a chance to add a few more words to this stimulating collection of letters.
>
> As I was reading the diverse reactions, I often found myself siding more with the people who were sharply critical of my research than with those who acclaimed it. Critical comments are extremely helpful for

shaping the next phases of the work that people like me are doing, as we search for the proper ways to utilize the new printing technologies.

Several of the writers mention my citation of George Forsythe, and your readers may be interested in further details about what he said. George was one of the first people to perceive the real importance of computer science, as opposed to the mere use of computers, and the remark I cited is taken from the introduction of an invited address on Computer Science and Education that he gave in 1968 at the Congress of the International Federation for Information Processing, held in Edinburgh. I wish I could have quoted his entire article; the best I can do is urge people to look for it in their libraries [*Information Processing 68*, Volume 2 (North-Holland, 1969), 1025–1039].

Perhaps I may be forgiven for citing also another article of my own, entitled "Computer programming as an art" [*Communications of the ACM* **17** (1974), 667–673; *L'Informatique Nouvelle*, no. 64 (June 1975), 20–27]. In this essay I attempt to show that the essential difference between science and art is that science has been codified (and in this sense "automated"), while art is what human beings achieve with their mysterious intuition. My main point is that science never catches up to art, since the advances in science are always accompanied by artistic leaps.

Thus, my hope is that the advent of computers will help us to understand exactly how little we really know about letter forms. Then, as we attempt to explain the principles in such concrete terms that even a machine can obey them, we will be learning a great deal more about the subject, so that we and the coming generations will be able to raise the artistic level even higher.

Meanwhile my experiences since publishing the article in *Visible Language* have been quite encouraging. Several leading designers have generously given me specific pointers on how to improve the Computer Modern fonts, and I spent the month of April making extensive refinements under the tutelage of Richard Southall. The number of parameters has grown from 28 to 45, but all the parameters still seem to make sense; and the careful incorporation of such subtleties is already yielding significantly better results. Much remains to be done, including further development of the mathematics of shapes, but there now is some evidence that the tools we are developing will not be inadequate to the task. I hope to publish a book that captures the things these people have taught me, so that such knowledge can be widely appreciated, apprehended, and appropriated, not merely applied.

Donald E. Knuth
Computer Science Department
Stanford University
12 October 1982

*The design and character of this type
have received both favourable and unfavourable criticism,
but inasmuch as bibliographers have, to my knowledge,
written about it in seven languages
and in sixteen countries of the world,
I feel that the accomplishment has at least created interest.*

— DARD HUNTER, *Primitive Papermaking* (1927)

Chapter 16

Lessons Learned from METAFONT

[A keynote address presented on 1 August 1983 at the Fifth Working Seminar in Letterform Education and Research, held under the auspices of the Association Typographique Internationale (ATypI). Originally published in Visible Language **19** *(1985), 35–53.]*

Type designers today face an important problem, the problem of constructing digitized patterns for printing. The central question is, "What is the right way to create such patterns?" Or, rather, "What *will* be the right way?" — since we are concerned primarily with long term issues that are different from the problems of meeting today's deadlines. In this paper, I shall try to convey some of my excitement about exploratory research that has been going on here at Stanford, since I think we have found a small part of the answer.

Let me state at the outset that I do not foresee the problem ever becoming simple. Indeed, when I ponder what lessons I have learned so far, the main lesson turns out to be that the problem is quite difficult! In a way, this is not surprising. For more than thirty years, computers have been oversold by salesmen who claim that computing machines are easy to use, while the truth is quite the opposite: Computer programming requires more attention to detail than anything else that human beings have ever done. Moreover, the problems of letterform design are extremely subtle, much more complex than most people think, because our machines and our eyes interact with the shapes in complicated ways. I am convinced that digital alphabet design is an extremely challenging problem, and that it is significant enough to deserve the attention of our best scientific minds and our best artistic skills and sensitivities. Furthermore, I believe that the world will be a better place to live in after we learn more about the subject.

There is also another point I want to make before getting into the details of my work: I am a mathematician, well aware that I am no artist. I do not believe that mathematical methods will resolve all the problems of digital typography; but I do believe that mathematics will help. Indeed, it is almost inconceivable that more than 2000 years of accumulated knowledge about geometry and curves will prove to be irrelevant to alphabet design. Yet mathematics is a threat to people whose love for letters is partly due to their hatred of (or, let us say, lack of attraction to) algebra. I am sorry that "math anxiety" exists, but I know that it is widespread. I am well aware that the injection of mathematics into a previously untainted area can be considered unfair to the leaders of that discipline, since they suddenly have to learn an enormous amount of new material in order to stay on top of their subject. However, I do not think there is really cause for alarm; it is not unusual for a subject to be so complex that no one person can understand it all. The most fascinating thing about recent developments in typography is, in fact, the emerging collaboration between scientists and artists: the bridges that are being built between C. P. Snow's "two cultures." I am not proposing that letter designers suddenly abandon their traditional ways and learn all about computer programming; I am proposing that they team up with computer scientists the way they used to collaborate with punchcutters. On the other hand, I am also pleased to see students growing up with feet solidly grounded in both worlds.

But what specifically is it that I think is so interesting? During the past few years I have been developing a computer system called METAFONT, which has three somewhat unusual characteristics:

(1) METAFONT understands a special language for drawing shapes with simulated *pens* that have *thicknesses*. For example, consider Figure 1, which shows a valentine-like curve traced by a slightly broad-edged pen. METAFONT drew this figure with ease, given only six points on the "spine" of the curve; the actual edge of the curve is quite complex and difficult to describe, but the pen motion is quite simple.

(2) The METAFONT language also encourages the construction of designs with explicit parameters, so that a large family of shapes can be described, rather than a single shape. For example, Figure 2 shows one of the sketches that Matthew Carter made when he was developing *Galliard*; METAFONT aims to facilitate the incorporation of variations into a design. This, in fact, accounts for the prefix "meta-" in METAFONT; the approach is "meta-" in the sense that it deals with fonts from outside, at a higher level, somewhat as "metamathematics" is the theory of mathematical proof techniques. Meta-concepts are proliferating these days: For example, I recently learned of a new game called "metagame" [7] in which the first move is to choose a game to play. (An interesting problem arises when the first player says, "Let's play metagame!")

FIGURE 1.   FIGURE 2.

I have written elsewhere about the concept of a meta-font [6], which is a high-level description that transcends any of the individual fonts it describes. This concept is to be distinguished from the METAFONT system itself, which is merely one way to describe meta-fonts. Figure 3 (due to Scott Kim) illustrates some of the parameter variations possible in an early version of a meta-font called Computer Modern; each variable has been pushed to extremes for the sake of example. Figure 3a shows changes in the slant of characters, and Figure 3b shows changes in the width; in both cases the pens stay the same but the path is different, hence the changes in image could not be done by optical transformations.

(a)	(b)	(c)
-1/6 slant Typography	condensed by .4 Typography	weight = -1 Typography
(normal Roman) 0 slant Typography	condensed by .6 Typography	(regular) weight = 0 Typography
(normal Slanted) 1/6 slant Typography	condensed by .8 Typography	weight = 1/4 Typography
1/4 slant Typography	normal Typography	weight = 1/2 Typography
1/3 slant Typography	extended by 1.2 Typography	weight = 3/4 Typography
1/2 slant Typography	extended by 1.5 Typography	(bold) weight = 1 Typography
1/1 slant Typography	extended by 2 Typography	weight = 2 **Typography**
serifs scaled by 0 Typography	sqrttwo = 2↑1 Typography	18 point Typography
serifs scaled by 1/4 Typography	sqrttwo = 2↑(4/5) Typography	(normal) 10 point Typography
serifs scaled by 1/2 Typography	sqrttwo = 2↑(3/5) Typography	9 point Typography
serifs scaled by 3/4 Typography	sqrttwo = 2↑(1/2) (produces perfect circles) Typography	8 point Typography
(normal) serifs scaled by 1 Typography	sqrttwo = 2↑(2/5) (produces superellipses) Typography	7 point Typography
serifs scaled by 2 Typography	sqrttwo = 2↑(1/5) Typography	6 point Typography
serifs scaled by 4 Typography	sqrttwo = 2↑0 Typography	5 point Typography

(d)   (e)   (f)

FIGURE 3.

Figure 3c shows what happens when the pen motion stays almost unchanged but the pen size varies. The lengths of serifs can be varied too (Figure 3d). A more unusual transformation is shown in Figure 3e, where alterations are made in the "constant" that is used to compute curves; this changes the bowl shapes. Figure 3f shows several parameters changing simultaneously to keep the letters readable as the type size changes; this is one of the main reasons for having parameters in a design. (The letters have been scaled here so that the x-heights are the same, thereby making the other changes more evident.) In each case the letters have been generated from an identical METAFONT description; the changes were caused only by changing parameters that apply to a font as a whole.

(3) In order to support characteristics 1 and 2, METAFONT descriptions of letterforms are given as *programs*. For example, Figure 4 shows two of the programs in an early version of a meta-font called CHEL, developed by Thom Hickey in 1982 (see [1]). Sample letters produced by these programs, for various settings of the parameters, appear at the top of the figure. The program for 'b' is quite short because most of the work is done by a *subroutine* — an auxiliary program that is used to construct parts of several different letters. In this case, Hickey devised a subroutine to draw a small bowl, and he used the same subroutine also in the 'd' and 'p', etc.

METAFONT programs are quite different from ordinary computer programs because they are largely "declarative" rather than "imperative." In other words, they state relationships that are supposed to hold; they do not tell the computer how to satisfy those conditions. For example, a METAFONT description might declare that the left edge of a stem line should occur one unit from the left; the program does not need to state that the center of the pen should be positioned one unit from the left, plus half of the stem width, because the computer can figure that out. Similarly, it is possible to state that a certain point lies on the intersection of two lines; it is not necessary to specify how to compute the intersection point. Most of the mathematical complexities can therefore be handled by the computer, behind the scenes.

Since METAFONT programs include all of the information about how to draw each letter in a wide variety of circumstances, the programs are able to record the "intelligence" that lies behind a design. I believe that this aspect of METAFONT — its ability to capture the designer's intentions rather than just the drawings that result from those intentions — will prove to be much more important than anything else. The ability to draw infinitely many alphabets by the variation of parameters is not

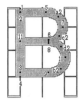
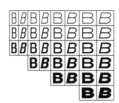

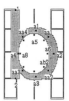

```
                                        "The letter B";
call charbegin(`B, 2, .76, ph, 0, ¹/₂[px, ph]slant);          % italic corr high for condensed
cpen;
x₁ = x₂ = x₃ = x₄ = x₁₁;   lft₁₉x₁ = ucin;
y₁ = h;  y₄ = 0;
new topindent, botoftop, topofbot, w₉₉;
topindent = round(¹/₂₈ʳ);                          % indent top even on condensed
w₉₉ = ³/₈[w₁₁₅, w₃₁₅];                              % a slow-grow pen for middle bar
botoftop = round(²/₅[bot₉₉chbar, top₉₉chbar]);      % bottom of top outer arc
topofbot = round(⁴/₅[bot₉₉chbar, top₉₉chbar]);      % top of lower outer arc
rt₁₉x₁₀ = round(r − ucin + ho);   rt₁₉x₇ = rt₁₉x₁₀ − topindent;
x₅ = ⁵/₈[rt₁₉x₁, lft₁₉x₇];   x₃ = ²/₅[rt₁₉x₁, lft₁₉x₁₀];         % based on counter widths
x₆ = x₈ = x₃;
top₁₁₇y₂ = h;  y₆ = y₂;  bot₁₁₇y₈ = 0;  y₉ = y₅;
new w₉₆, w₉₇;
w₉₆ = round(top₉₉chbar − botoftop);  call checkpen(98);          % used for top and bottom arcs
w₉₇ = round(topofbot − bot₉₉chbar);  call checkpen(97);          % to control thinning
top₉₈y₆ = top₉₇y₈ = bot₉₇y₉ = bot₉₆chbar;
if bot₉₈y₆ > top₉₇y₈: new w₉₆;  w₉₆ = w₉₈;  new w₉₈;  w₉₈ = w₉₆ + 1; fi;
yᵣ = ¹/₂[bot₁₁₇y₅, top₉₉chbar];  y₁₀ = ¹/₂[top₁₁₇y₉, bot₉₉chbar];  % ¹/₂ of counters
y₁₁ = y₁₂ = chbar;  z₁₂ = x₈;                         % height of bar same as cap H
vpen; vpenwd 1;
w₁₁₇ draw 2..5;                                      % top level
     draw 3..9;                                      % bot level
w₉₉ draw 11..12;                                     % mid level
hpen; hpenht 1;
w₁₉ draw 1..4;                                       % stem
call `a nqarc(5, 7, w₁₁₇, w₁₉);                       % upper upper
call `b nqarc(9, 10, w₁₁₇, w₁₉);                      % lower lower
call `c nqarc(6, 7, w₉₈, w₁₉);                        % lower upper
call `d nqarc(8, 10, w₉₇, w₁₉).                       % upper lower
```

```
                                        "The letter b";
call charbegin(`b, 2, .65, ph, 0, ³/₄px · slant);
x₁ = x₂ = lchoff;
y₁ = h;  y₂ = 0;
hpenht 1;  hpen;
w₁₇ draw 1..2;                                       % stem
call `a smallbowl(left).
```

FIGURE 4.

usually an important goal by itself; but the ability to explain a design in precise terms is highly instructive both to designers and to those who read their programs. The computer can enforce a discipline that helps its users to clarify their own knowledge; this educational experience is really the rewarding thing.

Now to return to my main theme, of lessons that I have learned so far. I think it is best to start in the summer of 1977, when I began this work; at that time I had no idea that I would ever be designing a language for letterforms, much less ever getting to know artists and typographers. I had been unable to obtain good drawings of the outlines of the letters that I wanted to typeset, so I was virtually forced to develop computer techniques for alphabet design, starting from scratch. My publishers supplied me with high quality letterpress proof pages that had been used to make the plates for the first printing of my book, but otherwise I had to work with extremely primitive equipment. Experiments with television cameras hooked up to computers proved to be a total failure, since the TV lenses caused considerable distortion when they were used to magnify a small image, and since a slight change in the brightness of the studio lighting caused enormous changes in the televised shapes. The best results I could get were obtained by making 35 mm slides of the letterpress proofs, and by projecting them about

8 meters onto a wall in my house, where I could make pencil sketches of somewhat blurry images about 5 cm high.

The three p's of METAFONT — drawing with *pens* and *parameters* via *programs* — popped into my mind within an hour or so after I had started to make those sketches. It suddenly dawned on me that I should not simply try to copy the shapes. A human being had originally drawn them, so I really wanted to learn as much as possible about what was in that person's mind at the time, and I wanted to incorporate that knowledge into a computer program.

The programs I wrote in 1977 were done in a traditional "imperative" programming language called SAIL, which is very much like an international computer language called ALGOL. Every time I changed anything in the program for any letter, I would have to recompile the changes into the machine's language; the idea of a declarative, interpretable language like METAFONT did not occur to me until it was suggested by Robert Filman a few months later. But the lack of such a language was not actually a bottleneck in 1977; the main problem was my ignorance about how to represent shapes in a decent way.

To illustrate these early difficulties, I have decided to show you something that I have never dared to show anyone else before: the very first results that I had in 1977 when I began to attempt drawing Arabic numerals. After I had translated my first rough sketches into a computer program, the machine presented me with Figure 5, in which each column represents a different setting of the main parameters (normal, bold, small-caps, sans-serif, and typewriter, respectively). The digit '8' had a special problem that — mercifully — prevented its appearance in all but one style; but my initial errors in the '2', '5', '6', and '7' were repeated fivefold. I am showing these early results because similar problems can be expected even with today's METAFONT; it is not easy to describe the essence of shapes to a machine.

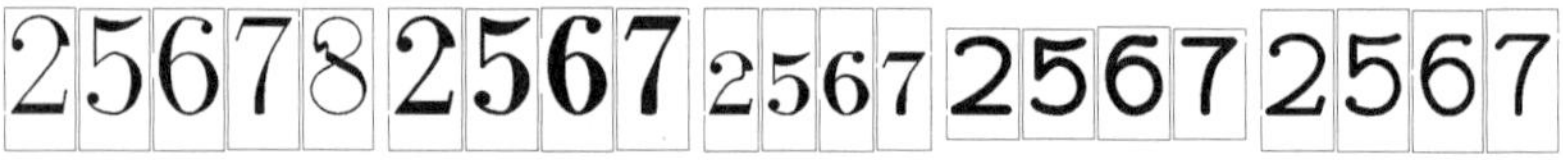

FIGURE 5.

Figure 5 is obviously riddled with errors, and it is instructive to look at them more closely. In a few cases I simply blundered: For example, I forgot to use a thick enough pen when starting the diagonal of the '2'. The strange glitch in the third '2' was due to a bad specification of the angle at the bottom; I had specified the same angle for small caps as for the normal size, even though a smaller figure was being drawn. Another bad angle occurs at the top of the bowl in each '5'. But other errors were more serious: The difficulties at the bottoms of the '5's are exhibited more severely at the tops of the '6's, where the bulbs are too high and they are joined badly to the rest of the shape. Even worse things occur at the bottoms of the '6's, where my whole approach was completely mistaken and had to be redone several times in subsequent experiments. The top of the rightmost '7' exhibits a problem that I did not resolve adequately until five years later, when I finally realized that the upper left portion of '7' (and the lower right of '2') could be regarded as an "arm" and "beak," analogous to parts of a letter like 'T' or 'E'.

01234567
01234567
01234567
01234567
01234567

FIGURE 6.

By the end of 1977, the numerals in my experimental meta-font had evolved to the point shown in Figure 6. I was satisfied with them at the time, so I spent most of 1978 working on the TEX typesetting system and doing other sorts of computer science research. In 1979 I decided to design a symbolic language for letterforms that would reflect at a higher level what I had been thinking about when writing my ALGOL programs in 1977; this new language became the original METAFONT system [4]. Considerable work was necessary in 1980 to build an interface between METAFONT's output and a high-resolution phototypesetter; during this time I was preoccupied with software problems and unable to do much with the font designs. Then finally I reached the goal that I had hoped to achieve two years earlier: I completed the second edition of my book *Seminumerical Algorithms* [5], a 700-page work in which everything but the illustrations had been done entirely by new computer methods. Altogether 35 fonts were used in that book — seven sizes of roman, six of italic, and three each of bold and slanted and typewriter styles, with each size drawn separately; there were six versions of sans-serif, and seven pi fonts for math symbols. All of these were created with the first METAFONT, and the sheets looked mighty good to me when they came out of the typesetter.

But I cannot adequately describe the enormous letdown I had when *Seminumerical Algorithms* finally appeared in print at the beginning of 1981. That was the first time I had seen the result of the entire process, including printing and binding; up to then I had been working almost entirely with low resolution equipment, and of course the high resolution output was much nicer, so I was eagerly anticipating a beautiful book. When I received the first copy and opened the covers, I burned with disappointment: Everything looked wrong! The main shock was due to the fact that I now was seeing the fonts as they looked after printing and — just as important — after binding the pages in buff covers just as the first edition had been bound. The fact that the new format was encased in the old context exaggerated the deficiencies of the new format. Sure, the new text was readable, and I could console myself a little with the thought that it was not as bad as some other books that were being printed at the time; but it was not at all what I was hoping to achieve. The sans-serif was totally wrong; the weights of roman versus italic versus numerals were not quite right; and the high resolution revealed unsuspected deficiencies in many individual characters. I developed a strong antipathy for the shapes of the numerals, especially the '2' and '6'. When using the book for reference or teaching, I was forced to look at the numbers on each page, and this would distract my thoughts; I wanted to think about elegant mathematics, but it was impossible to ignore the ugly typography.

My profound disappointment was not completely discouraging, however. For one thing, I had been reading a lot of biographies, and I knew about mid-life crises; since I was 40 years old in 1978, I had sort of been expecting to make at least one big mistake. My idea had always been to follow my intuition but to be ready for failure. I knew that METAFONT was quite different from what anybody else had done or was doing, and it certainly occurred to me that all of my ideas might simply be stupid: No wonder nobody else had tried them! On the other hand, it still seemed to me that the basic ideas of pens, parameters, and programs were still valid; the deficiencies in my published book were due to my faulty execution, but the ideas themselves seemed right. So I decided to persevere.

Two more years have gone by since then. In the meantime my colleagues and I have accumulated a lot of experience with the first METAFONT. I plan to spend the next year making a completely new system, starting over from scratch, based on this experience; the new system should therefore remove many of the deficiencies of the old. Since the new language will be ready in 1984 we are wondering if we should follow George Orwell and call it NEWSPEAK. Our plan is to make METAFONT84 widely available and to design it so that it can be used on all but the smallest computers.

Please forgive me for inserting so many biographical remarks into this paper. My main purpose is to explain the lessons I have been learning during this work, and it is high time that I give some more concrete details.

One of the first important things that I learned was that the computer deserves to be treated as a new medium. When we approach the problem of digital type design, we should not expect to do everything exactly as it was done before; we should rather expect that we can learn to guide a computer as people have traditionally learned to guide a brush or a chisel. When using the machine, it is best to hold back and to relinquish some of our own control—to let the machine "have its own head" as we find out what works and what does not. The ideal is to work together with the tool; we specify the important details, but we are willing to accept help as we do.

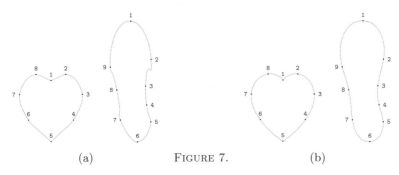

(a)   FIGURE 7.   (b)

Of course, this idea makes sense only if the computer is a decent medium, only if the curves that it draws are aesthetically pleasing. Consider, for example, Figure 7a; it turns out that today's METAFONT will produce these horrid shapes if the user simply specifies eight or nine points as shown without giving any additional instructions. A person soon learns how to overcome such problems and to obtain pleasing curves with METAFONT79, but the new system will be much better: John Hobby has recently done some important mathematical work that makes it possible to obtain Figure 7b from the same data that produced Figure 7a, and his new approach will be adopted in METAFONT84. This is quite important not only because it makes the system simpler to use and more responsive, but also because curves need to be adjusted when low-resolution characters are drawn; Hobby's method makes it more likely that such adjustments will not destroy the shapes of the curves.

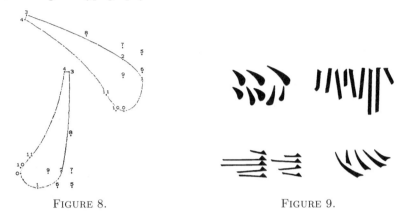

FIGURE 8.   FIGURE 9.

Figures 8 and 9 illustrate another important sense in which a designer might find that computers can provide an expressive medium. The "teardrop" shapes in Figure 8 were drawn by a METAFONT subroutine in which only a few points needed to be specified (one at the top, one at the bottom, and the horizontal coordinate at the edge of the bulb); all of the other points were determined by mathematical calculations inside the subroutine. John Hobby worked hard to create that subroutine, but a designer can learn to use teardrops effectively without worrying about exactly how the subroutine actually computes them. Figure 9 shows some of the strokes drawn by the teardrop subroutine and by three other subroutines in Hobby and Gu's early experiments on East Asian character design [2]. Further work by Hobby and Gu has led to another set of subroutines that may well be adequate for drawing a complete set of Chinese and Japanese characters in a variety of styles [3].

The second chief lesson I learned while using METAFONT was that it is best to let different parts of a design interact, rather than to specify them independently. For example, it is better to say that one point is midway between two others, instead of giving explicit coordinates to all three points. One way to illustrate this is shown in Figure 10, which is the result of an experiment with random numbers that I tried in 1977: I changed my early programs so that key points of the design were not specified exactly; the computer was supposed to pretend that it was a bit tipsy when placing those points. The top line shows perfect placement, but the second line shows what happened when the points were placed randomly with a standard deviation of about 1%; the third line shows a standard deviation of 2%, and so on. The chief thing I learned from this experiment was that the resulting letters seemed to be "warmer"

mathematics
mathematics
mathematics
mathematics
mathematics
mathematics

FIGURE 10.

when a little bit of randomness entered into the design. But the reason I am including Figure 10 is that it demonstrates that different parts of a design can be interrelated so that they depend on each other. For example, when the stems move, the serifs move with them; the individual points are not independently random.

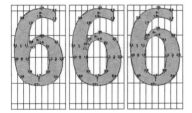

FIGURE 11.

Figure 11 exhibits a similar dependence; I made these three '6's by varying the position of only one point in the specification (point 6, which is at the top of the bowl). Many of the other points changed their position when point 6 moved, because my METAFONT program specified their positions relative to other points rather than with absolute coordinates.

FIGURE 12.

Another example of interdependence appears in Figure 12; again a series of letters has been drawn with only one parameter of the program changing. In the upper line I changed the slope at the middle of the S; in the lower line I changed the weight. In both cases a number of points changed their position in order to accommodate other changes, because I defined the positions by formulas instead of using numbers.

(a)   (b)

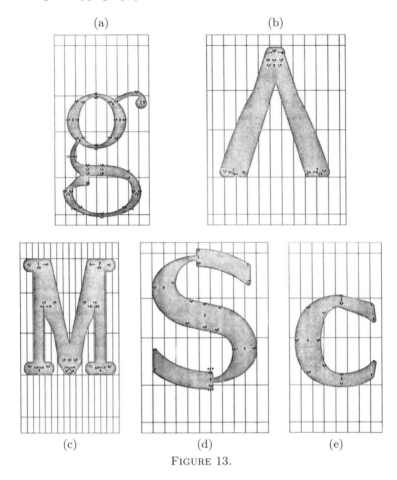

(c)   (d)   (e)

FIGURE 13.

Perhaps the best way for me to convey the flavor of METAFONT work is to show you some of my "META-flops": things that came out in quite unexpected ways. In fact, the computer is full of surprises, and this is where a lot of the fun comes in. For example, one of my programming mistakes caused a link in the 'g' to fold over in an interesting way (Figure 13a); and one of my attempts to draw a sans-serif 'A' came out looking more like an ad for Levi's western jeans (Figure 13b). Fallacious formulas led to a marvelous 'M' (Figure 13c), a sparky 'S' (Figure 13d), and a cruel 'C' (Figure 13e). When I misplaced the serif in Figure 13f, I swear that I was not thinking about Japanese yen; the currency connection was purely coincidental!

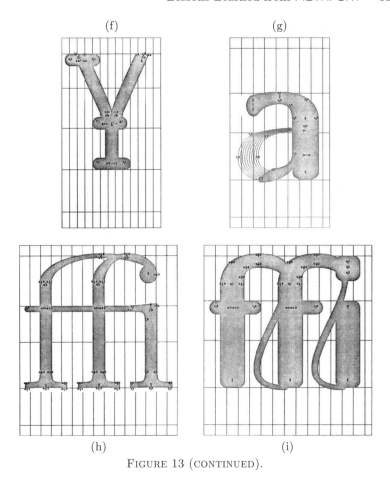

(f)   (g)

(h)   (i)

FIGURE 13 (CONTINUED).

Figure 13g came about when I was trying to discover why META-
FONT was drawing the wrong curve in an 'a'; I wanted to see more
details of the underlying strokes, because I suspected a computer error.
In this case it turned out that METAFONT was not at fault — I had made
a mathematical mistake when I specified the slope at the critical point.

To complete this exhibition of meta-flops, Figure 13h illustrates a
ligature in which I unwittingly told the computer to make *both* of the
'f's aim at the dot on the 'i'. And Figure 13i is what I like to call the
"ffilling station."

Since 1980 I have been enormously fortunate in this research, because people like Chuck Bigelow, Matthew Carter, Kris Holmes, Richard

Southall, and Hermann Zapf have generously been helping me to refine the crude tools I began with. In particular, Richard and I spent three weeks intensively going over each letter, and our preliminary studies were quite encouraging. He taught me many important lessons, and I would like to give some indication of what kinds of things we did.

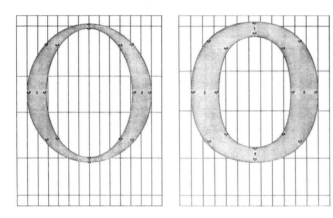

FIGURE 14.

Figure 14 shows two of the 'O's we drew. The image is slightly heavier at the bottom than at the top, and we added a parameter that makes it possible to have different curves on the inside and outside without losing the properties of a meta-font. Simply drawing two independent superellipses with different degrees of "superness" doesn't work, because the inner curve sometimes gets too close to the outer curve or even crosses it; our solution was to draw two superellipses from the same family and then to "pull" the inner curve a certain fraction of the way towards the outer one.

Some of Richard's corrections, made as we were revising the 'P', are shown in Figure 15. Notice, for example, that we took a little weight away from the stem inside the counter. In order to retain the spirit of a meta-font while making such refinements, we introduced a "stem correction" parameter that could be used for stem-weight changes in other letters. Sometimes a stem weight is changed by two or even three times the stem correction.

We were pleased to discover that METAFONT is good at notching the inside of diagonal strokes that fill in if they are not treated carefully. For example, the inside top of a bold sans-serif 'A' has been opened up in Figure 16a, so that the counter has an appropriate amount of white space while giving the illusion of straight thick stems. Our METAFONT

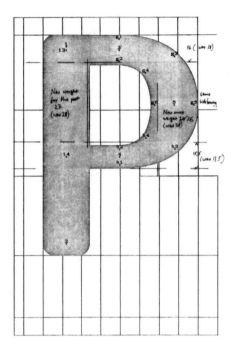

FIGURE 15.

programs are designed to give this effect in low resolutions as well as high. Figure 16b shows that the same idea applies to the typewriter-style 'A'.

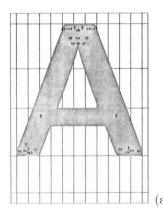 (a)   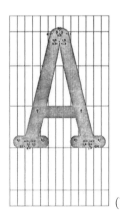 (b)   FIGURE 16.

I can summarize this recent work by saying that we are now paying a great deal of attention to the edges; the new version of METAFONT will differ from the old one primarily in this respect. I realize now that I was extremely naïve in 1977 when I believed that the edges would take care of themselves if I simply drew with a pen that had the right shape. On the other hand, we are not abandoning the pen metaphor, because it gives the correct "first-order" insights about how letters are drawn; the edge details are important second-order corrections that refine the designs, but they should not distract us from the chief characteristics of the forms.

FIGURE 17.

Figure 17 is a test palette that I made in 1980 when first experimenting with METAFONT programs to simulate broad-edged pens with varying pressure, based on the advice of Hermann Zapf. (In fact, this was the first thing Hermann wanted to try when he initially encountered METAFONT.) Although these particular strokes were all drawn by holding the pen at a fixed angle, in this case 25°, further experiments showed that a varying pen angle could also be imitated.

I would like to conclude by inviting you to participate with me in a thought experiment: Let us consider the letters 'ATYPI' that Sumner Stone has prepared as the symbol of our conference [8], and let us try to imagine how they could be incorporated into a new meta-font. Of course we could simply trace the outlines of the letters; but that would not be any fun, and it would not give us any insights. Let us rather try to embed the principles of Sumner's design into a specification that will produce lots of beautiful letters.

Take first the 'A' (Figure 18a): This is clearly made up of three strokes, two of which are thin and the other is thick. The thin strokes

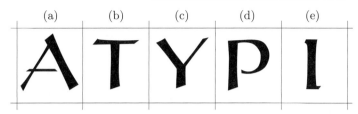

(a)   (b)   (c)   (d)   (e)

FIGURE 18.

appear to have been drawn with a narrower pen than was used to produce the thick stroke. Immediately we are led to introduce parameters for the width of those two pens. The strokes also taper gracefully; we can add a third parameter to govern the amount of tapering. (By varying this parameter we can experiment with letters that do not taper at all and with letters that taper too much.)

Turning to the 'T' (Figure 18b), we see that its crossbar is neither thin nor thick. We can either introduce a new parameter, or we can assign it an intermediate weight (for example, halfway between the narrow and wide pens in the 'A'). Tapering is present here but not quite so prominently as before; again we need not introduce a new parameter if we decide, for example, that the stem of the 'T' tapers half as much as that of the 'A'. Another parameter of the design is the angle at which the stem stroke terminates at the baseline; looking ahead, we can relate this to analogous features of the 'Y' and the 'P'.

The 'Y' itself (Figure 18c) will probably be difficult, because we will need to work out the principles that underlie a rather complex joining of three strokes at the center. This part of the letter looks simple, when it is done right, but I would expect to spend three or four hours trying different things before I found a scheme that would work properly as the parameters were varied.

The 'P' (Figure 18d) has an interesting little taper at the top of the bowl, but its most prominent feature is the gap at the bottom of the bowl. We should probably introduce a "gap" parameter, which can be used also in the 'A'.

Finally there is the "hungry I" (Figure 18e), which I do not really understand. Probably I would understand it more after actually trying to incorporate it into a meta-font, but I would want to ask Sumner for more information first. Then my METAFONT program would be able to reflect the designer's true intentions.

Looking to the future, I have not got any good insights about how new alphabets will actually be designed in, say, the year 2000. I certainly hope that none of the computer methods we are using today will still be in use; at the moment we are just beginning to explore the subject, and we should have lots of better ideas by then. But I have a hunch that METAFONT's notions of pens, parameters, and programs will find a place as part of what is eventually perceived to be the most suitable way to apply computers in digital alphabet design.

Appendix

[I could not resist actually trying the ATYPI experiment. I hope that the following detailed example, worked out after the lecture above was delivered, helps to clarify some of the points that I was trying to make.]

METAFONT can simulate broad-edged pen writing if we represent the pen's position by three points: left edge, middle, and right edge. The middle point is halfway between the other two. In the existing META-FONT, it is convenient to give numbers to the points by numbering the midpoint and adding 100 for the left edge and 200 for the right edge; thus, three points $(101, 1, 201)$ correspond to pen position 1. [In the new METAFONT I plan to work things out so that the points can be called $(1L, 1, 1R)$ instead.]

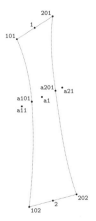

Figure 19.

It is easy to write a METAFONT subroutine that draws a simple stroke with such pens, allowing for the possibility of tapering. For example, Figure 19 illustrates a subroutine that I am currently exploring. Two pen positions are given — in this case they are called $(101, 1, 201)$ and $(102, 2, 202)$ — together with three fractions λ, ρ, and α; the fractions λ and ρ represent an amount of taper at the left and the right, while α represents the position of maximum taper. The stroke is drawn as follows: First the computer constructs points (a11, a1, a21) that are α of the way from (101, 1, 201) to (102, 2, 202). [In Figure 19, for example, α is 0.4; thus a straight line drawn from 101 to 102 passes through a11, and the distance from a11 to 101 is 0.4 times the distance from 102 to 101. The three points (a11, a1, a21) constructed in this way will lie on a straight line.] Next the computer constructs point a101 by going λ of the way from a11 to a1, and it constructs a201 by going ρ of the way from a21 to a1; this determines the amount of taper. Finally the edges of the stroke are determined as follows: A curve starts at 101, aiming towards a1; it passes through a101, at which time it is traveling in the direction parallel to a straight line from 101 to 102; then it finishes at 102, as if coming from a1. This determines the left edge; the right edge is similar.

By changing the widths and angles at the endpoints, and by changing the fractions λ, ρ, and α, it is possible to achieve a great variety of strokes. And it is possible to learn the use of these strokes without knowing or caring about the geometrical construction that produced them. Much more elaborate stroke subroutines are obviously possible, but at the moment I am getting familiar with simple ones like this. In particular, I have found that it is not difficult to get a fairly good approximation to Sumner's 'A' with just three such meta-strokes, even when everything is parameterized so that the construction works in quite general circumstances.

Figure 20 shows the meta-A that I came up with. It was drawn by a METAFONT program that can be paraphrased as follows: "The character will be 13 units wide; its height will be 1.1 times the cap height of the font, and its depth will be zero. Pen position 1 is at the baseline, with its left edge a half unit from the left of the entire character. Pen position 4 is at the baseline with its right edge a half unit from the right of the character. Pen position 2 is at 1.1 times the cap height and at the horizontal midpoint of the character. Pen position 3 is at the cap height and on a straight line between positions 2 and 4. The width of the pen at position 1 is the thin width; at positions 2 and 4 it is the thick width; and at position 3 it is 2/3 of the way from thin to thick. The pen angle at 3 and 4 is 15 degrees more than the normal "cut angle" in a vertical stem, and the angle at 2 exceeds the cut angle by 30 degrees. The bar line is determined by pen positions 5 and 6, whose top is at 3/7 of the cap height; the angle at 5 is 45°, the angle at 6 is 135°, and the width at both positions is a fraction of the thin width, determined by a given "aspect ratio" parameter. Position 5 is offset to the left of where a straight line

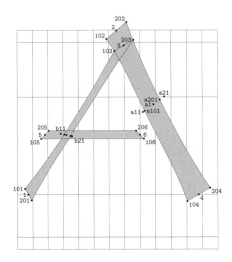

FIGURE 20.

from 5 to 6 intersects a straight line from 3 to 1; the amount of offset is the "gap amount" plus half the thin pen width. Similarly position 6 is offset from where a straight line from 5 to 6 intersects a straight line from 2 to 4; the amount of offset is the gap amount plus half the thick width. Let τ be the value of the taper parameter. The diagonal stroke from 2 to 4 is drawn with $\lambda = \tau^2$, $\rho = \tau$, and $\alpha = .45$; the diagonal stroke from 3 to 1 is drawn with $\lambda = \tau^{1/2}$, $\rho = \tau^{3/2}$, and $\alpha = .6$. The horizontal stroke has no taper."

In order to complete the specification, we need to define the parameter values. Figure 20 was obtained by letting the unit width be $26x$ (where x is an arbitrary scale factor); the cap height was $245x$; the thin width and thick width were $22x$ and $44x$, respectively. The aspect ratio was 0.85; the cut angle was 15 degrees; the gap amount was one unit; and the taper parameter was $\tau = 0.4$.

Figure 21 shows five 'A's drawn with the same parameters except that the unit widths were $17x$, $20x$, $23x$, $26x$, and $29x$. Figure 22 shows the effects of increasing weight: $(thin, thick) = (11x, 33x)$, $(22x, 44x)$, $(33x, 55x)$, and $(44x, 66x)$. Finally, Figure 23 illustrates a few other variations: (a) stem weights $(55x, 55x)$; (b) taper parameter increased to 0.6; (c) cut angle reduced to $5°$ and gap amount reduced to 0.1 unit; (d) all of the above. It is doubtful, of course, that Sumner would approve of these particular examples, which were obtained by extrapolation from a single drawing. But I think the two of us together could work out something that is quite satisfactory.

FIGURE 21.

FIGURE 22.

FIGURE 23.

Since this is an appendix, I shall conclude by appending the actual METAFONT programs, for the benefit of people who would like to see the complete details. I have used hh in the program below to stand for cap height in pixels, phh for cap height in points; r denotes the right edge of the character, and u denotes the unit width, in pixels; $charbegin(character\_code, unit\_width, height\_in\_points, depth\_in\_points)$ is a subroutine that sets up values like r and u, and tells where to put the result in a complete font. The last half of this program, following "The letter A", is what was paraphrased above. Equivalent programs will be much simpler and more readable in next year's METAFONT.

minvr 0; **minvs** 0;   % shut off velocity corrections
$fill = 1$;   % width of pen used to fill the strokes

subroutine $penpos($**index** i,   % set pen position i
     var $angle$, **var** $d)$:   % with given angle and width
$x_i = .5[x_{i+100}, x_{i+200}]$; $y_i = .5[y_{i+100}, y_{i+200}]$;
$x_{i+200} - x_{i+100} = d \cdot$ **cosd** $angle$;
$y_{i+200} - y_{i+100} = d \cdot$ **sind** $angle$.

subroutine $stroke($**index** i, **index** j,   % draw a stroke from i to j
     var $lambda$, **var** rho,   % with given left and right taper amounts
     var $alpha)$:   % and position of maximum taper
$x_1 = alpha[x_i, x_j]$; $y_1 = alpha[y_i, y_j]$;
$x_{11} = alpha[x_{i+100}, x_{j+100}]$; $x_{21} = alpha[x_{i+200}, x_{j+200}]$;
$y_{11} = alpha[y_{i+100}, y_{j+100}]$; $y_{21} = alpha[y_{i+200}, y_{j+200}]$;
$x_{101} = lambda[x_{11}, x_1]$; $y_{101} = lambda[y_{11}, y_1]$;
$x_{201} = rho[x_{21}, x_1]$; $y_{201} = rho[y_{21}, y_1]$;

cpen; *fill* **ddraw**
$$i + 100 \{x_1 - x_{i+100}, y_1 - y_{i+100}\}$$
$$..101 \{x_{j+100} - x_{i+100}, y_{j+100} - y_{i+100}\}$$
$$..j + 100 \{x_{j+100} - x_1, y_{j+100} - y_1\} ,$$
$$i + 200 \{x_1 - x_{i+200}, y_1 - y_{i+200}\}$$
$$..201 \{x_{j+200} - x_{i+200}, y_{j+200} - y_{i+200}\}$$
$$..j + 200 \{x_{j+200} - x_1, y_{j+200} - y_1\} .$$

```
"The letter A";
```
call *charbegin*(`A, 13, 1.1*phh*, 0);
$y_1 = 0$; $x_{101} = .5u$;
$y_4 = 0$; $x_{204} = r - .5u$;
$y_2 = 1.1hh$; $x_2 = .5r$;
$y_3 = hh$; **new** aa; $y_3 = $ aa$[y_2, y_4]$; $x_3 = $ aa$[x_2, x_4]$;
call *penpos*$(1, -cut - 45, thin)$;
call *penpos*$(2, cut + 25, thick)$;
call *penpos*$(3, cut + 15, {}^{2}\!/_{3}[thin, thick])$;
call *penpos*$(4, cut + 15, thick)$;
$y_{205} = y_{206} = {}^{3}\!/_{7}hh$;
call *penpos*$(5, 45, aspect \cdot thin)$;
call *penpos*$(6, 135, aspect \cdot thin)$;
new aa; $y_5 = $ aa$[y_1, y_3]$; $x_5 + gap \cdot u + .5thin = $ aa$[x_1, x_3]$;
new aa; $y_6 = $ aa$[y_2, y_4]$; $x_6 + gap \cdot u + .5thick = $ aa$[x_2, x_4]$;
call `a *stroke*$(2, 4, tau \cdot tau, tau, .45)$;   % right diagonal
call `b *stroke*$(3, 1, \textbf{sqrt } tau, tau \cdot \textbf{sqrt } tau, .6)$;   % left diagonal
fill **ddraw** $105 .. 106, 205 .. 206$.   % bar line

It is possible for point 203 to stick out of the stem, for certain values of the parameters (including, just barely, some of the examples in Figures 22 and 23). Therefore I subsequently modified the program so that it draws the left diagonal stroke first; then it says

rpen#; thick draw 2..4;

thereby erasing everything to the right of a straight line from 2 to 4. Then it draws the right diagonal and the bar line.

This research was supported in part by National Science Foundation grant IST-820-1926, and by the System Development Foundation.

Addendum

Readers who are interested in exploring this example further with the current version of METAFONT (which was called "next year's META-FONT" in 1983) can now use the following version of the program:

% Sumner Stone's A for ATypI, cut for METAFONT84 by Don Knuth
mode_setup;

$u^\# := {}^{26}/_{36}pt^\#$;	% basic unit
$cap\_height^\# := {}^{245}/_{36}pt^\#$;	% height of uppercase
$thin^\# := {}^{22}/_{36}pt^\#$;	% weight of thin strokes
$thick^\# := {}^{44}/_{36}pt^\#$;	% weight of thick strokes
$tau := 0.4$;	% typical amount of tapering
$gap := 1$;	% units of stroke separation
$cut := 15$;	% degrees of tilt at stroke edge
$aspect := 0.85$;	% vertical / horizontal weight ratio

define_pixels(u);
define_blacker_pixels$(thin, thick)$;

vardef $penpos_{@\#}(\textbf{expr } angle, d) =$ % set pen position
  $z_{@\#} = .5[z_{@\#l}, z_{@\#r}]$; $z_{@\#r} - z_{@\#l} = (d, 0)$ rotated $angle$;
enddef;

vardef $stroke(\textbf{suffix } \$, \$\$, @)(\textbf{expr } lambda, rho, alpha) =$ % tapered stroke
  $z_@ = alpha[z_\$, z_{\$\$}]$; $z_{@l} = alpha[z_{\$l}, z_{\$\$l}]$; $z_{@r} = alpha[z_{\$r}, z_{\$\$r}]$;
  $z_{@l'} = lambda[z_{@l}, z_@]$; $z_{@r'} = rho[z_{@r}, z_@]$;   % pull in for tapering
  labels$(@, @l, @r, @l', @r')$;
  $z_{\$l}\{z_@ - z_{\$l}\} .. z_{@l'}\{z_{\$\$l} - z_{\$l}\} .. z_{\$\$l}\{z_{\$\$l} - z_@\}$ --
      $z_{\$\$r}\{z_@ - z_{\$\$r}\} .. z_{@r'}\{z_{\$r} - z_{\$\$r}\} .. z_{\$r}\{z_{\$r} - z_@\}$ -- cycle
enddef;

`"The letter A"`;
beginchar$(\texttt{"A"}, 13u^\#, 1.1cap\_height^\#, 0)$;
$penpos_1(-cut - 45, thin)$;
$penpos_2(cut + 25, thick)$;
$penpos_3(cut + 15, {}^2/_3[thin, thick])$;
$penpos_4(cut + 15, thick)$;
$penpos_5(45, aspect * thin)$;
$penpos_6(135, aspect * thin)$;
$y_1 = 0$; $x_{1l} = .5u$;
$y_4 = 0$; $x_{4r} = w - .5u$;
$y_2 = 1.1h$; $x_2 = .5w$;
$y_3 = h$; $z_3 = whatever[z_2, z_4]$;
$y_{5r} = {}^3/_7h$; $z_5 + (gap * u + .5thin, 0) = whatever[z_1, z_3]$;
$y_{6r} = {}^3/_7h$; $z_6 + (gap * u + .5thick, 0) = whatever[z_2, z_4]$;
fill $stroke(3, 1, b, \text{sqrt } tau, tau * \text{sqrt } tau, .6)$;   % left diagonal
unfill z_2 -- z_4 -- $(z_4 + (thick, 0))$ -- $(z_2 + (thick, 0))$ -- cycle;   % erase excess
cullit;   % normalize after erasing
fill $stroke(2, 4, a, tau * tau, tau, .45)$;   % right diagonal
fill z_{5l} -- z_{6l} -- z_{6r} -- z_{5r} -- cycle;   % bar line
penlabels(**range** 1 **thru** 6); **endchar**;
end.

References

[1] Thomas B. Hickey and Georgia K. M. Tobin, *The Book of Chels* (Dublin, Ohio: 1982), privately printed.

[2] John D. Hobby and Gu Guoan, "Using METAFONT to design Chinese characters," *Computer Processing of Chinese and Oriental Languages* **1** (July 1983), 4–23. A preliminary version appeared in the proceedings of the 1982 International Conference of the Chinese-Language Computer Society (September 1982), 18–36.

[3] John D. Hobby and Gu Guoan, "A Chinese meta-font," *TUGboat* **5** (1984), 119–136. A preliminary version appeared in the proceedings of ICTP'83, the 1983 International Conference on Text Processing with a Large Character Set (Tokyo: 17–19 October 1983), 62–67.

[4] Donald E. Knuth, "METAFONT, a system for alphabet design," Stanford Artificial Intelligence Memo AIM–332 (September 1979). Reprinted as part 3 of *TEX and METAFONT: New Directions in Typesetting* (Bedford, Massachusetts: Digital Press and American Mathematical Society, 1979).

[5] Donald E. Knuth, *Seminumerical Algorithms*, Volume 2 of *The Art of Computer Programming*, second edition (Reading, Massachusetts: Addison–Wesley, 1981).

[6] Donald E. Knuth, "The concept of a meta-font," *Visible Language* **18** (1982), 3–27. [Reprinted with revisions as Chapter 15 of the present volume.]

[7] Raymond Smullyan, "Miscellanea: Metagame," *American Mathematical Monthly* **90** (1983), 390.

[8] Sumner Stone, "The ATypI logotype: A digital design process," presented at Fifth ATypI Working Seminar, Stanford, California (August 1983).

Chapter 17

AMS Euler — A New Typeface for Mathematics

*[Written with Hermann Zapf. Originally published in Scholarly Publishing **20** (1989), 131–157.]*

A collaboration between scientists and artists is helping to bring more beauty to the pages of mathematical journals and textbooks.

The printing of mathematics has become faster, simpler, and less expensive than ever before because of recent technological developments. Pages are now composed from millions of tiny dots of ink positioned by computers. Systems like TeX [14] can be used to specify where the letters and symbols should be placed on a page; companion systems like METAFONT [16] can be used to specify the dots of ink that produce those letters and symbols. TeX and METAFONT, completed in 1986, are already in use by tens of thousands of people on more than a hundred different kinds of computers, from PCs and Macintoshes to giant Cray machines. These systems are designed to give equivalent results on all computing devices and all digital output devices, although the quality will naturally vary with the quality of the typesetting machine being used. Furthermore, TeX and METAFONT are designed to be fully archival, in the sense that manuscripts preserved today in electronic form as files of text can be expected to produce identical output several generations from now.

Such trends were foreseeable ten years ago [12], but it has taken considerable time to dot all the i's and cross all the t's (literally) that were necessary to obtain sufficiently flexible and refined systems. The American Mathematical Society (AMS), one of the world's largest publishers of mathematics, formed a font committee in 1979 to help plan for the future by taking appropriate advantage of the emerging technology. The initial members of this committee were Richard Palais (chair), a professor of mathematics at Brandeis University; Barbara Beeton, an editor from AMS headquarters; Peter Renz, the mathematics editor for W. H. Freeman & Co.; and the two authors of the present article (DEK and HZ).

At that time DEK and HZ knew each other only through their respective publications. We both secretly wished to meet, but were afraid to ask, knowing that the other was extremely busy. Fortunately the AMS served as matchmaker, and we were able to begin a stimulating collaboration between mathematician and artist that we hope will have a beneficial effect on scholarly publishing. Our goal in this article is to record some aspects of our collaboration that we think are particularly noteworthy, as they bring out issues about mathematical publishing that are rarely discussed in print.

It seems best to tell our story by quoting directly from the letters that we wrote to each other and received from others at the time. (A complete record of this correspondence, with all the accompanying drawings, has been deposited in the Stanford University Archives, collection SC 362.)

Richard Palais explained the original goals of our work admirably in his initial invitation letter:

> 11 September 1979
> R. Palais to HZ
> Dear Professor Zapf,
> [Introductory remarks ...] It is therefore now feasible for the AMS to design a comprehensive and compatible family of alphabetic and symbolic fonts, organized following the TEX pattern and meant not only for use in the publication of the AMS journals and books, but also for the use of the mathematical and scientific community at large. Clearly this is a project that has long term value, a project that should be carried out with planning, care, and the best professional advice available.

At about the same time DEK wrote to HZ inviting him to get acquainted with METAFONT by visiting Stanford in February 1980. Already the germs of a design were beginning to emerge:

> 7 October 1979
> HZ to DEK
> Dear Dr. Knuth,
> ... We should work out carefully with METAFONT the basic structure for a standard scientific alphabet, neutral in its forms, and the best solution for all sorts of typesetting devices — to be printed later by commercial offset or low-quality office equipment, then xeroxed from printed sheets, etc., etc.

... I would prefer for a scientific basic alphabet the vertical structure, for you have not as many problems as with the slanted forms. For we want at the end a really good alphabet with many possibilities of special characters for all kinds of scientific publications. An alphabet with all the necessary symbols and extra forms fitting ideally together as a total design.

25 October 1979
DEK to HZ
Dear Prof. Zapf,
... I must explain that typography is not my life's work; I am primarily an educator, doing and guiding research in computer science and mathematics, and writing books that attempt to bring some unity into those subjects. Meanwhile, while solving a problem related to the publishing of such books, I seem to have stumbled onto some ideas of value in the printing industry, so I want to make sure that I have explained these ideas properly and gotten them off to a good start. If the ideas have merit, they should survive without my pushing for them; if not, they should die anyway.

... Now what about a set of fonts for AMS? At present they use Times New Roman for text, Times Italic for formulas and for emphasis. The use of Times Italic for formulas is very unfortunate in my opinion (and I'm not alone!), since the formulas become too crowded; there never was a good reason to use Times Italic except that it was a fashionable font for *text* work at the time AMS switched compositors.

The right thing to do seems obvious: to take an existing text and italic face for the text and emphasized text, and to design a compatible *new* face for use in mathematical formulas that go with the text. For example, we could start with Times Roman and Italic; but of course we should really use Zapf Book, or Optima, or some other beautiful font that you have given to the world.

The new mathematical typeface should be readily distinguishable from the text faces, in a subliminal way; furthermore it must include Greek and Fraktur and Script alphabets as well as roman letters and digits. Different letters and symbols must be readily distinguishable ('a' from alpha, 'v' from nu, zero from Oh, etc.), but it's not necessary to distinguish Greek letters that correspond exactly to Roman ones (upper case A, B, E, H, I, K, O, P, T, U, X, Z; lower case o and possibly u).

Your idea to design this face without a slant is very interesting, and I believe it is a good one in spite of the long traditional use of slanted symbols — especially because some mathematicians like to stack up accents like $\hat{\hat{a}}$.

Should the new font be different primarily because of the presence or absence of serifs? Or by its weight? Traditionally the letters of formulas have a slightly lighter weight than the text; for example, Computer Modern math italic has stems about $3/4$ as thick as the stems of the roman and slanted roman text fonts. Mathematicians attach significance to boldface symbols, so I believe it will be best to maintain this tradition of making non-bold symbols slightly lighter than the text.

One other characteristic might turn out to be important in planning the design, namely that mathematicians think of formulas as something they *write* on a blackboard or a piece of paper, while the text is something *typed*. Thus, the difference between text and math should probably be that the text is more mechanical, the math is more calligraphic.

The design should be psychologically right for mathematicians when they first see it, if possible; the mathematical meaning ideally will be perceived without conscious translation. Thus, the new font must be well aware of historic traditions even as it breaks new ground. ...

P.S. One other thought: Some mathematics seems to me inherently unbeautiful, no matter how it is set in type! We should choose test examples from books that have been well copy-edited.

To the authors' knowledge, similar attempts to design a compatible set of typefaces and symbols for mathematics have been made only twice before. The venerable typefoundry of Joh. Enschedé en Zonen, in Haarlem, Holland, asked Jan van Krimpen to undertake such a project in the late 1920s. Professor H. A. Lorentz, Nobel laureate in Physics (1902), lived in Haarlem and agreed to cooperate. But Lorentz died in 1928 and "the work involved proved to be even more extensive and intricate than had been anticipated" [4]; "as a consequence, the scheme was abandoned" [23, page 32]. The lone outcome of that project was a Greek typeface called Antigone, which van Krimpen says he designed quickly, following the fashion of Greek text types [23, page 35]. Antigone is an upright face, unlike the oblique Greek types traditionally used for mathematics; so it appears that he too was planning for a scientific alphabet with a vertical feeling.

A less abortive attempt was made by the American Mathematical Society beginning in 1962. Here the decision was to make all the mathematical alphabets slanted, to match Times Italic. This proved to be unfortunate in the case of Fraktur, because "the dignity and weight of the original was regrettably lost in many of the letters when they were tilted 18° [20]." The AMS Script capitals, designed as part of this

The first collaboration between DEK (seated) and HZ (standing), 14 February 1980. [Stanford News Service photo by Chuck Painter.]

project, were noteworthy as the first script letters specifically intended for mathematics. The difficulty was to create something that is "distinctly a script alphabet but with minimal ornamentation" [20], since the flowery hairlines of traditional script faces tend to disappear when used in small sizes as subscripts and superscripts.

HZ spent two weeks visiting DEK at Stanford in February 1980, two enormously exciting weeks for both of us. We were delighted to see how easily people from C. P. Snow's "two cultures" could work together; and we certainly did work intensely during that time. We studied the classic reference on mathematical typesetting [2], noting that even Oxford University Press did not have typefaces in which all the necessary characters were readily distinguishable in small sizes. Most of our days were devoted to tutorials by DEK about METAFONT and by HZ about type design and calligraphy. HZ explained how to get special effects by applying different amounts of "pen pressure," and DEK found a way to simulate such effects on a computer. We had very little time left to begin the design of a new typeface, but we did succeed in making a few trial characters. Here is a copy of the one and only proof we had time to make on a phototypesetting machine:

Consider the formula 66E − 77g.

Also consider the formula 66E − 77g ≥ α𝒳.

(We weren't happy with this script X, of course; we had been able to work on it for only a few minutes at the end of the day.)

> 24 February 1980
> HZ to DEK
> Dear Don,
> I want to tell you how much I appreciate the cordial reception you gave me. ... By separate mail I'm sending two broadsides, in case you have some space left on a wall. The Oppenheimer quotation [22, page 119; 25, page 220; 26, page 133] describes exactly my personal feelings about arts and science: The left part of the circles (in color) shows the world of the artist, the right side (abstract in lines only) the world of the scientist. In general (as demonstrated in the outer circle) they connect as human beings, but in other parts and thoughts they try always to get an agreement as an ideal dream.
>
> Let us take these two weeks in Stanford as a beginning.

> 17 March 1980
> DEK to HZ
> Dear Hermann,
> ... I now believe the proper name of the font would be "Euler"; or else we might choose to be dull and impersonal and call it "AMS Mathematics."
>
> In case "Euler" gets the nod, I tried to find examples of his handwriting ...

The name Euler had been suggested during an AMS Font Committee meeting on 23 February, because the Swiss mathematician Leonhard Euler (1707–1783) was one of the greatest and best loved mathematicians of all time [9]. Euler would surely have appreciated today's advances in technology, for the printing presses of his day could not keep up with his prodigious output. (Indeed, the St. Petersburg academy continued regular publication of the manuscripts in their "Euler backlog" for more than thirty years after his death!)

Leonhard Euler was primarily responsible for introducing the wide variety of alphabets now found in printed mathematics. John Wallis had occasionally mixed Greek and Italic letters in the formulas of his *Algebra* [24], but Euler carried this idea much further and made use also of the Fraktur alphabet. Here, for example, is an extract from an article he published in 1765 [6, §33]:

$$\text{Ind.} \quad v \, , \; a \, , \; b$$
$$\text{Fra\d{c}t.} \; \tfrac{1}{0} \, , \; \tfrac{\mathfrak{A}}{a} \, , \; \tfrac{\mathfrak{B}}{b} \, , \; \tfrac{\mathfrak{C}}{c}$$
$$\text{vbi} \quad \mathfrak{A} = v, \mathfrak{B} = a\mathfrak{A} + 1 ; \mathfrak{C} = b\mathfrak{B} + \mathfrak{A}$$
$$\text{et} \quad \mathfrak{a} = 1, \mathfrak{b} = a\mathfrak{a} + 0 ; \mathfrak{c} = b\mathfrak{b} + \mathfrak{a}$$

Euler's textbook on integral calculus (1769) contained formulas that combine Roman, Italic, Fraktur, and Greek all at once [7, §1130]:

$$e^{\frac{-f x \, cof. \, \zeta}{g}} \left\{ \begin{array}{l} (\mathfrak{A} + \mathfrak{B}x + \mathfrak{C}xx) cof. \frac{f x fin. \zeta}{g} \\ (\mathfrak{a} + \mathfrak{b}x + \mathfrak{c}xx) fin. \frac{f x fin. \zeta}{g} \end{array} \right\}$$

If he had used Cyrillic letters in his publications, today's mathematicians would probably know Cyrillic as well as Greek! But Euler did occasionally resort to notational novelties that did not survive him. Here is a formula in which he combined the astronomical symbols for Sun, Saturn, Jupiter, and Mars [8, §6]:

$$\odot = 2\,\saturn + 2\,\jupiter + \mars = \tfrac{\pi}{4}$$

By March 1980, DEK and HZ had decided that the new font should have a "handwritten" flavor. Hence there was a chance that Euler's own handwriting would inspire some feature of the design. And indeed, it turned out that Euler often made the top of the numeral zero pointed instead of round [3]:

However, this is a common characteristic of handwriting in general, and it didn't directly influence the design of AMS Euler; HZ had already been experimenting with pointed zeros before he had seen Euler's writing, after looking at mathematical manuscripts by Einstein, Newton,

Ramanujan, and DEK. The "point" of this point was to distinguish zero from Oh in a natural way.

20 March 1980
HZ to DEK
Dear Don:
Enclosed are a few sketches of some characters and symbols together with alternates, to get first your opinion and corrections before I make the sketches for AMS.

$$E = mc^2$$
$$\bar{x}' = \mathfrak{P}(x') = \alpha\bar{x} \quad g(\lambda v + \mu w)$$
$$f(\lambda p + \mu q) = \lambda^2 \dot{p} \, \mathfrak{A} p + 2\lambda \mu^2 - \alpha_{10}$$
$$[\sqrt{(1 + \sigma_\omega / \sigma_\gamma)^4}]$$
$$\mathcal{ELDFHKIJTCSGSSVWXYZT}$$
$$\gamma = 0.577216 \quad (\lambda + \tfrac{i\pi}{2})$$

[These drawings have been reduced to 50% of their original size. Many more sketches were enclosed, not shown here.]

4 April 1980
DEK to HZ
Dear Hermann,
The samples you sent contain a lot of marvelous touches, and I'm quite enthusiastic about the prospects for this design. However, in order to save space, I will restrict my remarks below to the problem areas and things that I *don't* like instead of exclaiming over what I *do* like very much; so this letter might seem to have too negative a tone. I apologize in advance for this, and I hope you can get the proper balance by imagining that I have written a much, much longer letter in which there is glowing praise for everything I don't mention below. ...

1 / The hooks at the beginning and end of the Roman lowercase letters must be more rounded so that they are more free and quite distinct from the Fraktur. Let the abrupt angle be a "trademark" of Fraktur, and let the Roman letters flow smoothly.

2 / For handwritten mathematics I much prefer a 'y' with a curved bowl, relating it to 'u' rather than to 'v'. ...

4 / I don't like the script K, but I'm not sure how to keep it from looking funny and at the same time to make it quite distinct from script H and X. Please do your best to find a nice K, as it is a very important letter to me (as Z is to you)! ...

7 / The tear-drop zero is very successful, and I really would like to see it used in this font. ...

9 / The upper left stroke of a 5 should be exactly vertical, not slightly slanted as you have it. Otherwise it will look horrible when digitized on the coarse rasters that many people will have in their laboratories.

Seven compatible alphabets were necessary altogether: lowercase Roman, uppercase Roman, uppercase Script, lowercase Greek, uppercase Greek, lowercase Fraktur, and uppercase Fraktur. (Script alphabets in the Italian style were invented by the Belgian punchcutter Jacques-François Rosart in 1753 [5]; but they apparently did not find their way to Berlin or St. Petersburg during Euler's lifetime, because he never used them. Mathematicians became enamored of script capital letters much later, during the 20th century. Script lowercase has never been commonly used in mathematics except for the letter 'ℓ'.)

23 April 1980
HZ to DEK
Dear Don:
Let me thank you especially for all the care you put into your corrections; it took quite a lot of your spare time. For a new font of such importance, this is exactly the way I like to work. You should not at all think I would be unhappy about any honest and constructive criticism or corrections of special or difficult characters.

Enclosed you will find the proposals which Dr. LeVeque wanted for the AMS Board of Trustees meeting in May.

Uem Pid Gro Mag Rvy Auf Vtl Dxh Jc 𝔎 𝔑 ℱ ℛ ℬ 𝒩 𝒜 𝒫 𝒰 ℛ − 𝒰 𝒜 𝒜 𝒴 𝒮 ?
ℰ ℒ 𝒮 ℱ 𝒢 𝒳 𝒵 𝒟 𝒦 𝒱 𝒴 ℋ 𝒲 𝒥 𝒥 ℳ 𝒪 𝒬 𝒯 𝒞 1752048639 13725490 = + ← [{ (
Σμκαγιεβυνλπωχσφδψθη ζ ρ ξ ϑ ο Π Γ Δ Θ Υ Ω Ξ Λ Φ Ψ Λ Θ Σ Γ Φ Ω ζ ξ
𝔅𝔣𝔞 𝔊𝔭𝔢 𝔐𝔬𝔣 𝔎𝔦𝔰 𝔗𝔲𝔤 𝔓𝔯𝔥 𝔚𝔥𝔮 𝔛𝔢𝔫 ℭ C Z F S L N Q B W I X K Y H T I E=mc²

William LeVeque, executive director of the American Mathematical Society, was carefully monitoring this activity. (He even came to Stanford during January 1981, and learned to design several Cyrillic characters with METAFONT.)

9 May 1980
W. J. LeVeque to HZ

Dear Professor Zapf:

I am very pleased to tell you that the Board of Trustees, at its meeting of 3 May, agreed to accept your proposal.

... I think it is wise to be quite open about one matter at the outset. Mathematicians tend, on the whole, to be rather conservative esthetically, and to like what they are accustomed to. Due account must be taken of that fact if either the Society or other mathematics publishers are to adopt the new Euler font. The Trustees therefore want to be sure that the entire Font Committee, augmented by several mathematicians not now on that committee, will have an opportunity to react to your designs, before they are considered final.

... We are all looking forward to working with you and to having the beautiful collection of fonts that we know will come from your efforts.

```
Date: 09 May 1980 0819-PDT
From: Don Knuth <DEK at SU-AI>
To:   Palais at MIT-MC
Thanks for your message about the Trustees' vote. As
for proceeding, how about this: (1) You send me a letter
explaining full details of any criticisms of the current
draft by the committee, so that I can communicate them
to Zapf. (2) You write Zapf a brief note saying that the
committee's recommendations have been forwarded to me and
that he should be hearing from me soon. (3) After I write
to him, he will make sketches at the size we need to make
the METAFONT designs. I'll give these to Scott Kim, who
has agreed to do the METAFONTing as a preliminary to
his thesis work. Periodically I will check with Scott
and oversee what he is doing. (4) After Scott and I have
something done, we will send the results to Zapf and to
whoever else from AMS wants to participate in the review.
This final editing may go through a few iterations, but
we will be able to typeset a lot of sample material and
make changes easily once it is all in METAFONT form.
```

26 May 1980
HZ to DEK
Dear Don:

... Perhaps there may arise a few differences between members of the Font Committee for some special character designs. I would suggest coordinating these different opinions before starting with the designs, so as to get precise directions for the final drawings and to avoid excessive redesigns. The best would be if this could be done by you.

27 May 1980
DEK to HZ
Dear Hermann,
I was glad to learn that the AMS trustees have officially decided to commission your work on this important typeface. Now it "only" remains to bring the project to a successful conclusion!

Thanks for the beautiful work enclosed in your letter. Most of it is exactly right, and I'm amazed at how you've solved problems that I thought would be almost impossible, like the script Q.

There is one thing that still bothers me, and I would like to bring it up again because I *do* feel strongly about it. (However, if you really want to overrule me, you certainly are the boss!) I think the opening and closing hooklets on the lowercase Roman letters still turn too sharply, so I've enclosed a sketch of the way I think they should be.

Present form: I would prefer them more rounded:

This will not only distinguish them more clearly from the Fraktur, it also will make for a smoother, more flowing, feeling. You have captured this wonderful flow in the lowercase 'g' and 'x'; I would like the 'm' and 'y', etc., to have the same completely uncrotchety spirit.

Now for more detailed comments on the individual letters: ... Script 'I' is a problem; the letter you have drawn looks fine, when it is next to a 'J', but in mathematics that 'I' will be all by itself and few people will recognize what it is. ... The lowercase sigma has slightly too long a hook now; it would be very hard to typeset the formula '$|\sigma|$' without making it look off center. ... The question mark is beautiful but it won't be needed in these fonts — mathematicians use exclamation points but not question marks! ... The second lowercase zeta and xi are better than the first, but the main horizontal stroke at the bottom is too long and mathematicians are accustomed to more of a hook below the baseline.

How should we proceed from here? I've been thinking a lot about this, and your recent boldface examples have made something clear to me that I should have realized long ago. Namely, the best way to prepare designs for METAFONT will be somewhat different from the normal way of working. In the first place, it is not necessary for you to make extremely fine quality drawings with pen and ink; pencil sketches will do nicely. But what I really need is *two sketches for each letter*, one showing lightface and one showing boldface (perhaps slightly extrabold in fact). This is the crucial information necessary to instruct METAFONT how to vary the design as the specifications change. I would not have been able to predict the appearance of the beautiful boldface uppercase Greek letters you sent, if just given the lightface ones; both are therefore essential.

You should make two such sketches for each Fraktur letter, too, even though the standard fonts will probably include Fraktur only in one weight that is almost-but-not-quite bold. Then we'll be able to make experiments with lots of degrees of boldness without changing the design.

I suppose it will be best for you to do all of the alphabets at once, instead of trying to work on a few letters and send them to California and then to do a few more, etc.; consistency will surely be important. Scott Kim is working hard to finish his book about "DESIGNatures" [11], and I expect he will be ready to start META-FONTing your work by September or October.

Meanwhile, to get started, we would like sample designs in large size of say five characters: uppercase A, lowercase i, Greek Sigma, numeral zero, and Fraktur R. Please send two drawings of each, one bold and one light. I'll check to see that the designs you send give all the information that Scott and I need to prepare METAFONT specifications. Then I'll give you the "go-ahead" to do the main part of your design work. ... How does this sound to you?

16 August 1980
HZ to DEK
Dear Don:
... On July 27th I had lunch in Boston with Palais and LeVeque, but we all missed you.

By the end of next week I will finish two alphabets (handwritten Roman and Greek), and I should send them directly to Rhode Island to be photographed and delivered to all the participants in the project for their approval.

In the meantime you may test the enclosed large-size drawings at Stanford and tell me as soon as possible if they are OK for Scott.

After receiving the comments and corrections for the two alphabets from you — checking and melting together the ideas of all our other AMS friends — I could finish the final drawings in a short time.

5 September 1980
To: Font Committee
From: W. J. LeVeque
Enclosed are photocopies of Hermann Zapf's first completed alphabets ... These will be the faces used for mathematical symbols, in place of the traditionally used italics — e.g., the x in $\sin x$. You will notice that they are upright, which will provide great simplification in the placement of diacritical marks above, below, or beside them.

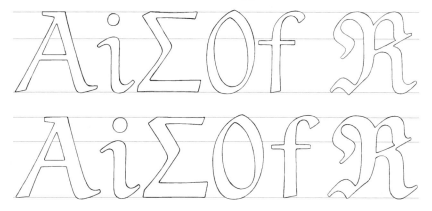

[These drawings, enclosed in HZ's letter of 16 August 1980, have been reduced to 33% of their original size.]

What is needed now are your criticisms or suggestions, as soon as you can supply them. Don Knuth will be visiting Providence on September 24, and it would be most convenient if you could return the enclosed sheets to me prior to that time.

abcdefghijklmnopqrstuv
wxyz1234567890 74fj
ABCDEGHIJLMNOP
QRSTUVWXYZKKFT
αβγδεζηθικλμνξοπρσς,
τυφχψω1234567890φ
ΓΔΘΛΞΠΣΦΨΩΛΞΨ

[Enlargements of these characters were distributed with identification numbers added, from 1 (for 'a') to 119 (for 'Ψ'). Each committee member received a five-page questionnaire asking for 119 ratings: Excellent/Satisfactory/Unsatisfactory/Comments.]

8 September 1980
DEK to HZ

Dear Hermann,

Thanks for your letter of August 16, and for the six sample letters (medium and bold) for METAFONT testing. I'm giving these immediately to Scott, although he is just now finishing up the last details on his book so it might be a few weeks before he can give this the concentrated attention it deserves. We might have a tough time keeping up with your productive pace!

The alphabet samples you sent to AMS are being circulated to the font committee, and I will do my best to see that we can gain the advantages of a committee's collective wisdom without suffering the disadvantages of "design by committee." Each member is independently filling out a questionnaire; this will be extremely valuable as an expression of what a mathematician's eyes perceive, especially when most of them independently make the same observations. There may also be cases where the committee is in complete disagreement (horrors!), but even then I think their input will be extremely valuable although we may not be able to please everybody.

P.S. The opening and closing hooklets on the letters now please me greatly. Thank you so much!

Questionnaires were filled out by William J. LeVeque, Richard Palais, Barbara Beeton, Peter Renz, DEK, and new committee members Ralph P. Boas (of Northwestern University), Lincoln K. Durst, Phœbe Murdock, Ellen Swanson, Samuel B. Whidden (all of the AMS), and William B. Woolf (of *Mathematical Reviews*). Here is an excerpt from a typical response:

16 September 1980
Ralph P. Boas to W. J. LeVeque
Dear Bill,
... People, including me, have been struggling for 50 years to get printers to distinguish $\in$ from ε. I thought the battle had been won — and now the AMS, at the stroke of an artist's pen, is about to lose it for us. Why does it matter? Because '$\varepsilon \in S$' is a perfectly possible combination. ... I do think the new alphabet is inherently quite attractive. However, I feel that the form 'α' fits better with the rest of the letters than 'a'.

The results were summarized in a long (13-page) epistle:

9 October 1980
DEK to HZ
Dear Hermann,
I hope you are having a pleasant autumn. School has just begun here and we have many fine new students. The trees are turning colors and the squirrels are gathering nuts; the birds are singing merrily.

But now to work! I went to AMS headquarters recently and we had a long and informative discussion relating to the Euler fonts. My purpose in this letter is to digest the committee's opinions so as to make your job as easy as possible. This committee is fairly well representative of the outlook of mathematicians who care about the quality of their papers, and I know that you appreciate such attention to details; so I will write you a little story about each character, based on their views.

The overall reaction was, of course, highly favorable, but we realize that there is a danger of confusing the mathematics font with the text font; more than half of the committee expressed concern about this problem. A little more "cursiveness" or "exuberance" in the shapes would be a noteworthy improvement in those letters that now involve only straight strokes. There was a general feeling that it's better to have a slightly less beautiful character if it is more distinguishable from ordinary Roman type, even when we love the looks of the Roman-like one.

Now for the individual "short stories," which are numbered according to the codes on the attached copy of the sample drawings. But before you read them, note that I think it would be best if you don't make the METAFONT-size drawings until Scott and I have finished with the test characters you already drew for us. Just look quickly through the comments now, so that you can get an idea of the committee's sentiments; then I think the next thing to do is to prepare samples of Script and Fraktur analogous to the Roman and Greek.

1 / Everyone likes the looks of this 'a', but we do feel strongly that the other style should be used instead. The italic 'α' is what mathematicians always write on the blackboard and it is more consistent with the other Euler letters. I apologize for not commenting on this before; I simply failed to notice the problem.

2, 3, 4, 5 / Everybody likes these, and they do seem sufficiently distinct from ordinary roman text.

6 / Here the question is whether to choose (6) or (39). The committee first split evenly over which was preferable, since (6) is quite elegant. However, after someone pointed out that (6) doesn't work well in the common case that 'f' is followed by a left parenthesis, the votes became unanimous in favor of (39), *not* (6).

7 / Excellent, unanimous approval.

. . .

119 / Form (119) should be used instead of (115), but add two serifs at the bottom, as in 'I' (48) and 'Φ' (114).

Above all I want to emphasize the committee's view that you should make your own decisions about what is best for the overall design. Our aim is to give you as many facts as we can about mathematicians' experiences, and about what issues are the most sensitive, but our separate opinions should not be allowed to mess up the whole. The general feeling so far is: "Altogether — what a beautiful piece of work!"

22 October 1980
R. Palais to DEK
Dear Don,
On behalf of all of us I want to thank you for the care and effort you obviously devoted to assimilating $n \times 119$ opinions on characters in the Zapf fonts. Your letter is in my mind a masterpiece. LeVeque was *very* impressed. I think he originally feared that you would let your own tastes dominate, but now he seems very enthusiastic about the project and the strategy you have devised for attaining the best of all worlds by bringing committee wisdom together with individual creativity. If this design project is a success — as I believe it will be — I think it will be as much due to your patience and æsthetic balance as to Zapf's wonderful taste and craftsmanship.

25 October 1980
HZ to DEK
Dear Don:
For me the whole Euler font story is an ideal example of teamwork. I agree with all the corrections you and your friends have made. And I am very happy that the new zeros are accepted.

5 December 1980
W. J. LeVeque to Font Committee [with enclosure above]

Dear Colleagues:

Enclosed is Sheet II of Hermann Zapf's work, along with comment sheets. In addition to Fraktur and Script alphabets, he has supplied new versions of the letters on Sheet I that required major modifications to take care of various criticisms. As before, please send your comments to me.

8 December 1980
R. P. Boas to HZ
Dear Professor Zapf:

... The new gamma is attractive, and I wouldn't worry if the loop does disappear in reproduction — after all, many Greek fonts don't show a loop.

I have just been reading a Russian paper that actually uses, more than once, $\varepsilon \in E$ (fortunately not $\varepsilon \in \mathcal{E}$), which points up the importance of distinguishing between the letter ε and the symbol $\in$.

5 February 1981
DEK to HZ
Dear Hermann,

Are you ready for another long letter about letters? Once again I'm going to try to digest the independent opinions of the font committee members. In general, people are feeling good about the way things are progressing. Everybody (except me) voiced a concern that the hairlines will drop out at small sizes; I should have explained to them that METAFONT will take care of hairlines, and that we needn't worry about such things at this stage.

Now to the individual letters by number, as before.

1 / There was one comment that the southwest corner of the bowl should bend at a slightly sharper angle (as in the $\mathfrak{b}$), so as to make this more distinctly Fraktur.

2, 3 / Unanimous approval: Bravo, bravo!

4 / Too much like a delta. I found a Fraktur $\mathfrak{d}$ in two mathematical reference books, and in both cases the diagonal stroke at the top came down more sharply (more nearly horizontal)

...

106 / Everyone likes this aleph; one person wondered if it were too bold, but we can always tune that later.

One more important change is necessary: I talked to a lot of people about my proposal to let one set of numerals be of variable width ... We should reverse that decision and make all ten digits have the same width, both in lining style and in old style.

So, that completes this round of comments. Clearly the Euler fonts are taking shape very nicely, and METAFONTing is going to be the next critical step.

Scott Kim, a graduate student of computer science working for DEK, had volunteered to encode the Euler designs with the METAFONT system in preparation for his thesis work, which was to address questions about the relationship between computers and visual thinking. His first experiments were quite successful:

17 February 1981

DEK to HZ

Dear Hermann,

Here are the first five sample Euler characters as they have been produced by METAFONT. Scott has done a considerable amount of excellent work to develop a new style of METAFONT programming that simulates pen rotation and pressure, and we are gradually learning how to control this medium. It isn't easy, but it's fun and instructive.

While preparing these examples, there were many times we wished you were right here to guide us! On the other hand, the fact that we are communicating in writing is very useful, since it forces us to be more precise and to get our ideas clearer.

Are the enclosed letters sufficiently close to your drawings that we can go ahead to the next stage? If not, please say so frankly, and send detailed comments about what refinements we should learn to make before we are ready to proceed to the real letters of AMS Euler.

Users of METAFONT write a "program" for each letter, expressing their intentions in a special language. The program tells the computer how to draw that letter, based on a number of parameters for things such as the height and unit width of the typeface, as well as the weights of different kinds of strokes. The program uses these parameters to define key points. For example, the crossbar stroke in the diagram shown here goes from key points 110–310 to key points 111–311.

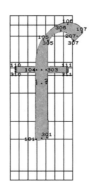

Such programs yield a "meta-font" [13], which can be used to generate a wide variety of specific fonts when the parameters are chosen appropriately. Here, for example, are six versions of the five test characters mentioned in DEK's letter of 17 February 1981:

$$Ai\Sigma 0f \quad Ai\Sigma 0f \quad Ai\Sigma 0f \quad Ai\Sigma 0f \quad Ai\Sigma 0f \quad Ai\Sigma 0f$$

The second and fifth examples correspond to HZ's drawings of 16 August 1980; the middle two are interpolations; the outer two are extrapolations (which are more dangerous).

A meta-font allows designers to experiment with many different possibilities. For example, the height or width of a character can be changed without altering the thickness of the strokes:

$$oooooo \qquad AAAAAA$$

23 February 1981
W. J. LeVeque to Scott Kim
Dear Scott,
I was very glad to hear that you expect to be able to complete the metafonting of the Roman, Greek, Fraktur, and Script alphabets this spring. . . .

Yes, those were euphoric days; everything seemed to be proceeding splendidly. But then came a big dose of reality, which threatened to jeopardize the entire project. Meta-design is more difficult than ordinary design, and it is not yet a well-understood concept (especially not for fonts such as this). DEK had forgotten that he had needed more than a year to learn the principles of meta-design. Furthermore there were more than 200 characters to be done, each drawn with two weights. It was impossible to expect that HZ had been precisely consistent in the way he changed each stroke of each character from medium weight to bold; hence no computer-generated meta-font could be expected to match HZ's drawings perfectly. Considerable judgment was necessary to distinguish the really critical aspects of the drawings from things that HZ himself would have changed if he were the meta-designer. Kim's assignment was therefore much more challenging than DEK or HZ realized at the time.

DEK asked if HZ would go so far as to give him and Scott the following freedom: "If it is difficult to coerce METAFONT to produce a faithful copy of your drawing, and if there is something nearly like your drawing that is easy for METAFONT and that looks OK to us, may we deliberately change your design to what is most natural for META-FONT? (This would of course be subject to your eventual approval of our results.)" HZ replied in the affirmative: "I trust you. There will be in several characters some compromise necessary between my drawings and the structure pattern of METAFONT. Don't be too anxious; I know you both will do your best."

> 26 May 1981
> DEK to HZ
> Dear Hermann,
> The postman brought three delicious treats from you last week! By now we have received complete sets of numerals together with lower and upper case Roman and Greek, in both normal and bold weights.
> So there is plenty of work for Scott to do now. He is planning to give top priority to Euler during the summer.

Alas, however, the summer saw only the completion of 26 lowercase Roman letters. There was no simple way to convert the drawings to computer code; each letter took a day's thought, a day's tedious measurements and typing, then another day's fighting with METAFONT. It turned out that the first METAFONT system was not at all suited for a project such as this; a completely new system was called for [15]. But DEK was already committed to other projects that kept him busy more than full time. We gradually learned that the necessary work would require several years.

> 19 April 1982
> DEK to HZ
> Dear Hermann,
> ... I have absolutely no doubt that Euler will some day live up to our expectations, but that day is much further off than I once believed.

To the rescue came Stanford's new program in Digital Typography, launched in the autumn of 1982 under the direction of Prof. Charles A. Bigelow. New students John Hobby, Dan Mills, David Siegel, and Carol Twombly combined a variety of skills to encapsulate all of HZ's drawings in computable form, just as DEK was finishing the brand-new META-FONT system in September 1985. The complete saga of these instructive developments has been told in a well-illustrated booklet by David Siegel [21].

> The group produced 484 characters in less than 484 working days, including all the programming. Total disk space consumed by the project was over 80 million characters stored on two computers. ... Equations set in Euler must endure the smudge of the over-inked press onto the flimsiest of papers. They must not fade away on

the drum of a laserprinter, nor under the not-so-bright lights of the ancient photocopiers in the math library. The letters must not blur under the dimmest of lighting near the periodicals through the foggiest of trifocals; they must shine clearly through the forest of hen scratchings during proofreading. The Euler typeface is ready to meet these challenges at the AMS.

Even after the fonts had been digitized, the work was not complete. Appropriate amounts of "white space" needed to be specified at the left, right, above, and below each character. Information needed to be supplied for positioning of accents and subscripts. (The mathematicians' original hopes that this would be unnecessary in an upright font were not realized; the actual advantage of uprightness was more subtle, namely that upright letters blend better with parentheses, plus signs, and the other symbols of mathematics.) New "macros" needed to be written so that authors and their computers would be able to refer to the new fonts in appropriate ways. And — most significantly — experience was needed to test and fine-tune the new designs in a variety of mathematical contexts. We needed to live with the new conventions and learn their basic properties before foisting them on a larger community.

The obvious next step was to make the Fraktur fonts widely available, as a supplement to existing typefaces, because there was an immediate need for mathematical Fraktur. This portion of AMS Euler was therefore the first to be used in actual publications, initially in a book typeset as an experiment at Stanford [19] and subsequently in many AMS journal articles.

AMS Euler finally reached its original design goals when all of its integrated alphabets were adopted for all of the mathematics in a substantial textbook. This text, called *Concrete Mathematics* [10], was in many ways an ideal launching pad for the new conventions. In the first place, *Concrete Mathematics* treated many different kinds of mathematics in its various chapters. Secondly, DEK was both typesetter and coauthor of this book, so he could examine the formulas carefully and make any necessary adjustments. And finally, the subject matter of *Concrete Mathematics* was a perfect match for the name AMS Euler, because DEK and his coauthors had already decided to dedicate their book to Leonhard Euler! "Leonhard Euler's spirit truly lives on every page: Concrete mathematics is Eulerian mathematics" [10, page ix].

When the book's designer, Roy Howard Brown, first saw the Eulerian fonts he noticed that they were slightly darker in color than traditional mathematical typefaces, so they called for a slightly stronger text face than normal. Based on these recommendations, DEK supplied a new typeface called Concrete Roman and Italic for the main text, using his Computer Modern meta-font [17] with somewhat "Egyptian" parameters [18]. The combination of AMS Euler and Concrete Roman proved to be a happy one throughout the 640 pages of *Concrete Mathematics*, so the Euler fonts now seem to have a bright future indeed.

One aspect of the switch from existing conventions to AMS Euler proved to be a surprise: There now are four distinct sets of numerals, namely "lining style" (with all digits above the baseline, having identical height: 0123456789) and "old style" (0123456789), in both the text face and in the mathematics face. Therefore the authors needed to distinguish for the first time between numbers that are part of the text (like '1988') and numbers that are part of the mathematics (like '3.1416'). This distinction proved to be rather effective and it was easily implemented with TeX. Lining numerals of the text face were used for such phrases as 'Chapter 2'; oldstyle numerals of the text face were used for equation numbers. Lining numerals of AMS Euler were used within mathematical formulas, and AMS Euler's oldstyle numerals would have been appropriate for numerical tables (not needed in this book).

The use of AMS Euler in *Concrete Mathematics* was otherwise fairly routine, except in one passage on pages 142–143, where the authors wanted to have a sequence of ever-more-complex-looking q's (because the mathematics was going from a "first-level" q to second, third, and higher levels). In the first draft the sequence was lowercase Roman, then uppercase Roman, then Script, then boldface Script: q Q 𝒬 𝓠. This sequence didn't work, because AMS Euler's script Q is actually smaller and less imposing than its Roman Q. Changing from the double use of script to bold Roman followed by uppercase Fraktur gave a sequence with the desired flavor: q Q **Q** ℚ. (Of course, script letters proved to be useful in other contexts; the goal of AMS Euler Script was always to avoid the excesses of commercial fonts that are typically designed for wedding invitations, not mathematics.)

While DEK was typesetting the book, during the period 1987–1988, he soon became accustomed to the new "upright" look, and he noticed that the traditional integral sign was no longer appropriate. So he introduced upright integral signs in the auxiliary math symbol fonts: $\int$ became $\int$. He also made a final change to the Euler alphabets (with HZ's approval), converting

$$\mathcal{L} \quad \text{to} \quad \mathcal{L}$$

by using transformation capabilities of the new METAFONT. Now there was a consistently vertical feeling in all of the mathematical formulas; the ideal of a unified design was realized at last!

If these new typefaces find favor in the mathematical community at large, more work should still be done. The present AMS Euler is not really a meta-font; its characters have merely been digitized in two weights from HZ's original drawings. Thus the fonts cannot easily be made wider for better readability in small sizes, nor can they easily be adapted to typesetting devices that produce darker or lighter images than the ideal. The new METAFONT, which was itself strongly inspired by early experiences with AMS Euler, should prove to be an appropriate tool for creating an Euler meta-font; therefore DEK and HZ both hope that someone will rise to this challenge. We can assure whoever tries it that the experience will be extremely stimulating and instructive.

Here are the major characters of Euler, shown in 12-point size with Concrete Roman as the accompanying text.

Numerals: 0123456789 : **0123456789**
    & 0123456789 : **0123456789**

Uppercase Roman: $|A|+|B|+|C|+|D|+|E|+|F|+|G|+|H|+$
$|I|+|J|+|K|+|L|+|M|+|N|+|O|+|P|+|Q|+|R|+|S|+$
$|T|+|U|+|V|+|W|+|X|+|Y|+|Z|+|A|+|B|+|C|+|D|+$
$|E|+|F|+|G|+|H|+|I|+|J|+|K|+|L|+|M|+|N|+|O|+$
$|P|+|Q|+|R|+|S|+|T|+|U|+|V|+|W|+|X|+|Y|+|Z|$

Lowercase Roman: $|a| + |b| + |c| + |d| + |e| + |f| + |g| + |h| + |i| + |j| + |k| + |l| + |m| + |n| + |o| + |p| + |q| + |r| + |s| + |t| + |u| + |v| + |w| + |x| + |y| + |z| + |a| + |b| + |c| + |d| + |e| + |f| + |g| + |h| + |i| + |j| + |k| + |l| + |m| + |n| + |o| + |p| + |q| + |r| + |s| + |t| + |u| + |v| + |w| + |x| + |y| + |z|$

Uppercase Greek: $|\Gamma| + |\Delta| + |\Theta| + |\Lambda| + |\Xi| + |\Pi| + |\Sigma| + |\Upsilon| + |\Phi| + |\Psi| + |\Omega| + |\Gamma| + |\Delta| + |\Theta| + |\Lambda| + |\Xi| + |\Pi| + |\Sigma| + |\Upsilon| + |\Phi| + |\Psi| + |\Omega|$

Lowercase Greek: $|\alpha| + |\beta| + |\gamma| + |\delta| + |\epsilon| + |\zeta| + |\eta| + |\theta| + |\iota| + |\kappa| + |\lambda| + |\mu| + |\nu| + |\xi| + |\pi| + |\rho| + |\sigma| + |\tau| + |\upsilon| + |\phi| + |\chi| + |\psi| + |\omega| + |\alpha| + |\beta| + |\gamma| + |\delta| + |\epsilon| + |\zeta| + |\eta| + |\theta| + |\iota| + |\kappa| + |\lambda| + |\mu| + |\nu| + |\xi| + |\pi| + |\rho| + |\sigma| + |\tau| + |\upsilon| + |\phi| + |\chi| + |\psi| + |\omega|$

Uppercase Fraktur: $|\mathfrak{A}| + |\mathfrak{B}| + |\mathfrak{C}| + |\mathfrak{D}| + |\mathfrak{E}| + |\mathfrak{F}| + |\mathfrak{G}| + |\mathfrak{H}| + |\mathfrak{I}| + |\mathfrak{J}| + |\mathfrak{K}| + |\mathfrak{L}| + |\mathfrak{M}| + |\mathfrak{N}| + |\mathfrak{O}| + |\mathfrak{P}| + |\mathfrak{Q}| + |\mathfrak{R}| + |\mathfrak{S}| + |\mathfrak{T}| + |\mathfrak{U}| + |\mathfrak{V}| + |\mathfrak{W}| + |\mathfrak{X}| + |\mathfrak{Y}| + |\mathfrak{Z}| + |\mathfrak{A}| + |\mathfrak{B}| + |\mathfrak{C}| + |\mathfrak{D}| + |\mathfrak{E}| + |\mathfrak{F}| + |\mathfrak{G}| + |\mathfrak{H}| + |\mathfrak{I}| + |\mathfrak{J}| + |\mathfrak{K}| + |\mathfrak{L}| + |\mathfrak{M}| + |\mathfrak{N}| + |\mathfrak{O}| + |\mathfrak{P}| + |\mathfrak{Q}| + |\mathfrak{R}| + |\mathfrak{S}| + |\mathfrak{T}| + |\mathfrak{U}| + |\mathfrak{V}| + |\mathfrak{W}| + |\mathfrak{X}| + |\mathfrak{Y}| + |\mathfrak{Z}|$

Lowercase Fraktur: $|a| + |b| + |c| + |d| + |e| + |f| + |g| + |h| + |i| + |j| + |k| + |l| + |m| + |n| + |o| + |p| + |q| + |r| + |s| + |t| + |u| + |v| + |w| + |x| + |y| + |z| + |a| + |b| + |c| + |d| + |e| + |f| + |g| + |h| + |i| + |j| + |k| + |l| + |m| + |n| + |o| + |p| + |q| + |r| + |s| + |t| + |u| + |v| + |w| + |x| + |y| + |z|$

Uppercase Script: $|\mathcal{A}| + |\mathcal{B}| + |\mathcal{C}| + |\mathcal{D}| + |\mathcal{E}| + |\mathcal{F}| + |\mathcal{G}| + |\mathcal{H}| + |\mathcal{I}| + |\mathcal{J}| + |\mathcal{K}| + |\mathcal{L}| + |\mathcal{M}| + |\mathcal{N}| + |\mathcal{O}| + |\mathcal{P}| + |\mathcal{Q}| + |\mathcal{R}| + |\mathcal{S}| + |\mathcal{T}| + |\mathcal{U}| + |\mathcal{V}| + |\mathcal{W}| + |\mathcal{X}| + |\mathcal{Y}| + |\mathcal{Z}| + |\mathcal{A}| + |\mathcal{B}| + |\mathcal{C}| + |\mathcal{D}| + |\mathcal{E}| + |\mathcal{F}| + |\mathcal{G}| + |\mathcal{H}| + |\mathcal{I}| + |\mathcal{J}| + |\mathcal{K}| + |\mathcal{L}| + |\mathcal{M}| + |\mathcal{N}| + |\mathcal{O}| + |\mathcal{P}| + |\mathcal{Q}| + |\mathcal{R}| + |\mathcal{S}| + |\mathcal{T}| + |\mathcal{U}| + |\mathcal{V}| + |\mathcal{W}| + |\mathcal{X}| + |\mathcal{Y}| + |\mathcal{Z}|$

Additional letters: $|\aleph| + |\ell| + |\wp| + |\imath| + |\jmath| + |\varepsilon| + |\vartheta| + |\varpi| + |\varphi| + |\aleph| + |\ell| + |\wp| + |\imath| + |\jmath| + |\varepsilon| + |\vartheta| + |\varpi| + |\varphi|$

(The special p on the bottom line is noteworthy as being designed by the eminent nineteenth-century mathematician Karl Weierstrass, who taught "Schönschrift" as a youth [1].)

Let us close by showing how three sets of formulas discussed above now appear in their new Eulerian garb:

$$\text{Ind.} \qquad \nu, \; \mathfrak{a}, \; \mathfrak{b}$$

$$\text{Fract.} \qquad \frac{1}{0}, \; \frac{\mathfrak{A}}{\mathfrak{a}}, \; \frac{\mathfrak{B}}{\mathfrak{b}}, \; \frac{\mathfrak{C}}{\mathfrak{c}}$$

$$\text{where} \qquad \mathfrak{A} = \nu; \; \mathfrak{B} = \mathfrak{a}\mathfrak{A} + 1; \; \mathfrak{C} = \mathfrak{b}\mathfrak{B} + \mathfrak{A}$$

$$\text{and} \qquad \mathfrak{a} = 1; \; \mathfrak{b} = \mathfrak{a}\mathfrak{a} + 0; \; \mathfrak{c} = \mathfrak{b}\mathfrak{b} + \mathfrak{a}$$

$$\exp\left(\frac{-fx \cos \zeta}{g}\right) \left\{ \begin{array}{l} (\mathfrak{A} + \mathfrak{B}x + \mathfrak{C}xx) \cos \dfrac{fx \sin \zeta}{g} \\[2ex] (\mathfrak{a} + \mathfrak{b}x + \mathfrak{c}xx) \sin \dfrac{fx \sin \zeta}{g} \end{array} \right\}$$

$$\epsilon \in \mathcal{E} \quad \Longleftrightarrow \quad \varepsilon \in \mathcal{E}$$

The recent rise of desktop publishing has increased mathematicians' sensitivity to typographic quality. Therefore the authors have been most pleased by the favorable reception this new typeface has been receiving during the first months it has been on public view; the story of AMS Euler has a happy ending indeed:

```
Date: Wed, 28 Dec 88 12:59:07 CST
From: thisted@galton.uchicago.edu (Ronald A. Thisted)
To: dek@sail.stanford.edu
Subject: Concrete Mathematics
Don,
I just saw your new book in our bookstore, and
I impulsively bought a copy (a Christmas gift to
myself, perhaps). ...
Incidentally, I find the result of the typography and
design to be the most readable technical book I have
seen in some time.  I am usually fatigued after reading
a few pages of most books, but I was able to read all of
chapter 1 without my eyes wandering.
```

The drawings and characters of AMS Euler shown in this article are copyright by the American Mathematical Society and used with their permission. This research was supported in part by grants from the System Development Foundation and the National Science Foundation.

References

[1] Kurt-R. Biermann, "Karl Weierstraß," *Journal für die reine und angewandte Mathematik* **223** (1966), 191–220.

[2] T. W. Chaundy, P. R. Barrett, and Charles Batey, *The Printing of Mathematics* (Oxford: Oxford University Press, 1954).

[3] A. L. Crelle, editor, *Journal für die reine und angewandte Mathematik* **23** (1842), facsimile inserted between pages 104 and 105. (A dozen additional examples of Eulerian zeros can be seen on page 96 of reference 9.)

[4] John Dreyfus, *The Work of Jan van Krimpen* (London: Sylvan Press, Museum House, 1952).

[5] Charles Enschedé, *Typefounders in the Netherlands*; English translation with revisions and notes by Harry Carter (Haarlem: Stichting Museum Enschedé, 1978), 261–267.

[6] Leonhard Euler, "De usu novi algorithmi in problemati Pelliano solvendo," *Novi commentarii academiæ scientiarum Petropolitanæ* **11** (1765; printed in 1767), 28–66.

[7] Leonhard Euler, *Institutionum Calculi Integralis*, Volume 2 (St. Petersburg: Academiæ Imperialis Scientiarum, 1769).

[8] Leonhard Euler, "De novo genere serierum rationalium et valde convergentium quibus ratio peripheriæ ad diametrum exprimi potest," *Nova acta academiæ scientiarum Petropolitanæ* **11** (1793; printed in 1798), 150–154.

[9] *Leonhard Euler 1707–1783: Beiträge zu Leben und Werk* (Basel: Birkhäuser Verlag, 1983).

[10] Ronald L. Graham, Donald E. Knuth, and Oren Patashnik, *Concrete Mathematics* (Reading, Massachusetts: Addison–Wesley, 1989).

[11] Scott Kim, *Inversions* (Peterborough, New Hampshire: Byte Books, 1981).

[12] Donald E. Knuth, "Mathematical typography," *Bulletin of the American Mathematical Society* (new series) **1** (1979), 337–372. [Reprinted with corrections as Chapter 2 of the present volume.]

[13] Donald E. Knuth, "The concept of a meta-font," *Visible Language*, **16** (1982), 3–27. [Reprinted as Chapter 15 of the present volume.]

[14] Donald E. Knuth, *The TEXbook*, Volume A of *Computers & Typesetting* (Reading, Massachusetts: Addison–Wesley and American Mathematical Society, 1984).

[15] Donald E. Knuth, "Lessons learned from METAFONT," *Visible Language,* **19** (1985), 35–53. [Reprinted as Chapter 16 of the present volume.]

[16] Donald E. Knuth, *The METAFONTbook,* Volume C of *Computers & Typesetting* (Reading, Massachusetts: Addison–Wesley and American Mathematical Society, 1986).

[17] Donald E. Knuth, *Computer Modern Typefaces,* Volume E of *Computers & Typesetting* (Reading, Massachusetts: Addison–Wesley, 1986).

[18] Donald E. Knuth, "Typesetting concrete mathematics," *TUGboat* **10** (1989), 31–36, 342. [Reprinted as Chapter 18 of the present volume.]

[19] Ernst Kunz, *Introduction to Commutative Algebra and Algebraic Geometry* (Boston, Massachusetts: Birkhäuser Boston, 1985).

[20] Phœbe J. Murdock, "New alphabets and symbols for typesetting mathematics," *Scholarly Publishing* **8** (October 1976), 44–53.

[21] David R. Siegel, *The Euler Project at Stanford* (Stanford, California: Computer Science Department, Stanford University, 1985).

[22] Technische Hochschule Darmstadt, *Hermann Zapf: Ein Arbeitsbericht* (Hamburg: Maximilian-Gesellschaft, 1984).

[23] Jan van Krimpen, *On Designing and Devising Type* (New York: Typophile Chap Books, 1957).

[24] John Wallis, *A Treatise of Algebra* (Oxford: 1685).

[25] *Hermann Zapf and His Design Philosophy* (Chicago: Society of Typographic Arts, 1987).

[26] *Sammlung Hermann Zapf* (Wolfenbüttel: Herzog August Bibliothek, 1993).

Addendum

A shorter version of the text of this article was published in *ABC–XYZapf: Fifty Years in Alphabet Design,* edited by John Dreyfus and Knut Erichson (London: The Wynkyn de Worde Society, and Offenbach: Bund Deutscher Buchkünstler, 1989), pages 171–179. This version includes several additional drawings from the later stages of the work.

The second edition of [10], published in 1994, used METAFONT to improve the subscripts and superscripts by making them slightly more extended.

Chapter 18

Typesetting Concrete Mathematics

*[Originally published in TUGboat **10** (1989), 31–36, 342.]*

During 1987 and 1988 I prepared a textbook entitled *Concrete Mathematics* [1], written with coauthors Ron Graham and Oren Patashnik. I tried my best to make the book mathematically interesting, but I also knew that it would be typographically interesting—because it would be the first major use of a new typeface by Hermann Zapf, commissioned by the American Mathematical Society. This typeface, called AMS Euler, had been carefully digitized and put into METAFONT form by Stanford's digital typography students [9]; but it had not yet been "tuned up" for real applications. My new book served as an ideal test case, because (1) it involved a great variety of mathematical formulas; (2) I was highly motivated to make the book readable and attractive; (3) my experiences with tuning up Computer Modern gave me insights into how to set the mysterious font parameters used by TEX in math mode; and (4) the book was in fact being dedicated to Leonhard Euler, the great mathematician after whom the typeface was named.

The underlying philosophy of Zapf's Euler design was to capture the flavor of mathematics as it might be written by a mathematician with excellent handwriting. For example, one of the earmarks of AMS Euler is its zero, '0', which is slightly pointed at the top because a handwritten zero rarely closes together smoothly when the curve returns to its starting point. A handwritten rather than mechanical style is appropriate for mathematics because people generally create math with pen, pencil, or chalk. The Euler letters are upright, not italic, so that there is a general consistency with mathematical symbols like plus signs and parentheses, and so that built-up formulas fit together comfortably. AMS Euler includes seven alphabets: Uppercase Roman (ABC through XYZ), lowercase Roman (abc through xyz), uppercase Greek (ΑΒΓ through ΧΨΩ), lowercase Greek (αβγ through χψω), uppercase Fraktur (𝕬𝕭𝕮 through 𝔛𝔜𝔷), lowercase Fraktur (abc through xyz), and

367

uppercase Script ($\mathcal{ABC}$ through $\mathcal{XYZ}$). It also includes two sets of digits (0123456789 and 0123456789), as well as special characters like $\wp$, $\aleph$, and some punctuation marks. Details about its design are discussed in another article [7].

To refine the digitized characters for mathematical use, I began by correcting the way they appeared in their "boxes," from TeX's viewpoint. For this purpose I used the \math tests of the standard testfont routine [5, Appendix H]; these tests put the characters through their basic paces by typesetting formulas such as $|A| + |B| + |C| + \cdots + |Z|$, $a^2 + b^2 + c^2 + \cdots + z^2$, $a_2 + b_2 + c_2 + \cdots + \mathfrak{z}_2$, and $\widehat{A} + \widehat{B} + \widehat{C} + \cdots + \widehat{Z}$. I noticed among other things that the Fraktur characters had all been placed too high above the baseline, and that more blank space was needed at the left and right of the characters in subscript/superscript sizes. After fixing such problems I also needed to set the italic corrections so that subscripts and superscripts would have proper offsets; and I needed to define suitable kerns with a \skewchar so that accents would appear visually centered. AMS Euler contains more than 400 characters, and Hermann had made them beautiful; my job was to find the right adjustments to the spacing so that they would fit properly into mathematics.

The next step was to design a set of TeX macros so that AMS Euler could be used conveniently in math mode. This meant adding new "families" to the conventions I had defined in previous formats. Plain TeX typesets mathematics with four basic font families (namely, \fam0 for text, \fam1 for math italic, \fam2 for symbols, and \fam3 for large delimiters), plus a few others that are used less frequently (\fam4 for text italic, \fam5 for slanted text, \fam6 for boldface roman, and \fam7 for typewriter style). I added \fam8 for AMS Euler Script and \fam9 for AMS Euler Fraktur; the AMS Euler Greek and Roman went into the old position of math italic, \fam1. Hermann had designed new parentheses and brackets, which were bundled together with the Fraktur fonts; therefore my macro file changed plain TeX's conventions by defining, e.g., \mathcode'(="4928 and \delcode'(="928300. Similarly, Euler has the symbol '$\leqslant$' as an alternative to '$\leq$', packaged with the Script alphabet; to make TeX recognize this substitution I said \mathchardef\leq="3814 \let\le=\leq.

With such additions to the plain TeX macros I could type formulas like \$\tan(x+y)\$ as usual and get not '$\tan(x+y)$' but '$\tan(x+y)$'. There was, however, one significant difference between typing the manuscripts for *Concrete Mathematics* and for *The Art of Computer Programming*, caused by the fact that the Euler numerals 0123456789 are distinctly different from the numerals 0123456789 in ordinary text. In previous work, I used to "optimize" my typing by saying, e.g.,

x is either 1 or -1,

thereby omitting $'s around a mathematical constant unless I needed them to get a minus sign instead of a hyphen. After all, I reasoned, those extra $'s just make TEX work harder and the result looks the same; so why should I be logical? But in *Concrete Mathematics* I needed to type

x is either 1 or -1,

to keep x from being 'either 1 or −1'. The early drafts of my manuscript had been prepared in the old way; therefore I needed to spend several hours laboriously hunting down and correcting all instances where the new convention was necessary. This experience proved to be worthwhile, because it taught me that there is a useful and meaningful distinction between text numerals and mathematical numerals. Text numerals are used in contexts like '1776' and 'Chapter 5' and '41 ways', where the numbers are essentially part of the English language; mathematical numerals, by contrast, are used in contexts like 'the greatest common divisor of 12 and 18 is 6', where the numbers are part of the mathematics. (Authors of technical texts in languages like Japanese, where Hindu-Arabic numerals are used in formulas but not in ordinary text, have always been well aware of this distinction; now I had a chance to learn it too.)

As I was tooling up to begin using AMS Euler, my publishers were simultaneously showing the preliminary manuscript of *Concrete Mathematics* to a book designer, Roy Howard Brown. I had sent Roy a copy of the first Euler report [9] so that he could see examples of the typeface we planned to use for mathematics. Our original intention, based on Zapf's original plans when he began the design in 1980, was to use Computer Modern Roman for the text and AMS Euler for the mathematics. But Roy noticed that AMS Euler was somewhat darker in color than a traditional mathematical italic, so he decided that the text face should be correspondingly heavier. He sent me several samples of typefaces with more suitable weights, so that I could prepare a special font compatible with AMS Euler. (One of my basic premises when I had developed the Computer Modern meta-font was that it should be readily adaptable to new situations like this.) When I saw Roy's samples, I decided to pursue something that I'd wanted an excuse to do for several years, namely to find settings for the parameters of Computer Modern that would produce an "Egyptian" (square-serif) style.

The cover designs for *Computers & Typesetting*, Volumes A–E, show a gradual transition of the respective letter pairs Aa, Bb, Cc, Dd, and Ee from the style of standard Computer Modern Roman to an Egyptian style. I had made these cover designs just for fun, at the suggestion of Marshall Henrichs, but I had never had time to experiment with a complete text face in that style. Now I had a good reason to indulge that whim, and after a pleasant afternoon of experiments I found a combination of parameters that looked reasonably attractive, at least when I examined samples produced by our laserprinter. (I magnified the fonts and viewed them from a distance, to overcome the effects of 300-dot-per-inch resolution.) Then I made more elaborate samples of text and printed them on Stanford's APS phototypesetter, to see if the new fonts would really pass muster. Some characters needed to be adjusted — for example, the 'w' was too dark — but I was happy with the result and so was Roy.

I decided to call the resulting font Concrete Roman, because of its general solid appearance and because it was first used in the book *Concrete Mathematics*. (In case you haven't guessed, the text you are now reading is set in Concrete Roman.) *There also is Concrete Italic, a companion face that is used for emphasis in the book.* EVEN STRONGER EMPHASIS IS OCCASIONALLY ACHIEVED BY USING A CONCRETE ROMAN CAPS AND SMALL CAPS FONT. Anybody who has the METAFONT sources for Computer Modern can make the Concrete fonts rather easily by preparing parameter files such as `ccr10.mf`, analogous to `cmr10.mf`; you just need to change certain parameter values as shown in the accompanying table.

Here are some samples of Concrete Roman in the 9-point, 8-point, 7-point, 6-point, and 5-point sizes:

Mathematics books and journals do not look as beautiful as they used to. It is not that their mathematical content is unsatisfactory, rather that the old and well-developed traditions of typesetting have become too expensive. Fortunately, it now appears that mathematics itself can be used to solve this problem.

A first step in the solution is to devise a method for unambiguously specifying mathematical manuscripts in such a way that they can easily be manipulated by machines. Such languages, when properly designed, can be learned quickly by authors and their typists; yet manuscripts in this form will lead directly to high quality plates for the printer with little or no human intervention.

A second step in the solution makes use of classical mathematics to design the shapes of the letters and symbols themselves. It is possible to give a rigorous definition of the exact shape of the letter 'a', for example, in such a way that infinitely many styles — bold, extended, sans-serif, italic, etc. — are obtained from a single definition by changing only a few parameters. When the same is done for the other letters and symbols, we obtain a mathematical definition of type fonts, a definition that can be used on all machines both now and in the future. The main significance of this approach is that new symbols can readily be added in such a way that they are automatically consistent with the old ones.

Of course it is necessary that the mathematically-defined letters be beautiful according to traditional notions of aesthetics. Given a sequence of points in the plane, what is the most pleasing curve that connects them? This question leads to interesting mathematics, and one solution based on a novel family of spline curves has produced excellent [sic] fonts of type in the author's preliminary experiments.

We may conclude that a mathematical approach to the design of alphabets does not eliminate the artists who have been doing the job for so many years; on the contrary, it gives them an exciting new medium to work with. [2, page 337]

Heavier weight makes the type more resilient to xeroxing and easier to read in a poorly lighted library, so these new typefaces may help solve some of the legibility problems we all know too well. But a typeface that is too bold can also make a book tiresome to read. To avoid this problem, Roy decided to use a \baselineskip of 13 points with 10-point type. This gives an additional advantage for mathematical work, because it prevents formulas like '$\sum_{0 \leqslant k < n} a_k^d$' in the body of the text from interfering with each other; the normal 12 pt baselineskip used in most mathematics books can get uncomfortably tight. Of course, the increased space between lines also increases the number of pages by about 8%; this seems a reasonable price to pay for increased readability.

Is the extra weight of Concrete Roman really necessary for compatibility with AMS Euler? Here is a small sample that uses ordinary cmr10 as the text font, so that readers can judge this question for themselves:

The set S is, by definition, all points that can be written as $\sum_{k \geqslant 1} a_k (i-1)^k$, for an infinite sequence $a_1, a_2, a_3, \ldots$ of zeros and ones. Figure 1 shows that S can be decomposed into 256 pieces congruent to $\frac{1}{16}S$; notice that if the diagram is rotated counterclockwise by 135°, we obtain two adjacent sets congruent to $(1/\sqrt{2})S$, since $(i-1)S = S \cup (S+1)$. [3, page 190]

And now let's replay the same text again, using Concrete Roman and \baselineskip=13pt:

The set S is, by definition, all points that can be written as $\sum_{k \geqslant 1} a_k (i-1)^k$, for an infinite sequence $a_1, a_2, a_3, \ldots$ of zeros and ones. Figure 1 shows that S can be decomposed into 256 pieces congruent to $\frac{1}{16}S$; notice that if the diagram is rotated counterclockwise by 135°, we obtain two adjacent sets congruent to $(1/\sqrt{2})S$, since $(i-1)S = S \cup (S+1)$. [3, page 190]

TABLE OF PARAMETER VALUES FOR CONCRETE FONTS

name	cmr10	ccr10	ccr9	ccr8	ccr7
font_identifier	CMR	CCR	CCR	CCR	CCR
serif_fit	0	1	1	1	1
cap_serif_fit	5	3	2.8	2.6	2.4
x_height	155	165	148.5	132	115.5
bar_height	87	92	78.3	69.6	60.9
tiny	8	11	10	9	8
fine	7	6	6	6	6
thin_join	7	17	17	15	13
hair	9	21	20	19	17
stem	25	25	24	22	20
curve	30	27	26	24	21.5
ess	27	25	24	22	20
flare	33	29	26	24	23
cap_hair	11	21	20	19	17
cap_stem	32	27	26	24	21.5
cap_curve	37	28	27	25	22.5
cap_ess	35	27	24	22	21.5
bracket	20	5	5	4	4
jut	28	30	27	24	21
cap_jut	37	32	29	26	23
vair	8	21	20	19	17
notch_cut	10	5/6	3/4	2/3	7/12
*bar, etc.**	11	21	20	19	17
cap_notch_cut	10	1	.9	.8	.7
serif_drop	4	5	3.6	3.2	2.8
o	8	4	4	3	3
apex_o	8	3	3	3	3
beak_darkness	11/30	4/30	4/30	4/30	4/30
other values from		cmr10	cmr9	cmr8	cmr7

*The measurements for *bar* apply also to *slab*, *cap_bar*, and *cap_band*. All of the Concrete fonts have *dish* = 0, *fudge* = .95, *superness* = 8/11, and *superpull* = 1/15, except that ccslc9 has *fudge* = 1. Parameters not mentioned here are inherited from the corresponding cm fonts,

(This table uses the conventions found on pages 12–31 of [6].)

ccr6	ccr5	ccslc9	ccti10	ccmi10	cccsc10	*lower*
CCR	CCR	CCSLC	CCTI	CCMI	CCCSC	
1	1	0	1	1	1	
2.2	2	2	3	3	3	2
99	82.5	155	165	165	155	116
52.2	43.5	85	92	92	87	65
7	6	9	11	11	11	
6	5	6	6	6	6	
12	11	13	17	17	17	
15	14	16	21	21	21	
18	16	22	24	25	25	23
19	17	23	26	27	27	
17	12	25	24	25	25	
20	18	28	28	29	29	22
15	14	16	21	21	21	21
19	17	23	26	27	27	24
20	18	24	27	28	28	26
19	14	23	26	27	27	24
3	3	5	5	5	5	
19	17	15	30	30	30	
20	18	16	32	32	32	24
15	14	15	21	21	21	
1/2	5/12	3/4	5/6	5/6	5/6	
15	14	15	21	21	21	21
.6	.5	.9	1	1	1	3/4
2.4	2	3.6	5	5	5	
3	3	4	4	4	4	3
3	2	3	3	3	3	3
4/30	4/30	5/30	4/30	4/30	4/30	
cmr6	cmr5	cmsl9	cmti10	cmmi10	cmcsc10	

except that cccsc10 has *lower.fudge* = .93; ccti10 has the u value 20 not 18.4, and the *crisp* value 11 not 8; ccmi10 has the *crisp* value 0 not 8 and its *math_fitting* is *false*. Font ccsl10 is the same as ccr10 except for its **font_identifier** and the fact that its *slant* is 1/6.

Equation numbers presented Roy and me with one of the most perplexing design questions. Should those numbers be typeset in Euler or cast in Concrete? After several experiments we hit on a solution that must be right, because it seems so obvious in retrospect: We decided to set equation numbers in an "oldstyle" variant of Concrete Roman, using the digits '0123456789'. The result—e.g., '(3.14)'—was surprisingly effective.

After I had been using AMS Euler for several months and was totally conditioned to "upright mathematics," I began to work on a chapter of the book where integral signs appear frequently. It suddenly struck me that the traditional integral sign is visually incompatible with AMS Euler, because it slopes like an italic letter. Such a slope was now quite out of character with the rest of the formulas. So I designed a new, upright integral sign to match the spirit of the new fonts. Then I could typeset

$$\int_a^b f(x)\,dx - \frac{1}{2\pi i}\oint_{|z|=r} \frac{g(z)\,dz}{z^n}$$

and $\int_{-\infty}^{\infty} \cos x^2\,dx$, instead of

$$\int_a^b f(x)\,dx - \frac{1}{2\pi i}\oint_{|z|=r} \frac{g(z)\,dz}{z^n}$$

and $\int_{-\infty}^{\infty} \cos x^2\,dx$. The new integral signs went into a new font called euex10, which became \fam10 in math mode; I told TEX to get integral signs from the new font by simply saying

```
\mathchardef\intop="1A52
\mathchardef\ointop="1A48
```

in my macro file. Later I noticed that the infinity sign '∞' of Computer Modern was too light to be a good match for the Euler alphabets, so I created a darker version '∞' and put it into euex10 with the new integral signs.

Hermann Zapf was helping to advise me all during this time. For example, he approved a draft of Chapter 1 that had been phototypeset in Concrete Roman and AMS Euler, while I was tuning things up. Later, when he received a copy of the first printing of the actual book, he saw Chapter 2 and the other chapters for the first time; and this led him to suggest several improvements that he could not have anticipated from Chapter 1 alone.

Chapter 2 is about summation, and I had used the sign $\sum$ from Computer Modern's cmex10 font, together with its displaystyle counterpart

$$\sum_{k=0}^{n} f(k),$$

to typeset hundreds of formulas that involve summation. Hermann pointed out that the capital \Sigma of Euler looks quite different — it is 'Σ', without beaks — so he suggested changing my summation signs to look more like the Σ of Euler. I did this in the second printing of the book, using $\sum$ in text formulas and

$$\sum_{k=0}^{n} f(k)$$

in displays. Hermann also asked me to make the product symbols less narrow, more like Euler's 'Π'; so I changed them

from $\prod$ and $\prod$ to $\prod$ and $\prod$.

Moreover, he wanted the arrows to have longer and darker arrowheads: '→', not '→'. And he wanted curly braces to be lighter, so that

$$\left\{ \begin{array}{c} a \\ b \\ c \\ d \end{array} \right\} \quad \text{would become} \quad \left\{ \begin{array}{c} a \\ b \\ c \\ d \end{array} \right\}.$$

All of these new characters were easy to design, using the conventions of Computer Modern [6], so I added them to euex10 and used them in the second printing.

Readers of *Concrete Mathematics* will immediately notice one novel feature: Most pages have "graffiti" printed in the margins. My coauthors and I asked students who were testing the preliminary book drafts to write informal comments that might be printed with the text, thereby giving the book a friendly-contemporary-lifelike flavor. We weren't sure how such "remarks from the peanut gallery" should be typeset, but we knew that we did want to include them; in fact, we collected almost 500 marginal notes. Roy hit on the idea of putting them in the *inner* (gutter) margin, where they would not have too much prominence. He also sent a sample of a suitably informal typeface, on which I modeled "Concrete Roman Slanted Condensed" type.

To typeset such graffiti, I introduced a \g macro into my TEX format file, so that it was possible to type simply '\g Text of a graffito.\g' on whatever line of text I wanted the marginal comment to begin. I did a bit of positioning by hand to ensure that no two comments would overlap; but my \g macro did most of the work. For example, it automatically decided whether to put graffiti into the left margin or the right margin, based on an auxiliary 'grf' file that recorded the choice that would have been appropriate on the previous TEX run.

This 9 pt typeface has worked out very nicely for marginal graffiti, where it is typeset ragged right, 6 picas wide, with 10 pt between baselines.

My macros for *Concrete Mathematics* cause TEX to produce not only the usual dvi file and log file corresponding to the input, but also the grf file just mentioned and four other auxiliary files:

• The ans file contains the text of any answers to exercises that appeared in the material just typeset; such answers will be \input at an appropriate later time. (Page 422 of *The TEXbook* discusses a similar idea. The only difference between *Concrete Mathematics* and *The TEXbook* in this regard was that I used one file per chapter in *Concrete Mathematics*, while *The TEXbook* was typeset from a single long file.)

• The inx file contains raw material for preparing the index. After everything but the index was ready, I put all the inx files together, sorted them, and edited the results by hand. (See pages 423–425 of *The TEXbook*, where I describe similar index macros and explain why I don't believe in fully automatic index preparation.)

• There's also a ref file, which contains the symbolic names of equations, tables, and exercises that may be needed for cross references. (A ref file is analogous to an aux file in LATEX.)

• Finally, a bnx file records the page numbers of each bibliographic reference, so that I can include such information as a sort of index to the bibliography. That index was done automatically.

I wouldn't want to deal with so many auxiliary files if I were producing a simpler book or a system for more general consumption. But for the one-shot purposes of *Concrete Mathematics*, this multiple-file approach was most convenient.

My coauthors and I decided to use a nonstandard numbering system for tables, based on the way superhighway exits are numbered in some parts of America: Table 244, for example, refers to the table on page 244. (The idea wasn't original with us, but I don't remember who suggested it.) Macros to accommodate this convention, and to update the cross-references when the page numbers change, were not difficult to devise.

All of the macros I wrote for *Concrete Mathematics* appear in a file called gkpmac.tex, which (I'm sorry to admit) includes very little documentation because it was intended only to do a single job. Macro writers may like to look at this file as a source of ideas, so I've made it publicly accessible [8]. But people who attempt to use these macros should be aware that I have not pretended to make them complete or extremely general. For example, I implemented a subset of LaTeX's picture environment, and used it to prepare all but one of the illustrations in the book; but I didn't include everything that LaTeX makes available. Moreover, I didn't need boldface type in the mathematical formulas of *Concrete Mathematics* (except for the Q on page 143 of the second printing); so I didn't include macros for accessing any of the bold fonts of AMS Euler in math mode. In this respect, the book was not a perfect test, because almost half of the Euler characters are boldface and therefore still untried. Macros for bold mathematics would be easy to add, following the pattern already established in gkpmac; but I must leave such tasks to others, as I return to my long-delayed project of writing the remaining volumes of *The Art of Computer Programming*.

References

[1] Ronald L. Graham, Donald E. Knuth, and Oren Patashnik, *Concrete Mathematics* (Reading, Massachusetts: Addison–Wesley, 1989). [Although the copyright date is 1989, I received my copy of the first printing on 29 August 1988 and used the book as a text during October–December of 1988. The second printing was dated January 1989. A second edition, with several major changes to the text but only minor changes to the typography — notably the fact that the AMS Euler characters in subscripts and superscripts became more extended — appeared in January 1994.]

[2] Donald E. Knuth, "Mathematical typography," *Bulletin of the American Mathematical Society* (new series) 1 (1979), 337–372. [Reprinted with corrections as Chapter 2 of the present volume.]

[3] Donald E. Knuth, *Seminumerical Algorithms*, Volume 2 of *The Art of Computer Programming*, second edition (Reading, Massachusetts: Addison–Wesley, 1981).

[4] Donald E. Knuth, *The TeXbook*, Volume A of *Computers & Typesetting* (Reading, Massachusetts: Addison–Wesley and American Mathematical Society, 1984).

[5] Donald E. Knuth, *The METAFONTbook*, Volume C of *Computers & Typesetting* (Reading, Massachusetts: Addison–Wesley and American Mathematical Society, 1986).

[6] Donald E. Knuth, *Computer Modern Typefaces*, Volume E of *Computers & Typesetting* (Reading, Massachusetts: Addison–Wesley, 1986).

[7] Donald E. Knuth and Hermann Zapf, "AMS Euler — A new typeface for mathematics," *Scholarly Publishing* **20** (1989), 131–157. [Reprinted as Chapter 17 of the present volume.]

[8] Donald E. Knuth, gkpmac.tex, available by anonymous ftp from ftp.cs.stanford.edu in directory pub/concretemath.errata/ (last updated in 2011). Also available from the Comprehensive TEX Archive Network (CTAN) in directory systems/knuth/local/lib/.

[9] David R. Siegel, *The Euler Project at Stanford* (Stanford, California: Computer Science Department, Stanford University, 1985).

Addendum

The Concrete Roman and AMS Euler fonts have by now been used together to typeset numerous technical books; the first of these, after *Concrete Mathematics*, was probably *Mindste Kvadraters Princip* by Kai Borre (Aalborg: Borre, 1992), ISBN 87-984210-1-8. In particular, the translations of *Concrete Mathematics* into French, Hungarian, Italian, and Polish have used essentially the conventions of the original English edition. The Russian translation uses "Concrete Cyrillic" fonts (a family analogous to Concrete Roman), developed by Olga Lapko.

Chapter 19

A Course on METAFONT Programming

*[Originally published in TUGboat **5** (1984), 105–118.]*

During the spring of 1984, four dozen brave students attended an unusual class at Stanford University, taught by two brave professors and by another reckless one. The subject of these lectures was type design in general and the use of the new METAFONT in particular. The course was necessarily improvisational, because METAFONT was still taking shape during the entire time; but I think it's fair to say that the lectures hung together quite well and that the experience was rewarding for all.

The main reason I can make this claim is that the two brave professors referred to above were Richard Southall and Charles Bigelow, who gave outstanding lectures in alternation with my own contributions. Southall's lectures covered the general subject of "Designing Typefaces," and he broke this down into five subtopics:

(1) Definitions — What is the difference between fonts and typefaces, between type design and calligraphy?

(2) Quality criteria — How can we objectively judge the success of text typefaces?

(3) Facets of the job — What does a type designer have to do?

(4) Methodology — How does traditional knowledge and practice teach us to tackle the problem of type design?

(5) "Ideal" designs — Can anyone tell us what shapes the characters ought to be?

Bigelow lectured on the history of letterforms, from ancient times to the present. It was instructive to see how character shapes have changed as the technology has changed: Alphabet designs were originally created by a "ductal" process, by the movements of a writing tool; then printing types were produced by a "glyptal" process, by carving in metal; and nowadays most letterforms are produced by a digital or "pictal" process, by specifying patterns on a discrete raster. The work of master type designers of all eras was presented and critically evaluated, and Bigelow concluded by discussing the current state of the art in commercial digital typefaces and in designs for CRT displays. All of the lectures by Southall and Bigelow were lavishly illustrated, in most cases by unique slides from their personal collections.

My job was to relate this all to the new METAFONT. My luck held good throughout the quarter, as new pieces of the language would begin to work just about two days before I needed to discuss them in class. That gave me one day to get some programming experience before I was supposed to teach everybody else how to write good programs themselves. I lectured about (1) coordinates, (2) curves, (3) equations, (4) digitizing, (5) pens, (6) transformations, and (7) the syntax of METAFONT.

The students did several instructive homework problems. First they were asked to do two assignments with cut paper, in order to illustrate the important differences between "what we see" and "what's there." Then came Homework #3, the first computer assignment, which was to write METAFONT code for Stanford's symbol, El Palo Alto (the tall tree); each student did just two of the branches, since it would have been too tedious to do all twelve of them, and I combined their solutions to obtain the following results:

(Each of these trees is different, although many of the individual branches appear in several different trees because some of the branches were worked on more often than others.) The purpose of this exercise was to help the students get used to the ideas of coordinates and simple curves, as they became familiar with the computer system and its text editor. An organic shape like a tree is very forgiving.

The fourth homework assignment was much more interesting, and we called it "Font 1." The class created a new typeface with a sans-serif, calligraphic flavor; we had just enough people who had completed Homework #3 so that everybody could be assigned the task of creating one uppercase letter and one lowercase letter. I presented an uppercase 'U' and lowercase 'l' as examples that would help to set the style;

but of course each student had a personal style that was reflected in the results, and there wasn't much unity in our final font. This fact was instructive in itself.

I had prepared two METAFONT macros to draw penlike strokes and arcs, and the students were required to draw everything with those two subroutines. This was a significant limitation, but it helped to focus everyone's attention by narrowing the possibilities. The students were also learning the concepts of meta-design at this time, because their programs were supposed to be written in terms of parameters so that three different fonts would be produced: normal, bold, and bold extended. This gave everyone a taste of METAFONT's algebraic capabilities, in which the computer plays a crucial role in the development.

The best way to describe the outcome of Homework #4 is to present the font that we made:

In every period there have been better or worse types employed in better or worse ways.
The better types employed in better ways
have been used by the educated printer
acquainted with standards and history,
directed by taste and a sense of the fitness of things,
and facing the industrial conditions of his time.
Such men have made of printing an art.
The poorer types and methods have been employed
by printers ignorant of standards
and caring alone for commercial success.
To these, printing has been simply a trade.
The typography of a nation has been good or bad,
as one or other of these classes had the supremacy.
And today any intelligent printer can educate his taste,
so to choose types for his work and so to use them,
that he will help printing to be an art rather than a trade.
There is not, as the sentimentalist would have us think,
a specially devilish spirit now abroad
that prevents good work from being done.
The old times were not so very good,
nor was human nature then so different,
nor is the modern spirit particularly devilish.
But it was, and is, hard to hold to a principle.
The principles of the men of those times
seem simple and glorious.
We do not dare to believe that we, too,
can go and do likewise.

DANIEL BERKELEY UPDIKE

ABCDEFGHIJKKLM
NOPQRSTTUVWXYZ
abcdefghijklm
nopqrstuvwxyz

This font of type, the first
to be produced by the new
METAFONT system, was
designed by Neenie Billawala,
Jean-Luc Bonnetain,
Jim Bratnober,
Malcolm Brown,
William Burley, Renata Byl,
Pavel Curtis, Bruce Fleischer,
Kanchi Gopinath,
John Hershberger,
Dikran Karagueuzian,
Don Knuth, Ann Lasko-Harvill,
Bruce Leban, Dan Mills,
Arnie Olds, Stan Osborne,
Kwang-Chun Park, Tuan Pham,
Theresa-Marie Rhyne,
Lynn Ruggles, Arthur Samuel,
New Wave Dave,
Alan Spragens, Nori Tokusue,
Joey Tuttle, and Ed Williams.

As I said, we didn't expect Font 1 to have any unity, but I was pleased that many of the individual characters turned out to be quite beautiful even when the parameters took on values that the students had not tried.

The fifth and final homework assignment was more interesting yet. Everybody was to design a set of eight characters that could be used to typeset border designs. These characters were called NW, NM, NE, ME, SE, SM, SW, and MW in clockwise order starting at the upper left; here 'N' means North, 'E' means East, 'S' means South, 'W' means West, and 'M' means Middle. The height of each character was determined by the first component of its name, and the width was determined by the other component. Thus, for example, NW and NM were required to have the same height; SE and ME were required to have the same width. As a consequence, the four characters with M's in their names could be used as repeatable extension modules to make arbitrarily large rectangles together with the four corner characters. But there were no other ground rules besides these mild restrictions on height and width, and the students were urged to let their creative minds dream up the greatest borders that they could program in METAFONT.

It was especially exciting for me to see the completed border projects, because I was impressed by the originality of the designs and (especially) because I was glad to see that the new version of METAFONT was working even better than I had dared to hope. We still need to wait awhile before we'll know how adequate METAFONT will be as a tool for letterform design, but already we can be sure that it's a super tool for borders! Here are the results of this experiment:

Ed Williams

Neenie Billawala

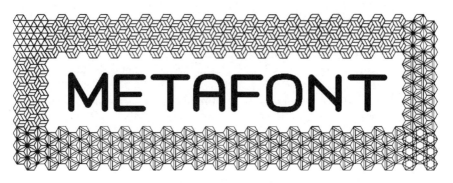

Jean-Luc Bonnetain

Jim Bratnober

William Burley

Renata Byl

Pavel Curtis

Bruce Fleischer

Kanchi Gopinath

John Hershberger

Dikran Karagueuzian

METAFONT

Don Knuth

METAFONT

Ann Lasko-Harvill

Bruce Leban

METAFONT

Dan Mills

Arnie Olds

Stan Osborne

Kwang-Chun Park

Tuan Pham

Lynn Ruggles

METAFONT

Arthur Samuel

New Wave Dave Siegel

Alan Spragens

Nori Tokusue

I should mention some of our experiences related to the "high tech" nature of a class like this. None of the computers accessible for classes at Stanford had a high-resolution screen with graphic capabilities, so we had ordered SUN workstations to fill the void. When those machines finally arrived — a week before the class was scheduled to begin — they were a new model for which new software needed to be written in order to put them into the campus network and connect them to various peripheral devices. The manufacturer balked at letting us see the source code of their software, but we needed it in order to get going. We also found that we couldn't use their version of UNIX anyway, because it allocated each file on our main disk to a specific workstation; that would have forced each student to log in at the same workstation each time! Furthermore their Pascal compiler was unusable on a program as large as METAFONT.

So we decided to use a locally developed operating system called the V-System or V-Kernel, due to Profs. David Cheriton and Keith Lantz and their students. Fortunately another grad student, Per Bothner, was a member of the TEX project, and he had also helped to develop a suitable Pascal compiler. Unfortunately, however, we couldn't use the V-System without connecting all of our SUNs to a more powerful machine like a VAX, and we didn't own such a computer. To make matters worse, the building in which we had planned to put our SUNs was being renovated; we were originally scheduled to occupy it in January, but each month another problem had delayed the construction, and it was clear by the end of March that we wouldn't have any place to put the SUNs until May at the earliest!

Here again Prof. Cheriton saved the situation for us, because he had independently been making plans to set up a teaching lab with graphic workstations in another building. His workstations hadn't arrived yet, so we were able to loan part-time use of our SUNs in return for the use of his lab. Furthermore he had a new VAX that we could install next door.

The actual timetable went something like this: On March 24 I had finished coding a subset of METAFONT that I hoped would be enough to use in the class, but I hadn't started to debug it yet. On April 1, I obtained the first successful output of that program on a small test case, and METAFONT also displayed a character correctly for the first time on my screen. (This was on the SAIL computer, a one-of-a-kind 36-bit machine on which I have done all of the development of TEX and META-FONT.) The next day, April 2, I learned about the possibility of using Cheriton's lab for our course; the room was still without furniture, computers, and air-conditioning, but David Fuchs and other people pitched in to help get things moving there. On April 3, Per Bothner success-fully transported METAFONT from SAIL to a SUN workstation using the V-System. And April 4 was the first day of class.

The V-Kernel system had previously been used only by hackers, so there was no decent manual for novices; furthermore none of us except Per knew how to use it. Arthur Samuel came to the rescue and began to prepare an introductory manual. Meanwhile, we had special meetings with Stanford's TV network technicians, because there was no adequate way to run METAFONT from a classroom so as to display the results online to the audience. On April 6 I began to write GFtoDVI, a fairly long program that is needed to get proofsheets from METAFONT's output; I knew that it would take at least two weeks to complete that program. Lynn Ruggles had already made progress on another utility routine, GFtoQMS, which produces fonts suitable for a new laserprinter that we had just received. (But that printer wasn't installed yet.)

Bigelow and Southall knew that it would be a miracle if the computers were all in place on time, so they were prepared to "vamp" until

I was ready. I gave my first lecture on Friday, April 13, one day after Lynn had been able to typeset the first METAFONT-made character on our QMS. The students had plenty of non-computer homework to do, as mentioned above, so we were able to make it seem natural that the first computer assignment was not distributed until April 27.

Well, the month of May was a long story, too—the computers broke down frequently because of inadequate air-conditioning, which took weeks to install—and there were plenty of software problems as I kept making new versions of METAFONT. But people were good natured and they tolerated the intolerable conditions; I rewarded them for this by cancelling a planned Homework #6. Teaching assistants Dan Mills and Dave Siegel did yeoman service to keep everything running as smoothly as possible throughout the nine weeks of the class.

Finally the course came to a glorious finish as we took a field trip to San Francisco. We had a picnic on Font Boulevard, then toured the fascinating MacKenzie–Harris type foundry and the Bigelow & Holmes design studio. I can best convey the jubilation of that memorable day by showing a picture of the "italic" font that we all made just after lunch:

Photo by Jill Knuth

Back row (left to right): Per Bothner, Bruce Fleischer, John Hobby, Rachel Hewson, Don Knuth, Neenie Billawala, Arnie Olds, Alan Spragens, Bruce Leban, Joey Tuttle, Stan Osborne, Dave Siegel, David Fuchs. Front row: John Hershberger, Jacques Désarménien, Dikran Karagueuzian, Nori Tokusue, Malcolm Brown, Kanchi Gopinath, Pavel Curtis, Jean-Luc Bonnetain, Renata Byl, Kwang-Chun Park, Richard Southall, Michael Weisenberg.

Chapter 20

A Punk Meta-Font

*[Originally published in TUGboat **9** (1988), 152–168.]*

In February 1985, Gerard and Marjan Unger gave a series of nine evening lectures at Stanford, in which they surveyed the evolution of styles in art, architecture, clothing, product design, and typography during the past 75 years. The lectures were especially interesting because of the way in which changes in typographic fashions were juxtaposed with the changes in other kinds of fashions; the Ungers demonstrated a remarkable fact: *Typography tends to lag behind other kinds of stylistic changes by about ten years.*

When I woke up on the morning of their final lecture, I suddenly realized that there was an obvious corollary of what they had been saying during the previous eight evenings: It was now about time to design a typeface based on trends that had emerged during the late 70s! Furthermore, I also had a reasonably clear idea of what such a design might be like, because the lectures had turned up a strong similarity between some "punk" graphics exhibited in London and a certain lines-and-dots motif found in the upholstery of some "punk" furniture designed in Italy.

A lines-and-dots motif is trivially easy for METAFONT to handle, so I decided to create a new family of trendy typefaces called PUNK. I spent several pleasant hours at the computer terminal that afternoon; and by evening I was able to present everybody in the audience with an up-to-the-minute souvenir of the Ungers' lectures, laserprinted in PUNK10 and PUNK20.

The idea of PUNK was to start with more-or-less traditional stick-letter shapes, but to ask METAFONT to perturb the key points by random amounts so that the letters look a bit deranged. Here, for example, are several texts set with a few varieties of PUNK fonts:

ABCDEFGHIJKLMNOPQRSTUVWXYZ ABCDEFGHIJKLMNOPQRSTUV
WXYZ 0123456789 ÆŒØ ΓΔΘΛΞΠΣΤΦΨΩ ÆŒØıȷ
.,;:?¡!#$%&—--*()[]↑↓†/⟨≠⟩

_____ PUNK10

'HUMPH!' SAID ARTIE. HIS FACE WAS RED AND HE WAS CER-
TAINLY FLUSTERED. 'IT'D BE A DEAD LUCKY THING IF SOME
MORE PEOPLE AROUND THE SHOP'D CHANGE A LITTLE. THEY
COULD N'T BE ANY PUNKER 'N THEY ARE NOW.'   [1]

_____

ABCDEFGHIJKLMNOPQRSTUVWXYZ ABCDEFGHIJKLMNO
PQRSTUVWXYZ 0123456789 ÆŒØ ΓΔΘΛΞΠΣΤΦΨΩ ÆŒØı
ȷ .,;:?¡!#$%&—--*()[]↑↓
†/⟨≠⟩

_____ PUNK12

A FORKED VEIN BEGAN TO SWELL IN SPADE'S FORE-
HEAD. ... HIS VOICE BECAME PERSUASIVE AGAIN.
'LISTEN, GUTMAN, WE'VE ABSOLUTELY GOT TO GIVE
THEM A VICTIM. THERE'S NO WAY OUT OF IT. LET'S
GIVE THEM THE PUNK.' HE NODDED PLEASANTLY AT
THE BOY IN THE DOORWAY.   [2]

_____

ABCDEFGHIJKLMNOPQRSTUVWXYZ
ABCDEFGHIJKLMNOPQRSTUVWXYZ 01
23456789 ÆŒØΓΔΘΛΞΠΣΤΦΨΩ ÆŒØı
ȷ .,;:?¡!#$%
&—--*()[]↑↓†/⟨≠⟩

_____ PUNK20

PISTOL. [ASIDE.] THIS PUNK IS
ONE OF CUPID'S CARRIERS. CLAP
ON MORE SAILS, PURSUE; UP WITH

YOUR FIGHTS; GIVE FIRE! SHE IS
MY PRIZE, OR OCEAN WHELM THEM
ALL! [EXIT.]   [6]

ABCDEFGHIJKLMNOPQRSTUVWXYZ

ABCDEFGHIJKLMNOPQRSTUVWXYZ δ1

23451789 ΛϾΟΓΔΘΛΞΠΣΥΦΨΩ ΛϾΘⅅI

♩ ˘ ˇ ˘ ° ˙ ¸ ˜ ˜ ˑ ° ´ .,;:ʒ!¡'"''" #$%

Ƙℜ~~~ ∧ ()[]↑↓†/⟨∺⟩

PUNKSL20

PUNK ROCK IS THE GENERIC TERM
FOR THE LATEST MUSICAL GARBAGE
BRED BY OUR TROUBLED CULTURE,
BRITISH AND AMERICAN. ...
JOHNNY ROTTEN AND THE SEX PIS-
TOLS ARE PUNKS. THEY SING 'AN-
ARCHY IN THE UK,' WHICH ENDS
WITH A SCREAM: 'DESTROY.' CLASH
AND DAMNED ARE OTHER BANDS.

... PUNK WILL FADE.   ITS
APOLOGISTS ARE LUDICROUS.
THERE ARE WAYS TO PROTEST
ABOUT THE PUTRID FACES OF

ЪOTH POP AND SOCIETY WITH-
OUT RELAPSING INTO ЪAR-
ЪARISM. PUNK IS ANTI-LIFE,
ANTI-HUMANITY. [3]

ABCDEFGHIJKLMNOPQRSTUV
WXYZ ABCDEFGHIJKLMNOPQR
STUVWXYZ 0123456789
ÆŒØΓΔΘΛΞΠΣΥΦΨΩ æœøßıȷ`
ʼ ˇ ˘ ¯ ˌ ˆ ˙ ˚ ˝ ˜   ̣ ˊ . , ; : ¿ ? ¡ ! ʻ ʼ ʼ ˏ ˎ ˏ
#$%⅋&-–—* ()[]↑↓‡/‹≈›

PUNKBX20

At the time I "designed" these typefaces, I had just begun to make the
final version of the Computer Modern fonts by converting my Almost
Computer Modern code to the conventions of METAFONT 84. The letters
'A', 'B', 'C', and 'D' had been debugged so far, and I was planning to
tackle 'E' soon; but I felt like taking a break. So I made sketches of
some punkish forms, as follows:

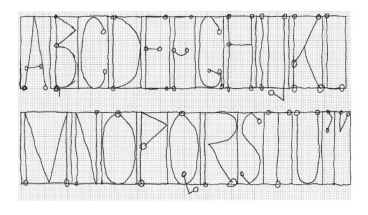

(I used a large sheet of graph paper; this illustration has been reduced to 25% of the original size. Needless to say, I had no idea that I would ever show these sketches to anyone else.)

At 1 pm I went to the computer and began to compose a simple base file. Not much needed to be done, since plain METAFONT already included most of the basic routines; so I had my first proof output twenty minutes later:

METAFONT output 1985.02.28:1320 Page 1 Character 65

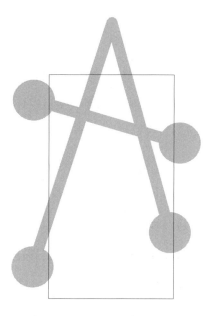

(45% of original size)

The letter 'A' seemed to be working, so I proceeded to type the META-FONT programs for 'B' through 'Z'. I decided to type everything before looking at any proofs; so I simply translated the sketches into META-FONT constructions, composing everything at the keyboard. It wasn't necessary to make accurate measurements, because random perturbations to the points were going to be made anyway. Thus I soon got used to the conventions of this font, and I was limited only by typing speed. I didn't even need sketches of the letters 'V' through 'Z', because their algebraic formulation was easy to imagine after I had done 21 other letters. At 3:04 pm the typing was done, and I was able to run META-FONT and get proofs of all 26 uppercase letters. I also had thrown in a few punctuation marks (period, comma, opening and closing single and double quotes).

Of course there were bugs in my code. For example, the first few letters came out looking like this on the initial proofsheets:

METAFONT output 1985.02.28:1504

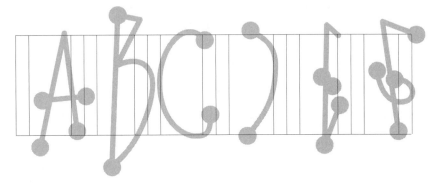

(I refuse to show you the first form of the letter '6'.) But by 4 pm I was ready to make the first trial setting of text:

THIS "PUNK" ALPHABET, INSPIRED BY
MARJAN'S LECTURE LAST NIGHT, WAS
DESIGNED BY METAFONT'S RANDOM NUM-
BER GENERATOR. THE QUICK BROWN FOX
JUMPED OVER THE LAZY HAMBURGEFONS.

At this point an unexpected glitch slowed things down a bit. The letters of this font had some unusual characteristics that hadn't arisen in GF files before, so a bug showed up in our METAFONT-to-laserprinter software when I tried to print out a 40-point test sample. I made copies of the offending files, for later reference, and I was able to get around the bug by choosing another random seed and generating the font again. After another half hour of tuning things up (and toning the randomness down), I was able to go home for supper.

During the supper hour, I realized that a proper keepsake for that evening would include the typeset date. So I gulped down my meal, quickly sketched a set of numerals, and raced back to my office. Soon I had a font of 43 characters — 26 letters, 10 numerals, and 7 punctuation marks. Whew! I was ready to hand out a sample sheet to everybody at 7 pm, hot off the copy machine.

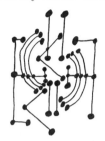

A year or so later, I was wandering around in Boston's Museum of Fine Arts and I came across a drawing made by Picasso in 1924 [5]; see the illustration at the right. This made me wonder if the PUNK fonts weren't really *sixty* years behind the times, not just ten. But I did find a striking confirmation of the relevance of at least part of the PUNK design in October 1986, when I chanced to see the following typography on a billboard in the Paris Métro(!):

In February of 1987 I decided to extend the original 43-character font to the full TeX character set. The extra programming didn't take long, since I chose to generate the lowercase letters as "small caps," and since only one or two minutes were needed to type each new character into the computer. About one third of the characters had to be revised after I saw proofsheets, since they looked either too punk or not punk enough; and one-third of the revised characters had to be revised again; and so on. But after about six hours of additional work, a complete PUNK meta-font with 128 characters was ready for use, in case anybody wanted it.

In the remainder of this paper, I'll present complete details of the METAFONT code, since this may be the shortest nontrivial example of METAFONT programs that produce all 128 characters used by plain TeX.

The programs appear in several different kinds of files, as explained in Appendix E of [4]: There are parameter files, to specify specific fonts of the family; there is a driver file, which controls most of the font generation process; and there are program files, which contain the code for individual characters. (I didn't need a base file, since the special macros for these fonts could all be included in the driver file.)

Here is a typical parameter file, PUNK20.MF:

% 20-point PUNK font:
designsize := 20*pt*#; **font_identifier** := "PUNK";

$ht^\# := 14pt^\#;$	% height of characters
$u^\# := {}^4/_9pt^\#;$	% unit width
$s^\# := 2pt^\#;$	% extra sidebar
$px^\# := .8pt^\#;$	% horizontal thickness of pen
$py^\# := .6pt^\#;$	% vertical thickness of pen
$dot^\# := 2.7pt^\#;$	% diameter of dots
$dev^\# := .5pt^\#;$	% standard deviation of punk points
$slant := 0;$	% obliqueness
$seed := 2.71828;$	% seed for random number generator
input PUNK	% switch to the driver file

Its purpose is to customize the meta-design to a particular selection of sizes and weights. The parameters used to define the five fonts exhibited earlier in this article are:

	PUNK10	PUNK12	PUNK20	PUNKSL20	PUNKBX20
designsize	$10pt^\#$	$12pt^\#$	$20pt^\#$	$20pt^\#$	$20pt^\#$
font_identifier	"PUNK"	"PUNK"	"PUNK"	"PUNKSL"	"PUNKBX"
$ht^\#$	$7pt^\#$	$8.4pt^\#$	$14pt^\#$	$14pt^\#$	$14pt^\#$
$u^\#$	$^1/_4pt^\#$	$.3pt^\#$	$^4/_9pt^\#$	$^4/_9pt^\#$	$.6pt^\#$
$s^\#$	$1.2pt^\#$	$1.4pt^\#$	$2pt^\#$	$2pt^\#$	$2.2pt^\#$
$px^\#$	$.6pt^\#$	$.75pt^\#$	$.8pt^\#$	$.8pt^\#$	$2pt^\#$
$py^\#$	$.5pt^\#$	$.62pt^\#$	$.6pt^\#$	$.6pt^\#$	$1.6pt^\#$
$dot^\#$	$1.3pt^\#$	$1.6pt^\#$	$2.7pt^\#$	$2.7pt^\#$	$3.5pt^\#$
$dev^\#$	$.3pt^\#$	$.36pt^\#$	$.5pt^\#$	$.5pt^\#$	$.5pt^\#$
slant	0	0	0	$^1/_3$	0
seed	sqrt 2	sqrt 3	2.71828	3.14159	0.57722

The driver file PUNK.MF was the most difficult to write, because it contains the "essence" of the design. The various parts of this file grew one step at a time. For example, the last two parameters of the '**beginpunkchar**' macro were added after I noticed that some characters can't tolerate as much random deviation in their points as a normal character can; too much displacement makes them unrecognizable.

% This is P U N K
% a meta-font inspired by Gerard and Marjan Unger's lectures, February 1985
mode_setup;

randomseed $:= seed;$

define_pixels$(u, dev);$
define_blacker_pixels$(px, py, dot);$
define_whole_pixels$(s);$
$xoffset := s;$
pickup pencircle xscaled px yscaled $py;$ $punk\_pen := savepen;$

pickup pencircle scaled *dot*; *def_pen_path_*;
path *dot_pen_path*; *dot_pen_path* := *currentpen_path*;
currenttransform := *identity* slanted *slant* yscaled *aspect_ratio*;

def beginpunkchar(**expr** *c*, *n*, *h*, *v*) =   % code *c*; width is *n* units
   hdev := *h* * *dev*;   % modify horizontal and
   vdev := *v* * *dev*;   % vertical amounts of deviation
   beginchar(*c*, *n* * $u^\#$, $ht^\#$, 0);
   italcorr $ht^\#$ * *slant*; **pickup** *punk_pen* **enddef**;
extra_endchar := *extra_endchar* & `"w:=w+2s;charwd:=charwd+2s#"`;

def ↑ = transformed *currenttransform* **enddef**;
def *makebox*(**text** *rule*) =
  for *y* = 0, *h*:
    rule((−*s*, *y*)↑, (*w* − *s*, *y*)↑); **endfor**   % horizontals
    for *x* = −*s*, 0, *w* − 2*s*, *w* − *s*: *rule*((*x*, 0)↑, (*x*, *h*)↑); **endfor**   % verticals
  enddef;
rulepen := *pensquare*;

vardef *pp* **expr** *z* = *z*+(*hdev**normaldeviate, *vdev**normaldeviate) **enddef**;

def pd expr *z* = *addto_currentpicture* **contour**
     dot_pen_path shifted z_{t_-} **withpen** *penspeck* **enddef**;   % **drawdot**

input PUNKL   % uppercase letters
input PUNKAE   % uppercase Æ, Œ, Ø
input PUNKG   % uppercase greek
input PUNKP   % punctuation
input PUNKD   % digits
input PUNKA   % accents

$ht^\#$:= .6$ht^\#$; *dev* := .7*dev*;
input PUNKSL   % special lowercase
extra_beginchar := *extra_beginchar* & `"charcode:=charcode+32;"`;
input PUNKL   % lowercase letters
extra_beginchar := *extra_beginchar* & `"charcode:=charcode-35;"`;
input PUNKAE   % lowercase æ, œ, ø

font_slant := *slant*;
font_quad := 18$u^\#$ + 2$s^\#$;
font_normal_space := 9$u^\#$ + 2$s^\#$;
font_normal_stretch := 6$u^\#$;
font_normal_shrink := 4$u^\#$;
font_x_height := $ht^\#$;
font_coding_scheme := `"TeX text without f-ligatures"`;
end

The 128 characters generated by PUNK.MF have the same font positions as the characters in fonts like cmr5 and cmcsc10 that don't have f-ligatures. Here, for example, is the layout of the font PUNKZ20, which is like PUNK20 except that *dev* = 0 (so that there is no randomness):

	'0	'1	'2	'3	'4	'5	'6	'7	
'00x	Γ	Δ	Θ	Λ	⋮	Π	Σ	Υ	"0x
'01x	Φ	Ψ	Ω	↑	↓	ı	ȷ	̀	
'02x	́	̌	̆	̇	̆	̊	̄	̧	"1x
'03x	̤	ß	æ	œ	ø	Æ	Œ	Ø	
'04x	̷	!	ˮ	#	$	%	&	ʼ	"2x
'05x	(	)	*	+	,	-	.	/	
'06x	0	1	2	3	4	5	6	7	"3x
'07x	8	9	:	;	<	=	>	?	
'10x	@	A	B	C	D	E	F	G	"4x
'11x	H	I	J	K	L	M	N	O	
'12x	P	Q	R	S	T	U	V	W	"5x
'13x	X	Y	Z	[	\	]	^	˙	
'14x	̔	A	B	C	D	E	F	G	"6x
'15x	H	I	J	K	L	M	N	O	
'16x	P	Q	R	S	T	U	V	W	"7x
'17x	X	Y	Z	̋	̄	̈	̆	̈	
	"8	"9	"A	"B	"C	"D	"E	"F	

Let's look now at the program files. The first one I wrote was PUNKL.MF, which defines all the letters from A to Z:

% Punk letters:

beginpunkchar("A", 13, 1, 2);
$z_1 = pp(1.5u, 0)$; $z_2 = (.5w, 1.1h)$; $z_3 = pp(w - 1.5u, 0)$;
pd z_1; **pd** z_3; **draw** z_1 -- z_2 -- z_3;   % left and right diagonals
$z_4 = pp.3[z_1, z_2]$; $z_5 = pp.3[z_3, z_2]$;
pd z_4; **pd** z_5; **draw** z_4 -- z_5;   % crossbar
endchar;

beginpunkchar("B", 12, 1, 1);
$z_1 = pp(2u, 0)$; $z_2 = pp(2u, .6h)$; $z_3 = pp(2u, h)$;
pd z_1; **pd** z_3; **draw** z_1 -- z_3;   % stem
$z_{1.5} = pp(w - u, .5y_2)$; $z_{2.5} = pp(w - u, .5[y_2, y_3])$;
draw z_2 -- $z_{2.5}$ -- z_3;   % upper lobe
draw flex($z_2, z_{1.5}, z_1$);   % lower lobe
endchar;

beginpunkchar("C", 13, 1, 2);
$z_1 = pp(w - 2u, .8h)$; $z_2 = pp(.6w, h)$; $z_3 = pp(u, .5h)$;
$z_4 = (.6w, 0)$; $z_5 = (w - 2u, .2h)$;
pd z_1; **pd** z_5; **draw** z_1 .. z_2 .. z_3 .. z_4 .. z_5;   % arc
endchar;

beginpunkchar("D", 14, 1, 2);
$z_1 = pp(2u, 0)$; $z_2 = pp(2u, h)$; $z_3 = pp(w - u, .6h)$;
pd z_1; **pd** z_2; **draw** flex(z_1, z_3, z_2);   % lobe
draw z_1 -- z_2;   % stem
endchar;

beginpunkchar("E", 12, .5, 1);
$z_1 = pp(2u, 0)$; $z_2 = pp(2u, h)$; $z_3 = pp(w - 2.5u, h)$; $z_4 = pp(w - 2u, 0)$;
pd z_3; **pd** z_4; **draw** z_4 -- z_1 -- z_2 -- z_3;   % stem and arms
$z_5 = pp(2u, .6h)$; $z_6 = pp(w - 3u, .6h)$;
pd z_5; **pd** z_6; **draw** z_5 -- z_6;   % crossbar
endchar;

beginpunkchar("F", 12, .5, 2);
$z_1 = pp(2u, 0)$; $z_2 = pp(2u, h)$; $z_3 = pp(w - 2u, h)$;
pd z_1; **pd** z_3; **draw** z_1 -- z_2 -- z_3;   % stem and arm
$z_5 = pp(2u, .6h)$; $z_6 = pp(w - 3u, .6h)$; $z_4 = pp.5[z_5, z_6] - (0, .1h)$;
pd z_5; **pd** z_6; **draw** flex(z_5, z_4, z_6);   % crossbar
endchar;

beginpunkchar("G", 13, .5, .5);
$z_1 = pp(w - 2u, .8h)$; $z_2 = pp(.6w, h)$; $z_3 = pp(u, .5h)$;
$z_4 = pp(.6w, 0)$; $z_5 = (w - 2u, 0)$;
pd z_1; **draw** z_1 .. z_2 .. z_3 .. z_4 --- z_5;   % arc
$z_6 = pp(.5[u, x_5], .4h)$; **pd** z_6; **pd** z_5; **draw** z_6 -- $(pp(x_5, y_6))$ -- z_5; % spur
endchar;

beginpunkchar("H", 14, 1, .5);
$z_1 = pp(2u, 0)$; $z_2 = pp(2u, h)$; $z_3 = pp(w - 2u, 0)$; $z_4 = pp(w - 2u, h)$;
$z_5 = pp(2u, .6h)$; $z_6 = pp(w - 2u, .6h)$;
pd z_1; **pd** z_2; **pd** z_3; **pd** z_4;
draw $z_1 \text{ -- } z_2$; **draw** flex(z_3, z_6, z_4);   % stems
pd z_5; **draw** $z_5 \text{ -- } z_6$;   % crossbar
endchar;

beginpunkchar("I", 5, 1, 2);
$z_1 = pp(.5w, 0)$; $z_2 = (.5w, \frac{1}{3}h)$; $z_3 = (.5w, \frac{2}{3}h)$; $z_4 = (.5w, h)$;
pd z_1; **pd** z_4; **draw** flex(z_1, z_2, z_3, z_4);   % stem
endchar;

beginpunkchar("J", 9, 1, 2);
$z_1 = pp(w - 2u, h)$; $z_2 = pp(w - 2u, -.1h)$; $z_3 = pp(u, 0)$;
pd z_1; **pd** z_3; **draw** $z_1 \text{ -- } z_2 \text{ -- } z_3$;   % arc
endchar;

beginpunkchar("K", 14, 1, 2);
$z_1 = pp(2u, 0)$; $z_2 = pp(2u, h)$; $z_3 = pp(2u, \frac{1}{3}h)$; $z_4 = pp(w - 1.5u, h)$;
pd z_1; **pd** z_2; **draw** $z_1 \text{ -- } z_2$;   % stem
pd z_3; **pd** z_4; **draw** $z_3 \text{ -- } z_4$;   % upper diagonal
$z_6 = pp(w - u, 0)$; $z_5 = \frac{1}{3}[z_3, z_4]$;
pd z_6; **draw** flex$(z_5, .8[z_1, \frac{2}{3}[z_5, z_6]], z_6)$;   % lower diagonal
endchar;

beginpunkchar("L", 11, 1, 2);
$z_1 = pp(2u, h)$; $z_2 = pp(2u, 0)$; $z_3 = pp(w - 1.5u, 0)$;
pd z_1; **pd** z_3; **draw** $z_1 \text{ -- } z_2 \text{ -- } z_3$;   % stem and arm
endchar;

beginpunkchar("M", 17, .5, 2);
$z_1 = pp(2u, 0)$; $z_2 = pp(2u, h)$; $z_3 = pp(.5w, 0)$;
$z_4 = pp(w - 2u, h)$; $z_5 = pp(w - 2u, 0)$;
pd z_1; **pd** z_5; **draw** $z_1 \text{ -- } z_2 \text{ -- } z_3 \text{ -- } z_4 \text{ -- } z_5$;   % stems and diagonals
endchar;

beginpunkchar("N", 13, .75, 2);
$z_1 = pp(2u, 0)$; $z_2 = pp(2u, h)$; $z_3 = pp(w - 2u, 0)$; $z_4 = pp(w - 2u, h)$;
pd z_1; **pd** z_4; **draw** $z_1 \text{ -- } z_2 \text{ -- } z_3 \text{ -- } z_4$;   % stems and diagonals
endchar;

beginpunkchar("O", 12, .5, 2);
$z_1 = pp(.5w, h)$; $z_2 = pp(u, .55h)$; $z_3 = pp(.5w, 0)$; $z_4 = pp(w - u, .55h)$;
pd z_1; **draw** $z_1\{left\} .. z_2 .. z_3 .. z_4 .. z_1$;   % bowl
endchar;

beginpunkchar("P", 13, 1, 2);
$z_1 = pp(2u, 0)$; $z_2 = pp(2u, 1.1h)$; $z_3 = pp(2u, .5h)$; $z_4 = pp(w, .6[y_3, y_2])$;
pd z_1; **pd** z_3; **draw** $z_1 \text{ -- } z_2 \text{ -- } z_4 \text{ -- } z_3$;   % stem and bowl
endchar;

beginpunkchar("Q", 14, .5, 2);
$z_1 = pp(.5w, h)$; $z_2 = pp(u, .55h)$; $z_3 = pp(.5w, 0)$; $z_4 = pp(w - u, .55h)$;
pd z_1; **draw** $z_1\{$curl 2$\}$ .. z_2 .. z_3 .. z_4 .. z_1;   % bowl
$z_5 = pp(.4w, .2h)$; $z_6 = pp(w - u, -.1h)$; $z_7 = pp(.5[x_5, x_6], -.2h)$;
pd z_5; **pd** z_6; **draw** z_5 -- z_7 -- z_6;   % tail
endchar;

beginpunkchar("R", 16, 1, 2);
$z_1 = pp(2u, 0)$; $z_2 = pp(2u, h)$; $z_3 = pp(w - u, .6[y_2, y_4])$;
$z_4 = pp(2u, .5h)$; $z_5 = pp(w - 1.5u, 0)$;
pd z_1; **pd** z_2; **pd** z_5;
draw z_1 -- flex(z_2, z_3, z_4) -- z_5;   % stem, bowl, and diagonal
endchar;

beginpunkchar("S", 11, .3, 1);
$z_1 = pp(w - 2u, .9h)$; $z_2 = pp(.5w, h)$; $z_3 = pp(u, .7h)$; $z_4 = .6[z_6, z_2]$;
$z_5 = pp(w - u, .35h)$; $z_6 = pp(.5w, u)$; $z_7 = pp(u, .2h)$;
pd z_1; **pd** z_7; **draw** z_1 -- z_2 ... z_3 .. z_4 .. z_5 ... z_6 -- z_7;   % stroke
endchar;

beginpunkchar("T", 13, .75, 2);
$z_1 = pp(u, h)$; $z_2 = pp(w - u, h)$; $z_3 = pp(.5w, 0)$;
pd z_1; **pd** z_2; **pd** z_3; **draw** z_1 -- z_2;   % arms
draw $.5[z_1, z_2]$ -- z_3;   % stem
endchar;

beginpunkchar("U", 13, .3, 2);
$z_1 = pp(2u, h)$; $z_2 = pp(2u, .2h)$; $z_3 = pp(.5w, 0)$;
$z_4 = pp(w - 2u, .2h)$; $z_5 = pp(w - 2u, h)$;
pd z_1; **pd** z_5; **draw** z_1 --- z_2 ... $z_3\{z_4 - z_2\}$ ... z_4 --- z_5;   % stroke
endchar;

beginpunkchar("V", 13, 1, 2);
$z_1 = pp(1.5u, h)$; $z_2 = pp(.5w, 0)$; $z_3 = pp(w - 1.5u, h)$;
pd z_1; **pd** z_3; **draw** z_1 -- z_2 -- z_3;   % diagonals
endchar;

beginpunkchar("W", 18, 1, 2);
$z_1 = pp(1.5u, h)$; $z_2 = pp(.5[x_1, x_3], 0)$; $z_3 = pp(.5w, .8h)$;
$z_4 = pp(.5[x_3, x_5], 0)$; $z_5 = pp(w - 1.5u, h)$;
pd z_1; **pd** z_5; **draw** z_1 -- z_2 -- z_3 -- z_4 -- z_5;   % diagonals
endchar;

beginpunkchar("X", 13, 1, 1);
$z_1 = pp(1.5u, h)$; $z_2 = pp(w - 1.5u, 0)$; $z_3 = pp(1.5u, 0)$;
$z_4 = pp(w - 2.5u, h)$;
pd z_1; **pd** z_2; **draw** z_1 -- z_2;   % main diagonal
pd z_3; **pd** z_4; **draw** z_3 -- z_4;   % cross diagonal
endchar;

beginpunkchar("Y", 13, 1, 2);
$z_1 = pp(1.5u, h)$; $z_2 = pp(w - 1.5u, h)$; $z_3 = pp(.5w, .5h)$; $z_4 = pp(.5w, 0)$;
pd z_1; **pd** z_2; **pd** z_4; **draw** z_1 -- z_3 -- z_4;   % stem and left diagonal
draw z_2 -- z_3;   % right diagonal
endchar;

beginpunkchar("Z", 11, 1, 2);
$z_1 = pp(1.5u, h)$; $z_2 = pp(w - 2.5u, h)$; $z_3 = pp(1.5u, 0)$;
$z_4 = pp(w - 1.5u, 0)$;
pd z_1; **pd** z_4; **draw** z_1 -- z_2 -- z_3 -- z_4;   % diagonals
endchar;

(It slowed me down a little to type the comments that identify the strokes. But such comments are enormously valuable when characters are being revised, so I knew that I should include them right from the beginning.)

Three of the letters go into a special file, **PUNKAE.MF**, because the character codes of these uppercase letters have a nonstandard relation to the character codes of the corresponding lowercase equivalents:

beginpunkchar(oct "035", 16, 1, 2);   % Æ
$z_1 = pp(1.5u, 0)$; $z_2 = pp(.6w, h)$; $z_3 = pp(w - 1.5u, h)$;
pd z_1; **pd** z_3; **draw** z_1 -- z_2 -- z_3;   % left diagonal and upper arm
$z_4 = pp.3[z_1, z_2]$; $z_5 = pp(.6w, 0)$; $z_6 = pp(w - 2u, .3h)$;
pd z_4; **pd** z_6; **draw** z_4 -- z_6;   % crossbar
$z_7 = pp(w - u, 0)$; **pd** z_2; **pd** z_7;
draw z_2 -- z_5 -- z_7;   % stem and lower arm
endchar;

beginpunkchar(oct "036", 18, 1, 2);   % Œ
$z_1 = pp(.5w, h)$; $z_2 = pp(u, .4h)$; $z_3 = pp(.5w, 0)$;
pd z_1; **draw** z_1 .. z_2 .. $\{right\}z_3$;   % bowl
$z_4 = pp(w - 1.5u, h)$; $z_5 = pp(w - 2u, .4h)$; $z_6 = pp(w - u, 0)$;
pd z_4; **pd** z_6; **draw** z_4 -- z_1 -- z_3 -- z_6;   % arms and stem
pd z_5; **draw** z_5 -- $.4[z_3, z_1]$;   % crossbar
endchar;

beginpunkchar(oct "037", 14, 1, 1);   % Ø
$z_1 = pp(.5w, h)$; $z_2 = pp(u, .5h)$; $z_3 = pp(.5w, 0)$; $z_4 = pp(w - u, .5h)$;
$z_5 = pp(w - 2u, 1.1h)$; $z_6 = pp(2u, -.1h)$;
pd z_1; **pd** z_6; **draw** z_1 .. z_2 .. z_3 .. z_4 .. z_5 -- z_6;   % bowl and diagonal
endchar;

There's also a special file **PUNKSL.MF** for lowercase letters with no matching uppercase:

beginpunkchar(oct "020", 5, 1, 2);   % dotless I
$z_1 = pp(.5w, 0)$; $z_2 = (.5w, \frac{1}{3}h)$; $z_3 = (.5w, \frac{2}{3}h)$; $z_4 = (.5w, h)$;

pd z_1; **pd** z_4; **draw** flex(z_1, z_2, z_3, z_4);   % stem
endchar;
beginpunkchar(oct "021", 9, 1, 2);   % dotless J
$z_1 = pp(w - 2u, h)$; $z_2 = pp(w - 2u, -.1h)$; $z_3 = pp(u, 0)$;
pd z_1; **pd** z_3; **draw** z_1 -- z_2 -- z_3;   % arc
endchar;
beginpunkchar(oct "031", 18, .3, 1);   % German sharp S
$z_1 = pp(.5w - u, .9h)$; $z_2 = pp(\frac{1}{3}w, h)$; $z_3 = pp(u, .7h)$; $z_4 = .6[z_6, z_2]$;
$z_5 = pp(.5w, .35h)$; $z_6 = pp(\frac{1}{3}w, u)$; $z_7 = pp(u, .2h)$;
pd z_1; **pd** z_7; **draw** z_1 -- z_2 ... z_3 .. z_4 .. z_5 ... z_6 -- z_7;   % left stroke
for $i = 1$ **upto** 7: $z[i + 10] = pp(z[i]$ shifted $(.5w - u, 0))$; **endfor**
pd z_{11}; **pd** z_{17};
draw z_{11} -- z_{12} ... z_{13} .. z_{14} .. z_{15} ... z_{16} -- z_{17};   % right stroke
endchar;

The uppercase Greek letters in file PUNKG.MF may have a slightly different style than those of PUNKL, because I wrote them two years later. Is there an obvious difference?

beginpunkchar(oct "000", 11, 1, 2);   % Γ
$z_1 = pp(2u, 0)$; $z_2 = pp(2u, h)$; $z_3 = pp(w - 1.5u, h)$;
pd z_1; **pd** z_3; **draw** z_1 -- z_2 -- z_3;   % stem and arm
endchar;
beginpunkchar(oct "001", 15, 1, 2);   % Δ
$z_1 = pp(u, 0)$; $z_2 = pp(.5w, h)$; $z_3 = pp(w - u, 0)$;
pd z_1; **draw** z_1 -- z_2 .. tension 5 .. z_3 .. tension 5 .. z_1;   % triangle
endchar;
beginpunkchar(oct "002", 15, .5, 2);   % Θ
$z_1 = pp(.5w, h)$; $z_2 = pp(u, .6h)$; $z_3 = pp(.5w, 0)$; $z_4 = pp(w - u, .6h)$;
pd z_1; **draw** z_1 .. tension .8 .. z_2 .. z_3 .. z_4 .. tension .8 .. z_1;   % bowl
$z_5 = pp(x_2 + 2u, .4h)$; $z_6 = pp(x_4 - 2u, .4h)$;
pd z_5; **pd** z_6; **draw** z_5 -- z_6;   % bar
endchar;
beginpunkchar(oct "003", 12, 1, 2);   % Λ
$z_1 = pp(u, 0)$; $z_2 = pp(.5w, h)$; $z_3 = pp(w - u, 0)$;
pd z_1; **pd** z_3; **draw** z_1 -- z_2 -- z_3;   % diagonals
endchar;
beginpunkchar(oct "004", 12, 1, 1);   % Ξ
$z_1 = pp(u, h)$; $z_2 = pp(w - u, h)$;
pd z_1; **pd** z_2; **draw** z_1 -- z_2;   % upper arm
$z_3 = pp(2u, .55h)$; $z_4 = pp(w - 2u, .55h)$;
pd z_3; **pd** z_4; **draw** z_3 -- z_4;   % bar
$z_5 = pp(u, 0)$; $z_6 = pp(w - u, 0)$;
pd z_5; **pd** z_6; **draw** z_5 -- z_6;   % lower arm

endchar;

beginpunkchar(oct "005", 13, 1, .5);   % Π
$z_1 = pp(1.5u, 0)$; $z_2 = pp(1.5u, h)$; $z_3 = pp(w - 1.5u, h)$;
$z_4 = pp(w - 1.5u, 0)$;
pd z_1; **pd** z_4; **draw** z_1 -- z_2 -- z_3 -- z_4;   % stems and bar
endchar;

beginpunkchar(oct "006", 13, 1, 1);   % Σ
$z_1 = pp(w - u, h)$; $z_2 = pp(u, h)$; $z_3 = pp(.5w - u, .5h)$;
$z_4 = pp(u, 0)$; $z_5 = pp(w - u, 0)$;
pd z_1; **pd** z_5; **draw** z_1 -- $z_2\{.5[z_4, z_5] - z_2\}$ .. z_3 -- z_4 -- z_5;   % arms and diagonals
endchar;

beginpunkchar(oct "007", 15, 1, .5);   % Υ
$z_1 = pp(u, .8h)$; $z_2 = pp(.3w, h)$; $z_3 = pp(.5w, .5h)$; $z_4 = pp(.5w, 0)$;
pd z_1; **pd** z_4; **draw** z_1 .. z_2 .. tension 2 .. z_3 --- z_4;   % left arc and stem
$z_5 = pp(w - u, .8h)$; $z_6 = pp(.7w, h)$;
pd z_5; **draw** z_5 .. z_6 .. tension 2 .. $\{z_4 - z_3\}z_3$;   % right arc
endchar;

beginpunkchar(oct "010", 13, 1, 2);   % Φ
$z_1 = pp(.5w, h)$; $z_2 = pp(.5w, 0)$; **pd** z_1; **pd** z_2; **draw** z_1 -- z_2;   % stem
$z_3 = pp(.5w, {}^2/_3 h)$; $z_4 = pp(u, .5h)$; $z_5 = pp(.5w, {}^1/_4 h)$; $z_6 = pp(w - u, .5h)$;
pd z_3; **draw** z_3 .. z_4 .. z_5 .. z_6 .. z_3;   % bowl
endchar;

beginpunkchar(oct "011", 14, 1, 1);   % Ψ
$z_1 = pp(.5w, h)$; $z_2 = pp(.5w, 0)$; **pd** z_1; **pd** z_2; **draw** z_1 -- z_2;   % stem
$z_3 = pp(u, .8h)$; $z_4 = pp(.5w, .2h)$; $z_5 = pp(w - u, .8h)$;
pd z_3; **pd** z_5;
draw $z_3\{.4[z_1, z_2] - z_3\}$ .. $z_4\{right\}$ .. $\{z_5 - .4[z_1, z_2]\}z_5$;   % stroke
endchar;

beginpunkchar(oct "012", 13, 1, 2);   % Ω
$z_1 = pp(u, 0)$; $z_2 = pp({}^1/_3 w, 0)$; $z_3 = pp(u, {}^2/_3 h)$; $z_4 = pp(.5w, h)$;
$z_5 = pp(w - u, {}^2/_3 h)$; $z_6 = pp({}^2/_3 w, 0)$; $z_7 = pp(w - u, 0)$;
pd z_1; **pd** z_7;
draw z_1 -- $z_2\{up\}$ .. z_3 .. z_4 .. z_5 .. $\{down\}z_6$ -- z_7;   % bowl and arms
endchar;

The next program file, PUNKD.MF, defines the ten punk digits. I ran out of time while typing this, so the comments at the end are somewhat uninspired.

---

beginpunkchar("0", 9, .5, 1);
$z_1 = pp(.5w, h)$; $z_2 = pp(u, .55h)$; $z_3 = pp(.5w, 0)$; $z_4 = pp(w - u, .55h)$;
pd z_1; **draw** $z_1\{curl 2\}$ .. z_2 .. z_3 .. z_4 .. z_1;   % bowl
endchar;

beginpunkchar("1", 9, .3, 1);
$z_1 = pp(2u, .7h)$; $z_2 = pp(.6w, h)$; $z_3 = pp(.6w, 0)$;
pd z_1; **pd** z_3; **draw** $z_1 \text{ -- } z_2 \text{ -- } z_3$;   % serif and stem
endchar;

beginpunkchar("2", 9, 1, 1);
$z_1 = pp(2u, .7h)$; $z_2 = pp(.5w, h)$; $z_3 = pp(w - u, .6h)$;
$z_4 = pp(u, 0)$; $z_5 = pp(w - 2u, 0)$;
pd z_1; **pd** z_5; **draw** $z_1 \text{ .. } z_2 \text{ .. } z_3 \text{ .. } z_4 \text{ -- } z_5$;   % stroke
endchar;

beginpunkchar("3", 9, .5, .5);
$z_1 = pp(2u, .7h)$; $z_2 = pp(.5w, h)$; $z_3 = pp(w - u, .5[y_2, y_4])$;
$z_4 = pp(.5w - u, .55h)$; $z_5 = pp(w - u, .5[y_4, y_6])$;
$z_6 = pp(.5w, 0)$; $z_7 = pp(1.5u, .2h)$;
pd z_1; **pd** z_7; **draw** $z_1 \text{ .. } z_2 \text{ .. } z_3 \text{ .. } z_4 \& z_4 \text{ .. } z_5 \text{ .. } z_6 \text{ .. } z_7$;   % arcs
endchar;

beginpunkchar("4", 9, 1, 1);
$z_1 = pp(w - u, .3h)$; $z_2 = pp(u, .3h)$; $z_3 = pp(\text{\textonehalf}\!\!{}^2\!/\!_3 w, h)$; $z_4 = pp(\!{}^2\!/\!_3 w, 0)$;
pd z_1; **pd** z_4; **draw** $z_1 \text{ -- } z_2 \text{ -- } z_3 \text{ -- } z_4$;   % stem and diagonals
endchar;

beginpunkchar("5", 9, .5, .5);
$z_1 = pp(w - 2u, h)$; $z_2 = pp(2u, h)$; $z_3 = pp(u, .7h)$;
$z_4 = pp(w - u, .5[y_3, y_5])$; $z_5 = pp(.5w, 0)$; $z_6 = pp(u, .2h)$;
pd z_1; **pd** z_6; **draw** $z_1 \text{ -- } z_2 \text{ -- } z_3 \text{ .. } z_4 \text{ .. } z_5 \text{ .. } z_6$;   % stroke
endchar;

beginpunkchar("6", 9, 1, 1);
$z_1 = pp(\!{}^2\!/\!_3 w, h)$; $z_2 = pp(u, .3h)$; $z_3 = pp(.5w, 0)$;
$z_4 = pp(w - u, .3h)$; $z_5 = pp(.6w, .6h)$; $z_6 = pp.z\,2$;
pd z_1; **pd** z_6; **draw** $z_1 \text{ .. } z_2 \text{ .. } z_3 \text{ .. } z_4 \text{ .. } z_5 \text{ -- } z_6$;   % stroke
endchar;

beginpunkchar("7", 9, .5, 1);
$z_1 = pp(2u, h)$; $z_2 = pp(w - .5u, h)$; $z_3 = pp(.4w, 0)$;
pd z_1; **pd** z_3; **draw** $z_1 \text{ -- } z_2 \& z_2 \text{ .. } z_3\{down\}$;   % stroke
endchar;

beginpunkchar("8", 9, .5, .5);
$z_1 = pp(.5w, h)$; $z_2 = pp(u, .5[y_1, y_3])$; $z_3 = pp(.5w, .6h)$;
$z_4 = pp(w - u, .5[y_3, y_5])$; $z_5 = pp(.5w, 0)$;
$z_6 = pp(u, .5[y_5, y_3])$; $z_7 = pp(w - u, .5[y_1, y_3])$;
pd z_1; **draw** $z_1\{curl\,8\} \text{ .. } z_2 \text{ .. } z_3 \text{ .. } z_4 \text{ .. } z_5 \text{ .. } z_6 \text{ .. } z_3 \text{ .. } z_7 \text{ .. } z_1$; % stroke
endchar;

beginpunkchar("9", 9, 1, 1);
$z_1 = pp(\!{}^1\!/\!_3 w, 0)$; $z_2 = pp(w - u, .7h)$; $z_3 = pp(.5w, h)$;
$z_4 = pp(u, .7h)$; $z_5 = pp(.5w, .4h)$;

pd z_1; **pd** z_5; **draw** $z_1 \mathrel{..} z_2 \mathrel{..} z_3 \mathrel{..} z_4 \mathrel{..} z_5$;   % stroke
endchar;

The program file `PUNKP.MF` defines "punk punctuation." This was one of the most difficult to write — although most of the characters are very simple — because there are so **DARN** many punctuation marks.

beginpunkchar(".", 5, 1, 2);
pd $pp(.5w, 0)$;   % dot
endchar;

beginpunkchar(",", 5, .5, .5);
$z_1 = pp(.5w, 0)$; $z_2 = pp(w - u, -.1h)$; $z_3 = pp(.5w, -.3h)$;
pd z_1; **pd** z_3; **draw** $z_1 \mathrel{--} z_2 \mathrel{--} z_3$;   % stroke
endchar;

beginpunkchar(":", 5, 1, .5);
pd $pp(.5w, 0)$; **pd** $pp(.5w, .4h)$;   % dots
endchar;

beginpunkchar(";", 5, .5, .5);
$z_1 = pp(.5w, 0)$; $z_2 = pp(w - u, -.1h)$; $z_3 = pp(.5w, -.3h)$;
pd z_1; **pd** z_3; **draw** $z_1 \mathrel{--} z_2 \mathrel{--} z_3$;   % stroke
pd $pp(.5w, .4h)$;   % dot
endchar;

beginpunkchar("!", 5, .5, .5);
pd $pp(.5w, 0)$;   % dot
$z_1 = pp(.5w, 1.05h)$; $z_2 = pp(.5w, .3h)$;
pd z_1; **pd** z_2; **draw** $z_1 \mathrel{--} z_2$;   % stem
endchar;
ligtable "!": "‘" =: oct "016";

beginpunkchar(oct "016", 5, .5, .5);   % Spanish inverted !
pd $pp(.5w, .9h)$;   % dot
$z_1 = pp(.5w, -.1h)$; $z_2 = pp(.5w, .6h)$;
pd z_1; **pd** z_2; **draw** $z_1 \mathrel{--} z_2$;   % stem
endchar;

beginpunkchar("?", 9, 1, .5);
$z_1 = pp(1.5u, .8h)$; $z_2 = pp(.5w, h)$; $z_3 = pp(w - u, .8h)$; $z_4 = pp(.5w, .3h)$;
pd z_1; **pd** z_4; **draw** $z_1 \mathrel{..} z_2 \mathrel{..} z_3 \mathrel{..} \{down\}z_4$;   % arc and stem
pd $pp(.5w, 0)$;   % dot
endchar;
ligtable "?": "‘" =: oct "017";

beginpunkchar(oct "017", 9, 1, .5);   % Spanish inverted ?
$z_1 = pp(1.5u, .1h)$; $z_2 = pp(.5w, -.1h)$;
$z_3 = pp(w - u, .1h)$; $z_4 = pp(.5w, .6h)$;
pd z_1; **pd** z_4; **draw** $z_1 \mathrel{..} z_2 \mathrel{..} z_3 \mathrel{..} \{up\}z_4$;   % arc and stem

pd $pp(.5w, .9h)$; % dot
endchar;

beginpunkchar("&", 14, .5, .5);
$z_1 = pp(w - 2u, h)$; $z_2 = pp(u, h)$; $z_3 = pp(3u, 0)$;
$z_5 = pp(w - u, .6h)$; $z_6 = pp(w - 2u, 0)$;
pd z_1; **pd** z_5; **draw** z_1 -- z_2 -- z_3 -- z_5; % arms and stem
draw z_1 -- $.5[z_2, z_3]$; **pd** z_6; **draw** z_6 -- $.6[z_3, z_5]$; % diagonals
endchar;

beginpunkchar("$", 12, .5, .5);
$z_1 = pp(w - 1.5u, .7h)$; $z_2 = pp(.5w, h)$; $z_3 = pp(u, .7h)$; $z_4 = .5[z_3, z_5]$;
$z_5 = pp(w - u, .3h)$; $z_6 = pp(.5w, 0)$; $z_7 = pp(u, .3h)$;
pd z_1; **pd** z_7; **draw** $z_1 .. z_2 .. z_3 .. z_4 .. z_5 .. z_6 .. z_7$; % stroke
$z_8 = z_2 + (0, .1h)$; **pd** z_8; **draw** z_8 -- z_6; % stem
endchar;

beginpunkchar("%", 18, .5, .5);
$z_1 = pp(3.5u, 1.1h)$; $z_2 = pp(u, .8h)$; $z_3 = pp(3.5u, .5h)$; $z_4 = pp(6u, .8h)$;
$z_5 = pp(w - 3.5u, .5h)$; $z_6 = pp(w - 6u, .2h)$;
$z_7 = pp(w - 3.5u, -.1h)$; $z_8 = pp(w - u, .2h)$;
pd z_1; **draw** $z_1 .. z_2 .. z_3 .. z_4 .. z_1$; % upper bowl
pd z_5; **draw** $z_5 .. z_6 .. z_7 .. z_8 .. z_5$; % lower bowl
$z_9 = pp(w - 3u, 1.1h)$; $z_0 = pp(3u, -.1h)$;
pd z_0; **draw** z_9 -- z_0; % diagonal
draw $z_1\{z_5 - z_1\} .. z_9$; % link
endchar;

beginpunkchar("@", 18, 1, .5);
$z_1 = pp(2u, 0)$; $z_2 = pp(\frac{1}{3}w, .7h)$; $z_3 = pp(w - 6u, 0)$;
$z_4 = pp(w, .3h)$; $z_5 = pp(\frac{1}{3}w, h)$; $z_6 = pp(u, .5h)$; $z_7 = .7[z_2, z_3]$;
pd z_1; **pd** z_7;
draw z_1 -- z_2 -- $z_3\{right\} .. z_4 .. z_5 .. z_6 .. z_7$; % diagonals and stroke
endchar;

beginpunkchar("-", 7, .5, .5);
$z_1 = pp(u, .4h)$; $z_2 = pp(w - u, .5h)$; **pd** z_1; **pd** z_2; **draw** z_1 -- z_2; % bar
endchar;
ligtable "-": "-" =: oct "173";

beginpunkchar(oct "173", 9, .5, .5); % –
$z_1 = pp(0, .5h)$; $z_2 = pp(w, .4h)$; **pd** z_1; **pd** z_2; **draw** z_1 -- z_2; % bar
endchar;
ligtable oct "173": "-" =: oct "174";

beginpunkchar(oct "174", 18, .5, .5); % —
$z_1 = pp(0, .5h)$; $z_2 = pp(w, .4h)$; **pd** z_1; **pd** z_2; **draw** z_1 -- z_2; % bar
endchar;

beginpunkchar("+", 9, .5, 1);
$z_1 = pp(0, .5h)$; $z_2 = pp(w, .5h)$; **pd** z_1; **pd** z_2; **draw** z_1 -- z_2;   % bar
$z_3 = pp(.5w, .1h)$; $z_4 = pp(.5w, .9h)$; **pd** z_3; **pd** z_4; **draw** z_3 -- z_4; % stem
endchar;

beginpunkchar("*", 13, .5, 1);
$z_0 = pp(.5w, 1.1h)$; $z_1 = pp(u, .9h)$; $z_2 = pp(2u, .3h)$;
$z_3 = pp(w - u, .3h)$; $z_4 = pp(w - u, .9h)$;
pd z_0; **draw** z_0 -- z_2 .. $\frac{1}{3}[.5[z_2, z_4], z_0]$ .. z_4 -- z_1 -- z_3 -- z_0;   % star
endchar;

beginpunkchar("'", 5, .3, .5);
$z_1 = pp(1.5u, h)$; $z_2 = pp(w - u, .85h)$; $z_3 = pp(u, \frac{2}{3}h)$;
pd z_1; **pd** z_3; **draw** z_1 -- z_2 -- z_3;   % stroke
endchar;
ligtable "'": "'" =: oct "042";

beginpunkchar(oct "042", 9, .3, .5);   % "
$z_1 = pp(.5w - .5u, h)$; $z_2 = pp(u, .6h)$; $z_3 = pp(w - u, .95h)$;
pd z_1; **pd** z_3; **draw** z_1 -- z_2 -- z_3;   % stroke
endchar;

beginpunkchar("'", 5, .3, .5);
$z_1 = pp(w - 1.5u, h)$; $z_2 = pp(u, .85h)$; $z_3 = pp(w - u, \frac{2}{3}h)$;
pd z_1; **pd** z_3; **draw** z_1 -- z_2 -- z_3;   % stroke
endchar;
ligtable "'": "'" =: oct "134";

beginpunkchar(oct "134", 9, .3, .5);   % "
$z_1 = pp(.5w + .5u, h)$; $z_2 = pp(w - u, .6h)$; $z_3 = pp(u, .95h)$;
pd z_1; **pd** z_3; **draw** z_1 -- z_2 -- z_3;   % stroke
endchar;

beginpunkchar(oct "015", 9, .3, .5);   % '
$z_1 = pp(.5w, h)$; $z_2 = pp(.5w, .6h)$; **pd** z_1; **pd** z_2; **draw** z_1 -- z_2; % stem
endchar;

beginpunkchar("(", 7, .5, .5);
$z_1 = pp(w - u, h)$; $z_2 = pp(u, .5h)$; $z_3 = pp(w - u, 0)$;
pd z_1; **pd** z_3; **draw** z_1 .. z_2 .. z_3;   % stroke
endchar;

beginpunkchar(")", 7, .5, .5);
$z_1 = pp(u, h)$; $z_2 = pp(w - u, .5h)$; $z_3 = pp(u, 0)$;
pd z_1; **pd** z_3; **draw** z_1 .. z_2 .. z_3;   % stroke
endchar;

beginpunkchar("[", 8, .5, .5);
$z_1 = pp(w - u, h)$; $z_2 = pp(.5w, h)$; $z_3 = pp(.5w, 0)$; $z_4 = pp(w - u, 0)$;
pd z_1; **pd** z_4; **draw** z_1 -- z_2 -- z_3 -- z_4;   % bars and stem
endchar;

beginpunkchar("]", 8, .5, .5);
$z_1 = pp(u, h)$; $z_2 = pp(.5w, h)$; $z_3 = pp(.5w, 0)$; $z_4 = pp(u, 0)$;
pd z_1; **pd** z_4; **draw** $z_1 \, \text{--} \, z_2 \, \text{--} \, z_3 \, \text{--} \, z_4$;   % bars and stem
endchar;

beginpunkchar("<", 9, .5, .5);
$z_1 = pp(w - u, .9h)$; $z_2 = pp(u, .5h)$; $z_3 = pp(w - u, .1h)$;
pd z_1; **pd** z_3; **draw** $z_1 \, \text{--} \, z_2 \, \text{--} \, z_3$;   % diagonals
endchar;

beginpunkchar(">", 9, .5, .5);
$z_1 = pp(u, .9h)$; $z_2 = pp(w - u, .5h)$; $z_3 = pp(u, .1h)$;
pd z_1; **pd** z_3; **draw** $z_1 \, \text{--} \, z_2 \, \text{--} \, z_3$;   % diagonals
endchar;

beginpunkchar("=", 9, .5, .5);
$z_5 = pp(u, {}^2\!/_3 h)$; $z_6 = pp(w - u, {}^2\!/_3 h)$;
pd z_5; **pd** z_6; **draw** $z_5 \, \text{--} \, z_6$;   % upper bar
$z_7 = pp(u, {}^1\!/_3 h)$; $z_8 = pp(w - u, {}^1\!/_3 h)$;
pd z_7; **pd** z_8; **draw** $z_7 \, \text{--} \, z_8$;   % lower bar
endchar;

beginpunkchar("#", 15, .5, .5);
$z_1 = pp(.5w, h)$; $z_2 = pp(3u, 0)$; $z_3 = pp(w - 3u, h)$; $z_4 = pp(.5w, 0)$;
pd z_2; **pd** z_3;
draw $z_3 \, \text{--} \, z_1 \, \text{--} \, z_2$; **draw** $z_3 \, \text{--} \, z_4 \, \text{--} \, z_2$;   % diagonals (linked)
$z_5 = pp(u, {}^2\!/_3 h)$; $z_6 = pp(w - u, {}^2\!/_3 h)$;
pd z_5; **pd** z_6; **draw** $z_5 \, \text{--} \, z_6$;   % upper bar
$z_7 = pp(u, {}^1\!/_3 h)$; $z_8 = pp(w - u, {}^1\!/_3 h)$;
pd z_7; **pd** z_8; **draw** $z_7 \, \text{--} \, z_8$;   % lower bar
endchar;

beginpunkchar("/", 9, 1, 1);
$z_1 = pp(1.5u, -.05h)$; $z_2 = pp(w - 1.5u, 1.05h)$;
pd z_1; **pd** z_2; **draw** $z_1 \, \text{--} \, z_2$;   % diagonal
endchar;

beginpunkchar(oct "013", 12, .5, .5);   % ↑
$z_1 = pp(u, .7h)$; $z_2 = pp(.5w, h)$; $z_3 = pp(w - u, .7h)$; $z_4 = pp(.5w, 0)$;
pd z_1; **pd** z_3; **pd** z_4;
draw $z_1 \, \text{--} \, z_2 \, \text{--} \, z_4$; **draw** $z_3 \, \text{--} \, z_2$;   % stem and diagonals
endchar;

beginpunkchar(oct "014", 12, .5, .5);   % ↓
$z_1 = pp(u, .3h)$; $z_2 = pp(.5w, 0)$; $z_3 = pp(w - u, .3h)$; $z_4 = pp(.5w, h)$;
pd z_1; **pd** z_3; **pd** z_4;
draw $z_1 \, \text{--} \, z_2 \, \text{--} \, z_4$; **draw** $z_3 \, \text{--} \, z_2$;   % stem and diagonals
endchar;

The final program file, `PUNKA.MF`, defines accents in a form that TEX likes. The TEX input

```
\def\AA{\accent'27A}
{\AA}ngel\aa\ Beatrice Claire Diana \'Erica Fran\c{c}oise
Ginette H\'el\'ene Iris Jackie K\=aren {\L}au\.ra
Mar{\'\i}a N\H{a}ta{\l}{\u\i}e {\O}ctave Pauline
Qu\^eneau Roxanne Sabine T\~a{\'\j}a Ur\v{s}ula Vivian
Wendy Xanthippe Yv{\o}nne Z\"azilie
```

causes accents to be positioned as follows, in the font PUNKSL20:

Angel 'Abeatrice Claire
Diana Érica Fran.coise
Ginette H'el 'eneris
Jackie K"aren·laura
Mar'ia N'ata·l 'i octave
Pauline Qu^eneauRoxanne
Sabine T~a 'iaur 'sula
Vivian Wendy Xanthippe
Yvønne Z"azilie

(Notice that the macro `\AA` needs to be redefined, but the other accents of plain TEX work without change.)

Here is the way accents are drawn:

```
beginpunkchar(oct "022", 9, 1, 1);                        % `
z1 = pp(2.5u, h);  z2 = pp(.6w, .8h);
pd z1;  pd z2;  draw z1 -- z2;                             % diagonal
endchar;
beginpunkchar(oct "023", 9, 1, 1);                        % ´
z1 = pp(w - 2.5u, h);  z2 = pp(.4w, .8h);
pd z1;  pd z2;  draw z1 -- z2;                             % diagonal
endchar;
```

beginpunkchar(oct "136", 13, 1, 1);   % ^
$z_1 = pp(2.5u, .8h)$; $z_2 = pp(.5w, h)$; $z_3 = (w - 2.5u, .8h)$;
pd z_1; **pd** z_3; **draw** z_1 -- z_2 -- z_3;   % diagonals
endchar;

beginpunkchar(oct "024", 13, 1, 1);   % ~
$z_1 = pp(2.5u, .9h)$; $z_2 = pp(.5w, .7h)$; $z_3 = pp(w - 2.5u, .9h)$;
pd z_1; **pd** z_3; **draw** z_1 -- z_2 -- z_3;   % diagonals
endchar;

beginpunkchar(oct "025", 11, 1, 1);   % ˘
$z_1 = pp(2u, h)$; $z_2 = pp(.5w, .75h)$; $z_3 = pp(w - 2u, h)$;
pd z_1; **pd** z_3; **draw** flex(z_1, z_2, z_3);   % stroke
endchar;

beginpunkchar(oct "026", 12, 1, 1);   % ¯
$z_1 = pp(u, .8h)$; $z_2 = pp(w - u, .8h)$; **pd** z_1; **pd** z_2; **draw** z_1 -- z_2; % bar
endchar;

beginpunkchar(oct "137", 5, 1, 1);   % ˙
pd $pp(.5w, .9h)$;   % dot
endchar;

beginpunkchar(oct "177", 13, 1, 1);   % ¨
pd $pp(^1/_5w, .9h)$; **pd** $pp(^4/_5w, .9h)$;   % dots
endchar;

beginpunkchar(oct "176", 13, 1, 1);   % ~
$z_1 = pp(u, .75h)$; $z_2 = pp(w - u, .9h)$;
pd z_1; **pd** z_2; **draw** $z_1\{up\}$ .. $\{up\}z_2$;   % stroke
endchar;

beginpunkchar(oct "175", 13, 1, 1);   % ˝
$z_1 = pp(4u, h)$; $z_2 = pp(2.5u, .7h)$;
$z_3 = pp(w - 2u, h)$; $z_4 = pp(w - 3.5u, .7h)$;
pd z_1; **pd** z_3; **draw** z_1 -- z_2 -- z_4 -- z_3;   % diagonals (linked)
endchar;

beginpunkchar(oct "027", 13, 0, 0);   % Scandinavian loop, for Å and å
$z_0 = (.5w, .66h)$;   % point z_2 of lowercase A
$z_1 = (.5w, .9h)$;
draw $z_0\{z_0 - (1.5u, 0)\}$ .. z_1 .. $\{(w - 1.5u, 0) - z_0\}z_0$;   % loop
endchar;

beginpunkchar(oct "030", 13, .5, .5);   % Cedilla, for ç
$z_1 = (.6w, 0)$; $z_2 = pp(.6w, -.1h)$; $z_3 = pp(2.5u, -.1h)$;
pd z_3; **draw** z_1 -- z_2 -- z_3;   % stroke
endchar;

beginpunkchar(oct "040", 11, .5, .5);   % Polish cross, for L and ł
$z_1 = pp(0, .25h)$; $z_2 = pp(4u, .4h)$;
pd z_1; **pd** z_2; **draw** z_1 -- z_2;   % diagonal
endchar;
ligtable oct "040": "l" kern $-charwd$, "L" kern $-charwd$;

References

[1] George Ade, *Artie: A Story of the Streets and Town* (Chicago: H. S. Stone, 1896), Chapter 19.

[2] Dashiell Hammett, *The Maltese Falcon* (New York: A. A. Knopf, 1930), Chapter 18.

[3] Derek Jewell, music review in the *Sunday Times* (28 November 1976), 37.

[4] Donald E. Knuth, *The METAFONTbook*, Volume C of *Computers & Typesetting* (Reading, Massachusetts: Addison–Wesley and American Mathematical Society, 1986).

[5] Pablo Picasso, pen drawing from Sketchbook 86. (This drawing was later used as an illustration in Vollard's de luxe edition of *Le Chef-d'Œuvre Inconnu* by Honoré de Balzac, 1931.)

[6] William Shakespeare, *The Merry Wives of Windsor*, Act 2, Scene 2, lines 135–137. (The *First Folio* has the spelling 'Puncke'.)

Addendum

Further proof that punkish characters were in the air at the time was provided by J. Daniel Smith of Michigan State University, who sent me the following example he found in the campus newspaper *State News* **83**, 152 (25 October 1988):

And Peter Flynn points out that similar letterforms were developed by the British cartoonist Norman Thelwell, who signed his name ꭨhₑₗᵥₑˡˡˑ. Thelwell was a frequent contributor to *Punch*, beginning in the 1950s — a magazine whose name is curiously similar to *Punk*.

Chapter 21

Fonts for Digital Halftones

[Revision of an article that was originally published in TUGboat **8** *(1987), 135–160.]*

Small pictures can be "typeset" on raster devices in a way that simulates the screens used to print fine books on photography. The purpose of this note is to discuss some experiments in which METAFONT has created fonts from which halftones can be generated easily on laserprinters. High levels of quality are not possible at low resolution, and large pictures will overflow TeX's memory at high resolution; moreover, a number of effective ways to deal directly with halftone images have been widely available since 1990. Yet the fonts discussed below have proved to be useful in several applications, and their design involves a number of interesting issues that remain relevant.

I began this investigation at the beginning of 1985, when fifteen of Stanford's grad students were working on a project to create "high-tech self-portraits" (see [4, pages 88–103]). The students were manipulating digitized graphic images in many ingenious ways, but at that time Stanford had no output devices by which the computed images could be converted to hardcopy. Therefore I decided to create a font by which halftones could be produced using TeX.

Such a font is necessarily device-dependent. For example, a laserprinter with 300 pixels per inch cannot mimic the behavior of another with 240 pixels per inch, if we are trying to control the patterns of pixels. I decided to use our 300-per-inch Imagen laserprinter (also known as the Canon LBP-CX engine), because it gave better control over pixel quality than any other machine available for student use.

It seemed best at first to design a font whose "characters" were tiny 8×8 squares of pixels. The idea was to have 65 characters for 65 different levels of brightness: For $0 \le k \le 64$ there would be one character with exactly k black pixels and $64 - k$ white pixels.

Indeed, it seemed best to find some permutation p of the 64 pixels in an 8×8 square so that the black pixels of character k would be p_0, p_1, ..., p_{k-1}. My first instinct was to try to keep positions p_0, p_1, p_2, ... as far apart from each other as possible. So my first METAFONT program painted pixels black by ordering the positions as follows:

$$
\begin{array}{|cc|cc|cc|cc|}
\hline
45 & 29 & 34 & 18 & 46 & 30 & 33 & 17 \\
13 & 61 & 2 & 50 & 14 & 62 & 1 & 49 \\
39 & 23 & 40 & 24 & 36 & 20 & 43 & 27 \\
7 & 55 & 8 & 56 & 4 & 52 & 11 & 59 \\
47 & 31 & 32 & 16 & 44 & 28 & 35 & 19 \\
15 & 63 & 0 & 48 & 12 & 60 & 3 & 51 \\
37 & 21 & 42 & 26 & 38 & 22 & 41 & 25 \\
5 & 53 & 10 & 58 & 6 & 54 & 9 & 57 \\
\hline
\end{array}
\tag{1}
$$

(This is essentially the "ordered dither" matrix of B. E. Bayer; see [5].)

It turns out to be easy to create such a font with METAFONT:

```
% Halftone font with 65 levels of gray via "ordered dither"
% using characters "0" (white) to "p" (black)

pair p[]; % the pixels in order
          % (first p0 becomes black, then p1, etc.)
pair d[]; % dither control
d[0]=(0,0); d[1]=(1,1); d[2]=(0,1); d[3]=(1,0);
def wrap(expr z)=(xpart z mod 8,ypart z mod 8) enddef;
for i=0 upto 3: for j=0 upto 3: for k=0 upto 3:
 p[16i+4j+k]=wrap(4d[k]+2d[j]+d[i]+(2,2));
endfor endfor endfor

w#:=8/pt; % that's 8 pixels
font_quad:=w#; designsize:=w#;

picture prevchar; % the pixels blackened so far
prevchar=nullpicture;
for i=0 upto 64:
 beginchar(i+ASCII"0",w#,w#,0); currentpicture:=prevchar;
 if i>0:
  addto currentpicture also unitpixel shifted p[i-1];
 fi
 prevchar:=currentpicture; endchar;
endfor
```

This file was called `odith.mf`; I used it to make a font called `odith300` by applying METAFONT in the usual way to the following file called `odith300.mf`, which enforces the device-dependence of the font:

```
% Halftone font for Imagen, via ordered dither
mode_setup;
if (pixels_per_inch<>300) or (mag<>1):
  errmessage "Sorry, this font is only for resolution 300";
  errmessage "Abort the run now or you'll " &
                      "clobber the TFM file";
  forever: endfor                % go into an infinite loop
else: input odith fi
end.
```

It's fairly easy to typeset pictures with `odith300` if you input the following macro file `ht.tex` in a TeX document:

```
% Macros for typesetting halftones

% Example of use:
% \input ht                               % input this file
% \font\htfont=<your favorite halftone font> % load a font
% \beginhalftone
% chars for top line of picture.
% chars for second line of picture.
% ...
% chars for bottom line of picture.
% \endhalftone
% Now the picture is in a box of the appropriate size.
% You can also say \setbox0=\beginhalftone...\endhalftone.

\chardef\other=12
\def\beginhalftone{\vbox\bgroup\offinterlineskip\htfont
  \catcode`\\=\other \catcode`\^=\other \catcode`\_=\other
  \catcode`\.=\active \starthalftone}
{\catcode`\.=\active \catcode`\/=0 \catcode`\\=\other
  /gdef/starthalftone#1\endhalftone{/let.=/endhalftoneline
    /beginhalftoneline#1/endhalftone/ignorespaces}}
\def\beginhalftoneline{\hbox\bgroup\ignorespaces}
\def\endhalftoneline{\egroup\beginhalftoneline}
\def\endhalftone{\egroup\setbox0=\lastbox\unskip\egroup}
```

(These macros are a bit tricky because '\' is one of the legal characters in odith300, but the 't' of \endhalftone is not; we must make backslashes revert temporarily to the status of ordinary symbols.)

Unfortunately, the results obtained with odith300 weren't very good; the images were too blatantly based on binary recursion, too computery. For example, here are three typical pictures, shown full size as they came off the machine:*

The squareness of the 8 × 8 characters is much too prominent.

Moreover, the laserprinter did strange things when it was given pixel patterns like those in odith300:*

Although character k has more black pixels than character $k - 1$, the characters did not increase their darkness monotonically in our experiments. Character 6 seemed darker than character 7; this was an optical illusion. Character 32 was darker than many of the characters that followed, and in this case the effect was not illusory: Examination with a magnifying glass showed that the machine deposited its toner in a very curious fashion.

---

* Asterisks are used in this paper to denote places where I am simulating the output of a 300-pixels-per-inch laserprinter with the offset printing process, using plates that were produced photographically from 1200-pixels-per-inch PostScript output. Vagaries of printing have probably made these images look rather different than they did on the Imagen of 1985, but I hope the basic ideas remain clear.

Another defect of the ordered-dither approach was that most of the characters were quite dark. Measurements with a densitometer showed that 50% density was reached already at about character number 16. Hence `odith300` overemphasized the light tones.

My next attempt was to look at halftone pictures in books and newspapers, in order to discover the secret of their success. Aha! These were done by making bigger and bigger black dots; in other words, the order of pixels p_0, p_1, ... was designed to keep black pixels *close together* instead of far apart. Also, the dots usually appear in a grid that has been rotated 45°, since human eyes don't notice the dottiness at this angle as much as they do when a grid is rectilinear. Therefore I decided to blacken pixels in the following order:

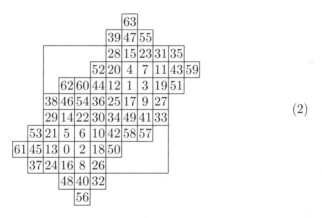

$$(2)$$

Here I decided not to stick to an 8×8 square; this nonsquare set of pixel positions still "tiles" the plane in Escher-like fashion, if we replicate it at 8-pixel intervals. The characters are considered to be 8 pixels wide and 8 pixels tall, as before, but they are no longer confined to an 8×8 bounding box. The reference point is the lower left corner of position 24.

The matrix above is actually better than the one I first came up with, but I've forgotten what that one was. John Hobby took a look at mine and suggested this alternative, because he wanted the pattern of *black* pixels in character k to be essentially the same as the pattern of *white* pixels in character $64-k$. (Commercial halftone schemes start with small black dots on a white background; then the dots grow until they form a checkerboard of black and white; then the white dots begin to shrink into their black background.) The matrix (2) has this symmetry property, because the sum of the entries in positions (x, y) and $(x+4, y)$ is 63 for all x and y, if you consider "wraparound" by computing indices modulo 8. Other interesting symmetries are present too, if you study the relative positions of the cells that are numbered 0–7, 8–15, 16–23, 24–31, 32–39, 40–47, 48–55, and 56–63; each group of eight is formed in essentially the same way.

John and I used this new ordering of pixel positions to make a "dot dither" font called `ddith300`, analogous to `odith300`. It yielded the following sequence of gray levels:*

Now we had a pleasantly uniform gradation, except for anomalies at characters near 62 that were unavoidable on a xerographic printer. The density reached 50% somewhere around character number 22, and we could compensate for this by preprocessing the data to be printed (using a "transfer function").

The three images that were displayed with `odith300` above look like this when `ddith300` is substituted:*

My students were able to use `ddith300` successfully, by making suitably large images, so I stopped working on halftones and resumed my normal activities.

However, I realized later that `ddith300` can easily be improved, because each of its characters is made up of two dots that are about the same size. There's no reason why the dots of a halftone image need to be paired up in such a way. With just a bit more work, we can typeset each dot independently.

Thus, I made a font `sdith300` for "single-dot dithering" with just 33 characters (not 65 as before), using the matrix

$$
\begin{array}{ccccccc}
 & & & 31 & & & \\
 & & 19 & 23 & 27 & & \\
 & & 14 & 7 & 11 & 15 & 17 \\
 & 26 & 10 & 2 & 3 & 5 & 21 & 29 \\
30 & 22 & 6 & 0 & 1 & 9 & 25 \\
 & 18 & 12 & 8 & 4 & 13 \\
 & & 24 & 20 & 16 \\
 & & & 28 \\
\end{array}
\tag{3}
$$

to control the order in which pixels are blackened. (This matrix corresponds to just one of the two dots in the larger matrix above, if we divide each entry by 2 and discard the remainder.) The characters are still regarded as 8 pixels wide, but they are now only 4 pixels tall. When a picture is typeset, the odd-numbered rows are to be offset horizontally by 4 pixels.

Here is the METAFONT file `sdith.mf` that was used to generate the single-dot font. Notice that the regularity of pattern (3) allows us to avoid listing all 32 elements of the matrix explicitly:

```
% Halftone font with 33 gray levels via "single-dot dither"
% using characters "0" (white) to "P" (black)
pair p[]; % the pixels in order
          % (first p0 becomes black, then p1, etc.)
p0=(1,1); p4=(2,0); p8=(1,0); p12=(0,0);
p16=(3,-1); p20=(2,-1); p24=(1,-1); p28=(2,-2);
transform r; r=identity rotatedaround ((1.5,1.5),90);

for i=0 step 4 until 28:
 p[i+1]=p[i] transformed r;
 p[i+3]=p[i+1] transformed r;
 p[i+2]=p[i+3] transformed r;
endfor

w#:=8/pt; % that's 8 pixels
font_quad:=w#; designsize:=w#;

picture prevchar; % the pixels blackened so far
prevchar=nullpicture;
for i=0 upto 32:
 beginchar(i+ASCII"0",w#,.5w#,0);
 currentpicture:=prevchar;
```

```
if i>0:
 addto currentpicture also unitpixel shifted p[i-1];
fi
prevchar:=currentpicture; endchar;
endfor
```

(There's also a file `sdith300.mf` to enforce device-dependence, analogous to the file `odith300.mf` considered earlier.)

Here's how the three example images look when they're rendered by font `sdith300` — a clear improvement:*

The TeX macros `ht.tex` presented earlier must be replaced by an alternative set `altht.tex` when independent dots are used:

```
% Alternative macros for typesetting halftones
% Example of use:
% \input altht                        % input this file
% \font\althtfont=<alternative halftone font> % load a font
% \beginalthalftone
% chars for top halfline of picture. (half-shifted right)
% chars for second halfline of picture. (not shifted right)
% ...
% chars for bottom halfline of picture. (possibly shifted)
% \endhalftone
% Now the picture is in a box of the appropriate size.
% You can also \setbox0=\beginalthalftone...\endhalftone.
\chardef\other=12
\newif\ifshifted \newdimen\hfm
\def\beginalthalftone{\vbox\bgroup\offinterlineskip
 \shiftedtrue \althtfont \hfm=.5em
```

```
\catcode'\.=\active \moveright\hfm\hbox\bgroup}
{\catcode'\.=\active \gdef.{\ifshifted\kern-\hfm\egroup
 \shiftedfalse\else\egroup\shiftedtrue\moveright\hfm\fi
 \hbox\bgroup\ignorespaces}}
\def\endhalftone{\egroup\setbox0=\lastbox\unskip\egroup}
```

These macros are much simpler than those of ht.tex, because the 33 ASCII characters "0" to "P" have no special meaning to plain TeX.

I learned in 1987 that a related, but more clever, technique had already been introduced in 1976 by Robert L. Gard [3]. The methods we have considered so far have been based either on (a) a halftone font with 65 levels of gray, in which each 8×8 character essentially contributes two dots to a picture, or (b) a halftone font with 33 levels of gray, in which each 4×8 character contributes one dot to a picture. Gard's method yields (c) a halftone font with 17 levels of gray, in which each 4×4 character contributes half of a dot (actually two quarter-dots) to a picture.

The kth level of gray in Gard's half-dot scheme is obtained by blackening cells 0 to $k - 1$ in the array

$$
\begin{array}{|c|c|c|c|}
\hline
1 & 5 & 10 & 14 \\
\hline
3 & 7 & 8 & 12 \\
\hline
13 & 9 & 6 & 2 \\
\hline
15 & 11 & 4 & 0 \\
\hline
\end{array}
\quad \text{or} \quad
\begin{array}{|c|c|c|c|}
\hline
14 & 10 & 5 & 1 \\
\hline
12 & 8 & 7 & 3 \\
\hline
2 & 6 & 9 & 13 \\
\hline
0 & 4 & 11 & 15 \\
\hline
\end{array}
\tag{4}
$$

(We actually make two sets of characters, one the mirror image of the other, and alternate between them as a picture is typeset.) The following METAFONT file hdith.mf will generate such a font hdith300, in essentially the same way that the other fonts ddith300 and sdith300 were generated earlier:

```
% Halftone font with 17 gray levels via "half-dot dither"
% using characters "A" (white) to "Q" (black) as well as
% the mirror-reflected versions "a" (white) to "q" (black)
pair p[]; % the pixels in order
          % (first p0 becomes black, then p1, etc.)
p0=(3,0); p4=(2,0); p8=(2,2); p12=(3,2);
transform r; r=identity rotatedaround ((1.5,1.5),180);
for i=0 step 4 until 12:
 p[i+1]=p[i] transformed r;
 p[i+2]=p[i] shifted (0,1);
 p[i+3]=p[i+2] transformed r;
endfor
```

```
w#:=4/pt; % that's 4 pixels
font_quad:=w#; designsize:=w#;

r:=identity reflectedabout ((2,0),(2,3));
picture prevchar; % the pixels blackened so far
prevchar=nullpicture;
for i=0 upto 16:
 beginchar(i+ASCII"A",w#,w#,0); currentpicture:=prevchar;
 if i>0:
  addto currentpicture also unitpixel shifted p[i-1];
 fi
 prevchar:=currentpicture; endchar;
 beginchar(i+ASCII"a",w#,w#,0);
 currentpicture:=prevchar transformed r; endchar;
endfor
```

To typeset with such a font, we can say for example

```
\input ht
\font\htfont=hdith300
\beginhalftone
iIjJjKkJjJkJkKkKkJjJjJiIiJkJkJjJjJjIhHhJjIjHjIgHhIiIiGhF
    hGiIhGhHhIjJjJjJjKkKkKkKkKkKkKkKiIjJkKkLkKlKlLlLlLlL.
IjJjKjJjJjJkKkKkJjJjJkHiHiJkJkJjJjJiHhHiIiIgHhGgGgIgGgFe
    FfGfGhHhHhIhIiJkKkKkKlKkKkKkKkKkJkJkKkKkLkKkLlLlKkLl.
iIjJiKjJjKkJkKkKkJkJjJjJjJjJiJjJjIiHhIhIhHiGgFgFfGfGiIjK
    jIiHgGfGhHhJjIjKkKkJkLkLkKkLkKlKkKjKkKkKlKkKkKkLlLlLlL.
HhIiJjJjKjJkJjKkKkKkJjJjJjJjIiJjJjJiIiIhIhIhGfFeFkMnOoOo
    OoOnNlJhGgHiIjJjJjJjKkLlKkKkKkKkJkKkKkLkKlKkKkLkKlKkLl.
iJiIiIhIjKjJiJjKkKjKjJjJjJjIjJjJjIiIiHhIiIiIfFgLnOoOoOoO
    oOoPoOoNkGfGhHiJjJjJlKkKkKkKkLjKkKjKjKkKkKkJjKkKkKlLkL.
IjIiIhHiJjKiJjJjKjKjJjJjIjIjJjIiJiHhIiHhIjIgGkOoOoOoOoOo
    OpOoOpPpOoJgFgIjJjIjJkKkJkJjJkKkKjJjJjKkKkJjJjKkKlLkKl.
      ⋮
\endhalftone
```

Uppercase and lowercase letters alternate in checkerboard fashion, so that the reflected characters will appear in the correct positions. Lines can be broken if desired, because space characters have no width in font hdith300. The \beginhalftone macro is the same for half dots as for double dots; only the font name and the data encoding scheme are different.

Here are nine pictures for comparison, showing all three dot-dither methods applied to all three images:*

double dot   single dot   half dot

Gard's half-dot method clearly improves the quality of single-dot pictures, in spite of its limitation to 17 levels of gray; it also has the advantage that its characters are square instead of diamond-shaped, hence the data is easier to compute. But it does ask TEX to typeset twice as much data. Indeed, the double-dot pictures shown here were typeset from 64 rows of 55 characters each; the single-dot pictures came from 128 rows of 55 characters each; and the half-dot pictures came from 128 rows of 110 characters each. Small versions of TEX are able to handle at most about 50,000 characters per page.

(The macro \beginhalftone reads the entire image into TEX's memory before it typesets the first line; and TEX does not release this information until there is no chance of needing to use it in an error message. Thus the net effect is to double the amount of memory TEX needs, until after a picture has been converted to a box. A simpler version of \beginhalftone would, however, suffice for the half-dot case, because the 17-level font uses only alphabetic letters.)

Given a printer with higher resolution, say 635 pixels per inch (which is equivalent to 25 pixels per millimeter), we could create analogous fonts ddith635, sdith635, and hdith635. Then the nine pictures would come out looking like this:

Now the pictures are smaller, because the characters are still 8 pixels wide, and the pixels have gotten smaller. At this resolution the halftones should look pretty much like those obtained by professional printers, except that they tend to be too dark due to "ink squash"; such problems can be cured by adjusting the densities in a preprocessing program.

These example images were prepared from 256-level data by using a special preprocessing routine, which is presented in Appendix 1. The preprocessor uses a generalization of the Floyd–Steinberg algorithm [2] to ameliorate the effects of limited gray levels. Indeed, if we had tried the same experiments *without* error diffusion, by setting the preprocessor's *dampening* parameter to zero, the nine example images would have looked like this:*

Diffusion makes little difference in Mona Lisa or in the high-frequency details of the Lincoln and Liberty images, but it is important for background areas that change only gradually. Without error diffusion, a distracting "paint by number" effect can easily become too prominent, especially when only 17 shades of gray are available.

What resolution is needed? People traditionally measure the quality of a halftone screen by counting how many lines of dots appear per inch in the corresponding unrotated grid, and it's easy to do this with a magnifying glass. The photographs in a newspaper like the *International Herald Tribune* use a 72-line screen, rotated 45°; this is approximately the resolution $50\sqrt{2}$ that we would obtain with a font like sdith400 on a laserprinter with 400 pixels per inch. (Our 300-per-inch fonts ddith300, sdith300, and hdith300 give a rotated screen with only $37.5\sqrt{2} \approx 53$ lines per inch.) The photographs on the book jackets of the *Computers & Typesetting* volumes have a 133-line screen, again rotated 45°; this is slightly better than the 635-pixels-per-inch examples shown earlier, which have about 112 lpi. But 133 is not the upper limit: A book that reproduces photographs with exceptionally high quality, such as [1], has a "duotone" screen of about 270 lines per inch.

Let's turn now to another problem: Suppose we have an image for which we want to obtain the best possible representation on a laserprinter of medium resolution, because we will be using that image many times—for example, in a letterhead. In such cases we get optimum results by creating a special font for that image alone; instead of using a general-purpose font for halftones, we'll want to control every pixel. The desired image can then be typeset from a special-purpose font of "characters" that represent rectangular subsections of the whole.

The examples above were first typeset on an Imagen printer as 64 lines of 55 columns per line, with 8 pixels in each line and each column. To get an equivalent picture with every pixel selected individually, we can make a font that has, say, 80 characters, each 64 pixels tall and 44 pixels wide. By typesetting eight rows of ten characters each, we'll have the desired image. For example, the following picture was done in that way:*

T_EX will typeset such an image if we say \gioconda after making the
following definitions:

```
\font\lisa=lisa300

\newcount\m \newcount\n
\def\gioconda{\vbox{\lisa \offinterlineskip \n=0
  \loop \hbox{\m=0 \loop \char\n \global\advance\n by 1
    \advance\m by 1 \ifnum\m<10 \repeat}
  \ifnum\n<80 \repeat}}
```

And once we have the individual pieces, we can combine them to get
unusual effects:*

The font lisa300 shown above was generated from a file lisa.mf
that began like this:

```
row 1; data "ffffffffffffffffffffffffffffffffffffffffffffffffffff"
            & "ffffffffffffffffffffffffffffffffffffffffffffffffffff"
            & "ffffffffffffffffffffffffffff";
row 2; data "80808000900010008000209012101010201000009000"
            & "900000109080200000101 0a0000002291000002"
            & "0920090010089008050 92080011";
row 3; data "8010f0d000d050f0a0910080a0a0a04080c0805000b0"
```

```
        & "8080c08020200050808040a0b19090a040a050a"
        & "0405100b050003010404021b0c3";
row 4; data "a8d00120b891308080a0a93100e12190a8005120a080"
        & "2060945080a0a024a060a0284060204029a5a0c"
        & "89020508134a850a159c8b065d9";
```

... and so on, until 512 rows had been specified; this file was generated by the program in Appendix 2, using a method called *dot diffusion* [7]. The parameter file lisa300.mf was

```
% Mona Lisa for Imagen 300
mode_setup;
if (pixels_per_inch<>300) or (mag<>1):
    ...  ⟨error messages as before⟩
else: input picfont
 width:=44; height:=64; n:=10; filename:="lisa";
 do_it; fi
end.
```

and the driver file picfont.mf was

```
string filename; picture pic[];
pic0=nullpicture; pic8=unitpixel;
for j=0 upto 1: pic[4+8j]=pic[8j];
 addto pic[4+8j] also unitpixel shifted (1,0); endfor
for j=0 upto 3: pic[2+4j]=pic[4j];
 addto pic[2+4j] also unitpixel shifted (2,0); endfor
for j=0 upto 7: pic[1+2j]=pic[2j];
 addto pic[1+2j] also unitpixel shifted (3,0); endfor
def do_it= ww:=width/4;
 for j=0 upto n-1: jj:=ww*j;
 scantokens("input "&filename); endfor enddef;

vardef row expr x =
 cc:=(x-1)div height; rr:=height-1-((x-1)mod height);
 if rr=height-1:
  beginchar(cc*n+jj/ww,width/pt,height/pt,0); fi enddef;

vardef data expr s =
 for k=0 upto ww-1: addto currentpicture also
  pic[hex substring(jj+k,jj+k+1) of s]
    shifted (4(jj+k),rr); endfor
 if rr=0: xoffset:=-4jj; endchar; fi enddef;
```

This is not very efficient, but it's interesting and it seems to work. The trick, of course, is to avoid overflowing METAFONT's memory, by trading time for space. (Some statistics: The file lisa.mf was 65428 bytes long; METAFONT produced a generic font file lisa300.300gf of 103088 bytes, which compressed down to a packed font file lisa300.300pk of 29044 bytes. The generation process occupied only 11256 words of META-FONT's memory, and used space for only 466 string characters.)

Ken Knowlton and Leon Harmon have shown that surprising effects are possible once a picture has been digitized (see [6]). Continuing this tradition, I found that it's fun to combine the TEX macros above with new fonts that frankly acknowledge their digital nature. One needn't always try to compete with commercial halftone screens!

For example, we can use ht.tex with a 'negdot' font that makes negative images out of square dots:

The METAFONT file negdot.mf that generated this font is quite simple:

```
% negative pseudo-halftone font: 65 sizes of square dots
% using characters "0" (large) to "p" (small)
mode_setup;
w#:=8/300in#; font_quad:=w#; designsize:=w#;
for i=0 upto 64: beginchar(i+ASCII"0",w#,w#,0);
 r#:=sqrt(.9w#*(1-i/80)); define_pixels(r);
 fill unitsquare scaled r shifted(.5w,.5h); endchar;
endfor end.
```

Unlike the previous fonts we have been considering, this one is device-independent (it works at all resolutions). Its "gray levels" are

We can, in fact, perceive images even when each character of the halftone font has *exactly the same number of black pixels*. Here, for example, is what happens when the three images above are typeset with a font in which each character consists of a vertical line and a horizontal line; the lines move up and to the right as the pixel gets darker, but they retain a uniform thickness. We perceive lighter and darker features only because adjacent lines get closer together or further apart.

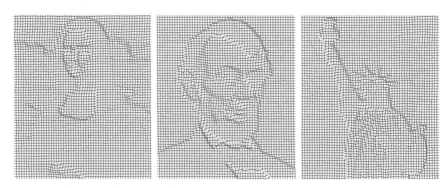

The METAFONT file `lines.mf` for this device-independent font is:

```
% pseudo-halftone font: 65 lines that move right and up
% using characters "0" (left/down) to "p" (right/up)
mode_setup; pickup pencircle scaled .3pt; q:=savepen;
w#:=8/300in#; font_quad:=w#; designsize:=w#;
for i=0 upto 64: beginchar(i+ASCII"0",w#,w#,0);
 pickup q; draw (0,h*i/64)--(w,h*i/64);
 draw (w*i/64,0)--(w*i/64,h); endchar;
endfor end.
```

Yet another possibility is the font produced by `angles.mf`; here each character is a single line of fixed radius that rotates from horizontal to vertical as the density increases:

```
% pseudo-halftone font: 65 radii that change direction
% using characters "0" (horizontal) to "p" (vertical)
mode_setup; pickup pencircle scaled .3pt; q:=savepen;
w#:=8/300in#; font_quad:=w#; designsize:=w#;
```

```
for i=0 upto 64:
 beginchar(i+ASCII"0",w#,w#,0); pickup q;
 draw ((0,0)--(w,0)) rotated (90*i/64); endchar;
endfor end.
```

The images are still amazingly easy to identify:

(We can think of a large array of dials whose hands record the local light levels.) It is amusing to view these images by tilting the page up until your eyes are almost parallel to the paper.

As a final example, let's consider a 33-character font that's designed to be used with `altht.tex` instead of `ht.tex`. Readers who like puzzles are invited to try to guess what this METAFONT code will do, before looking at the image of Mona Lisa that was typeset with the corresponding font. [*Hint:* The name of the METAFONT file is `hex.mf`.]

```
% alternate pseudo-halftone font: 33 secret patterns
% using characters "0" to "P"

mode_setup; q:=savepen;
w#:=6pt#; font_quad:=w#; designsize:=w#;

for i=0 upto 32: beginchar(i+ASCII"0",w#,.5w#,0);
 pickup q; alpha:=.5-i/72; z0=(.5w,.5h);
 z1=alpha[(5/6w,.5h),z0]; z2=alpha[(2/3w,-.5h),z0];
 z0=.5[z2,z5]=.5[z3,z6]=.5[z1,z4]; x2=x6; y5=y6;
 draw z1--z2; draw .5[z1,z2]--z0;
 draw z3--z4; draw .5[z3,z4]--z0;
 draw z5--z6; draw .5[z5,z6]--z0; endchar;
endfor end.
```

The answer to this puzzle can be seen in the illustration at the very end of this chapter (following the appendices and references).

Appendix 1: Preprocessing the Image Data

The following **CWEB** program illustrates how to convert digitized pictures into the form required by the fonts and macros described above. (The source file **halftone.w** and several data files are downloadable from `http://www-cs-faculty.stanford.edu/~knuth/programs.html`.)

1. Introduction. This program prepares data for images in the form needed by the fonts and macros above. The input file (*stdin*) is assumed to be an EPS file output by Adobe Photoshop™ on a Macintosh with the binary EPS option, having a resolution of 72 pixels per inch. This file either has m rows of n columns each, or $m + n - 1$ rows of $m + n - 1$ columns each, or $2m$ rows of $2n$ columns each; in the second case the image has been rotated 45° clockwise. (Such images can be obtained by starting with a given $km \times kn$ image, optionally rotating it 45°, and then using Photoshop's Image Size operation to reduce to the desired number of pixel units. In my experiments I took $k = 8$, so that I could also use the dot diffusion method of Appendix 2; but k need not be an integer. Larger values of k tend to make the reduced images more accurate than smaller values do.)

The output file (*stdout*) is a sequence of ASCII characters that can be placed into TEX files leading to typeset output images of size $8m \times 8n$, using fonts like those described in the paper. In the first case, we output m lines of 65-level pixel data. In the second (rotated) case, we output $2m$ lines of 33-level pixel data. In the third case, we output $2m$ lines of 17-level pixel data.

```
#define m  64    /* base number of rows */
#define n  55    /* base number of columns */
#define r  64    /* max(m, n) */
#include <stdio.h>
  float a[m + m + 2][n + r];    /* darknesses: 0.0 is white, 1.0 is black */
  ⟨ Global variables 4 ⟩;
  void main(int argc, char *argv[])
  { register int i, j, k, l, p;
    int levels, trash, ii, jj;
    float dampening = 1.0, brightness = 1.0;
    ⟨ Check for nonstandard dampening and brightness factors 2 ⟩;
    ⟨ Determine the type of input by looking at the bounding box 3 ⟩;
    fprintf(stderr, "Making_%d_lines_of_%d-level_data\n",
        (levels < 65 ? m + m : m), levels);
```

$printf$ ("\\begin%shalftone\n", $levels \equiv 33$? "alt" : "");
⟨ Input the graphic data 5 ⟩;
⟨ Translate input to output 12 ⟩;
}

2. Optional command-line arguments allow the user to multiply the diffusion constants by a *dampening* factor and/or to multiply the brightness levels by a *brightness* factor.

⟨ Check for nonstandard *dampening* and *brightness* factors 2 ⟩ ≡
   if $(argc > 1 \wedge sscanf(argv[1],$ "%g"$, \& dampening) \equiv 1)$ {
      $fprintf(stderr,$ "Using␣dampening␣factor␣%g\n"$, dampening);$
      if $(argc > 2 \wedge sscanf(argv[2],$ "%g"$, \& brightness) \equiv 1)$
         $fprintf(stderr,$ "␣␣and␣brightness␣factor␣%g\n"$, brightness);$
   }
This code is used in section 1.

3. Macintosh conventions indicate the end of a line by the ASCII ⟨ carriage return ⟩ character (i.e., control-M, aka \r); but the C library is set up to work best with newlines (i.e., control-J, aka \n). We aren't worried about efficiency, so we simply input one character at a time. This program assumes Macintosh conventions.

   The job here is to look for the sequence 'Box:' in the input, followed by 0, 0, the number of columns, and the number of rows.

#define $panic(s)$ { $fprintf(stderr, s);$ $exit(-1);$ }

⟨ Determine the type of input by looking at the bounding box 3 ⟩ ≡
   $k = 0;$
$scan:$
   if $(k\mathord{+}\mathord{+} > 1000)$ $panic($"Couldn't␣find␣the␣bounding␣box␣info!\n"$);$
   if $(getchar() \neq$ 'B'$)$ **goto** $scan;$
   if $(getchar() \neq$ 'o'$)$ **goto** $scan;$
   if $(getchar() \neq$ 'x'$)$ **goto** $scan;$
   if $(getchar() \neq$ ':'$)$ **goto** $scan;$
   if $(scanf($"%d␣%d␣%d␣%d"$, \& llx, \& lly, \& urx, \& ury) \neq 4 \vee llx \neq 0 \vee lly \neq 0)$
      $panic($"Bad␣bounding␣box␣data!\n"$);$
   if $(urx \equiv n \wedge ury \equiv m)$ $levels = 65;$
   else if $(urx \equiv n + n \wedge ury \equiv m + m)$ $levels = 17;$
   else if $(urx \equiv m + n - 1 \wedge ury \equiv urx)$ $levels = 33;$
   else $panic($"Bounding␣box␣doesn't␣match␣the␣formats␣I␣know!\n"$);$
This code is used in section 1.

4. ⟨ Global variables 4 ⟩ ≡
   int $llx, lly, urx, ury;$ /* bounding box parameters */
See also section 8.
This code is used in section 1.

5.   After we've seen the bounding box, we look for the string of characters 'beginimage\r'; this will be followed by the pixel data, one character per byte.

⟨ Input the graphic data 5 ⟩ ≡
  $k = 0$;
skan:
  if $(k{+}{+} > 10000)$
    panic("Couldn'␣t␣find␣the␣pixel␣data!\n");
  if $(getchar() \neq \text{'b'})$ **goto** *skan*;
  if $(getchar() \neq \text{'e'})$ **goto** *skan*;
  if $(getchar() \neq \text{'g'})$ **goto** *skan*;
  if $(getchar() \neq \text{'i'})$ **goto** *skan*;
  if $(getchar() \neq \text{'n'})$ **goto** *skan*;
  if $(getchar() \neq \text{'i'})$ **goto** *skan*;
  if $(getchar() \neq \text{'m'})$ **goto** *skan*;
  if $(getchar() \neq \text{'a'})$ **goto** *skan*;
  if $(getchar() \neq \text{'g'})$ **goto** *skan*;
  if $(getchar() \neq \text{'e'})$ **goto** *skan*;
  if $(getchar() \neq \text{'\r'})$ **goto** *skan*;
  if $(levels \equiv 33)$ ⟨ Input rotated pixel data 7 ⟩
  else ⟨ Input rectangular pixel data 6 ⟩;
  if $(getchar() \neq \text{'\r'})$
    panic("Wrong␣amount␣of␣pixel␣data!\n");
This code is used in section 1.

6.   Photoshop follows the conventions of photographers who consider 0 to be black and 1 to be white; but we follow the conventions of computer scientists who tend to regard 0 as devoid of ink (white) and 1 as full of ink (black).

We use the fact that global arrays are initially zero to assume that there are all-white rows of 0s above and below the input data in the rectangular case.

⟨ Input rectangular pixel data 6 ⟩ ≡
  for $(i = 1;\ i \leq ury;\ i{+}{+})$
    for $(j = 0;\ j < urx;\ j{+}{+})$
      $a[i][j] = 1.0 - brightness * getchar()/255.0$;
This code is used in section 5.

7.   In the rotated case, we transpose and partially shift the input so that the eventual *i*th row spans positions $a[i][j + \lfloor i/2 \rfloor]$ for $0 \leq j < n$. This nonobvious arrangement will turn out to be most convenient for the output phase, because of the error-diffusion algorithm that we will be applying to the transposed output.

For example, suppose $m = 5$ and $n = 3$; the input is a 7×7 array that can be expressed in the form

$$\begin{pmatrix} 0 & 0 & 0 & a & A & l & 0 \\ 0 & 0 & b & B & F & J & k \\ 0 & c & C & G & K & O & S \\ d & D & H & L & P & T & j \\ E & I & M & Q & U & i & 0 \\ e & N & R & V & h & 0 & 0 \\ 0 & f & W & g & 0 & 0 & 0 \end{pmatrix}.$$

In practice the boundary values a, b, c, d, e, f, g, h, i, j, k, l are very small, so they are essentially "white" and of little importance ink-wise. In this step we transform the input to the configuration

$$\begin{pmatrix} l & k & 0 & 0 & 0 & 0 & 0 \\ A & J & S & 0 & 0 & 0 & 0 \\ a & F & O & j & 0 & 0 & 0 \\ 0 & B & K & T & 0 & 0 & 0 \\ 0 & b & G & P & i & 0 & 0 \\ 0 & 0 & C & L & U & 0 & 0 \\ 0 & 0 & c & H & Q & h & 0 \\ 0 & 0 & 0 & D & M & V & 0 \\ 0 & 0 & 0 & d & I & R & g \\ 0 & 0 & 0 & 0 & E & N & W \end{pmatrix}$$

and later we will output

$$\begin{pmatrix} & l & & k & & 0 \\ A & & J & & S & \\ & F & & O & & j \\ B & & K & & T & \\ & G & & P & & i \\ C & & L & & U & \\ & H & & Q & & h \\ D & & M & & V & \\ & I & & R & & g \\ E & & N & & W & \end{pmatrix}.$$

$\langle$ Input rotated pixel data $7 \rangle \equiv$
   $\{$ **for** $(i = 0;\ i < ury;\ i\mbox{+}\mbox{+})$ **for** $(j = 0;\ j < urx;\ j\mbox{+}\mbox{+})$ $\{$
     $ii = m + i - j;\ jj = i + j + 1 - m;$

> **if** $(ii \geq 0 \wedge ii < m + m \wedge jj \geq 0 \wedge jj < n + n)$
> $a[ii][i] = 1.0 - brightness * getchar\,(\,)/255.0;$
> **else** $trash = getchar\,(\,);$
> }
> $a[0][n-1] = 1.0 - brightness;$ /* restore "lost value" */
> }

This code is used in section 5.

8. Diffusing the error.   We convert the darkness values to 65, 33, or 17 levels by generalizing the Floyd–Steinberg algorithm for adaptive grayscale [2]. The idea is to sweep through the image one pixel at a time, finding the best available density value at the currently scanned position and diffusing the error into adjacent pixels that haven't yet been processed.

Given a font with k black dots in character k for $0 \leq k \leq l$, we might assume that the apparent density of the kth character would be k/l. But physical properties of output devices make the actual density nonlinear. The following table is based on measurements from observations on font `ddith300` with a Canon LBP-CX laserprinter, and it should be accurate enough for practical purposes on similar machines. But in fact the measurements could not be terribly precise, because the readings were not strictly monotone, and because the amount of toner was found to vary between the top and bottom of a page. Users should make their own measurements before adapting this routine to other equipment.

⟨ Global variables 4 ⟩ +≡
  float $d[65] = \{$
    $0.000, 0.060, 0.114, 0.162, 0.205, 0.243, 0.276, 0.306, 0.332, 0.355,$
    $0.375, 0.393, 0.408, 0.422, 0.435, 0.446, 0.456, 0.465, 0.474, 0.482,$
    $0.490, 0.498, 0.505, 0.512, 0.520, 0.527, 0.535, 0.543, 0.551, 0.559,$
    $0.568, 0.577, 0.586, 0.596, 0.605, 0.615, 0.625, 0.635, 0.646, 0.656,$
    $0.667, 0.677, 0.688, 0.699, 0.710, 0.720, 0.731, 0.742, 0.753, 0.764,$
    $0.775, 0.787, 0.798, 0.810, 0.822, 0.835, 0.849, 0.863, 0.878, 0.894,$
    $0.912, 0.931, 0.952, 0.975, 1.000\};$

9.   In the main loop, we will want to find the best approximation to $a[i][j]$ from among the available densities $d[0]$, $d[p]$, $d[2p]$, $d[3p]$, $\ldots$, where p is 1, 2, or 4. A straightforward modification of binary search works well for this purpose:

⟨ Find l so that $d[l]$ is as close as possible to $a[i][j]$ 9 ⟩ ≡
  if $(a[i][j] \leq 0.0)$ $l = 0;$
  else if $(a[i][j] \geq 1.0)$ $l = 64;$
  else { **register int** $lo\_l = 0,\ hi\_l = 64;$

while $(hi\_l - lo\_l > p)$ { **register int** $mid\_l = (lo\_l + hi\_l) \gg 1$;
   /* $hi\_l - lo\_l$ is halved each time, so mid_l is a multiple of p */
   if $(a[i][j] \geq d[mid\_l])$ $lo\_l = mid\_l$;
   else $hi\_l = mid\_l$;
}
if $(a[i][j] - d[lo\_l] \leq d[hi\_l] - a[i][j])$ $l = lo\_l$;
else $l = hi\_l$;
}

This code is used in sections 10 and 11.

10. The rectangular case is simplest, so we consider it first. Our strategy will be to go down each column, starting at the left, and to disperse the error to the four unprocessed neighbors.

#define $alpha$ 0.4375   /* 7/16, error diffusion to S neighbor */
#define $beta$ 0.1875   /* 3/16, error diffusion to NE neighbor */
#define $gamma$ 0.3125   /* 5/16, error diffusion to E neighbor */
#define $delta$ 0.0625   /* 1/16, error diffusion to SE neighbor */

⟨ Process $a[i][j]$ in the rectangular case 10 ⟩ ≡
  { **register float** err;
    if $(i \equiv 0 \vee i > ury)$ $l = 0$;
         /* must use white outside the output region */
    else ⟨ Find l so that $d[l]$ is as close as possible to $a[i][j]$ 9 ⟩;
    $err = a[i][j] - d[l]$;
    $a[i][j] = ($**float**$)$ (l/p);   /* henceforth $a[i][j]$ is a level not a density */
    if $(i \leq ury)$ $a[i+1][j]$ += $alpha * dampening * err$;
    if $(j < urx - 1)$ {
      if $(i > 0)$ $a[i-1][j+1]$ += $beta * dampening * err$;
      $a[i][j+1]$ += $gamma * dampening * err$;
      if $(i \leq ury)$ $a[i+1][j+1]$ += $delta * dampening * err$;
    }
  }

This code is used in section 12.

11. The rotated case is essentially the same, but the unprocessed neighbors of $a[i][j]$ are now $a[i+1][j]$, $a[i][j+1]$, $a[i+1][j+1]$, and $a[i+2][j+1]$. (For example, the eight neighbors of K in the matrices of section 7 are B, F, J, O, T, P, L, G.)

  Some of the computation in this step is redundant because the values are known to be zero.

⟨ Process $a[i][j]$ in the rotated case 11 ⟩ ≡
  { **register float** err;
    if $((i \gg 1) \leq j - n \vee (i \gg 1) > j)$ $l = 0$;
         /* must use white outside the output region */

else ⟨Find l so that $d[l]$ is as close as possible to $a[i][j]$ 9⟩;
$err = a[i][j] - d[l]$;
$a[i][j] = ($**float**$) (l/p)$;   /* henceforth $a[i][j]$ is a level not a density */
if $(i < m + m - 1)$ $a[i + 1][j] \mathrel{+}= alpha * dampening * err$;
if $(j < m + n - 2)$ {
  $a[i][j + 1] \mathrel{+}= beta * dampening * err$;
  if $(i < m + m - 1)$ $a[i + 1][j + 1] \mathrel{+}= gamma * dampening * err$;
  if $(i < m + m - 2)$ $a[i + 2][j + 1] \mathrel{+}= delta * dampening * err$;
}
}

This code is used in section 12.

12.   Finally we are ready to put everything together.

⟨Translate input to output 12⟩ ≡
  $p = 64/(levels - 1)$;
  if $(p \neq 2)$ {
    for $(j = 0;\ j < urx;\ j{+}{+})$
      for $(i = 0;\ i \leq ury + 1;\ i{+}{+})$
        ⟨Process $a[i][j]$ in the rectangular case 10⟩;
    for $(i = 1;\ i \leq ury;\ i{+}{+})$ {
      for $(j = 0;\ j < urx;\ j{+}{+})$
        $printf ($`"%c"`$, (p \equiv 1\ ?\ $`'0'`$: ((i + j)\ \&\ 1)\ ?\ $`'a'`$: $`'A'`$) + ($**int**$)\ a[i][j])$;
      $printf ($`".\n"`$)$;
    }
  }
  else {
    for $(j = 0;\ j < m + n - 1;\ j{+}{+})$
      for $(i = 0;\ i < m + m;\ i{+}{+})$ ⟨Process $a[i][j]$ in the rotated case 11⟩;
    for $(i = 0;\ i < m + m;\ i{+}{+})$ {
      for $(j = 0;\ j < n;\ j{+}{+})$ $printf ($`"%c"`$,$`'0'`$ + ($**int**$)\ a[i][j + (i \gg 1)])$;
      $printf ($`".\n"`$)$;
    }
  }
  $printf ($`"\\endhalftone\n"`$)$;

This code is used in section 1.

Appendix 2: Pixel Optimization

Here is another short CWEB program. It was used to generate the special font for Mona Lisa.

1.   Introduction.   This program prepares a METAFONT file for a special-purpose font that will approximate a given picture. The input file (*stdin*) is assumed to be an EPS file output by Adobe Photoshop™ on a Macintosh with the binary EPS option, containing m rows of n columns each; in Photoshop terminology the image is m pixels high and n pixels wide, in grayscale mode, with a resolution of 72 pixels per inch. The output file ($stdout$) will be a sequence of m lines like

```
row 4; data "e8...d9";
```

this means that the pixel data for row 4 is the string of n bits $11101000\ldots11011001$ encoded as a hexadecimal string of length $n/4$.

For simplicity, we shall assume that $m = 512$ and $n = 440$.

```
#define  m  512      /* this many rows */
#define  n  440      /* this many columns */
#include <stdio.h>
  float a[m + 2][n + 2];      /* darknesses: 0.0 is white, 1.0 is black */
  ⟨ Global variables 4 ⟩
  ⟨ Subroutines 12 ⟩

  void main(int argc, char *argv[])
  { register int i, j, k, l, ii, jj, w;
    register float err;
    float zeta = 0.2, sharpening = 0.9;

    ⟨ Check for nonstandard zeta and sharpening factors 2 ⟩;
    ⟨ Check the beginning lines of the input file 3 ⟩;
    ⟨ Input the graphic data 5 ⟩;
    ⟨ Translate input to output 15 ⟩;
    ⟨ Spew out the answers 17 ⟩;
  }
```

2–6. [Sections 2–6 of this program are entirely analogous to the corresponding sections of the program in Appendix 1, but slightly simpler; let's cut to the end of section 6, where the interesting differences begin.]

We use the fact that global arrays are initially zero to assume that all-white rows of 0s appear above, below, and to the left and right of the input data.

```
⟨ Input rectangular pixel data 6 ⟩ ≡
  for (i = 1; i ≤ ury; i++)
    for (j = 1; j ≤ urx; j++) a[i][j] = 1.0 − getchar( )/255.0;
This code is used in section 5.
```

7. Dot diffusion. Our job is to go from eight-bit pixels to one-bit pixels; that is, from 256 shades of gray to an approximation that uses only black and white. The method used here is called *dot diffusion* (see [7]); it works as follows: The pixels are divided into 64 classes, numbered from 0 to 63. We convert the pixel values to 0s and 1s by assigning values first to all the pixels of class 0, then to all the pixels of class 1, etc. The error incurred at each step is distributed to the neighbors whose class numbers are higher. This is done by means of precomputed tables *class_row*, *class_col*, *start*, *del_i*, *del_j*, and *alpha* whose function is easy to deduce from the following code segment.

⟨ Choose pixel values and diffuse the errors in the buffer 7 ⟩ ≡
```
  for (k = 0;  k < 64;  k++)
    for (i = class_row [k];  i ≤ m;  i += 8)
      for (j = class_col [k];  j ≤ n;  j += 8)  {
        ⟨ Decide the color of pixel [i, j] and the resulting err 9 ⟩;
        for (l = start [k];  l < start [k + 1];  l++)
          a[i + del_i [l]][j + del_j [l]] += err * alpha [l];
      }
```
This code is used in section 15.

8.   We will use the following model for estimating the effect of a given bit pattern in the output: If a pixel is black, its darkness is 1.0; if it is white but at least one of its four neighbors is black, its darkness is *zeta*; if it is white and has four white neighbors, its darkness is 0.0. Laserprinters of the 1980s tended to spatter toner in a way that could be approximated roughly by taking *zeta* = 0.2 in this model. The value of *zeta* should be between −0.25 and +1.0.

An auxiliary array *aa* holds code values *white*, *gray*, or *black* to facilitate computations in this model. All cells are initially *white*; but when we decide to make a pixel *black*, we change its *white* neighbors (if any) to *gray*.

```
#define  white  0     /* code for a white pixel with all white neighbors */
#define  gray   1     /* a white pixel with 1, 2, 3, or 4 black neighbors */
#define  black  2     /* code for a black pixel */
```
⟨ Global variables 4 ⟩ +≡
```
  char aa [m + 2][n + 2];     /* white, gray, or black status of final pixels */
```

9.   In this step the current pixel's final one-bit value is determined. The pixel presently is either *white* or *gray*; we either leave it as is, or we blacken it and gray its white neighbors, whichever minimizes the magnitude of the error.

Potentially *gray* values near the newly chosen pixel make this calculation slightly tricky. [Translation: I got it wrong the first two times I tried.] Notice, for example, that the very first black pixel to be created will increase the local darkness of the image by $1 + 4zeta$. Suppose the original image is entirely black, so that $a[i][j]$ is 1.0 for $1 \le i \le m$ and $1 \le j \le n$. If a pixel of class 0 is set to *white*, the error (i.e., the darkness that needs to be diffused to its upperclass neighbors) is 1.0; but if it is set to *black*, the error is $-4zeta$. The algorithm will choose *black* unless $zeta \geq .25$.

⟨ Decide the color of pixel $[i, j]$ and the resulting *err* 9 ⟩ ≡
  if $(aa[i][j] \equiv white)$ $err = a[i][j] - 1.0 - 4 * zeta$;
  else {   /* $aa[i][j] \equiv gray$ */
    $err = a[i][j] - 1.0 + zeta$;
    if $(aa[i-1][j] \equiv white)$ $err -= zeta$;
    if $(aa[i+1][j] \equiv white)$ $err -= zeta$;
    if $(aa[i][j-1] \equiv white)$ $err -= zeta$;
    if $(aa[i][j+1] \equiv white)$ $err -= zeta$;
  }
  if $(err + a[i][j] > 0)$ {   /* black is better */
    $aa[i][j] = black$;
    if $(aa[i-1][j] \equiv white)$ $aa[i-1][j] = gray$;
    if $(aa[i+1][j] \equiv white)$ $aa[i+1][j] = gray$;
    if $(aa[i][j-1] \equiv white)$ $aa[i][j-1] = gray$;
    if $(aa[i][j+1] \equiv white)$ $aa[i][j+1] = gray$;
  }
  else $err = a[i][j]$;   /* keep it white or gray */
This code is used in section 7.

10. Computing the diffusion tables.   The tables for dot diffusion could be specified by a large number of boring assignment statements, but it is more fun to compute them by a method that reveals some of the mysterious underlying structure.

⟨ Initialize the diffusion tables 10 ⟩ ≡
  ⟨ Initialize the class number matrix 13 ⟩;
  ⟨ Compile "instructions" for the diffusion operations 14 ⟩;
This code is used in section 15.

11.   ⟨ Global variables 4 ⟩ +≡
  char *class_row*[64], *class_col*[64];
    /* first row and column for a given class */
  char *class_number*[10][10];   /* the number of a given position */
  int $kk = 0$;   /* how many classes have been done so far */
  int *start*[65];   /* the first instruction for a given class */
  int *del_i*[256], *del_j*[256];   /* relative location of a neighbor */
  float *alpha*[256];   /* diffusion coefficient for a neighbor */

12.   The order of classes used here is the order in which pixels might be blackened in a font for halftones based on dots in a 45° grid. In fact, it is precisely the pattern used in matrix (2) for the font ddith300, discussed earlier in this paper.

⟨ Subroutines 12 ⟩ ≡
```
void store (int i, int j)
{
    if (i < 1)  i += 8;  else if (i > 8)  i -= 8;
    if (j < 1)  j += 8;  else if (j > 8)  j -= 8;
    class_number [i][j] = kk;
    class_row [kk] = i;  class_col [kk] = j;
    kk ++;
}

void store_eight (int i, int j)
{
    store (i, j);  store (i - 4, j + 4);  store (1 - j, i - 4);  store (5 - j, i);
    store (j, 5 - i);  store (4 + j, 1 - i);  store (5 - i, 5 - j);  store (1 - i, 1 - j);
}
```
This code is used in section 1.

13.   ⟨ Initialize the class number matrix 13 ⟩ ≡
```
store_eight (7, 2);  store_eight (8, 3);  store_eight (8, 2);  store_eight (8, 1);
store_eight (1, 4);  store_eight (1, 3);  store_eight (1, 2);  store_eight (2, 3);
for (i = 1;  i ≤ 8;  i++)  class_number [i][0] = class_number [i][8],
        class_number [i][9] = class_number [i][1];
for (j = 0;  j ≤ 9;  j++)  class_number [0][j] = class_number [8][j],
        class_number [9][j] = class_number [1][j];
```
This code is used in section 10.

14.   The "compilation" in this step simulates going through the diffusion process the slow way, recording the actions it performs. Then those actions can all be done at high speed later.

⟨ Compile "instructions" for the diffusion operations 14 ⟩ ≡
```
for (k = 0, l = 0;  k < 64;  k++) {
    start [k] = l;      /* l is the number of instructions compiled so far */
    i = class_row [k];  j = class_col [k];  w = 0;
    for (ii = i - 1;  ii ≤ i + 1;  ii++)
        for (jj = j - 1;  jj ≤ j + 1;  jj++)
            if (class_number [ii][jj] > k) {
                del_i [l] = ii - i;  del_j [l] = jj - j;  l++;
                if (ii ≠ i ∧ jj ≠ j)  w++;
                    /* diagonal neighbors get weight 1 */
                else  w += 2;      /* orthogonal neighbors get weight 2 */
            }
    for (jj = start [k];  jj < l;  jj++)
        if (del_i [jj] ≠ 0 ∧ del_j [jj] ≠ 0)  alpha [jj] = 1.0/w;
        else  alpha [jj] = 2.0/w;
}
```

$start[64] = l;$ /* at this point l will be 256 */

This code is used in section 10.

15. Synthesis. Now we're ready to put the pieces together.

⟨ Translate input to output 15 ⟩ ≡
  ⟨ Initialize the diffusion tables 10 ⟩;
  if (*sharpening*) ⟨ Sharpen the input 16 ⟩;
  ⟨ Choose pixel values and diffuse the errors in the buffer 7 ⟩;

This code is used in section 1.

16. Experience shows that dot diffusion often does a better job if we apply a filtering operation that exaggerates the differences between the intensities of a pixel and its neighbors:

$$a_{ij} \leftarrow \frac{a_{ij} - \alpha \bar{a}_{ij}}{1 - \alpha},$$

where

$$\bar{a}_{ij} = \frac{1}{9} \sum_{\delta=-1}^{+1} \sum_{\epsilon=-1}^{+1} a_{(i+\delta)(j+\epsilon)}$$

is the average value of a_{ij} and its eight neighbors. (See the discussion in [7]. The parameter α is the *sharpening* value, which had better be less than 1.0.)

We could use a buffering scheme to apply this transformation in place, but it's easier to store the new value of a_{ij} in $a_{(i-1)(j-1)}$ and then shift everything back into position afterwards. The values of a_{i0} and a_{0j} don't have to be restored to zero after this step, because they will not be examined again.

⟨ Sharpen the input 16 ⟩ ≡
  {
    for ($i = 1$; $i \le m$; i++) **for** ($j = 1$; $j \le n$; j++)
    { **float** *abar*;
      $abar = (a[i-1][j-1] + a[i-1][j] + a[i-1][j+1] + a[i][j-1] + $
          $a[i][j] + a[i][j+1] + a[i+1][j-1] + a[i+1][j] + a[i+1][j+1])/9.0;$
      $a[i-1][j-1] = (a[i][j] - sharpening * abar)/(1.0 - sharpening);$
    }
    for ($i = m$; $i > 0$; i--) **for** ($j = n$; $j > 0$; j--)
        $a[i][j] = (a[i-1][j-1] \le 0.0 ? 0.0 : a[i-1][j-1] \ge 1.0 ? 1.0 :$
          $a[i-1][j-1]);$
  }

This code is used in section 15.

17.   Here I'm assuming that n is a multiple of 4.

⟨ Spew out the answers 17 ⟩ ≡
```
  for (i = 1; i ≤ m; i++) {
    printf ("row␣%d;␣data␣\"", i);
    for (j = 1; j ≤ n; j += 4) {
      for (k = 0, w = 0; k < 4; k++)
        w = w + w + (aa[i][j + k] ≡ black ? 1 : 0);
      printf ("%x", w);
    }
    printf ("\";\n");
  }
```
This code is used in section 1.

18.   The following examples indicate the effect of parameters `zeta` and `sharpening` on this algorithm:*

no sharpening, $\zeta = .2$ sharpening, $\zeta = .2$ sharpening, $\zeta = 0$

The research described in this paper was supported in part by the System Development Foundation and in part by National Science Foundation grants IST-8201926, MCS-8300984, and DCR-8308109.

References

[1] Carolyn Caddes, *Portraits of Success* (Portola Valley: Tioga Press, 1986).

[2] Robert W. Floyd and Louis Steinberg, "An adaptive algorithm for spatial greyscale," *Proceedings of the Society for Information Display* **17** (1976), 75–77. An earlier version appeared in *SID 75 Digest* (1975), 36–37.

[3] Robert L. Gard, "Digital picture processing techniques for the publishing industry," *Computer Graphics and Image Processing* **5** (1976), 151–171.

[4] Ramsey W. Haddad and Donald E. Knuth, *A Programming and Problem-Solving Seminar*, Stanford Computer Science Department report STAN-CS-85-1055 (Stanford, California: June 1985). This seminar was also recorded on videotapes under the title "Problem solving with Donald Knuth," *The Stanford Video Journal* **1** (Stanford, California: Stanford Instructional Television Network, 1985).

[5] J. F. Jarvis, C. N. Judice, and W. H. Ninke, "A survey of techniques for the display of continuous tone pictures on bilevel displays," *Computer Graphics and Image Processing* **5** (1976), 13–40.

[6] Ken Knowlton and Leon Harmon, "Computer-produced grey scales," *Computer Graphics and Image Processing* **1** (1972), 1–20.

[7] Donald E. Knuth, "Digital halftones by dot diffusion," *ACM Transactions on Graphics* **6** (1987), 245–273. [A revised form of this article appears as Chapter 22 of the present volume.]

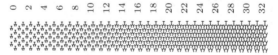

Chapter 22

Digital Halftones by Dot Diffusion

*[Revision of an article that was originally published in ACM Transactions on Graphics **6** (1987), 245–273.]*

This note describes a technique for approximating real-valued pixels by two-valued pixels. The new method, called dot diffusion, appears to avoid some deficiencies of other commonly used techniques. It requires approximately the same total number of arithmetic operations as the Floyd–Steinberg method of adaptive grayscale, and it is well suited to parallel computation; but it requires more buffers and more complex program logic than other methods when implemented sequentially on a machine with limited memory. A "smooth" variant of the method may prove to be useful in high resolution printing.

Given an $m \times n$ array A of real values between 0 and 1, we wish to construct an $m \times n$ array B of zeros and ones such that the average value of the entries $B[i,j]$ when (i,j) is near (i_0, j_0) is approximately equal to $A[i_0, j_0]$. In applications, A represents the light intensities in an image that has been scanned by some sort of camera; B represents a binary approximation to the image that might appear on printed pages.

Error Diffusion

An interesting solution to this problem was introduced by Floyd and Steinberg [7], who computed B from A as follows:

> **for** $i := 1$ **to** m **do for** $j := 1$ **to** n **do**
> **begin if** $A[i,j] < 0.5$ **then** $B[i,j] := 0$ **else** $B[i,j] := 1$;
> $err := A[i,j] - B[i,j]$;
> $A[i,j+1] := A[i,j+1] + err * alpha$;
> $A[i+1,j-1] := A[i+1,j-1] + err * beta$;
> $A[i+1,j] := A[i+1,j] + err * gamma$;
> $A[i+1,j+1] := A[i+1,j+1] + err * delta$;
> **end**.

449

Here α, β, γ, and δ are constants chosen to diffuse the error, which is directed proportionately to nearby elements whose B values have not yet been computed. Floyd and Steinberg suggested taking $(\alpha, \beta, \gamma, \delta) = (7, 3, 5, 1)/16$. A similar but more complex method had previously been published by Manfred R. Schroeder [23].

The Floyd–Steinberg method often gives excellent results, but it has drawbacks. In the first place, it is an inherently serial method; the value of $B[m, n]$ depends on all mn of the entries of A. Furthermore, it sometimes puts "ghosts" into the picture; for example, when faces are treated by this approach, echoes of people's hairlines can occasionally be seen in the middle of their foreheads. Several other difficulties will be discussed below.

The ghosting problem can be ameliorated by choosing $(\alpha, \beta, \gamma, \delta)$ so that their sum is less than 1; then the influence of $A[i, j]$ on remote elements decays exponentially. However, the ghosts cannot be exorcised completely in this manner. Suppose, for example, that $A[i, j]$ has the constant value a for all i and j, and let $\theta = (\beta + \gamma + \delta)/(1 - \alpha) \leq 1$. If a is very small, the entries of $B[i, j]$ for small i will all be zero, and the entries of $A[i, j]$ will build up to the limiting value

$$a(1 + \theta + \cdots + \theta^{i-1})(1 + \alpha + \alpha^2 + \cdots) = \frac{a(1 + \theta + \cdots + \theta^{i-1})}{1 - \alpha}$$

for large j. If we choose a so that this value is just slightly less than $1/2$, the $(i + 1)$st row will suddenly have many of its B values set to 1, after they had been 0 in all previous rows.

Floyd [8] has found that ghosts disappear if the intensities $A[i, j]$ are rescaled. For example, we can replace each $A[i, j]$ by $0.1 + 0.8 A[i, j]$. This works because the human eye is more sensitive to contrast than to absolute signal levels.

Ordered Dither

A second approach to the problem is the interesting technique of *ordered dither* [4, 17, 18]. Here we divide the set of all pairs (i, j) into, say, 64 classes numbered from 0 to 63, based on the values of i and j modulo 8 as shown in Table 1. If (i, j) belongs to class k, bit $B[i, j]$ is set to 1 if and only if $A[i, j] \geq (k + .5)/64$. In other words, each pixel is thresholded, based on the value in the corresponding position of the dither matrix. Notice that if $A[i, j]$ has a constant value a, this method will turn on t pixels in every 8×8 submatrix of B, where $|t/64 - a| \leq 1/128$.

45	29	34	18	46	30	33	17
13	61	2	50	14	62	1	49
39	23	40	24	36	20	43	27
7	55	8	56	4	52	11	59
47	31	32	16	44	28	35	19
15	63	0	48	12	60	3	51
37	21	42	26	38	22	41	25
5	53	10	58	6	54	9	57

TABLE 1. Class numbers for ordered dithering.

Dot Diffusion

The technique of ordered dither is completely parallel and ghost-free, but it tends to blur the images. It would be nice to have a solution that retains both the sharpness of Floyd–Steinberg and the parallelism of ordered dither.

The following technique seems to have the desired properties. Let us divide the positions (i, j) into 64 classes according to i and j modulo 8 as before, but replacing the matrix of Table 1 by the matrix of Table 2 on the next page. (The intuition that suggested Table 2 will be explained later; for now, let us simply consider it to be an arbitrary permutation of the numbers $\{0, 1, \ldots, 63\}$.)

Given any such matrix, we can perform the following diffusion algorithm:

for $k := 0$ **to** 63 **do**
   for all (i, j) of class k **do**
      begin if $A[i, j] < 0.5$ **then** $B[i, j] := 0$ **else** $B[i, j] := 1$;
      $err := A[i, j] - B[i, j]$;
      ⟨Distribute err to the neighbors of (i, j)
                   whose class numbers exceed k⟩;
   end.

Pixels of class 0 are computed first, then those of class 1, etc.; errors are passed to neighboring elements yet to be computed.

Each position (i, j) has four orthogonal neighbors (u, v) such that $(u - i)^2 + (v - j)^2 = 1$, and four diagonal neighbors (u, v) such that $(u - i)^2 + (v - j)^2 = 2$. One feasible way to do the error distribution in

35	48	40	32	28	15	23	31
43	59	56	52	20	4	7	11
51	62	60	44	12	1	3	19
38	46	54	36	25	17	9	27
29	14	22	30	34	49	41	33
21	5	6	10	42	58	57	53
13	0	2	18	50	63	61	45
24	16	8	26	39	47	55	37

TABLE 2. Class numbers for dot diffusion.

the diffusion algorithm is to proceed as follows:

⟨Distribute *err* to the neighbors of (i, j)
whose class numbers exceed k⟩ =
$w := 0$;
for all neighbors (u, v) of (i, j) **do**
  if class$(u, v) > k$ **then** $w := w + \text{weight}(u - i, v - j)$;
for all neighbors (u, v) of (i, j) **do**
  $A[u, v] := A[u, v] + err * \text{weight}(u - i, v - j)/w$.

We can choose the weight function to be weight$(x, y) = 3 - x^2 - y^2$; this weighs orthogonal neighbors twice as heavily as diagonal neighbors. For efficiency, the weights and the lists of relevant neighbors should be precomputed, once and for all, since the class numbers are independent of the A values.

A detailed implementation of this method appears in [14]. The program in that paper considers also a generalization in which white pixels orthogonally adjacent to black pixels are assumed to contribute some gray value to the total darkness; this approximates the dot gain characteristics of certain output devices.

Error Bounds

Let us say that position (i, j) is a *baron* if it has only low-class neighbors. Barons are undesirable in the diffusion algorithm because they absorb all of the local error. In fact, "near-baron" positions, which have only one high-class neighbor, are also comparatively undesirable because they direct all the error to one place. The class structure of the matrix in

Table 2 has only two barons (62 and 63), and only two near-barons (60 and 61). By contrast, the class structure of the matrix for ordered dither, Table 1, would be much less successful for diffusion, since it has sixteen barons (48 to 63).

The average error per pixel in the dot diffusion method will usually be less than the number of barons divided by twice the number of classes, if we average over a region that contains one pixel in each class. For example, we expect to absorb at most $2/128$ units of intensity per pixel in any 8×8 region if we use the matrix above, since the error committed at each pixel is compensated elsewhere except at the two baron positions, where we usually make an error of at most $1/2$.

However, it is possible to construct bad examples in which the entries of the matrix became negative or greater than 1; hence the maximum error does not simply depend on the number of barons. The worst case can be bounded as follows:

> **for** $k := 0$ **to** 62 **do**
>   **for** $l := k + 1$ **to** 63 **do**
> $\text{bound}[l] := \text{bound}[l] + \alpha_{kl} * \max(0.5, \text{bound}[k])$.

Here α_{kl} is the error diffusion constant from class k to class l as defined above, or zero if class l is not a neighbor of class k. It follows that $\text{bound}[l]$ is the maximum error that can be passed to positions of class l from positions of lower classes. The maximum total error in a region containing one position of each class is the sum of $\max(0.5, \text{bound}[k])$ over all baron classes k. Equivalently, it is the sum over *all* classes k of the quantity $\max(0, 0.5 - \text{bound}[k])$. (*Proof:* We have

$$\sum_k \max\big(0, 0.5 - \text{bound}[k]\big)$$

$$= \sum_k \max\big(\text{bound}[k], 0.5\big) - S$$

$$= \sum_k \max\big(\text{bound}[k], 0.5\big)\Big([k \text{ is a baron}] + \sum_{l>k} \alpha_{kl}\Big) - S$$

$$= \sum_{k \text{ is a baron}} \max\big(\text{bound}[k], 0.5\big) + \sum_l \text{bound}[l] - S$$

where $S = \sum_k \text{bound}[k]$.) In the matrix of Table 2, we have $\text{bound}[62] = \text{bound}[63] \approx 4.3365$; hence the average error per pixel is always less than $8.674/64 < 0.136$.

The original data must be chosen by a nasty adversary if the error is going to be this bad. (The adversary sets $A[i,j] = 0.5 + \text{bound}[k]$ if (i,j) belongs to class k where $\text{bound}[k] < 0.5$; otherwise $A[i,j] = 0$.) On the other hand, an adversary who wants to defeat the ordered dither algorithm can make it commit errors of 0.5 per pixel in every 8×8 block. (When (i,j) is of class k, let $A[i,j]$ be $(k + .5)/64$; then $B[i,j] = 1$ for all i and j, but the A's have average density 0.5.)

The Floyd–Steinberg method has near-zero error by this criterion, because all of its errors occur at the boundary, which has negligible area.

25	21	13	39	47	57	53	45
48	32	29	43	55	63	61	56
40	30	35	51	59	62	60	52
36	14	22	26	46	54	58	44
16	6	10	18	38	42	50	24
8	0	2	7	15	31	34	20
4	1	3	11	23	33	28	12
17	9	5	19	27	49	41	37

TABLE 3. A single-baron arrangement.

The matrix of Table 3 has only one baron and one near-baron; moreover, it leads to $\text{bound}[63] \approx 7.1457$. Therefore it might be better for dot diffusion than the matrix of Table 2. However, the barons in a large image based on Table 3 would all line up rectilinearly, and this would lead to a more noticeable visual texture. Human eyes tend to notice rectilinear dot patterns, while they are less prone to notice the dots of a halftone grid when the pattern has been rotated 45° (see [13]). If all entries of A are approximately $1/64$, the arrangement of Table 2 produces two pixels with $B = 1$ in every 8×8 submatrix, while Table 3 produces only one; one is the correct number, yet Table 3 yields a less satisfactory texture.

Table 2 was, in fact, suggested by dot patterns that are commercially used in halftone grids. If we imagine starting with a completely white matrix, and if we successively blacken all positions of classes $0, 1, \ldots$, we obtain 45° grids of black dots that gradually grow larger and larger. When all classes < 32 have been blackened, we have a checkerboard; from this point on, the blackening process essentially yields 45° grids of *white* dots that gradually grow smaller and smaller. Since the class number of (i, j) plus the class number of $(i, j + 4)$ is always equal to 63, the grid pattern of $63 - k$ white dots after k steps is exactly the same as the grid pattern of $63 - k$ black dots after $63 - k$ steps, shifted right 4. This connection of dot patterns to the diffusion pattern makes it reasonable to call the new method *dot diffusion*.

Dot diffusion can also be tried on a smaller scale, with the 4×4 class matrix

14	13	1	2
4	6	11	9
0	3	15	12
10	8	5	7

It can also be used with dots aligned at different angles, using patterns like those of Holladay [10], or with dots that are elliptical instead of circular.

Enhancing the Edges

Jarvis and Roberts [11, 12] discovered that ordered dither can be improved substantially if the edges of the original image are emphasized. Their idea, in essence, is to replace $A[i, j]$ by

$$A'[i, j] = \frac{A[i, j] - \alpha \overline{A}[i, j]}{1 - \alpha}$$

where $\overline{A}[i, j]$ is the average value of $A[i, j]$ and its eight neighbors:

$$\overline{A}[i, j] = \frac{1}{9} \sum_{u=i-1}^{i+1} \sum_{v=j-1}^{j+1} A[u, v].$$

The new values $A'[i, j]$ have the same average intensities as the old, but when $\alpha > 0$ they increase the difference of $A[i, j]$ from the neighboring pixels. If $\alpha = 0.9$ these formulas simplify to a well-known equation (see [19], Eq. 12.4–3):

$$A'[i, j] = 9A[i, j] - \sum_{0 < (u-i)^2 + (v-j)^2 < 3} A[u, v].$$

The sum here is over all eight neighbors of (i, j).

Jarvis and Roberts formulated this "constrained average" method in another way, which made it seem inherently tied to the ordered dither technique. However, the equations above make it clear that edge enhancement can be used with any halftoning method.

Actually we should also adjust $A'[i,j]$ to ensure that it lies between 0 and 1, by clipping it to 0 or 1 whenever it lies outside those extreme values. Otherwise too much of an "error" might need to be diffused.

Examples

The illustrations on the next few pages show what happens when the three methods discussed so far are applied to two different images, with and without edge enhancement. The data sets are deliberately rather small so that the details can be studied: Each image has 360 rows of data, with 250 pixels per row.

The first image is a digitized version of Mona Lisa, which is widely available because it is part of the Stanford GraphBase [15]; the Graph-Base function call $lisa(m, n, 255, 0, 0, 0, 0, 0, 0, workplace)$ returns an array of 360×250 bytes in which each pixel corresponds to a one-byte value, from 0 (black) to 255 (white). We want black to be represented by 1, so we could change the byte value r to the fraction $(255.5 - r)/256$. But the GraphBase image turns out to be rather dark, because of the lacquer coating on Leonardo's old painting; better results for our purposes are obtained by *squaring* the density to make it lighter. Thus the data entries $A[i,j]$ for the first image all have the form $\big((255.5 - r)/256\big)^2$, where r is the GraphBase byte for the pixel in row i and column j.

The second image was computed artificially by formulas: Given i and j in the range $1 \le i \le 360$ and $1 \le j \le 250$, let $x = (i - 120)/111.5$ and $y = (j - 120)/111.5$. If $x^2 + y^2 < 1$, the value of $A[i,j]$ is $(9 + x - 4y - 8\sqrt{1 - x^2 - y^2})/18$; otherwise $A[i,j]$ is simply $(1500i + j^2)/1000000$.

Edge-enhanced data $A'[i,j]$ was obtained from the original values by applying the simple formula above for the case $\alpha = 0.9$. Notice that this is amazingly effective in bringing out details of the Mona Lisa image, in spite of the comparatively low resolution we are working with; one can almost see the arches of the distant aqueduct in the background at the right of the picture and the curls in Mona Lisa's hair. The transformation may, however, have broadened her mysterious smile.

When dot diffusion was applied to the enhanced Mona Lisa data (Figure 10), the magnitude of the error absorbed at baron positions was only $704.1/2835 \approx 0.248$ on the average. The values of $A[i,j]$ stayed between -0.65 and 1.96 throughout the processing. Although we have observed that a dot diffusion baron might be stuck with nearly 4.34

FIGURE 1 (without edge enhancement)   FIGURE 2 (with enhanced edges)

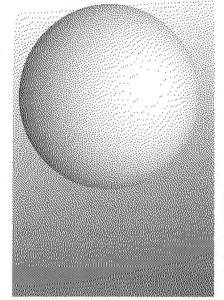

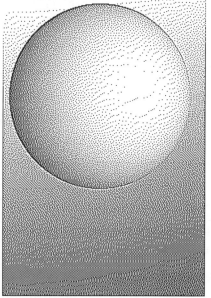

FIGURE 3 (without edge enhancement)   FIGURE 4 (with enhanced edges)

Images digitized by the Floyd–Steinberg algorithm.

FIGURE 5 (without edge enhancement)   FIGURE 6 (with enhanced edges)

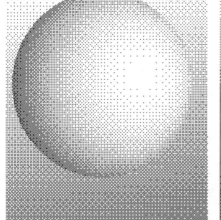
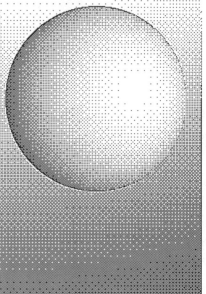

FIGURE 7 (without edge enhancement)   FIGURE 8 (with enhanced edges)

Images digitized by the ordered dither algorithm.

FIGURE 9 (without edge enhancement)   FIGURE 10 (with enhanced edges)

FIGURE 11 (without edge enhancement)   FIGURE 12 (with enhanced edges)

Images digitized by the dot diffusion algorithm.

units of error in the worst case, only 26 of the 2835 baron positions were "bad" in the sense that they absorbed an error whose magnitude was more than 0.5; those included the cases where $A[i, j]$ reached the extreme values -0.65 and 1.96. In addition to baronial error, 24.14 units of pixel intensity leaked out at the boundaries; this is the sum of $|A[i, j]|$ for $i = 0$ or $i = m + 1$ or $j = 0$ or $j = n + 1$ after the diffusion algorithm has done its work. Thus the total undiffused error came to $704.10 + 24.14 = 728.24$ among $360 \times 250 = 90000$ pixels, about 0.008 per pixel.

Similar results occurred in Figures 9, 11, and 12; the statistics can be summarized as follows:

	$\min A[i, j]$	$\max A[i, j]$	bad barons	total undiffused error
Figure 9	-0.575	1.640	22	$707.65 + 72.78 = 780.43$
Figure 10	-0.649	1.957	26	$704.10 + 24.14 = 728.24$
Figure 11	-0.630	1.656	13	$719.27 + 62.79 = 782.06$
Figure 12	-0.773	1.913	22	$725.08 + 41.44 = 766.52$

The Floyd–Steinberg algorithm had undiffused errors only at the boundaries:

	$\min A[i, j]$	$\max A[i, j]$	total undiffused error
Figure 1	-0.276	1.163	116.53
Figure 2	-0.331	1.405	66.14
Figure 3	-0.246	1.039	86.64
Figure 4	-0.324	1.483	48.20

By contrast, the ordered dither algorithm diffuses errors only in the sense that it tries to make each 8×8 block approximately correct. The relevant statistics for such a method are

$$\sum_{i=1}^{\lceil 360/8 \rceil} \sum_{j=1}^{\lceil 250/8 \rceil} \left| \sum_{k=0}^{7} \sum_{l=0}^{7} A[8i - k, 8j - l] - B[8i - k, 8j - l] \right|;$$

these sums came to $(1000.72, 1655.19, 608.62, 678.94)$, respectively, in Figures 5, 6, 7, and 8. Thus ordered dithering was roughly twice as bad as dot diffusion in the case of Mona Lisa, while it was slightly more accurate in the case of the sphere. But the absolute error did exceed 1.0 in respectively $(325, 710, 103, 150)$ of the 1440 blocks.

Figures 1–12 have been shown with relatively large square pixels, measuring 0.22 mm on a side, so that the reader can plainly discern the on/off patterns. We would have to reduce the illustrations by a factor of 6 to get the equivalent of a medium-quality commercial screen for photographic halftones.

Problems

The ordered dither method produces a binary-recursive texture that is unsuitable for most applications to publishing; such "cold" patterns are probably useful only when the underlying technology is intentionally being emphasized. The Floyd–Steinberg method usually gives much more pleasing results, but it too has occasional lapses where intrusive snake-like patterns call attention to themselves. The dot diffusion method, likewise, introduces a grainy texture of its own. Thus none of these approaches is wholly satisfactory, in the sense that a viewer presented with the illustrations at this size would instinctively find them attractive. Neither does any other halftoning method look great, when viewed at this scale. We must stand back a few yards and squint, before a continuous-tone effect can be perceived. When such experiments are conducted, the Floyd–Steinberg examples tend to look better than the others.

But the picture changes when we consider applications to printing. The author experimented with variations of these images on a conventional 300-pixel-per-inch laserprinter (roughly a 38% reduction from the present size of the illustrations), and the results of Floyd–Steinberg and ordered dither proved to be quite unsatisfactory. Nonlinear effects of the xerographic process caused large dark blotches to appear in places where white pixels were fairly rare; there was a sharp jump between gray and black areas. In the author's experiments, the best laserprinted Mona Lisa was produced by dot diffusion (see [14]); all other methods tried were significantly inferior.

Of course, laserprinters are only a crude approximation to the high-resolution devices used in quality printing. Modern digital phototypesetters, with pixel sizes of say 20 μm (1270 pixels per inch), can produce excellent halftones by simulating the analog screening method that was used on older equipment. Indeed, the method of ordered dither — but with the 8 × 8 dot diffusion matrix of Table 2 in place of the 8 × 8 binary-recursive matrix of Table 1 — is essentially a simulation of the traditional approach to halftones.

It is natural to suppose that we should be able to do an even better job than before, if only we could think of how to use the new machines in a more clever way, because so many things are now possible that could not be done with analog devices. One might hope, for example, that the Floyd–Steinberg method (with sufficiently high resolution) might be able to reproduce Ansel Adams's photographs better than any previous method of printing has been able to achieve.

But a moment's reflection makes it clear that the Floyd–Steinberg approach will be of no use at high resolution, because of physical limitations. Tiny droplets of ink are simply unable to arrange themselves in patterns like those of Figures 1–4. The worst case probably occurs in the case that $A[i, j] = 1/2$ for all i and j; then the Floyd–Steinberg algorithm produces a checkerboard of alternating black and white squares, and a typical printing machine will convert this into a splotch of ink like this: ■ . Ordered dither, as in Figures 5–8, will fail for the same reason. Both of these methods favor isolated black or white pixels.

Could dot diffusion, as described above, be useful at high resolution? Let's explore this by looking at a 27% reduction of Figures 9–12:

In this reduced form each pixel occupies .06 mm, so there are about 423 pixels per inch. If we rotate by 45° and divide by $4\sqrt{2}$ (which is the distance between "barons"), we see that the effect is analogous to a 75-line screen, which is about newspaper quality. These images are very small, and they would be even smaller on devices of higher resolution; a medium-quality commercial screen has about 130 screen dots per inch, or about 735 unrotated bilevel pixels per inch. A real illustration of Mona Lisa would therefore have hundreds of times as much data; we must keep this scale factor in mind.

Mona Lisa doesn't look bad in this example, but there are serious deficiencies in the reproduction of the sphere. Our eyes will not notice a regular pattern of dots, if the dots are small enough, but we are quick to perceive changes in texture. The background tones of gray behind the sphere should be changing very gradually, but false contours show up because a slight change in intensity can make a large change in the pattern computed by dot diffusion. (Similar but less prominent false contours can be seen in the background of the Floyd–Steinberg output, Figures 3 and 4, especially where the intensities $A[i, j]$ are nearly 1/2.)

Error diffusion methods are good at capturing the sharp details of a picture, but a successful method must also be "quiet" where the data shows little activity. The preparer of a digital halftone must be willing to compose background music as well as the occasional fanfare. This example demonstrates that dot diffusion, as defined above, is unsuitable for general use at high resolution.

In fact, there's another good reason why dot diffusion breaks down. It can be shown that if $A[i,j]$ has the constant value $1/2$ for all (i,j), the dot diffusion algorithm defined above will produce a perfect checkerboard of alternating black and white. (Small checkerboard patches can be perceived in portions of Figures 11 and 12.)

These observations lead us to conclude that our initial criterion, that the average of $B[i,j]$ near (i_0, j_0) should be approximately $A[i_0, j_0]$, is not sufficient, in spite of its mathematical appeal. What we really want is a criterion that takes into account the distortions produced by a printing process, as well as the subsequent distortions and illusions produced by our optic nerves. In other words, human perception of $B[i,j]$ near (i_0, j_0), after printing, should be approximately the same as human perception of $A[i,j]$ near (i_0, j_0). Some steps in this direction have been taken by Allebach and Dalton [2, 6], who include a visual model in their experimental algorithms.

Smooth Error Diffusion

The discussion in the previous section seems to indicate that methods based on error diffusion are doomed, as far as applications to high-resolution printing are concerned. But we haven't considered the full power of error diffusion. An important discovery was made by Billotet-Hoffmann and Bryngdahl [5], who realized that the Floyd–Steinberg method reproduces average gray levels even when the constant '0.5' is replaced by any other value! For example, if we set $B[i,j] := 1$ only when $A[i,j] > 0.6$, we will be setting the upper left corner element $B[1,1]$ to zero more often than before; but if we do, we'll be distributing a larger error value, hence the neighboring pixels will be more likely to become 1. Billotet-Hoffman and Bryngdahl found that the resulting textures are improved if the thresholds vary slightly as a function of i and j.

Let us therefore consider a parallel algorithm that has a more general form than dot diffusion. All pixel positions (i,j) are divided into r classes, numbered 0 to $r - 1$, and we proceed as follows:

```
for k := 0 to r − 1 do for all (i, j) of class k do
   begin if A[i, j] < θ_k then B[i, j] := 0 else B[i, j] := 1;
   err := A[i, j] − B[i, j];
   for l := k + 1 to r − 1 do
      begin let (u, v) be nearest to (i, j) such that class(u, v) = l;
      A[u, v] := A[u, v] + err * α_kl;
      end;
   end.
```

A diffusion algorithm that will be useful at high resolution must have some sort of smoothness property. This means, intuitively, that small changes to the given pixel values $A[i,j]$ should produce small changes in the resulting binary values $B[i,j]$. For example, if all the A's increase, it would be nice if the B's all would stay the same or increase. Let us therefore ask: Is there a sequence of parameter values θ_k and α_{kl}, for $0 \le k < l < r$, such that the general diffusion algorithm above has the following property?

> If $A[i,j] = a$ initially, for all i and j,
> and if $(m - .5)/r < a < (m + .5)/r$ for some integer m,
> then the above algorithm should set
> $$B[i,j] := \begin{cases} 1, & \text{if } 0 \le \text{class}(i,j) < m; \\ 0, & \text{if } m \le \text{class}(i,j) < r. \end{cases}$$

This condition states that the diffusion algorithm should act like a dither algorithm, when the data is constant.

Surprisingly, there is a simple solution to these nonlinear constraints. We may take

$$\theta_k = .5/(r - k), \qquad \alpha_{kl} = 1/(r - k - 1), \qquad \text{for all } 0 \le k < l < r.$$

In particular, this threshold θ_k is strictly less than $1/2$, until we reach the baron class $k = r - 1$. For all smaller classes, the error is distributed *equally* to the higher-class neighbors; that is, it does not depend on l.

Here's the proof: Suppose that each $A[i,j]$ has the initial value $a = a_0$ and that $(m - 0.5)/r < a_0 < (m + 0.5)/r$. If $m > 0$, the algorithm sets all $B[i,j]$ of class 0 to 1, and it sets all $A[i,j]$ of classes > 0 to the value $a_1 = a_0 + (a_0 - 1)/(r - 1) = (ra_0 - 1)/(r - 1)$. Now we have $(m - 1.5)/(r - 1) < a_1 < (m - 0.5)/(r - 1)$. If $m > 1$, the algorithm sets all $B[i,j]$ of class 1 to 1, and it sets all $A[i,j]$ of classes > 1 to $a_2 = a_1 + (a_1 - 1)/(r - 2)$. Hence $(m - 2.5)/(r - 2) < a_2 < (m - 1.5)/(r - 2)$; the process continues until we come to class m, with $A[i,j] = a_m$ and $-0.5/(r - m) < a_m < 0.5/(r - m)$. The algorithm now sets all $B[i,j]$ of class m to 0, and it sets all $A[i,j]$ of higher classes to $a_{m+1} = a_m + a_m/(r - m - 1)$. At this point we have $-0.5/(r - m - 1) < a_{m+1} < 0.5/(r - m - 1)$, hence the pattern persists; Q.E.D.

Although these threshold values θ_k appear to be very unsymmetrical with respect to 0 and 1, the stated smoothness property is symmetrical. Therefore the method is not as biased toward $B[i,j] = 1$ as it may seem. But there is a small bias. It can be shown, for example, that if

$r = 2$ and if the continuous A values for classes 0 and 1 are chosen independently and uniformly at random, then the resulting binary B values will be $(00, 01, 10, 11)$ with the respective probabilities $(3, 5, 20, 4)/32$; hence the total expected binary weight is $(5 + 20 + 8)/32 = 33/32$, slightly more than 1. If $r = 3$ the probabilities for the eight possible outcomes $B = 000, 001, 010, 011, 100, 101, 110, 111$, when the A values are independently and uniformly random, are respectively $(57, 123, 536, 148, 1423, 557, 2232, 108)/5184$; and the expected number of 1s is $115/72 \approx 1.597$, slightly more than $r/2$. In general the probability that all r of the B values are set to 1 is $1/(2^r r!)$, and the probability that they are all set to 0 is

$$\frac{1}{2^r r!} \left(1 - \left(\frac{0}{1}\right)^1 \right) \left(1 - \left(\frac{1}{2}\right)^2 \right) \cdots \left(1 - \left(\frac{r-1}{r}\right)^r \right).$$

But of course the assumption of independently random A values is not a good model for actual image data.

We can apply this method in the case $r = 32$, using the class matrix of Table 2 but with all class numbers divided by 2 (discarding the remainder). Indeed, the ordinary dot diffusion method discussed earlier would have given precisely the same results if we had considered it to be a 32-class method instead of a 64-class method. But now we want to expand the neighborhood of each pixel from size 9 to size 32; we regard cell (i, j) as having 32 neighbors (u, v) that form a diamond-like pattern, defined by

$$-3 + |v - j| \le u - i \le 4 - |v - j|;$$

these 32 neighbors (including (i, j) itself) contain one element from each class. The neighbor relation isn't symmetrical — for example, $(4, 1)$ is a neighbor of $(1, 2)$ but $(1, 2)$ is not a neighbor of $(4, 1)$; that's not a problem.

Let us call the resulting algorithm *smooth dot diffusion*. The previously described dot diffusion method requires no more arithmetic operations than the ordinary Floyd–Steinberg algorithm, since 256 additions and 256 multiplications are needed to process each 8×8 block. By contrast, the smooth dot diffusion algorithm needs only 62 divisions per 8×8 block, since it distributes errors equally; but it performs 992 additions, so it is slightly more expensive.

The maximum value of $A[i, j]$ during the smooth diffusion algorithm with r classes will occur when the $A[i, j]$ are as large as possible subject to the condition that $B[i, j]$ is set to 0 for all classes $< r - 1$; this allows the baron to grow arbitrarily near to its upper limit, $1.5 - 0.5/r$.

The minimum possible value of $A[i,j]$ is more difficult to describe. When $r = 32$ it occurs when we choose A values as small as possible so that $B = 1$ for classes 0 to 19, while $B = 0$ for classes 20 to 30. This extreme case will make the baron's value $-6(\frac{1}{12} + \frac{2}{13} + \frac{2}{14} + \cdots + \frac{2}{30} + \frac{2}{31} + \frac{1}{32}) \approx -11.776$. For general r, let k be minimal such that the harmonic sum $1/(r-k) + \cdots + 1/(r-1)$ exceeds $1 - 0.5/r$; then $k = r - r/e + O(1)$, and the least value that any $A[i,j]$ can assume is

$$\frac{k-r}{2} \left(\frac{1}{r-k} + \frac{2}{r-k-1} + \frac{2}{r-k-2} + \cdots + \frac{2}{r-2} + \frac{2}{r-1} + \frac{1}{r} \right)$$

$$= -\frac{r}{e} + O(1).$$

Since smooth dot diffusion deals with rather large neighborhoods, an error can move to positions quite far from its source. For example, there is a propagation path from class 7 to 9 to 14 to 16 to 18 to 20 to 23 to 27 to 29 to 30 to 32 to 36 to 42 to 45 to 48 to 51 to 53 to 55 in the matrix of Table 2 (before the class numbers have been divided by 2); this moves downward 30 rows below the starting point! However, the error is multiplied by small constants, so it is considerably dampened by the time it reaches the end of its journey. Other paths can move upward as many as 11 rows (for example, from 16 to 18 to 22 to 25 to 28 to 39 to 42 to 49). The only significant effect of such long paths is that an optimized sequential implementation, which keeps only a few consecutive rows of the image in memory at a time, requires a buffer of 16 rows; ordinary dot diffusion needs only 7 rows.

Comparison with Other Methods

Paul Roetling [21, 22] has developed a somewhat similar parallel algorithm for high-resolution halftones. His method, called ARIES (which means Alias-Reducing Image-Enhancing Screener), is essentially a modification of a dithering scheme in which the threshold levels are adjusted for each dot. ARIES first forms the set of all values $A[i,j] - k/r$ that contribute to a single dot, where position (i,j) corresponds to level k in the dither matrix and r is the total number of pixels per dot; then ARIES sets $B[i,j] := 1$ in the m positions (i,j) that score highest by this criterion, where m is chosen to equal the average intensity of the dot.

Figures 13 and 14 show the results of ARIES on our two sample images. Here 32-pixel dots were used, based again on the class matrix of Table 2 with all class numbers divided by 2. (If (i_0, j_0) is a pixel of class 0, the 32 pixels of a dot are its 32 neighbors as defined above,

FIGURE 13   (digitized by ARIES)   FIGURE 14

FIGURE 15   (digitized by smooth dot diffusion)   FIGURE 16

namely $(i_0 + \delta, j_0 + \epsilon)$ where $-3 + |\delta| \leq \epsilon \leq 4 - |\delta|$.) Figures 15 and 16 are the corresponding results of smooth error diffusion. The problematic false contours of Figure 12 have disappeared, but there is a small residual effect since each dot has only 32 pixels and can represent only 33 shades of gray. Both algorithms yield images that should make excellent halftones; at 423 pixels per inch they look like this:

The results of smooth dot diffusion may perhaps be slightly more crisp than those of ARIES; they are also slightly darker (although, paradoxically, Figure 16 appears to be somewhat lighter than Figure 12 on a low resolution device).

The error made by ARIES is guaranteed to be at most 0.5 in each dot position, and it should be about 0.25 per dot on the average. Our sample images include 2943 dots or partial dots; sure enough, the total error of ARIES was 723.42 in Figure 13 and 721.49 in Figure 14.

In Figures 15 and 16 the values of $A[i][j]$ remained less than 1.0007 throughout the smooth diffusion algorithm. But negative errors tended to accumulate, reaching a low of -4.555 in Mona Lisa and -3.703 in the sphere (both in baron positions). The 2835 barons absorbed 2337.15 units of error in Mona Lisa and 977.23 in the sphere, mostly negative as the algorithm tried to make the image a bit lighter. Altogether 1349 of the barons in Figure 15 were "bad," and 595 in Figure 16, in each case absorbing errors that were more negative than -0.5. The 32-cell neighborhoods also caused substantially more leakage at the boundaries: 2072.49 and a whopping 4150.88. Thus the total amounts of error per pixel in Figures 15 and 16 came to 0.049 and 0.057, respectively, compared to 0.008 for ARIES. The boundary errors would, of course, become negligible in a sufficiently large image.

A generalization of ARIES was suggested by Algie [1], who proposed a rank function of the form

$$A[i,j] - \alpha\,k$$

where α is a tunable parameter. The ARIES scheme is the special case $\alpha = 1/r$; another scheme, called "structured pels" by Pryor, Cinque, and Rubenstein [20], is the special case $\alpha = 0$. If we let $\alpha \to \infty$ we get methods in which each dot is chosen from a fixed repertoire of shapes. Satisfactory results from such schemes have been obtained by Robert L. Gard [9], who used alternating patterns of half-dots. Another related algorithm has been described by Anastassiou and Pennington [3].

Printers traditionally distinguish between "halftones" and "line art"; each is treated differently. *But we should not have to make this distinction when high-resolution digital typesetting equipment is used.* For example, a photograph might well contain textual information (such as a picture of a sign); why should that text have to be screened, when it could be made more legible? Methods like ARIES and smooth dot diffusion are able to adapt to whatever an image requires.

We could, of course, construct input data for which the output of smooth dot diffusion will be unsuitable for printing. For example, if each of the $A[i,j]$ values is already 0 or 1, smooth dot diffusion will simply set $B[i,j] := A[i,j]$ for all (i,j); we might be faced with values $A[i,j]$ that are unprintable, like a checkerboard. But we can assume that no such data will arise in practice. Such noise can be filtered out before the digitization process begins.

At present the author knows of no method that produces images of better quality for high-resolution digital phototypesetting than those produced by the smooth dot diffusion algorithm. However, it is obviously premature to make extravagant claims for this new method; computational experience so far has been very limited. If smooth dot diffusion lives up to its promise, a hardware implementation — possibly integrated with a scanning engine — might be an attractive possibility.

Acknowledgments

The referees were extremely helpful in pointing me to literature of which I was unaware. Their advice led to substantial improvements of the methods and the exposition in this paper. I also wish to thank B. K. P. Horn for letting me study the results of his many experiments with computer-generated halftones.

The preparation of this paper was supported in part by NSF grant CCR-8610181.

References

[1] Stephen H. Algie, "Resolution and tonal continuity in bilevel printed picture quality," *Computer Vision, Graphics, and Image Processing* **24** (1983), 329–346.

[2] J. P. Allebach, "Visual model-based algorithms for halftoning images," *Proceedings of SPIE, the Society of Photo-Optical Instrumentation Engineers* **310** (1981), 151–157.

[3] Dimitris Anastassiou and Keith S. Pennington, "Digital halftoning of images," *IBM Journal Research and Development* **26** (1982), 687–697.

[4] B. E. Bayer, "An optimum method for two-level rendition of continuous-tone pictures," *Conference Record of the IEEE International Conference on Communications* **1** (1973), (26-11)–(26-15).

[5] C. Billotet-Hoffmann and O. Bryngdahl, "On the error diffusion technique for electronic halftoning," *Proceedings of the Society for Information Display* **24** (1983), 253–258.

[6] J. C. Dalton, *Visual model based image halftoning using Markov random field error diffusion*, thesis, University of Delaware (December 1983). See also J. C. Dalton, G. R. Arce, and J. P. Allebach, "Error diffusion using random field models," *Proceedings of SPIE, the International Society for Optical Engineering* **432** (1983), 333–339; John Dalton, "Perception of binary texture and the generation of stochastic halftone screens," *Proceedings of SPIE, the International Society for Optical Engineering* **2411** (1995), 207–220.

[7] Robert W. Floyd and Louis Steinberg, "An adaptive algorithm for spatial greyscale," *Proceedings of the Society for Information Display* **17** (1976), 75–77. An earlier version appeared in *SID 75 Digest* (1975), 36–37.

[8] R. W. Floyd, Personal communication (21 May 1987).

[9] Robert L. Gard, "Digital picture processing techniques for the publishing industry," *Computer Graphics and Image Processing* **5** (1976), 151–171.

[10] Thomas M. Holladay, "An optimum algorithm for halftone generation for displays and hard copies," *Proceedings of the Society for Information Display* **21** (1980), 185–192.

[11] J. F. Jarvis and C. S. Roberts, "A new technique for displaying continuous tone images on a bilevel display," *IEEE Transactions on Communications* **COM-24** (1976), 891–898.

[12] J. F. Jarvis, C. N. Judice, and W. H. Ninke, "A survey of techniques for the display of continuous tone pictures on bilevel displays," *Computer Graphics and Image Processing* **5** (1976), 13–40.

[13] R. J. Klensch, Dietrich Meyerhofer, and J. J. Walsh, "Electronically generated halftone pictures," *RCA Review* **31** (1970), 517–533.

[14] Donald E. Knuth, "Fonts for digital halftones," *TUGboat* **8** (1987), 135–160. [A revised form of this article appears as Chapter 21 of the present volume.]

[15] Donald E. Knuth, *The Stanford GraphBase* (New York: ACM Press, 1994). Mona Lisa is shown on page 28.

[16] Kurt E. Knuth, James M. Berry, and Gary B. Ollendick, "An ink jet facsimile recorder," *IEEE Transactions on Industrial Applications* **IA-14** (1978), 156–161.

[17] J. O. Limb, "Design of dither waveforms for quantized visual signals," *Bell System Technical Journal* **48** (1969), 2555–2582.

[18] Bernard Lippel and Marvin Kurland, "The effect of dither on luminance quantization of pictures," *IEEE Transactions on Communication Technology* **COM-19** (1971), 879–888.

[19] William K. Pratt, *Digital Image Processing* (New York: Wiley, 1978).

[20] R. W. Pryor, G. M. Cinque, and A. Rubenstein, "Bilevel image displays — a new approach," *Proceedings of the Society for Information Display* **19** (1978), 127–131.

[21] Paul G. Roetling, "Halftone method with edge enhancement and Moiré suppression," *Journal of the Optical Society of America* **66** (1976), 985–989.

[22] Paul G. Roetling, "Binary approximation of continuous tone images," *Photographic Science and Engineering* **21** (1977), 60–65.

[23] M. R. Schroeder, "Images from computers," *IEEE Spectrum* **6**, 3 (March 1969), 66–78. See also *Communications of the ACM* **12** (1969), 95–101.

Chapter 23

A Note on Digitized Angles

[Originally published in Electronic Publishing — Origination, Dissemination, and Design **3** *(1990), 99–104.]*

We study the configurations of pixels that occur when two digitized straight lines meet each other. The exact number of different configurations is calculated when the lines have rational slopes. This theory helps to explain the empirically observed phenomenon that the two "halves" of an arrowhead don't look the same.

About ten years ago I was supervising the Ph.D. thesis of Christopher Van Wyk [4], which introduced the IDEAL language for describing pictures [5]. Two of his example illustrations showed arrows constructed from straight lines something like this:

When I looked at them, I was sure that there must be a bug either in IDEAL or in the *troff* processor that typeset the IDEAL output, because the long shafts of the arrows did not properly bisect the angle made by the two short lines of the arrowheads. The shafts seemed to be drawn one pixel too high or too low. Chris spent many hours together with Brian Kernighan trying to find out what was wrong, but no errors could be pinned down. Eventually his thesis was printed on a high-resolution phototypesetter, and the problem became much less noticeable than it had been on the laserprinted proofs. There still was a glitch, but I decided not to hold up Chris's graduation for the sake of a misplaced pixel.

I remembered this incident at the end of 1983, when I was getting ready to write a new version of the METAFONT system for digital

473

art [3]. I didn't want my system to have such a flaw. But to my surprise, I learned that the problem is actually *unavoidable* in raster output: Digitized angles can almost never be bisected exactly, except in very special circumstances. The two "halves" of the angle will necessarily appear somewhat different from each other, unless the resolution is quite high. Therefore Van Wyk (and Kernighan) were vindicated. Similar problems are bound to occur in MacDraw and in any other drawing package.

For example, one of the things I noticed was the following curious fact. Consider the 45° angle that is made when a straight line segment of slope 2 comes up to a point (x_0, y_0) and then goes down along another line of slope -3:

$$(x_0, y_0)$$
$$(x_0 - t, y_0 - 2t) \qquad (x_0 + u, y_0 - 3u)$$

If we digitize this angular path, the upper contour will take one of five different shapes, depending on the value of the intersection point (x_0, y_0), whose coordinates are not necessarily integers. The possibilities are

$$P_0: \qquad P_1: \qquad P_2: \qquad P_3: \qquad P_4:$$

Now suppose that this 45° angle provides the left half of an arrowhead. The right half of the arrowhead will then be a 45° angle made by a line of slope -3 meeting a line of slope $-1/2$:

$$(x_1, y_1)$$
$$(x_1 + 2u, y_1 - u)$$
$$(x_1 + t, y_1 - 3t)$$

For this angle there are, similarly, five possibilities after digitization, namely

$$Q_0: \qquad Q_1: \qquad Q_2: \qquad Q_3: \qquad Q_4:$$

To complete the arrowhead, we should match the left angle P_i with an appropriate Q_j. But none of the Q's has the same shape as any of the P's. And this is the point: Human eyes tend to judge the magnitude of an angle by its appearance at the tip. By this criterion, some of these angles appear to be quite a bit larger than others (except at high resolutions). Hence it is not surprising that a correctly drawn angle of type P would appear to be unequal to a correctly drawn angle of type Q, even though both angles would really be $45°$ when drawn with infinite resolution. (The patterns of white pixels, not black pixels, are the source of the inconsistency.) Here, for example, are four quite properly digitized arrows with shafts of increasing thickness:

We might also want to know the probability that the digitized shape will be of a particular type P_k, when the corner point (x_0, y_0) is chosen at random in the plane. Is one of the patterns more likely to occur than the others? The answer is no, when we use the most natural method of digitization; each P_k will be obtained with probability $1/5$. Similarly, each of the five shapes Q_k turns out to be equally likely, as (x_1, y_1) varies.

The main purpose of this note is to prove that the facts just stated are special cases of a general phenomenon:

Theorem. *When a line of slope a/b meets a line of slope c/d at a point (x_0, y_0), the number of different digital shapes it can produce as (x_0, y_0) varies is $|ad - bc|$. Moreover, each of these shapes is equally likely to occur, if (x_0, y_0) is chosen uniformly in the plane.*

We assume that a/b and c/d are rational numbers in lowest terms. Two digitized shapes are considered to be equal if they are identical after translation; rotation and reflection are not allowed.

Before we can prove the theorem, we need to define exactly what it means to digitize a curve. For this, we follow a general idea that is explained, for example, in [3, Chapter 24]. We consider the plane to be tiled with pixels, which are the unit squares whose corners have integer coordinates. Our goal is to modify a given curve so that it travels entirely on the boundaries between pixels. If the curve is given in parametric form by the function $z(t) = \big(x(t), y(t)\big)$ as t varies, its digitization is essentially defined by the formula

$$\text{round } z(t) = \big(\text{round } x(t), \ \text{round } y(t)\big)$$

as t varies, where $\text{round}(\alpha)$ is the integer nearest α.

We need to be careful, of course, when rounding values that are halfway between integers, because $\text{round}(\alpha)$ is undefined in such cases.

Let us assume for convenience that the path $z(t)$ does not go through any pixel centers; in other words, we will assume that $z(t)$ is never equal to $(m + \frac{1}{2}, n + \frac{1}{2})$ for integers m and n. (Exact hits on pixel centers occur with probability zero, so they can be ignored in the theorem we wish to prove. An infinitesimal shift of the path can be used to avoid pixel centers in general, therefore avoiding the ambiguities pointed out in Bresenham's interesting discussion [1]; but we need not deal with such complications.) Under this assumption, whenever we have $x(t) = m + \frac{1}{2}$ so that 'round $x(t)$' is ambiguous, the value of round $y(t) = n$ will be unambiguous, and we can include the entire line segment from (m, n) to $(m + 1, n)$ in the digitized path. Similarly, when t reaches a value such that round $x(t) = m$ but round $y(t) = n$ or $n + 1$, we include the entire segment from (m, n) to $(m, n + 1)$. This convention defines the desired digitized path, round $z(t)$.

When the path $z(t)$ returns to its starting point or begins and ends at infinity, without intersecting itself, it defines a region in the plane. The corresponding digitized path, round $z(t)$, also defines a region; and this digitized region turns out to have a simple characterization, when we apply standard mathematical conventions about "winding numbers": *The pixel with corners at* (m, n), $(m + 1, n)$, $(m, n + 1)$, $(m + 1, n + 1)$ *belongs to the digitized region defined by* round $z(t)$ *if and only if its center point* $(m + \frac{1}{2}, n + \frac{1}{2})$ *belongs to the undigitized region defined by* $z(t)$. (This beautiful property of digital curves is fairly easy to verify in simple cases, but a rigorous proof is difficult because it relies ultimately on things like the Jordan Curve Theorem. The necessary details appear in an appendix to John Hobby's thesis [2], Theorem A.4.1.)

Now we are ready to begin proving the desired result. The region defined by an angle at (x_0, y_0) with lines of slopes a/b and c/d can be characterized by the inequalities

$$a(x - x_0) - b(y - y_0) \geq 0; \qquad c(x - x_0) - d(y - y_0) \geq 0.$$

(We may need to reverse the signs, depending on which of the four regions defined by two lines through (x_0, y_0) are assumed to be defined by the given angular path; this can be done by changing (a, b) to $(-a, -b)$ and/or (c, d) to $(-c, -d)$.) The stated region contains the pixel with lower left corner (m, n) if and only if

$$a(m + \tfrac{1}{2} - x_0) - b(n + \tfrac{1}{2} - y_0) \geq 0; \qquad c(m + \tfrac{1}{2} - x_0) - d(n + \tfrac{1}{2} - y_0) \geq 0.$$

We can simplify the notation by combining several constants, letting $\alpha = a(x_0 - \frac{1}{2}) - b(y_0 - \frac{1}{2})$ and $\beta = c(x_0 - \frac{1}{2}) - d(y_0 - \frac{1}{2})$:

$$am - bn \geq \alpha; \qquad cm - dn \geq \beta.$$

Let $R(\alpha, \beta)$ be the digitized region consisting of all integer pairs (m, n) satisfying this condition; these are the pixels in the digitized angle corresponding to (x_0, y_0).

As noted above, it is safe to assume that the pixel centers do not exactly touch the lines forming the angle; thus we are free to stipulate that $am - bn \neq \alpha$ and $cm - dn \neq \beta$ for all pairs of integers (m, n). However, if equality does occur, we might as well define the digitized region $R(\alpha, \beta)$ by the general inequalities $am - bn \geq \alpha$ and $cm - dn \geq \beta$, as stated, instead of treating this circumstance as a special case. Notice that $R(\alpha, \beta)$ is equal to $R(\lceil \alpha \rceil, \lceil \beta \rceil)$; therefore we can assume that α and β are integers in the following discussion.

Another corner point (x_0', y_0') will lead to parameters (α', β') defining another region $R(\alpha', \beta')$ in the same way. The two regions $R(\alpha, \beta)$ and $R(\alpha', \beta')$ have the same shape if and only if one is a translation of the other; i.e., $R(\alpha, \beta) \equiv R(\alpha', \beta')$ if and only if there exist integers (k, l) such that

$$(m, n) \in R(\alpha, \beta) \Longleftrightarrow (m - k, n - l) \in R(\alpha', \beta').$$

Our main goal is to prove that the number of distinct region shapes, according this notion of equivalence, is exactly $|ad - bc|$.

Lemma. Let α, β, α', β' be integers. Then $R(\alpha, \beta) \equiv R(\alpha', \beta')$ with respect to slopes a/b and c/d if and only if $\alpha - \alpha' = ka - lb$ and $\beta - \beta' = kc - ld$ for some integers (k, l).

Proof. Assume that $R(\alpha, \beta) \equiv R(\alpha', \beta')$ with respect to a/b and c/d, and let (k, l) be the corresponding translation amounts. Thus we have

$$\left\{ \begin{array}{l} am - bn \geq \alpha \\ cm - dn \geq \beta \end{array} \right\} \Longleftrightarrow \left\{ \begin{array}{l} a(m - k) - b(n - l) \geq \alpha' \\ c(m - k) - d(n - l) \geq \beta' \end{array} \right\}$$

for all integer pairs (m, n). Let $\alpha'' = \alpha' + ka - lb$ and $\beta'' = \beta' + kc - ld$, so that

$$\left\{ \begin{array}{l} am - bn \geq \alpha \\ cm - dn \geq \beta \end{array} \right\} \Longleftrightarrow \left\{ \begin{array}{l} am - bn \geq \alpha'' \\ cm - dn \geq \beta'' \end{array} \right\}$$

for all integers (m, n). This implies that $\alpha = \alpha''$ and $\beta = \beta''$. For if, say, we had $\alpha < \alpha''$, we could find integers m and n such that $am - bn = \alpha$ and $cm - dn \geq \beta$, because a and b are relatively prime; this would satisfy the inequalities on the left but not on the right. (More precisely, we could use Euclid's algorithm to find integers a' and b' such that $aa' - bb' = 1$. Then the values $(m, n) = (\alpha a' + bx, \alpha b' + ax)$ would satisfy the left inequalities but not the right, for infinitely many integers x, because $ad - bc \neq 0$.)

Thus $R(\alpha, \beta) \equiv R(\alpha', \beta')$ implies that $\alpha - \alpha' = ka - lb$ and $\beta - \beta' = kc - ld$. The converse is trivial. $\square$

Let k and l be integers such that $\alpha = ka - lb$. The lemma tells us that $R(\alpha, \beta) \equiv R(0, \beta - kc + ld)$; hence every digitized region $R(\alpha, \beta)$ has the same shape as some digitized region $R(\alpha', \beta')$ in which $\alpha' = 0$.

It remains to count the inequivalent regions $R(0, \beta)$ when β is an integer. According to the lemma we have $R(0, \beta) \equiv R(0, \beta')$ if and only if there exist integers (k, l) with $0 = ka - lb$ and $\beta - \beta' = kc - ld$. But $ka = lb$ if and only if $k = bx$ and $l = ax$ for some integer x; hence the condition reduces to $\beta - \beta' = bxc - axd = x(bc - ad)$. In other words, $R(0, \beta) \equiv R(0, \beta')$ if and only if $\beta - \beta'$ is a multiple of $ad - bc$. The number of inequivalent regions is therefore $|ad - bc|$, as claimed.

To complete the proof of the theorem, we must also verify that each of the equivalence classes is equally likely to be the class of the digitized angular region, when the intersection point (x_0, y_0) is chosen at random in the plane. The notational change from (x_0, y_0) to (α, β) maps equal areas into equal areas; so we want to prove that the equivalence class of $R(\alpha, \beta)$ is uniformly distributed among the $|ad - bc|$ possibilities, when the real numbers (α, β) are chosen at random. Choosing real numbers (α, β) at random leads to uniformly distributed pairs of integers $(\lceil \alpha \rceil, \lceil \beta \rceil)$. And if $\lceil \alpha \rceil$ has any fixed value and $\lceil \beta \rceil$ runs through all integers, the equivalence class of $R(\alpha, \beta)$ runs cyclically through all $|ad - bc|$ possibilities. $\square$

A close inspection of this proof shows that we can give explicit formulas for the sets of intersection points (x_0, y_0) that produce equivalent shapes. Let $D = |ad - bc|$ and let R_j denote the shape corresponding to region $R(0, j)$ in the proof, where $0 \leq j < D$. Then the digitized angle will have shape R_j if and only if (x_0, y_0) lies in the parallelogram whose corners are $\left(1/2 - bj/D, 1/2 - aj/D\right)$ plus

$$\left((b - d)/D, (a - c)/D\right), \quad (-d/D, -c/D), \quad (b/D, a/D), \quad (0, 0),$$

or in a parallelogram obtained by shifting this one by integer amounts.

In the special case $a/b = 2/1$ and $c/d = (-3)/1$, the shapes R_j are what we called P_j above; in the special case $a/b = 3/(-1)$ and $c/d = (-1)/2$, the R_j are what we called Q_j. The shapes that appear in the digitized angles depend on the values of $(x_0 \bmod 1, y_0 \bmod 1)$ in the unit square, according to the following diagrams:

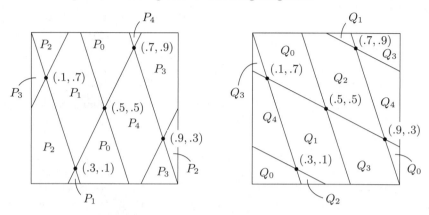

Notice that the parallelograms "wrap around" modulo 1, each taking up an area of $1/5$. Half of P_j corresponds to half of Q_{6-j}; the other half corresponds to half of Q_{7-j}.

When the slope of either line forming an angle is irrational, the number of possible shapes is infinite (indeed, uncountable). But we can still study such digitizations by investigating the shape only in the immediate neighborhood of the intersection point; after all, those pixels are the most critical for human perception. For example, exercises 24.7 through 24.9 of The METAFONTbook [3] discuss the proper way to adjust the vertices of an equilateral triangle so that it will digitize well.

The moral of this story, assuming that stories ought to have a moral, is probably this: If you want to bisect an angle in such a way that both halves of the bisected angle are visually equivalent, then the line of bisection should be such that reflections about this line always map pixels into pixels. Thus, the bisecting line should be horizontal or vertical or at a 45° diagonal, and it should pass through pixel corners and/or pixel centers. Furthermore, your line-rendering algorithm should produce symmetrical results about the line of reflection (see [1]).

This subject is clearly ripe for a good deal of further investigation.

Acknowledgments

I wish to thank the referees and the editor for their comments. In particular, one of the referees suggested the present proof of the theorem; my original version was much more complicated.

The preparation of this note was supported in part by National Science Foundation grant CCR-8610181.

References

[1] Jack E. Bresenham, "Ambiguities in incremental line rastering," *IEEE Computer Graphics and Applications* **7**, 5 (May 1987), 31–43.

[2] John Douglas Hobby, *Digitized Brush Trajectories*, Ph.D. thesis, Stanford University (1985). Published also as Stanford Computer Science Department report STAN-CS-85-1070 (April 1985).

[3] Donald E. Knuth, *The METAFONTbook*, Volume C of *Computers & Typesetting* (Reading, Massachusetts: Addison–Wesley and American Mathematical Society, 1986).

[4] Christopher John Van Wyk, *A Language For Typesetting Graphics*, Ph.D. thesis, Stanford University, (1980). Published also as Stanford Computer Science Department report STAN-CS-80-803 (June 1980). The "arrow" illustrations that prompted this research appear on page 20.

[5] Christopher J. Van Wyk, "A graphics typesetting language," *SIGPLAN Notices* **16**, 6 (June 1981), 99–107.

Chapter 24

TEXDR.AFT

This chapter and the next are for readers who share my fascination with original source documents. None of this material was intended for public consumption when first written, but we can read it today and get a good idea about how TeX and METAFONT came to exist in the first place.

The best way to establish the context for the genesis of TeX and META-FONT is probably to reproduce several entries from my diary of 1977.

7 Feb: Didn't sleep very well.
Did some correspondence; A & P committee meeting approves Tarjan promotion
Finished grading comprehensive exam and memo to next committee
Bed early

8 Feb: Rehearsal with chamber group
Debugging "Boolean evaluation on MIX" program
Discussion of computer typesetting with fonts in my book.
Read Reiser's thesis
Choir

Most of my working days during that winter were devoted either to teaching an introductory class on data structures — 170 students showed up for the first lecture on January 5, and 80 of them actually did all the work and passed the course on March 18; or to administrative work — I chaired the department's comprehensive exam committee, supervised research projects in the analysis of algorithms, and served on Stanford's Appointments and Promotions committee; or to writing portions of *The Art of Computer Programming* — during that period I prepared new material about bilinear forms for Section 4.6.4 of Volume 2, and new material about bitwise manipulations for Section 7.1 of Volume 4. But on February 7, while composing a memo for our department's next comprehensive exam committee, I looked at preview copies of new textbooks and had the opportunity to see high-resolution digital typography for the first time. That experience changed my life. Already on February 8 I began to talk to colleagues about the possibilities of using such machines to typeset my own books.

My diary of 1977 says nothing more about typographic matters until March 30; on that day, however, the die was cast.

30 Mar:
Galley proofs for vol. 2 finally arrive, they look awful ... I decide I have to solve the problem myself.   ‾typographically
Seder supper at church, is a bright spot in dull week.

I had to devote the month of April to finishing the other projects I had started. But by the beginning of May I had decided to create a program called 'TEX', and I was gearing up to embark on a new adventure.

2 May: Section 7.1 finished tonight at 1:00 a.m. — Hurray!

3 May: To San Jose with Jill, looking at church records from town near Heidelberg, figuring out old German handwriting

4 May: Cleaned up office, got 7.1 all put away.
Went through first 30 galleys until Belfast typesetting system understood

5 May: Read about Bell Labs typesetting system
Major design of TeX started.

6 May: More TEX

7 May: Long Test program for TeX constructed.
Went to movies AIRPORT 77 & Earthquake (to escape)

8 May: Mother's Day. Took Jill to brunch and fair and stitchery exhibit
Met Komloses at airport
Rested from technical work, went to bed early

9 May: Caught up on correspondence
Seminar here by Komlos

10 May: *Worked with Jill on design of hanging etc.*
Thought about TEX.

11 May: *Kombs luncheon seminar*
Sketched TGR programs

12 May: *Wrote draft report on TEX, stayed up till 5 am typing it into machine*

The draft report I wrote during the first third of May was entitled TEXDR.AFT, because the computer I was using did not allow a file to be named TEX.DRAFT. Here is what I typed on the night of May 12 and 13, mostly as a memo to myself:

Preliminary preliminary description of TEX

D Knuth, May 13, 1977

In this memo I will try to explain the TEX system for preparing publishable documents and how it is proposed to implement the system. Even though I don't understand TEX very well myself yet, I think the best way for me to get started is by trying to explain it to somebody else.

TEX is for technical text. Insiders pronounce the X as a Greek Chi (cf. the Scottish 'ch' sound in 'Loch Ness') since the word 'technical' stems from a Greek root meaning art as well as technology. I am preparing the system primarily for use in publishing my series The Art of Computer Programming-- the initial system will be tuned for my books, but it will not be difficult to extend it for other purposes if anybody wants to do so.

The input to TEX is a file in say TVeditor format at the Stanford AI lab. The output is a sequence of pages, produced in "one pass," suitable for printing on various devices. This report tries to explain how to get from input to output. The main idea is to consider the process as an operation on two-dimensional "boxes"; roughly speaking, the input is a long string of characters culled from a variety of fonts, where each character may be thought of as occupying a small rectangular box, and the output is obtained by gluing these boxes together either horizontally or vertically with various conventions about centering and justification, finally arriving at big rectangular boxes which are the desired pages. While LISP works with one-dimensional character strings, TEX works with two-dimensional box patterns; TEX has both horizontal and vertical 'cons' operations. Furthermore, TEX has another important basic concept of elastic glue between boxes, a type of mortar that stretches and shrinks at different specified rates so that box patterns will fit together in flexible ways.

In order to explain TEX more fully, I will alternate between very low-level descriptions of exactly how the processing takes place and very high-level descriptions of what you type to get complex effects.

First, at the very lowest level, we must realize that the input to TEX is not really a string of boxes, it is a file of 7-bit characters. This file is called an "external input file". The first thing TEX does is convert it to an "internal input file" by essentially obeying the following rules:

      1.Delete the first TVeditor directory page, if it exists.

      2.Delete the first line (title line) of every remaining page, and replace the end-of-page marks ('14) by carriage-returns ('15). Delete all line-feed symbols ('12). Delete all % marks and the sequences of characters following them up to (but not including) the next carriage-return.

      3.Delete all blank spaces following carriage-returns.

      4.If two or more carriage returns occur in sequence, replace all but the first by vertical-tab characters ('13). These are used to specify end of paragraphs in TEX; in other words, the user specifies end of paragraph by hitting two carriage returns in a row, or by a page break following a carriage return.

      5.Replace all remaining carriage-returns by blank spaces.

      6.If two or more blank spaces occur in a row, replace them by a single blank space.

      7.Add infinitely many } symbols at the right.

The reason for rule 7 is that TEX uses { and } for grouping, and the trailing }'s will match up with any {'s the user erroneously forgot to match in the external input file. By following the above rules, TEX obtains an internal input file containing no carriage-returns, line-feeds, %'s, or form-feeds (page marks), and with no two blank spaces in a row. Spacing in the output document is controlled by other features of TEX. (Actually TEX changes { and } internally to '14 and '15, but this does not affect the user so I will continue to write this report as if they were { and }.)

Now let's shift to a high level and show how the user can specify complex typesetting requirements to TEX. The following example is rather long and it deserves to be skimmed rather than studied in detail; I devised it mainly to serve as test data during initial development of the system. It is taken from the opening pages of my book Seminumerical Algorithms, skipping over the copy when the typesetting presents no essentially new challenges to the system. The reader might find it most useful to have the book in hand for comparison purposes. The line numbers at the left are not part of the TEX input, they are included only for purposes of cross reference so that I can refer to line so-and-so later on in this document.

    1 %Example TEX input related to Seminumerical Algorithms using ACPdefs
    2 ACPpages starting at page 1{
    3 titlepage %This tells the page format routine not to put page number at top
    4 sectionnumber 3
    5 runninglefthead{RANDOM NUMBERS}

6 hexpand 11 pt {fnt cmg11 CHAPTER hskip 10 pt THREE}
7 vskip 1 cm plus 30 pt minus 10 pt
8 rjustline {fnt cmgb20 RANDOM NUMBERS}
9 vskip .5 cm plus 1 pc minus 5 pt
10 quoteformat {Anyone who considers arithmetical \cr
11 methods of producing random digits \cr is, of course,
12 in a state of sin. \cr} author {JOHN VON NEUMANN (1951)}
13 quoteformat {Round numbers are always false.}
14 author{SAMUEL JOHNSON (c. 1750)}
15 vskip 1 cm plus 1 pc minus 5 pt
16 sectionnumber 3.1
17 sectionbegin {3.1. INTRODUCTION}
18 runningrighthead {INTRODUCTION}
19 Numbers which are ''chosen at random'' are useful in a wide variety of
20 applications. For example:
21   %This blank line specifies end of paragraph
22 yskip   %This means an extra space between paragraphs
23 textindent{a)}{\sl Simulation.}xskip When a computer is used to simulate natural
24 phenomena, random numbers are required to make things realistic. Simulation
25 covers many fields, from the study of nuclear physics (where particles are
26 subject to random collisions) to systems engineering (where people come into,
27 say, a bank at random intervals). \par
28 yskip textindent{b)}{\sl Sampling.} xskip It is often impractical to examine
29 all cases, but a random sample will provide insight into what constitutes
30 ''typical'' behavior.
31
32 yskip It is not easy to invent a foolproof random-number generator. This fact
33 was convincingly impressed upon the author several years ago, when he attempted
34 to create a fantastically good random-number generator using the following
35 peculiar method:
36
37 yskip yskip noindent {\bf Algorithm K} xskip({\sl ''Super-random'' number
38 generator}). xskip Given a 10-digit decimal number X, this algorithm may be
39 used to change X to the number which should come next in a supposedly random
40 sequence. \par
41 algstep K1.[Choose number of iterations.]Set $Y\leftarrow lfloor X/10 sup 9 rfloor$, i.e.,
42 the most significant digit of X. (We will execute steps K2 through K13 $Y+1$
43 times; that is, we will randomize the digits a {\sl random} number of times.)
44
45 algstep K10. [99999 modify.] If $X<10 sup 5$, set $X\leftarrow X sup 2 + 99999$;
46 otherwise set $X \leftarrow X - 99999$. xskip blackslug
47
48 boxinsert{ctrline{fnt cmgb10 Table 10}
49 ctrline{fnt cm9 A COLOSSAL COINCIDENCE: THE NUMBER 6065038420}
50 ctrline{fnt cm9 IS TRANSFORMED INTO ITSELF BY ALGORITHM K.}
51 blankline 3 pt vskip ruled
52 hjust to 12 pc{blankline vskip 6 pt
53 tabalign{#•quad#•quad$#$\cr
54 Step•ctr{X (after)}\cr

```
55 vskip 10 pt plus 10 pt minus 5 pt
56 K1•6065038420\cr K12•1905867781•Y=5\cr
57 vskip 10 pt plus 10 pt minus 5 pt blankline}
58 hskip 3 pc ruled align top
59 hjust to 12 pc{blankline vskip 6 pt
60 tabalign{#•quad #•quad $#$\cr
61 Step•ctr{$X$ (after)}\cr
62 vskip 10 pt plus 10 pt minus 5 pt
63 K10•1620063735\cr K11•1620063735\cr K12•6065038420•Y=0\cr
64 vskip 10 pt plus 10 pt minus 5 pt blankline}
65 vskip ruled blankline}  %end of the boxinsert
66 yskip yskip The moral to this story is that {\sl random numbers should not be
67 generated with a method chosen at random}. Some theory should be used.
68
69 exbegin
70 exno tr 1. [20] Suppose that you wish to obtain a decimal digit at random, not
71 using a computer. Shifting to exercise 16, let $f(x,y)$ be a function such that
72 if $0≤x,y<m$, then $0≤f(x,y)<m$. The sequence is constructed by selecting
73 $X sub 0$ and $X sub 1$ arbitrarily, and then letting$$
74 X sub{n+1} = f(X sub n, X sub {n-1}) quad for quad n>0.$$
75 What is the maximum period conceivably attainable in this case?
76
77 exno 17. [10] Generalize the situation in the previous exercise so that
78 $X sub {n+1}$ depends on the preceding $k$ values of the sequence.
79 \ff
80 sectionnumber 3.2 sectionbegin{3.2. GENERATING UNIFORM RANDOM NUMBERS}
81 runningrighthead {GENERATING UNIFORM RANDOM NUMBERS}
82 In this section we shall consider methods for generating a sequence of random
83 fractions, i.e., random {\sl real numbers $U sub n$, uniformly distributed
84 between zero and one}. Since a computer can represent a real number with only
85 finite accuracy, we shall actually be generating integers $X sub n$ between
86 zero and some number $m$; the fraction$$U sub n=X sub n/m eqno 1$$ will
87 then lie between zero and one.
88
89 vskip .4 in plus .2 in minus .2 in
90 sectionnumber 3.2.1 sectionbegin{3.2.1. The Linear Congruential Method}
91 runningrighthead{THE LINEAR CONGRUENTIAL METHOD}
92 By far the most successful random number generators known today are special
93 cases of the following scheme, introduced by D. H. Lehmer in 1948. [See
94 {\sl Annals Harvard Comp. Lab.} {\bf 26} (1951), 141-146.] We choose four
95 ''magic numbers'':$$
96 tabalign{rjust#•quad mathoff # quad•rjust #•ljust #\cr
97 X sub 0,•the starting value;•X sub 0•≥0. \cr
98 m,•the modulus;•m•>X sub 0, quad m>a, quad m>c. \cr} eqno 1$$
99 The desired sequence of random numbers $langle X sub n rangle$ is then obtained
100 by setting $$X sub{n+1}=(aX sub n+c)mod m,quad n≥0.eqno 2$$This is called
101 a {\sl linear congruential sequence}.
102
103 Let $w$ be the computer's word size. The following program computes $(aX+c)
```

104 mod(w+1)$ efficiently:$$tabalign{\it#quad⊛hjust to 50 pt{\tt#}}\cr
105 01⊛LDAN⊛X\cr
106 02⊛MUL⊛A\cr
107 05⊛JANN⊛*+3\cr
108 07⊛ADD⊛=W-1= quad blackslug\cr} eqno 2$$
109 {\sl Proof.} xskip We have $x=1+qp sup e$ for some integer q which is not a
110 multiple of p. By the binomial formula$$
111 eqalign{x sup p⊛=1+{p choose 1}qp sup e + cdots +{p choose p-1}q sup
112 {p-1}p sup{(p-1)e}+q sup p p sup {pe}\cr
113 ⊛=1+qp sup{e+1} big(){1 + 1 over p {p choose 2} q p sup e + 1 over p
114 {p choose 3} q sup 2 p sup {2e} + cdots + 1 over p {p choose p} q sup {p-1}
115 p sup {(p-1)e}.\cr$$ By repeated application of Lemma P, we find that$$
116 eqalign{(a sup p sup g - 1)/(a-1)⊛equiv 0'(modulo p sup g), \cr
117 (a sup p sup g - 1)/(a-1)⊛inequiv 0'(modulo p sup {g+1}). \cr}eqno 6$$
118 If $1<k<p$, $p choose k$ is divisible by p. {biglpren}{\sl Note:} xskip A
119 generalization of this result appears in exercise 3.2.2-11(a).{bigrpren} By
120 Euler's theorem (exercise 1.2.4-48), $a sup{varphi(p sup{e-f})} equiv 1'
121 (modulo p sup{e-f}); hence $lambda$ is a divisor of$$
122 lambda(p sub 1 sup e sub 1 ldots p sub t sup e sub t)=lcm paren{lambda(p sub 1
123 sup e sub 1), ldots, lambda(p sub t sup e sub t)}. eqno 9$$
124
125 This algorithm in MIX is simply$$
126 tabalign{hjust to 50 pt{\tt#}⊛{\tt#}} quad⊛ \cr
127 J6NN⊛*+2⊛underline{\it A1. j<0?}\cr
128 STA⊛Z⊛quad quad $→Z$.\cr} eqno 7$$
129 That was on page 26. If we skip to page 49, $Y sub 1 + cdots + Y sub k$ will
130 equal n with probability$$
131 sum over{y sub 1 + cdots + y sub k = n}atop{y sub 1, ldots, y sub k ≥ 0}
132 prod over {1≤s≤k}
133 {e sup{-np sub s}(np sub s)sup y sub s}over y sub s!
134 ={e sup -n n sup n}over n!.$$
135 This is not hard to express in terms of n-dimensional integrals$$
136 textsize{int from alpha sub n to n dY sub n int from alpha sub{n-1} to
137 Y sub n dY sub{n-1} ldots int from alpha sub 1 to Y sub 2 dY sub 1} over
138 textsize{int from 0 to n dY sub n int from 0 to Y sub n dY sub{n-1} ldots
139 int from 0 to Y sub 2 dY sub 1}, quad {\rm where} quad alpha sub j =
140 max(j-t,0). eqno 24$$
141 This together with (25) implies that$$ def rtn{sqrt n}
142 lim over {n→inf} s over rtn
143 sum over{rtn s<k≤n}{n choose k} big(){k over n - s over rtn} sup k
144 big(){s over rtn + 1 - k over n} sup{n-k-1} = e sup {-2s} sup 2, quad s≥0,
145 eqno 27$$ a limiting relationship which appears to be quite difficult to
146 prove directly.
147
148 exbegin exno 17. [HM26] Let t be a fixed real number. For $0≤k≤n$, let$$
149 P sub nk(x)=int from{n-t}to x dx sub n int from{n-1-t} to x sub n dx sub
150 {n-1}ldots int from {k+1-t} to x sub{k+2} dx sub{k+1} int from 0 to
151 x sub {k+1} dx sub k ldots int from 0 to x sub 2 dx sub 1;$$
152 Eq. (24) is equal to$$def sumk{sum over{1≤k≤n}}

153 sumk X prime sub k Y prime sub k big/{sqrt{sumk X prime sub k sup 2}
154 sqrt{sumk Y prime sub k sup 2}}.$$
155 sectionnumber 3.3.3.3 subsectionbegin{3.3.3.3. This subsection doesn't exist}
156 runningrighthead{A BIG MATRIX DISPLAY} Finally, look at page 91.$$
157 def diagdots{raise . by 10 pt hskip 4 pt raise . by 5 pt hskip 4 pt .}
158 eqalign{U∗=big(){tabalign{ctr#∗ctr#∗ctr#∗ctr#∗ctr#∗ctr#\cr
159 1\cr∗diagdots\cr∗∗1\cr
160 c sub 1∗ldots∗c sub{k-1}∗1∗c sub{k+1}∗c sub n\cr
161 ∗∗∗∗1\cr∗∗∗∗∗diagdots\cr∗∗∗∗∗∗1\cr}},\cr
162 U sup{-1}∗=big(){tabalign{ctr#∗ctr#∗ctr#∗ctr#∗ctr#∗ctr#\cr
163 1\cr∗diagdots\cr∗∗1\cr
164 -c sub 1∗ldots∗-c sub{k-1}∗1∗-c sub{k+1}∗-c sub n\cr
165 ∗∗∗∗1\cr∗∗∗∗∗diagdots\cr∗∗∗∗∗∗1\cr}}$$
166 This ends the test data, fortunately TEX is working fine.}

The first thing that must be emphasized about this example is that it is written
in an extension of TEX, not in the basic language itself. For example, "ACPpages"
in line 2 is a special routine that calls TEX's basic page-building routine but uses
it to prepare pages in the format of The Art of Computer Programming. The words
titlepage, sectionnumber, runninglefthead, quoteformat, author, sectionbegin,
runningrighthead, xskip, yskip, textindent, algstep, exbegin, exno, and
subsectionbegin are specific to my books and they have been defined in terms of
lower-level TEX primitives as we shall see below. Furthermore most of the fonts
used are embedded in these hidden definitions; for example, "sectionbegin" defines
the 10 point fonts used in the text of a section, while "exbegin" defines the
9 point fonts used in the exercises. Such keywords are chosen so that they do not
match English words, since they can appear intermixed with normal text. For
example, another definition is that the word MIX always is to be set in the
"typewriter type" font; the hidden definition
          def MIX|{{\tt \{MIX}}}
causes this to happen automatically in line 125. We shall study TEX's macro
definition mechanism later; three simple examples appear in lines 141, 152,
and 157 of the sample program, where a common idiom was given a short
definition just to save space. The construction \{string} is used to transmit
a string without interpreting its words according to existing definitions;
this device is used in the above definition of the keyword MIX. For curious
people who want to see a more complex definition, here is the definition of
quoteformat:
          def quoteformat #1 author #2 {lineskip 3 pt plus .5 pt minus 1 pt
                vskip 6 pt plus 5 pt minus 2 pt
                def \rm {fnt cmg8} def \sl {fnt cmgi8}
                {\sl tabalign{rjust##\cr #1}}
                vskip 6 pt plus 5 pt minus 2 pt \rm rjustline #2
                vskip 11 pt plus 5 pt minus 2 pt}
Please don't expect to understand this mess now, TEX is really very simple;
trust me. The word ''author'' which appears in this definition is given special
interpretation only in the context of quoteformat, otherwise it is treated as
usual; that is why I didn't use a non-English word like ''quoteauthor'' in
lines 12 and 14 of the example.

The specifications of sectionnumber and runninglefthead in lines 4 and 5 are to
be used in the top lines of pages in the book. Line 6 contains the first actual
text to appear on the page; but look first at line 8, which is simpler:
Line 8 says to use font cmgb20 (namely, "Computer Modern Gothic Bold 20 point",
which I plan to design shortly) for the words RANDOM NUMBERS, and to right-justify
them on the line (rjustline). Line 6 is similar but it uses the 11-point font
cmg11; ''hskip 10 pt'' stands for 10 points of horizontal space, and
''hexpand 11 pt'' means to take the line and stretch it 11 points wider than
it would ordinarily be. Note that font definitions within {...} disappear
outside the braces. So do all other definitions.

It is time to explain TEX's mechanism for stretching and shrinking.
Sizes in TEX can be specified in terms of points, picas, inches, centimeters,
or millimeters, using the abbreviations pt, pc, in, cm, mm respectively;
these abbreviations are meaningful only in contexts where physical lengths
are used, and one of these units must always be supplied in such contexts
even when the length is 0. (One inch equals 6 picas equals 72 points equals
2.54 centimeters equals 25.4 millimeters.) The glue between boxes has three
components:
>   the fixed component, x
>   the plus component, y
>   the minus component, z
The x part is "normal" spacing; when expanding a sequence of boxes to more
than their normal length, as on line 6, each x part in the glue is increased
by some multiple of the y part. When shrinking, each x part is decreased by
some multiple of the corresponding z part.

For example, given four boxes bound together by glue of specifications
>   (x1,y1,z1), (x2,y2,z2), (x3,y3,z3),
expansion of the line by an amount w is achieved by using the spacing
>   x1 + y1 w', x2 + y2 w', x3 + y3 w',
where $w' = w/(y1+y2+y3)$. The expansion is impossible if w>0 and y1+y2+y3=0.
The system tries hard to minimize bad-looking expansions, by having a
reasonably intelligent justification routine (described below). When
shrinking a line, the maximum amount of contraction is the sum of the z's, no
tighter fit will be attempted; thus, one should define the z width so that
x-z is the minimum space tolerated. The proper setting of y is such that x+y
is a reasonable spacing but x+3y is about at the threshold of intolerability.
Parameters y and z must be nonnegative, but x may be negative (for backspacing
and overlap) if care is used.

The notation ''hskip 10 pt'' in line 6 means that x = 10 pt, y = 0, and z = 0
in the horizontal glue between CHAPTER and THREE. If this hskip hadn't been
used, the normal conventions would have applied. Namely, the glue between
CHAPTER and THREE would have had x equal to the normal spacing for the font,
and y = x, z = x/2. The glue between letters has (say) x = 0, y = 1/10 of the
normal spacing for the font, z = 0; thus the expansion without using hskip
would have gone mostly into the space between CHAPTER and THREE, but by using
hskip as shown the expansion spreads out the individual letters. Fonts to

be used with TEX will have such letter spacing indicated as an additional feature;
TEX will also recognize things like the end of sentences, giving slightly more
white space after punctuation marks where appropriate. Symbols like + and =
conventionally are surrounded by spaces, while symbol pairs like '' and := are
moved closer together; the symbols + and = are not surrounded by spaces when
they appear in subscripts. Such things are taken care of in the same way that
ligatures are handled, by making the fonts a little smarter under TEX's control,
as described in more detail later.

Much of TEX is symmetrical between horizontal and vertical, although the basic
idea of building lines first rather than columns first is asymmetrically built
in to the standard routines (because of the way we normally write). The
specification ''vskip'' on line 7 specifies vertical glue analogous to
horizontal glue. When the page justification routine tries to fill the first
page of the example text (by breaking between pages ideally at the end of a
paragraph, or in a place where at least two lines of a paragraph appear on
both pages), this glue will expand or shrink in the vertical dimension using
$x = 1$ centimeter, $y = 30$ points, $z = 10$ points. Further variable glue is
specified in the definition of quoteformat: lineskip is the inter-line spacing,
and the vskips give special additional spacing between quotation and author
lines.   In the main text, the printer would refer to the type as "10 on 12",
meaning 10 point type with 12 points between corresponding parts of adjacent
lines; TEX will use a 10 point font with

     lineskip 2 pt plus .5 pt minus .25 pt

so that its line spacing is somewhat more flexible. Additional spacing between
paragraphs is given by

     parskip 0 pt plus 1 pt minus 0 pt

and there is other spacing between exercises, steps in algorithms, etc. The
definition

     def yskip {vskip 3 pt plus 2 pt minus 2 pt}

is used for special vertical spacing, for example in lines 22 and 37. A horizontal
skip

     def xskip {hskip 6 pt plus 10 pt minus 3.5 pt}

is used in lines 23, 37, etc. in contexts where a larger than normal space is
psychologically acceptable; for such purposes, flexible glue is especially
useful. A larger horizontal space called ''quad'' is used for example in line
74; this is "two ems" of space, a unit frequently used in mathematical typesetting.

Another nice feature of flexible glue occurs when you consider the case

     def hfill {hskip 0 cm plus 1000 cm minus 0 cm}.

In other words, y is essentially infinite (10 meters long). When this symbol
appears as an hskip at the beginning of a line, it right justifies that line; when
it appears at both the beginning and end, it centers the line; when it appears
in the middle it neatly partitions the line; and so on. These features of
TEX's variable glue seem to make it superior to existing justification
systems, because it provides new features in a rather simple way and at the
same time reduces the old features to a common pattern.

Once a list of boxes has been justified, all the glue is permanently set and the
overall box becomes rigid. Justification is either horizontal or vertical.

Horizontal justification of long lines includes some automatic hyphenation; further details about justification appear later in this memo.

Now let's look at more of the example. Lines 21 and 32, etc., are blank lines indicating the end of a paragraph; another way to specify this is ''\par'' in line 27. Line 124 is the end of a paragraph that ends with a displayed formula. Paragraphs are normally indented; one of the TEX commands subsumed under "sectionbegin" in line 17 is
>   parindent 20 pt
which affects the first line of every paragraph unless ''noindent'' appears as on line 37. The "sectionbegin" routine also specifies ''noindent'' on the very first paragraph of the section, since this is the standard format in my books. On line 23 we have ''textindent{a)}'', which creates a box of width parindent containing the characters a) followed by a blank space, right justified in this box.

In line 23 the "\sl" means "use slanted font." I have tentatively decided to replace italics by a slanted version of the normal "Roman" typeface, for emphasized words in the text, while variable symbols in math formulas will still be in italics as usual. I will have to experiment with this, but my guess is that it will look a lot better, since typical italic fonts do not tie together into words very beautifully. At any rate I will be distinguishing slanted from italic, in case it becomes desirable to use two different fonts for these different purposes. The "\bf" in line 37 stands for boldface. All these fonts are defined in sectionbegin, whose definition is hidden to you.

Mathematical formulas all appear between $...$ pairs, cf. lines 38 and 41, or between $$...$$ pairs (displayed equations). A special syntax is used in formulas, modeled on that of Kernighan and Cherry, Comm. ACM 18 (March 1975), 151-157. For example, ''sup 9'' in line 41 specifies a superscript 9, ''sub {n+1}'' in line 74 specifies a subscript n+1. Keywords like sup and sub are active only within $'s; the same applies to greek letter names like lambda (line 122) and varphi ("variant phi", the rounded version of this letter, which appears in a superscript in line 120), as well as to words like lim (line 142), max (line 140), lcm (line 122). All letters in formulas are set in italics unless they form part of a recognized word or are surrounded by "mathoff{...}" or "{\rm ...}".

All spacing within formulas is chosen by TEX, independent of spaces actually typed; the symbol ' (cf. line 117) denotes an inserted space, for cases when TEX's rules are unsatisfactory. In line 117, for example, extra space is wanted before "(modulo...)" since space before parentheses is usually omitted but not here. The later parts of the example text are largely concerned with complicated formulas, which will appear as shown in the corresponding parts of volume 2. The code "eqno 24" (cf. line 140) will insert "(24)" at the right margin, vertically centered on the corresponding displayed formula, if there is room, otherwise the "(24)" is stuck on a new line at the bottom right.

The algorithm-step-format keyword "algstep" used on lines 41 and 45 is defined as follows:

```
        def algstep #1. [#2] {vskip 3 pt plus 1 pt minus 1 pt
                noindent rjust in 20 pt{#1.} [#2] xskip hangindent 20 pt}
```
This sets vertical spacing glue before the text for the algorithm step, and it
also set up an appropriate "textindent", etc. The new feature here is the
hanging indent, which affects all but the first line of the following
paragraph.

The keyword "exno" used on lines 70, 77, etc. has a definition somewhat
similar to algstep; such definitions of format that are needed frequently in
my books will help to ensure consistency. The ''tr'' in line 70 will insert
a triangle in the left margin, using negative glue spacing so that the
character actually appears to the left of the box it is in.

Line 48 begins a "boxinsert", one of the important features needed in page layout.
The box defined within the {...} after boxinsert is set aside and placed on top
of either the present page or the following page (followed by vertical glue
specified by
```
                boxskip 20 pt plus 10 pt minus 5 pt,
```
this being another thing subsumed by "sectionbegin"). This is used for figures and
tables, in this case a table. The table caption appears in lines 48-50;
the table itself (cf. page 6 of the book) is rather complicated, so we will
defer explanation of lines 52-65 until after we have studied the simpler example
of tabalign in lines 96-98.

In general, a tabalign command takes the form
```
        tabalign{ u1#v1 ⊛ ... ⊛ un#vn \cr
                x11 ⊛ ... ⊛ x1n \cr
                  . . . . . . .
                xm1 ⊛ ... ⊛ xmn \cr}
```
Here the ⊛'s represent <TAB>'s on the keyboard and in the input file, but they
are shown here explicitly as printed characters to make their appearance plain.
The "\cr" is not a carriage-return, however, it is the sequence of three
characters \, c, r. The meaning is to form the mn boxes
```
                u1{x11}v1   ...   un{x1n}vn
                  . . . . . . . .
                u1{xm1}v1   ...   un{xmn}vn
```
and, for each k, to determine the maximum width of box uk{xik}vk for i = 1,...,m.
Then each uk{xik}vk is hjustified to the size of this maximum width, and each
line xi1⊛...⊛xin\cr is replaced by the horizontal concatenation of the resulting
boxes, separated by
```
                tabskip 0 pt plus 1 pt minus 0 pt.
```
If less than n entries appear on any line before the \cr, the remaining entries
are left blank.

In the example of tabalign on lines 96-98 we have n=4; the first column is to be
right justified, the second is to be treated as "mathoff" and surrounded by quad
spaces, the third again is right justified, the fourth is simply left-justified.
The result is shown on page 9 of the book, although with TEX the formula number
"(1)" will be centered. Note: Eventually I will put in an "omittab" feature which
will allow portions of a line to span several columns when desired.

Now let's look at lines 52-65 and compare with Table 1 on page 6 of the book.
A box of width 12 picas is built up using tabalign, and placed beside another
such box. The words "ruled" modifying vskip or hskip mean that the glue between
boxes also appears with a horizontal or vertical ruled line in its center.

The ''eqalign'' feature (cf. lines 111, 116) is used to line up operators in
different displayed formulas. Actually this is simply a special case of
tabalign:

      def eqalign #1 {tabalign{rjust##⊛ljust##\cr #1}}.

Note that line 113 begins with <TAB>.

The ''big(){...}'' in lines 113, 143, etc. and the ''big/{...}'' in line 152
is used to choose suitably large versions of parentheses and slashes, forming
''(...)'' and ''/...'', respectively; the size of the symbols is determined
by the height of the enclosed formula box. This type of operation is available
for [], <>, ||, and left and right braces signified by \[and \]. TEX will
provide the best size available in its repertoire. Parentheses, brackets,
braces, and vertical lines will be made in arbitrarily large sizes, but slashes
will not, at least not in this year's TEX. Some very large parentheses will be
generated for the big matrices in lines 158ff.

The ''biglpren'' and ''bigrpren'' on lines 118-119 are not really so big,
they are simply 12-point parentheses instead of 10-point ones, used to set
off the enclosed normal-size parentheses in the text's "(a)".

The summation signs produced by ''sum over...'' in lines 131, 143, will be
large, since these summations occur in displayed formulas; but between $...$
a smaller sign will be used and the quantity summed over will be attached
as a subscript. Similarly, the size of an integral sign will change, and
fractions ''...over...'' do too, as does the binomial coefficient
(cf. "$p choose k$" in line 118). The keyword ''textsize'' in lines 136 and
138 says to use smaller integral signs in this formula even though it is
displayed.

The \ff in line 79 means to eject a page (top justified) before continuing.
This again is part of the format of my books, a major section always should
begin on a new page.

I think the above comments on the example give the flavor of TEX. The example
was intended to show a variety of changing constructions of unusual complexity;
in general, most of a book will be comparatively routine, and it is only the
occasional formula or table which proves intricate. Such intricacies were
purposely emphasized in the example.

The next step in understanding TEX is to go back to the low level and see
what happens to an internal input file as it is being read in. What happens is
that it is massaged once again, converted to a sequence of "tokens", which are
either single characters or words. In general, adjacent letters and digits are
grouped together to form words; also periods and commas immediately followed
by digits are treated as letters, as are \ signs that are not preceded by

letters or digits. More precisely, the following finite-state machine
defines the token-building process.

State 0. Let x be the next character of the internal input file.
If x is \ or one of the 52 letters or 10 digits, set w←x and go to state 1.
If x is period or comma, set y←x, set w←null, go to state 2.
Otherwise output x as the next token.

State 1. Let x be the next character of the internal input file.
If x is a letter or digit, set w←w&x (w followed by x).
If x is period or comma, set y←x and go to state 2.
If x is \, output w as the next token, set w←x.
Otherwise output w as the next token, then output x as the next token,
and go to state 0.

State 2. Let x be the next character of the internal input file.
If x is a digit, set w←w&y&x, go to state 1.
Otherwise if w is nonempty, output w as the next token; then output y
as the next token; then go to state 0 but without resetting x at the
beginning of the instructions for that state.

For example, the sequence
Abc\de 5,000 plus-or-minus ''2.5 \per cent'' are ... here.
would be transformed into a sequence of 28 tokens:

Abc	\de	<space>	5,000	<space>	plus	-	or	-
minus	<space>	'	'	2.5	\per	<space>	cent	'	'
<space> are	<space>	.	.	.	<space> here	.		

TEX works on sequences of tokens. If a token has been defined (using ''def''), a
<space> before this token is removed. The remaining portion of the definition is
plugged in; the same process is repeated on the resulting sequence of tokens.
Definitions disappear after the } or $ or $$ which closes the group they are in;
they also are inoperative between \{ and its matching }. If the keyword MIX
had been defined as
        def MIX{{\tt MIX}}
instead of
        def MIX{{\tt\{MIX}}},
TEX would have looped endlessly while emitting {\tt {\tt {\tt {\tt ....

By now the reader will probably understand everything or nothing about the
definition process; but anyway I will try to spell out its rules more carefully.
One writes in general
        def token string0 #1 string1 #2 string2 ... #k stringk {right-hand side}
where "token" is any token except { or }, and where string0 ... stringk are
strings of zero or more tokens not including { or } or # or |; spaces are
ignored in these strings. I am describing the general case; the above definition
of MIX is the simplest case of the general form, where k is zero and string0 is
empty.

When the defined token is recognized, a matching process ensues until the
left-hand side is completely matched: tokens in string0...stringk must match
exactly with corresponding tokens of the input text (removing all spaces),
with error messages if a failure to match occurs. The #j's are matched to
tokens or to {...} groups. No expansion is done on the {...} groups, they are

merely treated as an uninterrupted sequence of tokens. There is at most one
definition active per token at any time. Once the matching process is
complete, TEX will have found the ingredients to be substituted for #1 through
#k in the right-hand side. These are simply copied into the positions
occupied by #1 ... #k in the right-hand sequence. And one further change is
made: the first # is removed from any sequence of two or more #'s. This is
done so that definitions can be made in the right-hand side without causing
confusion with the current definition.

For example, consider what happens when the following definition is active:
        def A #1 B C {def E ##1{##1 #1 #1}}.
If the internal input file contains
        A {X-y} B C D
the resulting sequence after expanding the definition will be
        def E #1{#1 {X-y} {X-Y}}D
(note the spacing).

If the character | appears just before the { which introduces the right-hand
side of a definition, the space if any after the last token matched will
be preserved. Thus, in the above example if we had written
        def A #1 B C|{def E ##1{##1 #1 #1}}
the result would have been
        def E #1{#1 {X-y} {X-y}} D.
This feature was used in our definition of MIX on a previous page, because
it will preserve the space that comes after MIX in mid-sentence; on the
other hand, most definitions (for example, xskip) would not use this feature.

The above is not the most general sort of macro definition facility, but I
have applied Occam's razor. A much more general capability is available via
TEX "routines" which are explained later; routines are for the more
experienced users. The reader should now be able to look back at the
definitions given above for quoteformat, algstep, and eqalign, discovering
that they are really quite simple after all.

Some tokens are not defined as macros but stand for actions to be carried out.
For example, "fnt" means the following non-space token is to be the name
of the current font of type, and "def" means that TEX is supposed to absorb
a new definition. Thus we have four mutually exclusive sorts of tokens:
        defined tokens
        action tokens
        { and }
        other tokens.
The { and } denote grouping and separate levels of context; definitions and
assignment actions made inside {...} do not have any effect outside.

Assignment actions affect TEX's transformation of the input. They are:
        fnt token   to change the current font
        hsize length   normal width of generated lines of text
        vsize length   normal height of generated pages of text
        hmargin length distance from left edge of paper to generated lines

vmargin length	distance from top edge of paper to generated pages
lineskip glue	spacing between generated lines
parskip glue	additional spacing between paragraphs (added to lineskip)
dispskip glue	additional spacing above and below displayed formulas
boxskip glue	additional spacing below an inserted box
noteskip glue	additional spacing above footnotes
tabskip glue	horizontal spacing between tabaligned columns
parindent length	indentation on first line of paragraphs
hangindent length	indentation on all but first line of paragraph
	(hangindent reset to zero after every paragraph)

All of these quantities will have default values, which I will choose after
TEX is up and running; the default values will apply whenever a quantity has
not been respecified. In the above, ''length'' is of the form

  token unit   or   - token unit

where the token is a digit string or a digit string containing a period (decimal
point), and where ''unit'' is either pt, pc, in, cm, or mm. Furthermore ''glue''
is of the form

  length plus length minus length

where the plus and minus parts cannot be negative; any of the three lengths
can be omitted if zero.

For example, standard XGP conventions at the moment are to produce 8 1/2 by 11
inch pages with one-inch margins and interline spacing of 4 pixels; this would
be specified by

  hsize 6.5 in vsize 9 in hmargin 1 in vmargin 1 in lineskip .02 in

At the outermost level, TEX has implicitly preceded the input by "TEXpublish{",
where TEXpublish is a routine that repeatedly calls on the page-builder, the
page-builder is a routine that repeatedly calls on the paragraph-builder,
and the paragraph-builder is a routine that reads the input and emits strings
of justified lines of text. TEXpublish simply prints each page that it gets;
our example text input substitutes the more sophisticated routine ACPpages for
TEXpublish.

In the first implementation of TEX, routines like ACPpages will be written in
SAIL code and loaded with TEX. I have had some notion of adding an interpretive
system to TEX and a mini-programming language so that such extensions are
easier to make without penetrating into TEX's innards, but on second thought
it seems much better to assume that TEX's code will be sufficiently clean
that it will best be extended using SAIL code. This will save the implementors
considerable time and make the system run faster.

Let's continue the outside-in approach by sketching the SAIL code for ACPpages.
Remember that this is not basic TEX, but the code resembles the internal program
of TEX. It is at the moment only an initial approximation to the real SAIL
code, since I will have to think more about how TEX will look inside before I
can be more specific.

```
if scan("starting") then
        begin scanreqd("at"); scanreqd("page"); spage←nextnonspacetoken;
        end else spage←"1";
```

{Here "scan" is a TEX routine which looks at the next nonspace token from the input; if it equals the specified token, scan returns true and discards the token, otherwise the current input token is not passed over and false is returned. The routine "scanreqd" is similar, but instead of returning false it will produce an error message like "Syntax error, I will insert missing #". The net result of the above code is to set spage to the string representing the specified starting page, or by default to set it to "1".}

```
        if spage = "r" then
                begin rnumeral←true; lop(spage);
                end;
        pageno←intscan(spage, brchar);
```

{Roman numeral page numbers are indicated by r1, r2, etc. Now pageno is the integer number of the desired first page and rnumeral is true if and only if roman numeral page numbers are desired.}

```
        scanreqd(leftbrace);
        put_on_stack_something_to_make_matching_right_brace_end_the_input;
        while true do
                begin cpage←nextpage;
                if not cpage then done;
```

{Here cpage is a pointer to a box or the null record pointer when the input has terminated.}

```
        if rnumeral then spage←cvrom(pageno) else spage←cvs(pageno);
        if omithead then {this would be set by "titlepage" routine}
                begin omithead←false;
                output_cpage_with_blanks_for_top_headline_and_with_spage_in_
                9_point_type_centered_as_a_new_line_at_the_bottom;
                end
        else    begin if pageno land 1 then {right-hand page}
                        begin texta←the_running_right_head;
                        textb←attr(sectno,cpage);
```

{texta and textb are record pointers to sequences of tokens; "attr" gets the sectno attribute of box cpage, as explained below}

```
                        line←pointer_to_box_which_TEX_would_make_from_the_input
                        "{textb} hfill {texta} rjust to .375 in {spage}"
                        end else
                        begin texta←the_running_left_head;
                        textb←attr(sectno,first(cpage));
                        line←pointer_to_box_which_TEX_would_make_from_the_input
                        "ljust to .375 in {spage} texta hfill textb"
                        end;
                place_line_above_cpage_with_14_pt_glue_and_output_the_result;
                end;
        pageno←pageno+1;
        end;
```

{In other words, odd-numbered pages get the sectionnumber attribute of cpage and the running right headline followed by a right-justified page number, as the title line; even-number pages get a left-justified page number followed by the running left headline followed by the sectionnumber attribute of the first component of cpage. Note that the section number is supposed to represent the top of a left-hand page but the bottom of a right-hand page.}

The above example indicates that we need to discuss another basic feature of TEX, namely the "attributes" which can be attached to its boxes. One such attribute is the section number; another is the height, another is the width; still others, used in math formulas, are the amounts of space available inside the box, if any, that may be used to attach subscripts and superscripts. For each attribute, two routines are supplied, explaining how to produce the attribute of a box formed from two boxes placed together horizontally or vertically. For example, the height attribute is replaced by max(h1,h2) when two boxes are joined horizontally but by h1+h2 when they are joined vertically. The section-number attribute is s1 if s2 is null, otherwise it is s2; and so on.

Now let's consider the page-building routine "nextpage"; this gives us a chance to study the process TEX uses for vertical justification, which introduces some of the concepts we will need in the more complicated routine used for horizontal justification.

The first idea is the concept of "badness." This is a number computed on the basis of the amount of stretching or shrinking necessary when setting the glue. Suppose we have a list of n boxes (either a horizontal list or a vertical list), separated by n-1 specifications of glue. Let w be the desired total length of the list (i.e., the desired width or height, depending on which dimension we are justifying); let x be the actual total length of boxes and glue; and let y,z be the total amount of glue parameters for expansion and contraction. The badness of this situation is defined to be

infinite, if $x > w - z + \epsilon$, where ϵ is a small tolerance to compensate
for floating-point rounding;

$100((x-w)/z)^3$, if $w - z + \epsilon \geq x > w$;

0, if $x = w$;

$100((w-x)/3y)^3$, if $w > x$;

plus penalties charged for breaking lines in comparatively undesirable places.

According to these formulas, stretching by y has a badness rating of 100/27, or about 3.7; stretching by 2y is rated about 30; stretching by 3y is rated 100 units of badness, and so is shrinking by the maximum amount z. I plan to charge a penalty of something like 80 units for breaking a paragraph or displayed formula in such a way that only one line comes by itself on a page; thus, for instance, a five-line paragraph gets a penalty of 80 if we break after the first or fourth line, but no penalty if we break after two or three lines. I will of course be tuning these formulas to make them correspond as well as I can to my aesthetic perceptions of bad layout. The user will be able to specify his own additional penalty points for undesirable breaking between specific lines (e.g. in a MIX program to break before an instruction that refers to *-1). A penalty is also made for break at "ruled" vertical glue.

The nextpage routine forms a list of lines (and the connecting vertical glue) which it receives from the nextparagraph routine; the nextparagraph routine returns a sequence g1 h1 ... gk hk alternating between vertical glue and boxes representing horizontally justified lines of text. The individual h's are not broken up or examined by nextpage, except to look at their attributes. Also \ff and end-of-input codes will be transmitted by nextparagraph to the nextpage routine.

The nextpage routine accumulates lines until its previous accumulation plus
the new paragraph is greater than or equal to the specified page height, vsize.
Then it breaks the new paragraph just after the jth line, for $0{\le}j{\le}k$, whichever
value of j has the minimum badness; if this minimum occurs for more than one
j, the largest such j is used. Then the glue g(j+1) is discarded, and the
remaining k-j lines are carried over to the next page. (They are immediately
checked to ensure that they don't already overfill the new page, and they are
broken in the same way if necessary.)

A boxinsert interrupts this otherwise straightforward procedure. The box to
be inserted is computed, off to the side, and then an attempt is made to place
it over the current accumulated page. If it fits, well and good, we leave it
there. If not, it is carried over to the next page, and placed in front of any
carryover from the present page. Additional box-inserts are inserted below
the first one, in a natural but hard-to-explain manner.

Footnotes: I have used footnotes only three times in over 2000 pages of The Art of
Computer Programming, and personally I believe they should usually be avoided, so
I am not planning an elaborate footnoting mechanism (e.g. to break long footnotes
between pages or to mark the first footnote per page with an asterisk and the
second with a dagger, etc.). They can otherwise be satisfactorily handled by
attaching a footnote attribute to any line referring to a footnote, and by
requiring the nextpage routine to put the footnote on the page containing that
line. This, together with the badness ratings, will solve the problem about
footnote references on the bottom line preempting the space needed for the
footnote itself, etc. A user will be able to get fancier footnotes if he doesn't
mind rewriting a few of TEX's routines.

On \ff or end-of-input, the nextpage routine simulates "vfill blankline" and
clears its page buffers, unless they were already empty. After end-of-input it
returns a null page, to signal the end of its activity; after \ff it asks
nextparagraph for more.

The nextparagraph routine assembles lines of width hsize, pausing to
transmit them
  a) at end of paragraph ('13);
  b) at beginning of display formula ($$);
  c) at end of display formula ($$);
  d) just before vskip operation;
  e) just before and after blankline, ctrline, ljustline, rjustline, hjustline;
  f) at \ff or end-of-input.
The operations in (e) produce independent lines of width hsize that are not
part of a paragraph, and such lines are merely transmitted without change.
Display formulas are also passed without change, except that appropriate glue
is attached above and below them. (The glue above a displayed equation is
reduced from dispskip to lineskip if the text on the preceding line does not
overhang the displayed formula after centering.)

The text of a paragraph, or of the portion of a paragraph beginning and/or ending
at $$, is indented (if appropriate) and passed to the hjust routine. The hjust

routine attempts to break the text into lines of length hsize in the least bad
way, taking proper account of hangindent. The "least bad" way is a way which
minimizes the maximum badness of any of the breaks made. At this point in the
process, the text consists of a possibly long sequence of boxes, separated by
glue, and these boxes will not be changed by the hjust routine. The hjust
routine has a new feature which makes it superior to existing justification
systems, besides the idea of variable-weight glue, namely it effectively "looks
ahead" so that the situation in the later lines of a paragraph can influence
the breaks in the earlier lines. I have noticed quite a few places where such
a justification routine will provide substantially better output. This
lookahead is accomplished by applying the principles of "dynamic programming,"
as I will try to explain below.

First let's understand what the boxes processed by hjust usually look like. They
might be large complicated boxes, which are to be treated as black boxes
essentially as the nextpage routine treats its lines; but mostly the individual
boxes at this point will be individual letters from one or more fonts. When
a text token comes along, the current font indicator is attached to it (so that
the 7-bit code becomes a 12-bit code), and the token is broken into its
individual characters. Pairs of adjacent characters are examined, from left
to right, using tables associated with the font; this is used to compute
changes in the glue between characters, and to produce ligatures if they are
present, etc. For example, on most fonts the sequence `''` will want to have
specially narrow glue between the two characters. We get ligatures by
replacing

f f	by	\<ff\>
f i	by	\<fi\>
f l	by	\<fl\>
\<ff\> i	by	\<ffi\>
\<ff\> l	by	\<ffl\>.

Such ligature formation and glue adjustment takes place when the character boxes
are being appended to the current line, before hyphenation etc.; this means that
we lose the chance to break "shuffling" into "shuff-ling", but so what.

The \<space\> token is changed into glue between boxes, with y=x and z=x/2 as
explained earlier. The hskip and quad actions also produce variable glue. Whenever
this glue has x or y greater than or equal to the spacing width of the current
font, it is an acceptable place to break the line with no penalty. Another
acceptable place is after an explicit hyphen. (Some hskips, used for backspacing,
have negative x; they are, of course, unacceptable breaks.) TEX will give double
y glue to the first space that follows a period, exclamation point, question mark,
or colon, unless letters or digits intervene before this space. A semicolon and
comma are treated similarly, but with 1.5 and 1.25 as the relative amounts of
y glue.

The math formula routine which processes $...$ will yield a sequence of boxes in
format compatible with the text strings outside of formulas; acceptable places
to break in formulas will be marked just after binary operators and relations.
A penalty is attached to such breaks; I will have to tune the parameters, but the
following idea appears to be best: Relations like =, $\leq$, $\equiv$, etc. have only a small

penalty, operations like +, -, x, / have a larger penalty, with - larger than
the others. Superscripts and subscripts and function arguments and the like will
be attached unbreakably to their boxes.

There are three "discretionary" symbols used to provide or inhibit breaks:
>   \-   OK to hyphenate this word here;
>   \+   do not hyphenate here;
>   *   OK to break here, but insert a times sign not a hyphen.

The last of these would be used in a long product like $(n+1)*(n+2)*(n+3)*(n+4)$.

Besides using the permissible breaks, TEX will try to hyphenate words.
It will do this only in a sequence of lower-case letters that is preceded and
followed by anything other than a letter, digit, -, \-, or \+. Note that,
for example, already-hyphenated compound words will not be broken. If a
permissible hyphenation break is discovered, a penalty of say 30 units of badness
will be paid, but this may be better than not hyphenating at all. An additional
20 units of badness is charged for breaking a word or formula in the last
line of a paragraph.

There is no point in finding all possible places to hyphenate. For one thing,
the problem is extremely difficult, since e.g. the word "record" is supposed to
be broken as "rec-ord" when it is a noun but "re-cord" when it is a verb.
Consider the word "hyphenation" itself, which is rather an exception:
>   hy-phen-a-tion   vs.   co-or-di-na-tion

Why does the n go with the a in one case and not the other? Starting at letter
a in the dictionary and trying to find rigorous rules for hyphenation without
much knowledge, we come up against a-part vs. ap-er-ture, aph-o-rism vs. a-pha-sia,
etc. It becomes clear that what we want is not an accurate but ponderously slow
routine that consumes a lot of memory space and processing time, instead we want
a set of hyphenation rules that are
>   a) simple;
>   b) almost always safe;
>   c) powerful enough to find say 80% of the words already hyphenated in
>   The Art of Computer Programming.

To justify point (c), I find that there are about 2 hyphenated words per page
in the books, and the places where the rules I shall propose do not find the
identical hyphenation only very rarely would cause a really bad break. The
time needed to handle the remaining exceptions is therefore insignificant by
comparison with what I already do when proof-reading.

So here are the rules I came up with.
1. Consider only breaks in which both parts contain a vowel other than final e.
(Vowels are a,e,i,o,u,y.)
2. Subject to 1, break before the following "safe" suffixes:
-cious -gion -ly -ment -mial -nary -ness -nomial -sion -tion -ture -vious
and also -tive preceded by a vowel, -ed preceded by d or t.
Break before -ing except in -bling -pling or when preceded by a double letter
other than ll or ss or zz; for other double letters, break between them.
If the word ends in s or ly, strip off this ending and apply these rules again.
Suffixes recognized by this rule must not be further broken except vi-ous.

3. Subject to 1 and 2, break after the following "safe" prefixes:
algo- equi- ex- hyper- ini- intro- lex- lexi- math- mathe- max- maxi- mini- multi-
out- over- pseudo- semi- some- sub- super- there- under-
Also be- followed by c,h,s,w; dis- followed by anything but h,y; trans- followed
by a,f,g,l,m; tri- followed by a,f,p,u.
4. Subject to 1 and 2, combine an h with the previous letter if it is a consonant,
treating the combination as a consonant; then it's OK to break between the two
consonants in the pattern vc-cv except when the pair of consonants is
    bl ck cl cr dr ght gl gr lk ll nd ng pl rch rd rm rt sch sp ss st thr zz
(I may have to revise this list.)

There will be rare exceptions (e.g., equivocate, minister, somersault, triphammer),
but these will be so infrequent as to be unimportant. Looking through quite a few
pages of volume 3, I found 48 hyphenations, and the above rules were satisfactory
except in the three cases
            de-gree   hap-hazard   re-placement.
Of course, these rules are biased toward my vocabulary and subject matter, but a
few extensions should make it work well enough for nearly everybody.

Now for the dynamic programming algorithm which minimizes the maximum badness of
breaks. The badness formula is the same as before; thus for each break after a given
point we can compute the resulting badness. In this way, for each permissible
break position, we will minimize the maximum badness that can occur counting this
and previous breaks. The running time will be approximately linear in the
number of possible breaks.

However, this will be rather slow since it tries breaking all words when in practice
only a few candidate words really need to be considered. Thus the following
approximate method should run about ten times faster: Given the best three ways to
break the kth line, use these to find the best three ways to break the (k+1)st
line. The breaks found will almost certainly be optimum unless the situation
is very bad anyway.

To conclude this memo, I should explain how TEX is going to work on
math formulas. However, I will have to sketch out the code in more detail
and it is only fuzzy in my mind at the moment. My plan is to use the
top-down precedence parsing approach introduced by Vaughan Pratt in his
1973 POPL paper, and used so successfully by him in CGOL (for example).
Further details will be forthcoming; I hope to do the box pasting in
one pass, but it may be necessary to build the parse tree first as
Kernighan and Cherry do.

(end of the file TEXDR.AFT)

---

13 May: Prepared for Bit Fiddling lecture. Bed early

14 May: To Sacramento with Jill (Library associates' tour)
Saw examples of fine printing

---

15 May: Completion of tour.
Finished preparing talk for tomorrow

16 May: Got typography books from library
Began teaching 1-week course about writing.
Also gave hour lecture on "Bit Fiddling"
Went to organ lecture in evening; also movie `Anna & King of Siam"

17 May: Unsuccessful attempt to replace splines by "squines" (piecewise quadratics)

18 May: Took slides of 20 pp from vols 1 & 2
Sketched programs for font generation
Dinner with Kai Yuen and Shahid. Bed early

19 May: Using slides, found out how the lower case works. Up during the night continuing to build up information re fonts.

20 May: More font building, at 5 a.m. had rough draft of l.c. and u.c.
Roman and italics and digits 0-9.

21 May: Completed notes on standard fonts, prepared computer programs for spline plotting

22 May: Sawed bamboo for music room hanging
de Bruijn arrives. We go to potluck dinner at church and then talk mathematics

⋮

13 Jun: Moved out of office at school: Sabbatical begins!
Went to movies (Network and Lenny)

14 Jun: Some debugging on fonts,
ran into snag not knowing what magnitude to give the derivatives.

15 Jun: All day trying to find right way to define derivatives —
all night
breakthrough came about 1 am : final solution very beautiful (4am)!
Went to bed at 7am

16 Jun: Up at 11
At AI lab debugging new spline program, after lunch with Jill's Uncle Don
Got "kinks" out of the program (see the first letters and you will
see what I mean)
Went to bed at 4am

17 Jun: Hanging the new macrame in music room
Made crucial refinements to spline-font program

18 Jun: Rehearse with orchestra for tomorrow's cantata performance (Bach 103)
Entered changes to font program and split it into separately-compiled parts

19 Jun: A Happy Father's Day.
Went bike riding (all four of us) on Cañada Road past the
water temple
Played "Bermuda Triangle" with John and Jenny

20 Jun: Correspondence catchup day. Talked to Lyle Ramshaw about splines
Chinese banquet arranged by Gene Golub's numerical analysis symposium
Then went to AI lab and got font program 'working' 4am

21 Jun: Experiments with smaller and smaller resolution reveal new
things to fix.
Set up TV camera in lab for font experiments

Chapter 25

TEX.ONE

When we left our hero at the end of Chapter 24, he was wrestling intensely with the problem of font generation by computational methods, having more-or-less disposed of the typesetting problem with his memo TEXDR.AFT. He had circulated that memo to several colleagues in May; now July was approaching, and so was a month-long trip to Southeast Asia. It was time to revise the draft of 13 May so that research assistants Michael Plass and Frank Liang could prepare a prototype implementation while he was away.

---

30 Jun: up late Wednesday, tried again for eight hours to finish the letter "s".
Not feeling very good, will not go onto this kind of goofy schedule any more.

---

1 Jul: Hurray, success on ess after 4 hrs. calculations (4:30 am today). Made me feel better.
Got typhoid & cholera shots for China trip.

---

2 Jul: Cleaned up font program, added punctuation, put it away.
Slept and slept

---

3 Jul: Read PUB manual and III manuals

---

4 Jul: to Wiederholds for Wirth goodbye party
Then watched fireworks at Draper mansion
A day of needed rest!

---

5 Jul: Slept late, then thought about data structures for TEX

---

6 Jul:	Measured the way formulas are set Dinner party at Wreden mansion, met interesting people
7 Jul:	Got many of TEX's data structures specified; redesigned the language and rewrote 3/4 of the draft MS.
8 Jul:	Went shopping with Jill More TEX writing
9 Jul:	Finished writing up "TEX.ONE", went to AI lab to type in first 8 pp
10 Jul:	John plays in Little League all star game, gets two hits Finished typing TEX.ONE at 2am
11 Jul:	Two weeks' correspondence — not bad, actually, finished in two or three hours Began to write program that converts Belfast form to near-TEX
12 Jul:	Long meeting with Mike and Frank to discuss plans for TEX implementation. Edited TEX.ONE draft making various improvements to the language

Here then is the file TEX.ONE:

Preliminary description of TEX   D Knuth, July 12, 1977

In this memo I will try to explain the proposed TEX system for preparing
publishable documents. Some of its rules are still undergoing change, but
for the most part this memo defines the system being implemented, for the
benefit of the implementors. [Note: If you already have read the preliminary
version of this preliminary description, please forget everything that was
in that document and try to forget that it ever existed. Major changes have
occurred, based on the valuable feedback received after circulating that
document, so now let's move on to the real thing.]

TEX is for technical text. Insiders pronounce the X as a Greek Chi (cf. the
Scottish 'ch' sound in 'Loch Ness') since the word 'technical' stems from a
Greek root meaning art as well as technology. I am preparing the system
primarily for use in publishing my series The Art of Computer Programming--
the initial system will be tuned for my books, but it will not be difficult to
extend it for other purposes if anybody wants to do so.

The input to TEX is a file in say TVeditor format at the Stanford AI lab.
The output is a sequence of pages, produced in "one pass," suitable for
printing on various devices. This report tries to explain how to get from
input to output. The main idea is to consider the process as an operation on
two-dimensional "boxes"; roughly speaking, the input is a long string of
characters culled from a variety of fonts, where each character may be
thought of as occupying a small rectangular box, and the output is obtained
by gluing these boxes together either horizontally or vertically with
various conventions about centering and justification, finally arriving at
big rectangular boxes which are the desired pages. While LISP works with
one-dimensional character strings, TEX works with two-dimensional box patterns;
TEX has both horizontal and vertical 'cons' operations. Furthermore, TEX has
another important basic concept of elastic glue between boxes, a type of
mortar that stretches and shrinks at different specified rates so that box
patterns will fit together in flexible ways. (I should really use the word
"mortar" instead of "glue" throughout this document; the only trouble is,
the extra syllable makes mortar harder to pronounce, and it takes longer
to type the word besides. Maybe the user's manual will say "mortar" consistently;
the present document is emphatically NOT a user's manual.)

In order to explain TEX more fully, I will alternate between very low-level
descriptions of exactly how the processing takes place and very high-level
descriptions of what you type to get complex effects.

First, at the very lowest level, we must realize that the input to TEX is not
really a string of boxes, it is a file of 7-bit characters. This file is called
an "external input file". Seven of the visible printing characters will have
special uses in such files; throughout this memo I will use the symbols
\{}$⊛%# for them, but there will be a way to dedicate other symbols to these
purposes if desired. The seven basic delimiters are
  \ the escape character used to indicate control mode rather than text mode
  { beginning of a group
  } ending of a group
  $ beginning and ending of math formulas
  ⊛ alignment tab
  % beginning of comment
  # macro parameter
The first thing TEX does is convert an external input file to an "internal
input file" by essentially obeying the following rules:

    1. Delete the first TVeditor directory page, if it exists.
    2. Replace the end-of-page marks ('14) on every remaining page by
carriage returns ('15). Delete all line-feed symbols ('12), null symbols ('00),
deletion codes ('177), and vertical tabs ('13). Replace all horizontal tabs ('11)
by spaces ('40). Delete all % marks and the sequences of characters following
them up to (but not including) the next carriage return.
    3. Delete all blank spaces ('40) following carriage-returns.
    4. If two or more carriage returns occur in sequence, replace all
of them by vertical-tab characters ('13). These are used to specify

end of paragraphs in TEX; in other words, the user specifies end of paragraph by hitting two carriage returns in a row, or by end of page following a carriage return.

    5. Replace all remaining carriage-returns by blank spaces.

    6. If two or more blank spaces occur in a row, replace them by a single blank space.

    7. Replace \ by '00, ⊛ by '11, \$ by '12, { by '14, } by '15, # by '177 (assuming that these are the basic delimiters mentioned above).

    8. Add infinitely many '15 symbols at the right.

The reason for rule 8 is that TEX uses { and } for grouping, and the trailing '15's (which are equivalents of }'s) will match up with any {'s the user erroneously forgot to match in the external input file. By following the above rules, TEX obtains an internal input file containing no appearances of the seven basic delimiters, and with no two blank spaces in a row. Spacing in the output document is controlled by other features of TEX, and the seven basic delimiters can be snuck in if necessary by using e.g. \ascii'173 for the symbol {.

[Actually there are nine basic delimiters; the other two are ↑ and ↓, for superscripts and subscripts respectively, but only within math formulas. Due to the discrepancies between various vintages of ASCII codes, Stanford codes are not universal; in particular, code '13 at MIT is the character ↑. There is a way to specify ↑ as one of the nine basic delimiters, even at MIT, and TEX will treat it properly -- not deleting it in rule 2 and not confusing it with the character inserted in rule 4. TEX doesn't really apply rules 1-8 as stated, it uses an efficient algorithm which has the net effect of these rules.]

Now let's shift to a high level and show how the user can specify complex typesetting requirements to TEX. The following example is rather long and it deserves to be skimmed rather than studied in detail; I devised it mainly to serve as test data during initial development of the system. Don't study it now, just glance at it and move to the next part of the memo. (Note: I based the example on the opening pages of my book Seminumerical Algorithms, but I skipped over lots of copy when the typesetting presented no essentially new challenges to the system. Thus, the example concentrates on difficult constructions, and it is by no means typical. The reader who eventually does dig into its fine points might find it useful to have the book in hand for comparison purposes.)

```
\require ACPhdr                                                            % 1
%Example TEX input related to Seminumerical Algorithms                     % 2
\ACPpages starting at page 1:                                             % 3
\titlepage %This tells the page format routine not to put a page number on top  % 4
\runninglefthead{RANDOM NUMBERS}                                          % 5
\ljustline{\hexpand 11 pt {\:p CHAPTER \hskip 10 pt THREE}}               % 6
\vskip 1 cm plus 30 pt minus 10 pt                                        % 7
\rjustline{\:q RANDOM NUMBERS}                                            % 8
\vskip .5 cm plus 1 pc minus 5 pt                                         % 9
\quoteformat{Anyone who considers arithmetical \cr                        % 10
```

```
methods of producing random digits \cr is, of course,              % 11
in a state of sin. \cr} author{JOHN VON NEUMANN (1951)}            % 12
\quoteformat{Round numbers are always false.\cr}                   % 13
author {SAMUEL JOHNSON (c. 1750)}                                  % 14
\vskip 1 cm plus 1 pc minus 5 pt                                   % 15
\runningrighthead{INTRODUCTION} section{3.1}                       % 16
\sectionbegin{3.1.                                                 % 17
INTRODUCTION}                                                      % 18
Numbers which are ``chosen at random'' are useful in a wide variety of   % 19
applications. For example:                                        % 20
     % This blank line specifies end of paragraph                 % 21
\yskip  % This means a bit of extra space between paragraphs       % 22
\textindent{a)}{\sl Simulation.}\xskip When a computer is used to simulate  % 23
natural phenomena, random numbers are required to make things realistic.   % 24
Simulation covers many fields, from the study of nuclear physics (where    % 25
particles are subject to random collisions) to systems engineering (where  % 26
people come into, say, a bank at random intervals).\par            % 27
\yskip\textindent{b)}{\sl Sampling.}\xskip It is often impractical to examine  % 28
all cases, but a random sample will provide insight into what constitutes  % 29
``typical'' behavior.                                             % 30
                                                                  % 31
\yskip It is not easy to invent a foolproof random-number generator. This fact  % 32
was convincingly impressed upon the author several years ago, when he attempted % 33
to create a fantastically good random-number generator using the following  % 34
peculiar method:                                                 % 35
                                                                  % 36
\yskip\yskip\noindent{\bf Algorithm K}\xskip(\sl``Super-random'' number  % 37
generator.}).\xskip Given a 10-digit decimal number $X$, this algorithm may be  % 38
used to change $X$ to the number which should come next in a supposedly random  % 39
sequence.\par                                                    % 40
\algstep K1. [Choose number of iterations.] Set $Y←\lfloor X/10↑9 \rfloor$,  % 41
i.e., the most significant digit of $X$. (We will execute steps K2 through K13  % 42
$Y+1$ times; that is, we will randomize the digits a {\sl random} number of  % 43
times.\par                                                        % 44
\algstep K10. [99999 modify.] If $X<10↑5$, set $X←X↑2 + 99999$;   % 45
otherwise set $X←X-99999$.\xskip\blackslug                        % 46
                                                                  % 47
\topinsert{\ctrline{\:r Table 1}                                   % 48
\ctrline{\:d A COLOSSAL COINCIDENCE: THE NUMBER 6065038420}       % 49
\ctrline{\:d IS TRANSFORMED INTO ITSELF BY ALGORITHM K.}          % 50
\vskip 3 pt \hrule                                                % 51
\ctrline{\valign{\vskip 6pt\top{#}®\vskip 6pt\top{#}\cr           % 52
\halign{\left{#}\quad®\ctr{#}®\left{#}\cr                         % 53
Step®\$X$ (after)\cr                                              % 54
\vskip 10 pt plus 10 pt minus 5 pt                                % 55
K1®6065038420\cr K12®190586778®Y=5\cr}      %end of \halign on line 53   % 56
\vskip 10 pt plus 10 pt minus 5pt \cr   %end of first column to be \valigned  % 57
\vrule                                  %vertical rule between columns   % 58
\halign{\left{#}\quad®\ctr{#}®\left{#}\cr                         % 59
```

```
Step®$X$ (after)\cr                                                        % 60
\vskip 10 pt plus 10 pt minus 5 pt                                        % 61
K10®1620063735\cr                                                         % 62
K11®1620063735\cr K12®6065038420®Y=0\cr}%end of \halign on line 59        % 63
\vskip 10 pt plus 10 pt minus 5pt \cr}} %end of 2nd \valigned column,\ctrline % 64
\hrule}                         %end of the \topinsert on line 48         % 65
\yskip\yskip The moral to this story is that {\sl random numbers should not be % 66
generated with a method chosen at random.} Some theory should be used.    % 67
                                                                          % 68
\exbegin                                                                  % 69
\tr\exno 1. [20] Suppose that you wish to obtain a decimal digit at random, not % 70
using a computer. Shifting to exercise 16, let $f(x,y)$ be a function such that % 71
if $0≤x,y<m$, then $0≤f(x,y)<m$. The sequence is constructed by selecting  % 72
$X↓0$ and $X↓1$ arbitrarily, and then letting $$                          % 73
X↓{n+1} = f(X↓n,X↓{n-1}) \qquad {\rm for} \qquad n>0.$$                    % 74
What is the maximum period conceivably attainable in this case?           % 75
                                                                          % 76
\exno 17. [10] Generalize the situation in the previous exercise so that  % 77
$X↓{n+1}$ depends on the preceding $k$ values of the sequence.            % 78
\par\vskip plus 100 cm\eject                                             % 79
\runningrighthead{GENERATING UNIFORM RANDOM NUMBERS} section{3.2}         % 80
\sectionbegin{3.2. GENERATING UNIFORM RANDOM NUMBERS}                     % 81
In this section we shall consider methods for generating a sequence of random % 82
fractions, i.e., random {\sl real numbers $U↓n$, uniformly distributed    % 83
between zero and one.} Since a computer can represent a real number with only % 84
finite accuracy, we shall actually be generating integers $X↓n$ between    % 85
zero and some number $m$; the fraction$$U↓n = X↓n/m \eqno(1)$$ will        % 86
then lie between zero and one.                                            % 87
                                                                          % 88
\vskip.4in plus.2in minus.2in                                            % 89
\runningrighthead{THE LINEAR CONGRUENTIAL METHOD} section{3.2.1}          % 90
\sectionbegin{3.2.1. The Linear Congruential Method}                     % 91
By far the most successful random number generators known today are special % 92
cases of the following scheme, introduced by D. H. Lehmer in 1948. [See   % 93
{\sl Annals Harvard Comp. Lab.} {\bf 26}(1951), 141-146.] We choose four  % 94
''magic numbers'':$$                                                      % 95
\halign{\right{#}®\left{\quad\rm{#}\qquad}®\right{#}®\left{#}\cr           % 96
X↓0,®the starting value;®X↓0≥0.\cr                                        % 97
m,®the modulus;®m®>X↓,\quad m>a,\quad m>c.\cr}\eqno(1)$$                   % 98
The desired sequence of random numbers $\langle X↓n \rangle$ is then      % 99
obtained by setting$$X↓{n+1}=(aX↓n+c)\mod m,\qquad n≥0.\eqno(2)$$This is   %100
called a {\sl linear congruential sequence.}                             %101
                                                                          %102
Let $w$ be the computer's word size. The following program computes $(aX+c)$ %103
\mod(w+1)$ efficiently:$$\halign{{\it#}\qquad®\hjust to 25pt{\left{#}}®     %104
\left{\tt#}\cr                                                            %105
01®LDAN®X\cr                                                              %106
02®MUL®A\cr 05®JANN®*+3\cr                                                %107
07®ADD®=W-1=\qquad\blackslug\cr}\eqno(2)$$                                %108
```

{\sl Proof.}\xskip We have $x=1+qp\uparrow e$ for some integer q which is not a   %109
multiple of p. By the binomial formula$$ %110
\eqalign{x\uparrow p*=1+{p\choose 1}qp\uparrow e+\cdots+{p\choose{p-1}}q\uparrow{p-1}   %111
p\uparrow{(p-1)e}+q\uparrow p\ p\uparrow{pe}}\cr   %112
*=1+qp\uparrow{e+1}\group(){1+1\over p{p\choose 2}qp\uparrow e + 1\over p   %113
{p\choose 3}q\uparrow 2\ p\uparrow{2e}+\cdots+1\over p{p\choose p}q\uparrow{p-1}   %114
p\uparrow{(p-1)e}.\cr}$$ By repeated application of Lemma P, we find that   %115
\def\mlo#1{\ ({\rm modulo}\ #1)}$$\eqalign{{(a\uparrow p\uparrow g - 1)/(a-1)*\equiv 0 \mlo   %116
{p\uparrow g},\cr(a\uparrow p\uparrow g-1)/(a-1)*\neqv 0 \mlo{p\uparrow{g+1}}.\cr}\eqno(6)$$ %117
If $1<k<p$, $p\choose k$ is divisible by p. \biglpren{\sl Note: }\xskip A   %118
generalization of this result appears in exercise 3.2.2-11(a).\bigrpren\ By   %119
Euler's theorem (exercise 1.2.4-48), $a\uparrow{\varphi(p\uparrow{e-f})}\equiv 1 \mlo   %120
{p\uparrow{e-f}}$; hence λ is a divisor of$$ %121
\lambda(p\downarrow 1\uparrow{e\downarrow 1} \ldots p\downarrow t\uparrow{e\downarrow t}) = {\rm lcm}\group()   %122
{\lambda(p\downarrow 1\uparrow{e\downarrow 1}),\ldots,\lambda(p\downarrow t\uparrow{e\downarrow t})}.\eqno(9)$$ %123
    %124
This algorithm in \MIX\ is simply$$ %125
\halign{\hjust to 25pt{\left{\tt#}}*\left{\tt#\qquad}*\left{#}\cr   %126
J6NN*\ast+2*\underline{\it A1. }j<0?}\cr   %127
STA*Z*\qquad\qquad\rightarrow Z.\cr}\eqno(7)$$ %128
That was on page 26. If we skip to page 49, $Y\downarrow 1 +\cdots+ Y\downarrow k$ will   %129
equal n with probability$$ %130
\sum\downarrow{{y\downarrow 1+\cdots+y\downarrow k=n}\atop{y\downarrow 1,\ldots,y\downarrow k\geq 0}}   %131
\prod\downarrow{1\leq s\leq k}   %132
{e\uparrow{-np\downarrow s}\group(){np\downarrow s}\uparrow{y\downarrow s}}\over{y\downarrow s!}}   %133
={e\uparrow{-n}n\uparrow n}\over{n!}.$$ %134
This is not hard to express in terms of n-dimensional integrals,$$ %135
{\int\downarrow{a\downarrow n}\uparrow n\ dY\downarrow n \int\downarrow{a\downarrow{n-1}}\uparrow{Y\downarrow n}   %136
dY\downarrow{n-1}\ldots\int\downarrow{a\downarrow 1}\uparrow{Y\downarrow 2}dY\downarrow 1} \over   %137
{\int\downarrow 0\uparrow n\ dY\downarrow n \int\downarrow 0\uparrow{Y\downarrow n} dY\downarrow{n-1}\ldots   %138
\int\downarrow 0\uparrow{Y\downarrow 2}dY\downarrow 1},\qquad{\rm where}\qquad a\downarrow j=   %139
\max(j-t,0).\eqno(24)$$ %140
This together with (25) implies that $$\def\rtn{\sqrt n}   %141
\mathop{lim}\downarrow{n\rightarrow\infty} s \over \rtn   %142
\sum\downarrow{\rtn s<k\leq n}{n\choose k}\group(){k\over n - s\over rtn}\uparrow k   %143
\group(){s\over\rtn + 1 - k \over n}\uparrow{n-k-1} = e\uparrow{-2s}\uparrow 2,\qquad s\geq 0,   %144
\eqno(27)$$ a limiting relationship which appears to be quite difficult to   %145
prove directly.   %146
    %147
\exbegin\exno 17. [HM26] Let t be a fixed real number. For $0\leq k\leq n$, let$$ %148
P\downarrow{nk}(x)=\int\uparrow x\downarrow{n-t}dx\downarrow n\int\downarrow{n-1-t}\uparrow t{x\downarrow n}dx\downarrow{n-1}   %149
\ldots\int\downarrow{k+1-t}\uparrow t{x\downarrow{k+2}}dx\downarrow{k+1}\int\downarrow 0\uparrow t{x\downarrow{k+1}}   %150
dx\downarrow k\ldots\int\downarrow 0\uparrow t{x\downarrow 2}dx\downarrow 1;$$ %151
Eq. (24) is equal to$$\def\sumk{\sum\downarrow{1\leq k\leq n}}   %152
\sumk X\prime\downarrow k Y\prime\downarrow k \group/.{\sqrt{\sumk{X\prime\downarrow k}\uparrow 2}   %153
\sqrt{\sumk{Y\prime\downarrow k}\uparrow 2}}.$$\par   %154
\runningrighthead{A BIG MATRIX DISPLAY} section{3.3.3.3}   %155
\subsectionbegin{3.3.3.3. This subsection doesn't exist}Finally, look at page   %156
91.$$\def\diagdots{\raise 10pt .\hskip 4pt \raise 5pt .\hskip 4pt .}   %157

```
\eqalign{U⊗=\group(){\halign{\ctr{#}⊗\ctr{#}⊗\ctr{#}⊗\ctr{#}⊗\ctr{#}⊗\ctr{#}⊗     %158
\ctr{#}\cr   1\cr   ⊗\diagdots\cr   ⊗⊗1\cr                                          %159
c↓1⊗\ldots⊗c↓{k-1}⊗1⊗c↓{k+1}⊗c↓n\cr                                                %160
⊗⊗⊗⊗1\cr⊗⊗⊗⊗⊗\diagdots\cr⊗⊗⊗⊗⊗⊗1\cr}},\cr                                          %161
U↑{-1}⊗=\group(){\halign{\ctr{#}⊗\ctr{#}⊗\ctr{#}⊗\ctr{#}⊗\ctr{#}⊗\ctr{#}⊗          %162
\ctr{#}\cr   1\cr   ⊗\diagdots\cr   ⊗⊗1\cr                                          %163
-c↓1⊗\ldots⊗-c↓{k-1}⊗1⊗-c↓{k+1}⊗-c↓n\cr                                            %164
⊗⊗⊗⊗1\cr⊗⊗⊗⊗⊗\diagdots\cr⊗⊗⊗⊗⊗⊗1\cr}}}$$                                           %165
```
This ends the test data, fortunately TEX is working fine.   %166

The first thing that must be emphasized about this example is that it is much more
complicated than ordinary TEX input, for reasons stated above. The second thing
that should be emphasized is that it is written in an extension of TEX,
not in the basic language itself. For example, "\ACPpages" in line 3 is a
special routine that prepares pages in the format of The Art of Computer
Programming. The codewords \ACPpages, \titlepage, \runninglefthead,
\runningrighthead, \quoteformat, \sectionbegin, \xskip, \yskip,
\textindent, \algstep, \exbegin, \exno, and \subsectionbegin are specific to
my books and they have been defined in terms of lower-level TEX primitives
as we shall see below. Furthermore most of the fonts used are embedded in these
hidden definitions; for example, "\sectionbegin" defines the 10 point fonts used
in the text of a section, while "\exbegin" sets up for 9 point type which is used
in the exercises. Another definition is that the word MIX is usually to be set
in the ''typewriter type'' font; the hidden definition
        \def\MIX{{\tt MIX}}
causes this to happen automatically in line 125. We shall study TEX's macro
definition mechanism later; three simple examples appear in lines 141, 152,
and 157 of the sample program, where a common idiom was given a short
definition just to save space. For curious people who want to see a more
complicated definition, here is the way \quoteformat is defined:
        \def\quoteformat#1 author#2{\lineskip 11 pt plus .5 pt minus 1 pt
                \vskip 6 pt plus 2 pt minus 2 pt
                \def\rm{\:s} \def\sl{\:t}
                {\sl \halign{\right{##}\cr#1}}
                \vskip 6 pt plus 2 pt minus 2 pt
                \rm \rjustline{#2}
                \vskip 11 pt plus 4 pt minus 2 pt}
The word "author" which appears in this definition is not preceded by the
escape character \ since it is scanned as part of the \quoteformat macro.
Please don't expect to understand this mess now, TEX is really very simple;
trust me.

In fact, let's forget all the complications for a moment and try to imagine
TEX at its simplest. Consider the following alternative to the above examples:
A file containing no occurrences of the symbol "\" is preceded by the code
        "\deffnt a METS".
Then TEX will output this file in the METS font, with all paragraphs justified.

The very first nonblank character in the external input file is taken by TEX

to be the user's escape character. The user thinks of this character pretty much as he or she thinks of the "control" key in the editor, since it precedes system instructions. Normally the file will start with
\require FILENAME
where FILENAME sets up the user's favorite default values; this has been done in line 1 of our big example. File ACPhdr begins with the sequence
\chcode'173←2. \chcode'176←3. \chcode'44←4.
\chcode'26←5. \chcode'45←6. \chcode'43←7.
\chcode'136←8. \chcode'1←9.
which, at Stanford, defines the characters {}$%# to be the basic delimiters 2,3,4,5,6,7,8, and 9, respectively; but most users won't ever deal with such low-level trivia since they will be using somebody else's \require file. The \ACPhdr file also defines codewords like \quoteformat and other standard Art of Computer Programming conventions.

Now let's penetrate past line 1 of the example and see if we can figure out any more. The beginning of a chapter is generally complex from a typographic standpoint, and lines 3-18 of the example are devoted to getting through these initial complications; the chapter really starts at line 19. Let us now muster up enough courage to tackle lines 3-18.

The specification of \runninglefthead in line 5 gives the copy that is to appear in the top line of left-hand pages in the book. Line 6 contains the first actual text to appear on the page; but look first at line 8, which is simpler: Line 8 says to use font q (which ACPhdr has defined to be "Computer Modern Gothic Bold 20 point", a font that I am currently designing) for the words RANDOM NUMBERS, and to right-justify them on the line (\rjustline). Line 6 is similar but it uses a different font, font p (which turns out to be Computer Modern Gothic 11 point type); a TEX user can have up to 32 fonts, named @, A or a, B or b, ..., Z or z, [, | or <,], ↑, and ← respectively (cf. ascii code, any character can be used and its low five bits are relevant). Font @ is special, it is the only font whose characters are allowed to have different heights and baselines; the other fonts will define constant baseline and box height for each of their characters. Furthermore, TEX assumes that some of its math symbols are on font @.

Continuing in line 6, "\hskip 10 pt" stands for 10 points of horizontal space, and "\hexpand 11 pt" means to take the line and stretch it 11 points wider than it would ordinarily be. Note that font definitions within {...} disappear outside the braces. So do all other definitions.

It is time to explain TEX's mechanism for stretching and shrinking. Sizes in TEX can be specified in terms of points, picas, inches, centimeters, or millimeters, using the abbreviations pt, pc, in, cm, mm respectively; these abbreviations are meaningful only in contexts where physical lengths are used, and one of these units must always be supplied in such contexts even when the length is 0. (One inch equals 6 picas equals 72 points equals 2.54 centimeters equals 25.4 millimeters.) The glue between boxes has three components:
the fixed component, x

the plus component, y
the minus component, z
The x part is "normal" spacing which is used when boxes are strung together
without modification. When expanding a sequence of boxes to more
than their normal length, as on line 6, each x part in the glue is increased
by some multiple of the y part. When shrinking, each x part is decreased by
some multiple of the corresponding z part.

For example, given four boxes bound together by glue of specifications
(x1,y1,z1), (x2,y2,z2), (x3,y3,z3),
expansion of the line by an amount w is achieved by using the spacing
x1 + y1 w', x2 + y2 w', x3 + y3 w',
where w' = w/(y1+y2+y3). The expansion is impossible if w>0 and y1+y2+y3=0.
The system tries hard to minimize bad-looking expansions, by having a
reasonably intelligent justification routine (described below). When
shrinking a line, the maximum amount of contraction is the sum of the z's, no
tighter fit will be attempted; thus, one should define the z width so that
x-z is the minimum space tolerated. The proper setting of y is such that x+y
is a reasonable spacing but x+3y is about at the threshold of intolerability.
Parameters y and z must be nonnegative, but x may be negative (for backspacing
and overlap) if care is used.

The notation "\hskip 10 pt" in line 6 means that x = 10 pt, y = 0, and z = 0
in the horizontal glue between CHAPTER and THREE. If this \hskip hadn't been
used, the normal conventions would have applied. Namely, the glue between
CHAPTER and THREE would have had x=w (the normal interword spacing for the font),
and y = w/8, z = w/2. The glue between letters has (say) x = 0, y = w/18,
and z = w/6; thus the expansion without using \hskip would have
gone mostly into the space between CHAPTER and THREE, but by using
\hskip as shown the expansion spreads out the individual letters. Fonts to
be used with TEX will have such letter spacing indicated as an additional feature;
TEX will also recognize things like the end of sentences, giving slightly more
white space after punctuation marks where appropriate. Symbols like + and =
conventionally are surrounded by spaces, while symbol pairs like '' and := are
moved closer together; the symbols + and = are not surrounded by spaces when
they appear in subscripts. Such things are taken care of in the same way that
ligatures are handled, by making the fonts a little smarter under TEX's control,
as described in more detail later.

Much of TEX is symmetrical between horizontal and vertical, although the basic
idea of building lines first rather than columns first is asymmetrically built
in to the standard routines (because of the way we normally write). The
specification "\vskip" on line 7 specifies vertical glue analogous to
horizontal glue. When the page justification routine tries to fill the first
page of the example text (by breaking between pages ideally at the end of a
paragraph, or in a place where at least two lines of a paragraph appear on
both pages), this glue will expand or shrink in the vertical dimension using
x = 1 centimeter, y = 30 points, z = 10 points. Further variable glue is
specified in the definition of \quoteformat: \lineskip is the inter-line spacing,
and the \vskips give special additional spacing between quotation and author

lines. In the main text, the printer would refer to the type as "10 on 12", meaning 10 point type with 12 points between corresponding parts of adjacent lines; TEX will use a 10 point font with

\lineskip 12 pt plus .25 pt minus .25 pt

so that its line spacing is somewhat more flexible. Additional spacing between paragraphs is given by

\parskip 0 pt plus 1 pt minus 0 pt

and there is other spacing between exercises, steps in algorithms, etc. The definition

\def\yskip {\vskip 3 pt plus 2 pt minus 2 pt}

is used for special vertical spacing, for example in lines 22 and 37. A horizontal skip

\def\xskip {\hskip 6 pt plus 3.5 pt minus 3.5 pt}

is used in lines 23, 37, etc. in contexts where a larger than normal space is psychologically acceptable; for such purposes, flexible glue is especially useful. Larger horizontal spaces called \quad and \qquad are used for example in line 96; these are "one em" and "two ems" of space, respectively, units frequently used in mathematical typesetting.

The generality of flexible glue can be appreciated when you consider the hypothetical definition

\def\hfill {\hskip 0 cm plus 1000 cm minus 0 cm}.

In this case, y is essentially infinite (10 meters long). When such an \hfill code appears at the beginning of a line, it right justifies that line; when it appears at both the beginning and end, it centers the line; when it appears in the middle it neatly partitions the line; and so on. These aspects of TEX's variable glue seem to make it superior to existing justification systems, because it provides new features in a rather simple way and at the same time reduces the old features to a common pattern.

Once a list of boxes has been justified, all the glue is permanently set and the overall box becomes rigid. Justification is either horizontal or vertical. Horizontal justification of long lines includes some automatic hyphenation; further details about justification appear later in this memo.

Now let's look at more of the example. Lines 21 and 31, etc., are blank lines indicating the end of a paragraph; another way to specify this is ''\par'' in line 27. Line 124 is an end of a paragraph that ends with a displayed formula. Paragraphs are normally indented; one of the TEX commands subsumed under "\sectionbegin" in line 17 is

\parindent 20 pt

which affects the first line of every paragraph unless "\noindent" appears as on line 37. The "\sectionbegin" routine also specifies "\noindent" on the very first paragraph of the section, since this is the standard format in my books. On line 23 we have "\textindent{a)}", which creates a box of width \parindent containing the characters "a)" followed by a blank space, right-justified in this box.

In line 23 the "\sl" means "use slanted font." I have tentatively decided to replace italics by a slanted version of the normal "Roman" typeface, for

emphasized words in the text, while variable symbols in math formulas will
still be in italics as usual. I will have to experiment with this, but my
guess is that it will look a lot better, since typical italic fonts do not
tie together into words very beautifully. At any rate I will be distinguishing
slanted from italic, in case it becomes desirable to use two different fonts
for these different purposes. The "\bf" in line 37 stands for boldface. All
these fonts are defined in \sectionbegin, whose definition is hidden to you.
The periods in lines 84 and 101 are ''slanted''; this places them properly
close to the preceding letter, since a little space usually will intervene
when slant mode goes off.

Mathematical formulas all appear between $...$ pairs, cf. lines 38 and 41,
or between $$...$$ pairs (displayed equations). A special syntax is used in
formulas, modeled on that of Kernighan and Cherry, Comm. ACM 18 (March 1975),
151-157. For example, "↑9" in line 41 specifies a superscript 9, "↓{n+1}"
in line 74 specifies a subscript n+1. Math-structure operators like
↑ and ↓ take action only within $'s. All letters in formulas
are set in italics unless they form part of a recognized word or are
surrounded by "{\rm ...}" or "\hjust...", etc. Digits and
punctuation marks like semicolons or parentheses, etc., come out in roman
type in math mode unless specified {\it...} as in line 127. The "1" on that
line will be italic, as will the "j", but the "0" and "?" will be roman.

Spacing within formulas is chosen by TEX, independent of spaces actually
typed, although it is possible to insert space in cases when
TEX's rules are unsatisfactory. In line 116, for example, extra space
has been specified before and after "(modulo" using the code "\ ";
space before parentheses is usually omitted, but it should not be omitted
here. The later parts of the example text are largely concerned with
complicated formulas, which will appear as shown in the corresponding parts
of volume 2. The code "\eqno(24)" (cf. line 140) will insert "(24)" at the right
margin, vertically centered on the corresponding displayed formula, if there
is room, otherwise an attempt is made to move the formula left off-center to
insert "(24)", otherwise the "(24)" is stuck on a new line at the bottom right.

The algorithm-step-format keyword "\algstep" used on lines 41 and 45 is defined
as follows:

```
\def\algstep #1. [#2] {\vskip 3 pt plus 1 pt minus 1 pt
       \noindent \hjust to 20 pt{\right{#1.}} [#2]\xskip
       \hangindent 20 pt}
```

This sets vertical spacing glue before the text for the algorithm step, and it
also sets up an appropriate "textindent", etc. The new feature here is the
hanging indent, which affects all but the first line of the following
paragraph.

The keyword "\exno" used on lines 70, 77, etc. has a definition somewhat
similar to \algstep; such definitions of formats that are needed frequently in
my books will help to ensure consistency. The "\tr" in line 70 will insert
a triangle in the left margin, using negative glue spacing so that the
character actually appears to the left of the box it is in.

Line 48 begins a "\topinsert", one of the important features needed in page layout.
The box defined within the {...} after \topinsert is set aside and placed on top
of either the present page or the following page (followed by vertical glue
specified by
        \topskip 20 pt plus 10 pt minus 5 pt,
this being another thing subsumed by "\sectionbegin"). Box inserts are used for
figures and tables, in this case a table. The table caption appears in lines 48-50;
the table itself (cf. page 6 of the book) is rather complicated, so we will
defer explanation of lines 52-65 until after we have studied the simpler example
of \halign in lines 96-98.

In general, an \halign command takes the form
        \halign{ u1#v1 ⊛ ... ⊛ un#vn \cr
                 x11 ⊛ ... ⊛ x1n \cr
                      . . . .
                 xm1 ⊛ ... ⊛ xmn \cr}
(In addition, \vskip's, \hrule's, and displayed-equation-mode \eqno's are allowed
after the \cr's.) The "\cr" is not a carriage-return, it is the sequence of three
characters \, c, r. The u's and v's are any sequences of characters not including
#, ⊛, or \cr. The meaning is to form the mn horizontal lists ("hlists")
of boxes
        u1{x11}v1   ...   un{x1n}vn
             . . . .
        u1{xm1}v1   ...   un{xmn}vn
and, for each k, to determine the maximum width of hlist uk{xik}vk for i = 1,...,m.
Then each uk{xik}vk is hjustified to the size of this maximum width, and each
line xi1⊛...⊛xin\cr is replaced by the horizontal concatenation of the resulting
boxes, separated by horizontal glue specified by
        \htabskip 0 pt plus 1 pt minus 0 pt.
If less than n entries appear on any line before the \cr, the remaining entries
are left blank. When the \halign appears inside $'s, each of the individual
uk{xik}vk hlists is considered to be a separate independent formula.

In the example of \halign on lines 96-98 we have n=4; the first column is to
be right-justified, the second is to be treated as "\rm" and surrounded by
quad spaces, then placed flush left in its column,
the third again is right-justified, the fourth is simply left-justified.
The result is shown on page 9 of the book, although with TEX the formula number
"(1)" will be centered. Note: Eventually I will put in an "\omittab" feature which
will allow portions of a line to span several columns when desired.

Now let's look at lines 52-65 and compare with Table 1 on page 6 of the book.
Two boxes are built up using \halign and its vertical dual \valign.

The "\eqalign" feature (cf. lines 111, 116) is used to line up operators in
different displayed formulas. Actually this is simply a special case of
\halign:
        \def\eqalign #1{\halign{right{##}⊛left{##}\cr#1}}.
Note that line 113 begins with ⊛.

The "\group(){...}" in lines 113, 143, etc. and the "\group/.{...}" in line 153 are used to choose suitably large versions of parentheses and slashes, forming "(...)" and "/...", respectively; the size of the symbols is determined by the height of the enclosed formula box. This type of operation is available for [], <>, ||, left and right braces or floor/ceiling brackets. TEX will provide the best size available in its repertoire. Parenthesis, brackets, braces, and vertical lines will be made in arbitrarily large sizes, but slashes will not, at least not in this year's TEX. Some very large parentheses will be generated for the big matrices in lines 158ff.

The "\biglpren" and "\bigrpren" on lines 118-119 are not really so big, but they are larger than the normal ones. The \group() operation will use these in lines 122-123.

The summation signs produced by "\sum ..." in lines 131, 143, will be large, since these summations occur in displayed formulas; but between $...$ a smaller sign will be used and the quantity summed over will be attached as a subscript. Similarly, the size of an integral sign will change, and fractions "...\over..." do too, as does the binomial coefficient (cf. "$p \choose k$" in line 118). More about this later.

The \eject in line 79 means to eject a page before continuing. This again is part of the format of my books, a major section always should begin on a new page.

I think the above comments on the example give the flavor of TEX. The example was intended to show a variety of challenging constructions of unusual complexity; in general, most of a book will be comparatively routine, and it is only the occasional formula or table which proves intricate. Such intricacies were purposely emphasized in the example.

The next step in understanding TEX is to go back to the low level and see what happens to an internal input file as it is being read in. What happens is that it is massaged once again, converted to a sequence of "tokens", which are either single characters or "control sequences" which stimulate TEX to do some work. A control sequence is either \ followed by a single nonletter nondelimiter, or \ followed by one or more letters (and terminated by the first nonletter). For example, "\vsize" and "\]" are control sequences; the font-change action "\:a" is two tokens, the control sequence \: followed by the character a; the string "\ascii'147" is five tokens, the control sequence \ascii followed by ',1,4,7. If the character following \ is a letter, and if the control sequence is terminated by a blank space, this blank space is ignored, effectively removed from the input file -- its purpose was simply to mark the end of the control sequence. Thus, for example, "\yskip \yskip" and "\yskip\yskip" are equivalent. I had to write "\MIX\ " instead of simply "\MIX " on line 125, in order to obtain the two tokens \MIX and "\ ", the latter space now counting as a real one. For appearance's sake, TEX also ignores a space following a font-identification character; e.g. "\:aNow is the time" is equivalent to "\:a Now is the time".

When the control sequence consists of \ and a single character, all printing

characters are distinguished, but when the control sequence consists of \ and a
letter string no distinction is made between upper and lower case letters,
except on the very first letter of the sequence; thus, "\GAMMA" and "\Gamma" are
considered identical, but they are not the same as "\gamma". Furthermore,
letter sequences are considered different only if they differ in the
first seven characters (six if TEX is implemented on a 32-bit machine) or if
they have different lengths mod 8. For example, "\qUotefOmmmm" and
"\quOTEfoxxxxxxxxxxxx" are both equivalent to "\quoteformat". The total number of
different control sequences is therefore approximately

$$128\text{-}14 + 2*(26^2 + 26^3 + 26^4 + 26^5 + 26^6 + 8*26^7)$$

and this should be enough.

A control sequence is, of course, invalid unless TEX knows its meaning.
TEX knows certain primitive control sequences like "\vsize" and "\ " and "\def",
and the macro facility provided by \def enables it to learn (and forget) other
control sequences like "\MIX" and "\quoteformat".

Here are the precise rules by which TEX reduces the internal input file
to ''pure input'' consisting of tokens in which every control sequence is primitive
and distinct from "\def" and "\require". We already mentioned that \require simply
inserts another batch of input from a file. In the case of \def, one writes in
general

    \def<ctrl-seq><string0>#1<string1> ... #k<stringk>{<right-hand side>}

where <string0> ... <stringk> are sequences of zero or more characters not
including { or } or #; spaces are significant in these strings, except the
first character after the defined control sequence is ignored if it is a delimiting
space following a letter string. The <right-hand side> is any sequence of
characters with matching { and }'s, again with significant spaces. I am
describing the general case; in simple situations such as the definition of
\rtn in line 141, k is zero and <string0> is empty. The value of k must be ≤9.

When the defined <ctrl-seq> is recognized, later in the input, a matching
process ensues until the left-hand side is completely matched:
characters in string0...stringk must match exactly with corresponding characters
of the input text, with error messages if a failure to match occurs. Once the
matching process is complete, TEX will have found the ingredients to be
substituted for parameters #1 thru #k in the right-hand side, in the following
way: If <stringj> is empty, #j is the next single character of the input, or
(if this character is "{"), the next group of characters up to the matching "}".
If <stringj> is not empty, #j is 0 or more characters or {...} groups until the
next character of the input equals the first character of <stringj>. No macro
expansion is done during this matching process, and no backing up is done
if a failure occurs; the succeeding characters of the input string must
match the remaining characters of <stringj>. If the parameter #j turns out to be
a single {...} group, the exterior { and } are removed from the group. Note
that the matching process operates on characters of the internal input file,
not on tokens; it is possible, for example, that #j might turn out to be a
single delimiter character like "\".

Once #1 ... #k have been discovered by these rules, they are simply
copied into the positions occupied by #1 ... #k in the right-hand sequence.
And one further change is made to the right-hand side:
the first # is removed from any sequence of two or more #'s. This is

done so that definitions can be made in the right-hand side without causing confusion with the current definition.

For example, consider what happens when the following definition is active:
\def\A#1 BC {\def\E ##1{##1#1 #1}}.
If the internal input file contains
\A {X-y} BC D
the resulting sequence after expanding the definition will be
\def\E #1{#1X-y X-y}D
(note the spacing).

The above is not the most general sort of macro definition facility, but I have applied Occam's razor. The reader should now be able to look back at the definitions given above for \quoteformat, \algstep, and \eqalign, discovering that they are really quite simple after all.

Assignment actions: I mentioned that the ''pure input'' contains codes for primitive actions that can be carried out, as well as the characters being transmitted to the final document. Some of these actions are simple assignment actions which set parameters informing TEX how to transform the subsequent input. Like macro definitions, assignment actions have an effect only until leaving the current {...} or $...$ or $$...$$ group, or until a reassignment occurs.

Here is a list of TEX's assignment actions:

> \chcode'<octal>←<number>   defines basic delimiter
> \deffnt <char><filename>   the real font name corr. to its nickname
> \:<char>   the current font to be used
> \mathrm   the font to be used for math functions like log
> \mathit   the font to be used for math variables like x
> \mathsy   the font to be used for math symbols like \mu
> \ragged or \justified   appearance of right margins
> \hsize <length> normal width of generated lines of text
> \vsize <length> normal height of generated pages of text
> \parindent <glue>   indentation on first line of paragraphs
> \hangindent <glue>   indentation on all but first line of paragraph
>   (hangindent reset to zero after every paragraph)
> \lineskip <glue>   vertical spacing between generated baselines
> \parskip <glue> additional spacing between paragraphs (added to lineskip)
> \dispskip <glue>additional spacing above and below displayed formulas
> \topskip <glue> additional spacing below an inserted box at top
> \botskip <glue> additional spacing above an inserted box at bottom
> \htabskip <glue>horizontal spacing between \haligned columns
> \vtabskip <glue>   vertical spacing between \valigned rows
> \output <routine> what to do with filled pages

All of these quantities will have default values, which I will choose after TEX is up and running; the default values will apply whenever a quantity has not been respecified. In the above, <length> is of the form

<number><unit>   or   -<number><unit>

where the <number> is a digit string or a digit string containing a period (decimal point), and where <unit> is either pt, pc, in, cm, or mm. Furthermore <glue> is of the form

<length> plus <length> minus <length>

where the plus and minus parts cannot be negative; any of the three lengths can be omitted if zero, as long as at least one of the three is present. A blank space after <number> or <unit> is removed from the input.

For example, standard XGP conventions at the moment are to produce 8 1/2 by 11 inch pages with one-inch margins and interline spacing of 4 pixels; in a font 30 pixels high, this would be specified by

\hsize 6.5 in \vsize 9 in \lineskip .17 in

and you could also say

\def\hmargin{1 in}   \def\vmargin{1 in}

for the benefit of TEX's default \output routine. (I will explain \output later.)

In a future extension I will include the additional assignment action

\tempmeas <length> next <number> lines

so that TEX can set narrow measure for small illustrations (cf. vol. 1 page 52).

In order to keep from confusing TEX's page-builder and paragraph-builder, changes made to \hsize and \vsize will take effect only when TEX puts the first line onto a fresh page or the first item into a fresh paragraph.

The assignment actions \chcode and \deffnt do not follow scope rules; they have ''global'' effect.

Control structure: It is now high time to consider TEX's paragraph-building and page-building mechanisms, and the other aspects of its control structure. In fact I probably should have started with this explanation long ago, it might have saved both you and me a lot of confusion.

Internally TEX deals with boxes and ''hlists'' (which are horizontal lists of boxes separated by horizontal glue) and ''vlists'' (which are vertical lists of boxes separated by vertical glue). The two kinds of lists are not allowed to mingle, and TEX must know at any time whether it is building an hlist or a vlist.

We say that TEX is in ''horizontal mode'' when it is working on an hlist -- intuitively, when it is in the middle of a line -- otherwise it is in ''vertical mode.'' More formally, let us write "h..." for legal TEX input beginning in horizontal mode, and "v..." for legal TEX input beginning in vertical mode. Assignment actions don't affect the mode, so they are ignored in the present discussion.

When in vertical mode, the next token of the (pure) input, not counting assignment actions, should be one of the following:

v... =

\vskip <glue> v...
          (vertical glue, appended to current vlist)
\ljustline{h...}v...,\ctrline{h...}v..., or \rjustline{h...}v...
          (append box of width \hsize to current vlist)

\hrule [height <length>] [width <length>]
    (append a horizontal rule to current vlist, this is like a
    solid black box, default height is .5 pt and default width
    is the eventual width of this vlist, namely from the left of
    its leftmost box to the right of its rightmost box)
\moveleft <length> v... or \moveright <length> v...
    (the next box in the current vlist is to be shifted
    wrt the normal left edge, this applies to one box only)
\topinsert{v...}v... or \botinsert{v...}v...
    (insert vlist into current page, or onto the next page if
    it doesn't fit on the current one)
\halign{...}v...
    (returns a vlist of m boxes formed from mn hlists as described
    above; the vlist is appended to the current one)
\top{v...}v..., \mid{v...}v..., or \bot{v...}v...
    (used mostly in \valign, returns a vlist that \vjust will
    top justify, center vertically, or bottom justify)
*   \mark{...}v...
    (associates titles, etc., with the following lines of text)
*   \penalty <number>v...
    (additional units of badness if a page break comes here)
    <blank space>v... or \ v... or \par v...
    (ignored)
*   \noindent h...
    (initiates a nonindented paragraph)
*   <box> h...
    (initiates an indented paragraph beginning with this box)
*   \eject v...
    (ejects the current page unless it is empty)
**   \eqno(<number>)v...
    (attaches equation number at right of displayed equation)
Here * designates options which are legal only if the current vlist is
being maintained by the page builder, and ** designates an option legal only
in displayed formula mode. The page builder is active at the beginning of
the program but not within other routines (e.g. \topinsert) that construct
vlists.

A box specification is one of the following:
<box> =
    <nonblank character>
        (the box consisting of that character, in the current font)
    \ascii'<octal>
        (equivalent to the character, which may be hard to enter otherwise)
    \hjust to <length>{h...}
        (the hlist converted to box of specified length, if necessary
        by breaking it into several lines as in the paragraph routine)
    \hjust{h...} or \hexpand <length>{h...}
        (the hlist converted to box of its natural line length plus the
        specified length... here \hjust is like \hexpand 0 pt)
    \vjust to <length>{v...}

         (the vlist converted to a box of the specified length,
         in this case without the ability to break it apart, sorry)
\vjust{v...} or \vexpand <length>{v...}
         (the vlist converted to box of its natural height plus the
         specified amount... here \vjust is like \vexpand 0 pt)
\page
         (the page just completed, should be used only in \output routine)
\box0, \box1, ... \box9
         (the ''global'' box most recently stored by \save0,...,\save9)
In the cases of \page and \boxk, the box is destructively read, not copied,
the next attempt to read it will be an error. Box construction routines and
\output routines may use the designation \savek ($0 \leq k \leq 9$) to store a box into
one of the ten global save areas; again, this box is not copied, it is
manufactured from the current hlist or vlist and the current hlist or vlist
is emptied.

When in horizontal mode, the next token of the (pure) input, not counting
assignment actions, should be one of the following:
h... =
        \hskip <glue> h...
         (horizontal glue, appended to hlist)
        \tjustcol{v...}h...,\midcol{v...}h..., or \bjustcol{v...}h...
         (append box of height \vsize to current hlist)
        \vrule [height <length>] [width <length>]
         (append vertical rule to current hlist, this is analogous to
         \hrule but the defaults are .5 pt width and hlist height;
         if the height is specified, the rule goes up by this much
         starting at the baseline)
        \raise <length> h... or \lower <length> h...
         (the next box or rule in the current hlist is to be shifted
         wrt the normal base line, this applies to one box only)
 *   \topinsert{v...}h... or \botinsert{v...}h...
         (insert vlist into precisely the page that contains the previous
         box in the current hlist, e.g. a footnote)
        \valign{...}h...
         (returns an hlist of m boxes formed from mn vlists as described
         above; the hlist is appended to the current one)
        \left{h...}h..., \ctr{h...}h..., or \right{h...}h...
         (used mostly in \halign, returns an hlist that \hjust will
         left justify, center horizontally, or right justify)
        \penalty <number>h...
         (additional units of badness if a line break comes here)
        <blank space>h...
         (variable spacing-between-words glue in the current font, but
         ignored in math mode)
        \ h...
         (same as blank space but not ignored in math mode)
        <box> h...
         (in particular, a nonblank character... the box is appended
         to the current hlist)

$...$ h...
> (hlist determined in math mode is appended to current hlist)

* $$...$$ h...
> (interrupts the current paragraph, which is sent to the page
> builder, but \hangindent is not cleared... the paragraph resumes
> after the closing $$... within the $$'s is a single math
> formula or a bunch of them specified by \eqalign or \halign,
> they will be centered and appended to the vlist of the page
> builder according to the conventions for displayed equations...
> appropriate vertical glue is also passed to the page builder...
> the additional glue above a displayed equation (\dispskip)
> is not added if the text on the preceding line of the paragraph
> does not overhang the first displayed equation after centering)

*   \par v... or <two consecutive carriage-returns in external input> v...
> (end of paragraph, the current hlist is broken into lines
> as explained later; the lines are appended to the vlist of
> the page-builder)

*   \eject h...
> (terminates the current ''paragraph'' and the current page, but
> the final line of the current ''paragraph'' is justified as
> if in mid-paragraph; the text resumes with a new ''paragraph''
> which is not indented, nor is \hangindent cleared)

Here * designates options which are legal only if the current hlist is
being maintained by the paragraph builder, which is called into action by the
page builder as explained above.

Boxes have a reference point on their left edge, and this reference point is
used when gluing two boxes together. If the box is a simple character from a
font, the reference point is at the left of the character at the baseline
(i.e., at the bottom of letters like x but not like y; the box extends below
the baseline to accommodate the descending parts of letters). When boxes are
concatenated horizontally, their baselines are lined up (unless otherwise
specified by \raise or \lower). The maximum height above the baseline and the
maximum depth below the baseline are also remembered, in order to determine
the height of the resulting box. When boxes are concatenated vertically, their
left edges are lined up (unless otherwise specified by \moveright or \moveleft).
The distance between consecutive baselines is taken to be \lineskip plus any
additional vertical glue specified by \vskip or \parskip, etc., unless this is too
small to prevent overlap of boxes; in the latter case the boxes are butted
together with zero glue. The baseline of the result is taken to be the baseline
of the bottom line. The maximum distance to the right of the reference edge
is taken to be the width of the resulting box.

The quantity \lineskip is ignored before and after \hrule's. Thus, one may
write for example
> \vskip 3pt \hrule \vskip 2pt \hrule \vskip 3pt
to get a double horizontal rule with 2 points of space in between and with
3 points of space separating the double rule from the adjacent lines, regardless
of the current value of \lineskip.

When two consecutive elements of an hlist are simply characters from the same
font, TEX looks at a table associated with that font to see whether or not
special symbols should be specified for this pair of characters. For example,
some of my standard fonts will make the following substitutions:

ff	→	\<ff\>
fi	→	\<fi\>
fl	→	\<fl\>
\<ff\>i	→	\<ffi\>
\<ff\>l	→	\<ffl\>
``	→	\<``\>
''	→	\<''\>
--	→	\<en-dash\>
\<en-dash\>-	→	\<em-dash\>

I will use the codes '11, '12, '13, '14, '15, '175, '177 for the first seven
combinations, since TEX will not confuse them with basic delimiters at
this stage. (Other suggestions for combinations are   := → \<:=\> and, for
fancy coffee-table books that are to be set in an expensive-looking oldstyle type,
ligatures for ct and st.)

Note the en-dash and em-dash here; there are actually four different characters
involved in mathematical publishing,

the hyphen (for hyphenating words),
the en-dash (for contexts like "13--20"),
the minus sign (for subtraction),
and   the em-dash (for punctuation dashes).

These are specified in TEX as -, --, - within $'s, and ---, respectively.

The above rules for v... and h... summarize most TEX commands, except for the
assignment actions already summarized and for the operations of interest in
page output or math mode.

Here now is the code for \ACPpages which shows complex page layout. The code
uses ''variables'' \tpage and \rhead which are not part of TEX, I am making
use of TEX's macro capability to ''assign'' values to these symbols. Readers
who are not familiar with such a trick may find it amusing, and I guess it
won't be terribly inefficient since pages come along comparatively rarely.

```
\def \titlepage {\def \tpage{T}} % causes \tpage to be set to T for ''true''
\def \runninglefthead#1 {\def \rhead{{\:m#1}}}
\def \runningrighthead#1 section#2 {\mark
        {\ifeven{\hjust to .375 in {\left{\cpage}}\left{\rhead}#2}
        \else{#2\right{\:m#1}\hjust to .375 in {\right{\cpage}}}}}
\def \ACPpages starting at page #1:
{\setcpage #1          % sets current page number for next page
\output{\lineskip 12 pt % beginning of output routine, resets \lineskip
\vskip \vmargin        % skips top margin (\vmargin is defined by user)
\ifT \tpage            % the next is used when \tpage is T
     {\def \tpage{F} % resets \tpage
     \topline          % user's special line for top of title pages
     \moveright \hmargin     % adjust for left margin
```

```
        \ljustline{\page}
        \vskip 3 pt
        \moveright \hmargin
        \ljustline{\hjust to 29 pc{\:c \ctr{\cpage}}}}   % center page no. at bottom
\else   {\moveright \hmargin    % this format used when \tpage ≠ T
        \ljustline{\hjust to 29 pc{\:a \ifeven{\topmark}\else{\botmark}}}
        \vskip 12 pt
        \moveright \hmargin \ljustline{\page}}
\advcpage}              % increase current page number by 1
```

The \output code is activated whenever the page builder has completed a page.
TEX is then in vertical mode, and the settings of \hsize, \lineskip, etc. are
unpredictable so such things should be reset if they are used. The box defined
by the vlist constructed by the \output routine is output, unless it is
empty (e.g. if it were \save'd).

The TEX actions used in the above code and not explained already are:

\setcpage <number>	Sets the current page to a given integer; if negative, denotes roman numerals.
\advcpage	Increases the absolute value of current page number by one.
\cpage	A character string showing the value of the current page is inserted into the input, as a decimal number with leading zeroes suppressed or as a roman numeral (lower case).
\ifeven{α}\else{β}	Uses α if current page is even otherwise uses β (TEX's scanner skips over the other one one character at a time).
\ifT <char> {α}\else{β}	Uses α if <char> is T otherwise uses β.
\topmark, \botmark	The \mark operation associates an uninterpreted string of characters with the set of subsequent lines received by the page builder, until the next mark; "\topmark" inserts into TEX's input the mark associated with the first line on the current \page, and "\botmark" the mark associated with the last line, not counting any \topinserted or \botinserted lines.

I propose to use the following as the default output routine for TEX. It uses
five more actions, namely \day, \month, \year, \time, and \file, corresponding
to the environment which called TEX.

```
\def \hfill{\hskip plus 100 cm}          %''infinite'' stretchability
\lineskip 0 pt                           %reset space between lines
\:\font                                  %resets to default font character
\vskip \vmargin                          %skips over top margin
\ifT \notitle {} \else{                  %optionally skips title
        \ljustline{\hjust to 7.5 in{     %title line has pageno 1 inch from right
        \hskip\hmargin                   %skip left margin
        \day\ \month\ \year\hfill        %date
        \time\hfill                      %starting time
```

```
\file\hfill                              %principal input file name
\cpage}}                                 %page number
\vskip 12 pt}                            %one pica skip after title line
\moveright \hmargin \ljustline{\cpage}   %insert body of page, skipping left margin
\advcpage                                %increase page number
```

\hmargin, \vmargin, \font, \notitle are settable by the user (or SNAIL), and
they in turn have default values.

Now let's consider the page-building routine more closely; this gives us a chance
to study the process TEX uses for vertical justification, which introduces some of
the concepts we will need in the more complicated routine used for horizontal
justification.

The first idea is the concept of ''badness.'' This is a number computed on the
basis of the amount of stretching or shrinking necessary when setting the glue.
Suppose we have a list of n boxes (either a horizontal list or a vertical list),
separated by n-1 specifications of glue. Let w be the desired total length
of the list (i.e., the desired width or height, depending on which dimension we
are justifying); let x be the actual total length of boxes and glue; and let
y,z be the total amount of glue parameters for expansion and contraction. The
badness of this situation is defined to be

infinite, if $x - z > w + \epsilon$, where ϵ is a small tolerance to compensate
        for floating-point rounding;
$100((x-w)/z)\char94 3$, if $w + z + \epsilon \geq x > w$;
0,   if $x = w$;
$100((w-x)/3y)\char94 3$, if $w > x$;

plus penalties charged for breaking lines in comparatively undesirable places.

According to these formulas, stretching by y has a badness rating of 100/27,
or about 3.7; stretching by 2y is rated about 30; stretching by 3y is rated
100 units of badness, and so is shrinking by the maximum amount z. I plan to
charge a penalty of something like 80 units for breaking a paragraph or sequence of
displayed formulas in such a way that only one line comes by itself on a page;
thus, for instance, a five-line paragraph gets a penalty of 80 if we break
after the first or fourth line, but no penalty if we break after two or three
lines. I will of course be tuning these formulas to make them correspond as
well as I can to my aesthetic perceptions of bad layout. The user will be
able to specify his own additional \penalty points for undesirable breaking
between specific lines (e.g. in a MIX program to break before an instruction
that refers to *-1).

Breaks are not allowed before or after line rules.

The page-building routine forms a vlist as explained above, accumulating lines of
text and vertical glue until the natural height of its previous accumulation, plus
the k new lines, is greater than or equal to the specified page height, \vsize.
Then it breaks the new paragraph just after the jth line, for some $0 \leq j \leq k$, whichever
value of j has the minimum badness; if this minimum occurs for more than one
j, the largest such j is used. Then the glue between lines j and j+1 is discarded,

and the remaining k-j lines are carried over to the next page. (They are immediately checked to ensure that they don't already overfill the new page, and they are broken in the same way if necessary.) The \output routine is invoked whenever a full page has been generated.

A \topinsert or \botinsert interrupts this otherwise straightforward procedure. The box to be inserted is computed, off to the side, and then an attempt is made to place it in the current accumulated page. If it fits, well and good, we leave it there. If not, it is carried over to the next page, in a natural but hard-to-explain manner, unless the requirement about coming on the same page as a specific line has to be met (i.e., box insertion in horizontal mode). Then the least bad legitimate solution will be used.

Footnotes: I have used footnotes only three times in over 2000 pages of The Art of Computer Programming, and personally I believe they should usually be avoided, so I am not planning an elaborate footnoting mechanism (e.g. to break long footnotes between pages or to mark the first footnote per page with an asterisk and the second with a dagger, etc.). They can otherwise be satisfactorily handled by \botinsert as defined here. A user will be able to get fancier footnotes if he or she doesn't mind rewriting a few of TEX's subroutines.

The paragraph-building routine assembles an hlist as described above, and must break it into lines of width \hsize for transmission to the page-builder. (Note: There is only one page-builder, in spite of TEX's largely recursive nature, and there is only one paragraph-builder. However, there can be arbitrarily many \hjust to <length> routines active at once, and these are analogous to the paragraph builder in most ways, since they have to break their hlists into lines too. The discussion about line-breaking applies to such routines too, but for convenience I will write this as if only the paragraph-builder has to worry about breaking lines.)

The elements of the paragraph-builder's hlist are usually sequences of text characters or fragments of math formulas, but they also may be indivisible boxes constructed by TEX's higher level box operators. In my fonts there is a small amount of variable glue between the individual text characters (between the letters a and b, for instance, we would use the glue obtained as a sum of right-glue for a and left-glue for b, as specified in font tables); furthermore the spaces between words have more elastic glue as explained earlier. TEX will give double y glue (but won't change the x glue) to the first space that follows a period, exclamation point, question mark, or colon, unless letters or digits or commas or semicolons or boxes intervene before this space. A semicolon and a comma are treated similarly, but with 1.5 and 1.25 as the relative amounts of y glue.

The main problem of the paragraph builder is to decide where to break a long hlist. Again TEX uses the concept of ''badness'' discussed under the page building routine, but this time it improves on what was done by providing a ''lookahead'' feature by which the situation in the later lines of a paragraph can influence the breaks in the earlier lines; in practice this often provides substantially better output.

Before discussing the lookahead feature, we need to define the location of
all permissible breaks. Every \hskip whose x or y glue exceeds the
spacing width of the current font is an acceptable place to break (and to
omit the horizontal glue) with no penalty. Adjacent \hskips are merged
together, incidentally, by adding the three glue components. Another acceptable
place to break without penalty is after an explicit hyphen or dash.
(Some \hskips, used for backspacing, have negative x; they are, of course,
unacceptable breaks.) The math formula routine which processes $...$ will allow
breaks just after binary operators and relations at the top level; relations
like =, $\leq$, $\equiv$, etc. have only a small penalty, say 10; operators like +,-,x,/,
mod have a larger penalty, with - and mod larger than the others (say 30, 70, 30,
40, 80, respectively). Superscripts and subscripts are attached unbreakably to
their boxes.

There are four "discretionary" symbols used to provide or inhibit breaks.
First is the \penalty <number> command, which specifies that a break is
admissible if the stated penalty is considered, then there are three more:
>   \-   OK to hyphenate this word here (penalty 30);
>   \+   do not break here;
>   *   OK to break here (penalty 30), but insert
>   a times sign, not a hyphen.
The last of these would be used in a long product like $(n+1)*(n+2)*(n+3)*(n+4)$.

In a minute I will discuss TEX's way of doing automatic hyphenation, but for
the moment let's suppose we know all the candidate places to break lines; now
what is the best way to break up an entire paragraph? I think it is best to define
''best'' as the way that minimizes the sum of the squares of the badnesses of all
the individual breaks. This will tend to minimize the maximum badness as well
as to handle second-order and third-order badnesses, etc. As before, badness
is based on the amount of stretching or shrinking, plus penalty points.

To find the best breaks by this criterion, we don't have an exponentially hard
problem; a dynamic programming algorithm will find the absolutely best way to
break in time $O(n^2)$, where n is the number of permissible places to break.
Namely, let f(m) be the minimum sum of badness-squareds for the paragraph up
to break position m, then f(m) is the minimum over k<m of f(k) plus the square of
the badness of breaking the text (k,m].

Actually a near-linear approximation to this quadratic algorithm will be
satisfactory: Given the best three places to break the k-th line, we use these
to find the best three places to break the (k+1)st line. When the end of
the paragraph is reached, or if the paragraph is so long that we don't have
enough buffer space (say more than 15 lines long), we clear out our buffers
by backtracking through the f(m) calculation to find the best-known breaking
sequence. In \ragged mode, the lines are not expanded or shrunk to \hsize, but
in \justified mode they are.

Built-in hyphenation:
Besides using the permissible breaks, TEX will try to hyphenate words.
It will do this only in a sequence of lower-case letters that is preceded and

followed by anything other than a letter, digit, -, or discretionary symbol. Note that, for example, already-hyphenated compound words will not be broken. If a permissible hyphenation break is discovered, a penalty of say 30 units of badness will be paid, but this may be better than not hyphenating at all. An additional 20 units of badness is charged for breaking a word or formula in the last line of a paragraph (more precisely, one which is followed by less text than half of \hsize).

There is no point in finding all possible places to hyphenate. For one thing, the problem is extremely difficult, since e.g. the word "record" is supposed to be broken as "rec-ord" when it is a noun but "re-cord" when it is a verb. Consider the word "hyphenation" itself, which is rather an exception:

> hy-phen-a-tion   vs.   con-cat-e-na-tion

Why does the n go with the a in one case and not the other? Starting at letter a in the dictionary and trying to find rigorous rules for hyphenation without much knowledge, we come up against a-part vs. ap-er-ture, aph-o-rism vs. a-pha-sia, etc. It becomes clear that what we want is not an accurate but ponderously slow routine that consumes a lot of memory space and processing time, instead we want a set of hyphenation rules that are

> a) simple;
> b) almost always safe;
> c) powerful enough to find a close enough approximation to, say,

80% of the words already hyphenated in The Art of Computer Programming. To justify point (c), I find that there are about 2 hyphenated words per page in the books, and the places where the rules I shall propose do not find the identical hyphenation only very rarely would cause a really bad break. The time needed to handle the remaining exceptions is therefore insignificant by comparison with what I already do when proof-reading.

(Five pages of detailed rules for English hyphenation followed in this place; they are omitted here because they are of little interest and they can be found in the 1979 user manuals for TEX. Frank Liang subsequently found a significantly better procedure, which applies to many more languages.)

To conclude this memo, I should explain how TEX is going to work on math formulas. I can at least sketch this.

The main operators that need to be discussed are ↓, ↑, \over, \groupxy, and \sqrt; others are reduced to minor variations on these themes (e.g., \int and \sum are converted to something similar to ↓ and ↑, \atop is an unruled \over, \underline is like \group, and \vinc (overline) is like \sqrt). Each math formula is first parsed into a tree, actually a modified hlist which I shall call a tlist. A tlist is a list of trees possibly separated by horizontal glue, and a tree is one of the following:

> a box (if not a character box then it was constructed with mathmode off);
> the node \sub with a tree as left son and a tlist as right son;
> the node \sup with a tree as left son and a tlist as right son;
> the node \subsup with a tree as left son, tlists as middle and right sons;
> the node \over with tlists as left and right sons;

the node \sqrt with tlist as son;
the node \group with bracket characters as left and middle sons and
with a tlist as right son.

Best results will be obtained when using a family of three fonts of varying
sizes. The definition
\fntfam <char><char><char>
defines such a family in decreasing order of size. For example, TEX will be
initially tuned to work with the following set of font definitions:

\deffnt a cm10	\deffnt g cmi10	\deffnt u cmath10
\deffnt b cm9	\deffnt h cmi9	\deffnt v cmath9
\deffnt c cm8	\deffnt i cmi8	\deffnt w cmath8
\deffnt d cm7	\deffnt j cmi7	\deffnt x cmath7
\deffnt e cm6	\deffnt k cmi6	\deffnt y cmath6
\deffnt f cm5	\deffnt l cmi5	\deffnt z cmath5

\fntfam adf \fntfam bef \fntfam gjl \fntfam hkl \fntfam uxz \fntfam vyz
\mathrm a   \mathit g   \mathsy u (in the text)
\mathrm b   \mathit h   \mathsy v (in the exercises)
These are 10 pt thru 5 pt fonts of "Computer Modern" and "Computer Modern Italic";
8 pt type actually doesn't get used in formulas, only at the bottom of title
pages and in the index.

Characters within math formulas will be adjusted to use the appropriate font
from a family if the current font appears as the first (largest) of some
declared family; otherwise the single font by itself will be treated as
a ''family'' of three identical fonts (i.e., using the same size in
subscripts as elsewhere).

After a math formula has been completely parsed into a tlist, TEX goes from
top to bottom assigning one of five modes to the individual trees:
    A   display mode
    B   text mode
    C   text mode with lower superscripts
    D   script mode
    E   scriptscript mode
Later on, modes ABC will use the size of the first of a font family, while
D and E will use the sizes of the second and third, respectively. The following
table shows how TEX determines the modes of the sons of a tree node, given the
mode of the father:

father	\sub	\sup	\subsup	\over	\sqrt	\group
A	AD	AD	ADD	BC	C	A
B	BD	BD	BDD	DD	C	B
C	CD	CD	CDD	DD	C	C
D	DE	DE	DEE	EE	D	D
E	EE	EE	EEE	EE	E	E

Large summation and integral signs, etc., are used only in mode A.

Once the modes are assigned, TEX goes through bottom up, converting all trees
to boxes by setting the glue everywhere except at the highest level tlist,
which becomes an hlist (passed to the paragraph-builder or whatever). Incidentally,
if you want to understand why TEX does a top-down pass and then a bottom-up

pass, note that for example the numerator of \over isn't known to be a
numerator at first; consider "1 \over 1", where the "1" is supposed to be
mode D. Furthermore the \subsup nodes can originate either from

$$\ldots\downarrow\ldots\uparrow\ldots \quad \text{or from} \quad \ldots\uparrow\ldots\downarrow\ldots$$

since I found that some typists like to do subscripts first and others like
to do superscripts first. Incidentally, when TEX parses a formula, $\downarrow$ and
$\uparrow$ have highest precedence, then \sqrt, then \over;

$$x \downarrow y \downarrow z \quad \text{and} \quad x \uparrow y \uparrow z$$

are treated as

$$x \downarrow\{y \downarrow z\} \quad \text{and} \quad x \uparrow\{y \uparrow z\},$$

while constructions such as

$$x \downarrow y \uparrow z \downarrow w$$

are illegal.

The first font of a family should possess tables that tell TEX how much to
raise the baseline of superscripts, lower the baseline of subscripts, and
position the various baselines of the \over construct, as a function of the mode
and the node. For example, in the fonts I am designing, the 7-point superscript
of an unsubscripted 10-point box will have its baseline raise 11/3 pt in B mode,
26/9 pt in C mode; the subscript of an unsuperscripted box will have baseline
lowered 3/2 pt in both B and C modes; and when both sub- and super-scripts are
present the subscript will be lowered 11/4 pt and the superscript raised
11/3 pt or 26/9 pt (or more if necessary to appear above a complex subscript).
Subscripts and superscripts on more complex boxes (e.g. groups) are positioned
based on the lower and upper edges of the box.

Displayed formulas are never broken between lines by TEX; the user is supposed
to figure out the psychologically best place to break them. Since TEX has
negative glue components, it will be possible to squeeze longish formulas onto
a line. Multiple displayed formulas should be separated by the \cr's of
\halign or \eqalign.

(end of the file TEX.ONE)

And they all lived happily ever after.

Chapter 26

TEX Incunabula

[Originally published in TUGboat 5 (1984), 4–11.]

Several people have asked me for a list of the "first" books ever typeset by TEX. Bibliophiles might some day enjoy tracing the early history of this particular method of book production; I have therefore tried to record the publications known to me, before my memory of those exciting moments fades away. The following list is confined to works that were actually published, although my files also include dozens of concert programs, church programs, newsletters, and such things that my wife and I have been putting together ever since TEX began to be operational.

The first edition of the TEX manual is already quite rare, although I believe several hundred copies were printed. It was called "Tau Epsilon Chi, a system for technical text," Stanford Computer Science Report STAN-CS-78-675 = Artificial Intelligence Laboratory Memo AIM-317 (September 1978), 198 pp. The American Mathematical Society published a corrected version of this manual in June 1979; my wife Jill designed the cover of this edition, of which I believe approximately 1000 copies were sold. If you have a "clean" copy you will be able to distinguish a subtle TEXture on the cover (quite similar to the example on page 225 of *The TEXbook*).

Most people learned about the prototype version of TEX by reading the third edition of the manual, which appeared as part 2 of *TEX and METAFONT*, co-published by AMS and Digital Press in the latter part of 1979. Approximately 15,000 copies of this book were printed.

The type for all three editions was produced on experimental low-resolution equipment that was not available commercially. The first edition used a Xerox Graphics Printer (XGP) that had been donated to Stanford's Artificial Intelligence Laboratory; the second used a one-of-a-kind "Colorado" printer at Xerox Electro-Optical Systems in Pasadena, California; and the third used a "Penguin" printer at Xerox's Advanced Systems Development group in Palo Alto. These machines had

LENA BERNICE

Her Christmas in Wood County, 1895

Lena Bernice was our grandmother.
She told us about her first Christmas
tree. She told us many things while
the snow fell.

Elizabeth Ann and Jill
Christmas 1978

FIGURE 1. The title page of TEX's first book.

variable resolution, which was set to 200 pixels/inch on the XGP and
384 pixels/inch on the others. Dale Green and Leo Guibas were instrumental in getting the latter two editions printed.

The METAFONT manual had a similar printing history: It first came
out on the XGP as "METAFONT, a system for alphabet design," Stanford Computer Science Report STAN-CS-79-762 = Artificial Intelligence

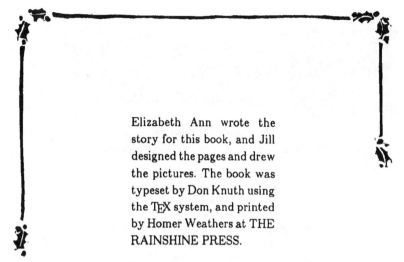

Elizabeth Ann wrote the story for this book, and Jill designed the pages and drew the pictures. The book was typeset by Don Knuth using the TEX system, and printed by Homer Weathers at THE RAINSHINE PRESS.

28

FIGURE 2. The colophon at the end of TEX's first book.

Laboratory Memo AIM-332 (September 1979), 105 pp.; then it was reprinted on a Penguin, with minor corrections, in the Digital Press book mentioned earlier.

Of course, user manuals don't count as significant milestones in publishing. I like to think that the first *real* book to be printed with TEX was a 28-page keepsake that was made for my wife's relatives at

he snow began around three o'clock. Aunt Sally had the little ones turn to the window and recite their lesson.

"See the snow softly fall
over barns and churches tall."

Gussie was trying to teach Horace at home, so she copied it down. She wanted Horace to be a member of the state legislature, like Ben James who was her uncle and the greatest orator in Wood County.

Lena Bernice thought about little Jimmy Reed in the lesson book and how he wondered if the snow tasted of sugar. She thought about the brave dog, Cæsar, who had protected his mistress during the blizzard in Old Kentucky. She thought about the layer of ice on Rock Pond.

Aunt Sally took up the *Illustrated Geography* and showed The Entire Class a picture of the Alps and of the dear Saint Bernards who saved many a folk from certain death.

2

FIGURE 3. The opening pages of *Lena Bernice*.

Christmastime, 1978. This book included eighteen original linoleum block illustrations, into which we pasted XGP-produced text set in a special 14-point extended variant of the prototype Computer Modern font. In order to compensate for the XGP's limited resolution, we prepared magnified copy and the printer reduced it to 70%; the effective resolution was therefore about 286 pixels/inch. The title, opening pages,

3

and colophon are illustrated here (reduced another 61% from the published size). About 100 copies were printed, of which roughly 25 were sold and the remaining 75 were given as gifts. A complete library citation for this book would read as follows: "*Lena Bernice: Her Christmas in Wood County, 1895*. By Elizabeth Ann James, with illustrations by Jill Carter Knuth. Columbus, Ohio: Rainshine Press, 1978."

David W. Wall made an unusual application of TEX and METAFONT in his Ph.D. thesis, "Mechanisms for broadcast and selective broadcast," Stanford Computer Science Report STAN-CS-82-919 = Stanford Computer Systems Laboratory Technical Report No. 190 (June 1980), 120 pp. He considered each illustration to be a "character" in a new "typeface," and he drew these large characters with METAFONT; then he superimposed textual labels using TEX. This approach would defeat our current METAFONT software if the figures were to be drawn at high resolution, but he got away with it because he was using the XGP. (See the samples attached, which have been reduced to 65% of their original size.) In David's words, "I fear I've opened a Pandora's box; this isn't exactly what METAFONT was designed for. But ain't it purty?"

On the other hand, if w looks at its own fragment state and finds a *better* edge than the one v selected, then w must know about a vertex in the fragment of v and w that v did not know was present. Thus as soon as w merged its fragment state with that of v it had a larger fragment state than v. Its fragment state may even have been larger than v's beforehand.

Endpoint Disagrees with v

$\vdots$

We observe that x precedes y on this path p. For if $x = y$ then this single vertex is on both path q_1 and path q_2, which are represented by edges without a common endpoint. This violates Lemma 4. Similarly, if x follows y then y is on the portion of path p from m to x and so by Lemma 2 it must also be on the portion of path q_1 from m to x. Thus y is on both q_1 and q_2, which again contradicts Lemma 4. So x precedes y.

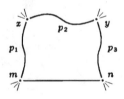

Replacing $\{m, n\}$ with p

FIGURE 4. Excerpts from David Wall's thesis.

All during this time we were without any access to a high-resolution phototypesetter, but after several months of work David Fuchs and I successfully built an interface to an Alphatype CRS machine in the winter and spring of 1980. (Most of our effort was directed to making a complete revision of the microcode inside the CRS, because of the machine's limited font storage.) My notes show that we produced the first decent sample pages on 1 April 1980; and the first page of output that was eventually published was my one-page poem entitled "Disappearances," which appeared on page 264 of *The Mathematical Gardner*, edited by David Klarner (Belmont, California: Wadsworth, 1981). In May I sent off a longer paper, "The Letter S," which was published in *The Mathematical Intelligencer* **2** (1980), 114–122 [reprinted as Chapter 13 of the present volume].

Most of my time during April, May, June, and July of 1980 was spent making the final revisions to the big book that was TEX's *raison d'être*, the book that had been the original impetus for all of my work on TEX and METAFONT. The text of that volume had already been typeset during 1976 at The Universities Press, Belfast, using Monophoto systems called Cora and Maths; but the results were not satisfactory. I received the paper tapes from Belfast and converted them to pseudo-TEX so that the re-keyboarding would be easier. (It isn't clear that I actually saved any time by this maneuver!) All 700 pages of the book finally fell into place; and the camera-ready copy for *Seminumerical Algorithms*, Volume 2 of *The Art of Computer Programming*, second edition (Reading, Massachusetts: Addison–Wesley, 1981) was completed at 2 am on Tuesday morning, 29 July 1980. On the 22nd of October I had to remake page iv (so that it contained Library of Congress information). A bound copy of the book actually appeared in my hands on 4 January 1981. It seems most appropriate to regard the emergence of this book as the actual birth of TEX in the world of publishing. My publishers prepared a limited edition of 256 copies, hand bound in leather, to commemorate the occasion. (I believe that only a few people ever purchased these special copies, because computer scientists didn't want to pay for leather binding, while lovers of fine printing didn't cherish the invasion of computers. However, about 11,000 copies of *Seminumerical Algorithms* were sold in its regular binding during 1981.)

Meanwhile other people at Stanford had been getting books ready for publication, using TEX and the Alphatype in our lab. The first of these to be finished was *KAREL the ROBOT: A Gentle Introduction to the Art of Programming* by Richard E. Pattis (New York: Wiley, 1981), 120 pp. Many of the illustrations in this book were typeset using special symbols METAFONTed for the occasion with David Wall's help. The next book of this kind was *Practical Optimization* by Philip E. Gill, Walter Murray, and Margaret H. Wright (New York: Academic Press, 1981), 417 pp. Speaking of optimization, a paper by Bengt Aspvall and Yossi Shiloach, "A polynomial time algorithm for solving systems of linear inequalities with two variables per inequality," *SIAM Journal on Computing* **9** (1980), 827–845, was also produced on the Alphatype in our lab that year.

Scott Kim was the first to use our Alphatype together with TEX to produce copy with non-METAFONT typefaces, in his *Inversions: A Catalog of Calligraphic Cartwheels* (Peterborough, New Hampshire: Byte Books, 1981), 124 pp. He later METAFONTed some special symbols that are featured in Arthur Keller's *A First Course in Computer Programming using PASCAL* (New York: McGraw–Hill, 1982), 319 pp. (It's interesting to note that the Italian translation of this text, *Programmare in PASCAL* (Bologna: Zanichelli, 1983), 303 pp., was one of the first books to be published from TEX output in Italy. The Italian translators [G. Canzii, A. Pilenga, A. Consolandi] worked independently of the American author, and produced camera-ready copy on a Versatec machine in Milano — unfortunately without Scott's symbols.)

Terry Winograd was one of the first TEX users and (therefore) one of the first to complain about its original limitations; for example, I added \xdef at his request on 28 November 1978. He had begun writing a book with a system called PUB [Larry Tesler, "PUB, The Document Compiler," Stanford Artificial Intelligence Project Operating Note 70 (March 1973), 84 pp.], then had converted all the files to BRAVO [Butler W. Lampson, "Bravo Manual," in *Alto User's Handbook*, Xerox Palo Alto Research Center (1978), 32–62], before converting again to TEX. Winograd contributed macros for indexing to the first issue of *TUGboat*, and his struggles with the early TEX finally led to the completed book *Language as a Cognitive Process*, Volume 1: *Syntax* (Reading, Massachusetts: Addison–Wesley, 1983), 654 pp. He used Computer Modern fonts, but substituted Optima for the (awful) sans-serifs that I had been using at the time.

Gio Wiederhold modified ACME files that he had used to prepare the first edition of his database book so that he could typeset the second edition with TEX. He says that it took about six months to do the final formatting (e.g., writing extra copy so that page breaks would occur in desirable places). The resulting volume holds the current record for the longest book to be produced in our lab: *Database Design*, second edition (New York: McGraw–Hill, 1983), 767 pp.

Another faculty colleague, Jeffrey D. Ullman, converted first-edition *troff* files to TEX files for his book *Principles of Database Systems*, second edition (Rockville, Maryland: Computer Science Press, 1982), 491 pp. Then he used TEX directly to write *Computational Aspects of VLSI* (Rockville, Maryland: Computer Science Press, 1984), 505 pp.

Jeff's 13-year-old son, Peter, helped by using METAFONT to create special fonts for the typesetting of VLSI stipple patterns.

My coauthor Daniel H. Greene TEXed our book *Mathematics for the Analysis of Algorithms* (Boston: Birkhäuser, 1981), 107 pp. It's interesting to compare the first edition to the second (1982, 123 pp.), because the fonts were significantly tuned up during the year that intervened between editions. [The third and "ultimate" edition (1990, 132 pp.) was destined to exhibit further typographical progress.]

The books and articles mentioned so far were all typeset by their authors; this is to be expected in a computer science department. But a few experiments were also undertaken in a more traditional way, where the TEX composition was done by people who were skilled at keyboard entry but not intimately familiar with the subject matter. I think the first such books to be done in our lab were the *Handbook of Artificial Intelligence*, Volume 2, edited by Avron Barr and Edward A. Feigenbaum (Los Altos, California: William Kaufman, 1982), 441 pp.; *Handbook of Artificial Intelligence*, Volume 3, edited by Paul R. Cohen and Edward A. Feigenbaum (Los Altos, California: William Kaufman, 1982), 652 pp.; *Introduction to Arithmetic for Digital Systems Designers* by Shlomo Waser and Michael J. Flynn (New York: Holt, Rinehart and Winston, 1982), 326 pp.; *Introduction to Stochastic Integration* by Kai Lai Chung and Ruth J. Williams (Boston: Birkhäuser, 1983), 204 pp.; *Hands-on Basic: For the IBM Personal Computer*, by Herbert Peckham (New York: McGraw–Hill, 1983), 320 pp.; *Hands-on Basic: For the Apple II*, by Herbert Peckham with Wade Ellis, Jr., and Ed Lodi (New York: McGraw–Hill, 1983), 332 pp.; *Hands-on Basic: For the TRS-80 Color Computer*, by Herbert Peckham with Wade Ellis, Jr., and Ed Lodi (New York: McGraw–Hill, 1983), 354 pp.; *Hands-on Basic: For the Atari 400/800/1200XL*, by Herbert Peckham with Wade Ellis, Jr., and Ed Lodi (New York: McGraw–Hill, 1983), 319 pp.; and *Probability in Social Science* by Samuel Goldberg (Boston: Birkhäuser, 1983), 131 pp. Incidentally, the typesetting of this last book was done by my son John during the summer of 1982, before he had learned anything about computers. I helped him with a few \halign constructions, but otherwise he worked essentially without supervision. At that time he was about to be a senior in high school; I know of at least three other children in his high school who were typesetting books with TEX. [*Introduction to Commutative Algebra and Algebraic Geometry* by Ernst Kunz (Boston: Birkhäuser, 1985), 237 pp., typeset by Amy and Michael Wang; *Social Dynamics* by Nancy Brandon Tuma and Michael T. Hannan (Orlando, Florida: Academic Press, 1984), 578 pp., typeset by Katie Tuma.]

It may be of interest to note that the first volume of the *Handbook of Artificial Intelligence* (1981) was done with early Computer Modern fonts on our Alphatype, but the typesetting was by PUB rather than TEX. In particular, all hyphenation in that book was done by hand.

Members of Stanford's Space, Telecommunications and Radioscience Laboratory began to use TEX for articles that were typeset on our Alphatype and published in journals and conference proceedings. I believe the first of these were "Photographic observations of earth's airglow from space," by S. B. Mende, P. M. Banks, R. Nobles, O. K. Garriott, and J. Hoffman, *Geophysical Research Letters* **10** (1983), 1108–1111; "Solar wind control of the low-latitude asymmetric magnetic disturbance field," by C. Robert Clauer, Robert L. McPherron, and Craig Searls, *Journal of Geophysical Research* **88** (1983), 2123–2130; "VLF wave injections from the ground," by Robert A. Helliwell, in *Active Experiments in Space* (Paris: European Space Agency, 1983), 3–9; "Electron beam experiments aboard the space shuttle," by P. M. Banks, P. R. Williamson, W. J. Raitt, S. D. Shawhan, and G. Murphy, *ibid.*, 171–175. Dozens more are currently (1983) in press.

Students who knew what they were doing were allowed to use our Alphatype at their own discretion and without my knowledge. For example, I remember being surprised one evening to see the Computer Modern fonts used in an advertisement for "Earth Shoes," in the program of a musical comedy put on by Stanford undergraduates. Surely the most surprising thing to come out of our laboratory, and by far the most significant in financial terms, was the hardware for the first Sun workstation (or at least a key part of it): Andreas von Bechtolsheim "typeset" the printed circuit board for Sun Microsystems' first product on our Alphatype in 1981, using special-purpose fonts that he created with METAFONT.

The software we used to interface between TEX and the Alphatype CRS was used at three other sites: The American Mathematical Society (Providence, Rhode Island), the Royal Institute of Technology (Stockholm, Sweden), and Bell Northern Research (Mountain View, California). I have only sketchy information about what books were produced with TEX at other installations, but I'll give a partial list so that people at those sites might be moved to provide a more correct history.

The first AMS use of TEX and the Alphatype in my collection is an article entitled "1980 Wiener & Steele Prizes Awarded," *Notices of the American Mathematical Society* **27** (1980), 528–533. (Since then an ever-growing percentage of the *Notices* has been TEXed.) The SIAM-AMS-MAA Combined Membership List for 1981–1982 was another early production, as was the AMS *Catalog of Publications* for 1981–1982. The Society first put TEX's mathematical abilities to the test in the pre-preliminary edition of Michael Spivak's *The Joy of TEX*, 134 pp., which was distributed at the AMS meeting in San Francisco (January 1981). There are many instances of TEX usage in the subsequent *Proceedings* [Volume 85 (1982), pp. 141–488, 567–595, 643–665, 673–674; Volume 86 (1982), pp. 12–14, 19–86, 103–125, 133–142, 148–150, 153–183, 186–188, 253–274, 305–306, 321–327, 363–374, 391, 459–490, 511–524, 574–598, 609–624, 632–637, 641–648, 679–684]. David J. Eck's thesis, "Gauge-natural bundles and generalized gauge theories," was published in *Memoirs of the American Mathematical Society* **33**, number 247 (September 1981), 54 pp.; this memoir includes an interesting preface by Richard Palais, pointing out that David was pleased to be the first guinea pig for $\mathcal{A}_{\mathcal{M}}\mathcal{S}$-TEX when he typeset the thesis.

Before the AMS publishing team began using the Alphatype, they produced several things from photo-reduced Varian output. The indexes to individual issues of *Mathematical Reviews* have been done with TEX since November 1979 (Volume 58, #5); the *Combined Membership List* for 1980–1981 also came off the Varian.

Several books composed elsewhere were also typeset with the facilities at AMS, notably Oregon Software's *PASCAL–2: Version 2.0 for RSX-11* (1981), 186 pp.; *Turtle Geometry* by Harold Abelson and Andrea diSessa (Cambridge, Massachusetts: M.I.T. Press, 1981), 497 pp.; and *History of Ophthalmology* by George Gorin (Wilmington, Delaware: Publish or Perish, 1982), 646 pp.

At Bell Northern, I think TEX was used mostly (or entirely?) for company-confidential reports. But I have seen several excellent publications from the Swedish Royal Institute of Technology — notably a 46-page monograph on *Non-linear Inverse Problems* by Gerd Eriksson, Report TR17A-NA-8209 (1983) — and I would like to know more about their independent experiences with TEX.

The University of Wisconsin Press sent me a copy of their *1981 Fall Catalog*, which they told me was typeset by TEX. I don't know if TEX actually helped to produce any of the books listed in the catalog.

When Computer Modern fonts are not used, it isn't so easy to tell that TEX was behind the formatting. But I have been assured that the book *Guide to International Commerce Law* by Paul H. Vishny (Colorado Springs, Colorado: Shepard's/McGraw–Hill, 1981), 782 pp., was entirely typeset by TEX, using an IBM 370/3081 coupled to an APS 5 phototypesetter.

Some books have been published directly from Xerox Dover output (384 dots/inch resolution) that was printed at Stanford. In particular, the original hardcover edition of Joseph Deken's *The Electronic Cottage* (New York: William Morrow, 1982), 334 pp., was produced in this way, because of tight publication deadlines, and so were the books *Arithmetic and Geometry: Papers Dedicated to I. R. Shafarevich on the Occasion of His Sixtieth Birthday*, edited by Michael Artin and John Tate (Boston: Birkhäuser, 1983); Volume 1, 359 pp., Volume 2, 481 pp.

Max Díaz was instrumental in setting up a TEX installation at the Instituto de Investigaciones en Matemáticas Aplicadas y en Sistemas of the Universidad Nacional Autónoma de México (i.e., at IIMAS-UNAM). The first TEX-produced book to be done entirely in Mexico was *Nonlinear Phenomena*, edited by Kurt Bernardo Wolf, *Lecture Notes in Physics* **189** (1983), 464 pp. Max's *Fácil TEX* macros [*TUGboat* **2**, 2 (July 1981), A-1–A-91] were, of course, the basis of this production, which was photoreduced from low-resolution output.

I began to work on TEX shortly after seeing galley proofs of Pat Winston's book *Artificial Intelligence* (Reading, Massachusetts: Addison–Wesley, 1977), 444 pp., which was the first technical book to be typeset with high-resolution phototypesetting equipment. Now I've just learned that the new edition of his book is being typeset with TEX, so a circle is being closed. [Patrick Henry Winston, *Artificial Intelligence*, second edition (Reading, Massachusetts: Addison–Wesley, 1984), 527 pp.]

The *AI Magazine* (an official publication of the American Association for Artificial Intelligence) has been typeset with TEX in our laboratory since volume 3, number 2 (Spring 1982). Actually nobody told me anything about this until 16 June 1983, when I received the following unsolicited letter from the managing editor, Claudia C. Mazzetti: "The production time of the magazine has decreased almost in half because of TEX. We just want to express our thanks for creating such a marvelous system!"

Well, by 1983 I was unable to understand why anybody would think the old version of TEX was easy to use, since I had just spent two years removing hundreds of deficiencies. (All of the work reported above was produced by the old proto-TEX system.) Furthermore I'm still not entirely happy with the Computer Modern fonts, although the "Almost Computer Modern" version of July 1983 is much better than the fonts that we were using in 1980. I expect to make further improvements during the next two years, as I complete my research on typography. My goal is to have a new METAFONT in 1984 and a new Computer Modern in 1985. Meanwhile, we do have a new, permanent

TEX in 1983, and I'll conclude this list by mentioning the first three publications that have flowed from the new TEX together with our new APS Micro-5 phototypesetter: *The TEXbook* (Reading, Massachusetts: Addison–Wesley, 1983), 496 pp., was the first; it was sent to the publisher on October 12. *Coordinated Computing: Tools and Techniques for Distributed Software* by Robert E. Filman and Daniel P. Friedman (New York: McGraw–Hill, 1984), 390 pp., was the second. And my paper "Literate Programming" (15 pp.) was the third; this paper — which discusses WEB — combines Times Roman and Univers type with Computer Modern, and it will be published in volume 27 of *The Computer Journal*.

I like to think that the use of TEX has not only produced books that are well formatted; TEX also seems to have helped produce books whose content is significantly better than books that were written in the old way. Part of this change is due simply to the advantages of word processing and computer editing, since changes are so much easier; but part of it is due to the fact that authors are able to choose the notations and formatting that they want, once they are free from the worries of communicating through several levels of other people to whom such notations might be unfamiliar. I believe that a large number of the books listed above show such improvements in scientific exposition. In particular, my own books have been greatly improved because I've been able to control the typesetting. I still rely heavily on the advice of professional editors and book designers, but I can be much more sure of the final quality than ever before, because there now is comparatively little chance that misunderstandings will introduce any errors. This, to me, is the "bottom line" that has made all of my work on TEX worth while.

Addendum

Additional information on early TEX use at the Royal Institute of Technology was subsequently published by Hans Riesel, "Report on experience with TEX80," *TUGboat* **6** (1985), 76–79.

Chapter 27

Icons for TEX and METAFONT

[Originally published in TUGboat 14 (1993), 387–389.]

Macintosh users have long been accustomed to seeing their files displayed graphically in "iconic" form. I recently acquired a workstation with a window system and file management software that gave me a similar opportunity to visualize my own UNIX files; so naturally I wanted my TEX-related material to be represented by suitable icons. The purpose of this note is to present the icons I came up with, in hopes that other users might enjoy working with them and/or enhancing them.

The file manager on my new machine, a Sun SPARCstation, invokes a "classing engine," which looks at each file's name and/or contents to decide what kind of file it is. Every file type is then represented by a 32 × 32 bitmap called its *icon*, together with another 32 × 32 bitmap called its *icon mask*. In bit positions where the icon mask is 1, the file manager displays one of two pixel colors, called the foreground and background colors, depending on whether the icon has 1 or 0 in that position. (The foreground and background colors may be different for each file type.) In other positions of the bitmap, where the icon mask is 0, the file manager displays its own background color.

For example, each file whose name ends with .tex or .mf is now iconified with the bitmaps

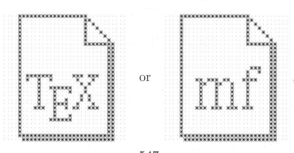

or   ,

respectively on my machine; these are compatible with the existing scheme in which C program source and header files, identified by suffixes .c and .h, have

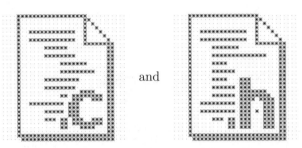

and

as icons. Similarly, a file named *.ltx will get the icon

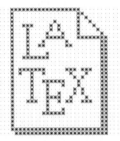

All I had to do was tell the classing engine how to identify TEX and METAFONT files, and to provide the bitmaps for icons and masks. In each case mentioned so far, the corresponding icon mask is one that the file manager already has built in as the `Generic_Doc_glyph_mask`, namely

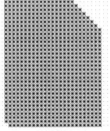

The transcript files output by TEX and METAFONT provided me with a more interesting design problem. They're both named *.log on my system, so they can't be distinguished by file name. I decided that any file whose first 12 bytes are the ASCII characters 'This␣is␣TeX,'

should be considered a TEX transcript, and any file that begins with 'This␣is␣METAFONT,' should be considered a METAFONT transcript. The corresponding icons were fun to make; I based them on the illustrations Duane Bibby had drawn for the user manuals:

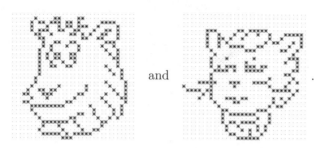

and .

The icon masks for transcript files are then

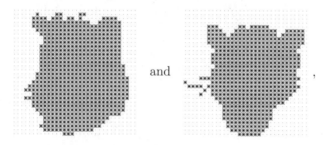

and ,

respectively.

TEX's main output is, of course, a device-independent (DVI) file, and METAFONT produces generic font (GF) files. I decided to represent such files by

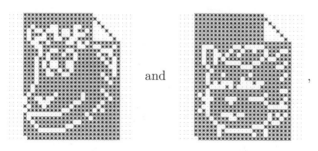

and ,

because they are analogous to photographic "negatives" that need to be "developed" by other software. When a GF file has been packed into a

PK file, its icon changes to

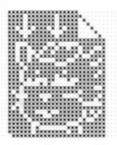

Virtual font files are represented by an analogous

These file types are identifiable by the respective names *.dvi, *gf, *pk, *.vf, and they can also be identified by content: The first byte always has the numerical value 247 (octal *367*), then the next byte is respectively 2, 131, 89, 202 (octal *002, 203, 131, 312*) for dvi, gf, pk, or vf.

The other principal output of METAFONT is a font metric file, which can be identified by the suffix .tfm in its name. I assigned the following icon and mask to such files:

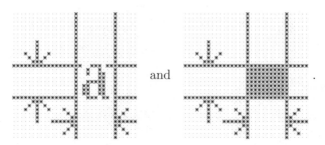

and

I do all my programming nowadays in the CWEB language [1, 2, 3, 4], hence I also accumulate lots of files of two additional types. CWEB source

files are identified by the suffix .w, and CWEB change files have the suffix
.ch; the corresponding icons

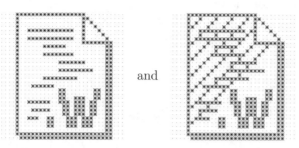 and

are intended to blend with the system's existing conventions for .c and
.h files, mentioned above.

What foreground colors and background colors should be assigned
to these icons? I'm not sure. At the moment I have a grayscale monitor,
not color, so I don't have enough experience to recommend particular
choices. Setting all the foreground colors equal to basic black (RGB values $\langle 0, 0, 0 \rangle$) has worked fine; but I don't want all the background colors
to be pure white (RGB $\langle 255, 255, 255 \rangle$). I'm tentatively using pure white
for the background color of the "negative" icons (dvi, gf, pk, and vf), and
off-white (RGB $\langle 230, 230, 230 \rangle$) for the background of transcript icons.
The TEX and METAFONT source file icons currently have background
RGB values $\langle 200, 200, 255 \rangle$, corresponding to light blue; font metric icons
and LATEX source icons have background RGB values $\langle 255, 200, 200 \rangle$,
light red. I should probably have given METAFONT source files an orange hue, more in keeping with the cover of *The METAFONTbook*. On
my grayscale monitor I had to lighten the background color assigned
by the system software to C object files and to coredump files (*.o and
core*); otherwise it was impossible for me to see the detail of the system
icons

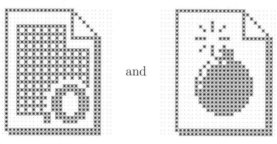 and

on my grayscale display. I expect other users will need to adjust foreground and background colors to go with the decor of their own desktops.

In 1989 I had my first opportunity to work with a personal graphic workstation, and I immediately decided to make 64×64-bit icons for TEX and METAFONT — for the programs, not for the files. But I've always found it more convenient to run TEX and METAFONT from UNIX shells, so I never have used those early icons. Here they are, still waiting for their proper raison d'être:

All of the icons shown above, except for those already present in directory /usr/openwin/share/include/images of the OpenWindows distribution from Sun Microsystems, can be obtained via anonymous ftp from directory `pub/tex/icons` at `ftp.cs.stanford.edu` on the Internet. That directory also contains a file called `cetex.ascii`, which can be used to install the icons into OpenWindows by saying '`ce_db_merge system -from_ascii cetex.ascii`'.

References

[1] `CWEB` public distribution, available by anonymous ftp from directory `pub/cweb` at `ftp.cs.stanford.edu`.

[2] Donald E. Knuth, *Literate Programming*, CSLI Lecture Notes 27 (Stanford, California: Center for the Study of Language and Information, 1992). Distributed by Cambridge University Press.

[3] Donald E. Knuth, *The Stanford GraphBase: A Platform for Combinatorial Computing* (New York: ACM Press, 1994).

[4] Donald E. Knuth and Silvio Levy, *The CWEB System of Structured Documentation*, Version 3.0 (Reading, Massachusetts: Addison–Wesley, 1993). An up-to-date version is available online in [1].

Addendum

The icons developed for OpenWindows have now been adapted to other window systems by several volunteers. They can be found, for example, in directory `support/icons/` of the CTAN archives.

Chapter 28

Computers and Typesetting

[Remarks presented at the Computer Museum, Boston, Massachusetts, on 21 May 1986, as part of a "coming-out party" to celebrate the completion of TₑX. Originally published in TUGboat 7 (1986), 95–98.]

The title of the books we're celebrating today is *Computers & Typesetting*, and since we're meeting here in the Computer Museum I think it's appropriate to point out that computers have been intimately associated with typesetting ever since the very beginning.

Anybody who reads about the history of computers will soon learn that many of the key ideas go back to 19th century England, where Charles Babbage designed a so-called Difference Engine and went on from there to plan his Analytical Engine. Babbage's machines were never completed, but a Swedish author and publisher named Georg Scheutz read about them and was so fascinated that he and his son Edvard actually built a working difference engine. Thus it was that the first sophisticated computing device came to be built in Sweden. And the most interesting thing, to me at least, was that the output of the Scheutz machine was not punched cards or anything like that; their machine actually produced stereotype molds from which books could be printed![1]

---

[1] Babbage had been planning all along to typeset the output of his Difference Engine; for this purpose he had experimented with movable type, stereotyping, and copper punches, but he never exhibited the results of those experiments. His Analytical Engine, which was to be controlled by punched cards, was supposedly going to be able to print its results as well as to punch them on cards. See Charles Babbage, *Passages From the Life of a Philosopher* (London: Longman, Green, Longman, Roberts, & Green, 1864), Chapters 5 and 8; reprinted in *Charles Babbage and His Calculating Engines*, edited by Philip and Emily Morrison (New York: Dover, 1961), 35–37, 61.

Even earlier, J. H. Müller had planned to add a printing apparatus to the mechanical calculator he had invented: "If the calculator sells well, I'll

Several books were, indeed, printed from the output of the early Swedish machine. It was demonstrated in 1856 at the Universal Exposition in Paris, and the souvenir album of that exposition contains the following glowing tribute: "This nearly intelligent machine not only effects in seconds calculations that would demand an hour; it prints the results that it obtains, adding the merit of neat calligraphy to the merit of calculation without possible error."[2] I have copied a small part of a page from the first computer-produced book — printed in 1857 — so that you can see how far we've come since then:[3]

$$
\begin{array}{c|c}
2405 & 38112 \\
2406 & 38130 \\
2407 & 38148 \\
2408 & 38166 \\
2409 & 38184 \\
\end{array}
$$

As far as I know, the tables in this book represent the first extant output of an automatic calculator.[4]

go on to make a machine that prints any arbitrary arithmetical progression, either as a sequence of plain numbers or together with the argument separated by a line, on paper with printer's ink, stopping itself when the page is full." See his letter of 9 September 1784 in *Georg Christoph Lichtenberg Briefwechsel* **2**, edited by Ulrich Joost and Albrecht Schöne (Munich: C. H. Beck, 1985), 905.

[2] Léon Brisse, *Album de l'Exposition Universelle* (Paris, 1857), 194. (Cited in Uta C. Merzbach, *Georg Scheutz and the First Printing Calculator* [Washington: Smithsonian Institution Press, 1977].)

[3] George and Edward Scheutz, *Specimens of Tables, Calculated, Stereomoulded, and Printed by Machinery* (London: Longman, Brown, Green, Longmans, & Roberts, 1857), 50 pp. The example reproduced here comes from the main table on pages 13–42, which contains logarithms of the integers from 1 to 10,000. Fourteen other tables were also included to prove the versatility of such a machine, which produced its output at the rate of 120 numbers per hour. The Boston Public Library has two copies of this book, originally sent by Edvard Scheutz to Benjamin A. Gould (dated 1 May 1857) and to the Nathaniel Bowditch Library (dated 11 May).

[4] No; I learned later that Georg Scheutz had previously published a short table that was calculated and stereotyped on the first machine that he and his son had put together. Page 74 of his book *Nytt och Enkelt Sätt att Lösa*

I'd also like to say a few words about the history of my own work on computers and typesetting. Last week I went back to my diary of 1977 and found an entry from Thursday, May 5, where it says "Design of TEX started." My diary[5] says that I worked intensely on the design all day Thursday, Friday, and Saturday; then I went to see *Airport 77* and *Earthquake* to relax. The entry for the following Thursday says: "Wrote draft report on TEX, stayed up till 5 am typing it into machine." That weekend I went with my wife on a tour of the Sacramento area with Stanford's Library Associates. We saw many examples of fine printing during that trip, and this experience encouraged me to read a lot of books about font design during the following week. My diary entry for Saturday, 21 May 1977 — exactly nine years ago today — says that by 5 am I had completed a "rough draft of lowercase and uppercase Roman and italics and digits 0–9." After a few hours of sleep, I spent the rest of that Saturday writing computer programs to plot curves on a raster. Oh, how little I knew in those days about how difficult it would be to complete this work, which I had sketched out in about two weeks!

Why did I *start* working on TEX in 1977? The whole thing actually began long before, in connection with my books on *The Art of Computer Programming*. I had prepared a second edition of Volume 2, but when I received galley proofs they looked awful — because printing

---

Nummereqvationer af Högre och Lägre Grader (Stockholm: J. L. Brudins, 1849), contains the values of $x^3 - 3x^2 + 90037x$ for $1 \leq x \leq 25$, beginning as follows:

1	90035
2	180070
3	270111
4	360164
5	450235

This first-ever example of an automatically printed table was brought to the attention of computer science historians by Michael Lindgren, whose book *Glory and Failure* (Stockholm: Royal Institute of Technology Library, 1987), contains fascinating details about all aspects of the Scheutz machines. In particular, page 150 of Lindgren's book shows the actual stereotype plate that had been used to print the demonstration table in 1849; leading zeros had been scratched off by hand! (That was not true in 1857.) Notice that the individual digits of Scheutz's type were aligned much more neatly in 1849 than in 1857, presumably because a short demonstration table was less burdensome for the machine than a long production run.

[5] See Chapter 24 of the present volume.

technology had changed drastically since the first edition had been published. The books were now done with phototypesetting, instead of hot lead Monotype machines; and (alas!) they were being done with the help of computers instead of by hand. The result was poor spacing, especially in the math, and the fonts of type were terrible by comparison with the originals. I was quite discouraged by this, and didn't know what to do. Addison–Wesley offered to reset everything by the old Monotype method, but I knew that the old way was dying out fast; surely by the time I had finished Volume 4 the same problem would arise again, and I didn't want to write a book that would come out looking like the recent galleys I had seen.

Then a nice thing happened. I was on a committee to revise Stanford's reading list for our department's comprehensive exam, and one of the things we had to do was evaluate a book that Pat Winston had just written about *Artificial Intelligence.* We received galley proofs of that book, and the story we were told was that these galleys had been generated by a new machine in Southern California [at Information International, Inc.], all based on a discrete high-resolution raster. Apparently one of Winston's students at M.I.T. had flown to Los Angeles with that book on magnetic tape, and the galley proofs we saw were the result. Well, I had had lots of experience with rasterized printing, but only at low resolution, so I thought of bitmaps simply as amusing approximations to "real" typography. When I saw the galleys of Winston's book, I was astounded, because the resolution was so good I couldn't tell that the type was actually digital. In fact the digital type looked a lot better than what I had been getting in my own galley proofs.

Digital typesetting means patterns of 0s and 1s, and computer science can be thought of as the study of patterns of 0s and 1s. Therefore, it dawned on me for the first time that I, as a computer scientist, would be able to help solve the printing problem that was worrying me so much. I didn't need to know about metallurgy or optics or chemistry or anything scary like that; all I had to do was construct the right pattern of 0s and 1s and send it to a high-resolution digital typesetter like that machine in Southern California; then I'd have my books the way I wanted them. In other words, the problem of quality printing had been reduced to a problem about 0s and 1s. Therefore it was almost an *obligation* for a computer scientist like myself to study the problem carefully.

Within a week after seeing the galleys of Winston's book, I decided to drop everything else and to work on digital typography. Professor Winston unfortunately couldn't be present here today, but I have to say: Pat, I can't thank you enough for having written that book!

Ever since those beginnings in 1977, the TEX research project that I embarked on was driven by two major goals. The first goal was *quality*: we wanted to produce documents that were not just nice, but actually the best. Once upon a time, computers could deal only with numbers; then several years passed when they had numbers and uppercase letters; after awhile they became able to deal with both uppercase and lowercase; then they became capable of working with letters of variable width; and by 1977 there were several systems that could produce very attractive documents. My goal was to take the last step and go all the way, to the finest quality that had ever been achieved in printed documents.

It turned out that it was not hard to achieve this level of quality with respect to the formatting of text, after about two years of work. For example, we did experiments with *Time* magazine to prove that *Time* would look much better if it had been done with TEX. But it turned out that the design of typefaces was much more difficult than I had anticipated; seven years went by before I was able to generate letterforms that I began to like.

The second major design goal was to be *archival*: to create systems that would be independent of changes in printing technology as much as possible. When the next generations of printing devices came along, I wanted to be able to retain the same quality already achieved, instead of having to solve all the problems anew. I wanted to design something that would still be usable in 100 years. In other words, my goal was to arrange things so that, if book specifications were saved now, our descendants could produce an equivalent book in the year 2086. Although I expect that there will be a continual development of "front ends" to TEX and METAFONT, as well as a continual development of "back ends" or device drivers that operate on the output of the systems, I designed TEX and METAFONT themselves so that they will not have to change at all: They should be able to serve as useful *fixed points* in the middle, solid enough to build on and to rely on.

Today I'd like to brag a little, and say that I think that these goals of top quality and technology independence seem to be achieved; and Volumes A, B, C, D, E tell everything about how it was done. Today I'm seeing these books for the first time, and I'm happy that all of you can be here to help me celebrate this event. These books are somewhat unusual because they describe themselves: They describe exactly how they were typeset. All of the formatting was done by the TEX system described in Volumes A and B. Also every letter and every symbol that appears in all five volumes, as well as on the covers and book jackets, was done by the METAFONT system described in Volumes C and D.

Volume E tells how I dotted all the i's and crossed all the t's, literally. If copies of these books were sent to Mars, the Martians would be able to use them to recreate the patterns of 0s and 1s that were used in the typesetting. Essentially everything I learned during the past nine years is in here.

All of the methods described in these books are in the public domain; thus anybody can freely use any of the ideas. The only thing I'm retaining control of is the names, TEX and METAFONT: Products that go by either name are obliged to conform to the standard. If any changes are made, I won't complain, as long as the changed systems are not called TEX or METAFONT.

Volumes A and C are user manuals. I tried to write manuals that would suit users at all levels as they grow with the systems. And I also strove for a high standard of excellence in the choice of the quotations from other works that are included at the end of every chapter.

Volumes B and D contain the complete program listings of TEX and METAFONT. These books are specifically for computer scientists, not for casual users, but I'm especially pleased with how they came out because they represent an unexpected payoff of my research. This is something that I had no idea would be possible when I began nine years ago. As I wrote the programs for TEX and METAFONT, I wanted to produce systems that would represent the state of the art in computer programming, and this goal led to the so-called WEB system of structured documentation. I think that WEB might turn out to be the most important thing about all this research—more important in the long run than TEX and METAFONT themselves—because WEB represents a new way to write software that I think is really better than any other way. The use of WEB has made it possible to write programs that are so readable, I think there already are more people who understand the inner workings of TEX than now understand any other system of comparable size. Furthermore I think it's fair to claim that WEB has made TEX and METAFONT as portable, as maintainable, and as reliable as any other pieces of software in existence. The programs are now running and producing essentially identical results on almost all large computers; there are thousands of users, yet no bugs have been reported for more than half a year. I think there is at most one more bug in TEX, and I'm willing to pay $20.48 to the first person who finds it. (Next year the reward will double, to $40.96, etc.)[6]

---

[6] (Editor's note.) A listener asked, how much had it cost to pay off the finders of bugs in the programs and errors in the books? Depending on how many

Volumes B and D also contain another innovation that improves on the basic WEB system previously available: Every pair of facing pages has a mini-index on the right-hand page, for quick cross reference to anything that's referred to on either page; this saves a lot of time thumbing through the master index at the end.

In recent years I've been making a pitch for programs as works of *literature*. Although there still is no Pulitzer Prize for the best-written computer programs of the year, I tried to write Volumes B and D in such a way that I would be a candidate for such a prize if it were actually given! More seriously, I intended these books to be useful to computer scientists for self study as well as for study in college seminars. Volume D, in particular, should make a good text for a group of advanced students.

The fifth volume, Volume E, is the most fun of all. I hope you will all open a copy and riffle through the pages, so that you can see what I mean. METAFONT is a computer language that is not very much like any other, so my goal in this book was to provide lots of examples of how METAFONT can be used to produce fonts of reasonably good quality. Over 500 examples appear here; they cover nearly every letter, digit, punctuation mark, and other symbol that was used in printing these books.

The fonts you get from these programs have the general name "Computer Modern." My colleague Charles Bigelow has contributed an introduction that talks about Modern fonts in general. The book explains how you can make your own personal variations of the fonts, which are designed with many parameters so that they can be generated in almost limitless variety. At the end of the book there are sample pages that show specimens of 75 standard Computer Modern typefaces; and thousands of additional varieties could be generated with ease.

Even if you don't read the METAFONT programs in this book, I think it's appealing just to look at the pictures of these constructed alphabets,[7] and to "know" that the program on the page facing each letter was what "drew" that letter; it's all there. Somehow this gives a satisfying sense of completeness and order.

---

checks were actually cashed, Don estimated the total to be between $2,000 and $5,000. It is doubtful that the checkbook in question is easily balanced.

[7] (Editor's note.) The pictures, it was pointed out, were generated separately from the text of the examples, and pasted in. If both the raster images and the text had been incorporated at the same time, it would have exceeded the capacity of the machines used to produce the book in 1985.

The most important thing I want to talk about this morning is *HELP*. I had lots and lots of help — literally hundreds of people who volunteered to assist this project in significant ways — beginning with Hans Wolf of Addison–Wesley, who taught me the details of the Monotype systems that had been used to typeset *The Art of Computer Programming* in the 60s. I was especially fortunate in my work on font design to have had extensive help from world leaders like Hermann Zapf and Matthew Carter.

Another stroke of luck was to have outstanding research associates like David Fuchs and John Hobby. Furthermore my research project at Stanford had generous financial support, most notably from the National Science Foundation and the System Development Foundation. With so much help, it would have been very hard for my research to fail. And my wife Jill gave the most help of all. (Next month we will celebrate 25 years of marriage!)

One final note: People often ask me why TEX and METAFONT are symbolized in these books by a lion and a lioness. When Duane Bibby first came up with the lion idea, I instinctively felt that it was right, but I never understood exactly why this was, until about a month ago when I was in the Boston Public Library. I passed by the magnificent stone lions on the library's grand staircase, and I thought: "That's it! TEX and METAFONT try to be like these lions, fixtures that support a great library.[8] I love books, and lions represent books!" No wonder I'm so happy when I realize that TEX and METAFONT have already contributed to the making of several dozen books of fine quality: It makes me extremely pleased to think that this research will probably contribute to the making of many more fine books in years to come.

---

[8] (Editor's note.) One is also reminded of the lions that grandly guard the entrance to the New York Public Library, which celebrated its 75th anniversary during this same week.

Chapter 29

The New Versions of TeX and METAFONT

*[Originally published in TUGboat **10** (1989), 325–328; **11** (1990), 12.]*

For more than five years I held firm to my conviction that a stable system was far better than a system that continues to evolve. But during the TUG meeting at Stanford in August, 1989, I was persuaded to make one last set of changes, in order to bring TeX and METAFONT to a state of completion consistent with their overall philosophy and goals.

The main reason for the changes was the fact that I had guessed wrong about 7-bit character sets versus 8-bit character sets. I believed that standard text input would continue indefinitely to be confined to at most 128 characters, since I did not think a keyboard with 256 different outputs would be especially efficient. Needless to say, I was proved wrong, especially by developments in Europe and Asia. As soon as I realized that a text formatting program with 7-bit input would rapidly begin to seem as archaic as the 6-bit systems we once had, I knew that a fundamental revision was necessary.

But the 7-bit assumption pervaded everything, so I needed to take the programs apart and redo them thoroughly in 8-bit style. This put TeX onto the operating table and under the knife for the first time since 1984, and I had a final opportunity to include a few new features that had occurred to me or been suggested by users since then.

The new extensions are entirely upward compatible with previous versions of TeX and METAFONT (with a few small exceptions mentioned below). This means that error-free inputs to the old TeX and META-FONT will still be error-free inputs to the new systems, and they will still produce the same outputs.

However, anybody who dares to use the new extensions will be unable to get the desired results from old versions of TeX and METAFONT. I am therefore asking the TeX community to update all copies of the old versions as soon as possible. Let us root out and destroy the obsolete 7-bit systems, even though we were able to do many fine things with them.

In this note I'll discuss the changes, one by one; then I'll describe the exceptions to upward compatibility.

The Character Set

Up to 256 distinct characters are now allowed in input files. The codes that were formerly limited to the range $0 \mathinner{.\,.} 127$ are now in the range $0 \mathinner{.\,.} 255$. All characters are alike; you are free to use any character for any purpose in TEX, assigning appropriate values to its \catcode, \mathcode, \lccode, \uccode, \sfcode, and \delcode. Plain TEX initializes these code values for characters above 127 just as it initializes the codes for ordinary punctuation characters like '!'.

There's a new convention for inputting an arbitrary 8-bit character to TEX when you can't necessarily type it: The four consecutive characters ^^$\alpha\beta$, where α and β are any of the "lowercase hexadecimal digits" 0, 1, 2, 3, 4, 5, 6, 7, 8, 9, a, b, c, d, e, or f, are treated by TEX on input as if they were a single character with specified code digits. For example, ^^80 gives character code 128; the entire character set is available from ^^00 to ^^ff. The old convention discussed in Appendix C, under which character 0 was ^^@, character 1 (control-A) was ^^A, . . . , and character 127 was ^^?, still works for the first 128 character codes, except that the character following ^^ should not be a lowercase hexadecimal digit when the immediately following character is another such digit.

The existence of 8-bit characters has less effect in METAFONT than in TEX, because METAFONT's character classes are built in to each installation. The normal set of 95 printing characters described on page 51 of *The METAFONTbook* can be supplemented by extended characters as discussed on page 282, but this is rarely done because it leads to problems of portability. METAFONT's **char** operator is now redefined to operate modulo 256 instead of modulo 128.

Hyphenation Tables

Up to 256 distinct sets of rules for hyphenation are now allowed in TEX. There's a new integer parameter called \language, whose current value specifies the hyphenation convention in force. If \language is negative or greater than 255, TEX acts as if \language is zero.

When you list hyphenation exceptions with TEX's \hyphenation primitive, those exceptions apply to the current language only. Similarly, the \patterns primitive tells TEX to remember new hyphenation patterns for the current language; this operation is allowed only in the special "initialization" program called INITEX. Hyphenation exceptions can be added at any time, but new patterns cannot be added after a paragraph has been typeset.

When TEX reads the text of a paragraph, it automatically inserts "whatsit nodes" into the horizontal list for that paragraph whenever a character comes from a different \language than its predecessor. In that way TEX can tell what hyphenation rules to use on each word of the paragraph even if you switch frequently back and forth among many different languages.

The special whatsit nodes are inserted automatically in unrestricted horizontal mode (that is, when you are creating a paragraph, but not when you are specifying the contents of an hbox). You can insert a special whatsit yourself in restricted horizontal mode by saying \setlanguage⟨number⟩. This is needed only if you are doing something tricky, like unboxing some contribution to a paragraph.

Hyphenated Fragment Control

TEX has two new parameters \lefthyphenmin and \righthyphenmin, which specify the smallest word fragments that will appear at the beginning or end of a word that has been hyphenated. Previously the values \lefthyphenmin=2 and \righthyphenmin=3 were hard-wired into TEX and impossible to change. Now plain TEX format supplies the old values, which are still recommended for most American publications; but you can get more hyphens by decreasing these parameters, and you can get fewer hyphens by increasing them. If the sum of \lefthyphenmin and \righthyphenmin is 63 or more, all hyphenation is suppressed. (You can also suppress hyphenation by using a font with \hyphenchar=-1, or by switching to a \language that has no hyphenation patterns or exceptions.)

Smarter Ligatures

Now here's the most radical change. Previous versions of TEX had only one kind of ligature, in which two characters like 'f' and 'i' were changed into a single character like 'fi' when they appeared consecutively. The new TEX understands much more complex constructions by which, for example, we could change a 'j' following 'f' to a dotless 'ȷ' while the 'f' remains unchanged: 'fȷ'.

As before, you get ligatures only if they have been provided in the font you are using. Before we look at the new features of METAFONT, by which enhanced ligatures can be created, let's review the old conventions. A METAFONT programmer has always been able to specify a "ligature/kerning program" for any character of the font being created. If, for example, the 'fi' combination appears in font position 12, the replacement of 'f' and 'i' by 'fi' is specified by including the statement

   "i" =: 12

in the ligature/kerning program for "f"; this is METAFONT's present convention.

The new ligatures allow you to retain one or both of the original characters while inserting a new one. Instead of =: you can also write |=: if you wish to retain the left character, or =:| if you wish to retain the right character, or |=:| if you want to keep them both. For example, if the dotless 'ȷ' appears in font position 17, you can get the behavior mentioned above by putting

   "j" |=: 17

into f's ligature/kern program.

There also are four additional operators

$$ |=:>, \quad =:|>, \quad |=:|>, \quad |=:|>>, $$

where each > tells TEX to shift its focus one position to the right. For example, after f and j have been replaced by f and dotless ȷ as above, TEX will begin again to execute f's ligature/kern program, possibly inserting a kern before the dotless ȷ, or possibly changing the f to an entirely different character, etc. But if the instruction had been

   "j" |=:> 17

instead, TEX would turn immediately to the ligature/kern program for characters following character 17 (the dotless ȷ); no further change would be made between f and ȷ even if the font had something specified for that combination.

Boundary Ligatures

Every consecutive string of "characters" read by TEX in horizontal mode (after macro expansion) can be called a "word." (Technically we consider a "character" in this definition to be either a character whose \catcode is a letter or otherchar, or a control sequence that has been

\let equal to such a character, or a control sequence that has been defined by \chardef, or the construction \char⟨number⟩.) The new TEX
now imagines that there is an invisible "left boundary character" just
before every such word, and an invisible "right boundary character" just
after it. These boundary characters take effect if the font designer has
specified ligatures and/or kerning between them and the adjacent letters. Thus, the first or last character of a word can now be made to
change its shape automatically.

A ligature/kern program for the left boundary character is spec-
ified within METAFONT by using the special label || : in a **ligtable**
command. A ligature or kern with the right boundary character is specified by assigning a value to the new internal METAFONT parameter
boundarychar, and by specifying a ligature or kern with respect to this
character. The *boundarychar* may or may not exist as a real character
in the font.

For example, suppose we want to change the first letter of a word
from 'F' to 'ff' if we are doing some olde English. The METAFONT font
designer could then say

```
ligtable ||: "F" |=: 11
```

if character 11 is the 'ff'. The same ligtable instruction should appear
in the programs for characters like (and ' and " and - that can precede strings of letters; then 'Bassington-French' will yield 'Bassington-
ffrench'.

If the 's' of our font is the pre-19th century s that looks like a
mutilated 'f' (namely 'ſ'), and if we have a modern 's' in position 128,
we can convert the final s's as Ben Franklin did by introducing ligature
instructions such as

```
boundarychar := 255;
ligtable "s": 255 =:| 128,
             "." =:| 128,
             "," =:| 128,
             ")" =:| 128,
             "'" =:| 128,
```

and so on. (A true oldstyle font would also have ligatures for ss and si
and sl and ssi and ssl and sh and possibly st; it would be fun to create
a Computer Modern Oldſtyle, perhaps for a Chriſtmas newſletter.)

The implicit left boundary character is omitted by TEX if you say
\noboundary just before the word; the implicit right boundary is omitted
if you say \noboundary just after it.

More Compact Ligatures

Two or more ligtables can now share common code. To do this in META-
FONT, you say 'skipto ⟨*n*⟩' at the end of one **ligtable** command, then
you say '⟨*n*⟩::' within another. Such local labels can be reused; for
example, you can say **skipto** 1 again after 1:: has appeared, and this
skips to the *next* appearance of 1::. There are 256 local labels, numbered 0 to 255. *Restriction:* At most 128 ligature or kern commands
can intervene between a **skipto** and its matching label.

The TFM file format has been extended in an upwardly compatible way to allow more than 32,500 ligature/kern commands per font.
(Previously there was an effective limit of 256.)

Better Looking Sloppiness

There is now a better way to avoid overfull boxes, for people who
don't want to look at their documents to fix unfeasible line breaks
manually. Such people have previously tried to do this by setting
\tolerance=10000, but the result was terrible because TEX would tend
to consolidate all the badness in one truly horrible line. (TEX considers
all badness ≥ 10000 to be infinitely bad, and all such infinities are equal.)

A new dimension parameter called \emergencystretch provides
a better way. If \emergencystretch is positive and if TEX has been
unable to typeset a paragraph without exceeding the given tolerances,
another pass over the paragraph is made in which TEX pretends that
additional stretchability equal to \emergencystretch is present in every line. The effect of this is to scale down all the badnesses into a range
where previously infinite cases become finite; TEX will find an optimum
solution to the scaled-down problem, and this will be about as good
as possible in a practical sense. (The extra stretchability is not really
present; therefore underfull boxes will be reported in warning messages
unless \hbadness is increased.)

Looking at Badness

TEX has a new internal integer parameter called \badness that records
the badness of the box it has most recently constructed. If that box
was overfull, \badness will be 1000000; otherwise \badness will be between 0 and 10000.

Looking at the Line Number

TEX also has a new internal integer parameter called \inputlineno,
which contains the number of the line that TEX would show on an error

message if an error occurred now. (This parameter and \badness are
"read only" in the same way as \lastpenalty: You can use them in the
context of a ⟨number⟩, e.g., by saying 'ifnum\inputlineno>\badness
... \fi' or '\the\inputlineno', but you cannot set them to new values.)

Not Looking at Error Content

There's a new integer parameter called \errorcontextlines that specifies the maximum number of two-line pairs of context displayed with
TeX's error messages (in addition to the top and bottom lines, which
always appear). Plain TeX now sets \errorcontextlines=5, but
higher-level format packages might prefer \errorcontextlines=1 or
even \errorcontextlines=0. In the latter case, an error that previously involved three or more pairs of context would now appear as
follows:

```
! Error.
<somewhere> The \top
                    line
...
l.123 \The
          bottom line.
```

If \errorcontextlines<0 you wouldn't even see the '...' here.

Output Recycling

One more new integer parameter, called \holdinginserts, completes
the set. If \holdinginserts>0 when TeX is putting the current page
into \box255 for the \output routine, TeX will not move anything from
insertion nodes into the corresponding boxes; all insertion nodes will
stay in place. Designers of output routines can use this when they want
to put the contents of box 255 back into the current page to be rebroken
(because they might want to change \vsize or something).

Exceptions to Upward Compatibility

The new features of TeX and METAFONT imply that a few things work
differently than before. I will try to list all such cases here (except when
the previous behavior was erroneous due to a bug in TeX or META-
FONT). I don't know of any cases where users will actually be affected,
because all of these exceptions are pretty esoteric.

- TEX used to convert the character strings ˆˆ0, ˆˆ1, …, ˆˆ9, ˆˆa, ˆˆb, ˆˆc, ˆˆd, ˆˆe, ˆˆf into the respective single characters p, q, …, y, !, ", #, $, %, &. It will no longer do this if the following character is one of the hexadecimal digits 0123456789abcdef.

- TEX used to insert no character at the end of an input line if \endlinechar>127. It will now insert a character in that place unless \endlinechar>255. (As previously, \endlinechar<0 suppresses the end-of-line character. This character is normally 13 = ˆˆM = ASCII control-M = carriage return.)

- Some diagnostic messages from TEX used to have the notation ["80] .. ["FF] when referring to characters in the range 128..255 (for example when displaying the contents of an overfull box involving fonts that include such characters). The notation ˆˆ80 .. ˆˆff is now used instead.

- The expressions **char** 128 and **char** 0 used to be equivalent in METAFONT; now **char** is defined modulo 256 instead. Hence **char** −1 = **char** 255, etc.

- INITEX used to forget all previous hyphenation patterns each time you specified \patterns. Now all hyphenation pattern specifications are cumulative, and you are not permitted to use \patterns after a paragraph has been hyphenated by INITEX.

- TEX used to act a bit differently when you tried to typeset missing characters of a font. A missing character is now considered to be a word boundary, so you will get slightly more diagnostic output when \tracingcommands>0.

- TEX and METAFONT will report different statistics at the end of a run because they now have a different number of primitives.

- Programs that use the string pool feature of TANGLE will no longer run without changes, because the new TANGLE starts numbering multi-character strings at 256 instead of 128.

- INITEX programs must now set the values \lefthyphenmin=2 and \righthyphenmin=3 in order to reproduce their previous behavior.

Chapter 30

The Future of TeX and METAFONT

[Originally published in TUGboat **11** *(1990), 489.]*

My work on developing TeX, METAFONT, and Computer Modern has come to an end. I will make no further changes except to correct extremely serious bugs.

I have put these systems into the public domain so that people everywhere can use the ideas freely if they wish. I have also spent thousands of hours trying to ensure that the systems produce essentially identical results on all computers. I strongly believe that an unchanging system has great value, in spite of the fact that any complex system can be improved. Therefore I believe that it is unwise to make further "improvements" to the systems called TeX and METAFONT. Let us regard these systems as fixed points, which should give the same results 100 years from now that they produce today.

The current version number for TeX is 3.1, and for METAFONT it is 2.7. If corrections are necessary, the next versions of TeX will be 3.14, then 3.141, then 3.1415, ..., converging to the ratio of a circle's circumference to its diameter; for METAFONT the sequence will be 2.71, 2.718, ..., converging to the base of natural logarithms. I intend to be fully responsible for all changes to these systems for the rest of my life. I will periodically study reports of apparent bugs, and I will decide whether changes need to be made. Rewards will be paid to the first finders of any true bugs, at my discretion, but I can no longer afford to double the size of the reward each year. Whenever I have created a new version, I will put it in the official master TeX archive, which currently resides at Stanford University. At the time of my death, it is my intention that the then-current versions of TeX and METAFONT be forever left unchanged, except that the final version numbers to be reported in the "banner" lines of the programs should become

```
TeX, Version $\pi$
```

571

and

METAFONT, Version e

respectively. From that moment on, all "bugs" will be permanent "features."

As stated on the copyright pages of Volumes B, D, and E, anybody can make use of my programs in whatever way they wish, as long as they do not use the names TEX, METAFONT, or Computer Modern. In particular, any person or group who wants to produce a program superior to mine is free to do so. However, nobody is allowed to call a system TEX or METAFONT unless that system conforms 100% to my own programs, as I have specified in the manuals for the TRIP and TRAP tests. And nobody is allowed to use the names of the Computer Modern fonts in Volume E for any fonts that do not produce identical tfm files. This prohibition applies to all people or machines, whether appointed by TUG or by any other organization. I do not intend to delegate the responsibility for maintenance of TEX, METAFONT, or Computer Modern to anybody else, ever.

Of course I do not claim to have found the best solution to every problem. I simply claim that it is a great advantage to have a fixed point as a building block. Improved macro packages can be added on the input side; improved device drivers can be added on the output side. I welcome continued research that will lead to alternative systems that can typeset documents better than TEX is able to do. But the authors of such systems must think of another name.

That is all I ask, after devoting a substantial portion of my life to the creation of these systems and making them available to everybody in the world. I sincerely hope that the members of TUG will help me to enforce these wishes, by putting severe pressure on any person or group who produces any incompatible system and calls it TEX or META-FONT or Computer Modern — no matter how slight the incompatibility might seem.

Chapter 31

Questions and Answers, I

*[Q&A Session at the annual meeting of the TₑX Users Group, on 25 July 1995 in St. Petersburg, Florida. Originally published in TUGboat **17** (1996), 7–22; edited by Christina Thiele, based on tape recordings by Calvin W. Jackson and Jeremy Gibbons. The session was called to order by Barbara Beeton.]*

Barbara: I've had the pleasure of knowing Don for quite a long time. I'd like to start off with the first question ... the obvious question, *other* than what the T-shirt means: How's Volume 4 doing? [*laughter*]

Don Knuth: Thank you very much, Barbara. You said that I'm the reason most of you are here. I think that Barbara is just as much a part of the reason, as me or anyone, about why we're here. She's done wonderful work for us all these years as editor of *TUGboat* and coordinator of many other activities.

You know, the reason I came to this meeting is that, after the tenth TUG conference, I promised I would come to the 16th because that was the most important number for a computer scientist. Sixteen is not only a power of two, it's two to a power of two:

$$16 \; = \; 2^{2^{2^{2^{2^{-\infty}}}}} \; .$$

[*laughter*] It's about as binary a number as you can get, until 65,536. Numbers are important to me. So this is a momentous meeting for the whole TeX project.

I looked up what was I doing exactly 16 years ago today. And I found out that, of all things, I was working with Barbara Beeton, who had come to Stanford for 2 or 3 weeks on behalf of the American Math Society. She and some colleagues were showing me the problems they were having with making the index to *Math Reviews*. So on 25 July 1979, Barbara and I were trying to figure out how to do a *Math Reviews* index. Our work led to more powerful facilities for leaders and things like that, because the index to *Math Reviews* occasionally presents lots of problems where you have to run the dots in a certain way, based on how many references there are. It was very interesting because I found two bugs in TeX that day — they were numbers 413 and 414 in the history of the development of TeX. Something to do with an error message in case you get to an end-of-file in the middle of something else . . . I think it was that kind of error. That was sixteen years ago today.

Barbara asked, "Why do I have this T-shirt on?" The T-shirt says:

$$x^n + y^n = z^n \quad \dots \; Not!$$

That's a mathematical formula which I could show you how to do in TeX, if you're interested . . . [*laughter*]

I'm wearing this T-shirt because I had a thrill a month ago. It's continually exciting for me to see the uses that people are making of TeX all over the world. Very exciting. One of the most important somehow to me was last month when I went to the library and saw Andrew Wiles's solution to Fermat's Last Theorem. I think a lot of you know that it was front-page news.[1] For a while, there was some doubt whether there was maybe still a gap in his proof, and then it was fixed up. This is the most

---

[1] Wiles proved that the equation $x^n + y^n = z^n$ has no integer solutions when $n > 2$ and $xyz > 0$.

famous by far of all results in mathematics. Just as people can remember where they were when they heard about Kennedy being assassinated, I know mathematicians can all remember where they were when they first heard that Fermat's Theorem was solved. The paper came out in the *Annals of Mathematics* last month;[2] it arrived in our library and I saw it sitting there, and I looked at it and it was just wonderful for me because it was done with TEX and it looked gorgeous! [*laughter*] This to me was the ... you know, it was so ... I mean, I almost felt like I had helped to prove the Theorem myself! [*more laughter*] So now, I'm also very glad to find out that the people who were responsible are here this week. In the back row, we have the editor of *Annals of Mathematics*[3] and also Geraldine Pecht, who was the typesetter. Another thrill for me. Let's give them a hand. [*applause*]

But I didn't want to talk today about anything prepared in advance, I wanted to answer questions.

So, Barbara asked the first question: "What about Volume 4 of *The Art of Computer Programming?*" Now, I usually only answer that question on special occasions. [*laughter*] These days I'm a full-time writer and I'm working very hard on *The Art of Computer Programming*. We have, uh ... let me just see if I can find a scratch page to work on ... [went to overhead projector with live Emacs screen, running at Stanford and transmitted to Florida via the Internet]. This is just to remind me about what to talk about ....

Now, it used to be that we used *"ACP"* as the abbreviation for *The Art of Computer Programming*. But someone else suggested that it should be called *TAOCP*. So now this is the new abbreviation for it: *TAOCP*. *TAOCP* is my life's work; this is what I embarked on in 1962, and I think I have about 20 years of work to go on it yet, after which I'll be 77 years old. So you see why I retired early — in order to be able to work very hard on this.

Bart Childs: Should that be *TAOCP?* [there was a typo on the Emacs screen, which showed '`TOACP`']

Don: It is. You want me to enlarge this font? I only have three or four screen fonts ... Oh! [*sees typo*]

Bart: Does that mean I get a check for five dollars and twelve cents? [*laughter*]

---

[2] Andrew Wiles, "Modular elliptic curves and Fermat's Last Theorem," *Annals of Mathematics* (2) **141** (1995), 443–551.

[3] Maureen Schupsky, Managing Editor, Princeton University Press.

Don: Not for you!! [*laughter*] ... You know I did that on purpose just to see if anybody was looking. [*laughter*] Alright ... Then there's this *other* book I'm working on, called *The Art of Computer Programming* [*laughter*] ... OK, so ... Boy, am I nervous. [*laughter*]

Anyway, in order to finish this project, I have to work very hard, because computer science people keep discovering new things. Originally, my idea was that I was going to be able to summarize *all* of the good stuff in computer science; but now I have to say that I just have to work very hard in order to summarize all the *classical* good stuff in computer science. I'm working especially to get all the history correct and to lay the right foundation for the specialized things. But I can't go up to the frontiers in everything as I could have in the 60s, when I began the project. I worked on TEX for about 10 years total, I guess, and I'm hoping that those 10 years actually will save me about 6 or 7 years of the time I would have had to put into *TAOCP*, because I can now do my other work more efficiently.

The Art of Computer Programming is sort of what I view as the thing that I'm most uniquely able to do in my life. I'm feeling very healthy now and happy, and I feel that what I'm accomplishing every week is about as much as I've ever been able to do in my life in a week. So, I hope I can keep it up for a while. But I know that it takes a lot of time. That's why I'm retired and I'm working full-time on this.

I spent last year building infrastructure for the project, which meant making large computer files of what has accumulated in my house. So I have thousands and thousands of items that I've indexed and put into place so that I know how to find things.

Right now, my current project is to finish answering mail about *The Art of Computer Programming* that came in since I was working on TEX. You know that if anybody found errors in *The TEXbook*, I answered the mail eventually and paid for the errors and so on. Well, people also get a reward for finding errors in *The Art of Computer Programming*. But the fact is, the last time I wrote a check for that was July of 1981. [*laughter*] In August of 1981, my secretary started issuing a form letter, typeset with TEX, saying "I will get back to you soon." [*laughter*] I started putting these letters into a little pile. Then the pile got to be a bigger pile, and it got mixed with all the other preprints I was receiving, until the pile grew to 260 inches high! Now, convert that to centimeters ... well, anyways, it's a lot! [*laughter*] It was about seven to eight meters of material. I went through all that and I am now answering those letters. Actually, the number of letters that I hadn't answered was less than 500 — something like 450 letters — and I'm now answering those letters

von Neumann, John [=Margittai Neumann
    János], 18, 225, 456.
Wadler, Philip Lee, 594.
Wall, Hubert Stanley, 481.
Wallis, John, product, 50, 112, 480.
Wang, Hao (王浩), 382–384.
Wang, Paul Shyh-Horng (王士弘), 436, 631.
Watson, Dan Caldwell, 248.
Wedderburn, Joseph Henry Maclagan, 583.
Wegbreit, Eliot Ben, 603.
Weierstrass, Karl Theodor Wilhelm, 381.
Wiles, Andrew John, 465.
Wilf, Herbert Saul, 92, 483.
Windley, Peter F., 518.
Wise, David Stephen, 420, 434, 595.
Wiseman, Neil Ernest, 420.
Yao, Andrew Chi-chih (姚期智), 538.
Young Tanner, Rosalind Cecilia
    Hildegard, 75.
Zave, Derek Alan, 90, 603.
Zeilberger, Doron, 64.

FIGURE 1. Excerpt from the end of the errata to Volume 1.

and hoping that the checks will reach the people at the addresses from where they sent me their comments.

I'll show you the errata because I'm working on it now. Here's an example (Figure 1), just so you can see what I'm talking about. [*display changes from Emacs to output of* xdvi] This is part of the errata to the index of Volume 1.[4] This is 8pt type being enlarged a lot. I want to show you one of the things I'm working on right now .... For all the authors that I cite in *The Art of Computer Programming*, when they have a non-Western name, I'm building a big database of the names in their native script, for example, Chinese or Japanese. (I haven't put in the Indian names yet, but I'm working with people in India to get that solved.) ... Right now, I have most up-to-date stuff on the Chinese part of it ... I have bitmap fonts for all the Unicode characters — especially the Chinese characters — and I now have a pretty good database of these things, hopefully. In a few years Unicode software should be ready and available, and I'll be able to typeset the various names properly.

I built some interesting Emacs macros that help me with the Unicode characters even though I don't have any software yet for Unicode. I can

---

[4] The PostScript files for these errata can now be downloaded from the Web page http://www-cs-faculty.stanford.edu/~knuth/taocp.html, near the bottom. (Incidentally, I realized later that the index entry for Paul Wang really belongs in the errata to Volume 2.)

type in four hexadecimal digits and then say M-x unic to Emacs; magically the hexadecimal digits are converted into the Chinese character—
the bitmap of it—which is then part of the document. [*demonstrates
by typing 59da*M-x unic] There's Andy Yao's surname in Chinese:

```
\Uni1.08:24:24:-1:20% Unicode char "59da
<1c0770180660018066018066018066019466effb66c339e78%
33167033066033066033066030e7066366c66e666764666%
6e06600c06600e0c601b0c6219986231b06360607f80803e>%
```

I just have 24-by-24 bitmaps of all the characters, but it's enough for
proofreading purposes. I have my workstation set up so that it's very
easy to get these bitmaps. The unic macro tells Emacs to invoke a
little program that looks up the hex code in a file, finds the bitmap, and
inserts it into the TEX file. The stuff between angle brackets is sent by
TEX to PostScript, using the macro

```
\def\Uni#1:#2:#3:#4:#5<#6>%
    % \Uni ems:cols:rows:-hoff:rows+voff<hexbitmap>
  {\leavevmode \hbox to#1\unicodeptsize
    {\special{" 0 0 moveto currentpoint translate
      \unic@deptsize \unic@deptsize scale #2 #3 true
      [24 0 0 -24 #4 #5] {<#6>} imagemask}\hss}}
```

At the end of the year, I'm planning to announce this errata list,
which will be finished by that time. Right now I've accumulated about
180 pages for all three volumes, and I'm still building the list while
answering those old letters.

Then my publishers are going to issue Volume 4 in fascicles, about
128 pages at a time. The idea is to do that about twice a year for the
next 10 years. My steady state, I figure, is going to be about 256 pages
a year of output. We're going to have three or four fascicles in hand
before we actually start this publication. The first four fascicles—one
of them will be extra large, containing the update errata to Volumes 1, 2
and 3; the other three—the second one will be the design of a computer
called MMIX which will be replacing the MIX computer. MMIX is a RISC
machine, very much like the computers that we're all converging to these
days. It's a 64-bit RISC computer that I might even *own*, some day, if
anybody likes it enough to actually build it. Several experts in the field
are helping me design it. Dick Sites, who was the architect of the Alpha
chip, was one of my students and has promised to work on all the final
steps of the design. Also John Hennessy (who designed the MIPS chip),

and some of the people from SPARC. So MMIX is going to be a nice clean RISC computer, which will help us make experiments on algorithms, to see how well the different cache management schemes work with different sorting algorithms and so on.

The second fascicle will be to replace MIX by MMIX and I'm hoping that, eventually, every time I have a MIX program in *The Art of Computer Programming*, it will be replaced by an MMIX program. I'm not going to do that until I finish Volumes 4 and 5. But I'm hoping that a lot of other people will have done that work already by the time I get there. People have already promised me that they're going to have a C-compiler up for MMIX next year, and we're trying to get operating systems written for it.

The other two initial fascicles? One of them will be the first part of Volume 4, which talks about bit-fiddling. This section discusses techniques that are mostly in folklore about efficient methods for computers where you're using bitwise logical operations of a machine — exclusive-or, masking, and complementation, as well as addition, subtraction, multiplication, and division — to gain great efficiency. I've got that material pretty much written already. In fact, it was what I had drafted just before I started working on TEX — I wrote the first draft about bit-fiddling in the first months of 1977.

And then I get into the study of brute force enumeration techniques. The subject of Volume 4 is combinatorial algorithms, namely the methods that have been developed to deal with problems where you have zillions of cases; all kinds of ideas have been invented for speeding up, by many orders of magnitude, the obvious methods for dealing with cases of combinatorial importance. I begin the chapter by talking about bit-fiddling, and the next part talks about fast methods for listing all permutations, and listing all subsets of a set, and things like that. A vast literature about such things exists. Surprisingly, more people have written papers about generating permutations than about sorting. Sorting is the idea of putting into order; generating permutations is about putting into disorder. More people have explained how to unorder things than to order things. [*laughter*] Most of those papers are fairly repetitious and trivial, though, and not as interesting as the sorting papers, so the difficulty for me is mostly to survey this literature and put it all together. Most of the people writing on permutation generation were unaware that lots of other people were working on the same thing.

OK. Well, that's more than enough of an answer to your question, I hope, on the state of Volume 4. Every day I try to finish a page or so, and I think I've been going at about that rate for a while now.

Page xi replacement for exercise 3 ———————————————— 25 Mar 1995

3. [*34*] Leonhard Euler conjectured in 1772 that the equation $w^4 + x^4 + y^4 = z^4$ has no solution in positive integers, but Noam Elkies proved in 1987 that infinitely many solutions exist [see *Math. Comp.* **51** (1988), 825–835]. Find all integer solutions such that $0 \le w \le x \le y < z < 10^6$.

4. [*M50*] Prove that when n is an integer, $n > 4$, the equation $w^n + x^n + y^n = z^n$ has no solution in positive integers w, x, y, z.

FIGURE 2. Excerpt from the errata for the front matter of Volume 2.

While I've got this on the screen ... let's try going forward a couple of pages ... I really want to look at this equation here (Figure 2). I used to have Fermat's Last Theorem as a research problem at the beginning of the book. [*laughter*] In the errata it says now: "Prove that when n is an integer greater than 4, the equation $w^n + x^n + y^n = z^n$ has no solution in positive integers." So, now I've just added another variable to the equation and we've got another good research problem. And it turns out that for $n = 4$, there are infinitely many solutions. The proof of Fermat's Last Theorem caused a personal crisis for me, but I've now resolved it in this way. [*laughter*]

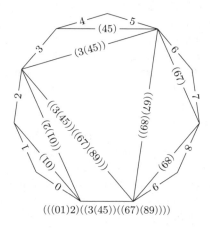

$((((01)2)((3(45))((67)(89))))$

FIGURE 3. METAPOST illustration in the errata to Volume 1.

I want to look also at page 61 of the errata as an example of new material (Figure 3). This page shows some very nice constructions that come out of studying trees. I put this up as an example of an illustration: I'm doing all the illustrations for the book in METAPOST, and this page

shows one of the ones that happen to be in the errata. I love META-
POST, and John [Hobby], in the next talk this morning, will show you
his system. It handles technical illustrations much better than anything
else. The great beauty of METAPOST from my point of view is that if
I have to modify any of my illustrations later on, maybe a year later, I
can see from the METAPOST source code exactly what I had in mind
when I made the original. METAPOST is a declarative language where
you state the characteristics that you want your illustration to have,
then it draws the diagram. The errata currently contain five or six
examples where I've either redrawn an old figure or, as in this case,
made a new one. Many, many other examples that I prepared when
I did the *Stanford GraphBase* book convinced me that METAPOST is
really ideal for technical illustrations. I don't think anything else will
ever be able to be much better.

METAPOST is not the answer for the kind of illustrations that people
do when they're preparing advertisements or things like that. But when
you're writing a technical book — yesterday Sebastian [Rahtz] made the
same point with respect to PSTricks — you have to produce diagrams
that satisfy certain mathematical properties. A Super MacDraw-type
of program doesn't very easily give you this ability, while METAPOST
does it, and very easily — all the technical things are correct, according
to the mathematics. It's kind of scandalous that the world's calculus
books, up until recent years, have never had a good picture of a cardioid.
Yesterday we saw a real cardioid on the screen [slide by Denis Girou].
Nobody ever knew what a cardioid looked like, when I took calculus,
because the illustrations were done by graphic artists who were trying
to imitate drawings by previous artists, without seeing the real thing.

OK — I've talked too much about this. Ask another question!

Robert McGaffey: Do you think the RSA algorithm will ever be
broken?

Don: Do I think the RSA algorithm will ever be broken? Now, the
RSA algorithm is the Rivest–Shamir–Adleman scheme for encryption.
People have just factored the key of the original cipher that was put up
by R, S, and A in 1977. That was a 140-digit number, which was a very
weak version of their general idea. But Rivest et al. said: "Here's our
secret message. Can you decode it?" By the time someone decoded it
last year, Ron [Rivest] had lost the original answer ... forgotten what
it was. But it turned out that, after decoding, the encoded message
was: "The secret word is squeamish ossifrage." That was the solution.
In order to break this cipher, people had to factor a 140-digit number,

and it was done with many thousands of hours of computer time last year. Now the thing is, though, if you go from a 140-digit number to a 141-digit number, already the problem gets much larger. So if you go to a 300-digit number, it would, as far as we know — all of the computers running now in the universe would not be able to do it. But there might still be advances in factoring, so Rivest himself predicts that a 300-digit encoding would last at least for about 30 years. A 500-digit number for a hundred years — he would rather confidently predict that's true.

We doubt if anyone's going to discover a magic way to factor numbers. But the big problem is that it's illegal to use the full power of RSA. I mean, the government wants to be sure that it can read secrets if necessary, because it doesn't want the Mafia to have the secrets. So we now have a peculiar situation where it's against the law to compute a certain mathematical equation, a mathematical formula. Well, I don't like confrontational issues. [*laughter*] I don't live in a secret way ... I mean, I'm not a secretive kind of guy. I spent a year of my life working in cryptanalysis and I've met a lot of wonderful people in that community, but I knew that the life wasn't for me. I like to be a college professor and tell what I know. So I'm not a good consultant on that kind of question. But it is possible to send secure information assuming that nobody can factor numbers. That's either a blessing or a threat, depending on your point of view. For me, I can see it from both sides.

In the back?

Michael Sofka: Is P $=$ NP, and if not, how far do you think we are from the proof?

Don: P $=$ NP is the most famous unsolved problem in computer science, analogous to Fermat's Last Theorem, although the P $=$ NP problem has only been around for about 30 years, 25 maybe. In the context of combinatorial algorithms, it says: Are we going to be able to solve problems that would require going through 2^n cases? Can we actually do those in n^{10}, or something like that, if we knew the best method? If P $=$ NP, the answer would be "yes," with some polynomial: we could reduce all these exponential problems to polynomial problems. If not, the answer is "no," we'll never be able to reduce them.

I have a feeling that someone might resolve the problem in the worst possible way, which is the following. Somebody will prove that P is equal to NP because there are only finitely many obstructions to it *not* being equal to NP. [*laughter*] The result would be that there is some polynomial such that we could solve all NP problems in polynomial time. However, we won't know what the polynomial is; we'll just know that it exists. So maybe the complexity will be n to the trillionth or something like that — but it'll be a polynomial. In such a scenario we'll never be able to figure it out because it would probably take too long to find out what the polynomial is. But it might exist. Which means that the whole question P = NP was the wrong question! [*laughter*] It might go that way. You see, even if you have a method that takes 2^n steps and you compare it to a method that takes n^{100}, then at least you can use the 2^n one for n up to 20 or 30. But the n^{100} you can't even do for $n = 2$. So the degree of that polynomial is very important. There are so many algorithms out there, the task of showing that no polynomial algorithms exist is going to be very hard. Still, I really thought that Fermat's Theorem was a similar kind of thing, where it was more important to have the problem than to solve it. Therefore, my real feeling about Wiles's Theorem is that he did a marvellous wonderful piece of work, but I wish he'd solved something else! [*laughter*]

A lot of people think that as soon as a problem is shown to be in this class NP, they shouldn't work on it, because it means that there's probably no polynomial way to solve the problem. But before we studied NP, we had *unsolvable* problems — problems for which there didn't exist any algorithms at all. No matter how long you worked, you could never solve the problem. To tell whether a given Turing machine ever stops: This problem is unsolvable by any algorithm, in general, no matter how long you give yourself. In the days before NP became famous, people would stop working on a problem as soon as it was proved to be unsolvable in general. But that was a bad strategy, because almost every problem we ever solve is a special case of some unsolvable problem.

Take calculus, for example — the problem of taking a formula, a function of n, and saying: "Is the limit as n goes to infinity equal to zero or not?" That's an unsolvable problem. But its unsolvability doesn't imply that we shouldn't study calculus. I mean, limits of lots of useful functions do go to zero, and therefore people were able to develop calculus. But the general problem is unsolvable. I mean, you could define f of n — it only takes a few lines to make a formula that is equal to zero if a given Turing machine is stopped at time n, and it's equal to 1 if the Turing machine is still going at time n. And so the limit is equal to zero if and only if that Turing machine stops. It's unsolvable.

A similar thing happens with NP. That is, we have lots of special cases of problems that are NP-hard that we can solve efficiently; just knowing that something is NP doesn't mean that it's a good idea to give up on it or to stop trying to get good heuristic methods for it.

Questions about TEX?! [*laughter*] Yes?

T. V. Raman: One of the nice things about TeX is that it gives authors the flexibility to define macros that sort of encode semantics, so if you're writing a paper about permutations you can define a thing called \permute and then write your contents using that. I rely heavily on this in my system AsTeR. What I wanted to know —

Don: Excuse me, you're going to be speaking later on ...?

Raman: Yes, I'll be talking tomorrow afternoon.

Don: So your system uses the TeX source as part of the semantics of the presentation of the document, while the author is thinking mostly of the convenience of writing.

Raman: Yes. So, what happens, in fact, is that everything turns into an object. And so, the more semantics there are in the markup, the better it is. Now, in normal documents, there is this tension between wanting to write things using a base level of markup where an author just writes 'x\over y' whenever he wants '$\frac{x}{y}$' versus an author defining, say, \inference as a macro that takes two things and then puts x over y with a horizontal bar between them. In the latter case, I win; in the earlier case I lose. My gut feeling is that, if you look at a large book, it's like a large computer program, and, sort of, in order to preserve your sanity, it seems to make more sense to read it that way.

Don: Can people hear what the question is? He's saying that if you're blind or handicapped, you can study the TeX source of a document. If it's properly done, it can even be better than if you had the hard-copy, because the document could have been written with a very logical markup scheme. In typography we try to reveal the structure by typographic means. But, in fact, we know even more of the structure when we're making our source files. So, an author with that in mind would maybe prepare the source files to have more information than just what you're going to see on the page afterwards.

When you're writing, you have an audience in mind. If you look at any book about how to write, or any course that deals with writing, the number one rule always is: *Keep your reader in mind.* If authors realize that they're writing something for hypertext, then they'll be planning their exposition to take best advantage of hypertext. When I wrote my first paper in a foreign language[5] it was published in Canada, where they spell "color" with a "u." [*laughter*] My second paper in a foreign

---

[5] "Another enumeration of trees," *Canadian Journal of Mathematics* **20** (1968), 1077–1086.

language[6] was Norwegian, and so when I was talking about variables for "left" and "right," I would say 'v' and 'h' instead of 'l' and 'r'. I mean, you plan as you're writing, you plan for the reader. These are very simple examples. So, if you expect that somebody is looking at your TEX source or that somebody will be able to click on part of your document and therefore it'll highlight something that is logically related, you might approach the whole process of exposition in a different way and you'll be able to reach more readers. So I try to make my ... I can show you the macro files developing for *The Art of Computer Programming* in the new style, but ...

Raman: I'd love to see that, because the other thing I'd like to do is run the system off the ...

```
% Macros for The Art of Computer Programming
% (STILL UNDER CONSTRUCTION!
%  I started with manmac.tex and am letting this evolve)
\input epsf
\input rotate
\input picmac
\input unicode
\catcode'@=11 % borrow the private macros of PLAIN (with care)
\font\ninerm=cmr9
    ⋮
```

FIGURE 4. The beginning of acpmac.tex.

Don: [*more screen maneuvers; see Fig. 4*] Let's just take a look at that file. It's still under construction, OK? [*laughter*] I input various macro files: The '`epsf`' is to get METAPOST figures; '`rotate`' allows PostScript to do rotation; '`picmac`' is my subset of LATEX picture mode; '`unicode`' is that thing that I told you about for getting Chinese names. OK, let's take a look at some formatting ... [*more pointing out of various codes for formatting*]

These are my composition macros (Figure 5) ... you can see some of the hyphenation exceptions I've put in. Equation numbers are going

---

[6] "Søking etter noe i en EDB-maskin," *Forskningsnytt* **18**, 4 (Norges Almenvitenskapelige Forskningsråd, 1973), 39–42.

⋮

```
% Composition macros
\hyphenation{logical Mac-Mahon hyper-geo-metric
   hyper-geo-met-rics Ber-noulli Greg-ory dis-trib-uted}
{\obeyspaces\gdef {\ }}
\def\hang{\hangindent\parindent}
\def\dash---{\thinspace---\hskip.16667em\relax}
\def\eq(#1){{\rm({\oldsty#1})}}
\let\EQNO=\eqno \def\eqno(#1){\EQNO\hbox{\eq(#1)}}
\def\star{\llap{*}}
\def\slug{\hbox{\kern1.5pt\vrule width2.5pt
   height6pt depth1.5pt\kern1.5pt}}
\let\:=\. % preserve a way to get the dot accent
\def\.#1{\leavevmode\hbox{\tt#1}}
\def\[#1]{[\hbox{$\mskip1mu\thickmuskip =
   \thinmuskip#1\mskip1mu$}]} % Iverson brackets
\def\bigi[#1]{\bigl[\begingroup\mskip1mu
   \thickmuskip=\thinmuskip #1\mskip1mu\endgroup\bigr]}
\def\AD{{\adbcfont A.D.}}
\def\BC{{\adbcfont B.C.}}
\def\og#1{\leavevmode\vtop{\baselineskip\z@skip
   \lineskip-.2ex \lineskiplimit\z@
   \ialign{##\cr\relax#1\cr
     \hidewidth\kern.3em\sh@ft{40}`\hidewidth\cr}
   \kern-1ex}} % ogonek
\def\em#1:{{\it#1:\/}} % \em Hint: or \em Caution: etc
```

⋮

```
\def\euler{\atopwithdelims<>}
\def\Euler#1#2{\mathchoice{\biggl<\mskip-7mu
     {#1\euler#2}\mskip-7mu\biggr>}%
   {\left<\!{#1\euler#2}\!\right>}{}{}}
\def\Choose#1#2{\mathchoice{\biggl(\mskip-7mu
     {#1\choose#2}\mskip-7mu\biggr)}%
   {\left(\!{#1\choose#2}\!\right)}{}{}}
\def\smsum{\mathop{\vcenter{\hbox{\tenrm\char6}}}}
   % small summation sign
\def\phihat{{\mkern5mu\hat{\vrule width0pt
   height1.2ex\smash{\mkern-5mu\phi}}}}
\def\umod{\nonscript\mskip-\medmuskip\mkern5mu
   \mathbin{\underline{\rm mod}}\penalty900\mkern5mu
   \nonscript\mskip-\medmuskip} % least remainder
```

⋮

FIGURE 5. Excerpts from acpmac.tex.

into oldstyle numerals. The control sequence \star is for a starred section, something that's advanced; \slug goes at the end of a proof — I might have to change it so it's not so black, because people see so many overfull boxes, they don't like to see the black slug anymore. [laughter] I'm redefining backslash dot — I make it \: so that I can use \. for typewriter type in the middle of math mode. There's an important notation due to Iverson, where you can put any formula in square brackets and that evaluates the formula to 0 or 1 — you can put that in the middle of equations, it's very useful. Here are macros for saying A.D. or B.C. And here's something I use for special emphasis, like a hint — I'm not using this to indicate italics, I say \it for that kind of emphasis. My \em#1: is a special format that I often use to say 'Note:' or something like that [walking through the macros, with comments on some of the more interesting ones] ... These are Eulerian numbers ... with angle brackets instead of the parentheses of binomial coefficients.

Raman: Do you have a macro called \euler there?

Don: Yeah, these are Eulerian numbers here. ... Capital \Euler is a similar notation that uses two delimiters and has the right amount of negative space between them so that you have two angle brackets next to each other; similarly, for binomial coefficients, the capital \Choose puts in two parentheses. Here's \smsum for a small summation sign — I don't remember where I used that. Now \phihat — this is a special symbol — the letter ϕ has to have the hat put just right, because '$\hat{\phi}$' is a common thing that arises when you're studying Fibonacci numbers. ... Then I have here the format for an algorithm ...; a whole bunch of macros for typesetting assembly code; underlining text in the comments ... etc. [remaining examples not included here]

My TEX files for errata show some of the structure that will be in *TAOCP* itself. As I said, I'm working day-by-day just now to put in new corrections. I have four kinds of errata: One is called an "amendment," which means new stuff that we didn't have before; one is called a "bug," something that has to be fixed; one is called a "plan," where I need to work out the details later but I want to note down in the file that it's in my mind to make the change; and then there's something called an "improvement," which is kind of trivial, but still I thought of it and I want to use it when we go to the final book.

For example (Figure 6), here's a quotation by Turing that I kind of like; it comes from 1945, which is before computers were even invented, but he'd been thinking about computing for a long time: "Up to a point, it's better to let the snags be there than to spend such time in design

```
\amendpage 1.189 insert quotation before the exercises (95.07.13)
{\quoteformat
\vskip-3pt
Up to a point it is better to let the snags [bugs]
be there than to spend such time in design that there are none
(how many decades would this course take?).
\author A. M. TURING, Proposals for ACE (1945)
% p18, quoted in Comp J 20(1977)273
}
\endchange
```

FIGURE 6. A recent addition to the errata.

```
\amendpage 2.xi replacement for exercise 3 (95.03.25)
\ex3. [34] Leonhard Euler conjectured in 1772 that the equation
$w^4+x^4+y^4=z^4$ has no solution in positive integers,

                   :
                   :

\improvepage 2.27 line 2 (81.08.13)
random, they \becomes random; they
\endchange
```

FIGURE 7. More examples of errata in TEX form.

that there are none. How many decades would this course take?" That
quotation is an amendment to Volume 1, made just twelve days ago.

Look, here (Figure 7) is the TEX source that generated Figure 2.
And here's an example where I changed a comma to a semicolon. The
way I use this is that trivial improvements don't usually get listed in the
hardcopy unless you work extra hard. There's a special way of getting
all the \improvepage entries to come out, but usually they only appear
in the file.

So that's the kind of thing I'm doing. This improvement, by the
way, is dated 1981. For 20 years, I've had copies of *The Art of Computer Programming* sitting in my office and I kept putting notes in the
margins, marking things that I want to improve. That's now all in these
files.

Other questions?

Silvio Levy: How come you don't use LATEX? [*laughter*]

Don: How come I don't use LATEX? [*laughter*] I'm scared of large
systems! [*louder laughter*] Bart?

Bart Childs: Your paper, "The errors of TeX," was great. Have you ever thought of one about "Mistakes of TeX"?

Don: "The *Mistakes* of TeX"?? [*laughter*]

Bart: I mean, I guess I'm kind of thinking of the changes you made when you went to TeX version 3. The 7-bit/8-bit and things there that might be thought of as mistakes. Are there any other things you can think of in that line?

Don: In the errors-of-TeX paper,[7] I think I listed everything that I would consider a mistake. I think I would have noted the misprediction of 7-bit versus 8-bit input if I had written that paper a year later, but of course, I wrote it before TeX3 came out. I've promised to put out a sequel to that paper when everything has cooled down and you know, when the last error in TeX has been found. [*laughter*] So the present state is this [*file manipulations on screen, bringing up the file* `errorlog.tex`[8]; *see Figure 8*]

```
* 26 June 1993
R928\>668. Avoid potential future bug (Peter Breitenlohner). @628,637
* 17 December 1993
S929\>881. Boundary character representation shouldn't depend on font
memory size (Berthold Horn). @549,1323
* 10 March 1994
R930. Huge font parameter number may exceed array bound (CET). @549
* 4 September 1994
F931\>926. Math kerns are explicit (Walter Carlip). @717
R932. Avoid overflow on huge real-to-integer conversion. @625,634
* 19 March 1995
R933. Avoid spurious reference counts in format files (PB). @1335
\relax
\bye
```

FIGURE 8. End of the file `errorlog.tex`.

---

[7] "The errors of TeX," *Software — Practice & Experience* **19** (1989), 607–685; reprinted with additions and corrections as Chapters 10 and 11 of *Literate Programming*. See also "Notes on the errors of TeX," *TUGboat* **10** (1989), 529–531; this was the keynote address at the 10th anniversary TUG meeting, held at Stanford in July 1989.

[8] The file `errorlog.tex` appears under `systems/knuth/errata/` in the *CTAN* archives. Other files mentioned below, like `tex82.bug`, can also be found in that directory.

The last change was on March 19. Well, no, that was the date the bug was reported. So, here's Peter Breitenlohner — he's here today — "Avoid spurious reference counts in format files." This was causing some problems ... He found you could break TEX if you kept saving format files and loading them again and saving them again and loading them again several hundred times; you would exceed memory capacity because the reference count could get larger than the total memory size. So that was a bug that we fixed, and he got \$327.68 for it — 2^{15} pennies.

What were the other most recent changes? Number 932, "Avoid overflow on huge real-to-integer conversion." Number 931, "Math kerns are explicit" — this was a bug introduced by change 926. Number 930, "Huge font parameter number may exceed array bound," a place where the implementation wasn't totally robust. Number 929, "Boundary character representation shouldn't depend on font memory size" — this was a fairly serious one that was fixed by the major implementors shortly after we put out the previous update in 1993.

These errors — the dates listed here are actually dates when the people found them. I fixed them all in March of this year [1995]. I plan to look again at reported bugs in TEX in 1997, and again in 2000, and then 2004 and 2009, hoping that each time I'll be able to do that in about a day. A lot of volunteers are out there filtering these reported bugs, and vetting the ones that really do seem to require my attention. Yesterday, when we were running test programs at Stanford, somebody noticed that Stanford was still using a very old version of TEX and it didn't seem to matter. [*laughter*] I believe the bugs are starting to taper off. The remaining ones are getting to be scenarios that can cause the system to break, but only if you really try hard.

There's one severe bug in the design that will have to remain as a feature, and it has to do with multilingual typesetting. I don't think I put it in the `errorlog` file, but it's noted at the end of another file called `tex82.bug` (Figure 9). Let's look there ... This file has complete details about every change since 1982. See this one? It's the "absolutely final change to TEX, to be made after my death." The version number changes to π. It's like my last will and testament here. [*laughter*] So I'll never see that change made. With version π, TEX is declared to have no more bugs. Anything that uses the name TEX should be fully compatible with everything else that uses that name.

After the final change, this file lists "possibly good ideas that I won't implement"; ... then come two "design errors that are too late to fix." The most serious one is multilingual. If you're using several languages in the same paragraph, I forgot to save some part of the

----

415. The absolutely final change (to be made after my death)
@x module 2
@d banner=='This is TeX, Version 3.14159' {printed when \TeX\ starts}
@y
@d banner=='This is TeX, Version π' {printed when \TeX\ starts}
@z
When this change is made, the corresponding line should be changed
in Volume B, and also on page 23 of The TeXbook. My last will and
testament for TeX is that no further changes be made under any
circumstances. Improved systems should not be called simply 'TeX';
that name, unqualified, should refer only to the program for which
I have taken personal responsibility. -- Don Knuth

* Possibly nice ideas that will not be implemented
. classes of marks analogous to classes of insertions

      .
      .
      .

* Design errors that are too late to fix
. additional parameters should be in symbol fonts to govern the
  space between rules and text in \over, \sqrt, etc.
. multilingual typesetting doesn't work properly when the \lccode
  changes within a paragraph

* Bad ideas that will not be implemented
. several people want to be able to remove arbitrary elements of
  lists, but that must never be done because some of those elements
  (e.g. kerns for accents) depend on floating point arithmetic
. if anybody wants letter spacing desperately they should put it in
  their own private version (e.g. generalize the hpack routine)
  and NOT call it TeX.

FIGURE 9. End of the file tex82.bug.

state information — I forget exactly what it is now,[9] but it was a serious
oversight and I should have thought about it. Now it's too late; this is
one glitch that's going to have to remain.

The only other thing I really wish I'd worked harder on was the
positioning of square root signs and fraction bars. I don't have enough
parameters in there to control the space between the barline and the text.
I made the mistake of solving a problem that needed two parameters by
using only one parameter: I got the amount of space by calculating it

---

[9] All languages within a paragraph have to use the same \lccode table.

as a multiple of the thickness of the barline, but I should have had the spacing as an independent parameter. Now I find that as I'm writing stuff and I have a square root that doesn't look right, I have to put a hidden strut in the exponent, to give more space there. I wish I'd done that better; but otherwise — considering the amount of inevitable compromise that has to go into any large system — I'm basically happy with the way things converged.

As I read papers typeset with TeX, the main thing that makes me unhappy, besides the way I typeset the square root sign, is the way that people have not updated to the improved Computer Modern fonts that I put out three or four years ago.[10] We're still seeing the old fonts and I don't know how long it's going to take before people change. Eberhard [Mattes] did make the switch two or three months ago [in his widely used emTeX implementation].

The font change is especially evident on lowercase Greek delta. I found myself four or five years ago writing a paper in which I was going out of my way to avoid using the letter δ. I tried to analyse, "Why am I not using that letter?" and I realized that I subconsciously *hated* my lowercase delta; I didn't like the look of it at all. But in this paper I really needed the delta, it was the natural letter to use, and so I said, "OK ... I'm gonna take a day off and redesign that letter, making a really beautiful delta." And I think I now have the best δ the human race has ever seen. [*laughter*] That was ages ago. Now, every time I see a paper using the old one, I cringe.

I also changed a few of the other letters, like some of the calligraphic capitals: I fixed the spacing on the barline of the '$\mathcal{H}$', and I didn't like the base of the '$\mathcal{T}$' so I changed it to '$\mathcal{T}$'. I see that the Dutch TeX Users Group uses the old $\mathcal{T}$ in their logo ... but I'm hoping everyone will switch over to the real `cmr` fonts. The `TFM` files have not changed. Oh, I've also made all the arrows heavier ('→' became '→'). Arrows were disappearing on xeroxes all over the place, so now the arrowheads are larger and darker.

Cameron Smith: Is there a date or version number we should look for to make sure ... ?

Don: Well, if the source file is dated '93 or after, it'll be OK.

Silvio: No! Change `cm` to `dm`! The update is never going to happen unless you do that.

---

[10] See `http://www-cs-faculty.stanford.edu/~knuth/cm.html`.

Don: It's happened in most places by now, but there still are pockets of people who haven't upgraded the old files. If you use DVIPS, all you have to do is delete the PK files and the system will make all the new fonts for you automatically.

Silvio: If you've got the new version of the source.

Don: Yeah, well, the sources are all there.

Silvio: Right, but it's very hard for the public to . . .

Don: Please, figure out a way to solve this, because it's frustrating. Every time I get a letter or a preprint from someone that has the old delta, I tell them to tell their computer operators to update, and then they send me back an upgraded paper and say, yes it's OK now. [*laughter*] As long as people are aware of it. It's not that much of a change. If we get the word around to the distributors and the math journals, it shouldn't take too long to converge.

Robin Fairbairns: Can I just make a comment on that? Eberhard Mattes is possibly the author of the version with the largest user base — he has just reissued everything, and a month back he produced an entirely new set of fonts. On the mailing list there is a continual whining about "we don't want to go to the trouble of updating our font files." I keep saying "You really *do* need to do this." But despite that, people say, "It costs computer time on our PCs."

Don: They'll get a new PC in five years. [*laughter*] It'll eventually happen. I'm just hoping that it will happen sooner rather than later.

Silvio: Look, I posted a copy for people in Australia. I can tell you the top priority will not be to update because of a delta. If you issue a new version, with its own number and a new name, and if you make it obligatory, otherwise, . . .

Don: It didn't change that much to make it obligatory.

Jeremy Gibbons: If you change the name, old DVI files won't work when you print them — there'll be lots of missing fonts.

Don: Right. And it's not tremendously important. I mean, I'm too much of a nit-picker; I'm just telling you it does offend me, but it apparently doesn't offend those other people. [*laughter*]

Silvio: It offends me, too!

Don: Oh, OK. Well, I don't want to change the names of my fonts. [*pause*] Nelson?

Nelson Beebe: Don, the world has changed a lot since 1978 —

```
\vfill
{\quoteformat
Things have changed in the past two decades.
\author BILL GATES (1995)
% "You, too, can start a software firm"
% International Herald Tribune 5 Jan 1995, pages 9 and 11
\bigskip
In addition to the errors listed here,
about half of the occurrences of 'which' in volumes one and three
should be changed to 'that'.
\author DONALD E. KNUTH ({\sl The Art of Computer Programming %
        Errata et Addenda}, 1981)
\eject
}
```

FIGURE 10. Another excerpt from the *TAOCP* errata.

Don: Yes, in fact I put a wonderful quote to that effect from Bill Gates at the beginning of my errata list this year (see Figure 10).

Nelson: Assuming you were 25 years younger and were sitting down to do TEX now, with the market full of word processors and PostScript laserprinters and so on — what would you do differently?

Don: Well, as far as I know, I would still do the same thing, pretty much.   So, anything that you don't like, I'd probably still put in! [*laughter*] It's just the way I do things ...

Cameron: I wanted to ask you about a particular point, related to that. You went to a lot of trouble to design a line-breaking paragraphing algorithm that looked over a wide range of possibilities for an optimal set of breaks. But I encountered in *The TEXbook* that computer memories being what they were, it wasn't practical to similarly accumulate several pages of material and look for optimal page breaks. And sort of related to that, there's the difficulty of communications between a line-breaking algorithm and a page-breaking algorithm, where, let's say you're doing a letter and there's a letterhead on the first page that forces you to have a different page width and you might need to have line breaks change in the middle of paragraphs. Things like that, which could have been simplified if there were the ability to defer the cut-off of the page and have better communications between the line-breaking and page-breaking algorithms. Would you redo something like that, now that we have multi-megabyte memory?

Don: OK, certainly the memory constraints are quite different now. Amazing how much — memory has changed more than anything else. There are also major changes in the way we — well, we've got many more years of experience. We understand these things now. At the time when I was working on TeX — I'm trying to put things in context — many things were experimental, so that we could learn about the territory. In any system design, whenever you go through a new generation, it turns out that you understand the previous generation and you clean up the previous generation, and then you also go into your new experiments, which have to be cleaned up by the next generation. That kind of traditional growth of understanding is the way the world works.

Now a lot of these things about what kind of communication would be useful and so on are becoming clearer. The idea of TeX was — and I think will remain for as long as it survives — to find the smallest number of primitives that would be able to handle the most important things. So that 99% of the work would be done by these primitives, and the other part would be done by tinkering. My attitude on these things is that when I have a job to get done, I don't ever expect to have a system that's going to do 100% of it for me, but I expect it'll do so much of it so that the tinkering is down to noise level. Adding spit and polish is no more than a small percentage of the time I've put into the other parts of the job. Of course, the noise level for one person is different from another.

For example, I prepared a book about the Bible[11] where I had a lot of illustrations. I spent 6 or 7 hours on each illustration: massaging it, making custom color separations, doing fat-bits editing to clean up joins and various things, retouching whatever I could improve. For me, that work was noise level, because I had already spent 40 hours writing the chapter that goes with the illustrations — so what's another 6 hours, I mean, it's a small percentage of the job, in some ways.

But if I'm going through a commercial establishment that's trying to get graphics in and out the door, somebody's paying for their work, and if I have 60 illustrations taking 6 hours each, that's a completely different story. So, my view is that different users will have different ideas as to how much really needs to be automated. Many things are relatively easy for an author to spend a little extra time doing, because much more time has already gone into writing the book. But people who work with the author might want such things to be automated; they'll

---

[11] Donald E. Knuth, *3:16 Bible Texts Illuminated* (Madison, Wisconsin: A–R Editions, 1990); reviewed in *TUGboat* **12** (1991), 233–235.

want such things to be part of a fancy system that the author doesn't want to take time to learn.

So, if I have a typographic task where I need to do something in 2 or 3 passes, well, I simply try it a couple of times and run it through the machine and look through the previewer and get it right. A week or two ago, my wife and I put out newsletters for our family. We do this every year; each of our four grandparents has an extended family of, I don't know, about 60 or 80 names. We write to them and say, "Would you like to send us your comments on this year?" and then we collect them all together in little booklets and send them out to four groups. Every year I fiddle with that for, I don't know, 6 to 8 hours just to do neat things; like a newsletter editor. ... You spend some time doing all kinds of prettying up, if you have the time to put in. The tools that you have available always change the expectations of what you try to accomplish.

So, I figure the next generation of systems will include a lot more complicated mechanisms to handle the general cases of everything, where I've considered only the cases that I thought were the 99%. Typesetting can lead to all kinds of complexities—maybe you want to have the reference point in the middle of a character instead of at the left edge, as you're going left and right, in color and rotated and in many columns, and so on. We now have more understanding of how to design such general mechanisms.

With respect to the memory situation ... I think the page-breaking business is still ... it's not so much memory-bound as maybe—you still want to do two passes, but the machines are fast enough for two passes—it isn't that slow anymore. So, I would say this kind of next generation thing is natural for other people to work on, with the understanding that they gained from the first system.

Pierre?

Pierre MacKay: Just going back to the question of upgrading the fonts. I was thinking about something that wouldn't break things. You stick a METAFONT **special** to identify the font version. Since people upgrade their drivers far more often than they upgrade their fonts, just have the driver recognize that **special** and say "Tut tut! You shouldn't be using this font!" [*laughter*]

Fred Bartlett: I think that everything the gentleman over here wants to do with line-breaking and page-breaking could be done fairly simply by writing moderately complex macros and new output routines, *if* there were a way to save the items that get discarded at the end of every page. You want to save the discardable items that get tossed out when TEX calls the output routine. I was wondering why, when you wrote TEX, you threw those away without making it possible to save them at all?

Don: The output routine can put it into a box — copy it into a box —

Fred: — but it can't save the skip that is thrown out.

Don: The skip that's thrown out, isn't that the value of one of the parameters that gets passed to the output routine?

Peter Breitenlohner: The penalty is passed, but the skip is thrown out after the page has been printed. And if nothing comes back, it is not thrown out.

Don: Somewhere in *The TEXbook* it gives a null output routine that's supposed to put everything back together again? And what — that doesn't work?

Peter: It works! Because then the skip is not at the top.

Fred: But you can't ship out a page, you can't save a page to a box and then go back, accumulate a new page and then push it through and save that to a second box, as for left and right-column setting, and then put the two boxes together and have them join smoothly, because then the skip in between will be missing, and you'll have ... you won't have the line skip in between, and it means that if you want to do complex 2-column setting, as for a couple of text books [I've done], then you have a problem with tables and figures and a whole bunch of other junk. It would be nice ... it's something I've wrestled with for, I don't know, 6 or 7 years, and the best I've been able to do is to have TEX warn me when it starts balancing columns, starting on the right-hand column, and because I probably don't have the right skip here. Almost everything else in TEX is parameterized: You can get to it, you can save it, you can inspect it, have TEX do tests — except the discardable items, and discardable skips. I'm just wondering why.

Don: I guess I didn't think of it. [*laughter*] The output routine was the most experimental part of TEX. We had no models to go by at all. We had 4 or 5 problems that we knew we had to solve, and we tried to find the smallest number of primitives that would handle those 4 or 5 problems. We got to the point where we could clarify the solutions to the problems. But we *knew* this was experimental. I'm sorry that your problem didn't occur before TEX 3.0 because then I might have been tempted ... [*laughter*]

Fred: I heard you say you expected more people to extend TEX than have done so.

Don: Yeah, absolutely. I expected extensions whenever someone had a special-purpose important project, like the *Encyclopedia Britannica* or making an Arabic–Chinese dictionary, or whatever — a large project. I never expected a single tool to be able to handle everybody's exotic projects. So I built a lot of hooks into the code so that it should be fairly easy for a computer science graduate to set up a new program for special occasions in a week or so. That was my thought. But I don't think people have done that very much.

It's certainly what I would have done. If I were putting out a Bible or something, if I were a publisher with some project that I wanted to do especially well, then I would want a special typesetting tool for it. Rewriting a typesetting system is fairly easy. [*laughter*]

I guess people haven't done it because they're afraid they'd break something. I don't think they would have. I think the caution is misplaced. So I tried to show how to do it, by implementing several of the features of TEX as if they *were* added on after, just to show how to use the hooks, as a demo. But that didn't get things going; many more people are working with TEX at the macro level. Of course, the big advantage is that then you can share your output with others — you can assume your source code is going to work on everybody else's systems. But still, I thought special projects would lead to a lot of custom versions of the program. That hasn't happened.

Jeremy: A related question is ... if you can take a vertical box apart into its components, and play with them and reassemble it, one thing you *can't* get is, if you have a box that has been moved left or moved right, when you disassemble the box, you lose that information. [Don: Oh really?] You can get \lastbox, and that gives you the box, but it doesn't tell you whether it was shifted. I thought I saw in your list of bad ideas that weren't going to have anything done with them, something to do with taking lists apart. Was that there?

Don: I'm not sure what that really referred to any more. There is some problem about making sure that no user can access the results of rounding errors, which are different on different machines. So I had to be very careful in TEX to keep it portable — any time you do a glue calculation. Still, I don't think that would happen in shift-left shift-right. One of the changes to TEX not so many years ago was to ... I don't remember. Maybe somebody can ... maybe Peter [Breitenlohner] can recall. I think it was you who suggested it: There was something in the *hlist_out* and *vlist_out* routines where it looked at the shift amount of the box and ... ?

Peter: It was in leaders. The leaderbox looked for the shift amount, but the shift amount in the data structure was always zero ... TEX took the shift amount, and added it and subtracted it back, or something like that.

Don: Yeah, so the thing is, I had some code in there that — it wasn't a bug because it could never cause any harm — but I was always adding zero to something. We took it out, so that people wouldn't be confused by it. The amount by which a box is shifted is stored with the box. If it's in a vertical list, that means so much is shifted towards the right and in a horizontal list, it means how much it's shifted up and down. The shift amount could never be nonzero in a leaders box. OK, if the shift amount is not restored properly, it might be a bug, something you could report, and in 1997, maybe you can get big money for it. [*laughter*]

Jeremy: I don't think it's a bug, it's just a problem, something you can't do — taking things apart and reassembling them .... It wasn't a design decision ... a deliberate one?

Don: Alright, well, the number of possible things like that was too huge to anticipate, so I just am glad that there weren't more, I guess. I'm sorry.

Cameron: A lot of the questions have been of the form "Why did you do X?" but I think maybe part of what the thrust really is, is: If you were doing it again, as some people are trying to do, and as you've suggested that more people *should* be doing, reading from TEX for special needs, are there things that you'd recommend to *those* people? Not so much why did you do it this way 20 years ago, but if someone else were doing it again what would you tell them is most important to think about?

Don: I just recommend putting extreme care into the design and checking things out and getting a wide number of users to help you with it, to show you the problems that they have and look at as many examples as possible. These are the things people are of course doing already. Dotting the i's and crossing the t's is the name of the game; you have to work very hard over a long period of time. The more you open or extend your vision as to how much you're going to solve, the longer it's going to take to get the whole package to be consistent.

The hardest struggle is the struggle towards convergence, instead of divergence. You need input from a tremendous variety of sources, but you also have to avoid the committee syndrome ... you have to have some small number of people who make the decisions, so that everything converges. Otherwise, you get the big problem of all committee projects — that everybody on the committee has to be proud of one part of the final thing. Then you have lots of incompatible stuff in there, mostly for political reasons. The hard thing is to do the detailed checking on as many things as you can for consistency and convergence. The steering problem was the toughest aspect of TEX's development.

If you study the paper "The Errors of TEX," you'll see how the process worked. First there was one user — and I took a lot of time to satisfy myself. Then I had ten users, and a whole new level of difficulties arose. Then I had a hundred users and another level of things happened. I had a thousand users, I had ten thousand — each of those were special phases in the development, important. I couldn't have gone with ten thousand until I'd done it with a thousand. But each time a new wave of changes came along, the idea was to have TEX get better, and not to let it get more diverse as it needed to handle new things. So, when I said I'd still do things pretty much the same way, what I meant is that I still think I would have horizontal lists and vertical lists; I still would have boxes and glue, and so on. Those basic structural principles seem to give a lot of mileage from a small number of concepts, to handle a tremendous variety of typesetting challenges. But I wasn't talking about whether I would do exactly the same with respect to a shift amount here and there. All those fine points are extremely important, but I'd still keep the same basic architecture.

Barbara: It's getting on to refreshment time. So, I would like to thank Don very much for taking time to answer everybody's questions. I will take the prerogative of one last question: Would you be willing to do this again in 2011? In 16 more years?

Don: Yeah, that sounds about right. [*laughter*] Thirty-two isn't quite as thrilling, but it should be OK. Thank you very much. [*wide applause*]

FIGURE 11. Past presidents of TUG who attended the sixteenth annual meeting: Pierre MacKay (1983–1985), Bart Childs (1985–1989), Don Knuth
(1977–1980), Nelson Beebe (1989–1991), Christina Thiele (1993–1995),
Michel Goossens (1995–1997). Photo by Luzia Dietsche.

Chapter 32

Questions and Answers, II

*[Q&A session at the Charles University in Prague on 9 March 1996. Originally published in TUGboat **17** (1996), 355–367; edited by Christina Thiele and Barbara Beeton.]*

Karel Horák: [Introductory remarks in Czech, then English.]

I'm very glad to have such a happy occasion to introduce you, Professor Knuth, to our audience, who are mostly members of $\mathcal{C}_{\mathcal{S}}TUG$, the Czech/Slovak TEX User Group, but also some academicians from Prague because this session is organized by $\mathcal{C}_{\mathcal{S}}TUG$ and the Mathematics Faculty of Charles University. We are very happy to have you here, and I would be happy, on behalf of Charles University, to give you a special medal. [*wide applause*]

Don Knuth: [*surprised*] Thank you very much.

Prof. Ivan Netuka: Professor Knuth, dear colleagues, dear friends, ladies and gentlemen. I feel really very much honored having the opportunity to greet Professor Donald Knuth, as well as most of you here sitting in this guildhall, on behalf of the Dean of the Faculty of Mathematics and Physics of Charles University, Professor Bedřich Sedlák.

As far as I know, Professor Knuth has come to Prague for the first time. Despite this fact, he has been known here, not only among *all* mathematicians, *all* computer scientists, but also many physicists, and even to people having nothing to do with our subjects. People here are fully aware of the significance of Donald Knuth's treatise, *The Art of Computer Programming*. Many of us have had the opportunity to be pleased by reading the charming booklet devoted to *Surreal Numbers*. We know that Donald Knuth's favorite way to describe computer science is to say that it is the study of algorithms. We share his opinion that the study of algorithms has opened up a fertile vein of interesting new mathematical problems and that it provides a stimulus for many areas of mathematics which have been suffering from a lack of new ideas.

601

Concave side of the Memorial Medal (actual size).

My personal experience — the personal experience of a mathematician — says that, for every mathematician, there exists a personality who has brought an extraordinarily great service to his field. Here we have a rare case where, in that statement, the order of the quantifiers may be reversed, maybe: There exists a personality who has brought a great service, an extraordinarily great service, to every mathematician. Here is my one-line proof: Donald Knuth — TₑX.

Professor Knuth, in acknowledgment of your achievements in computer science, in mathematics, as well as in computerized typography, which has given the whole of the community an excellent tool for presenting scientific results, the Faculty of Mathematics and Physics of Charles University has decided that you be awarded the Faculty's Memorial Medal. I am happy to make that presentation now. [*wide prolonged applause*]

Don: Well, this is quite a beautiful medal, and a wonderful surprise; I hope you can all come and look at it.

"Universitas Carolina Pragensis" — so we all speak Latin; maybe I should speak Latin today. [*laughter*]

Convex side, featuring the Charles University seal in the center.

I don't know much about the Czech language, but I've tried to learn some of it. On many doors this week I see the word "Sem." [*laughter*] And then as I came up to this lecture hall today, there were many other signs that said "TEX." [*laughter*] So I thought we could have an especially powerful version of TEX [*writes "SemTEX" on the blackboard*]; [*more laughter*] but perhaps it's dangerous;[1] I don't know . . . .

This morning I have no prepared lecture, but I want to say just what you want to hear, so I want to answer your questions. This is a tradition that I maintained in California: The very last session of every class that I taught at Stanford was devoted to questions and answers. I told the students they didn't have to come to that class if they didn't want to, but if they came I would answer any question that they hoped to have answered when they signed up for the class. I actually borrowed this tradition from Professor [Richard] Feynman at Caltech. And I decided

---

[1] "Sem" is the Czech word for "here, this way"; on a door it means "pull." "Semtex" is a powerful plastic explosive designed and manufactured in the Czech Republic (and also the name of several computer viruses).

I would do it in my classes, too; it's a wonderful idea that I recommend to all professors — to have open-ended question and answer sessions.

I've recently made some home pages on the World Wide Web that you can get via `http://www-cs-faculty.stanford.edu/~knuth` and there on those pages I have the answers to all frequently asked questions. But today, you can ask me the *in*frequently asked questions. [*laughter*] By the way, I'll tell you one more joke and then we'll get started. Do you know what the home page is of OJ — O. J. Simpson — in the United States? It's "`http colon slash slash slash backslash slash escape`." [*laughter*]

Now, please ask me questions. [*pause*]

Well, if there are no further questions, ... [*laughter*]. You may ask in Czech, and then someone will translate.

X: Maybe a question to start with. I learned TEX carefully, and I had a problem when someone asked me to take the integral with tilde accent. I found that maybe there isn't one with TEX because you can't specify an italic correction to boxes.

Don: The italic correction is .... With each character there's a limited amount of information that goes in the data structure for each character; we have [*drawing on blackboard*] the height, the depth, the width, and the italic correction.

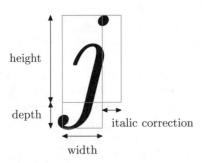

But those are the only numbers that are allowed, and in mathematics mode, the italic correction is used in a different way from outside of mathematics. In mathematics mode, the italic correction is actually used for subscripts; it's the amount by which you would bring the subscript to the left — without the italic correction, TEX would typeset "P sub n" (P_n) like this: P_n.

The italic correction on the integral sign might even be another case because the large operators use the italic correction to cover the offset between the lower limit and the upper limit. Anyway, there's only one number in there. If you want a special construction that demands many more numbers, the only way I know is to make a special macro for that. I would carry the information somewhere up in the TEX level, not in the inside, not with the character. You would have to build a structure that has this information in it. I don't know how general a solution you need, but certainly if you said the ... I can't even remember the name now ... my goodness, how do you get the ... like the same mechanism by which someone would take an equal sign and then put something over it, like $\stackrel{\text{def}}{=}$. It's defined in plain TEX by a macro[2] ... I would build it up out of the primitives, but if you had different integral signs, you would probably have to allow the person who specified the font to ...

X: I have a solution, but it is not a TEX solution: I used METAFONT to produce special characters, which have the ...

Don: Yes, using METAFONT would be the ideal way to get the correct artistic effect, but then everyone else has to get your METAFONT code and compile your font. Just by a combination of boxes and glue, you should be able to position the characters that you have. You could just make a \vbox or a \vcenter of something or other, and then you build the \hbox of ... with a kern and then a tilde and so on. Otherwise, I don't know any simple way of doing exactly that balancing because it's complicated by the visual proportions of the spacing with integral signs — it gets really complicated to handle *all* cases.

My general philosophy with TEX was to try to have a system that covers 99% of all cases easily [*laughter*]; and I knew there would always be a residual number. But I felt that this residual would only be needed by the people who really care about their papers, and then if they're only spending 1% of the time on this, they could enjoy feeling that they had contributed something special by adding their little signature, putting their special stamp on it. So I didn't try to do everything automatically. I still believe that it's worthwhile to think about how to do more automatically, but I don't believe you ever get all the way there.

Karel Horák: I would be very interested in your way of thinking — when you started thinking about making TEX and the typesetting system — when you realized that you also needed to produce some letters, to have not only TEX but also METAFONT. Because — I don't know too much about all typefaces of digital typography — but I think there weren't very many types which you *could* use with TEX, so probably

---

[2] \buildrel.

you started thinking about METAFONT, about something like that, from the first?

Don: Exactly.

Let's go back to May 1977. I sat down at a computer terminal and started writing a memorandum to myself about what I thought would be a good language for typesetting. And two weeks later, I began working on fonts. This was going to be my sabbatical year, where I would do no teaching through the end of 1977, and the beginning of 1978. I thought that I would write a typesetting system just for myself and my secretary. [*laughter*] I had no idea that I would ever be seeing TEX on, for example, the tram signs in Brno [*laughter*] or on signs posted in famous churches. TEX was just for my own purposes, and I had one year to do it. And I thought it would be easy. So, in May of 1977, I went to Xerox PARC, the place where the ideas of mouses and windows and interfaces and so on were being worked on, and I knew that they were playing with splines for letterforms. I saw Butler Lampson at a computer terminal, and he was adjusting splines around the edges of letters that he had magnified; so I thought, "good, I'll make an arrangement to work at Xerox PARC during my sabbatical year, and use their cameras and make the type."

I knew from the beginning that I wanted the type to be captured in a purely mathematical form; I wanted to have something that would adapt to technology as it kept changing, so that I would have a permanent mathematical description of the letters. Unfortunately, Xerox said, "Yes, you're welcome to use our equipment, but then we will own the designs, they will be the property of Xerox." I didn't want any of this work to be proprietary; I didn't want people to have to pay to use it. ... A mathematical formula is just numbers — why shouldn't everybody own those numbers?

So instead, I worked only at Stanford, at the Artificial Intelligence Laboratory, with the very primitive equipment there. We did have television cameras, and my publisher, Addison–Wesley, was very helpful — they sent me the original press-printed proofs of my book, from which *The Art of Computer Programming* had been made. The process in the 60s that I wanted to emulate was interesting: They would first print with metal type, Monotype, on to good paper, one copy. They made one copy with the metal, then they photographed that copy and printed from the photograph. Addison–Wesley gave me that original copy from which they had made the original photographs. So I could try putting the TV camera on that, and go from the TV camera to a computer screen to copy the letters. At that time, we could connect our display terminals to television and to movies on television; people were looking at the titles of movies, and capturing the frames from the movies and then making type. They would keep waiting for more episodes of *Star Trek* or something so that we would have the whole alphabet; eventually we would get a title with the letter "x" in it. That's how we were trying to get type by means of television at the time.

I thought it would be easy, but immediately I noticed that if I turned the brightness control down a very little bit, the letters would get much thicker. There was a tremendous variation, so that what I would see on my TV screen had absolutely no consistency between a letter that I did on Monday and a letter that I did on Tuesday, the following day. One letter would be fat and one letter would be thin, but it would be the same letter because the brightness sensitivity was extremely crude. This is still true now: If you scan a page of text and you change the threshold between black and white, a small change in the threshold changes the appearance of the letter drastically. So I couldn't use TV.

For the next attempt, my wife made photographs of the pages and then we took our projector at home and projected them down a long hallway. On the wall I would try to copy what the letters were. But at that point I realized that the people who had designed these typefaces actually had ideas in their mind when they were doing the design. There was some logic behind the letters. For example, consider the letters 'm', 'n', 'i', and 'l'. I noticed that the 'm' was 15 units wide, the 'n' was 10 units, and the 'i' was 5 units. Aha! A pattern! The 'l' was 5 units, the 'f' was 6 units, the 'fi' ligature was 10 units. So, if you cut off the tops of certain letters, you would see an exact rhythm of 5 units between stems. Great — there were regularities in the design! That's when it occurred to me that maybe I shouldn't just try to copy the letterforms, but I should somehow try to capture the intelligence, the logic, behind those letterforms. And then I could do my bold font with the same logic as the regular font.

The truth therefore is that at first I didn't know what to do about fonts; late May 1977 is when I started to have the idea of METAFONT.

I spent the summer of 1977 in China, and I left my students in California; I told them to implement TEX while I was gone. [*laughter*] I thought it would be very easy; I would come home and they would have TEX working, and then I could do the fonts. But when I got back, I realized that I had given them an impossible task. They actually had gotten enough of TEX running to typeset one character on one page, and it was a heroic achievement, because my specifications were very vague.[3]

---

[3] See Chapter 25 of the present volume.

I thought the specifications were precise, but nobody understands how imprecise a specification is until they try to explain it to a computer. And to write the program.

When I was not in China — in June, the first part of July, and September, October, November — I spent most of my time making fonts. And I had to, because there was no existing way to get a font that would be the same on different equipment. Plenty of good fonts existed, but they were designed specifically for each manufacturer's device. There was no font that would go to two devices. And the people at Xerox PARC — primarily John Warnock — were still developing their ideas; they eventually founded Adobe Systems in 1982. Now, with the help of many great designers, they have many beautiful fonts. But that came later, more than five years after I had an urgent need for device-independent type.

My lecture to the American Math Society was scheduled for January 1978. The transcript of the lecture that I gave, the Gibbs Lecture to the Society,[4] shows the work that I did with fonts in 1977. It was a much longer task than I ever believed possible. I thought it would be simple to make something that looked good — but it was maybe six years before I had anything that really looked satisfactory.

So, the first significant idea was to get fonts that would work on many different computers and typesetting machines, including future devices that had not been invented, by having everything defined in mathematics. The second idea was to try to record the intelligence of the design. I was not simply copying a shape, I also would specify the logic underlying that shape and its parts. My goal was to understand the designer's intention, not merely to copy the outcome of that intention.

Well, I didn't have TEX running until May of 1978; I drew the fonts first. For the article "Mathematical Typography," my talk to the American Math Society in January 1978, I made individual letters about 4 cm high and I pasted each one on a big sheet of paper and took a photograph of that.

That's a long answer. I hope I answered the question.

Karel: I have another question about this system; it is, when you started to learn typography, you had some knowledge before, or you started in the process, learning more and more? Because my experience with *The TEXbook* is that there is very much about typography. You can learn a lot about typography, much more than some people who are doing typesetting on the professional level, using those windows mouse

---

[4] See Chapter 2 of the present volume.

systems. They never can learn from the books which are supplied with those systems.

Don: Thank you. So, what was my background before 1977? When I was in secondary school — America's version of a European gymnasium — I had a part-time job setting type (so-called) on what was known as a mimeograph machine. I'm not sure what would be the equivalent here. On a mimeograph you had a sort of blue gelatinous material. The typewriter typed into it and it made a hole. I would also use a light table, and special pens, and try to make music or designs on the mimeograph stencil. I had a summer job where I would type, and then I would use my stylus to inscribe pictures on the gel. So I knew a little bit about typography. This was not fine printing, of course; it was very amateurish, but at least it gave me some idea that there was a process of printing that I could understand. After making the stencils, I would run the mimeograph, and cut the paper, and so on. I was doing this as a student.

Later, my father had a printing press in the basement of our house, and he did work for several schools of Milwaukee; this was to save money because the schools could not afford professional printing. He would also work for some architects that were friends of ours, to make their specification documents. Schools would need programs for concerts, or graduation ceremonies, and tickets for football games ... my father would do this in our basement. He started with a mimeograph machine, then he upgraded to something called a VariTyper, which was marvelous, because it had proportional spacing — some letters were wider than others. The fonts were terrible, but we had this machine, and I learned how to use it.

Still later, I started writing books, *The Art of Computer Programming*. So, by 1977, I had been proofreading thousands of pages of galley proofs. I certainly was looking at type. And you might say I was getting ink in my blood.

But I also knew that engineers often make the mistake of not looking at the traditions of the past. They think that they'll start everything over from scratch, and I knew that such attitudes were terrible. So actually, right during May of 1977, when I was thinking about starting my sabbatical year of typesetting, I took a trip with the Stanford Library Associates, a group of book lovers from Stanford.[5] We visited places in Sacramento, California, where other bibliophiles lived. We stopped at a typographic museum, which had a page from a Gutenberg Bible, and

---

[5] See pages 502–503.

so on. One man who lived in the mountains had his own hand press, and I had a chance to try it. Everywhere we went on this tour, I looked intently at all the letters that I saw, trying to imagine how a computer could draw them. And I saw people's collections of what they felt was the finest printing.

At Stanford Library there is a wonderful collection of typographic materials donated by Morgan and Aline Gunst, who spent a lifetime collecting fine printing. As soon as I got back from the library trip, I knew about the Gunst collection, so I spent May and June reading the works of Goudy and Zapf and everything else I could find, back through history. First of all, it was fascinating, it was wonderful, but I also wanted to make sure that I could capture as well as possible the knowledge of past generations in computer form.

The general idea I had at that time was the following. At the beginning, when I was young, people had computers that could deal only with numbers. Then we had computers that knew about numbers *and* capital letters, uppercase letters. So this greatly increased our ability to express ourselves. But even in Volume 1 of *The Art of Computer Programming* when I designed my MIX computer, I never expected that computers could do lowercase letters. [*laughter*] The Pascal language was developed in 1970; Pascal originally used only uppercase letters, and parentheses, commas, digits, altogether 64 characters.

Next, in the early 1970s, we had lowercase letters as well, and computers could make documents that looked almost like a typewriter. And then along came software like the *eqn* system of UNIX, which would make documents that approached printing. You probably know that *troff* and the *eqn* system for mathematics were developed at Bell Labs. Those systems actually were extensions of a program that began at M.I.T. in 1961, and it developed through a sequence of about five levels of improvement, finally to *eqn* in 1975.

So I knew that it was possible, all of a sudden, to get better and better documents from computers, looking almost like real books. When contemplating TEX I said, "Oh! Now it's time to go all the way. Let's not try to *approach* the best books, let's march all the way to the end — let's do it!" So my goal was to have a system that would make the best books that had ever been made, except, of course, when handmade additions of gold leaf and such things are added. [*laughter*] Why not? It was time to seek a standard solution to all the problems, to obtain the very best, and not just to approach better and better the real thing. That's why I read all the other works that I could, so that I would not miss any of the ideas. While reading every book I could find in the Gunst collection, to see what those books could tell me about typesetting and about letterforms, I tried to say, "Well, how does that apply today, how could I teach that to a computer?" Of course, I didn't succeed in everything, but I tried to find the powerful primitives that would support most of the ideas that have grown up over hundreds of years.

Now, of course, we have many more years of experience, so we can see how it is possible to go through many more subtle refinements that I couldn't possibly have foreseen in 1980. Well, my project took more than one year, and I had more than one user at the end. The subsequent evolution is described in my paper called "The errors of TEX," and the complete story after 1978 is told in that paper.[6]

In 1980, I was fortunate to meet many of the world leaders in typography. They could teach me, could fill in many of the gaps in my knowledge. Artisans and craftsmen usually don't write down what they know. They just do it. And so you can't find everything in books; I had to learn from a different kind of people. And with respect to type, the interesting thing is that there were two levels: There was the *type designer*, who would draw the shapes, and then there was the *punchcutter*, who would cut the actual type. And the designer would sometimes write a book, but the punchcutter would not write a book. I learned about optical illusions — what our eye thinks is there is not what's really on the page. And so the punchcutter would not actually follow the drawings perfectly, but the punchcutter would distort the drawings in such a way that after the printing process was done and after you looked at the letter at the right size, what you saw was what the designer drew. The punchcutter knew the tricks of making the right distortions.

Some of these tricks are not necessary any more on our laserprinters. Some of them were only for the old kind of type. But other tricks were important, to avoid blots of ink on the page and things like that. After I had done my first work on METAFONT, I invited Richard Southall to Stanford; he had been working at Reading University with the people who essentially are today's punchcutters. He gave me the extra knowledge that I needed to know. For example, when stems are supposed to look exactly the same, some of them are a little bit thinner, like the inside of a P — you don't want it to be quite as thick, you want it to be a little thinner; then, after you have the rest of the letter there, the lightened stem will look like it was correct. Richard taught me that kind

---

[6] *Software — Practice & Experience* **19** (1989), 607–681. Reprinted with additional material in *Literate Programming* (1992), 243–339.

of refinement. I learned similar things from Chuck Bigelow, Matthew Carter, Kris Holmes, Gerard Unger, Hermann Zapf, and others.

But we had very primitive equipment in those days, so that the fonts we could actually generate at low resolution did not look professional. They were just cheap approximations of the fine type. Stanford could not afford an expensive typesetting machine that would realize our designs at the time. Now I'm so happy that we have machines like the LaserJet 4, which make my type look the way I always wanted it to look, on an inexpensive machine.

X: Now that PostScript is becoming so widely used, do you think it is a good replacement for METAFONT — I mean, good enough? Right now, we can use TEX and PostScript ...

Don: The question is, is PostScript a good enough replacement for METAFONT? I believe that the available PostScript fonts are quite excellent quality, even though they don't use all of the refinements in METAFONT. They capture the artwork of top-quality designs. The multiple master fonts have only two or three parameters, while Computer Modern has more than sixty parameters; but even with only two or three, the Myriad and Minion fonts are excellent.

I'm working now with people at Adobe, so that we can more easily substitute their multiple master fonts for the fonts of public-domain TEX documents. The goal is to make the PDF files smaller. The Acrobat system has PDF files that are much larger — they're ten times as big as DVI files, but if you didn't have to download the fonts, they would only be three times as large as the DVI files. Acrobat formats allow us search commands and quite good electronic documents. So I'm trying to make it easier to substitute the multiple master fonts. They still aren't quite general enough, although I certainly like the quality there.

Adobe's font artists, like Carol Twombly and Robert Slimbach, are great; I was just an amateur. My designs as they now appear are good enough for me to use in my own books without embarrassment, but I wouldn't mind using the other ones. Yes, I like very much the fonts that other designers are doing.

Asking an artist to become enough of a mathematician to understand how to write a font with 60 parameters is too much. Computer scientists understand parameters, the rest of the world doesn't. Most people didn't even know the word "parameters" until five years ago — it's still a mysterious word. To a computer person, the most natural thing when you're automating something is to try to show how you would change your program according to different specifications. But this is not a natural concept to most people. Most people like to work from a given set of specifications and then answer a specific design problem. They don't want to give an answer to all possible design specifications that they might be given and explain how they would vary their solution to each specification. To a computer scientist, on the other hand, it's easy to understand the connection between variation of parameters and variation of programs.

In the back?

Láďa Lhotka: I have a problem for you. How did you decide to write and document the program for TEX in the structured way that you did?

Don: I was talking with Tony Hoare, who was editor of a series of books for Oxford University Press. I had a discussion with him in approximately ... 1980; I'm trying to remember the exact time, maybe 1979, yes, 1979, perhaps when I visited Newcastle? I don't recall the date exactly. He told me that I ought to *publish* my program for TEX.[7]

As I was writing TEX I was using for the second time in my life a set of ideas called "structured programming," which were revolutionizing the way computer programming was done in the middle 70s. I was teaching classes and I was aware that people were using structured programming, but I hadn't written a large computer program since 1971. In 1976 I wrote my first structured program; it was fairly good sized — maybe, I don't know, 50,000 lines of code, something like that. (That's another story I can tell you about sometime.) This gave me some experience with writing a program that was fairly easy to read. Then when I started writing TEX awhile later (I began the implementation of TEX in October of 1977, and finished it in May 78), it was consciously done with structured programming ideas.

Professor Hoare was looking for examples of fairly good-sized programs that people could read. Well, this was frightening — a very scary thing, for a professor of computer science to show someone a large program. At best, a professor might publish very small routines as examples of how to write programs. And we could polish those until ... well, every example in the literature about such programs had bugs in it. Tony Hoare was a great pioneer for proving the correctness of programs. But if you looked at the details ... I discovered from reading some of the articles, you know, I could find three bugs in a program that was proved

---

[7] I looked up the record later and found that my memory was gravely flawed. Hoare had heard rumors about my work and he wrote to Stanford suggesting that I keep publication in mind. I replied to his letter on 16 November 1977 — much earlier than I had remembered.

correct. [*laughter*] These were *small* programs. Now, he says, take my *large* program and reveal it to the world, with all its compromises. Of course, I developed TEX so that it would try to continue a history of hundreds of years of different ideas. There had to be compromises. So I was frightened by the notion that I would actually be expected to show someone my program. But then I also realized how much need there was for examples of fairly large programs that could be considered as reasonable models of good practice, not just small programs.

I had learned some important ideas from a Belgian man, who had a system that is explained in my paper on literate programming. He sent me a report, which was 150 pages long, about his system[8] — it was inspired by "The spirit in the machine." His 150-page report was very philosophical for the first 99 pages, then on page 100 he started with an example. That example opened my eyes to the notion that a program should be regarded as hypertext (as we would say today). He proposed a way of taking a complicated program and breaking it into small parts. Then, to understand the complicated whole, what you needed is just to understand the small parts, and to understand the relationship between each part and its neighbors.

In February of 1979, I developed a system called DOC and UNDOC ... something like the WEB system that came later. DOC was like WEAVE and UNDOC was like TANGLE, essentially. I played with DOC and UNDOC and did a mock-up with a small part of TEX. I didn't use DOC for a whole implementation but I took the inner part called *getnext*, which is a fairly complicated part of TEX's input routine, and I converted it to DOC. This gave me a little 20-page program that would show the *getnext* part of TEX written in DOC. And I showed that to Tony Hoare and to several other people, especially Luis Trabb Pardo, and got some feedback from them on the ideas and the format.

Then we had a student at Stanford whose name was Zabala — actually he's from Spain and he has two surnames — we called him Iñaki; Ignacio is his given name. He took the entire TEX that I'd written in a language called SAIL (Stanford Artificial Intelligence Language), and he converted it to Pascal in this DOC format. TEX-in-Pascal was distributed around the world by 1981. Then in 1982, when I was writing TEX82, I was able to use his experience and all the feedback he had from users, and I made the system that became WEB. There was a period of two weeks when we were trying different names for DOC and UNDOC, and the

---

[8] Pierre-Arnoul de Marneffe, *Holon Programming: A Survey* (Université de Liège, Service d'Informatique: December 1973).

winners were TANGLE and WEAVE. At that time, about 25 people would meet every Friday at Stanford to discuss digital typography. And we would play around with a whole bunch of ideas; this was the reason for most of the success of TEX and METAFONT.

Another program I wrote at the time was called Blaise, because it was a preprocessor to Pascal. [*laughter*]

Petr Olšák: I have two questions. What is your opinion of LATEX, as an extension of TEX at the macro level? I think that TEX was made for the plain TEX philosophy, which means that the user has read *The TEXbook* ... [*laughter*] while LATEX is done with macros, and takes plain TEX as its base. And the second question: Why is TEX not widely implemented and used in commercial places? They use only mouse and WYSIWYG-oriented programs.

Don: The first question was, what do I think about LATEX? I always wanted to have many different macro packages oriented to different classes of users, and LATEX is certainly the finest example of these macro packages. There were many others in the early days. But Leslie Lamport had the greatest vision as to how to do the job well. There's also *AMS*-TEX, and many mathematicians used Max Díaz's macros — originally known as MaxTEX but later officially called Fácil TEX — in the early days before we had LATEX. Mike Spivak and Leslie Lamport provided very important feedback to me on how I could improve TEX to support such packages. I didn't want to force ... I like the idea of a macro system that can adapt to special applications. I myself don't use LATEX because I don't have time to read the manual. [*laughter*] LATEX has more features than I need myself, in the way I do things. Also, of course, I understand TEX well enough that it's easier for me not to use high-level constructions beyond my control.

But for many people LATEX is a simpler system, and it automates many of the things that people feel naturally ought to be automated. For me, the things that it automates are largely things that I consider are a small percentage of my total work. The task of hand-tuning a bibliography doesn't bother me, but it bothers other people a lot. I can understand why a lot of people prefer their way of working.

Also, when you're writing in a system like LATEX you can more easily follow a discipline that makes it possible for other programs to find the structure of your document. If you work in plain TEX, you have the freedom to be completely unstructured in your approach and you can defeat any possible process that would try to automatically extract bibliographic entries and such things from your document. If you restrict yourself to some kind of a basic structure, then other processes become possible. So a disciplined use of TEX can be quite valuable. It allows translation into other structures, languages and so on.

But I use TEX for so many different purposes where it would be much harder to provide canned routines. LATEX is at a higher level; it's not easy to bend it to brand-new applications. Very often I find that, for the kind of things that I want to do, I wake up in the morning and I think of a project ... or my wife comes to me and says, "Don, can you make the following for me?" So I create ten lines of TEX macros and all of a sudden I have a new language specifically for that kind of a document. A lot of my electronic documents don't look like they have any markup whatsoever.

Now, your second question, why isn't TEX used more in commercial publication? In fact, I was quite pleasantly surprised to see how many commercial publishers in the Czech Republic are using TEX. Thursday night, I saw three or four Czech–English dictionaries that were done with TEX, and you know it's being used for the new Czech encyclopedia. And Petr Sojka showed me an avant garde novel that had been typeset with TEX with some nice tricks of its own very innovative page layout. In America, TEX is used heavily in legal publications, and behind the scenes in lots of large projects.

I never intended to have a system that would be universal and used by everybody. I always wanted to write a system that would be used for just the finest books. [*laughter*] Just the ones where the people had a more difficult than ordinary task, or they wanted to go the extra mile to have excellent typography. I never expected that it would compete with systems that are for the masses.

I'm not a competitive person, in fact. It made me very happy to think that I was making a system that would be primarily for mathematics. As far as I knew, there wasn't anybody in the world who would feel offended if I made it easier to typeset mathematics. Printers considered mathematics to be "penalty copy," something that they did only grudgingly. They charged a penalty for the extra horrible work of typesetting mathematics. I never expected that I would be replacing systems that are used in a newspaper office or anything like that. It turned out that after TEX got going, we found we could make improvements to non-mathematical typesetting; for example, in one experiment we re-typeset a page of *Time* magazine, to show how much better it would be if they had a good line-breaking algorithm.[9] But I never expected when I began

---

[9] See pages 140 and 141.

that such magazines would ever use what I was doing because, well, it was a billion-dollar industry and I didn't want to put anyone out of work or anything.

So it was very disturbing to me in the early 80s when I found there was one man who was very unhappy that I invented TEX. He had worked hard to develop a mathematical typesetting system that he was selling to people, and he was losing customers. So he wrote to the National Science Foundation in America, saying, "I'm a taxpayer and you're using my tax money to put me out of business." This made me very unhappy. I thought everything I was doing was for everybody's good. And here was a person I'd obviously hurt. But I also thought that I still should make TEX available to everyone, even though it had been developed with some help from the government. I don't think the government should give financial support only to things that are purely academic and not useful.

Yes?

X: I have a question about the usage of your typographic programs in commercial institutions like DTP studios and so on. I'd like to ask about using parts of the TEX source. You made clear that the programmers were free to incorporate parts of the TEX source into their own programs. There are some remarkable examples of this, do you know.

Don: That question came up also last summer when I had a question and answer session at the TUG meeting in Florida.[10] I thought it would be fairly common to have special versions of TEX. I designed TEX so that it has many hooks inside; you can write extensions and then have a much more powerful TEX system readily adapted.

I guess I was thinking that every publishing house using TEX would have an in-house programmer who would develop a special version of TEX if they wanted to do an edition of the Bible, or if they wanted to do an Arabic-to-Chinese dictionary or some other special job. If they were doing an encyclopedia, they could have their own version of TEX that would be used for this application.

A macro language is Turing-complete — it can do anything — but why should we try to do everything in a high-level language when some things are so easily done at a lower level? Therefore I built hooks into TEX and I implemented parts of TEX as demonstrations of those hooks, so that a person who read the code could see how to extend TEX to other things. We anticipated certain kinds of things for chemistry or

---

[10] See page 598 of the present volume.

for making change bars that would be done in the machine language for special applications.

Certainly, if I were in the publishing business myself, I would probably have had ten different versions of TEX by now for ten different complicated projects that had come in. They would all look almost the same as TEX, but no one else would have exactly the same program — they wouldn't need it, since they're not doing exactly the book that my publishing house was doing.

I thought such special versions would proliferate. And certainly, there was a point in the middle 80s when more than a thousand people in the world understood the implementation of TEX. They knew the intricacies of the program quite well; they had read it, and they would have been able to make many kinds of extensions if they had wanted to. But now I would say that the number of people with a working knowledge of TEX's innards is probably more than a hundred, but less than a thousand. It hasn't developed to the extent that I expected.

One of the most extensive such revisions is what I saw earlier this week in Brno — a student whose name is Thanh,[11] who has a system almost done that outputs PDF format instead of DVI format. If you specify a certain flag saying \PDFon, then the output comes out as a file that an Acrobat reader can read immediately. Ten years ago I also expected that people would go directly to PostScript; that hasn't happened yet as far as I know.

No one has done a special edition of the Bible using TEX in the way I expected. Some extensions were made in Iceland; I don't remember if they did it at the higher level — I think they worked mostly at the macro level, or maybe entirely.

Anyway, I made it possible to do very complicated things. When you have a special application, I was always expecting that you would want to have a specially tuned program there because that's where it's easiest to do these powerful things.

X: I want to ask which features of TEX were in the first version — for example, line-breaking, hyphenation, and macro processing — if all these things were in the first version?

Don: The very first version was designed in April 1977. I did have macros and the algorithm for line-breaking. It wasn't as well developed;

---

[11] Han The Thanh; see Petr Sojka, Han The Thanh, and Jiří Zlatuška, "The Joy of TEX2PDF — Acrobatics with an alternative to DVI format," *TUGboat* **17** (1996), 244–251.

I didn't have all the bells and whistles like `\parshape` at that time, but from the very beginning, from 1977 on, I knew I would treat the paragraph as a whole, not just line by line. The hyphenation algorithm I had in those days was not the one that we use now; it was based on removing prefixes and suffixes — it was a very peculiar method, but it seemed to catch about 80% of the hyphens. I worked on that just by looking at the dictionary: I would say, if the word starts with 'anti', then put a hyphen after the 'i'; similar rules applied at the end of a word. Or if a certain combination of letters occurred in the middle, there were natural breaks. I liked this better than the *troff* method, which had been published earlier. TEX's old hyphenation algorithm is described in the old TEX manual, which you can find in libraries.[12]

Now, you asked about line-breaking, hyphenation, macros, and so on; I developed the macro language in the following way. I took a look at Volume 2 of *The Art of Computer Programming* and I chose representative parts of it. I made a mock-up of about five pages of that book, and said, "How would I like that to look in a computer file?" And that was the whole source of the design.[13]

I stayed up late one night and created TEX. I went through Volume 2 and fantasized about natural-looking instructions — "here I'll say 'begin an algorithm', and then I'll say 'Algorithm K', and then I'll say 'algstep K1'," you know. This gave me a little file that represented the way I wanted the input to look for *The Art of Computer Programming*. The file also included some mathematical formulas. Formulas were based on the ideas of *eqn*; the *troff* language had demonstrated a way to represent mathematics that secretaries could learn easily. And that was the design. Then I had to implement a macro language to support those features.

The macro language developed during 1978, primarily with the influence of Terry Winograd. Terry was writing a book on linguistics, a book on English grammar.[14] He wanted to push macros much harder than I did, and so I added `\xdef` and fancier parameters for him.

The hyphenation algorithm we have now was Frank Liang's Ph.D. research. He worked with me on the original hyphenation method, and his experience led him to discover a much better way, which can adapt to

---

[12] *TEX and* METAFONT: *New Directions in Typesetting* (Bedford, Massachusetts: Digital Press, 1979).

[13] See pages 484–488 of the present volume.

[14] *Language as a Cognitive Process*, Volume 1: *Syntax* (Reading, Massachusetts: Addison–Wesley, 1983).

all languages — I mean, to all western languages, which are the languages that use hyphens.

To develop rules for proper spacing in mathematics, I chose three standards of excellence of mathematical typesetting. One was Addison–Wesley books, in particular *The Art of Computer Programming*. The people at Addison–Wesley, especially Hans Wolf (their main source for composition), had developed a style that I had always liked best in my textbooks as a college student. Secondly, I took *Acta Mathematica*, from 1910 approximately; this was a journal in Sweden ... Mittag-Leffler was the editor, and his wife was very rich, and they had the highest budget for quality mathematics printing, so the typography was especially good in *Acta Mathematica*. And the third source was a copy of *Indagationes Mathematicæ*, the Dutch journal. There's a long fine tradition of quality printing in the Netherlands, and I selected an issue from 1950 or thereabouts, where again I thought that the mathematics was particularly well done.

I took these three standards of excellence and looked at all of the mathematics formulas closely. I measured them, using the TV cameras at Stanford, to find out how far they dropped the subscripts and raised the superscripts, what styles of type they used, how they balanced fractions, and everything. I made detailed measurements, and I asked myself, "What is the smallest number of rules that I need to do what they were doing?" I learned that I could boil it down into a recursive construction that uses only seven types of objects in the formulas.

I'm glad to say that three years ago, *Acta Mathematica* adopted TEX. And so the circle has closed. Addison–Wesley has certainly adopted TEX, and I'm not sure about the Dutch yet — I'm going to visit them next week. [*laughter*] But anyway, I hope to continue the good old traditions of quality.

I have to call on people who haven't spoken. George?

Jiří Veselý: I have a question. You are asked every time carefully regarding all suggestions and things like that for improvements. Once I was asked about the possibility to make a list of all hyphenated words in the book. I was not able to find in your book a way to do this. I would like to know something about your philosophy what to include and what not to include. What would be in that special package, and what would be in TEX?

Don: The question is, what is the philosophy that I use to try to say what should be a basic part of TEX and what should be harder to do or special, or something like that. Of course, these decisions are all arbitrary. I think it was important, though, that the decisions were all made by one person, even though I'm not ... I certainly make a lot of mistakes. I tried the best to get input from many sources, but finally I took central responsibility to keep some unity. Whenever you have a committee of people designing a system, everyone in the committee has to feel proud that they have contributed something to the final language. But then you have a much less unified result because it reflects certain things that were there to please each person. I wanted to please as many people as I could but keep unity. So for many years we had a weekly meeting for about two hours every Friday noon, and we had visitors from all over the world who would drop in. I would listen to their comments and then I would try to incorporate the best ideas.

Now you ask specifically about why don't we have an easy way to list all the hyphenations that were made in the document. It sounds like a very nice suggestion, which I don't recall anyone raising during those weekly meetings. The words that actually get hyphenated, the decision to do that is made during the *hpack* routine, which is part of the line-breaking algorithm. But the fact that a hyphenation is performed by *hpack* doesn't mean that it's going to appear in the final document, because you could discard the box in which this hyphenation was done.

It's very easy in TEX to typeset something several times and then choose only one of those for the actual output. So, to get a definitive representative of the hyphenation, you'd have to catch it in the output routine, where the discretionary had appeared. This would be easy to do now in a module specially written for TEX. I would say that right now, in fact, you could get almost exactly what you want by writing a filter that says to TEX "Turn on all of the tracing options that cause it to list the page contents." Then a little filter program would take the trace information through a UNIX pipe and it would give you the hyphenated words. It would take an afternoon to write this program; well, maybe two afternoons ... and a morning. [*laughter*] You could get that now, but it was not something that I can recall I ever debated whether or not I should do at the time we were having those weekly discussions on TEX.

My paper on "The errors of TEX" has the complete record of all the changes that were made since 1979, with dates, and with references to the code, exactly where each change appears. And so you can see the way the evolution was taking place. Often the changes would occur as I was writing *The TEXbook* and realizing that some things were very hard for me to explain. I would change the language so it would be easier to explain how to use it. This was when we were having our most extensive meetings with users and other people in the group as sources of ideas; the part of the language I was writing about was the part that was changing at the moment.

During 1978, I myself was typesetting Volume 2, and this led naturally to improvements as I was doing the keyboarding. In fact, improvements occurred almost at a steady rate for about 500 pages: Every four pages I would get another idea how to make TeX a little better. But the number of ways to improve any complicated system is endless, and it's axiomatic that you never have a system that cannot be improved. So finally, I knew that the best thing I could do would be to make no more improvements — this would be better than a system that was improving all the time.

Let me explain. As I was first developing TeX at the Stanford Artificial Intelligence Laboratory, we had an operating system called WAITS, which I think is the best that the world has ever seen. Four system programmers were working full time making improvements to this operating system. And every day that operating system was getting better and better. And every day it was breaking down and impossible to use for long periods of time.

In fact I wrote the first draft of *The TeXbook* entirely during downtime. I would take a big tablet of paper to the Artificial Intelligence Laboratory in the morning and I would compute as long as I could. Then the machine would crash, and I would write another chapter. Then the machine would come up and I could type a little bit and get a little more done. Then, another hang-up; time to write another chapter. Our operating system was always getting better, but I couldn't get much computing done.

After awhile the money ran out; three of the programmers went to Lawrence Livermore Laboratory and worked on a new operating system there. We had only one man left to maintain the system, not to make any more improvements. And it was wonderful! [*laughter*] That year, I could be about as productive as anyone in the world.

So I knew that eventually I would have to get to the point where TeX would not improve anymore. It would be steady and reliable, and people would understand the warts it had ... the things that it couldn't do.

I still believe it's best to have a system that is not a moving target. After a certain point, people need something that is stable, not changing at all. Of course, if there's some catastrophic scenario that we don't want ever to happen, I still change TeX to avoid potential disasters. But I don't introduce nice new ideas any more.

Other people are working on extensions to TeX that will be useful for another generation. And they will also be well advised at a certain

point to say "Now we will stop, and not change our system any more."
Then there will be a chance for another group later.

Karel: I'd like to ask about the idea of the italic font in mathematics.
I never saw other textbooks that use different fonts for italics in text
and in mathematics, so I'm asking if it's your own idea or if it comes
also from these three sources?

Don: I didn't find in any of the other books the idea of having a text
italic and a math italic. I wanted the math italic to look as beautiful as
possible, and I started with that. But then I found that the text italic
was not as good; since I had METAFONT, it was easy to get text italic
that would look better. If I made the text italic good, then the math
would not position the subscripts and the superscripts as well.

It's partly because of what I explained before — TeX has only four
numbers to go with every character. Printers, in fact, in the old days,
had only three numbers; they didn't have the italic correction. So they
couldn't achieve TeX's spacing automatically; the better printers adjusted mathematical spacing by hand. But italic now, the italic fonts
of today by all the font designers are much better than they used to
be. We've seen a great improvement in italic typography during the last
ten, fifteen years. In fact, if you read older books you'll sometimes say,
"How could anybody read this italic?" or, "Why did they accept such
peculiar spacing?" The old fonts were based on the constraints of metal
type. The whole idea of italic correction was not in any other book, but
it was necessary for me to get the spacing that I wanted.

When I show mathematical formulas to type designers, they can
never understand why mathematicians want italic type in their equations. It seems you're combining a roman 2 with an italic x. And they
say, "Wouldn't the positioning be so much simpler if you had a regular,
non-sloped font in mathematics?" The type designer Jan van Krimpen
once worked with a famous physicist in the Netherlands, in Haarlem —
what was his name?[15] I think he was the second person to receive the
Nobel Prize in physics; he died in the 20s — anyway he and van Krimpen
were going to develop a new font for mathematics in the Netherlands,
and it wasn't going to have italics for mathematics. It was going to be
unified between the Greek letters and other symbols that mathematicians wanted. But the project stopped because the physicist died; van
Krimpen finished only the Greek, which became fairly popular.

---

[15] It was H. A. Lorentz. See John Dreyfus, *The Work of Jan van Krimpen*
(London: Sylvan Press, Museum House, 1952), page 28.

Several other font designers have visited Stanford. When they looked at mathematics, they said, "Well, why don't you use a non-sloping font?" Hermann Zapf made a proposal to the American Mathematical Society that we would create a new typeface for mathematics which would include the Fraktur alphabet, and Greek, and script, and special characters, as well as ordinary letters. One key idea was that it would not have sloped characters, so that x would be somehow straight up and down. Then it should be easier to do the positioning, the balancing. Hermann created a series of designs, and we had a large committee of mathematicians studying the designs and commenting on them and tuning them.[16]

This font, however, proved to be too radical a change for mathematicians. I've seen mathematicians actually writing their documents where they will write an x slanted twice as much — I mean, they make it look *very* italic; then it looks like a mathematical letter to them. So after 300 years of seeing italic math in print, it's something that many people feel is right. There are maybe two dozen books printed, well, maybe more, maybe a hundred, printed with the AMS Euler font in place of italics; but most mathematicians think it's too different. On the other hand, I find now that the Euler Fraktur font is used by almost everyone.

In Brno, I saw Euler Roman used as the text font for a beautiful book, a Czech translation of Dürer's *Apocalypse*.[17] I also saw Euler Roman a few days ago in some class notes. Once, when I was in Norway, I noticed that everyone's workstation was labeled with the workstation's name in AMS Euler, because people liked it. It's a beautiful font, but it hasn't been used as the typeface for mathematics in a large number of books.

Karel: If there are no other questions, I would thank Professor Knuth very much for this session. [*wide prolonged applause*]

Don: Thank you all for excellent questions.

Karel: [Closing comments in Czech.]

---

[16] "AMS Euler—A new typeface for mathematics," *Scholarly Publishing* **20** (1989), 131–157; reprinted as Chapter 17 of the present volume.

[17] See page 16 of the present volume.

Chapter 33

Questions and Answers, III

[On 6 January 1996, Kees van der Laan informed the NTG, the Dutch-language-oriented TₑX Users Group, that Donald Knuth would be in Holland in March. Knuth was invited by the Mathematisch Centrum (MC, nowadays called Centrum voor Wiskunde en Informatica, CWI) to speak at CWI's 50th anniversary. The NTG noticed that this was an exceptional occasion to organize a special meeting for all Dutch TₑX and METAFONT users who would like to meet the Grand Wizard himself. Fortunately Knuth accepted the NTG invitation and so a meeting was organized in "De Rode Hoed" in Amsterdam on March 13th. About 35 people from all over the country and even from Belgium came to the event. Everything was recorded on both video and audio tape by Gerard van Nes. Christina Thiele volunteered to write this transcript, first published in the journal of the NTG: MAPS (Minutes and APpendiceS) 16 (1996), 38–49.]

Erik Frambach: Welcome, everyone. This is a very special meeting on the occasion that Mr. Donald Knuth is in Holland. The NTG thought it would be a good idea to take the opportunity and ask him if he would be willing to answer our questions about TₑX, METAFONT, and anything else connected to the things we do with TₑX. Luckily, he has agreed. So we are very happy to welcome Mr. Donald Knuth here — thank you for coming.

Tonight we have time to ask him any questions that we have long been waiting to pose to him. [*laughter*] I'm sure that all of you have

many, many questions that you would like the Grand Wizard's opinion about. So, we could start now with questions.

Don Knuth: I get to ask questions too! [*laughter*]

Last Saturday I was in Prague and the Czech/Slovak TEX users had a session something like this. You'll be glad to know that I saw quite a few copies of *4TEX* CDROMs at that meeting.[1]

This trip is not my first time in Amsterdam: I visited Amsterdam in 1961. Therefore it's only been 35 years, and probably will be less than 35 years till the next time. I guess people are tape-recording these questions and answers to try to keep me honest, because they also did that in Prague. So in case the same question comes up, you'll have to take the average of the two answers. [*laughter*]

Wietse Dol: Did you know that Barbara Beeton does that? She mails you and says "Tape everything."

Don: Yes, that's what they said in Prague too! [*laughter*] I think she's desperate for things to publish, or maybe she just has a lot of questions. But before I open questions, let me say that one of the most interesting questions asked me in Prague was asked after the session, and I wish it would get into the record. The question was: How did I

---

[1] The popular *4TEX* distribution of TEX for PC-compatible computers was the result of collaboration by NTG members.

meet Duane Bibby, who did the illustrations for *The TEXbook* and *The METAFONTbook*? Somehow I always wanted people to know about that.

Here's the story. I had the idea that after writing math books for many years, I wanted to have a book that had weirder — well, anyway, different — illustrations in it. Here I was writing a book about books, and books have illustrations, so why shouldn't I have illustrations too? So I wrote to an artist called Edward Gorey. Does anyone know . . .

Frans Goddijn: Yup. *Amphigorey.* Beautiful.

Don: Yes, Edward Gorey. *Amphigorey.*[2] He makes very morbid drawings but with a wonderful sense of humor. I had used several of his books with my children. I thought he would be a natural person. I wrote him two letters but he never responded. Then I wrote to a Japanese artist called Anno, Mitsumasa Anno, who is really the logical successor to Escher. Anno does what Escher did, but in color; so I asked if he'd be able to illustrate my book. He sent back a nice letter, saying "I'm sorry I don't have time because I have so many other commitments, but here are five of my books full of pictures and if you want to use any of those, go ahead." Very nice, but I wanted personalized pictures.

Then I went to a party at Stanford where I met a lady who worked for a publisher. She'd just met a brilliant young artist who she'd begun to work with. I invited him to come to my house, and we spent some time together and he's a wonderful person. Duane lives now up in northern California, about 4 hours' drive from my house, so I only went up there once to see him. He sometimes comes down to the San Francisco area on business. First we discussed the book and then he sent me a bunch of drawings and all kinds of sketches that he had. Originally, TEX was going to be a Roman citizen, and Duane drew this man in a toga with olive branches on his head — which is why the lion has olive branches now. But all of a sudden he started doing sketches of his cat, which really seemed to click, and pretty soon he had drafted all 37 of the drawings, using a lion. Most of those eventually become the drawings in the book, and we adjusted half a dozen of the others. When I went to visit up at his house, I got to meet TEX the cat, who looks very much like the one you see in the book. So that's the story about Duane Bibby.

Erik: Thank you. Who would like to start with the first question? Please identify yourself when you ask one.

---

[2] *Amphigorey: Fifteen Books by Edward Gorey* (New York: G. P. Putnam, 1972). *Amphigorey Too* (New York: G. P. Putnam, 1975). *Amphigorey Also* (New York: Congdon & Weed, 1983).

Piet van Oostrum: My name is Piet van Oostrum. You have this wonderful lion on *The TEXbook*, the lioness on *The METAFONTbook*. What about baby lions?

Don: Oh, I see ... [*laughter*] Duane still does illustrations for special occasions. He's made new illustrations for the Japanese translations of both *The TEXbook* and *The METAFONTbook*, with TEX and META dressed up in Japanese costumes. So now, if there happens to be some kind of an offspring that would come out of somewhere, I imagine he would be glad to help draw it. But it would probably be a little bit of an illegitimate child, from my point of view. [*laughter*] I mean, I wouldn't take responsibility for anything those characters do. [*laughter*]

Piet: So what are your ideas about the offspring of TEX and META-FONT?

Don: Well, I think that no matter what system you have, there will be a way to improve it. If somebody wants to take the time to do a good, careful job, then as we learn more about typesetting, it will happen that something else will come along. I personally hope that I won't have to take time to learn a new system, because I have enough for my own needs. But I certainly never intended that my system would be the only tool that anybody would ever need for typesetting. I tried to make it as general as I could with a reasonably small program, and with what we knew and understood about typesetting at the time. So these other projects — I don't consider that they're a threat to me or anything. I hope that there will be some compatibility so that — I mean, I'd like to be immortal — so that the books I've written now could still be typeset 50 years from now without having to go through the files and edit stuff. I like the archival and machine-independent aspects of TEX especially, and I tried to set a model, a minimum standard of excellence for other people to follow.

Hans Hagen: But when you look in the future, ... you consider today's programming by a lot of people as an art, well a lot of art takes hundreds of years to be recognized as art. In about a hundred years there will be pretty different computers, the programming languages will be changed, the media on which we put all those things will be changed.

Real programs and everything related to them, will they ever have a chance to become immortal, as you see it?

Don: Did you state your name? [*laughter*]

Hans: I'm Hans Hagen.

Don: You're saying that it's pretty arrogant of us to assume that what we do now will last at all. Technology is changing so fast that we have absolutely no idea what people are going to think of next. One hundred years ago, physicists were saying there was nothing more to do in physics, except to get another decimal — a fifth decimal place for the fundamental constants — and then that would wrap up physics. Clearly there is no way to know about these things. But I do believe that once we have things in electronic form and we have mirror sites of them, there is a fair degree of immortality — whereas paper burns.

Have you heard about a project called "The Clock," being developed by Stewart Brand and his colleagues? He's the one who published the *Whole Earth Catalog*. They have a bunch of people that are considering if they could build something that would last for a thousand years ... I don't want to go on too much more about that. I do hope that the stability of TEX will make it possible to reproduce the things we're doing now, later. And since it's fairly easy to do that, I think it will happen — unless there's a nuclear holocaust. Some mathematicians have this debate about the Platonic view ... does everything in mathematics exist and we're just discovering it, or are we actually creating mathematics? In some sense, once something gets put into bits, it's mathematics and therefore it exists forever, even if the human race dies out — it's there, but so what?

Erik: Who's next?

Marc van Leeuwen: If I could extend a bit on the previous questions. The stability of TEX itself, I could imagine, might be a stumbling block for development of new things exactly *because* it's so stable and everybody's already using it. So if something comes along that is just a bit better, then people will not tend to use that because it's not available everywhere, and there are all kinds of reasons to keep on using the old thing.

Don: I guess I said in Florida that people are still trying to use old fonts that I'm trying to stamp out from the world. Four years ago I redesigned the Greek lowercase delta and I made the arrowheads darker. I didn't change anything in the way TEX operates — all the dimensions and the characters' heights and widths stayed exactly the same. But I did tune up a lot of the characters. Still I see lots of math journals are still using the old ones from four years ago, and I get letters and preprints from people with the old-style delta. I changed it because I just couldn't stand the old versions. [*laughter*] Now I've got home pages — if I ever have some errata to TEX or other news items I put them there: `http://www-cs-faculty.stanford.edu/~knuth`. This address gets to my home page, and there's a reference saying, "Important notice for all users of TEX"; and that page says "Look at the lowercase delta and if you have the wrong one, you die!" [*laughter*]

I understand that people have a reluctance to change from things they've become accustomed to. I know of two main successors to TEX: One is ε-TEX and the other is $\mathcal{N}\mathcal{T}\mathcal{S}$. ε-TEX is going to be apparently 100% compatible with TEX, so if somebody doesn't switch over to incompatible features, then they have a system that still works with old things. That will allow a gradual change-over. It'll take more space on a computer, of course, but that's not a big deal these days. The people who work on ε-TEX always sent me very reliable comments about TEX when they caught errors in my stuff, so I imagine they're going to be doing a careful job. So it'll be one of these things where you walk into a random installation of UNIX or whatever and you'll find ε-TEX there as the default, and you'll still have TEX. Then you also have certain other features that might be really important to you for your special applications.

Johannes Braams: You mentioned ε-TEX and $\mathcal{N}\mathcal{T}\mathcal{S}$. But are you also aware of the Omega project?

Don: Of course, the Ω project! Yes, I'm hoping to use that myself for the authors' names in *The Art of Computer Programming*. I've been collecting the names of Chinese, Japanese, Indian, Hebrew, Greek, Russian, Arabic authors and I want to typeset their names properly [*laughter*], not just in transliteration. I have some rudimentary software that will do this for proofing purposes, for getting my database going and for writing to people and saying, "Is this your name?" With the Ω system, I'm hoping that it'll be accompanied by good fonts that will make it possible for me to do this without a great deal of work. Right now, to get the Arabic names, I have to use ArabTEX; to get the Hebrew names ... I had a terrible time trying to find Hebrew fonts on CTAN

two weeks ago — I can tell you that whole story if you want to know
... I kept clicking on the different things and they would refer to files
that didn't exist and README files that were four years out of date and
inconsistent, so I couldn't find any Hebrew fonts. Maybe you have it on
your CD ...

Johannes: I could certainly point you to someone who could help you
with the Hebrew font — I know someone in Israel who's trying to do
Hebrew support within the Babel system. And they do do typesetting
in Israel with TEX.

Don: My own typesetting friend in Israel is Dan Berry, who unfortunately is fairly committed to *troff*. [*laughter*] I'm sure that I can get
good Hebrew through Yannis [Haralambous] and Ω. I sure hope Unicode is going to arrive sooner rather than later; it's much better than the
alternatives, for much the reasons that Marc [van Leeuwen] mentioned.

   I haven't found a great enthusiasm in Japan for Unicode, because
they have a system that seems to work pretty well for them, so why
change. Every time I ask Japanese people for their name in Unicode,
they say, "What's Unicode? Here's my JIS name." But the JIS characters don't include all the Chinese codes, and in fact, my own name —
I have a Chinese name — can't be expressed in JIS without changing it
slightly. There are two different Unicode characters, one for the Japanese
version and one for the Chinese.

   In the back? Kees?

Kees van der Laan: I have a lot of questions of course. But I would
like to start with some questions about METAFONT. The first one is:
How come macro writing in TEX and METAFONT is so different?

Don: Why are macros in TEX and METAFONT so different? I didn't
dare make TEX as extreme as METAFONT. These languages are of

completely different design. METAFONT is in some ways an incredible programming language — it basically consists of object-oriented macros. You have macros in the middle of record structures.

The way I designed these languages is fairly simple to describe. Let's take TEX. I wrote down one night what I thought would be a good source file for *The Art of Computer Programming*. I took a look at Volume 2, which I had to typeset. I started out on the first page, and when I got to any copy that looked very much like something I had already done I skipped that. Finally I had examples of all the different kinds of typesetting conventions that occur in Volume 2. It totalled 5 printed pages; and you can even see these pages — exactly what my original test program was — in a paper by David Fuchs and myself, where we talked about optimum font caching.[3] In there, we gave an example and we show these 5 pages, which illustrate what I wanted TEX to be able to do. I wrote out what I thought I would like to type — how my electronic file should look. And then, I said, OK, that's my input, and here's my output — how do I get from input to output? And for this, well, it looks like I need macros. [*laughter*]

Same thing for METAFONT. I went through my first draft of all the fonts that later became Computer Modern. I wrote actually in SAIL, an ALGOL-like compiler language; but SAIL had a macro capability, so I developed a few primitive macros in which I could say, "pick up the wide pen," "draw from point 1 to point 2," and things like that. These macros were compiled by the SAIL compiler into machine language, which would then draw the letters. I went through the entire alphabet, and by the end of the year I had some 300 little programs, each one drawing a letter. Then I realized what kind of a language I would want to write in, to describe the letters. So one day, on a family camping trip — I was in the Grand Canyon with my wife and kids — I took an hour off, sat under a tree and wrote out the program for the letter A, in a language that I thought would be a good algebraic language, reflecting at a high level what I had been doing with pretty primitive low-level instructions in my SAIL programs. I did the letter B, too; Capital A and B. Then I went back to the camping trip. These sheets of paper containing my original programs are now in Stanford's archives — the program for the letter B was reproduced in a Stanford library publication last year. The woman who's in charge of rare books and manuscript collections at Stanford is

---

[3] "Optimal prepaging and font caching," *ACM Transactions on Programming Languages and Systems* **7** (1985), 62–79. See also pages 484–488 of the present volume, for the first draft of TEX source code.

quite interested in METAFONT, so she wrote a little article about what they have.[4]

That program again implied that I wanted some macros to go with it. But these needed to be much more structured than the macros of TEX. It had to be that when I said z1' this would actually be equivalent to (x1',y1'); and I wanted to be able to write z1' without any delimiters. It turned out that in order to have a high-level language that would feel natural to me writing the program, it had to look completely different from TEX. So TEX and METAFONT share a common format for error messages and certain other data structures inside, but otherwise they're quite different systems. In order to have a good high-level language for fonts, I didn't want to have to waste time writing parentheses, brackets, commas, and other delimiters.

Kees: It's a nice introduction to my second question: [*laughter*] For the future of METAPOST, which allows markup of pictures, with encapsulated PostScript as the result, what is your attitude to higher-dimensional data for METAPOST and METAFONT? For example, adding a triple as an analogy of the **pair** data structure?

Don: METAPOST already has a data structure for triples because of **color**. So RGB expressions are actually triples of numbers.

Kees: Yes, but the triple as a data point in space?

Don: Ah, I see. I did write METAFONT in a way that has hooks in it so that it can be easily extended; for example, you might want to draw 3-dimensional pictures, for perspective and projective geometry instead of affine geometry. The program itself for METAFONT was written so that it could easily be changed by people who wanted to have a system that goes beyond the basics. I always wanted the systems that I would make widely available to be able to handle 99% of all applications that I knew. But I always felt there were going to be special applications where the easiest thing would be to change the program, and not write a macro.

I tried to make the programs so that they would have logical structure and it would be easy to throw in new features. This hasn't happened anywhere near as often as I thought, because people have turned out to be more interested, I think, in interchangeability of what they do; once you have your own program, then other people don't have it. Still, if I were a large publisher, and I were to get special projects — some

---

[4] Robin E. Rider, "Back to the future: High-tech history," *Imprint* **14**, 1 (Fall 1994), 9–18.

encyclopaedia, some new edition of the Bible, things like that — I would certainly think that the right thing to do would be to hire a good programmer and make a special computer system just for this project. At least, that was my idea about the way people would do it. It seems that hasn't happened very much, although in Brno I met a student who is well along on producing Acrobat format directly in TEX, by changing the code. And the Ω system that Johannes mentioned, that's 150,000 lines of change files. [*laughter*] I built in hooks so that every time TEX outputs a page, it could come to a *whatsit* node and a *whatsit* node could be something that was completely different in each version of TEX. So, when the program sees a *whatsit* node, it calls a special routine saying, "How do I typeset this *whatsit* node?" The special routine looks at the subtype, and the subtype might be another subtype put in as a demo or it might be a brand new subtype.

Similar hooks are in the METAFONT program. If people have extra time when they're not browsing the Web [*laughter*], I recommend as a great recreation to read the program for METAFONT. Some parts of it are pretty rough going and I hope that nobody ever finds a bug there because I'd hate to have to look at them again. [*laughter*] But those are the rasterization routines, the things that actually fill in the pixels. There are many other things in that program — the linear equation solver that it has and the data structure mechanisms ... lots of beautiful algorithms are in there — to take square roots in fixed point, and the intersection of two curves, and so on. METAFONT is full of little programs that were great fun to write and that I think are useful and interesting in their own right. I think when John Hobby wrote META-POST, he enjoyed it, because he could add his own nice little programs to the ones that are already there.

I'm a big fan of METAPOST for technical illustrations. I don't know anything that's near as good, so I'm doing all the illustrations of *The Art of Computer Programming* in METAPOST. Also, the technical papers I've written are going to be published in a series of eight volumes by Cambridge University Press, and all the illustrations, except the photographs, are going to be METAPOSTed. The first volume of these eight was the book *Literate Programming*; the second volume is going to come out this summer and is going to be called *Selected Papers in Computer Science*. It reprints a dozen or 15 papers that I wrote for general audiences, not for specialists in computer science — articles in *Scientific American* or *Science* magazine and things like that. The third volume will be about digital typography, and it'll reprint all my articles in *TUGboat* and things about TEX. What do you think, by the way — should

I publish in that third volume the memo that I wrote to myself the first night, when I designed TEX? I put it in a computer file and it's in the Stanford archives, but I've never shown it to anyone. [*round of "of course!" and "sure" and laughter from the audience*] Maybe it'd sell more books [*more laughter*].

Frans: You need to put it on your home page and we can then decide —

Don: No, no. That way we'd never sell the books. [*laughter*] Not that I'm a mercenary type of person, of course. It's in a file called `tex.one` — "teks dot one," actually. I have to admit I pronounced the name "teks" for a month or two — I was thinking of "technical texts." The name of the file was `tex.one`, and it would make interesting reading probably, someday.

   And your name is?

Jan Karman: In this company I will probably ask a very heretic question, but a little heresy makes a lot of fun — talking about META-FONT. There are probably many type foundries now that crank out lots of good-quality fonts and kerning tables. It's not clear whether Post-Script or True Type will survive. Do you think that METAFONT will survive text fonts? Not talking about the math fonts.

Don: I don't think the extra capabilities of METAFONT have proved to be necessary for good-quality type fonts, although I think that you can still make better-quality type fonts with it. Designers find it difficult to think as a computer person does, in the sense that when people in the computer business automate something, trying to make the computer do something, it's natural for us to have parameters and say that we're going to try to solve more than one problem. We try to solve a whole variety of problems based on the parameters that people set. But it's much easier if people gave us only a single problem with a single parameter setting, then we can make the computer do exactly the prescribed thing. Computer scientists have become accustomed to thinking of how we would change behavior as conditions change, but designers aren't at all accustomed to this. Designers are much happier if the boss says one month, "Give me a medium roman font," and the next month, "Give me a bold roman font." It's much more difficult if the boss says, "Show me how you would draw a roman font no matter how heavy I want the letters to be." METAFONT provides a way to solve that problem and to draw characters with parameters, but it's a rare designer who's comfortable with that notion. They can do multiple master fonts by making multiple drawings and then matching up points between the drawings and having the computer interpolate. The multiple master fonts in PostScript allow up to four parameters, and almost all of them have only one or two parameters. The most I know of is two; probably others have gone all the way to four. But then they have to provide drawings for all the extreme points of these parameters.

In spite of this limited use of parameters, what's available commercially is quite beautiful, as far as readability is concerned, although it doesn't really provide the quality that you guys had in the Netherlands in the 17th century. What's the man's name, the great punchcutter in Haarlem — he made 4.5 pt, 5 pt, up to 16 pt, and each letter was designed for its size, and his fonts had a nice uniform appearance. This doesn't happen at all with today's Type1 fonts. There were two guys who did most of the punchcutting for Enschedé and others in the 18th century: One of them, Fleischman, was a genius for really beautiful letters; the other, Rosart, was just good at making lots and lots of letters.[5] [*laughter*] They were fun. Rosart cut all kinds of highly decorated alphabets and things like that. I have a big coffee-table book that gives examples of all the fonts from Enschedé, which was translated into English by Matthew Carter's father. In this book, *Typefoundries in the Netherlands*, you can look at these typefaces and weep.[6]

Still, on a laserprinter, we get pretty good fonts now, and therefore it looks like there won't be that many professional type designers using METAFONT. Pandora was a good meta-design by a genuine graphic artist.[7] METAFONT has turned out to be wonderful for making border designs and special-purpose things for geometry. There's now a really neat system in Poland where they have TEX and METAFONT in a closed loop — TEX outputs something and then METAFONT draws a character and if that doesn't fit, TEX says, "go back and try it again." Jackowski and Ryćko understand TEX and METAFONT, and the programs are

---

[5] Johann Michael Fleischman, 1701–1768; Jacques-François Rosart, 1714–1777.

[6] *Typefoundries in the Netherlands from the Fifteenth to the Nineteenth Centuries*, by Charles Enschedé, translated by Harry Carter (Haarlem: Stichting Museum Enschedé, 1978), 477 pp. This magnificent book was composed by hand and printed by letterpress to commemorate the 275th anniversary of Joh. Enschedé en Zonen.

[7] Neenie Billawala, *Metamarks: Preliminary Studies for a Pandora's Box of Shapes*, Stanford Computer Science report STAN-CS-89-1256 (Stanford, California: July 1989), 132 pp.

well documented and can do these things. So METAFONT isn't going to disappear, for that reason; but it's never going to be taught in high school.

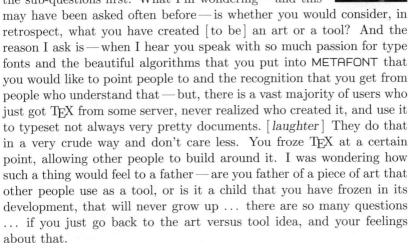

Frans: My name is Frans Goddijn and I have one question with some sub-questions. [*laughter*] I'd like to ask the sub-questions first. What I'm wondering — and this may have been asked often before — is whether you would consider, in retrospect, what you have created [to be] an art or a tool? And the reason I ask is — when I hear you speak with so much passion for type fonts and the beautiful algorithms that you put into METAFONT that you would like to point people to and the recognition that you get from people who understand that — but, there is a vast majority of users who just got TeX from some server, never realized who created it, and use it to typeset not always very pretty documents. [*laughter*] They do that in a very crude way and don't care less. You froze TeX at a certain point, allowing other people to build around it. I was wondering how such a thing would feel to a father — are you father of a piece of art that other people use as a tool, or is it a child that you have frozen in its development, that will never grow up ... there are so many questions ... if you just go back to the art versus tool idea, and your feelings about that.

Don: Obviously, if I write something that has a lot of power to do many different things, it'll be possible to make it do awful things. I just came from the Rijksmuseum, where they have an exhibit called "The Age of Ugliness," featuring a whole bunch of fancy silver bowls from the late 19th century .... When you say an art, I'm not sure I understand exactly what you mean. To me, art is used in two quite different senses, most often nowadays in the sense of fine art, while art (originally *Kunst*) once was anything that was not natural — so we have the word *artificial*, something that is made by people instead of by nature. The Greek word is τέχνη. [*laughter*] But then you refer to a tool as something that is maybe just a device that is the fastest way to get from here to there but maybe you don't care about elegance ... What I think people mean when they talk about art is the aesthetics — something about beauty and something with a little bit of love in it. With TeX, my idea was to make it possible to produce works that you are proud of; I assumed that people can enjoy actually spending a little extra time making the results better. I didn't expect that the whole world would be doing this. [*laughter*]

Incidentally, I can't understand the mentality of a person who writes graffiti on a beautiful building although I can see why drawing is fun. Why would you want to scrawl something — some kind of animal instinct for territory might account for it, I suppose, but it's really impossible for me to conceive of such actions.

When it comes to matters of aesthetics, you can't dictate taste. You can't say that your idea of beauty is going to match anyone else's idea of beauty. But I did want to have a tool where we could reach the highest levels of beauty according to our own tastes. I didn't allow people to have letterspacing very easily, but I tried to make everything else easy. [*laughter*] ...
Of course, I originally designed TEX just for myself, for *The Art of Computer Programming*; I thought my secretary and I were going to be the only users. And it wasn't until later that I was convinced that I should make it more general and so on. But I did want a tool for myself by which I could produce books that would make me feel good after spending almost all my life writing those books.

I started writing *The Art of Computer Programming* when I was 24 years old and I still have 20 years of work to do on it. That's a lot of time. I don't want to write those books if they're going to come out looking awful. I wanted a way to make it possible to produce good-looking books. Originally, when computers started out, they knew only numbers, digits. The 19th-century computers could print tables. Then we had computers that could do numbers and letters, but only on a Teletype machine; so you had some capital letters and a 32-character set. But then, after I graduated from college, we got ... let me see, I was probably ten years out of college before we could do lowercase letters on a computer. You know, the Pascal language, when it came out, it used all uppercase letters — there was never any consideration that there would be more than 64 characters in a computer's repertoire. Finally, we were beginning to see in the middle 70s that computers could actually do lowercase letters, and produce something that looked a little bit readable, a little bit like books. Wow! [*laughter*]

Simultaneously there was a development of typographic software starting at M.I.T. in 1961 and going through 4 or 5 generations, leading to *troff* and *eqn*, where even mathematics was being typeset. In 1977 I therefore knew an existence theorem: It was possible to typeset something that looked almost like good mathematics. The output of *eqn* was appearing in physics journals, and experience showed that secretaries could learn how to do the input. So I thought, "Why not go all the way to the end, to convergence?" What I wanted to do with TEX was not to provide a little refinement over *troff* and the other things; I was saying now, "Let's try to produce the best typography that has ever been achieved by mankind." Except for the illuminated gold-leaf type of lettering, I wanted to — at least when it came to black and white printing — I wanted to match the best possible quality. Computer typesetting had gone through this lengthy development, getting a little better and a little better. It was time to say, "OK, let's jump to the limit now." Of course, I didn't think this would be an activity that everybody would want to do. But there were enough people that would care about trying to get as much quality as possible, that they could be — well, that's why I finally made TEX more available. Leaders of the American Math Society were the first people, nearly the first people who convinced me that I should make the system do more than I originally intended.

Andries Lenstra: Why didn't you start from *troff*? It was completely inappropriate?

Don: Yes, yes. You see, *troff* was patched on top of ... I mean, there was a whole system, it was a fifth generation, each of which was a patch on another one. So it was time to scrap it and start all over again: "Here's what the language should be, so let's design some good data structures for it." Not "Let's try to be compatible." I had the advantage that I was not at Bell Labs, so I wouldn't be hurting anybody's feelings by saying, "Let's throw it all away." [*laughter*] It was naturally impossible for the people at Bell Labs to do such a thing — it wouldn't be nice. But it occurred to me that now we had proof that a higher goal was possible, so it was time to start over, and rethink how to get from input to output. Thus the program could be much more unified, much smaller, and it would also work. I mean, *troff* was collapsing all the time. A lot of the earliest users of TEX had been frustrated by *troff* breaking over and over again, as it had gotten unwieldy. But *troff* had also proved that there was light at the end of the tunnel.

I also had to scrap TEX, you know, and start over again; after five years, I decided that it would be best to go back and redo the program. But it would have been very hard to do that if my friend in the next office had written it. [*laughter*] So, I just have this philosophy that there will be always some people who are more interested in quality than others, and I wanted to make TEX good for them.

I don't know any good way to make it impossible to create a bad document, unless you have a system with only a small menu of options. Small menus are, of course, good enough for a large class of users — to make a system so simple that you can't possible do anything ugly in it.

Erik: I think it's time for a coffee break now — we'll take five or ten minutes.

Don: Johannes, you had a question that you had to ask, so let's get that over with. [*laughter*]

Johannes: It's about typesetting. What is your opinion about the skyline model of typesetting? In TEX, you talk about boxes: Each letter is inside a box, and we glue boxes together to make a line, and each line is viewed as a box, and the boxes are fitted together to form a paragraph. The skyline model tries to go a little bit further than the rigid box and line, and tries to take into account that some of the descenders in the upper line and the high parts in the lower line don't overlap, so that you could actually have lines much tighter together — especially in math typesetting, that could be an advantage.

Don: Hmmm, I guess you're talking about general principles of computer graphics where you have arbitrary rectangles in a picture, instead of having the rectangles strictly nested inside of other rectangles. ... This certainly would be a major change to all the data structures of TEX. You could go to a quadtree structure or something like that. All the things that people use to solve hidden-line problems and do rendering, to find out what's in front of something else, and all the algorithms they use to make movies like *Toy Story*. It would be most valuable, I imagine, for catching unusual cases in math formulas.

I have two feelings about such things. One is that I like to see people extending the problems that computers can solve automatically. People learn a lot when they try to do this. The whole field of artificial intelligence has been one of the areas that has had greatest spin-offs to computer science because they've tried to solve very hard problems. Especially in the early days, they came up with methods that turned out to be useful in many other parts of computer science. So, it's my feeling that when people are working on more ambitious goals, they develop powerful techniques that often have very relevant spin-offs. Even so, after they've solved that problem, they're going to think of something else which will be another refinement and so on — they'll never have a situation where they're going to create the most beautiful document automatically. There's going to be a time when you can look at the output and see that you can still improve it. Designers of the most automatic systems would be well advised to at least leave users a chance to move something up and down and fake out the automatic algorithm.

The philosophy that I had when I did TeX was that I would try to have a system that did 99% of everything automatically; then I would look at what remained and I would kludge the rest. But "kludging it" is only one way to describe this approach; another way of saying it is, "Tidy up the rest," or "Dot the i's and cross the t's." My feeling is that the non-automatic part gives me a little extra pride, knowing that I have put some spit and polish on the final product. If such extra work is excessive, it's a nuisance and I'm wasting time. But if I can really limit this to 1% — if I've spent 30 hours writing a paper and it takes me only another 15 minutes to clean up — then I'm happy to do another 15 minutes at the end. It's a small little extra that gives me a chance to celebrate the fact that I've finished the paper.

The spacing that TeX does worst right now, in my experience, is with respect to square root signs being a little too tight, with the operand either too close to the radical sign or too close to the bar line or both; I most often tend to be fiddling with that. In the book *Concrete Math* and also now in *The Art of Computer Programming*, I've adopted a convention where I put an @-sign into a math formula where I want one math unit of extra space. The @-sign is then defined to have a math code of hexadecimal 8000, and I've made the definition

```
{\catcode'\@=\active \gdef@{\mkern1mu}};
```

the effect is that, in math mode, an @-sign will be regarded as a macro that adds one math unit of space. For example, I'll type

```
\sqrt{@\log n}
```

because otherwise the space before the letter 'l' is a little bit too tight. [*laughter*] Now maybe even this skyline model wouldn't know that 'l' was too tight, maybe it would. But it's cases like this ...

The most common case really for spacing adjustment is where I have something like '$x^2/3$', with a simple superscript and then a slash, and then the denominator. There's almost always too much space before the slash. And this is true, I find, in all the books that I used to think were typeset perfectly by hand [*laughter*], but now I'm sensitive to such things. Nowadays I go through my books and papers, typically with Emacs, and look for all occurrences of a one-character exponent followed by a slash, and most of those look better with a negative thinspace before the slash: `$x^2\!/3$` yields $x^2/3$. It would be nicer if I didn't have to do that. But still, it's a small thing for me.

Would the skyline model help me much? Sometimes I run into cases where I'll add another word to the answer to an exercise in order to avoid a clash between lines. The lines are actually not getting spread apart too far, but they're so close together that a subscript like '$k \leq n$' will clash with a parenthesis in the next line. And I don't want the type to be quite so close together there. Now, if I had been smarter, I would have designed my $\leq$-sign to have a diagonal stroke under the $<$ instead of a horizontal bar, namely '$k \leqslant n$', and I wouldn't have had those clashes — too late for that now. [*laughter*]

Kees?

Kees van der Laan: May I ask you a question about your attitude to markup in general? And let me illustrate it by first telling a story. When we started with using TeX etc., we mean actually we start with LaTeX — I mean, that is the effect in Holland. And then I looked at the products of the markup and I did not like it. And then I was wondering, what is your attitude to that? I'm sorry to say so, I paged through *The TeXbook* source file `texbook.tex` and I looked at all the things in there and then I thought, "Well, I have some idea of what your ideas are of markup." And when you explained about METAFONT and all those things not in there, which you have implicit — am I wrong if I summarize this, that you adhere to something like minimal markup?

Don: Yes. For example, when I am reading Edsger Dijkstra's books, every time I get to a section where it says "End of Comment," it strikes me as redundant. And I always think, "Oh, yes, this is Edsger's style."

When I wrote a paper for his 60th birthday, I said at the end, "Acknowledgment, I want to thank Edsger for such-and-such," and "End of Acknowledgment." [*laughter*][8] But that's the only time in my life I'll ever do that. Maybe I'm an illogical person; but apparently half the people using HTML now type only the `<p>` at the beginning of a paragraph, and the other half type only a `</p>` at the end of a paragraph. [*laughter*] Hardly anybody uses both, according to what my spies tell me. And I don't know what the heck these systems actually do with the unbracketed material.

When I write HTML, I'm scrupulous with my markup. If you look at my home pages — I'll pay you $2.56 if you find any case where I started something and didn't close it with the right tag. I tried to be very careful in that, and to indent everything very well, and so on. But I found it a terrible nuisance, because it's not the way I think.

A high-level language, to me, is something that should reflect its structure in some visual way but not necessarily explicitly; so that, when I know the conventions, we can suppress some things. Parentheses are one such convention and mathematics got a lot better when people invented other notations like operator precedence that allow us to see structure without spelling it out in too much detail. A mathematician spends a lot of time choosing notations for things, and one of the things we try to avoid in mathematics is double subscripts. I read one French Ph.D. thesis where the author had five levels of subscripts [*laughter*] — he kept painting himself into a corner. He started out with a set $\{x_1, \ldots, x_n\}$, so then when he talked of a subset, it had to be $\{x_{i_1}, \ldots, x_{i_m}\}$, and then he wanted to take a subset of this; finally he had a theorem that referred to '$x_{i_{j_{k_1}}} \ldots x_{i_{j_{k_r}}}$'. [*laughter*] I try to choose notations that give me the economy of thought at a high level.

That's probably why I didn't believe in a great deal of markup in *The TEXbook*. I would begin typewriter type and end typewriter type for sections by saying `\begintt` and `\endtt`. I would also delimit the lines when presenting parts of the plain TEX macros, saying `\beginlines` and `\endlines` — those macros are in the file, since it's very important to me to see the structure. But in other cases, I left things as simple as possible, as long as I could visualize the beginning and end of stuff.

An analogous thing occurred when I was doing administrative work at Stanford. Sometimes after solving a problem, I stopped worrying about it, so I forgot to implement the solution! I was always a very bad committee chairman because I'm not very good at finishing that last

---

[8] *Beauty is Our Business* (Springer, 1990), 242.

ending line, I guess. Still, with HTML, the documents were short and I decided that my home pages were going to be used by many different kinds of browsing software so I had better be very rigorous.

While I was developing TEX, I attended one of the meetings of the committee that designed SGML and had a very good discussion with Charley Goldfarb and the other people on the committee — we only had that one meeting near Stanford. Certainly I appreciate the fact that rigorous markup makes it possible to build other kinds of programs around what you have. The more structure you have in a document, the easier it is to make a database that includes things about it, and knows what's going on. I never objected to SGML; I just always felt that in order to maximize my efficiency, I didn't want to mess around with full markup unless I had to.

X: SGML allows minimizations; that's why the end-paragraph is not necessary. So that's one of the reasons why it's so difficult sometimes. You have a formalization to minimize.

Don: But LATEX doesn't allow it.

Johannes: We do have some hooks, however, permitting omitted end-tags in LATEX3, but that's not far enough along.

Don: Well, Kees should talk to Johannes. [*laughter*]

Incidentally, I don't feel the need for a special editor to write HTML code — people are hyping fancy things where you can click on a tool and it'll put in the start and end tag together. But when I wrote my files, I did make up a simple Emacs keyboard macro that would take whatever tag I just typed and create the end-tag. All this macro had to do was search back till it found a less-than sign and then copy that string twice and put a slash in front of it; so I used that all the time — it was easy.

Johannes: A quite different type of question now, from someone who'd like to be here: Literally, he writes, "Why is the height of the minus sign in the cm symbol font the same as the height of the cmr plus sign?"

Don: Ah. A lot of people are wondering about that one. Where you have '$a - c$' or 'x^-' or something similar, why is it that the height and depth are greater than the actual shape of the minus sign? In fact, it's not just the $+$ and $-$, the same is true also for $\pm$, $\mp$, $\oplus$, $\ominus$, $\otimes$, $\oslash$, $\times$, and $\div$. If you look at the METAFONT code for these, there is a **beginarithchar** macro that begins all of the arithmetic characters in the font, guaranteeing that they will all have the same size.

Johannes: But it doesn't say why.

Don: That's right — it doesn't say why. And the reason is that early on, I wanted certain things to line up the same. For example, in the formula

$$\sqrt{x+y} + \sqrt{x-y}\,,$$

I wanted the square root signs to be placed in the same way. Otherwise you would get

$$\sqrt{x+y} + \sqrt{x-y}\,.$$

And there are many other cases where there's a plus sign in one part of a formula and a minus sign in the other part; for consistency of spacing, it ought to look symmetrical. There are other cases, I readily admit, where you have only a minus sign, without a similar counterpart involving a plus sign, and you wonder why extra space has been left there. So I say '\smash-' [*laughter*] in those cases.

Johannes: The particular application, why this question was asked — Michael Downes from the AMS —

Don: Yes, Michael Downes, he has more experience than any of us in this room; he's the chief typesetter of most of the mathematics in the world.

Johannes: He has a problem properly attaching a superscript on top of the \rightarrowfill ...

Don: The \rightarrowfill? OK ... The \rightarrowfill is this thing that makes a right arrow of any desired length, and then he wants to put a superscript on this. What's the macro for building that up? I haven't used that page in a long ... [*laughter*][9] The \rightarrowfill is made up of minus signs and so probably if I had known Michael ... known about Michael's problem in the old days, I would have changed the plain TEX macros so that it would not use the height of the minus sign in the \rightarrowfill operator.[10] Anyway, I've now told you the reason why it's there for the other ones.

Johannes: Another question, which is about multiple languages. There's a problem when you have one paragraph where you have different languages.

Don: Yes, the \lccode changes. This is the ...

---

[9] The macro is called \buildrel; see *The TEXbook*, page 437.

[10] In fact, the \leftarrowfill and \rightarrowfill now do omit the height and depth of the minus, in `plain.tex` version 3.14159 (March 1995).

Johannes: And I've been told that inside one paragraph you can only use one hyphenation table, which is the one that is active at the end of the paragraph. So, switching hyphenation tables inside paragraphs is a problem. Suppose, for example, you have a paragraph with English text, with a German quote inside it, the German quote being several lines long.

Don: No, I know that TEX will properly keep track of which hyphenation table to use. The glitch, the mistake that I didn't anticipate, occurs only if the two languages have different \lccode mappings — so that each has a different idea of which characters are lowercase. When you hyphenate, you need to hyphenate an uppercase word the same as a lowercase word, so TEX uses the \lccode of a character to convert every letter into the lowercase code of that letter. I didn't anticipate that people might, for different languages, have a different mapping from uppercase to lowercase. And so it's that mapping that, at the end of a paragraph, applies to all the languages in the paragraph. But otherwise, TEX is careful to keep track of what language is current at each point inside.

By the way, there's a file called `tex82.bug`. Go to the CTAN archives, and find subdirectory `systems/`, and under that `knuth/`, and under that `errata/`, and that's where `tex82.bug` is. At the end of `tex82.bug` this particular error about \lccode is mentioned as being an oversight that's too late to fix.

Marc van Leeuwen: Why is it too late to fix? It would conflict with other things?

Don: Yes. People are already using these things in lots of documents, and it's very hard to change. In fact, I don't see any way to fix it. [*laughter*] I would say that when you are faced with a situation where you're doing multiple languages with multiple \lccodes, this is a good reason to write your own version of TEX.

Andries Lenstra: Could I ask a question? Happily enough, I'm not the first person to mention LATEX, so I may mention it now. There's a situation that often arises when people try to write a Ph.D. thesis where they want to change LATEX code because they think they know better about things of beauty or typography, and unhappily enough they are not experts on LATEX, so they don't succeed or they succeed badly. In general, people who know about typography can't write beautiful LATEX code or other forms of code, and vice versa — people who know how to write these forms of code are no experts on typography. What do you think of the endeavors in the past to bring the two worlds together, for instance, as Victor Eijkhout has tried to do with his `lollipop` format, a machine to create other formats. I would have thought that it would have had a big success but the opposite seems to be the truth. What do you think of it?

Don: I'm not familiar with the details of `lollipop`. I suppose that it was based on a famous quotation from Alan Perlis, who said that, "If somebody tells you he wants a programming language that will only do the right thing, give him a lollipop."

Andries: Yes.

Don: I'm sure that the lollipop effort was instructive and worthwhile, but I don't know the details so I can't answer in great detail on this. Probably the type designers didn't find the language easy to learn. I do think that we're having much more communication now, as every month goes by, between the people that know about type and the people that know about macros. It's just a matter of time as we wait for these waves to continue moving — we're nowhere near a convergent stage, where TEX has reached its natural boundary and the type designers have reached their natural boundary. The boundaries are still moving toward each other. I don't think it's like a hyperbolic geometry, where they never will get together.

The main difficulty of course is that TEX is free, and so a lot of people will say, "Well, how could it be any good, if you're not charging money for it?" A lot of the people in the type design community will only work on things where there's money behind it; money proves to them that it's worth talking to people. So it just takes a little while till they see some good examples, which will make them more open for these discussions. And that's happening all the time in different countries.

In the Czech Republic I was quite delighted to learn that the new encyclopaedia in Czech, which is the first one for many years, is being done with TEX. And not only that, it's being done with a very high budget. The publishers made this decision because they tried all the other systems and were disgusted with them. They had good results with TEX. Many other commercial publishers are using it too because they talk to their friends at the big publishing houses. This will, I think, be solved with time. And products like `lollipop` are very worthwhile in the meanwhile to facilitate this. It takes time to bring different communities together. I think the financial factor is definitive for a lot of people.

Piet van Oostrum: I don't know if you have ever looked into the LᴬTᴇX code inside, but if you look into that, you get the impression that Tᴇχ is not the most appropriate programming language to design such a large system. Did you ever think of Tᴇχ being used to program such large systems and if not, would you think of giving it a better programming language?

Don: In some sense I put in many of Tᴇχ's programming features only after kicking and screaming; so I'll try to explain the background. I know how Leslie [Lamport] went about writing LᴬTᴇX — first he would write the algorithms out in a high-level programming language, with **while**'s and **if–then**'s and so on; then he would pretty much mechanically convert the high-level code to Tᴇχ macros. If I had suspected that such a style was going to be the most common use of Tᴇχ, I probably would have worried a lot about efficiency in those days. Now, computers are so fast that I don't worry so much about the running time, because the program still seems to go zip-zip!

In the 70s, I had a negative reaction to software that tried to be all things to all people. Every system I looked at had its own universal Turing machine built into it somehow, and everybody's machine was a little different from everybody else's. So I thought, "Well, I'm not going to design a programming language; I want to have just a typesetting language." Little by little, however, I needed more features and so the programming constructs grew. Guy Steele began lobbying for more capabilities early on, and I put many such things into the second version of Tᴇχ, Tᴇχ82, because of his urging. That made it possible to calculate prime numbers as well as do complicated things with page layout and figure placements. But the reason I didn't introduce programming features at first was because, as a programmer, I was tired of having to learn yet another almost-the-same programming language for every system I looked at; I was going to try to avoid that. Later, I realized that it was sort of inevitable, but I tried to stay as close as I could to the paradigm of Tᴇχ as a character-by-character macro language. As I said before, I was expecting that the really special applications would be done by changing things in the compiled code. But people didn't do that; they wanted to put low-level things in at a higher level.

Piet: What do you think, for example, of something like building in a programming language that is, from a software engineering point of view, easier to use?

Don: It would be nice if there were a well-understood standard for an interpretive programming language inside of an arbitrary application.

Take regular expressions—I define UNIX as "30 definitions of regular expressions living under one roof." [*laughter*] Every part of UNIX has a slightly different regular expression. Now, if there were a universal simple interpretive language that was common to other systems, naturally I would have latched onto that right away.

Piet: The Free Software Foundation is trying to do that and Sun is trying to do it and Microsoft is trying to ...

Don: The Free Software Foundation is trying actually to include also the solutions of Sun and Microsoft. In other words, to make all of the conventions work simultaneously as much as possible. And that conflicts with my own style, where I've tried to have unity rather than diversity ... I haven't provided ten ways to do one thing. C++ is similar— whenever members of the C++ committee would say, "Well, we could do it this way or this way," they did both. I haven't gone that route in my systems, because it is messy. But I admit that the messy way is the best that can presently be realized in practice.

Marc: I have a question about literate programming. I know you must be very fond of it, if I understand your interviews—

Don: Yes, I'm so fond of it that I could ... well ... OK. [*laughter*] You know, I'm really so fond of literate programming, it's one of the greatest joys of my life, just doing it.

Marc: My question was that obviously it's not nearly as popular as TEX is, and, what's more, there isn't much coherence in the world of literate programming. There are a dozen different systems being used— some people favor one way, some people favor another—and this worries me a bit. I too am very fond of this style of programming, but I would like to see it being used much more.

Don: Literate programming is so much better than any other style of programming it's hard to imagine why the world doesn't convert to it. But I think Jon Bentley put his finger on the reason and it was something like this: There aren't that many people in the world who are good programmers and there aren't that many people in the world who are good writers, and here we are expecting them to be both. That overstates the case but it touches the key point. I think that everyone who's looked at literate programming agrees that it's a really good way to go, but they aren't convinced that ordinary students can do it. Some experiments at Texas A&M are proving otherwise, and I've had similar experiences on a smaller scale at Stanford. It's a hypertext way of programming; and I imagine that with better hypertext systems like we're seeing now, and with people becoming so familiar with the Web, we're going to get a variety of new incompatible systems that will support literate programming. Hopefully somebody with time and talent, and taste, will put together a system of literate programming that is so charming it will captivate a lot of people. I believe that the potential is there, and it's just waiting for the right person to make that happen.

Marc: I think one problem might be that if you compare your programs with the average program that people write, there just aren't nearly as many interesting algorithms in the average program, so literate programming doesn't add too much to a program that is very dull by itself.

Don: Well, thank you for your comment. But maybe sometimes I make a non-interesting algorithm interesting just by putting in a joke here or there. I've taken production programs that I got from Sun Microsystems, for example, and as an exercise, spent the afternoon converting them to a literate form. There weren't any exciting algorithms in there, but still, you could look at the final program and it was better — it had better error diagnostics, better organization, it corrected a few bugs. I don't have time to go over to Sun and show them this, and say, "Why don't you rewrite your operating system?" [*laughter*] But I know that it would be much better. So all I ever published was the very simple rewrite of the wc word count routine in UNIX. That's not at all an exciting algorithm, but it's a demo of how good system programming can be done in a pleasant way.[11]

My approach to literate programming isn't the only one, of course. In the recent book by a group at Princeton, *A Retargetable C Compiler*, Chris Fraser and Dave Hanson used a variety of literate programming to describe their C compiler. Other books are coming out now that are using other flavors of literate programming. I was talking to someone at Microsoft who said that he thought literate programming was on the rise, and I said, "Does that mean the next version of Windows is going to be all done in literate programming?" ... "Well, no, not exactly." [*laughter*] The people who've experienced literate programming will never go back to the old way, and they'll probably gain influence gradually. The companies that use it are going to sell more products than their competitors, so pretty soon this will happen. I imagine that there are about ten thousand users of literate programming and a million users of TEX, so it's a factor of a hundred.

---

[11] D. E. Knuth, *Literate Programming* (1992), 341–348; this wc program is based on a prototype by Klaus Guntermann and Joachim Schrod, *TUGboat* **7** (1986), 135–137.

Marc: Do you think it still has to develop? I get the impression that with so many tools around, that it's not yet mature. The idea is mature, but the implementation still has to ...

Don: Yeah, that's true. There's great need for programming environments based on this idea. It's not at all easy to create these environments and to have the power to promote them and maybe the support to do it in a way that wouldn't make it too expensive or too hard for people to install. The most ideal thing would be if the Free Software Foundation were to adopt it, or something like that, or some of the people they work with. Actually, [Richard] Stallman [of the Free Software Foundation] designed a variant of literate programming for himself, and he has it well integrated with TEX, in his own style. He hasn't put it into too many of his programs, but he's getting there. It's one of those things that needs, as you say, to mature.

Marc: Do you believe literate programming should go in the direction of integrated systems, where you really have all the facilities you need in one system? Because I think the tendency is more towards very minimalistic systems that do not do any pretty printing because that gets you into too much trouble when you're switching programming languages. So it really boils down to something which is very flexible but not very convenient for someone to use.

Don: One programming language is good enough for me, so I'm not the right person to ask. For my own purposes, writing *The Art of Computer Programming* during the next twenty years, I'm pretty sure that CWEB is going to be as good as anything I'll need. I'll write programs for *Mathematica*™ and I'll write some programs for METAPOST; I could develop or use literate programming for those programs, but I don't think I will. I don't write so many lines that I would gain a great deal ... although I would get a better program afterwards. Unless somebody already presents me with a good system for it, I won't go ahead with MathWeb or MPWeb. But with CWEB, I'm going to write an average of five programs a week for the foreseeable future, and there, my productivity is infinitely better when I do it with literate programming.

One other thought flashed in my mind as I was talking just now ... I wrote a paper, last year I think it was, about mini-indexes for literate programs[12] and here I was trying to anticipate what sort of programming environment would help me. In the listings for TEX: The Program

---

[12] *Software — Concepts & Tools* **15** (1994), 2–11; reprinted as Chapter 11 of the present volume.

and *METAFONT: The Program*, and also for *The Stanford GraphBase*, on the right-hand page of each two-page spread you'll find an index to all the identifiers used on those two pages and where they were declared. My paper explains the system I used to get those indexes, and this kind of functionality would also be needed in any hypertext system. Such minimalistic systems are attractive primarily because a good programmer can write them in a couple of days, understand them and use them, and get a lot of mileage out of them. Once somebody writes a good hypertext system for literate programming, I think that'll attract a lot of people. We need a robust system that doesn't crash, and has a familiar user interface because it's like other hypertext systems that we're already using. The time for that will be ripe in about two years.

Erik: It's half past nine now and I think we'll have to stop here. I want to thank our special guest, Donald Knuth, for being with us. I think we've all learned a lot now. We're very happy that you were able to be here. Thank you very much.

Don: I really appreciate all the work you did to arrange for this special meeting room on rather short notice. [*applause*]

Erik: Also, thank you to Elsevier Science, who helped, in the person of Simon Pepping; and our English colleague, Sebastian Rahtz, who is not here, although I expected him. But he paid for the coffee and tea, so thanks. There's of course a little present that we have for you. I hope you like it! [*He presents a book about Dutch art called De Stijl.*[13]]

Don: Ah yes ... the Dutch type designer, Gerard Unger, came to Stanford for three weeks, he and his wife Marjan, and they talked about things like this to our type designers. They also related fashion of clothes and furniture and architecture to type styles as well. This book is great. Was it done with TEX?

Erik: I don't think so ... as we are in Holland now ... [*laughter*] [*he also presents a pair of wooden tulips*]

Don: A nice gift for my wife.

Erik: And of course a copy of the *EuroTEX'95* proceedings.[14] [*he presents the proceedings*]

---

[13] Carel Blotkamp et al., *De Stijl: The Formative Years* (M.I.T. Press, 1986); a translation of *De Beginjaren van De Stijl* (Utrecht: Uitgeverij Reflex, 1982).

[14] Wietse Dol, editor, *Proceedings of the Ninth European TEX Conference*, September 4–8, 1995, Arnhem, The Netherlands, 441 pp.

Don: Oh!! I thought you'd never ... [*laughter*] Yes, I was looking at this last week in the Czech Republic, so thank you everyone.

Erik: What is your opinion about the fonts we used?

Don: I think it's ... oh, you introduced the Computer Modern Brights. Yes, the only complaint I had was that the kerning in the word 'TEX' itself could be tuned a little bit.[15] On the whole the typography is quite attractive — thank you very much.

---

[15] "The TEX logo in various fonts," *TUGboat* **7** (1986), 101; reprinted as Chapter 6 of the present volume.

Chapter 34

The Final Errors of T_EX

[This chapter was written in August 1998.]

When I completed my article on "The errors of T_EX" in September of 1988 [2], I stated that "I plan to publish a brief note ten years from now, bringing the list to its absolutely final form." Here then is the brief note that was promised.

In September 1988 the error log of T_EX ended with item number 865. Sixteen items had entered the log since May 1987, so I had no reason to believe that T_EX would soon become completely quiescent. But I'm sure that I expected the final total number of entries to be less than 900.

Such hopes were dashed in 1989, when I realized that changes in technology had invalidated one of my early assumptions. I had believed that 7-bit character input would continue to be the norm; but the rapid rise of computer systems based on 8-bit bytes, and of workstations that used 8-bit characters for accented letters, made it clear that a decent T_EX system for a worldwide community would have to be retooled in order to deal more adequately with non-English languages. Therefore, after extensive discussions culminating at the 10th annual meeting of the T_EX Users Group, I decided to incorporate several significant new features into Version 3 of T_EX and Version 2 of METAFONT [4].

Of course the new extensions caused a flurry of activity in T_EX's error log, which reached 900 items already in January of 1990. A summary of all the log entries through the end of 1991 was published in [3], totalling 916 items. And still the story hadn't ended; my diary entry for 9 January 1992 said, "Alas, bad news from T_EXegetes: Three new bugs in T_EX, one in METAFONT."

Today, however, I'm pleased to report that the program for T_EX has been completely stable for the past three years, so it may have converged at last. The remaining log entries, from 1992 to the present, are shown in

10 January 1992

881 ↦ **917** Also avoid producing a double kern at boundary (CET).   §897   S
       918 Disallow \setbox where it doesn't work (Robert Hunt).   §1241, 1270   S
       919 Robustify \mskip and \mkern in presence of negative quad (WGS).   §716, 717   S
679 ↦ **920** Defend against '}{' in \read (Michael Downes).   §483   S
798 ↦ **921** Save string memory if font occurs repeatedly (Bogusław Jackowski).   §1260   E
784 ↦ **922** Don't let \newlinechar interrupt unprintable expansion (Bernd Raichle).   §59, 60   S

7 February 1992

881 ↦ **923** Restore *cur_l* properly when boundary character doesn't exist (Mattes and Raichle).   §1036   D

17 July 1992

892 ↦ **924** Use current language at beginning of horizontal mode (Rainer Schöpf and CET).   §1091, 1200   C

17 December 1992

879 ↦ **925** Avoid (harmless) range errors (Philip Taylor and CET).   §934, 960   R

25 February 1993

881 ↦ **926** Protect kerns inserted by boundary characters (William Baxter).   §837, 866   C
917 ↦ **927** Don't let boundary kern disappear after hyphenation.   §897   S

26 June 1993

668 ↦ **928** Avoid potential future bug (Peter Breitenlohner).   §628, 637   R

17 December 1993

881 ↦ **929** Boundary character representation shouldn't depend on the font memory size (Berthold Horn).   §549, 1323   S

10 March 1994

       930 Huge font parameter number may exceed array bound (CET).   §549   R

4 September 1994

926 ↦ **931** Math kerns are explicit (Walter Carlip).   §717   F
       932 Avoid overflow on huge real-to-integer conversion.   §625, 634   R

19 March 1995

       933 Avoid spurious reference counts in format files (PB).   §1335   R

FIGURE 1. The error log of TeX (1992–1998).

Figure 1; complete details of all changes, in the form of before-and-after listings of the affected lines of code, appear in a file called `tex82.bug`, which is part of the CTAN archives on the Internet.

The histogram in Figure 2 shows the rate at which the 68 items after September 1988 entered the error log, peaking in the latter half of 1989 and falling off thereafter, except for occasional spurts of activity as new kinds of users began to encounter new kinds of bugs. The shaded boxes stand for items that were spawned by previous entries in the log; if I had made the earlier corrections perfectly, these 34 items would not have been necessary.

Some entries in the log represent rather drastic changes to the program. For example, change number 878 — which converted the routines for 7-bit input/output to the new 8-bit conventions — replaced 195 lines of WEB Pascal by 213 new lines of code. Change 881, which introduced "smart ligatures," involved the replacement of 78 lines by 856 new lines.

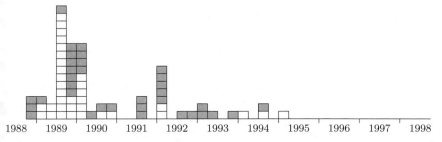

FIGURE 2. When the changes were made.

And changes 879–880, which provided for multilingual hyphenation, replaced 155 lines by 329.

But such drastic changes occurred only when the major new features of version 3.0 were added. Most of the log entries represent relatively small perturbations to the program. Indeed, about 57% of all changes since 1988 required the replacement of fewer than 10 lines of Pascal code by fewer than 10 new lines.

If we use the fifteen categories of [2] to classify the 68 log items of the past decade, we obtain the following totals:

- Type A (algorithmic anomaly), 0.
- Type B (blunder or botch), 0.
- Type C (cleanup for consistency or clarity), 4.
- Type D (data structure debacle), 6.
- Type E (efficiency enhancement), 2.
- Type F (forgotten functionality), 3.
- Type G (generalization or growth), 11.
- Type I (interactive improvement), 2.
- Type L (language liability), 0.
- Type M (module mismatch), 1.
- Type P (promotion of portability), 2.
- Type Q (quest for quality), 1.
- Type R (reinforcement of robustness), 10.
- Type S (surprising scenario), 24.
- Type T (trivial typo), 0.

Not surprisingly, surprises dominate the list.

Were any of these changes particularly instructive or noteworthy? Most of the lessons learned since 1988 were similar to those already enumerated in [2], only more so. Ten more years of experience confirm that we must expect to expend substantial effort if we want to debug a complex program thoroughly.

The Final Bug?

The most interesting of the recent errors may well be the last one, number 933 — which indeed is what I hope will turn out to be the "historic" last bug in TEX. This error, discovered in 1995 by Peter Breitenlohner, is rather esoteric and it has no effect on normal use; yet I believe he amply deserved the reward of $327.68 that I paid him on 20 March 1995.

The situation is this: TEX avoids garbage collection by using reference counts in key parts of its data structures. Reference counts are assumed to take no more computer space than a pointer does, because the number of references to a node cannot exceed the total number of nodes when TEX's conventions are followed.

Breitenlohner found a fallacy in that impeccable logic, by making use of a special version of TEX called INITEX. System wizards install macro packages with INITEX by invoking the \dump command, which stores the current contents of the data structures in a so-called format file; \dump is not permitted in ordinary incarnations of TEX. Commonly used fonts and macros can be preloaded quickly by TEX or by INITEX if they have previously been dumped into a format file.

When the \dump command occurs in the midst of macro expansions and/or conditional instructions, the data structures that control INITEX's input state are not saved as part of the format file, because such things are irrelevant to subsequent users. Unfortunately, however, those data structures might refer to objects that *are* saved — and ay, there's the rub. Before change number 933 was made, INITEX could dump reference counts that included references from nodes that would not be loaded later. Therefore a user with malice aforethought could repeatedly ask INITEX to load such files and dump new ones that were even worse; the reference counts could build up until they became arbitrarily large.

Change 933 added instructions to TEX's *final_cleanup* routine so that all references from nonrestored pointers were removed before dumping. A similar change was, of course, made to METAFONT.

Non-Bugs, But Close

I reserve the right to decide whether or not any purported flaw in TEX constitutes a bug that should be corrected.

Some people think that TEX is incorrect just because users can easily make it loop forever. But in fact, TEX is *supposed* to loop forever if you give it commands that specify endless activity. For example,

```
\def\x{\x}\x
```

causes infinite macro expansion. A more interesting example is

```
\let\par=\relax \noindent\vfill
```

which tells TEX to keep performing `\relax` until it gets into vertical mode — and that never happens! (See the rules on page 286 of *The TEXbook* [1].)

In general terms, I would say that TEX should not issue the error message "This can't happen" unless it has previously given some other error message. But this definition of buggy behavior has exceptions too, because the program for TEX explicitly acknowledges that certain kinds of run-time errors are possible yet unreasonable (because they won't occur in normal use).

For example, §798 of the program invokes the fatal this-can't-happen message when a user has tried to \span 256 or more columns of a table. The program of §798 includes the comment

{ this can happen, but won't }

— clearly admitting the fact that TEX's message in this remotely possible situation is false. You may call this an instance of my warped sense of humor; or you may understand that I did not want to issue an "overflow" error, because the maximum number of spans is not as easy to increase as the other quantities that are listed on page 300 of *The TEXbook* and reported by `\tracingstats`; but you cannot call it a bug that is worth $327.68. Implementors who disagree are free to change TEX's behavior in this case, because the TRIP test does not prescribe the action on fatal errors. For example, they could substitute a message analogous to the one for discretionary-list-too-long in §1120, if they really believe that an honest user will be misled by TEX's present treatment of humongous spanning. But I don't think it's an issue. Incidentally, David Kastrup found a deucedly clever way to invoke this false behavior of TEX in 1996, with the following remarkably short program:

```
\def\x#1{\if#1m\span\expandafter\x\fi}
\halign{&#\cr\expandafter\x\romannumeral256001\cr}
```

Another example of anomalous behavior that is explicitly known to be possible in extreme circumstances arises when numbers get large enough to cause arithmetic overflow. TEX tries to catch integer overflow before it happens, in situations that are likely to arise in practice (see, for example, §104, §445, and §1236); but §104 points out that I did not take the trouble to make the program thoroughly bulletproof against adversarial attacks.

For example, the TEX code

```
\hbox{\romannumeral\maxdimen}
```

creates a box that contains 1,073,741 occurrences of the letter m, followed by 'dcccxxiii'. With the default font cmr10, this box will be exactly 586,410,016,845 scaled points wide; that's about 1.954 miles (3.145 kilometers). Something's gotta give. In this case TEX's string pool, where roman numerals are formed, will overflow, but in smaller examples the integer arithmetic will fail instead. Although the compiler flags in §9 specify that integer overflow should be trapped by the hardware, contemporary implementations of TEX often ignore this recommendation; for example, a typical UNIX installation will report that \hbox{\romannumeral3932000} has width 32766.76666 pt, while the width in points of \hbox{\romannumeral3932001} is −32766.45555!

Integer overflow can occur in many ways, if you try hard enough to defeat the present setup. For example, one can concoct paragraphs that have more than 2^{31} demerits under certain feasible sequences of line breaks. But I do not regard such constructions as evidence of bugs in TEX, unless I can be convinced that a reasonable user would encounter such behavior. (Or unless, as with bug 933, one of the fundamental assumptions of TEX's design has been disproved.)

For reasons of portability, I do not believe that the maximum number of spanned columns in a table should be increased past 255, nor that the maximum size of an integer constant should exceed $2^{31} - 1 = 2147483647$ on computers with 64-bit arithmetic. After all, TEX is a language for typesetting. Who needs such gigantic numbers?

Design Flaws

The design of TEX has been frozen since 1990; therefore nobody can say any longer that TEX has a bug in its specifications. At present I do know of three things that I would have changed if I had thought of them before deciding to finalize the design:

(1) Additional parameters in symbol fonts could govern the minimum distance between ruled lines in fractions, \sqrt, \overline, and \underline; at present this minimum distance depends only on the thickness of the line.

(2) Only one setting of the internal code numbers that map upper-case letters to lowercase is used for hyphenation in a paragraph, even though that paragraph might involve several languages that have different mappings. Extensions of TEX that want to overcome this problem will probably have to introduce new kinds of whatsit nodes that record changes to \lccode values.

The problem can be avoided without extending TEX, if you use the following workaround: The \hyphenate macro defined by

```
\newbox\hyfbox \def\hyphenate#1{{\everyvbox{}\setbox0=
  \vbox{\pretolerance=-1\parfillskip=0pt\hsize=\maxdimen
    \rightskip=0pt\hbadness=10000\everypar{}
    \noindent\hskip-\leftskip #1\endgraf
    \global\setbox\hyfbox=\lastbox}}\unhbox\hyfbox}
```

will hyphenate whatever you give it, using hyphenation from the current language, returning a horizontal list that includes discretionary hyphens.

(3) Rule 12 in Appendix G of *The TEXbook* doesn't allow us to bring a large accent (from, say, font cmr17) close to a small letter in math mode, because of the formula $\delta \leftarrow \min\big(h(x), \chi\big)$. That formula allows us to lower the accent by at most the height of the box underneath, so the accent will not go lower than its original position in the font.

Problem (3) was brought to my attention by Vaughan Pratt in March 1998; he asked me how to typeset '$\check{r}$' (with an accent larger than the normal '$\check{r}$' from $\check r$), and my best solution in plain TEX was not beautiful:

```
\font\bigacc=cmr17 \textfont"F=\bigacc
\def\CHECK{\mathaccent"7F14 }
\setbox2=\hbox{$r$}\setbox4=\hbox{\raise3pt\copy2}\ht4=\ht2
\def\CHECKr{\lower3pt\hbox{$\CHECK{\copy4}$}}
```

I'm not sure what I would have done if he had asked me the same question in 1988; at that time I would have believed it to be a bug in TEX. Now it's just an unfortunate feature.

Conclusion

Any complex system can be improved; therefore the goal of absolute perfection and optimality is unattainable. Yet I think TEX can be said to have arrived at a reasonably satisfactory state, given that stability itself is highly desirable. I am deeply grateful to the many volunteers all over the world who have helped me to formulate many of the changes that have led TEX to its present embodiment, known as "Version 3.14159."

References

[1] Donald E. Knuth, *The TEXbook*, Volume A of *Computers & Typesetting* (Reading, Massachusetts: Addison–Wesley and American Mathematical Society, 1984).

[2] Donald E. Knuth, "The errors of TEX," *Software — Practice & Experience* **19** (1989), 607–685; reprinted with additions and corrections as Chapter 10 of *Literate Programming*. See also [3].

[3] Donald E. Knuth, "The error log of TEX (1978–1991)," Chapter 11 of *Literate Programming*, CSLI Lecture Notes 27 (Stanford, California: Center for the Study of Language and Information, 1992), 293–339.

[4] Donald E. Knuth, "The new versions of TEX and METAFONT," *TUGboat* **10** (1989), 325–328; **11** (1990), 12. Reprinted in *Die TEXnische Komödie* **2**, 1 (March 1990), 16–22. French translation by Alain Cousquer, "TEX 3.0 ou le TEX nouveau va arriver," *Cahiers GUTenberg*, n°4 (December 1989), 39–45. Also reprinted as Chapter 29 of the present volume.

Addendum (December 2002)

In 1998, TEX became certifiably Y2K-safe by printing the current year with four digits instead of two.

A bug in \xleaders was found in 1999; some tricky ways to defeat TEX's alignment algorithms were defeated in 2001; the rounding of glue was improved in 2002.

But I remain optimistic that no further changes will be needed.

Addendum (March 2008)

Following a substantial analysis of the entire program by David Fuchs, eight more changes were made in TEX version 3.1415926 — one each of Types B, F, I; two of Type E; and three of Type R. No major errors were found, but we wanted to make the program more robust and consistent. The most significant problem to be corrected was the fact that leaders with \mskip glue had never worked properly; that feature, which nobody could actually have used, is now disallowed. Further details about the changes, which bring the total number up to 946, appear in my note "The TEX tuneup of 2008," *TUGboat* **29** (2008), 233–238.

I remain optimistic that no further changes will be needed.

Addendum (January 2014)

Well, make that 947. [See "The TEX tuneup of 2014," *TUGboat* **35** (2014), 5–8.] Yet I remain optimistic.

Index

≨ versus ≤, 368, 642.
4TEX, 626.
8-bit characters, 563–564.
16-bit characters, 205–206,
   217–221, *see also* Unicode.
99% policy, 595–596, 605, 633,
   641–642.
∞, 71, 73, 78, 92, 103–104, 154.
∞ sign, 374.
ε versus ϵ and $\in$, 352, 355.
ε-TEX, 630.
π, 51, 571, 590.
Ω system, 630–631, 634.
@ for spacing, 641.

ABC book, 2.
Abelson, Harold, 543.
accents, 38, 247, 368, 412–414, 655,
   661.
ACM (Association for Computing
   Machinery), 60, 88–89.
ACME (Advanced Computer for
   Medical rEsearch), 540.
Acrobat, 612, 618, 634.
Acta Mathematica, 620.
active characters, 190.
active nodes, 105–106, 115–116.
Adams, Ansel Easton, 461.
Addison–Wesley Publishing
   Company, iv, 5, 7, 12, 35, 151,
   319, 558, 562, 606, 620.
Ade, George, 414.

adjustment ratio, 76–77, 115–117.
Adleman, Leonard Max, 581.
Adobe Acrobat, 612, 618, 634.
Adobe Photoshop, 434, 440.
Adobe Systems Incorporated, iv,
   248, 608, 612.
adversary, 454.
AFM (Adobe Font Metric) files, 248.
Aho, Alfred Vaino, 60.
Alamnehe, Abass Belay, 18.
Alavi, Yousef, 61.
Algie, Stephen H., 468–469.
ALGOL-like languages, 95–98, 320,
   632.
algorithms, 601, 634, 650.
Alice Through the Looking-Glass
   (əɔilA), 163–164.
Allebach, Jan Philip, 463, 470.
alphabets for mathematics,
   344–347, 367–368.
Alphatype CRS phototypesetter,
   286–287, 538–540, 542–543.
Amá, Ronaldo, 214.
American Institute of Physics, 59.
American Mathematical Society
   (AMS), iv, x–xii, 19, 25, 60–61,
   91, 247, 339–342, 347, 352–353,
   363, 367, 533, 542–543, 574,
   608, 624, 639.
   Transactions, 20–26, 64.
American Physical Society, 61.

663